HINDU PHILOSOPHY OF RELIGION

HINDU PHILOSOPHY
OF
RELIGION

PART- II
(MĪMAṀSĀ SŪTRA OF JAIMINI)

By

N.V. THADANI

BHARATIYA KALA PRAKASHAN
DELHI (INDIA)

First Edition : 1952
Revised Edition : 2007

Published by **C.P. Gautam**
BHARATIYA KALA PRAKASHAN
3421-A, IInd Floor Narang Colony, Tri Nagar,
Delhi-110035. Phone : 27393083, 32967505 (O), 32492129 (R)
E-Mail : bkp3421@yahoo.co.in

ISBN : 978-81-8090-166-9

Laser Type Setting by
A-ONE GRAPHICS
Pitampura, Delhi-110088

Printed By :
BDH Printer at Salasar Imaging Systems

असतो मा सद्गमय
तमसो मा ज्योतिर्गमय
मृत्योर्मामृतं गमय॥

**Lead us from falsehood into Truth;
From darkness into living Light;
From death to Immortality**

Bṛhadāraṇyaka Upaniṣad, I, iii, 27.

EDITOR'S NOTE

Mīmāṁsā means a reverent study leading to a scientific quest of Truth; and it was this search after Truth, leading to the solution of the great problem of life, that engaged the attention of the ancients in the past. The real problem of life is the attainment of happiness, and the avoidance of its opposite—misery and pain; and the ancients tried to examine it at all levels and from all points of view. They reflected for long, and realised that pleasure is but a passing episode in an endless course of pain, and permanent happiness can be attained only when there is a total extinction of pain. The author of the *Sāṅkhya*—so called because it signifies reflection— accordingly declared that the chief aim of a man's life is to secure freedom from sorrow and pain. But the great question was how to bring it about; and this meant a knowledge of the cause of pain and the means of attaining to happiness; and an inquiry into this problem gave rise to a harvest of speculations which are stored up in the different systems of Hindu Philosophy. They have their different points of view; but they are all agreed that Good is the source of happiness, and Evil of pain; and the one is called Dharma, and the other Adharma. Dharma is the law of life, and its breach is Adharma. But if this law (Dharma), the observance of which makes for a never-failing and perennial source of happiness, be really true and unerring, it cannot be laid down by mortal man, subject to all the infirmities of flesh and blood; and so it is said to emanate from an impersonal source, the Holy Vedas—the *apauruṣeya* (impersonal) revelation in the verbal form of *Brahman*.

The Veda is accordingly said to be the transcendent

authority, the sovereign voice *(nirapekṣa rava)* of the Primeval Being; and what it enjoins is Dharma, and what it prohibits is Adharma. It is believed to contain the ancient traditional knowledge of the Hindus, handed down to us from the immemorial past; but the contents and language of this mine of thought are difficult to understand. At places it is unintelligible, at others it is incongruous, and at others again it is self-contradictory and appears to be meaningless. This problem had faced a number of thinkers even in the past, and they tried to study the text carefully and to interpret it correctly. This was done in the best and most perfect manner in the *Mīmāṁsā,* which, because it formulated the principles of interpretation of the Veda, came to be regarded as the philosophy and art of interpretation. It is for this reason that it occupies, according to tradition, not only a pre-eminent place among the systems of Hindu Philosophy, but is believed to govern them all. Indeed, it is a common saying of the classical Paṇḍits that "Logic, Grammar and the like only grind the mill, but it is the *Mīmāṁsaka* (knower of *Mīmāṁsā)* alone who ordains the *Śāstras*."[1]

Tradition tells us that there are three avenues of scholarship, —study of words *(pada),* of sentences *(vākya),* and authority in regard to interpretation *(pramāṇa),* —and they relate to Grammar, Logic and *Mīmāṁsā* respectively—the last being the most important of all. The *Mīmāṁsaka* was accordingly given the pride of place in the assemblies of great thinkers in the past, and a number of panegyrics[2] have been composed in his honour by those who knew the importance of this system.

The reason why the *Mīmāṁsā* occupies such a pre-eminent position is not far to seek. It defines Dharma or the law of life; it lays down the correct method of interpretation of the Vedas

1. Anye ghārattikās sarve, nūnam śāstra-kṛto vayam.
2. There are well-known panegyrics like *Mīmāṁsā-śāstra-yugma-śrama-vimala-manā mārgyatām mādṛśo' nyāḥ*—
" Let one other like me be found whose mind is crystallised by his labours in the study of both parts of the *Mīmāṁsā.* "

and removes the conflict of authorities; and it gives a verdict on contentious issues and supplies maxims of universal application. This immense store of knowledge is contained in the *Sūtras* of *Jaimini,* popularly called the *Mīmāṁsā* (or *Pūrva-Mīmāṁsā) Sūtras*. Their language is simple and straightforward, though it differs a great deal from later classical *Sanskṛt,* which has undergone a number of changes with the lapse of time.

These *Sūtras* have been explained by *Sabara-svāmin,* who has been followed by a number of scholars. But, as they have all been led to believe that they refer to Vedic ceremonies and a system of ritualistic practices, they have tried to interpret the *Sūtras* in their light, with the result that the whole system has come to be regarded as dealing with ritual and the laws and practices of various sacrifices, while its more truly philosophic spirit and idea has been forgotten and lost. Indeed, what was meant to illustrate the method of interpretation of the Vedaṣ, has been taken to be the subject-matter of the system itself; and so we have been carried very far away from the original idea of its author. Thus, when in more recent years it has come to be studied again as a part of the principal systems of Hindu Philosophy, a great Indian thinker seriously maintains that "it is unnecessary to say much about the unsatisfactory character of the *Pūrva-Mīmāṁsā* as a system of Philosophy"[1]

All the six systems of Philosophy, of which the *Mīmāṁsā* is one, are closely connected together, and present an integrated development of thought: they are consistent in themselves and with one another, so that, when all their speculations are put together, they constitute a complete whole. But this becomes clear only when the *Sūtras* are interpreted in their proper perspective, and not with a particular bias or pre-possession. Indeed, it is this predilection of critics and commentators during several centuries in the past that has led the reader astray from the simple and direct treatment of their subject-matter, and caused so much confusion about their character.

---

1. *Indian Philosophy* by Dr. S. Radhakrishnan, Vol. II, p. 428.

It is possible to interpret the text of the Sacred Books in many ways; but there are three principal methods of interpretation—the grammatical method, the logical method, and a symbolic method. Every text should be approached by means of the first method, and the sense yielded by it should be put together in a logical manner. But if that does not yield a rational or consistent meaning, a resort may be had to the third method. Indeed, it has been observed that "the names occurring in them (the Vedas) are of universal applicability, and do not have any historical reference. *Viśvāmitra* means 'the all-friendly' and not any historical character[1];" and in view of the abstract character of the Sacred Books of the Hindus, it is essential that the different systems of Philosophy and other basic texts should be properly interpreted and made available to the reader.

The Bharati Research Institute, Delhi, has been started to fulfil this long-felt need, and to help in the advancement of a proper knowledge of the Sacred Books of the Hindus. It is proposed to bring out two series at present—entitled a Library of Hindu Philosophy and Religion, and a Library of Sanskṛt Classics. The first series opens with the present volume,—a rendering of the *Mīmāṁsā*—one of the six great systems of Hindu Philosophy, the importance of which need not be re-emphasised. It is a free, but an accurate, translation of *Jaimini's Mīmāṁsā Sūtras,* made without reliance on any *Bhāṣya, Vṛtti,* or school of thought of this system. The *Sanskṛt* text has also been appended for ready reference.

The whole work is purely original, and the author of this volume, Dr. N.V. Thadani, has devoted thirty years of life to a study of the Sacred Books. His earlier work in this field—*The Mystery of the Mahābhārata*— was published in five volumes about eighteen years ago; but it met with scant recognition on account of the novelty of its approach to the Epic, which it regarded as an account of the different systems of Hindu Philosophy and Religion in story-form, and tried to explain it as such in accordance with the method of interpretation now

1. *Indian Philosophy* by Dr. S. Radhakrishnan, Vol. II, p. 392.

discovered in the *Mīmāṁsā*. Dr. Thadani has since widened his field of inquiry, and translated the *Sūtras* of all the six systems of Hindu Philosophy, and the present volume is the first to be published in this series.

The present writer must admit that, as he had been initiated into *Śāstric* studies from the orthodox point of view, when he saw Dr. Thadani's rendering of the *Sūtras* for the first time, he was filled with no small misgiving about the possibility of its yielding any satisfactory results. But when he examined the entire method of rendering them more carefully, and found how close was its fidelity to grammatical rules, he felt that it could not be rejected out of hand; and before long he saw that the whole idea was consistent throughout, and maintained a uniform level of thought. He then remembered that there were suggestions of this line of thought even among ancient scholiasts, and felt that Dr. Thadani's translation could not in reason be set aside.

Indeed, the one thing that would be patent to even the most casual reader of this work is that it contains a complete unity of thought and expression throughout. According to the *Sāstras*[1] there is a fourfold consistency of interpretation: consistency as regards inter-related systems of thought *(Śāstra-saṅgatiḥ);* consistency within the system itself *(Adhyāya saṅgatiḥ);* consistency of each topic with the rest *(pāda saṅgatiḥ);* and consistency between all sections *(Adhikaraṇa saṅgatiḥ)*. The learned author has been chiefly concerned with consistency in all its aspects; and though he differs widely from the available interpretations of the various systems of thought recognised by the orthodox scholars, his work cannot fail to strike not only as grammatically correct, but also as wholly consistent in its own way.

Dr. Thadani has further amplified and illustrated his scheme of thought in an exhaustive Introduction, which too will be found to be equally consistent.

We believe that the work will bear fruit, and the devoted labours of many years will open a new vista for inquiry and

1. Introduction to Bhāṭṭa-dīpikā (N.S. Edition), p. 4.

research along new lines, and lead scholars to a fresh study of our Sacred Books, and to re-interpret them according to the method of interpretation explained by *Jaimini* in the *Mīmāṁsā*. The present volume will be followed by a rendering of the five remaining systems of Hindu Philosophy at an early date.

—S. N. Shastri

PREFACE

It is not without some hesitation that I am releasing the present work—a translation of the *Mīmāṁsā Sūtras* of *Jaimini*—the longest and, perhaps, the least understood of all the six principal systems of Hindu Philosophy, for a more regular course would have been to begin with the *Sāṅkhya,* and then go on to the other systems. But, for reasons explained in the Introduction, it has been necessary to do so, in order that the reader may be able to form an idea of the real character of the Sacred Books of the Hindus.

The present work is an attempt at a simple, but a reasonably accurate, translation of the original text. A purely literal rendering of a work, even in a modern language, would make difficult reading; and an English version of so simple a book as the *Bhagavad Gītā* has often to deviate from the original idiom to be understood. This difficulty is greatly increased in the case of the *Sūtras* of Hindu Philosophy; for they are not short, pithy, and independent utterances of great truths, as is commonly believed—but brief, exact, and clearly defined statements of great ideas, which are closely knit together and need to be properly understood. It would have been possible to translate each *Sūtra* literally and separately; but, while that may have been more exact and accurate, it would have broken up the unity of thought and continuity of expression of the work as a whole, and that was perhaps even more important. It was accordingly necessary to steer a middle course, and that has been attempted in the present work.

A correct translation of the text depends on three main factors: appropriate meanings of words used in the *Sūtras,* a just connection between the parts of a *Sūtra,* and a proper correlation between one *Sūtra* and another. But it is not always easy to satisfy these conditions, simple as they appear to be; for words in *Sanskṛt* have often a large number of meanings, out of which a proper selection has to be made; and a wrong choice can heap error on error without end. Indeed, the chief difficulty in getting at a properly connected meaning of the text would be due to this; and it is complicated by the idea, commonly held by scholars, that each *Sūtra* is complete or almost complete in itself. Nor is the language of the text always free from ambiguity, and extreme conciseness has often been gained at the expense of clarity of expression; while a total absence of punctuation within a *Sūtra* makes it difficult to disentangle its parts. But, even as the author of the *Vedānta Sūtras* tells us, it requires calmness, patience, and devotion to the task to be able to enter into the spirit of the text; and once we succeed in grasping its form and mode of expression, it is not difficult to get at the correct meaning; and the whole idea is then found to be consistent and continuous from end to end. This applies not only to the *Mīmāṁsā,* but to all systems of Philosophy composed in this form.

I should like to take this opportunity of thanking all those who have assisted me or lightened my task. I am very grateful to Dr. S. N. Shastri of Hindu College, who, at great cost of time and trouble, has gone through the entire rendering, *Sūtra* by *Sūtra,* and made some very valuable suggestions. He has also read some of the proofs and interested himself in the publication of the work. I am also very thankful to the authorities of the Sri Aurobindo Ashram at Pondicherry, for the assistance they have rendered in printing the book, – more specially the Mother, Dr. Indra Sen, and Mr. N. D. Gupta, Manager of the Press. But my deepest debt of gratitude is due to my wife who, with rare self-denial, has lightened my task, and enabled me to do my work. It was she who started me on the study of the *Mahābhārata* thirty years ago, and has throughout been a source of great comfort to me.

—N.V. Thadani

CONTENTS

ABBREVIATIONS

Adi P.	*Ādi Parva* of the *Māhābhārata*
Ait. Ar. Up.	*Aitareya Araṇyaka Upaniṣad*
AV.	*Atharva Veda*
BhG.	*Bhagavad Gītā*
Ch. Up.	*Chāndogya Upaniṣad*
Kauṣ. Up.	*Kauṣītakī Upaniṣad*
MBh.	*Mahābhārata*
MM.	*The Mystery of the Mahābhārata*
MS.	*Mimāṁsā Sūtras*
MWD.	Monier William's Sanskṛt English Dictionary
NS.	*Nyāya Sūtras*
RV.	*Ṛg Veda*
SBE.	The Sacred Books of the East
SK.	*Sānkhya Kārikā*
SS.	*Sānkhya Sūtras*
ŚBr.	*Śatapatha Brāhmaṇa*
Śānti P.	*Śānti Parva* of the *Mahābhārata*
Tait. Up.	*Taittīyak Upaniṣad*
Up.	*Upaniṣad*
VS.	*Vaiśeṣika Sūtras*
Ved. S.	*Vedānta Sūtras*
YS.	*Yoga Sūtras*

TRANSLITERATION CHART

The letters of the *Sanskṛt* alphabet are usually arranged as follows:—

Vowels a. ā; i, ī; u, ū; ṛ, ṛī;lṛ, lṛī; e, ai; o, au, Anusvāra (.); Visarga (:).

Consonants

Gutturals	*k*	kh	g	gh	ṅ
Palatals	*c*	ch	j	jh	ñ
Linguals	*ṭ*	ṭh	ḍ	ḍh	ṇ
Dentals	*t*	th	d	dh	n
Labials	*p*	ph	b	bh	m

Semi-vowels

Palatal y Lingual *r* Dental *l* Labial *v*

Sibilants

Palatal ś Lingual *ṣ* Dental *s* Aspirate *ḥ*

INTRODUCTION
THE SECRET OF THE SACRED BOOKS OF THE HINDUS

I

THE PROBLEM OF THE SACRED BOOKS

The Sacred Books of the Hindus

The sacred books of the Hindus present a number of problems which have yet to be solved. They have been tackled by various scholars from time to time, but their essential enigma remains. The nineteenth century, and more specially its latter half, witnessed a great awakening of interest in *Sanskṛt* among European scholars, and it has spread to America in more recent years. But the result has fallen short of expectation; and philosophy and religion have, for the most part, given place to history, philology, anthropology, archaeology and antiquarian research. The modern scholar would not indeed deny the moral and spiritual significance of the sacred books; but they are for him but relics of a bygone age, with values and problems entirely different from his own. The Vedas are believed to be the earliest record of the genius of man; but however important to the student of antiquity, it would not be easy to define their moral and spiritual worth, or contribution to the solution of the problems of life. They are said to be four in number—*Ṛk, Sāma, Yajur,* and *Atharva;* and of these the first, which is the oldest, appears to be but a collection of hymns addressed to a number of gods. Some of these are indeed unique in their search after the Infinite; and a number of them have all the characteristics of great poetry. But even a modern Indian philosopher is obliged to refer to them as consisting of "half-formed myths or crude allegories, obscure gropings or immature compositions", although he also finds "a freshness and simplicity and an intellectual charm, as of the breath of spring or the flowers of the morning, about these first efforts of the human mind to comprehend and express the mystery of the universe."[1] The *Sāma Veda* is said to be purely liturgical, containing a number of hymns taken from the *Ṛg Veda,* and meant to be sung at sacrifices. The *Yajur,* like the *Sāma,* is also said to serve the same purpose, and to contain a number of sacrificial formulae, even as its name is believed to imply; while the *Atharva,* which appears to be a later addition and was not included among the original set, is said to contain a number of incantations and charms against evil and disease.

The Difficulty of Understanding

The student of the Vedas has not found it easy to understand them; and both Indian and foreign scholars have formed their own opinions, ranging from their being but "primeval childlike naive prayer of the *Ṛg Veda"* to "allegorical representations of the attributes of the Supreme Deity"; while some would regard them as "sacrificial compositions of a primitive race which attributed great importance to ceremonial rites". At the same time the *Ṛg Veda* is said to be "a work representing the thought of successive generations of thinkers, and so contains within it different strata of thought." The late Sri Aurobindo Ghosh was one of the few among recent thinkers who believed that the Vedas are "replete with suggestions of secret doctrines and mystic philosophies, and looked upon the gods of the hymns as symbols of psychological functions". He was of the opinion that the *Ṛg Veda* belongs to the early period of human thought, "when the spiritual and psychological knowledge of the race was concealed, for reasons now difficult to determine, in a veil of concrete and material figures and symbols, which protected the sense from the profane, and revealed it to the initiated. One of the leading principles of the mystics was the sacredness and secrecy of self-knowledge, and the true knowledge of the gods.

This wisdom was, they thought, unfit for—perhaps even dangerous to—the ordinary human mind, or, in any case, liable to perversion and misuse and loss of virtue, if revealed to vulgar and unpurified spirits. Hence they favoured the existence of an outer worship, effective but imperfect, for the profane, but an inner discipline for the initiate, and clothed their language in words and images which had equally a spiritual sense for the elect, and a concrete sense for the mass of ordinary worshippers. The Vedic hymns are conceived and constructed on these principles." But Sri Aurobindo Ghosh did not explain how all this could be proved to be true, and modern scholars have not been able to follow his lead.[2]

Divisions of the Vedas

The Vedas are the earliest of the sacred books of the Hindus, and all other works are said to be derived from them. Each Veda is divided into two principal parts—*Mantra* and *Brāhmaṇa;* and of these the former is said to be a collection of hymns addressed to a number of gods, and is called *Saṁhitā;* while the latter consists of two parts—*Vidhi* or directions relating to sacrifices, and *Artha-vāda* or explanation of legends connected with the *Mantras*. It is said that out of the *Brāhmaṇa* part of the Vedas arose two sections of Vedic literature,—*Sūtras* or aphoristic rules relating to the performance of all kinds of sacrifices, and *Upaniṣads,* believed to be an exposition of the secret doctrine of the Vedas, and the source of all the great systems of Hindu Philosophy.

Śruti and Smṛti

The Vedas, with their *Mantra* and *Brāhmaṇa* parts, as well as the *Upaniṣads,* are called *śruti,* believed to be revealed knowledge orally communicated to some privileged persons by the Supreme Spirit himself. They are said to have heard and not composed it themselves, and it is for this reason that the works are called *śruti* or "that which is heard". This was succeeded by a vast body of literature, classified as *smṛti,* for it was believed to have been remembered, as the word signifies;

and it is said to include the six *Vedāṅgas* or 'limbs' of the Vedas, the *Sūtras,* including those of the six systems of philosophy, the Law-books of *Manu,* the great Epics of the *Rāmāyaṇa* and the *Mahābhārata,* the eighteen *Purāṇas,* and the *Nīti-śāstras.*

The Problem

But a great body of this literature is difficult to understand; and even when we are able to get what we believe to be the literal meaning of words, they do not appear to make much sense, or have a bearing on what we should regard as of some moral and spiritual value to human life. The *Upaniṣads* indeed contain a considerable body of matter of this kind, and the *Mahābhārata* includes the *Bhagavad Gītā* and a number of discourses on philosophy and religion; but a substantial portion of even these works is difficult to grasp. Nor is it easy to see in what sense the *Upaniṣads* can be described as an exposition of the secret doctrine of the Vedas, when we do not know what that doctrine is; and the Vedas themselves, as we understand them, do not appear to justify the claim that they are a revelation of truth made by the Supreme Spirit himself. The Epics and the *Purāṇas* have their own problems too. The *Rāmāyaṇa* has been described as a Veda; but it is difficult to see in what sense it can be regarded as such; nor is even the life *of Rāma,* believed to be an embodiment of perfection, free from criticism or blame when examined in the light of the text as composed by *Vālmīki.* The *Mahābhārata,* on the other hand, claims to be the fifth or the last of the Vedas; and we are told, in all seriousness, that "that which is in it, is elsewhere; and that which does not occur in it, occurs nowhere else". It would be difficult to conceive of a greater exaggeration if the Epic be as it is commonly understood. The problem of the *Purāṇas* is similar too. They are eighteen in number, and are said to be sacred, and to treat of five great topics—the creation of the universe, its destruction and renovation, the genealogy of gods and the patriarchs, the rule of the *Manus,* and the history of the Solar and the Lunar races; but it would be difficult to conceive of anything more fantastic than what they appear to contain.

The difficulty of understanding the ideas of the ancients is not limited to these works alone; and the *Sūtras* of the six principal systems of Hindu Philosophy are still, for the most part, believed to be unintelligible; and most of our present knowledge of these systems is based on certain commentaries of eminent scholars rather than their text.

All these books are believed to be sacred, and the orthodox are required to accept without question all that they contain; but no one has, so far, been able to explain in a clear, reasoned, and sustained manner what exactly they teach, or the basis of their claim to be regarded as sacred.

The Problem of Hinduism

The problem of Hinduism or the systems of religion that go under that name, is perhaps more difficult still. While there are a large number of gods of the Vedas, the principal deities of the Hindus are three—*Brahmā, Śiva* and *Viṣṇu*—said to be the great Trinity of the Creator, Destroyer, and Sustainer of the universe; but even this distinction is not based on any exact interpretation of the sacred books. Again, while there are innumerable temples dedicated to both *Śiva* and *Viṣṇu* still in existence in the country, the worship of *Brahmā,* believed to be the Creator, has all but disappeared. Then we have Jainism and Buddhism too as among the great systems of religion that had their origin in India; but while Jainism still remains, its more liberal counterpart, Buddhism, has but few traces left. *Buddha,* the reputed founder of Buddhism, is said to be an 'incarnation'or embodiment of the idea of *Viṣṇu,* the highest of the Hindu triad; and yet his *Hīnayāna* school is purely agnostic, and he himself is said to have remained silent when questioned about the existence of God.

The problem of castes, customs and religious laws—of rites, ceremonies and sacrifices—and of rules, forms and modes of worship—still prevalent among the Hindus, is equally intricate; and there are not a few who, finding no rational answer, maintain that Hinduism is but a general name for the life of the people of a country, with a common social order, and held together by common customs, traditions, and laws —culture and forms of worship— rather than a clearly defined system of thought and religion.

The Great Question

The problem, as stated above, is undoubtedly a difficult one, and there are not a few who believe that it cannot be solved. A number of attempts have from time to time been made in the past to answer these questions; but all that has been achieved is either an expression of high, but unsubstantiated, opinion regarding the greatness of the sacred books, or the formation of separate sects with simpler doctrine and more clearly definable creed. The modern thinker appears to have reconciled himself to the general decline of faith as an inevitable consequence of the scientific spirit of the present day; and the only religion he can accept is that which can transform science itself into philosophy, and reason into faith. And the great question is—Can there be such a system of religion? and have the sacred books of the Hindus any contribution to make to the formation of such a one?

REFERENCES

1. *Indian Philosophy* by Dr. S. Radhakrishnan, 1,66.
2. *Ibid* Vol. I, 68-70.

II

THE SECRET OF THE SACRED BOOKS

The Solution of the Problem

The solution of the problem of the sacred books can lie only in the contents of the sacred books themselves. If what we have been taught to understand of them be all that they contain, if the Vedas be but hymns of praise addressed to the gods, and the gods themselves the beings that they are; if the *Sūtras* must still remain unintelligible; and if the 'stories' of the Epics and the *Purāṇas* be nothing but impossible accounts of imaginary deeds, or, in any case, a record of events of a world far removed from our own—we must remain content with the estimate that is generally formed of these works, and cease to think of them as anything more than an exuberant flight of fancy of a 'primitive' people. Indeed, all that we can do in such a case is to sift the fine from the gross, and salvage what we can; and so there are not a few who, unable to find any connection between the 'story' of the *Mahābhārata* and the teachings of the *Bhagavad Gītā,* believe that the latter is but an interpolation, cleverly introduced into the Epic to enable it to partake of its popularity, and make it more current among the people; and so would separate it from the main work.

The Language of the Text

But have we really understood the language of the text of the sacred books, and is it impossible to get some other meaning out of it? This question may well be asked, for these books were composed in the *Sanskṛt* language long before modern nations learned the art of writing; and the earliest, the Vedas, are, according to some, believed to have been written more than five thousand years ago; while few would place them later than 1200 to -1500 B.C.

Language is a record of human thought in relation to ideas, objects, and actions; and the history of a number of modern languages shows that a thousand years are enough to bring about such a change in the human mind, that few, if any, can understand what has been written in the earliest works. This is true of the English language, whose record is unbroken by any great invasion or cataclasm; and there are few, if any, among Englishmen today who can understand the earliest works composed in the old Anglo-Saxon. The same is equally true of a number of modern Indian languages; and it should not be a matter for surprise if a similar change has taken place in *Sanskṛt* too. The earliest of the sacred books, the Vedas, are more than three thousand five hundred years old; and the difficulty of understanding the original sense of the language of the text can easily be grasped when we realise that the *Sūtras* or the 'aphorisms' of the six principal systems of philosophy, which are of a later date, are still 'unintelligible'. If this be the case with the *Sūtras,* the language of which appears to be simple and easy to grasp, there should be little wonder if the original meaning of words used in the earlier works has been forgotten or lost– specially as the country has been subjected to many invasions from time to time, and a number of ancient records must have been destroyed or defaced.

Indeed, if we could re-discover the original meaning of the text of the sacred books, we should be able to reveal their secret; and then it might well be that we find that the traditional view of their character is really true; and that the Vedas, even as the word literally signifies, are books of scientific knowledge, dealing with the laws of Nature and the life of man; and then the idea of their 'revelation' would be 'similar to that of modern discoveries when they are the result of accident or good fortune, rather than persistent human effort. The *Upaniṣads* may then appear to be a clearer exposition of these laws; the *Vedāṅgas* as the real 'limbs' or parts of the Vedas or the knowledge they contain; the six systems of philosophy as an expression of the same idea in a still clearer form; the Epics and the *Purāṇas* as an account of these systems in story-form; and the great systems of religion, which form part of Hinduism – with all its array of architectural design, statuary and carving, painting, music, and poetry – the essence of all the fine arts – together with their gods, forms of worship, ritual and 'sacrifices', but as a magnificent attempt to live in the light of the teachings of the sacred books – or science refined into philosophy, and both sublimated into religion or the art of perfect life. This may mean that the original idea of the sacred books and the different systems of philosophy and religion has been forgotten and lost, and what remains is very different from their ancient conception. But the question still remains – Can all this be proved?

A Retrospect

It is seventeen years since the last of the five volumes of *The Mystery of the Mahābhārata* was published; and I tried to show in that work that the gods of the Vedas represented the great forces of Nature, and their corresponding forms in man; and that their real meaning could be obtained by dividing their names into parts in the same manner as we obtain the meaning of the sacred syllable OM by dividing it into its letters, – A, U, M. I applied this method of interpretation to the story of the *Mahābhārata,* and showed how it transformed the whole of it into an account of the different systems of philosophy and religion; and explained that it was for this reason that the Epic claimed to contain all the great truths of life in the world. The essential character of the *Mahābhārata* is described in its opening chapter, where *Vyāsa,* its celebrated author, is said to have composed the 'story' after he had arranged the Vedas; and we are told that its ideas have been expressed in an intricate form, and it has to be understood in the light of the teachings of all the sacred books, – the *śruti* and the *smṛti*. I pointed out that the Epic is accordingly a 'story' of what is contained in the Vedas and later works, and should be understood in their light.

The work met with a mixed reception. While there were some who believed that this was the correct method of interpreting the sacred books, and there was adequate authority for it in the sacred books themselves – there were a number of those who were of the opinion that it was inconceivable that a whole work like the *Mahābhārata* – the longest in literature could have been composed in a form where the names of all the principal characters, and innumerable other words, had to be broken into parts to be understood. They were prepared to concede that a few of them could perhaps represent objects of Nature or ideas of philosophy, but could not imagine that this could be true of all. The European scholar found in it a great deal that ran counter to what he had learned to believe of the ancients and their life; while the Indian was not prepared to substitute his *Kṛṣṇa,* whom he had loved so well as a human being in real flesh and blood, for a deity who could to him be only an abstraction of an image or an idea, however perfectly personified.

I felt, however, that there were two principal tests applicable to a work of this kind – its character as described in the book itself, and consistency of explanation in accordance with it. There could indeed be no doubt that the *Mahābhārata* has been described in the Epic itself as a 'story' 'of the Vedas, and as containing the sense of all the sacred books. We are told that it explains their 'mystery', and deals with the problems of life and death, the great phenomena of Nature, the divisions of Time, and the language, customs and manners of the people.[1] But the main story, as we read it, narrating the rivalries of the *Kaurava* and *Pāṇḍava* princes – has little to do with these questions. The *Bhagavad Gītā* is indeed a part of the Epic; but it appears to have so little connection with the story, that there are not a few who believe that it is an interpolation; and the introductory statement in regard to the character of the Epic is believed to be an exaggeration, common to writers of that age, and intended only to impress the reader.

I felt, however, that this was not possible; and if there was a method of interpretation by means of which the 'story' itself could be transformed into a description of ideas, and consistently so throughout—and all its strange and fantastic notions disappeared, it could not lightly be rejected. The method of interpretation was based primarily on the division of words into parts, and was warranted by the practice of the ancients themselves; and I thought that there could not, in reason, be any objection to its application over the whole range of the *Mahābhārata* or even the entire body of the sacred books, provided the text remained unchanged and only made better and a more rational sense; and the meanings assigned to the parts of words—letters and syllables—were in general accord with admitted usage and consistent throughout. I realised, however, that if the characters who figure in the Epic were symbolic of ideas and objects, they should retain their attributes, wherever they appeared in any sacred work; and, as the *Mahābhārata* had a number of such characters—specially gods and the sages—who figure in a number of sacred books from the Vedas downwards, I felt that the Epic could not stand alone as a 'story' of different systems of philosophy and religion, and that all other similar works must be of the same kind. I had found that this method of interpretation had given a new meaning to the gods of the Vedas as well as the 'story' of the *Mahābhārata,* and thought that the real idea of the *Rāmāyaṇa* and the *Bhāgavat Purāṇa* must be similar too.

I accordingly applied the same method of interpretation to the *Rāmāyaṇa,* and found that it too was transformed into a 'story' of different systems of philosophy, though on a smaller scale than the *Mahābhārata;* and the conflict between *Rāvaṇa* and *Rāma* was changed into an exposition of the difference between the system of *Brahmā* and the dualistic school of *Viṣṇu*; and it was for this reason that *Rāvaṇa* has been described in the Epic as a 'descendant' of *Brahmā, and Rāma* as half an 'incarnation' or embodiment of the idea of *Viṣṇu.* I then desired to understand the idea of all the ten principal 'incarnations' of *Viṣṇu*—the Fish, the Tortoise, the Boar, the Man-Lion, the

Dwarf, *Paraśurāma, Rāmacandra, Kṛṣṇa, Buddha,* and *Kalki*—and studied the *Bhāgavat Purāṇa* for the purpose. I applied the same method of interpretation, and found that their idea was exactly the same, and that they described the evolution of the idea of God in the same manner as the *Mahābhārata* dealt with the progress of Man from Nature unto God.

All this was the result of this method of interpretation, based primarily on the division of words used in the text into their parts, so that the text itself remained unchanged; and it transformed a number of strange, extraordinary and fantastic 'stories' into simple and consistent accounts of different systems of philosophy and religion, and so placed the ideas of the ancients in an entirely new light. There were the same names, the same words, the same parts, and their meanings were throughout the same—transforming so many 'stories' in works believed to have been composed in different ages, into the same systems of philosophy and religion, with all their points of contact and conflict intact. It then occurred to me that, if all this was true, the main ideas of the Epics and the *Purāṇas* must be found in the systems of philosophy themselves. I had studied these systems in the original—all but the *Pūrva-Mīmāṁsā*—(for that is how the *Mīmāṁsā* is generally called), with such assistance as I could secure, before writing *The Mystery of the Mahābhārata;* but the *Sūtras* had, for the most part, remained unintelligible to me; and most of my conclusions were based on what I could gather from the *Upaniṣads* and the *Mahābhārata.*

I now believed that these *Sūtras* could not really be unintelligible. I also felt that there must be some mention somewhere of a method of interpretation which had yielded such extraordinary results, and had such a wide range of application from the Vedas to the Epics and the *Purāṇas*. Nor was I disappointed. I found that the *Sūtras,* though difficult in parts, yielded, on the whole, to an easy rendering, and contained even more than what I had expected. They were not separate utterances, as is commonly believed; nor was each *Sūtra* complete in itself—an idea which has caused so much confusion about them and rendered them unintelligible. I found that they were connected with one another, and could be grouped together into paragraphs, conveying correlated ideas; nor, with the exception of the *Mīmāṁsā,* did they require much of an explanation to understand them. They also contained a reference to the method of interpretation which I had followed in my study of the sacred books. While there is a broad mention of it in *Nyāya* and a passing reference in the *Vaiśeśika* and *Vedānta,* the *Mīmāṁsā* examines it at considerable length, and explains the reasons for its adoption. It tells us also of a number of other things, and constitutes, even as tradition has taught us to believe, an introduction to the real study of the Vedas; and, as the same ideas have been repeated or amplified in later works, it may be said to contain the secret of the sacred books. It describes the Law of Dharma or good and intelligent action, and tells us that that is the subject-matter of the Vedas, and that the gods are but personifications of the great forces of Nature acting in accordance with this law. It also points out that a number of the hymns of the Vedas make little sense as they are, and that not a few contain strange, extraordinary and inconsistent statements. That, it observes, has deliberately been done to invite special attention to the necessity of finding out a different method of interpretation of the text. It then goes on to explain that there is such a method, and if we understand the text in its light, the whole idea would be transformed into an exposition of the laws of life. It explains and illustrates this method at considerable length, and tells us that the same has to be applied to all sacred books—the *śruti* as well as the *smṛti*. It has accordingly been necessary to publish the whole of the *Mīmāṁsā* first, so as to enable the reader to grasp the fundamental idea of the sacred books, and the method of interpreting them; and the rest will follow in due course.

REFERENCE

1. *Ādi P. l, I,* 17-70; 80-87; 252-256.

III

THE SYSTEMS OF HINDŪ PHILOSOPHY

Connected Systems of Thought

But the *Mīmāṁsā* does not stand alone, and needs to be understood in its relation to the other systems of philosophy, each of which is called a *Darśana,* which means "a vision or a point of view". Indeed, it would be found on examination, that they are all but different points of view from which we can survey the great problem of life. Life is too large to be seen from a single angle; and so the ancients conceived of the idea of examining it from six different points of view, according to the instrument of knowledge used for the purpose; and it is for this reason that these systems are spoken of as *Darśanas*. We shall presently see what these points of view are; but it follows from this that each of them, taken by itself, should be incomplete; while all of them, taken together, include all that the ancients knew at the time. Unfortunately, however, each of them has been regarded as a complete system by itself; or they are at best taken in pairs—with the result that there has been a great deal of confusion and conflict of thought in regard to their real idea. Indeed, as has been observed, the original *Sūtras* are generally regarded as unintelligible; and the student has, for the most part, been obliged to be guided by the opinion of commentators who, though extremely learned and eminent in their own way, confined themselves to but a few of these systems, and regarded them as complete; but, finding that they did not fit into their own scheme of thought, imported their own ideas into them. Nor did they feel bound to limit their exposition to the language of the *Sūtras,* which they conceived to be but independent utterances, complete in themselves, and more like pivots of thought, round which a great body of ideas—their own and of the ancients— could move; and so they felt free to make their own contributions to these systems.

But a proper study of the *Sūtras* shows that they are not only not unintelligible, but that a single thread of thought runs through all of them; and that, while each system constitutes its own special body of thought, it serves as a stepping stone to the following one; and all of them, taken together, make a great indivisible whole—so that, as the *Sāṅkhya* is the first and *Vedānta* the last—the question posed in the first *Sūtra* of the former has its final answer in the last *Sūtra* of *Vedānta.*

This is not a mere statement of a personal opinion, for the character of the systems of philosophy has been described in the *Vedānta Sūtras* themselves, and the whole idea may be summarised as follows:

> All systems of philosophy are equally important, for no single system can be regarded as all-comprehensive; and the whole range of thought has been divided among them just as we may divide the number hundred into parts to enable us to understand it. At the same time each of them has its own point of view; and we approve of this division, for it enables us to appreciate them (III, iv, 9-14).
>
> But there are some who believe that these divisions are arbitrary, and this has led to a conflict of opinion (III, iv, 15-16).
>
> But, so far as we are aware, this is the view only of those who have a limited experience of the laws of life, and it is rejected by *Jaimini*[1]. According to *Bādarāyaṇa,*[2] we can prove our point, for this division is based on reason, and we can clearly explain its whole principle, which is not meant merely to glorify these systems (III, iv, 17-21).
>
> It is not difficult to do so, for we are able to get the meaning of the text from the words themselves. There is no uncertainty about them, because they are all properly described. Nor are there any symbolic expressions like 'kindling the fire', etc.; and there is a proper connection of cause and effect in

their ideas, which have their counterparts in the *śruti*. But it is necessary to have calmness and self-control to be able to understand them[3] (III, iv, 22-27).

Division of Thought in the Systems

A proper study of the systems of philosophy will show that they are characterised by clearly defined divisions of thought. Thus we might observe that all knowledge is from the known to the unknown; and the known is the world of Nature around us, while its knower is Man. All knowledge is accordingly based on the relation between the two—Nature and Man—out of which arises the idea of the Unknown, which we may describe as the Unmanifest or God. The *Sāṅkhya,* the first of these systems of philosophy, accordingly makes a rapid survey of all that the ancients knew of the great principles of Nature; and, assuming it to be the supreme creator of things, examines the different problems of life in its light. It has, therefore, no place for God as a creator in its scheme; and its final conclusion is that the soul of man is different from all that is in Nature, and that it can attain to freedom from sorrow and pain—the end of all our quest in the world—by devoting itself to pure self-knowledge, and refraining from all action which arises from Nature or *Prakṛti*.

The whole problem thus resolves itself into the attitude of man to knowledge and action on the one hand, and the idea of Nature or God as the supreme creator of the universe, on the other. As the knower of all this is man, we can examine it in the light of his different faculties,—his senses, mind, *ahaṅkāra*[4] (or the I-as-an-actor), intellect and the soul; and corresponding to these we have the five remaining systems of philosophy—*Nyāya, Vaiśeṣika, Mīmāṁsā, Yoga,* and *Vedānta*. As we shall presently see, *Nyāya* deals with the question in the light of the function of the senses, conceives of God as a mere on-looker of things, and lays special emphasis on knowledge as the goal of life. The *Vaiśeṣika* does so in the light of the character of the mind, conceives of an Unknown Power which has a share in the shaping of things, and, while stressing the importance of knowledge, brings out the idea of action too. The *Mīmāṁsā* considers it in the light of the character of *ahaṅkāra* or the I-as-an-actor, ever ready to act—conceives of action as of the essence of life, and as including knowledge itself, and speaks of the great forces of Nature as acting intelligently and for the benefit of all, and so sustaining the universe. *Yoga* examines it in the light of the character of the intellect, gives God a special place in the scheme of life, and, though it admits the importance of action, still concludes on knowledge as the final end. Lastly, *Vedānta* examines the whole problem in the light of the character of the soul itself which, unlike the *Sāṅkhya,* it does not regard as altogether different from all that is in Nature; and so it conceives of *Brahmā* or God as including all that is in the universe, and regards knowledge and action but as counterparts of the same energy of the soul; and tells us that real freedom is achieved only when a person attains to equilibrium in the midst of action and the experience of pleasure and pain. As will be observed, *Vedānta* contains the most trenchant criticism of the *Sāṅkhya,* and its last *Sūtra* provides an answer to the question raised in the opening *Sūtra* of that system.

Pairs of Systems

All human faculties are connected together, and some of them in a special way; and corresponding to this the six systems of philosophy are often grouped together into three pairs—*Sāṅkhya* and *Yoga, Nyāya* and *Vaiśeṣika,* and *Mīmāṁsā* and *Vedānta*—also called *Pūrva-Mīmāṁsā* and *Uttara-Mīmāṁsā* respectively. The *Sāṅkhya* and *Yoga* are grouped together, because, as we have observed, *Yoga* is based on the character of the intellect, and the *Sāṅkhya* too, though it has its own ideas of Nature, soul, and God—attempts to evolve a rational system of thought and to provide a rational soultion to the fundamental problem of life, freedom from sorrow and pain; and so both *Sāṅkhya* and *Yoga* are based on the character of the intellect, although their conclusions are not the same; and it is for this reason that the *Bhagavad Gītā* speaks of the basic identity of the two.[5]

Similarly, as *Nyāya* is based on the character of the senses, and *Vaiśeṣika* on that of the mind, and there is a vital connection between the two, there is a corresponding connection between these systems, and they too are often taken together.

There is a similar connection between *ahaṅkāra* and the soul. According to the *Sāṅkhya, ahaṅkāra* or the I-as-an-actor evolves out of the intellect, because action can take place only after there is a decision to act, and the latter is the function of the intellect. Again, the *Sāṅkhya* maintains that all things in the universe, including the intellect, *ahaṅkāra,* mind, the senses, the 'elements' and their properties—indeed everything except the soul—is a creation of Nature or *Prakṛti;* and so it attempts to make a clear distinction between *ahaṅkara* and the soul. But it does not succeed, because it is obliged to admit that, though the soul is, according to it, different from *ahaṅkāra,* it identifies itself with it through lack of knowledge, and imagines that it is an actor itself; and it cannot explain why, since it is really so different, it should be affected by ignorance, and do so. The question is really answered by *Vedānta,* which tells us that the soul is for ever linked up with a 'subtle body', which partakes of the character of the essence of the intellect, mind, and the senses, and so cannot be dissociated from all that is in Nature. It accordingly maintains that the soul and *ahaṅkāra* are but two aspects of the same entity; and when the soul is engaged in action, it is spoken of as *ahaṅkāra;* and when it is not, we speak of it as soul. And corresponding to this there is a close connection between the *Mīmāṁsā* and *Vedānta*—based on the character of *ahaṅkāra* and the soul respectively; and so the one is spoken of as *Pūrva* and the other as *Uttara-Mīmāṁsā*—the beginning and end of all philosophy.

A Joint Work

All this would, however, be possible only if all these systems of philosophy were composed at the same time, and their authors collaborated with one another; and an examination of their form and subject-matter warrants such a conclusion.[6] Indeed, there are clear references to *Nyāya, Vaiśeṣika* and *Yoga* in the *Sāṅkhya;* while *Vedānta* constitutes the most powerful criticism of this system. At the same time the opinions of *Jaimini* and *Bādarāyaṇa*—the celebrated authors of *Mīmāṁsā* and *Vedānta*—quoted freely in their respective systems, go clearly to show that they were contemporaries.

The Problem of Dates

It would indeed be difficult, if not impossible, to fix the chronology of the sacred books, even of the systems of philosophy—with any degree of accuracy, for the ancients had their own conception of Time; and so we have, for the most part, to depend on internal evidence, that of the works themselves. There are, however, not a few who would assign widely different dates to these systems, so that the question of their being a joint work of contemporaries cannot, so far as they are concerned, arise. Some of them would go so far as to maintain that the *Sāṅkhya,* in its present form, was composed in about the fourteenth century A.D., mainly on the ground that we have no certain knowledge of its reputed author, *Kapila;* and *Mādhava,* the author of the *Sarva-darśana-saṅgraha,* who lived in the sixteenth century A.D., makes no mention of the *Sāṅkhya,* and gives an account of the *Sāṅkhya-kārikā* of *Iśvara-Kṛṣṇa* instead.[7] In this connection it may be of interest to point out that *Iśvara-Kṛṣṇa* himself refers to the *Muni* (who can only be *Kapila*[8]), as the author of the work on which he had based his own; and states that it consists of sixty topics, and that he had written his own after a careful study and grasp of the original, and had omitted its short tales and subjects of controversy.[9] An examination of the *Sūtras* of the *Sāṅkhya* in its present form will show that the statement of *Iśvara-Kṛṣṇa* is true in every part,—for this system really consists of sixty topics, and the character of the *Sāṅkhya-kārikā* is indeed as its author has described it to be. As *Isvara-Kṛṣṇa* is believed to have lived in the first century A.D., this may enable us to fix the date of the *Sāṅkhya* and other systems, as also of still earlier works.

It has been stated by *Iśvara-Kṛṣṇa* that he had composed the *Kārikā* after properly understanding the original text, implying that it was not easy to understand the *Sāṅkhya* even in his days. These *Sūtras* are still believed to be largely unintelligible; but it may be presumed that they were not exactly so in his time, still not quite easy to grasp. The history of modern languages shows that it takes nearly a thousand years for the original forms of expression to lose their meaning; and, if we apply the same test to *Sanskṛt,* the *Sūtras* of the *Sāṅkhya,* which appeared to be difficult to understand even in the days of *Iśvara-Kṛṣṇa,* must have been composed before the eighth century B.C. Indeed, as all the six systems of philosophy must have been composed at the same time, the date of composition of all would be the same.

We can fix the approximate date of composition of the Vedas in the same manner. The *Mīmāṁsā* tells us that the original meaning of the Vedas had been lost in the days of *Jaimini,* that is, the eighth century B.C. Indeed, it appears from what has been stated in the *Mīmāṁsā,* that the original idea of even the *smṛtis*—the Epics and the *Purāṇas*—had all but disappeared. The latter works must accordingly have been composed a few hundred years earlier, that is, between 1500 and 2000 B.C., while the Vedas a few hundred years earlier still, that is, between 2000 and 2500 B.C. The Vedas may indeed belong to a still earlier period, for they have always been regarded as sacred, and persistent attempts must have been made not only to preserve their original form, but also their original meaning. In any case they are not likely to be earlier than about three thousand B.C., and there can be little wonder if their original meaning has been forgotten or lost.

An Essence of the Sacred Books—

As the systems of philosophy contain an essence of the sacred books, it would be convenient to give a summary of their *Sūtras,* as that will enable the reader not only to have a proper idea of the place of the *Mīmāṁsā,* but also to understand the range of thought of the ancients and the character of the sacred books.

REFERENCES

1. The celebrated author of the *Mīmāṁsā.*
2. The celebrated author of the *Vedānta Sūtras.*
3. It would be found on examination that this is the real character of the language of the *Sūtras.* They are accordingly not only not unintelligible, but, comparatively speaking, easy to understand.
4. The word *ahaṅkāra,—aham-kāra,* means literally "*(aham)* I as an *(kāra)* actor". This is the original idea of the word; and its meaning as egosim, or something that needs to be repressed, is a subsidiary one. It is sometimes

identified with *abhimāna,* which is said to be an erroneous conception regarding one's self or the soul – the meaning being that the soul is really not an actor, but when through an error of thought we regard it as such, it may be described as *ahaṅkāra. Ahaṅkāra* is thus the soul erroneously conceived to be an actor; but when we distinguish it from the soul, it may be said to be an instrument of action like the senses, mind, etc.

5. BhG. V. 4-5.
6. Dr. S. Radhakrishnan is of the opinion that the whole tone and manner of composition of the *Sūtras* suggests that they belong apparently to the same period, and believes that these systems must have existed in some form before the Christian era (*Indian Philosophy,* II, 23).
7. *Sāṅkhya-pravacana-bhāṣya* by Richard Garbe, Harvard Oriental Series, Vol. II, Preface, p. ix. Also *Indian Philosophy* by Dr. S. Radhakrishnan, II, 255-256.
8. Cf. BhG. X, 26.
9. *Sāṅkhya-kārikā,* LXIX-LXXIII.

IV

THE SĀṄKHYA SYSTEM

The Sāṅkhya

The *Sāṅkhya* is the first of the six principal systems of philosophy, and is said to have been composed by the celebrated ascetic *Kapila*. The word *Sāṅkhya* means 'relating to numbers', as well as 'rational, discriminative'; and this system partakes of both these characteristics, for it enumerates certain topics or categories of ideas, and at the same time is essentially rational in its outlook, maintaining that we can attain to freedom from the sorrows of life by means of pure knowledge or discrimination.

Six Chapters and Sixty Topics

It is divided into six chapters and, as the author of the *Sāṅkhya-kārikā* has observed, deals with sixty topics—twenty-seven in the first, nine in the second, six in the third, four in the fourth, twelve in the fifth, and two in the last. There is little repetition of thought in the first two chapters, and only a few points are re-emphasised in the following three; but the whole idea is summed up again in the last chapter, and so it contains only two new topics. It would be convenient to give a summary of the whole.

CHAPTER- I

THE PROBLEM OF LIFE

The object of a man's life is to put an end to all pain, for freedom from pain alone is real freedom. The soul is kept in bondage by *Prakṛti,* but it cannot be so for ever (1-33).

Life is governed by a number of laws—of change, of cause and effect, of death, and of action and actionlessness, all of which require knowledge to understand (34-59). But the knowledge of things not visible to the eye is acquired by means of inference. All knowledge has a bearing on *Prakṛti* or Nature; and we can know by means of inference that it is originally in a state of rest, and then evolves into its various forms of life,—intellect, *ahaṇkāra* or the I-as-an-actor, mind, the senses of knowledge and action, and the 'elements' and their properties (60-66).

Prakṛti is the first cause of things—including intellect, *ahaṅkāra* and the mind; and the first cause can neither be the atom, nor action, nor the soul (67-85).

It is necessary to have knowledge to understand all this; and, in order to have knowledge, we must know the means of acquiring it. There are three such means,—*pratyakṣa* or sense-perception, *anumāna* or inference, and *śabda* or the testimony of the true and the wise; and it is necessary to understand their scope and character (86-103).

In this connection we must remember that the soul is not an actor, but only an experiencer of the result of action. It is something real, for the unreal cannot exist (104-120).

In order to understand the problem of life, we must know the real significance of destruction and creation, the character of substances and the three *Guṇas,* and the function of the intellect and the soul; and this will enable us to understand the meaning of freedom and bondage (121-164).

I[1]. The Object of Human Life

The whole object of a man's life is to put an end to all kinds of pain; but the remedy for this is not physical (1-6).[2]

II. Freedom and its Importance

Freedom means freedom from pain; and it implies that a person should know what it is, and it should be possible for him to attain it (7-11).

III. The Soul and its Bondage

The soul is eternal—that is, it is not subject to time or place. But it is kept in bondage by *Prakṛti* or Nature; and it is not an actor, though it is associated with *Prakṛti*. But it cannot be kept in bondage for ever. The association of the soul with *Prakṛti* or Nature is its bondage; but it does not arise from ignorance, for ignorance does not inhere in the soul (12-33).

IV. The Law of Change

All things, except the soul, are subject to change (34-37).

V. The Law of Cause and Effect

It is necessary to understand the relation of cause and effect, and have a knowledge of the laws of Nature (38-41).

VI. The Law of Death

There is also the law of Death; but a knowledge of it cannot put an end to pain (42-47).

VII. The Law of Action and Actionlessness

The object of life—namely, cessation of pain, cannot be achieved by means of any course of action; and so we may conclude that we can succeed only by means of actionlessness or renunciation of all action (48-59).

VIII. Prakṛti and its Creation

The knowledge of things not visible to the eye is obtained by means of inference; and it is by its means that we understand that there is at first a state of equilibrium of the three *Guṇas;* and it is this that is called *Prakṛti.*[3] Then, when the course of life begins, we can understand that *Prakṛti* evolves into intellect, *ahaṅkāra* (the I-as-an-actor, which includes the mind),[4] the five subtle properties of the five great 'elements', the ten senses, and the five great 'elements'.[5] All these, together with the soul, make a total of twenty-five[6] (60-66).

IX. Prakṛti is the First Cause of Things

When we trace the origin of things through an uninterrupted series of objects, we find that the only conclusion at which we can arrive is that *Prakṛti* is the original cause of things (67-70).

X. Creation of Intellect, Ahaṅkāra, and Mind

From *Prakṛti* arises *Mahat* or the intellect, the first activity of which is the mind, and the last *ahaṅkāra*[7] and the latter acts by means of the senses of knowledge and action (71-73).

XI. The Atom is not the Original Cause of Things

When we trace the original cause of things through an uninterrupted series of objects, we come at last to the atom. But it cannot be regarded as the original cause of things, because it is derived from something else (74-80).

XII. Action is not the Original Cause

Action cannot be regarded as the original cause, for it has an origin itself (namely, the actor) (81).

XIII. The Individual Soul is not the Original Cause

Nor can we regard the individual soul as the original cause, because it is subject to birth, and it is only the perfect one that is not born again. Again, things give birth to their likes; and so, if the soul had been the original cause, it would have created only souls, and not the objects we see (82-85).

XIV. The Means of Acquiring Knowledge

It is necessary to have a correct notion of things, which requires proper means of acquiring definite knowledge. There are three such means, –*pratyakṣa* or the evidence of the senses, *anumāna* or inference, and *śabda* or the testimony of the true and the wise. We can prove anything by means of these (86-88).

XV. Pratyakṣa

Pratyakṣa is the knowledge of a real substance with a real form, acquired by means of impressions that it makes on us. However, it cannot prove the existence of God (89-92).

XVI. The Existence of God cannot be Proved

It is impossible to prove the existence of God – for we can conceive of Him only as free or not free, and in either case He cannot be regarded as the original creator of life. But His idea can correspond to that of a liberated soul; but that will only be a magnified conception of such a soul, which is itself not an actor, and can only be regarded as an on-looker of things (93-99).

XVII. Anumāna

Anumāna or inference consists in an uninterrupted appearance of certain things, which are known to be always connected with or dependent on one another (100).

XVIII. Sabda

Śabda or oral authority is the teaching of a true and trustworthy person, and is a valid means of acquiring knowledge like *anumāna* (101-103).

XIX. The Soul is not an Actor

Pleasure abides in the mind and not the soul; and the soul is not an actor, but only an experiencer of the result of action. Hence it cannot be an actor, for it cannot be both an actor and experiencer at the same time (104-107).

XX. The Unreal cannot Exist

If an object is out of reach of the senses or is minute, we can know of it by means of the effect it produces; but an unreal thing cannot be proved to exist like a man with horns. Nor can we say that there is action when there is apparently none (108-120).

XXI. The Meaning of Destruction

Destruction is really dissolution or absorption into the original cause or principle from which a thing emanates, and not annihilation or reduction to nothingness (121).

XXII. The Law of Birth

Things give birth to things like their own (122-123).

XXIII. Character of Substances

A thing that is produced out of something else cannot be eternal or all-pervading. It is subject to action or change, is distinct from and dependent on other things, and has its own characteristics and form; but it is not altogether different from all other things (124-125).

XXIV. The Three Guṇas

All created things are characterised by the three *Guṇas* and a state of unconsciousness, all of which belong to *Prakṛti,* which is accordingly the original cause of all. Love, hate, and insensibility are the different characteristics of the three *Guṇas,* which affect all creatures, though they may have different or opposite qualities in respect of one another (126-128).

XXV. The Function of the Intellect

There is a difference between cause and effect, though they have something in common too; and it is the function of the intellect to point out all this. But intellect has its own limitations too; and it is for this reason that we have to think of *Prakṛti* or the soul as superior to it. It is the function of the intellect to infer cause from effect; and we cannot deny its existence, nor that of Dharma or the moral law of life (129-138).

XXVI. The Character of the Soul

The soul is different from the body, which is dependent on it. It is different from the body because it is without any

Guṇas; and, as it is the latter that make for action, the soul cannot act. It can only be an experiencer or on-looker of things. It is different from the body, because a thing is said to be lifeless and is cast away when the soul ceases to abide in it. It is different from the intellect and the mind, for the latter partake of the *Guṇas,* whereas the soul does not. We cannot deny the existence of the soul—for it is the soul that feels pain, the removal of which is the chief object of a man's life. The state of sound sleep also proves the existence of the soul and its difference from the body (139-148).

There are an infinite number of souls, each different from the other, for the birth of each is different; but the same soul may occupy different bodies in different births, for it is born again and again. The form of the body can be changed, but not of the soul dwelling in it. In any case we must agree that it is the same soul that dwells in the same body during a life-time. The sacred books all agree that the same soul is born again and again; and that is so because of its attachment to the world; and the body in which it is born is the visible form of its bondage (149-159).

XXVII. Freedom and Bondage

The two states of existence—life in this world and freedom from bondage—are inconsistent with each other. We cannot deny that there is bondage; and the very idea of indifference to the world is a proof of its reality. But the soul is not an actor, and only believes that it is so under the influence of the intellect, to which it is closely allied, and which darkens its light of pure knowledge (160-164).

REFERENCES

1. The Roman figures refer to the numbers of topics in this system.
2. The figures in brackets refer to the numbers of *Sūtras* in the text.
3. We cannot understand the idea of action without reference to a state of rest Indeed, there has to be a state of rest, however brief, before there can be

action. The evolution of *Prakṛti* or Nature into different forms of life is a form of action; and so it must be preceded by a state of rest or equilibrium. As, however, we cannot know the original state of the substance out of which all life evolves, we come to the conclusion that it must be one of rest before it begins to act; and we do so by means of inference.

The *Sāṅkhya* does not explain the idea of the *Guṇas* in any detail; and that is done by the following systems.

4. The *Sāṅkhya* tells us that the mind arises out of *ahaṅkāra* (II, 18-19), but does not explain how. That is done by *Nyāya,* which tells us that "its origin lies in its connection with the result of previous action" (III, ii, 60).

5. The *Sāṅkhya* does not describe the 'elements' or their attributes, or the ten senses or their connection with the 'elements' and their attributes. That is done by the following systems. It may be explained as follows:

'ELEMENTS'.	ETHER	AIR	FIRE	WATER	EARTH
ATTRIBUTES:	Sound	Touch	From	Taste	Smell
SENSES OF KNOWLEDGE:	Ears	Skin	Eyes	Tongue	Nose
SENSES OF ACTION:	Legs	Arms	Tongue (for speech)	Organ of Creation	Organ of Excretion

The ancient idea of an "element" was different from that of the present-day science. It was conceived as a great "elemental" substance, or a great and fundamental object of Nature.

6. The total of twenty-five is made up of (i) *Prakṛti* in a state of rest or unmanifest form; (2-4) intellect, *ahaṅkāra,* and mind; (5-9) the five great 'elements'; (10-14) the five attributes of the 'elements'; (15-19) the five senses of knowledge; (20-24) the five senses of action; and (25) *puruṣa* or the individual soul.

This is the idea of *puruṣa* (individual soul) and *Prakṛti* in the *Sāṅkhya;* and it has no place for God as a creator in its scheme.

7. The special characteristic of the intellect is decision; of the mind desire; and of *ahaṅkāra* action. This statement of the *Sāṅkhya* means that decision and desire are closely connected together, and are followed by action. We have already been told that *ahaṅkāra* arises from the intellect; and the *Sāṅkhya* tells us more clearly in the following chapter (II, 18-19) that the mind is produced from *ahaṅkāra*. The present statement needs therefore to be understood in its proper light. How the mind arises from *ahaṅkāra* is explained by *Nyāya*.

CHAPTER-II

THE LAW OF ACTION

The whole world exists either for the sake of the soul or of *Prakṛti;* and the proof of it lies in the nature of desire and the character of *Prakṛti* (1-6).

Desire arises from the mind or the intellect; and we must know the nature of both, which involves that of *ahaṅkāra* or the I-as-an-actor too (7-19). At the same time we must safeguard against certain errors in regard to the idea of action and the character of the mind (20-27).

Action involves the function of the senses as well as of *prāṇa* or vital breath; and it is of many kinds. It can be painful as well as not painful; but it is only when all kinds of actions come to an end that a person feels happy and free (28-35).

There are a number of factors of action—the senses, mind, *ahaṅkāra,* intellect, as well as an Unseen Power (36-47).

XXVIII. The Purpose of the Universe

The whole world exists either for the sake of the soul or of *Prakṛti;* and the proof of it lies in the nature of desire and the real character *of Prakṛti* (1-6).

XXIX. The Origin and Scope of Desire

Desire of all kinds arises from the mind or the intellect, and creation itself is the result of desire. All this exists for the sake of the soul, as we find from an examination of country, time and place (7-12.)

XXX. Intellect

Intellect means the understanding of objects by means of mental effort, and its special function is to settle Dharma (13-15).

XXXI. Ahaṅkāra

Ahaṅkāra is an erroneous conception regarding one's self, and it acts in association with the ten senses and the mind and the five properties of the 'elements' (16-17).

XXXII. Mind

The mind is characterised by the quality of goodness, and is produced from *ahaṅkāra*. It dwells within, and functions through the senses of knowledge and action (18-19).

XXXIII. Certain Ideas and Errors

We see that *ahaṅkāra* can act, but not material things. We also know that a person must cease to act, but not at the commencement of his life, and the idea of it arises when he thinks of death. It is only confused people who mix up things and believe that, since the senses are different, there can be no unity in action; and they hold that the mind is of the nature of the senses. There are some who believe that the difference between things arises from the effect of the passage of time (20-27).

XXXIV. The Senses

The senses of knowledge and action have their respective attributes which do not change, and their special functions are to see, hear, etc. The whole manner of action is affected by *prāṇa* or vital breath; and the action of the senses can be regular as well as irregular (28-32).

XXXV. Action and its Cessation

There are five kinds of activity—painful and not painful; and when they all cease, a person attains to calmness, aversion to all desire, and health of body and mind, and his whole life becomes fragrant and beautiful (33-35).

XXXVI. The Factors of Action an Unseen Power, the Senses, Mind, Ahaṅkāra, and Intellect

There is an Unseen Power; and when we say that all action is for the sake of the soul, it is because we give prominence to the idea of this Power. Action consists of thirteen parts, the function of the ten senses—and the mind, *ahaṅkāra* and the intellect, which constitute an internal organ. Of these the most important is the intellect, for it puts together or arranges all things. We know this by means of memory and inference; but we cannot trace the origin of the intellect, for it is not self-illuminated. But it is the most powerful factor of action, and it is for that reason that it is honoured most (36-47).

CHAPTER- III

MAN AND THE UNIVERSE

There is a law of life according to which things with special characteristics arise from those which are without such special characteristics; and the whole world is subject to this law (1-5).

But the ultimate origin of all things is beyond what is differentiated or not differentiated. Nevertheless, the birth of a creature is the effect of a cause; for the soul is always accompanied by a 'subtle body', which is the cause of its birth and the difference between individuals that we see (6-13).

The soul is small like an atom, but all things exist for its sake; and this vast universe cannot be destroyed (14-22).

But the soul seeks freedom from its bondage, and that can arise only from knowledge, and the elimination of all desire (23-36). Desire is associated with objects, which can all be classified (37-45); and *Prakṛti* itself is said to consist of the three *Guṇas* (46-50).

Freedom consists in freedom from the action of *Prakṛti,* and the recurrence of birth and death; and it can be achieved only by refraining from all action (51-57). *Prakṛti* acts entirely for the sake of the soul; and the soul can make itself free by means of knowledge, and when the two become indifferent to each other (58-81). It is possible to achieve this freedom, for the impressions of previous actions made on the soul can become fainter and fainter, till at last they finally disappear, and the soul becomes free for ever. (82-84).

XXXVII. The Law of Evolution

Things with special characteristics arise from those which

are without such special characteristics. The body, with its differentiated parts, arises in the same manner, and so also the whole world out of its seed (1-5).

But the origin of things is beyond what is differentiated or not differentiated. It is said that a creature is born of its parents; but it is not so; for the birth of a body is an effect, the cause of which lies in a previous birth. There is a 'subtle body' which accompanies the soul through all its transmigrations, and it consists of seventeen parts; and the difference between individuals is due to their different actions in a previous state of existence (6-13).

XXXVIII. The Soul and the World

When we understand the nature of the soul we come to the conclusion that it must be small like an atom, and is covered by a body which is made up of food. We also find that the course of activity of all things is for the sake of the soul (14-16).

XXXIX. The Universe cannot be Destroyed

The body consists of the five 'elements', although there are some who say that it consists of only four, or even one. In any case we know that the 'elements' do not possess any consciousness, and that this vast universe cannot be destroyed (17-22).

Freedom and Bondage[1]

Freedom arises from knowledge, and bondage from its opposite. But events which occur in a normal, natural course, do not make for bondage; nor does freedom mean freedom from everything, real as well as unreal (23-28).

XL. Elimination of Desire

When a person has no desire to act, all his actions may be said to have been done. Desire is destroyed by means of meditation, which comes of restraint of action, concentration of mind, a certain posture of the body, and one's own effort. Control is effected by means of suspension of breath; the posture should be steady as well as comfortable; while effort should be in conformity with one's own stage of life. All this can be attained by means of indifference to worldly objects and constant discipline (29-36).

XLI. Different Divisions of Things

Bondage is of five kinds; the incapacity to act of twenty-eight kinds; satisfaction of nine kinds; attainment of eight kinds; while the intermediate divisions of these are of similar kinds; and we can describe all things in this manner. The attainment of objects is achieved by means of deliberation, inference, etc.; but there can be no freedom without renouncing everything (37-45).

XLII. Prakṛtii and its Guṇas

There are a number of divisions of what relates to the great forms and forces of Nature; and the whole universe has been created in this manner. It is characterised by the *Guṇas,* of which the highest is *Sattva,* the lowest *Tamas,* and the intermediate one *Rajas* (46-50).

The Problem of Freedom[2]

The action of *Prakṛti* is like that of a born slave for its master. There is a recurrence of birth and evolution into higher and higher forms of life by its means. It is in accordance with the same law that there is sorrow born of old age and death; and we can get rid of it not by plunging into action, but by refraining from it. He who does so attains to all knowledge, and may be said to have done all his deeds. It is possible to prove the existence of an *Iśvara* or God of this kind, namely, a soul that is free (51-57).

The Action of Prakṛti[3]

As *Prakṛti* cannot be the experiencer of its own actions, they are all performed for the sake of the soul, though unconsciously so. It acts without any self-interest of its own, like a servant for its master, because it is its nature to do so (58-62).

The Freedom of the Soul[4]

When the pure soul acquires knowledge, it ceases to have any interest in *Prakṛti;* and it attains to freedom either when it becomes indifferent to *Prakṛti,* or the latter becomes indifferent to it, or when both become indifferent to each other. But, in spite of the desire of the soul to make itself free, it continues in its bondage through lack of discrimination, because of the service rendered to it by *Prakṛti.* But there is always a cessation of action when the purpose of action has ceased to be served; and so when *Prakṛti* ceases to serve the purpose of the soul, the latter becomes free. The bondage and freedom of the soul do not arise by themselves; for there can be no bondage except through lack of discrimination on the part of the soul, and the devotion of *Prakṛti* to it; and freedom is attained by means of discrimination. In this way a person can make himself free even during his life-time (63-81).

The continued existence of the body is like a wheel that goes round and round for ever; and the proof of the possibility of freedom lies in the fact that the impressions of actions made on the soul can be made fainter and fainter,—till at last they finally disappear. But it is only when, as a result of discrimination, there is a complete end to sorrow, that a person can become free (82-84).

REFERENCES

1. This is not a new topic, and may be said to be a continuation of XXVII.
2. This is not a new topic, and is a continuation of XXVII.
3. This is not a new topic, and may be said to be a continuation of XXXVIII.
4. This is not a new topic, but a continuation of XXVII.

CHAPTER -IV

FUNCTION OF INTELLECT AND THE MIND

The function of the intellect is discrimination, and it has a bearing on the idea of pleasure and pain as well as desire. There is discrimination when we understand reality; pleasure arises on receiving, and pain in losing a thing; and association with objects makes for desire (1-10). But he who is without desire or hope is happy (11-12).

There are a number of ways of attaining to happiness; but it would be improper to refrain from performing necessary actions (13-21).

Desire is the cause of re-birth; but he who is without attachment attains to discrimination and freedom (22-28). However, good advice has little effect on an impure mind (29-32).

XLIII. Discrimination

There is discrimination when we understand reality, as in the case of the King's son.[1] We can also get it from instruction meant even for someone else. But it requires repeated teaching, and a fatherly regard of the preceptor for his pupil (1-4).

XLIV. Pleasure and Pain

A person becomes glad or sorry according as he gains or loses a thing. A serpent is relieved when it casts off its skin, and a person when he renounces all action (5-7).

Desire[2]

Thinking intently on an object makes for its bond, even though there be no means of attaining it. Association with objects, however trifling, is a hindrance in the path, because it creates desires; and that is so even if their number be only two (8-10).

XLV. The Cause of Happiness and the Means to Attain it

He who is without desire or hope is happy; and he continues to be so if he refrains from actions, and lives where he can (11-12).

There are a number of ways of attaining to happiness. In seeking knowledge from teachers or books, we should glean the very best; and concentration means one-pointedness. But it would be very improper to fail to perform necessary actions, —even through forgetfulness. A person should reflect, honour his teachers, and practise continence; and he can achieve success by devoting himself to whatever form or idea he wishes to pursue (13-21).

Desire is the cause of re-birth; and even if a person gains all he seeks, he is born again. But he who is without attachment attains to discrimination—for bondage arises from association with objects, and there can be no abatement of desire through indulgence (22-28).

XLVI. An impure Mind

Good advice has no effect on an impure mind,—at least not commensurate with the character of the advice. In any case, a person cannot realise his goal through wealth or power (29-32).

REFERENCES

1. There are a number of references to 'stories' in this chapter, to which a reference has been made by the author of the *Sāṅkhya-kārikā* (SK. LXII)
2. This is not a new topic, and is but a continuation of XXIX.

CHAPTER-V

GOD AND NATURE

Prayer has no necessary connection with the existence of God. If we believe that there is God who comes to our help in time of need, we must associate Him with desire; and if we do so, we cannot conceive of Him as free. We cannot associate Him with action, for all actions are not good (1-12).

Action is a characteristic of *Prakṛti* or Nature, and discrimination arises from knowledge (13-19). But if we believe that all action is performed by *Prakṛti,* it does not mean that we destroy the basis of Dharma (20-26). Dharma implies an idea of reality, which is produced by means of an innate power. We cannot properly describe or prove it, but its existence cannot be denied (27-38). It is also dealt with in the Vedas, which deal with the problem of action. The idea of the soul has a bearing on that of the intellect which, in its turn, refers to this innate power (39-51). All this means knowledge, and can be expressed by means of language (52-60).

The separate existence of the soul and Nature means that there can be no monistic conception of life (61-65).

Intellect is the first to arise from *Prakṛti;* but intellect and joy are two different things; and it is only by means of pure intellect or discrimination that a person can make himself free (66-68).

The intellect is not all-pervasive; nor is the mind (69-71); but it can enable us to understand the nature of freedom (72-86). It also enables us to understand the nature of an atom (87-90), and attain to peace in the midst of change

(91-101). It is by means of the intellect that we can understand the nature of our body and its functions (102-110); and the four different kinds of creatures that exist in the world (111-112); and it is also by its means that we can distinguish between the body and the soul, and understand the nature of action (113-125). But it makes us realise that there is nothing permanent in the world (126-129).

XLVII. Belief in God and Prayer

Prayer for success has no necessary connection with God. It really means pursuit of virtuous actions, understanding the effects of causes, and following the precepts of the sacred books. The fact that certain effects follow from certain causes does not require belief in the existence of God; for we can succeed through self-help. It is only when we do not think so, that we get the popular idea of God, one who helps in time of need. But we cannot believe in such a God without reference to desire, which is the basis of all action; and if we associate God with desire, we cannot conceive of Him as free. If we believe that His action arises out of association with the powers of Nature, even that postulates desire. If, however, we believe that there is an essence of goodness in desire, and so we can associate it with Him, we must regard everything as good or belonging to God. But that, as we know, cannot be proved. Indeed, we cannot associate God with action, for the sacred books agree that all action is a characteristic of Nature, and so is performed by it (1-12).

XLVIII. Importance of Knowledge

Detachment does not arise from ignorance, but from knowledge. Indeed, the origin of the world itself is from knowledge; and if we destroy knowledge, we destroy the whole world (13-19).

XLIX. Dharma and Belief in Prakṛti

If we believe that all action is performed by *Prakṛti,* it does not mean that we destroy the basis of Dharma. Those who understand Dharma know that it refers to the function of the inner organ; and there is no objection to this on the part of those who believe that it is *Prakṛti* who creates (20-26).

L. An Innate Power

The idea of reality is produced by means of an innate power; but it cannot be adequately described or specified. For instance, we know that it exists in the growth of a tree, but cannot easily prove it; but if we admit that it exists within a tree, we cannot deny it in the case of man. In every action there must be the association of two things, the signifier and the thing signified; but this does not mean that action is obligatory (27-38).

LI. The Character of the Vedas

We cannot easily understand the meaning of the Vedas; but we know that the idea of Dharma does not arise from sacrifices, and a person can be freed from bondage by developing his own inner energy. We cannot regard the Vedas as eternal, because they are said to deal with the problem of action; nor do they deal with the real problem of the soul. Indeed, the real state of the soul has a bearing on the function of the intellect, which may be seen in the manifestation of our inner energy, the existence of which cannot be denied (39-51)

LII. The Use of Language

There can be no real knowledge of that which does not exist or cannot be described in words. The meaning of a word is not self-explanatory; and a word is but an effect of a cause, and cannot be eternal. If, however, we agree that an effect follows a cause as a result of action, we must also agree that the action which produces the result must exist too (52-60).

LIII. Impossibility of Monism

When we understand the character of the soul as something different from all that is in Nature, we see that there can be no monistic conception of life. Indeed, there can be no such conception even if we deny the existence of the soul, for it would be contradictory to the evidence of the senses. But a monistic view is not possible if we agree that both Nature and the soul exist (61-65).

LIV. Intellect and Joy

Intellect and joy are two different things, and there is no necessary presence of joy in the exercise of the intellect. The primary object of action is the cessation of pain, and the idea of joy is a secondary one; and it is only by means of indifference to the world that a person can make himself free from the bondage of life (66-68).

The Mind and Intellect[1]

Whether we think of the mind as an instrument of action or an organ of sense, it cannot be regarded as all-pervasive; and the course of action of the intellect is similar too. The mind consists of parts, each of which is connected with an organ of sense (69-71).

LV. The Nature of Freedom

We cannot be certain about the existence of anything except Nature and the soul; and the latter is merely an experiencer of the result of action. At the same time we cannot identify freedom with joy. Freedom is not the elimination of some particular characteristic, or the destruction of some particular form, or even of all things; nor can it be attained by means of some particular mode of life by one who merely refrains from action. It does not consist in possession—of a kingdom, or good fortune, or even supernatural powers, or an *Indra* like state; nor does it consist in the knowledge of the 'elements', or of the six categories or sixteen kinds of things[2] (72-86).

The Atom[3]

The atom is not eternal, because it is the effect of a cause, and consists of parts. The law of *pratyakṣa* or the evidence of the senses does not require that a thing should have a physical form; and the primary measures are only two—small and large (87-90).

LVI. Impermanence

Although all things are transient, he who is tranquil can understand the totality of things by means of *Yoga* and his innate power (91-95).

Knowledge and the fact of possessing it are two different things, and there is no permanent bond between them because both of them are subject to change. There is thus no permanent bond between things, because the intellect itself, which perceives Dharma, is not permanent. When we have a proper understanding of things, we find that neither action nor an object of desire is permanent (96-101).

LVII. The Body and its Function

The body does not consist of the five 'elements' alone; for instance, it has a mind, without which the senses cannot act. The different senses perform different functions; and the function of an object is different from its parts—main as well as subsidiary. This, however, does not mean that a function is a substance. At the same time there is no difference in the material causes of things, even though the countries or places be different. Thus the meaning of a name arises from the explanation of the cause of a thing, and is the same everywhere (102-110).

LVIII. Four Kinds of Creatures

There are four kinds of creatures—germs, plants, creatures born of an egg, and creatures born from the womb. They are different from one another; but there is one thing common to all—the 'element' Earth (111-112).

The Body and the Soul[4]

The action of the body does not commence with the action of *prāṇa* or vital breath, but with the function of the senses. But the latter do not act of their own accord; and there is something within that experiences their function, because of which we get the idea of experience. That is the soul, which is the master, and the rest are its servants. The soul can understand its true character in a state of *Samādhi* or profound meditation, when the perceiver and the object perceived become identified, or in a state of deep dreamless slumber, or of freedom from worldly existence. The first two make for action again, but not the third; for he who is without attachment is reborn but once; the rest again and again (113-125).

Impermanence[5]

Everything in the world is impermanent; but this does not mean that we deny the powers that can be acquired by means *of Yoga*. However, no gross 'element' has any consciousness or intelligence either by itself or in combination with other things (126-129).

REFERENCES

1. This is not a new topic, and may be included in XXX and XXXII.
2. This is a reference to the *Vaiśeṣika* and *Nyāya* systems of thought. According to the former, supreme good is attained by means of a knowledge of six categories of things; and according to the latter by means of a knowledge of sixteen things.
3. This is not a new topic, and may be included in XI.
4. This is not a new topic, and may be included in XXVI and LVII.
5. This is not a new topic, and is included in LVI.

CHAPTER-VI

THE SOUL AND FREEDOM

We cannot deny the existence of the soul or its difference from the body (1-4); but it is only when there is a complete cessation of sorrow that a person can be said to be happy (5-9).

The soul is really without any attachment or *Guṇas;* and it is only want of discrimination that brings about its bondage (10-16). But it can become free; and he who is liberated is not bound again (17-23); and it can do so by means of discrimination (24-31).

Prakṛti is the original cause of all things,—all except the soul (32-44); and there is a multiplicity of souls, because we see that all creatures are different from one another (45-51). At the same time we cannot deny that the world is real, and that the actor is *ahaṅkāra* and not the soul (52-58). But it is the soul that understands, and is the principle of life within us (59-66).

Thus we conclude that the efficient cause of action is *Prakṛti,* and it is closely associated with the soul. But whatever the cause of this association, the chief object of a man's life is to put an end to it all, for it is the cause of our pain (67-70).

The Soul and the Body[1]

We cannot deny the existence of the soul or its difference from the body. The very idea of possession implies the existence of a possessor; and the latter can only be a living creature with a soul, and not a thing made of stone (1-4).

Pleasure and Pain[2]

It is only when there is a complete cessation of sorrow that a person can be said to be happy. Pain arises from sorrow;

but pleasure does not satisfy our desires; for we know that there is no one who is happy in this world. Sorrow is of many forms; and even pleasure may be said to be a kind of sorrow. But the absence of joy does not mean that action is not performed for the sake of the soul (5-9).

The Soul and the Guṇas[3]

If the soul can be without attachment, it means that it cannot have any *Guṇas* or the attributes of Nature, which do not belong to the soul, and are ascribed to it through want of discrimination (10-11).

Lack of Discrimination[4]

This absence of discrimination is without a beginning; but it is not eternal like the soul, and can be destroyed by means of knowledge, as darkness is by light. But it is the cause of the soul's bondage, which cannot be explained otherwise (12-16).

The Meaning of Freedom[5]

He who is liberated cannot be bound again, for otherwise there would be no difference between freedom and bondage. Liberation is the same thing as the removal of obstacles; and it is only the best who can be free (17-23).

LIX. Meditation

Meditation is more important than a particular posture of the body, for it alone can make for the suppression of the evil influences of our actions. Indeed, if there is want of discrimination, there can be a wrong course of action even if a person is without attachment; for discrimination alone can destroy attachment as well as confusion of thought (24-31).

Prakṛti and the Soul[6]

If we agree that *Prakṛti* is the original cause, it can only be the cause of all things other than the soul. When we examine and analyse objects up to the atom, we find that there is action similar to that of *Prakṛti* in every case; and so we conclude that it is *Prakṛti* that is supreme. But even when objects are combined with one another, we find that there is no destruction of any part—not even of an atom. But this does not mean that we should regard *Prakṛti* as superior to everything; for we see that all its actions are meant for the sake of the soul; and when the latter is liberated, there is no need for any of its things, not even experience (32-44).

Multiplicity of Souls and Dualism[7]

There is a multiplicity of souls, because we see that they are all different from one another; and we have to admit a state of dualism, *Prakṛti* and the souls. But this can lead to a conflict, for we cannot say which of the two comes first and which last. In any case we cannot regard the Universal Spirit, who is pure thought, as the creator of inanimate things; for were it possible, there would be no meaning in withdrawal from the objects of life (45-51).

LX. Reality of the World

We cannot deny that the world is a real one; that the actor is *ahaṅkāra* and not the soul; and that experience abides in thought, which partakes of its actions. The moon and other heavenly bodies revolve because the cause of their creation is real, and their knowledge arises as an inference of an effect from a cause. The reality of the world is proved by means of an uninterrupted series of events; and that is the very basis of the idea of release from the bondage of life (52-58).

The Soul[8]

There is an entity within us which understands the course of actions, and pervades everything; but, as it acts as a substitute for something else, it has knowledge of experience, place, and time. When it is not present, the body decays; and we cannot say that it is some unknown power, for we can easily know it. That is the soul; but, as it is without any *Guṇas,* it cannot act; and so we conclude that all actions are performed by *ahaṅkāra,* and have nothing to do with God (59-66).

Conclusion[9]

The efficient cause of action is *Prakṛti,* and its relation to the soul is like that of possession and possessor. There are some who say that the soul comes to be associated with *Prakṛti* through want of discrimination, while others believe that it is so because of the 'subtle body' which accompanies it throughout its series of births. But whatever the cause, the chief object of a man's life is to put an end to it (67-70).

REFERENCES

1. This is included in XXVI and LVII.
2. This is included in XLIV.
3. This is included in XXIV and XXVI.
4. This may be included in XLIII.
5. This is not a new topic, and is included in Freedom and Bondage and The Nature of Freedom, –XXVII, LV.
6. This is not a new topic, and is included in VIII, IX, XXI, etc.
7. This is included in XXVI and LIII.
8. This is not a new topic is included in XIX, XXVI, etc.
9. This is obviously not a new topic.

V

OBSERVATIONS ON THE SĀṄKHYA

The Sāṅkhya and Other Systems

Thus ends the *Sāṅkhya,* with its sixty topics, to which the author of the *Sāṅkhya-kārikā* has referred; and it constitutes the great foundation of thought upon which the remaining systems have been reared. Indeed, to understand the *Sāṅkhya* is to understand the basis of all these systems, for they too deal with the same topics, but from different points of view, and are but an amplification, commentary or criticism of its ideas and conclusions. For instance, the *Sāṅkhya* believes that the chief object of a man's life is to put an end to all kinds of pain, and that is possible only by means of pure knowledge and renunciation of action. As, however, the idea and scope of this knowledge has not been defined by the *Sāṅkhya, Nyāya* explains what it is, and tells us that it consists in the knowledge of sixteen categories of things, which are condensed into six by the *Vaiśeṣika.* The *Mīmāṁsā* correlates both knowledge and action in its idea of Dharma; and *Yoga,* while admitting that renunciation of action is the ultimate goal of life, seeks to reconcile knowledge with action so long as it lasts. But *Vedānta* attempts to eliminate the difference between the two by showing that knowledge itself is a form of action, and that there can be no action without knowledge; and so we have to look for a solution of the problem in some other direction.

Three Heads of Comparison

The different conclusions of the *Sāṅkhya* accordingly lend themselves to a variety of opinion, and it is this that is presented by the other systems. It would be convenient to group together the main ideas of the *Sāṅkhya* under three heads—*Prakṛti,* Soul, and God— and compare them briefly with those of other systems; and that will enable us to understand the latter in their proper perspective.

Prakṛti

With regard to *Prakṛti* or Nature, the *Sāṅkhya* tells us that it is the supreme creator of life—of all things except the soul; and the idea of its evolution is obtained by means of inference. It is necessary to understand what this means.

Man as a Microcosm

There can be no idea of existence without knowledge; and, according to the ancients, existence and knowledge are synonymous terms. Again, knowledge, so far as man is concerned, is limited to human knowledge— that is, all that it is possible for man to know; and it is conditioned by his faculties—the senses acting in association with their objects, mind, *ahaṅkāra* (I-as-an-actor or ego), intellect and the soul; and is limited to what they can grasp, and to the objects to which they can react. There may be many things in the universe; but if we are not aware of them, or they are beyond our reach—they do not exist so far as man is concerned. Hence, all of life that exists for man in the universe consists of what lies within and without him— the soul, intellect, *ahaṅkāra,* mind, senses and their objects; and it is for this reason that he was conceived to be a microcosm, a miniature of the universe.

Prakṛti as a Creator

The *Sāṅkhya* does not conceive of *Prakṛti* as a creator of the soul. Indeed, it could not do so, for it would have rendered nugatory its own conception of freedom from the bondage of life; and so its evolution is limited to the intellect and the rest, while the soul is said to have an independent existence of its own.

The Meaning of Prakṛti

The *Sāṅkhya* defines *Prakṛti* as a state of equilibrium or rest of the three *Guṇas* or the attributes of objects, which arise out of it; and this obviously means that, as evolution or creation is a kind of action, we can form a proper idea of it only with reference to a previous state of rest. *Prakṛti* may accordingly be said to be "a great action in the making", and that indeed is the literal meaning of the word[1]. It is also unmanifest in its original state, and becomes manifest when it evolves into different forms of life.

The Process of Action

We have observed that the evolution of *Prakṛti* into intellect and the rest is a form of action; and if, as the *Sāṅkhya* tells us, its idea is based on inference, it can only mean that it is based on the idea of the process of action from a state of rest in the case of man.

Now we find that before an action can take place, there must be a decision to act; and the latter is a function of the intellect. Thus, the first form of activity, following a state of equilibrium or rest, is that of the intellect; and so the *Sāṅkhya* tells us that *Mahat* or Intellect is the first to arise from *Prakṛti* in its state of equilibrium or rest.

The next stage in the process of action is the necessity of the existence of an actor; and that is *Ahaṅkāra* or the I-as-an-actor which, as the *Sāṅkhya* tells us, arises out of the Intellect.

But the actor cannot act without desire, which is an attribute of the mind; and so the Mind is said to arise out of *Ahaṅkāra* in the next order of creation.

Again, the mind cannot function without reference to the senses of knowledge and action; and so they are the next in order to arise.

Finally, as the senses cannot function without reference to their objects, we have the great 'elements' and their properties to complete the tale.

A General Agreement

That is how the idea of *Prakṛti* and its evolution may be said to have been obtained by means of inference; and, as there can be little difference of opinion on the subject, there is, except for some clarification on certain points, little reference to it in the remaining systems.

The Soul

The central idea of the *Sāṅkhya,* in connection with the chief problems of life, refers to the soul.

According to the *Sāṅkhya,* the soul exists, for we cannot deny its existence; and it is because of its existence in the body that all the other faculties of man are able to act. But it is altogether different from *Prakṛti* and all that arises from it; and we say so because we find that, at one time or another, it desires to make itself free from all association with the latter. Were it of the same kind, it would not have this desire.

The desire to become free postulates that the soul understands the nature of freedom; and that is possible only if it has been free at some time. Hence we may assume that the soul, before it is born for the first time or comes to be associated with *Prakṛti,* is free.

It is not possible to explain how the soul came to be associated with *Prakṛti* for the first time; but we cannot deny that it dwells in the body and so is associated with it, and desires to make itself free. Its chief problem accordingly is how to secure this freedom.

It is, however, possible to say that this association is caused by some inexplicable attraction between *Prakṛti* and the soul. But it is this that is the primary cause of all human sorrow and pain, which it is the object of a man's life to bring to an end.

The world is full of sorrow, for there is no one who is really happy. Indeed, there is no real joy in life; and pleasure itself may be said to be a form of pain, for it soon turns into it.

The principal cause of this sorrow and pain is action or

change,—conceived in its widest significance; and it is all due to *Prakṛti* or Nature, which is subject to incessant change.

The soul feels this pain because of its association with the body, which is a part of *Prakṛti* or Nature, and so subject to change. Indeed, it feels it still more because, through some strange misconception, it imagines itself to be an actor—though it is really not so—and so identifies itself with *ahaṅkāra* or the I-as-an-actor, which is a part of Nature and abides within the body like the intellect mind, and the senses, which too have been created by *Prakṛti*.

This being so, the soul can make itself free again only by understanding its true character as soul, as something altogether different from *ahaṅkāra* and all other faculties or organs of the body. Then, if it ceases to have any association with *ahaṅkāra* or the I-as-an-actor, and refrains from all action or association with action, it can make itself free from all that belongs to Nature or *Prakṛti*. There are thus two means of attaining to freedom, self-knowledge and a complete renunciation of action.

But this self-knowledge implies a perfect knowledge of all that is in Nature, for witout it the soul cannot come to regard itself as something altogether different from it. Further, a complete renunciation of action can be achieved only by stages or degrees, for a person must act so long as he lives; and, it is not possible to acquire perfect knowledge during one life-time, he must pass through many lives to be able to do so. Hence we must agree that the same soul is born again and again.

There is thus an almost endless continuity of life and its experiences; and death is only an interval between two lives.

We find that there are innumerable souls in innumerable bodies, and each is different from the other; and, if all this is in accordance with a law and not due to the arbitrary will of an irresponsible creator, the only explanation of this difference is that the same soul is born again and again; but each soul is at a different stage of its journey of life; and, as the actions and experiences of each are different, the souls are different too.

Life means action; and so there is action when a soul is born. Then, as the soul continues to live, it must associate itself with action all the time. Action arises out of desire, and is followed by a result; and so there are impressions produced by actions, which are followed by other actions. Hence, these impressions of action may be said to be the cause of other actions.

As the soul has to associate itself with actions, it must also associate itself with the impressions of these actions.

The soul is said to be without a body; but there is so only in its real essence, when it makes itself free. So long as it is associated with action, it remains encased in what may be called a 'subtle body',—which is composed of seventeen parts,—the intellect, mind, and the essence of the ten senses, and five properties of the great 'elements'. It is this 'subtle body' that contains a record of the experiences of the soul, the impressions of actions with which is has associated itself; and so it is by means of it that further actions take place.

As we have to agree that the same soul is born again and again, we must also agree that this 'subtle body' accompanies the soul even after death, and cannot be destroyed so long as the soul is born; for it is the cause of its future actions in the world; and it is by its means that it can acquire more and more knowledge or experience of Nature, whereby it can attain to perfection and become free. The soul accordingly commences its journey of life at the stage where it leaves it at the time of previous 'death'; and this continues till it acquires all knowledge or experience, becomes perfect, and is made free.

Now the question is how can the soul, passing through this series of births, attain to final freedom in the end? This, the *Sāṅkhya* tells us, is possible only when it acquires perfect knowledge of all that is in Nature or *Prakṛti*. But *Prakṛti* is an intelligent power, for its first form of life is *Mahat* or Intellect. It also acts, for it is the creator of *Ahaṅkāra* or the I-as-an-actor. At the same time it is characterised by goodness too—for it is the creator of the Mind, which has desire for its attribute, and there is an element of goodness inherent in all desire so far as the doer of the deed himself is concerned. The action of *Prakṛti* is, accordingly, intelligent, and is designed to do good–primarily to itself, and then to the soul.

According to the *Sāṅkhya* the object of the soul is to acquire perfect knowledge of all that is in Nature or *Prakṛti;* but this is possible only if *Prakṛti,* which is both intelligent and good, is willing to impart this knowledge to the soul; for the soul has no means of compelling it to do so. Indeed the instruments of intellect, mind, and the senses, by means of which the soul may be said to acquire this knowledge, are all a creation *of Prakṛti,* and so subject to its control; and so it is necessary that *Prakṛti* itself should help the soul to acquire knowledge of itself, and make it free. It may, therefore, be said to have an affection for the soul, by means of which it attracts it for the first time, and again and again when it is re-born; but finally makes it free.

All action begins with desire, and ends when it is satisfied; and when there is no further desire, there can be no further action. Thus, when *Prakṛti* has manifested all that it has to the soul, it has nothing more to show, and all its action towards the soul comes to an end. Similarly, when all desire of the soul to know more and more of *Prakṛti* is satisfied, it has nothing more to desire, and no further purpose in action. In this manner all mutual attraction and action and interaction between *Prakṛti* and the soul comes to an end, and the soul becomes for ever free.

But this process is gradual as more and more of knowledge means less and less of action, the soul associates itself with less and less of new actions during the latter part of its series of births; and in this manner the impressions of previous actions recorded on its 'subtle body' become fainter and fainter, till at last it comes to a stage when it is born for the last time, and associates itself with the least action. There are no new impressions of actions, and the old impressions made on its 'subtle body' have all died away; and so now the soul is pure soul in itself, and becomes for ever free, never again to be drawn into the tangles *of Prakṛti.*

A Criticism

This, in brief, is the main idea of the *Sāṅkhya* in regard to the character of the soul, and the manner of its attaining to freedom. But it contains a number of points which lend themselves to a sharp difference of opinion; and so it is small wonder that the remaining systems have apparently conflicting points of view. For instance, we find that the *Nyāya* idea of the soul is very vague; but the *Vaiśeṣika* goes to the other extreme, and conceives of as a substance, characterised by both desire and action, and no more eternal or non-eternal than the 'element' Air; and, consistently with this idea, it maintains that freedom from the bondage of life can be attained not by means of renunciation of action, but by means of action performed in accordance with the highest nature of the soul. The *Mīmāṁsā* and *Yoga* take us a step or two further, but the idea is still confused; and it is only when we come to *Vedānta* that we find that the soul, being inseparable from its 'subtle body', cannot be regarded as altogether different from all that is in *Prakṛti.* Again, we find that knowledge itself may be regarded as a form of action; and so knowledge and action may be said to be but counterparts of the same energy of the soul; and, as the latter has *prāṇa* or vital breath for its vehicle, we may be said to know as well as to act with each breath that we draw. Finally, we see that the very idea of freedom of the soul, as propounded by the *Sāṅkhya,* and the manner in which it is said to be achieved, is an impossible one; for it depends on the possibility of a total elimination of the impressions of all previous actions recorded on the 'subtle body'. This is inconceivable, for, though they might be made fainter and fainter, they can never be annihilated; for the last birth, whenever it takes place,—being a form of action, must leave an impression on the 'subtle body' of the soul, and result in a future birth again. Indeed, it is as impossible to conceive of a total destruction of action as it is of zero which, as we know, is essentially an imaginary number and, strictly speaking, inconceivable. Thus, the association of the soul with *Prakṛti,* however begun, can never come to an end. *Vedānta,* accordingly, gives us a pure monistic view of life, where *Prakṛti* itself is conceived to be but a form of *Brahmā* or God; and *puruṣa* and *Prakṛti,* or the soul and its 'subtle body' have always lived together and will do so for ever. Indeed, the soul is said to be born when, in addition to its 'subtle body' it comes to possess the 'gross' one too,—consisting of the five 'elements'. *Vedānta* accordingly maintains that the freedom of the soul is achieved not by breaking its bond with *Prakṛti,* as the *Sāṅkhya* would have us believe, but by a life of equanimity in the midst of all actions, and the experience of pleasure and pain.

The Idea of God in the Sāṅkhya

The idea of God can only correspond to that of our highest conception of the soul, for there is no other way of thinking of Him.

The highest conception of the soul, according to the *Sāṅkhya,* is that, in its purest state, it is characterised by knowledge alone, and is not an actor; and it is also something altogether different from all that is in *Prakṛti,* and has nothing to do with it.

The *Sāṅkhya* accordingly cannot conceive of God as an actor or creator, and realises that any other idea of the Deity would be irrelevant. It has accordingly no place for God as a creator in its scheme. It has, however, no objection to a God who is like a liberated soul—that is, one who exists, but has nothing to do with life and its problems: only such a God can be of little use to any one.

The Idea of God in other Systems

The idea of God in *Nyāya* and *Vaiśeṣika,* and, to a certain extent, even in *Yoga,* is an extension of what it is in the *Sāṅkhya.* *Nyāya* is prepared to admit that He exists, but believes that He can neither provide nor prevent the results of actions, which are really performed by man. The *Vaiśeṣika* does not refer to

Him by name as *Iśvara;* but, like the *Sāṅkhya,* mentions the existence of an Unseen Power, which acts in a variety of ways, specially in the case of extraordinary actions. The *Mīmāṁsā* like the *Vaiśeṣika,* does not refer to God – but rather to a number of gods who, unlike the Unseen Power, are manifest as the great forms and forces of Nature – governed by a law which is both intelligent and good. *Yoga,* on the other hand, tells us of an *Iśvara* or God who is omniscient and absolute, devotion to whom is essential for success in life as well as to attainment of freedom; but He is conceived to be a special kind of *puruṣa* or the individual soul, somewhat like the liberated soul of the *Sāṅkhya,* but with more clearly defined attributes – for *Yoga* does not state that He creates. It is only when we come to *Vedānta* that the *Mīmāṁsā* idea of the gods, and the *Sāṅkhya* idea of *Prakṛti* as a good and intelligent Power, are expanded into that of *Brahmā* or God, who is a good and intelligent creator – omniscient and absolute – and who includes all that is in Nature or *Prakṛti,* and yet is something more. Indeed, He is *Prakṛti* itself made divine by partaking of the character of goodness, intelligence as well as joy *(Sat-cit-ānanda),* and the fusion of its idea into that of God. According to the *Sāṅkhya,* there is a principle of goodness and intelligence, but not of joy, in the universe – not even in good or intelligent action; and what appears to be pleasure is but a form of pain. *Vedānta,* on the other hand, tells us that life is based fundamentally on the principle of joy; and there is joy both in the process of its creation and continuance; and death is but a door to another form of life; and so when we believe that the great forces of Nature partake of the character of goodness, intelligence, as well as joy in their working, we transform Nature itself into *Brahmā* or God. As the idea of goodness, intelligence, and joy is also expressed in terms of Sacrifice, we might say that Sacrifice transforms Nature itself into *Brahmā* or God. This is pure monism of God in *Vedānta* the highest conception of the Deity that the mind of man can grasp, and the culmination of all ancient thought on the subject.

The Basic Idea of Systems of Philosophy

We have observed that the different systems of philosophy examine the great problems of life from different points of view, and it is this that accounts for the difference between them. But a little reflection will show that there is a fundamental unity of thought underlying all of them. The *Sāṅkhya,* as we have seen, is an attempt at an all-inclusive survey of the many problems of life; but a study of the remaining systems shows that their approach is a more restricted onc. This can be explained on the assumption that each of them attempts to survey the same field from a limited angle. We have seen that the *Sāṅkhya* examines the problem of life in the light of its idea of *Prakṛti* as the supreme creator of things—all except the soul; but in the five remaining systems the centre of thought shifts from *Prakṛti* to Man and his faculties—the senses, mind, *ahaṅkāra,* intellect, and the soul respectively. Man indeed thinks and acts as a single unit, involving the function of all his faculties; but it is possible to lay special stress on any one of them at a particular moment of times, and say that he looks at things in the light of his intellect, or his desires (mind), or his senses. It is in this sense that *Nyāya* may be said to examine the problem of life in the light of the point of view of the senses; *Vaiśeṣika* of the mind; *Mīmāṁsā* of *ahaṅkāra* or the I-as-an-actor; *Yoga* of the intellect; and *Vedānta* of the soul. This would explain their differences and divisions, as well as their points of contact and conflict. This would also explain how the six systems can be grouped into three pairs—*Sāṅkhya* and *Yoga, Nyāya* and *Vaiśeṣika,* and *Mīmāṁsā* and *Vedānta* (also called *Pūrva-Mīmāṁsā* and *Uttara-Mīmāṁsā);* and a reference to this has already been made.[2]

This theory of the relation between the five systems of philosophy and the five faculties of man is based on the contents of the systems themselves. As they are all concerned with the chief problems of life, in which the soul occupies the most central place, we should be able to understand the basic idea of each in the light of its conception of the soul; and we find that *Nyāya* considers the idea of the soul with special reference to the function of the senses, *Vaiśeṣika* of the mind, *Mīmāṁsā* of *ahaṅkāra, Yoga* of the intellect, and *Vedānta* of the real character of the soul itself. According to *Nyāya* an object is perceived by means of the senses, but only when they function in direct contact with the soul. It is not anxious to specify who the 'director' of the senses is, and would be content to call it the 'knower', only to explain that the knower can only be the soul.[3] The *Vaiśeṣika* tells us that it is only when the mind functions in close connection with the soul, that we can get a clear idea of the soul.[4] The *Mīmāṁsā* speaks of the soul as an actor, and tells us at the same time that the main factor in action is *ahaṅkāra* or the I-as-an-actor, which may be regarded as an aspect of the soul when the latter is said to engage in action.[5] *Yoga* tells us that the idea of the soul can be grasped by means of reason and reflection, which are a special attribute of the intellect.[6] Finally, *Vedānta* bases its whole conception of life, including Nature as well as God, on its idea of the soul – regarded as inseparable from its 'subtle body', and as knower and actor combined together into one.[7]

It has been necessary to give a brief account of the different systems of philosophy in this form; and their text may now be summarised in some detail.

REFERENCES

1. *Prakṛti* or *pra-kṛti* means "*(pra)* great *(kṛti)* action"; or "*(kṛti)* action *(pra)* going forth". It may therefore be said to be a fountain of great action, or a great action about to 'go forth' or make things manifest.
2. See p. xix
3. NS. III, i, 1-3, 12-20.
4. VaiS. IX, i, ii.
5. MS. IX, iii, 21-24.
6. YS. I, 16-17.
7. This will be found to be the main subject-matter of *Vedānta*.

VI

THE NYĀYA SYSTEM

The Plan of Nyāya

The word *Nyāya* has a number of meanings in *Sanskṛt,* – "an original type, or that into which a thing goes back; a plan, system; a logical argument; etc."; and *Nyāya,* coming after the *Sāṅkhya,* may be said to give us a pattern of thought which serves as a model for all other systems. There is an undoubted plan underlying the sixty topics of the *Sāṅkhya;* but its treatment of the problems of life is not exactly systematic, and it keeps true to its own type, as indicated by its name.

Nyāya, on the other hand, though limited in its scope, is more systematic. The *Sāṅkhya* emphasises the importance of knowledge as a means of attaining to freedom from pain; and *Nyāya* tells us what kind of knowledge this should be. The highest happiness, it tells us in the opening *Sūtra* of the work, arises from a knowledge of the essence of sixteen 'categories' of things; and the rest of it is devoted to an examination of each one of them. It is divided into five chapters, with two parts to each chapter; and the subject-matter of the sixteen 'categories' is divided among them.

The plan of the whole work is simple in the extreme. The first *Sūtra* of the first part of the first chapter tells us 1what these sixteen "categories" are; and the next *Sūtra* tells us that the freedom of the soul arises when pain, natural activity, and faults arising from false knowledge disappear; and the remaining part of the whole chapter, with both its parts, is devoted to a definition of terms used in connection with these "categories."

The first of these 'categories' relates to the means of acquiring knowledge; and the first part of the second chapter is devoted to a detailed examination of the principal means, while the second part deals with some other problems of acquiring knowledge.

The second 'category' relates to the objects to be known, which are said to be twelve in number; and the first part of the third chapter deals with four, and the second part with three more, of these.

In the first part of the fourth chapter the remaining five of these 'objects' are dealt with; and then the author goes on to consider ten out of the fourteen remaining 'categories' in the second part of this chapter.

In the first part of the fifth chapter three more out of the remaining four 'categories' are dealt with; while the second part of this chapter ends with an examination of the last 'category'.

The text may now be summarised as follows :

CHAPTER - I

THE SIXTEEN CATEGORIES

PART I

The highest happiness arises from a knowledge of the sixteen 'categories' of things; and the freedom of the soul arises when pain, natural activity, and faults arising from false knowledge disappear (1-2).

There are four means of acquiring knowledge; and the objects to be proved are twelve in number (3-22). In the same manner we may define some more 'categories' of things (23-41).

The Subject-Matter of Nyaya–

The highest happiness arises from a knowledge of the essence of sixteen "categories" of things: (1) the means of acquiring knowledge; (2) the objects to be known; (3) doubt; (4) motive or purpose in action; (5) instances; (6) admitted or established truth; (7) different parts of an argument or syllogism; (8) the process of reasoning; (9) the art of drawing conclusions; (10) discussion; (11) disputation; (12) carping criticism; (13) fallacies; (14) quibbles; (15) the real nature of things; and (16) inability to carry on an argument because of impossibility of agreement on the first principles (1).

The Freedom of the Soul–

The freedom of the soul arises when pain, natural activity, and faults arising from false knowledge disappear (2).

1. The Means of Acquiring Knowledge

There are four means of acquiring knowledge–sense-perception, inference, analogy or instances,[1] and testimony of the trustworthy and the wise (3-8).

II. The Objects to be Proved

The objects to be proved are twelve in number—(i) soul; (ii) body; (iii) senses; (iv) objects of the senses; (v). intellect; (vi) mind; (vii) activity; (viii) faults; (ix) state after death; (x) fruit of action; (xi) pain; and (xii) emancipation of the soul (9-22).

III. Doubt

Doubt arises from a peculiar connection of cause and effect, a number of similar perceptions, contradictions, and irregularities of perception and non-perception (23).

IV. Purpose in Action

Purpose in action is the aim that causes action (24).

V. Instances

An instance is that which enables common people to understand a thing in the same manner as an expert (25).

VI. An Admitted Truth

An admitted truth means complete agreement in regard to an essential principle. It is of two kinds—universal and particular. A universal established truth is that in which each part of an idea or object is consistent with all its essential parts. A particular established truth is that which can be conclusively proved in connection with a similar idea too. An established truth by agreement is that which has been accepted after special examination (26-31).

VII. Different Parts of a Syllogism

There are five parts of a syllogism: (a) a statement of the proposition; (b) reason for the statement; (c) illustration; (d) drawing near to the conclusion; and (e) conclusion (32-39).

VIII. The Process of Reasoning

The process of reasoning is an examination of an object in order to understand its course of nature or character (40).

IX. The Art of Drawing Conclusions

The art of drawing conclusions consists in making a definite statement about an object after examining it from all sides (41).

PART II

The defination of Terms

We may define the remaining 'categories' in the same manner (1-20).

IX. Discussion

Discussion consists in a criticism of the means of acquiring knowledge, reasoning and proof (1).

XI. Disputation

Disputation includes all that is contained in discussion; and it is a censurable form of giving expression to quibbles, the real nature of a thing, and inability to carry on an argument for want of agreement on the first principles (2).

XII. Carping Criticism

Carping criticism consists in taking up a very strong attitude on the opposite side (3).

XIII. Fallacies

A fallacy consists in an argument which is wide of the mark, is inconsistent, is identical with the question itself, is similar to the thing to be proved, or is untimely—that is, when the reason for it has ceased to be applicable (4-9).

XIV. Quibbles

Quibbling consists in so breaking up the language of a statement as to produce a doubt in regard to its meaning. It is of three kinds: perverting the sense of language, of fundamental notions, and of the mode of treatment of the question (10-17).

XV. The Real Nature of a Thing

The real nature of a thing consists in understanding its original or essential nature from similar as well as dissimilar characteristics (18).

XVI. Inability to Carry on an Argument from Impossibility of Agreement on the First Principles

Inability to carry on an argument from impossibility of agreement on the first principles consists in erroneous notions and want of understanding; and it is of many kinds (19-20).

REFERENCE

1. The *Sāṅkhya* gives us only three means of acquiring knowledge—sense-perception, inference, and testimony of the trustworthy and the wise. *Nyāya* adds one more—analogy or instances.

CHAPTER - II

THE MEANS OF ACQUIRING KNOWLEDGE

PART-I

The first 'category' is the means of acquiring knowledge, and it is important, because it makes for disappearance of doubt; and when doubt disappears, we can understand the properties of things (1-7).

We cannot say that there are no proper means of acquiring knowledge (8-20); and they are really four in number—sense-perception, inference, analogy, and oral evidence or the testimony of the trustworthy and the wise; and it is necessary to understand their character and scope (21-68).

Doubt

Doubt disappears when we understand similar as well dissimilar properties of things. It disappears as a result of mental effort; but it is a mental effort itself, and so long as it continues, the mental effort continues too (1-7).

The Means of Acquiring Knowledge

It is sometimes said that there are no proper means of acquiring knowledge, because they cannot be valid for all time. But we have to make the best use of all the means we have; and the fact that we cannot have any that are valid for all time does not mean that we can deny their validity altogether. But it is even possible to show that certain things are true for all time. For instance, if it is proved that there is sound, it is also proved that there is an instrument that produces it; and that is true for all time. What is, however, required is that there should be a balance between a thing to be proved and its evidence (8-20).

Sense-Perception

There can be no sense-perception if the soul and the mind do not participate in it. As knowledge is a characteristic of the soul, it participates in sense-perception, which is a form of knowledge; and the mind participates in it too, because it is its characteristic to prevent simultaneousness of perception (21-25).

It is because of sense-perception that the connection between a sense-organ and its object is expressed by means of the same word (26-30).

Inference

Sense-perception has its own limitations, and cannot take us very far; whereas we wish to have perfect knowledge—the knowledge of the whole. Indeed, if there were no proof regarding the whole, we shall find that it is not possible to understand anything properly; and that is so because the mind is always attracted to the idea of the whole and dwells on it; and so it makes use of inference to understand things (31-38).

There are some who maintain that there is no such thing as present time. But were there no present time, we should be unable to grasp anything, not even the past and the future (39-43).

Analogy

There are some who believe that analogy is not a conclusive means of acquiring knowledge. But analogy, by its very definition, consists in the demonstration of what is not perceptible by means of what is perceptible; and so it would be of no value if the comparison were indistinct. Indeed, its special value consists in enabling us to sum up the whole idea, and to say that it is so and so in specific and not general terms (44-48).

Oral Aurhority or Testimony of the Trustworthy

There are some who believe that oral authority or testimony of the trustworthy is a kind of inference, because the object itself is not perceptible and has to be inferred. Indeed, so far as their practical application is concerned, the two'are not different; but the value of oral testimony consists in the fact that, because the information is conveyed by a trustworthy person, there is a firm conviction in regard to its import. There are certain things, like satisfaction, a burning heart and a splitting head, which cannot be perceived; and in such cases the testimony of a trustworthy person is our only means of acquiring knowledge. But there are some who believe that it is not worthy of being regarded as a means of acquiring knowledge because it is susceptible to a number of faults—falsehood, inconsistency of statement, and repetition. But this is not a valid objection, for these defects arise not from the nature of the means, but from the defect of the act, the actor, and the manner of producing a result. Its real defect, however, arises from a difference of time when a statement is made, as also from translation—for they may alter the whole idea. The Vedic hymns and the science of medicine are authoritative—but their authority is derived from the statements of trustworthy persons (49-68).

PART II

SOME MORE PROBLEMS OF KNOWLEDGE

There are some who believe that there are four other means of acquiring knowledge—traditional instruction, inference from circumstances, equivalence, and proof from non-existence. But these are really included in the original four (1-8).

In this connection it is necessary to have a proper idea of certain thing : existence and non-existence (9-14); essential and secondary, attributes (15-16); perception and non-perception (17-23)— including the atom (24-30); identity and difference (31-32); and existence and eternity (33-38). The use of language is important too-specially with reference to the language of the Vedas, and it is necessary to understand their method of interpretation (39-69).

Other Means of Acquiring Knowledge

There are some who believe that, in addition to these four, there are four other means of acquiring knowledge—traditional instruction, inference from circumstances, equivalence, and proof from non-existence. But all these are really included in the original four (1-8).

The Idea of Existence and Non-Existence

When we describe a thing as non-existent, it does not mean that it is devoid of everything—including non-existence. For instance, before a thing is born, it appears to be non-existent; but it is only in a metaphorical sense that we say that such a thing is non-existent. So long as the fundamental notion of a thing remains, we cannot say that it is non-existent; but we can speak of even eternal things as non-eternal in a metaphorical sense (9-14).

The Idea of Essential and Secondary Attributes

There is no contradiction between the essential and secondary attributes of a thing (15-16).

The Idea of Perception and Non-Perception—

Before we have spoken, a thing may be said to be unperceived; and the same effect is produced by means of covering or concealing; and so not speaking is like concealment so far as perception is concerned. But as non-perception is characterised by non-perceptibility, we cannot find its cause, for what cannot be perceived is intangible. It is, however, not correct to say that all intangible things are imperceptible (17-23).

The Atom

We know that the atom, which is intangible, exists and is eternal. It may be argued that since it is imperceptible, we cannot know what lies within it. But we know that something does, for we are taught about it; only we may not be able to know what exactly lies within it, for a further study may lead to something else (24-30).

Identity and Difference

The idea of difference arises from things that are different, and of identity from things that are identical. But there can be no real identity, because no two things are exactly alike (31-32).

Existence and Eternity

A thing is said to be eternal when we cannot perceive the cause of its destruction. But if a thing is perceivable, but is not perceived, it would be an invalid argument to say that it does not exist. But if we are unable to perceive the cause of the destruction of an object, and our inability to do so persists, we may conclude that it is permanent (33-38).

The Use of Language : The Language of the Sacred Books and the Method of their Interpretation – We find that there are separate parts of a word or a compound; and we are taught to make a change, and substitute one part for another, which may raise a doubt as to its exact idea. But if a word expressed the idea of an object exactly according to the requirements of each case, there would be no reason for changing its form. But when we find that the whole idea of the text has become unbalanced, and we are filled with a doubt as to its exact meaning, it implies that it is necessary to make a change.[1] For instance, when we find that there is an improper statement about a good man, we have the option to change the form of a word to understand its meaning. But this is not the only test; and a change of form may become necessary if we find that there is a conflict with the idea of Dharma; for when the form of words is changed, the objects described are found to conform to Dharma, and we do not find any transgression. There are, however, certain words like gold etc., the form of which does not require any change, because they are not connected with any transgression. There is a principle underlying this method of changing the form of words in order to understand their meaning: words expressing the idea of permanence do not require any change; those expressive of impermanence do. In certain cases, however, the form of words expressing even the idea of permanence may also be changed, if the objects described are beyond the grasp of the senses, and there is a doubt about their character as permanent. But in all cases where a state of transience is described, it is necessary to change the form of words. The reason for this change of form is that there is no restriction in respect of what may be described in the sacred books, and this absence of restriction is expressed in terms of absence of restriction in the use of words (39-56).

There are certain cases where the form of words must necessarily be changed; and such are expressions relating to unexpected characteristics, misfortune, destruction, deterioration, excess, diminution, ambiguity, or some secret matter; and this change becomes necessary because the idea or object deviates from a natural or normal state. A word is made up of two things—basic form and terminations; and we have to divide it into parts because the common meaning of words in their juxtaposition in the text gives rise to a doubt as to whether the outward form, the constituent parts, and the real nature of a thing have been properly described (57-69).

REFERENCE

1. The change of form of a word, as the *Mīmāṁsā* has explained at considerable length, means its division into parts—letters or syllables or both, as may be necessary. The *Mīmāṁsā* tells us that if we deal with the text of the Vedas in this manner, their hymns of praise would be transformed into laws of Nature; and, as this method applies to the *smṛti* too, it would transform 'stories' into systems of philosophy.

CHAPTER - III

THE OBJECTS TO BE KNOWN

PART I

The second 'category' refers to the objects to be known; and, in this connection, we must understand how an object can be perceived (1-3).

Then we must know the nature of the soul, the body, the senses, and the objects of the senses—the first four of the objects to be known (4-73).

An Object of Sense

An object of sense is commonly perceived by means of sight and touch; but it is not always so. We are able to perceive it because of its sphere of activity, and the existence of the soul (1-3).

The Soul and the Body

The existence of the soul is proved by the fact that there is no sin in burning a dead body, whereas we cannot burn a living body even though we believe that the soul is eternal. Indeed, he who ventures to do so is punished with death himself (4-6).

The Senses

When the left eye sees an object, it is grasped by the rest of our faculties, because there is recognition. But this recognition does not lie in the eye—for there is another entity that perceives it too, and that refers to our own self; and it is this that makes for unity of perception (7-11).

Whenever there is perception, the senses undergo some kind of change; but this change is not due to memory, even though it be regarded as an attribute of the soul (12-14).

While thinking of the problem of perception, it is not necessary to bring in the soul, because we have the mind; and the main point is that there should be a knower and, so far as perception is concerned, it is a mere matter of name whether we call it mind or the soul. We know that there is a knower, because of the experience of memory, joy, fear, and sorrow; but the knower does not change from time to time like a flower (15-20).

Desire is inborn within us, as we find from the desire of a new-born child drawn to its mother's breasts; and this act is natural like the attraction of iron towards a loadstone. Indeed, a child is born with its own characteristics like any other object that can be made, and it is possible to know its in herent qualities. Similarly, we can say that a body consists of earth, water, and fire from a perception of these qualities in it. It is in this manner that a body is said to consist of four or five 'elements' (21-31).

As there is perception with as well as without eyes, there is a doubt in regard to the idea of the perceiver. We can grasp things both great as well as small—even an atom— in this manner. An atom is perceived by means of a special close contact of a ray of light with an object; and even if we are unable to perceive it by means of our senses, it does not mean that it does not exist; for its existence can be inferred. This principle of perception is based on the knowledge of the nature and attributes of an object (32-38)

The essential feature of human effort is that there is an orderly arrangement of the senses brought about by action This is necessary for the removal of obstacles, both internal and external, that may lie in our way. A number of things can be seen or inferred in this way, and it would be irrelevant to deny their use (39-55).

The Objects of the Senses

The objects of the senses are of five kinds; and there is an identity between the senses and the objects to which they correspond. There are five properties of the 'elements',-smell, taste, form, touch and sound. Of these the first four, from smell to touch are the properties of Earth; the properties of Water are taste, form, and touch; of Fire form and touch, and of Air touch only; and of Ether only sound (56-63).

It may be argued that this is not so, on the ground that our senses tell us that each 'element' has but one attribute. But this is really not so; for bur senses tell us that Earth and Water have each more than one property,—only one of them is the most important, and predominates over the rest; and we believe that it is its only property because of its preponderance. This is also due to the fact that we perceive these properties by means of our senses, and only one of them can function at a time. There is, however, an exception in the case of sound; but that is due to heterogeneity in the different qualities of things (64-73).

PART II

The next three objects to be known are the intellect, mind, and activity. We must know the character and functions of the intellect (1-24); the character and functions of the mind (25-55); and the connection between them and activity (56-72).

A Case of Doubt

There may be a doubt in regard to the perception of sound, because Ether and Air have similar properties. At the same time they have their own special spheres of action, and so we do not perceive it (sound) arise in both simultaneously (1-4).

The Function of the Intellect

Perception occurs in regular succession, and not simultaneously; and absence of perception arises not so much because of pre-occupation with something else, as because of absence of a proper method of approach to an object. We do not judge as we see; and when we see that one thing is produced out of another and a different one, it is really a case of inference arising out of the disappearance of the first substance (5-16).

Even when an object disappears or is destroyed, knowledge remains; and, in any case, there is no destruction of the mind, for there is no simultaneous perception of objects, which is due to the existence of the mind. Even if knowledge be regarded as an attribute of the soul, our conclusion remains the same, namely, that it cannot be destroyed (17-20).

Absence of knowledge arises from inability to understand the cause of a thing. If we do not perceive the cause of the destruction of an object, and if it continues to exist, we may say that it is permanent; but when we recognise a state of impermanence, it means that one kind of perception is cancelled by another (21-24).

The Function of the Mind

The mind functions not in association with the soul, but within the body. It is characterised by quick motion, and so does not come into conflict with the function of the soul, which has memory for its attribute, but no fixed time for remembrance. The action of the soul consists in those forms of knowledge which are spontaneous and do not require any special association with anything; and there is no simultaneous recollection because there is no simultaneous attention or any other expression of any other form of knowledge (25-33).

There is commencement and cessation of action because of desire and aversion on the part of the knower; and the cause of desire and aversion is not the mind, but the soul (34-39).

Memory belongs to the soul because of its own nature as knower; and it arises from contemplation, intentness on an object, repeated study, awareness of characteristic marks, name, resemblance, possession, vicinity, dependence, association, sequence of things, performance of the same work, opposition, pre-eminence, occurrence, cessation, pleasure, pain, desire, aversion, fear, making a request, activity, love, and good deeds and evil deeds. It arises because we can, as it were, seize action, which is transient, in this way. When we remember a thing in this manner, we admit its existence which might otherwise have been denied (40-45).

There is no doubt about the character of a substance when we perceive its qualities as well as the qualities of other substances, and compare and contrast the two (46-55).

The Mind and its Activity

There is only one mind because there is no simultaneity of knowledge. It may sometimes appear as though we can perceive a number of actions simultaneously; but the perception of these actions is really like the sight of a circle of light made by a moving firebrand; and we imagine that they are simultaneous because of the quick movement of the mind. The mind is minute like an atom; and its origin lies in its connection with the result of previous action, and is not due to the character of the parents of the child or to food. Were it to arise in this manner, it could not be governed by a law—unless we admit that the origin of the body itself, like the origin of the union of the parents of the child, is action. This union is deliberate, and cannot be effected by some Unseen Power; for, were it so, the same Power should bring about emancipation too. This union is brought about by the activity of the mind; and, as it cannot be destroyed, it would appear as though birth must continue without end, and death itself become irrelevant, and it should be possible to conceive of an eternal state of existence. But it is not possible to argue in this manner, because we know that there is no such state (56-72).

CHAPTER - IV

THE OBJECTS TO BE KNOWN

PART - I

(Continued)

The five remaining objects to be known are faults, state after death, fruit of action, pain, and emancipation of the soul; and so we must understand the character of faults (1-9), state after death (10-18), the fruit of action (19-53), pain (54-61), and emancipation of the soul (62-67).

Faults

Faults may be classified under three heads—with reference to the different meanings of love, hate, and delusion. But, so far as the character of a large number of persons, like an army, is concerned, they may be of many kinds; and in the case of erroneous reasoning, they refer to lapses of reason. Of these delusion is the worst, because in the case of one who is not deluded, the rest do not arise (1-9).

State after Death

If we believe that the soul is eternal, it means that we believe that there is a future life. It is not manifest; but there is no inconsistency in it, because what is manifest arises from what is unmanifest; and things arise by means of an uninterrupted succession of events (10-18).

The Fruit of Action

When there is no fruit of the actions of a man, it is said that *Iśvara* or God is the cause of this failure. But we cannot say so, for there is no fruit or result in the absence of a man's actions; and since it is caused by his actions, there is no reason for any reference to God (19-21).

When people are unable to find the cause of a substance, they sometimes say that it has no cause. But that which appears to have no cause itself arises from something that has a cause; and the expressions 'having a cause' and 'having no cause' should be understood in their relative sense, and there is no necessary contradiction between them (22-24).

We cannot say that there is nothing eternal in the world, because, so far as we are aware, there is a regular order of things, which continues without end. However, we cannot say that all things are eternal, because we see that there is a cause of their birth and death. But when we understand the origin of things, we find that the idea of eternity is there too. Nevertheless, we cannot prove it, because all things that we see in the world are subject to change (25-33).

Even though things are different from one another, they have still a number of characteristics derived from a common source (34-40).

It is necessary for the intellect to devote itself to a single purpose in order to understand its cause (41-43).

As the result of some actions arises immediately, and of others after a time, it is possible to have a doubt in regard to the nature of result. There are some who believe that there can be no real result of an action after a lapse of time, because the cause itself has been destroyed. But the result of an action, before it has appeared, may be said to be like the fruit of a tree before it has appeared; and it cannot be said to be either existent, or non-existent, or existent-non-existent. What, however, our intellect can prove is that it is non-existent; but we have to understand the sense in which the term is used. Nor is there any inconsistency in comparing the result of an action with the fruit of a tree, for the term 'fruit' can refer to son, cattle, wife, and a number of other things (44-53).

Pain

We cannot say that the result of birth is unmixed pain, because there is joy too in its midst (54-55).

But there seems to be no end to pain in the world, so much so that it seems that it is not possible to attain to joy or emancipation from the bondage of life. But this is a mistaken view, and is not supported by the Vedas—only we have to interpret their text aright (56-61).

Emancipation from Bondage

Final joy or emancipation from the bondage of life is like the absence of pain of one who is in deep sleep and sees no dreams; and such a one is not inclined to associate himself with things again; for actions are caused by desire or deliberate intention; and so long as they last, so will pain (62-67).

PART II

TEN MORE CATEGORIES

We can now make a rapid survey of ten more 'categories'— motive (1-3), doubt (4-6), admitted truth and its instances (7-10), different parts of an argument, process of reasoning, art of drawing conclusions (11-15), discussion (16-49), disputation, and carping criticism (50-51).

Motive

Motive is associated with *ahaṅkāra*, which acts; and when we understand that action gives rise to faults, *ahaṅkāra* ceases to act. The cause of faults is attraction for the attributes of objects, as well as the objects of desire themselves; and the cause of this attraction is an erroneous conception of all things, taken as a whole as well as in parts (1-3).

Doubt

Doubt arises because of conflict between knowledge and ignorance, and it comes to an end when we understand the cause of things. Similarly, if there be no activity, there can be no doubt (4-6).

Admitted Truth and its Instances

The idea of admitted truth and its instances can easily be illustrated (7-10).

Different Parts of an Argument, Process of Reasoning, and the Art of Drawing Conclusions

All these are connectted together, and their idea can easily be illustrated (11-15).

Discussion

The idea of discussion can also be easily illustrated (16-49).

Disputation and Carping Criticism

Disputation and carping critcism art like a fence made of branches of thorn, designed to protect the growth of a seed; and they are meant for the purpose of preserving our understanding of reality (50-51).

CHAPTER - V

THREE CORE CATEGORIES

PART - I

The next three 'categories' are fallacies, quibbles, and the real nature of a thing; and it is necessary to understand them (1-43).

Fallacies, Quibbles, and the Real Nature of a thing

Fallacies and quibbles arise from similarities; and so also the idea of the real nature of a thing. These similarities are of twenty-four kinds; and they should be properly understood. (1-43).

PART - II

THE LAST CATEGORY

The last 'category' refers to inability to carry on an argument because of impossibility of agreement on the first principles; and we have to understand what that means (1-24).

Inability to Carry on an Argument for Want of Agreement on the First Principles

There are twenty-four situations of unfitness to carry on an argument because of impossibility of agreement on the first principles; and it is necessary to understand them (1-24).

VII

THE VAIŚEṢIKA SYSTEM

The Plan of the Vaiśeṣika

The plan of the *Vaiśeṣika* is similar to that of *Nyāya*. The word is derived from *viśeṣa*, and means "special, distinguished, etc."; and, as the two systems are closely allied, it may be regarded as a special form of presentation of the same ideas of *Nyāya*.

Division into Chapters

The whole work is divided into ten chapters, with two parts to each chapter; and, as in the case of *Nyāya*, the opening *Sūtras* give us an idea of its subject-matter. It is said to be Dharma, which is defined to be that which brings about the highest good; and this highest good is said to consist in the knowledge of six things— substance, attributes of a substance, action, the common properties of things, the special properties of things, and the intimate relation of objects by means of their similarities and dissimilarities; and the whole work is devoted to a detailed examination of each one of these questions in the same manner as in *Nyāya*.

In the first part of the first chapter we are told of the subject-matter of the *Vaiśeṣika*, and the six 'categories' of things, the knowledge of which makes for the highest good; and then the author proceeds to describe three of these—substance, attributes of a substance, and action. In the second part he goes on to consider the fourth—the common properties of things.

In the second chapter he deals with the fourth and fifth 'categories'—the common and special properties of things.

In the third chapter he examines the relation of objects through their similarities and differences—the last 'category' of knowledge.

In the fourth chapter he again examines the attributes of substances, and attempts to classify them; while in the fifth, he deals with the factors of action; and the sixth is devoted to a consideration of intelligent and good actions.

In the last four chapters we have a further examination of the attributes of things; and that completes this system.

It may now be summarised as follows:—

CHAPTER I

THE SUBJECT-MATTER OF THE VAIŚEṢIKA : SIX CATEGORIES OF THINGS

PART I

The subject-matter of the *Vaiśeṣika* is Dharma, and Dharma is that which makes for the highest good (1-3).

The highest happiness or good arises from a knowledge of the real nature of six things—substance, attributes of a substance. action, common properties of things, special properties of things, and the intimate relation of objects by means of their similarities and dissimilarities (4).

It is necessary to understand all this; and so let us deal with the characteristics of the first three—substance, attributes of a substance, and action (5-31).

Dharma

The subject-matter of the *Vaiśeṣika* is Dharma; and Dharma is that which enables us to ascertain the nature of prosperity and of the highest happiness or good (1-3).

Source of Highest Happiness

The highest happiness or good arises from a knowledge of the real nature of six things—substance, attribute, action, common properties of things, special properties of things, and the intimate relation of objects by means of their similarities and differences (4).

Substances

Substances are of nine kinds—Earth, Water, Fire, Air, Ether, Time, Space, Soul, and Mind (5).

Attributes

The attributes of things are colour or form, taste, smell, touch, name, measure or value, individuality, union and division, priority and posteriority, intelligent ideas, pleasure and pain, desire and aversion, and efforts (6).

Action

Action consists in throwing a thing up or down, bending, stretching out, and the manner of going (7).

Characteristics of Substance, Attribute and Action

The common characteristics of substance, attribute and action are that they exist, are not eternal, inhere in an object, are effect and cause, and possess general and special properties (8).

If a substance and attribute have the same origin, they are identical in character. Substances produce substances and attributes other attributes; but action cannot produce action (9-11).

A substance cannot destroy effect or cause; attributes can destroy both; and action can counteract effect (12-14).

The marks of a substance are that it is characterised by action and attributes, and is the material cause of other substances. The marks of an attribute are that it abides in a substance, is devoid of other attributes, is not the cause of combinations and divisions, and is the same in all cases. The marks of an action are that it abides in a single indivisible substance, and is the cause of combinations as well as divisions (15-17).

Substance and attribute are a common cause of substance, attribute and action; while action is the common cause of combination, separation, and quick motion, and is not a cause of substance (18-22).

One substance may be the common effect of many substances; but one action cannot be the effect of a number of actions (23-27).

Colour or form can be the joint effect of a number of colours or forms (28).

An act of throwing up implies weight, effort, and direct material contact (29).

Combinations and divisions are characteristic of action; but action is not the cause of substance or action (30-31).

PART II

THE COMMON PROPERTIES OF THINGS

After this we have to understand the idea of the common properties of things; and they refer to cause and effect (1-3), notion of reality (4-6), and the nature of existence (7-10). We have also to understand how we can get the idea of a substance (11-12), attribute of a substance, and action (13-16), as well as of existence (17).

Cause and Effect

If there be no cause, there can be no effect; but this does not mean that if there be no effect, there is no cause (1-3).

Notion of Reality

The notion of reality is a fundamental one, for we find that things have a continuous course of existence. But the characteristics of a substance, attributes of a substance, and action can be universal as well as special (4-6).

Existence

That is existence by which a substance, attributes of a substance, and action are said to be what they are. But existence is different from all these; and in spite of its presence in attributes and action, is neither an attribute nor an action (7-10).

A Substance

The idea of a substance can be explained by getting hold of a number of substances (11-12).

Attributes and Actions

In the same manner the nature of attribute and action can be explained by means of a number of attributes and actions (13-16).

State of Existence

We say that there is a state of existence, because objects that are said to exist possess certain common properties, and do not possess certain other properties, and are characterised by one common state, which is called existence (17).

CHAPTER - II

COMMON AND SPECIAL PROPERTIES OF SUBSTANCES

PART - I

We find that substances have common as well as special properties, and it is necessary to understand them. For instance, the great 'elements'—Earth, Water, Fire, Air and Ether—have such properties, and we should know what they are (1-31).

Properties of the 'Elements'

Earth has properties of form, taste, smell, and touch. Water has form, touch, and taste; Fire has form and touch; and Air has touch. These properties are not seen in Ether (1-5).

Special Attribute of Fire

We find that a number of things change their form when brought into contact with fire; and this enables us to understand the special attribute of Fire—namely, form (6-8).

Character of Air

Touch is the attribute of Air; but it is not the touch of visible things—for Air itself is not visible. It is a substance, but does not possess the state of a substance. It is a substance, because it is characterised by action and attributes; but, as it does not possess the state of a substance, it is sometimes said to be eternal. The expansion of Air is a mark of its variety of forms; but even in a close contact with Air, nothing visible can be seen (9-19).

Character of Ether

Going out and going in are the characteristic marks of

Ether; and they take place at the same time, because this is not a case of action, but only of contact—for Ether is only in contact with an object (20-23).

Sound is an attribute of Ether and of nothing else— neither Air, nor mind, nor the soul (24-27).

Ether is a substance like Air, and no more eternal (or non-eternal) than the latter. It is real because we know that it exists; and it exists because we know that sound is its special attribute (28-31).

PART - II

The 'elements' have their special properties too (1-5). In the same manner we can understand the character of Time (6-9), Space (10-20), and Sound (21-37).

Special Attributes of "Elements"

Smell is the special attribute of Earth, cold of Water, and heat of Fire (1-5).

Character of Time

The character of Time is that it belongs to the future, present, and the past,—and is swift. It is a substance like Air, and eternal (or non-eternal) like it. It is real because we know that it exists, and has certain definite characteristics. It is also a factor of action; and things that are not subject to Time are said to be permanent, and those that are, impermanent (6-9).

Character of Space

When we describe a thing from a particular point, it is a clear proof of the existence of Space. Space is a substance like Air, and eternal (or non-eternal) like it. It is real because it exists, and has certain definite characteristics, and produces certain effects. We form an idea of the East because of its permanent connection with the Sun; and it is with reference to that that we have the South, West, and North, and the intermediate spaces between them. There is, however, a possibility of doubt in this (10-20).

Sound

Sound is that which 'catches' the ears. There are different kinds of sounds to express different ideas of things. Sound is not a substance, though associated with one; nor is it action, though it has the character of one. It is only a perfect attribute. There is no mark of its permanence, for it is subject to constant change; and it is a mistake to suppose that it can be found in a manifest object (21-30).

Sound is produced by means of the meeting and separation of things, and by other sound. The first sound arises from soundlessness. There can be confusion or doubt in a multiplicity of sounds; but generally speaking, it is possible to separate and distinguish between them (31-37).

CHAPTER- III

RELATION OF OBJECTS THROUGH SIMILARITIES AND DIFFERENCES

PART I

The last and sixth subject of knowledge is the intimate relation of objects through their similarities and differences. These relations are different in different cases.

For instance, the objects of the senses are different from the result attained by means of them (1-8). An object may be united with one thing for one purpose, and with another for another; and an effect may be the effect of something different from what we believe it to be (9-14). Similar considerations arise in respect of what constitutes a valid argument (15-19).

The Objects of the Senses

The objects of the senses are well known; but when a person attains to them, the result achieved is different from the objects themselves (1-8).

An object which is closely connected or united with another, may be associated with it for one purpose, and opposed to it in another; and even so an effect may be the effect of something other than we believe it to be. That is due to the fact that the result is different from the object that produces it (9-14).

Conditions of a Valid Argument

That which is not proved, cannot be advanced as a valid

argument; nor that which does not exist, or is doubtful (15-17).

An argument bearing on what relates to the connection of the objects of the senses with the soul, is not invalid; but it can have its limitations (18-19).

PART - II

We can understand the character and function of the mind in the same manner, for it acts in association with the senses and the soul (1-3).

Similarly, we can know that the soul exists, because of the functions of the body, senses, and the mind, and the experience of pleasure and pain (4-5) and also the character of the 'I'within us (6-18).

All souls are alike so far as the experience of pleasure and pain, and the acquisition of knowledge are concerned; but otherwise the souls are really many, and different from one another (19-21).

Mind

We know that there is a mind when the soul comes into contact with the senses, and when there is knowledge or the absence of it. Mind is a substance like Air, and eternal (or non-eternal) like it. A creature has only one mind; and we say so because there is no simultaneity of knowledge or action (1-3).

Soul

Breathing in, breathing out, closing and opening the eyes, the manner of living, the course of the mind, the changes within the senses—pleasure, pain, desire, aversion, and efforts—all these show that there is a soul. It is a substance, and eternal (or non-eternal) like Air (4-5).

Proof of the Soul's Existence

When we are in physical contact with a person, we can

say that he is so and so; and it is for this reason that *pratyakṣa* or sense-perception is necessary for the purpose of acquiring scientific knowledge. But so far as the 'I' within us is concerned—since it is different from everything else that we see—sense-perception cannot be a proper means of acquiring its knowledge (6-10).

But we find that when we say 'I', it refers to the soul and soul alone; and that is as good a proof of the existence of the soul as *pratyakṣa* or sense-perception can provide; and so this knowledge of the soul may be said to be derived by means of a *pratyakṣa* of a different kind. When, however, we say from the peculiar manner of his going, that it is a particular person, what is perceptible is his *ahaṅkāra* or the I-as-an-actor, so far as his body is concerned (11-18).

Similarity and Difference between Souls

We find that the experience of pleasure, pain, and knowledge is common to all; and so we might say that, to this extent, the souls of all creatures are the same. But the souls are really many, and each is different according to the state in which it is born (19-21).

CHAPTER - IV

THE ATTRIBUTES OF SUBSTANCES

PART - I

Let us now consider the idea of attributes of substances.

Certain things are said to be eternal, while others non-eternal; and we need to understand that the eternal is that which exists; and that it is an effect, but an effect without a cause (1-5).

An attribute is something that is abstract, and we can understand its idea from what is concrete. For instance, we can understand the idea of largeness from a large number of substances and forms; and we can get the idea of form from a number of things having a form. It is in this manner that we can understand the idea of attributes and character of things (6-13).

The Eternal

The eternal is that which exists, but has no cause. Its proof is that it is an effect, but an effect without a cause. This is an exception to the common rule that there can be no effect without a cause, for the rule applies to things that are non-eternal, and not eternal (1-5).

From Concrete to Abstract

We can understand the idea of largeness when we have a large number of substances and forms. Similarly, we can have an idea of form, when we collect together a large number of substances with different forms; and we can form an idea of taste, smell, and touch in the same manner. It is in this way that we have a perception of names, measures, individual existence of objects, union and separation, priority and posteriority, and action—indeed all knowledge relating to the attributes and character of things (6-13).

PART - II

CHARACTERISTICS OF SUBSTANCES

All substances have three characteristics—body, sense-organs, and sphere of activity. All of them do not consist of the five 'elements'; but they are composed of atoms, which combine in them in different ways (1-4).

We may classify the bodies of creatures in two ways—those born of the womb, and those not born of the womb (5-11).

Characteristics of Substances

All substances made of the Earth and other 'elements' have three characteristics—body, sense-organs, and sphere of activity. There is no ocular evidence of the combinations of all substances; and all of them do not consist of the five 'elements'—for some consist of only three. This, however, does not mean that we deny that the atoms of which they are composed can combine in different ways (1-4).

Two Kinds of Creatures

The bodies of creatures may be said to be of two kinds—those born of the womb, and those not born of the womb. This is a universal rule of division, and is not restricted by country or place (5-11).

CHAPTER - V

THE FACTORS OF ACTION

PART - I

Let us now consider the problem of action.

The principal factors of action are the soul, the hand and its instruments (1-6); but it is necessary to have impulse and effort too (7-10); and we can explain all kinds of human actions in this manner (11-13). But there is also an Unseen Power which has its share in some actions (14-15); and there is also an element of deliberate intention in action (16-18).

The Soul, the Hand and its Instruments

The principal factors of action are the soul, and the hand and its instruments. The hand acts because it is connected with the soul; and the mace, its instrument, acts in the same manner—because it is connected with the hand. Were there no such connection, the mace would drop down because of its weight (1-6).

Action, Impulse and Effort

Action requires a special impulse and a special effort. Were there no special impulse, there would neither be upward nor oblique action. Again, there is a special impulse, because there is a special effort (7-10).

An Illustration

We can explain the action of a child in terms of the action of the hand—that is, as a result of special impulse and special effort; and we can explain the action of one who has been scorched, through the appearance of blisters, in the same manner. If there be no effort, there can be no action—even as a person who is fast asleep cannot walk (11-13).

Other Forms of Action: An Unseen Power

When a straw or a blade of grass moves, it does so because of the action of air; but the movement of a magnet and the approach of a needle towards it, is caused by an Unseen Power (14-15).

Deliberate Intention

There is also an element of deliberate intention in action (16-18).

PART - II

Action on this earth takes place in three ways—as a result of impulse, as a result of properly connected combination of things, and as a result of the presence of an Unseen Power (1-13). The action of the mind is caused by means of its association with the soul (14); and there is pleasure or pain when the two come into contact with the objects of the senses (15-16).

Attraction and repulsion, desire to eat and drink, and the connection of different results are all caused by an Unseen Power (17-18).

There can be no action without the existence of the soul (19-23); but we can conceive of the action of the *Guṇas* (or the inherent attributes of the objects of Nature) in the case of things which are not inseparably connected with the soul—*e.g.* Time (24-26).

The Factors of Action

We see that action on this earth takes place in three ways: as a result of impulse, as a result of properly connected combination of things— which includes the action of the forces of Nature which we can understand—and an Unseen Power, where it is performed in a special or extraordinary manner. For instance, water falls because of its weight when it is not supported by anything; it flows on because it is fluid; and it rises in a pipe or tube because of its contact with air. All these actions take place, not because of the pressure of impulse, but because of properly connected combination of things, and in accordance with the laws of Nature, which we can understand (1-6).

An Unseen Power

But we do not know how sap rises in a tree; and so its ascent may be said to be caused by an Unseen Power. On the other hand, we know that waters thicken or break when brought into contact with fire; and we can explain the action of Fire and Air by means of our knowledge. But there are some extraordinary actions—like the flaming of fire in the upper regions, or the oblique blowing of the wind, or the first action of the atoms or the mind—which we cannot explain; and so we say that they are caused by an Unseen Power (7-13).

Action of the Mind

The action of the mind can be explained in the same manner as that of the hand—that is, as a result of its association with the soul (14).

Pleasure and Pain

Pleasure and pain arise through the contact of the soul with the mind, senses, and the objects of the senses. But they do not arise when the mind abides in the soul, and is not associated with the senses and their objects (15-16).

Attraction, Repulsion, Desire, Result

Attraction, repulsion, desire to eat and drink, and the connection with different results—all these are caused by an Unseen Power. Were there no such Power, things would not cohere; nor would there be freedom from the bondage of life (17-18).

Ignorance

Ignorance is absence of existence, or a negation of things (19-20).

Region, Time, Ether, Guṇas

Region, Time, Ether are different from the soul, which alone can act; and they are actionless by themselves. The *Guṇas* (or the inherent attributes of the objects of Nature) too cannot act without reference to the soul. It is a law that things that are actionless in themselves cannot come together by means of their own action and produce an effect (21-23).

But it is possible to conceive of the action of the *Guṇas*—for they are said to be the original cause of things; but that is said of things which are not inseparably connected with something else (*e.g.* the soul). We can explain the idea of the creation of the regions and of Time in this manner—that is, by means of the action of the *Guṇas* (24-26).

CHAPTER - VI

INTELLIGENT ACTION

PART- I

Let us now consider the character of different kinds of actions.

Certain actions are intelligent actions, like the composition of the Vedas and the *Brāhmaṇas*, acts of charity, and actions that incline us to the best of men, and make us shun those who are hostile or dangerous (1-16).

Intelligent Action

The language of the Vedas is an instance of intelligent action, for the composition of words in the text follows a deliberate design; and that is true of the *Brāhmaṇas* too, for they give us a clear and correct idea of action in this manner (1-2).

An act of charity is also characterised by intelligence on the part of the giver as well as receiver (3-5). It is an intelligent act, because feeding the wicked is not called an act of charity. Thus we should always be inclined to those who are the best; and this is true of all classes of persons. Similarly, it is an intelligent act to shun those who are hostile or dangerous to us (6-16).

PART - II

GOOD ACTION

Certain actions may be classified as good actions, meant for the benefit of all (1-4). Certain actions are said to be pure and certain others impure. But a pure action must be characterised by restraint which, however, is not mere abstention from action (5-9).

Desire arises from a prospect of pleasure, and also when a person is absorbed in the objects of the senses. But it is also inherent in man (10-13). Desire and aversion are the cause of all things—just as well as unjust; and real freedom can be obtained not by means of renunciation of action, but by means of action performed in accordance with the highest nature of the soul (14-16).

Action and Motive: Good Action

There can be no action without a motive; and motive is of two kinds—seen and unseen. Where we are unable to discover any motive, we should take it that the proposed action is meant to secure the highest end, or is meant for the benefit of all (1).

Kinds of Good Actions

There are a number of actions of this kind (meant for the benefit of all)—such as initiation in good deeds, fast, continence, etc., as well as the observance of the four stages of life (2-4).

Pure and Impure: Restraint

That which has the desired form, taste, smell and touch, and is consecrated and washed, is said to be pure or clean; and the impure is the opposite of what is pure. But this is only a physical test, and is not enough; and we must take into consideration something else too, and that is restraint. But restraint is different from mere abstention; and we cannot understand the truth without knowing what it really means (5-9).

Birth of Desire

Desire arises from a prospect of pleasure, and also when a person is absorbed in the objects of the senses. But it owes its origin to an Unseen Power, because all are born with it, and it is a peculiar characteristic of the whole race (10-13).

Cause of Action

Desire and aversion are the cause of all action,—just as

well as unjust; and they bring about the union and parting of things (14-15).

Attainment of Freedom

But freedom from the bondage of life can be attained not by renunciation of action, but by means of action performed in accordance with the highest nature of the soul (16).

CHAPTER -VII

GUṆAS OR THE ATTRIBUTES OF THINGS

PART I

Let us now consider the character of *Guṇas* or the inherent attributes of the objects of Nature.

The different 'elements' have their own attributes; and they are not eternal because the substances themselves are not eternal (1-5).

All things are produced by means of a cause and through a process of development; and each is a separate entity (6-7).

The idea of small and large arises from certain special characteristics of things, and is obtained by means of comparison and contrast; so also that of eternal and non-eternal (8-20). In the same manner we can understand the idea of ignorance, ether, soul, mind, space, and Time (21-25).

The Attributes of the 'Elements'

The attributes of form, taste, smell and touch, belonging to the 'elements', are non-eternal, because the substances themselves are not eternal. The attributes of eternal things are eternal, and of non-eternal things non-eternal (1-5).

Production of Things

Preceded by the attributes of their cause, all things on earth are produced by means of a process of ripening or development; and each is a single substance (6-7).

The Idea of Small and Large

We can understand the idea of small and large in the same manner as that of the eternal. When we say that a particular thing is small or large, it is because it has certain special characteristics, and does not have certain other special characteristics (8-13).

Comparison and Contrast

The idea of smallness or largeness is obtained by means of comparison and contrast with other things. Similarly, actions can be explained by means of other actions, and attributes by means of other attributes. Even so we can explain the idea of what is non-eternal by means of what is non-eternal, and of eternal by means of what is eternal. The eternal may be described as something round or circular (14-20).

Ignorance, Ether, Soul, Mind, Space, Time

Ignorance or want of knowledge is itself a mark of knowledge (21). Ether is great because of its omnipresence; and so is the soul (22). The mind does not possess omnipresence, and is minute like an atom (23). Space (regions or the cardinal points of the compass) is explained by means of the idea of *Guṇas* or the inherent attributes of the objects of Nature (24); and Time can be understood by means of the idea of a cause or an action (25).

PART - II

We can get the idea of identity and separateness in the same manner—that is, by means of comparison and contrast (1-3). But there is no universal identity of actions and the attributes of things (4-8). We can understand the idea of the combination and division of things in the same manner (9-12). But it is not always possible to understand the combination and division of cause and effect (13-16).

Language is intended to express ideas correctly, and it is necessary to know how to interpret it (17-22). That will enable us to understand that the terms prior and posterior are relative terms; that actions can be understood by means of other actions, and attributes by means of other attributes; and we shall know the meaning of a thing being in a particular place, and the difference between substance and attribute (23-28).

The Idea of Identity and Separateness

The idea of identity and separateness can be understood by means of comparison and contrast in the same manner as that of smallness and largeness (1-3).

No Universal Identity

There is no universal identity of actions and attributes, because they are innumerable, and each is different from the other; and the idea of universal identity would only cause confusion (4-8).

Combination of Things

The combination of two things can be brought about in three ways—by the action of either of the two, of both separately, or of both together; and we can explain the idea of division in the same manner (9-10).

Means of Understanding Ideas

The idea of combination and division, as well as of action and attributes, can be obtained by means of comparison and contrast in the same manner as that of smallness and largeness (11-12).

Attributes and Knowledge

If there is no proof of the union of things, we cannot see the combination or division of cause and effect; and that is so because *Guṇas* (or the inherent attributes of things) are not the cause of the union or separation of things. But we can think of *Guṇas* in a state of rest[1] (13-16).

Language as a Means of Acquiring Knowledge

Language is intended to express ideas correctly; but a word and its meaning are not always connected together. The idea of things is sometimes expressed by means of the consonants of a word; and the meaning of a consonant in a combination of consonants is what has been put into it by the author; while that of a word used in the common way arises from its own special characteristics. The proof of the meaning of a word is that there should be general agreement about it (17-20).

Relation between Words and Ideas

When we use a number of words in a sentence, one must come earlier than another, because they lie in the same direction. It is also possible that there is a cause for this—namely, that one idea precedes another (21-22).

Relative Terms

The terms prior and posterior are relative terms, and can be understood in the same manner as small and large. Similarly, actions can be understood by means of other actions, and attributes by means of other attributes (23-25).

Relation of Cause and Effect

When we say that a particular thing is in a particular place, we get an idea of the inseparable relation of cause and effect (26).

Difference between Substance and Attribute

Substance and attribute are not the same thing, and we can understand the difference between them (27-28).

REFERENCE

1. This is called Prakṛti by the Sāṅkhya.

CHAPTER - VIII

GUṆAS OR THE ATTRIBUTES OF THINGS

PART - I

(Continued)

We can explain the idea of knowledge by means of substances, which include the soul and the mind, although they are not perceptible to the senses (1-2). But we should remember that the means of acquiring knowledge are part of the idea of knowledge (3). Indeed, attributes and actions are closely connected with substances (4-5); and the idea of what is general and special refers to all the three (6-8). Thus the idea of whiteness is closely connected with a white object; and we can get the idea of an object by means of a regular succession of a number of objects (9-11).

Knowledge and Substances

We can explain the idea of knowledge primarily by means of substances; and the soul and the mind are included among the substances, although they cannot be perceived by the senses (1-2).

Knowledge and the Means of Acquiring it

The manner of acquiring knowledge is part of the idea of knowledge (3).

Attributes, Actions, and Substances

Attributes and actions are closely connected with substances; and we can acquire their knowledge by means of substances (4-5).

The idea of what is general and special refers to substances, attributes, and actions; but the idea of substances, attributes and actions can be understood only by reference to substances (6-8).

Thus whiteness and the idea of whiteness are closely knit together in a white substance; and that gives us the idea of whiteness. As a white substance is the cause of the idea of whiteness, the two are related as cause and effect. But we get the idea of substances by means of a regular succession of a number of substances; and that is possible because actions do not occur simultaneously, but only in a regular order of succession (9-11).

PART II

It is our intellect that enables us to understand the ideas and attributes of things (1-4). But certain attributes inhere in substances,—*e.g.* smell in the 'element' Earth. Similarly, Water Fire and Air have their own attributes; and these 'elements' may be said to be like *Prakṛti* in respect of these attributes (5-6).

Function of the Intellect

When we say "this, that, done by you, feed him, etc.", we are able to do so because of the function of the intellect; and that is true of all things (1-4).

Prakṛti and the 'Elements'

So far as our knowledge of smell is concerned, the Earth may be said to be *Prakṛti* or its primary substance; and that is so because it is so large and possesses the attribute of smell. The same may be said of Water, Fire, and Air with reference to their respective attributes (5-6).

CHAPTER - IX

GUṆAS OR THE ATTRIBUTES OF THINGS

PART - I

(Continued)

We can understand the idea of existence and non-existence in the same manner (1-10).

Perception arises as a result of the union of the soul and the mind with a substance; and when substances are perceived, there can be a perception of attributes and actions. When there is perception of the soul, there can be a perception of its attributes too (11-15).

Existence and Non-Existence

When it is impossible to get any information regarding an action or an attribute, it is sometimes said to be non-existent. The whole universe that exists is also said to be originally non-existent. But it is really existent as well as non-existent even then; and there is no other meaning of *A-sat* or non-existence (1-5).

Existence and Perception

We say that the past does not exist because it is not perceptible to the senses; but as soon as we recollect it, it becomes perceptible at once. Similarly, that which is non-existent becomes existent if it comes to be perceived (6-10).

Perception

When there is a special union of the soul and the mind in the soul, there is a clear perception of the soul. In the same manner, when there is union of the soul and the mind in connection with other substances, there is perception of those substances. When substances are perceived, there can be a perception of their attributes and actions too; and so when there is a perception of the soul, there can also be a perception of its attributes (11-15).

PART - II

All this requires the use of language; and the purpose of language is to describe the real characteristics of an object in a strictly logical manner (1-4). But that requires the function of the intellect too (5); and we can understand by its means how memory and dreams arise (6-9), and know the difference between ignorance and knowledge (10-13).

The Purpose of Language

A true statement, based on the characteristics of an object, should tell us all about its cause and effect, and what is combined with, opposed to, and inherent in it. This is the real purpose of language—to describe the real characteristics of an object in a strictly logical manner; and cause, statement of reasons, inference, proof, and the instruments of action have no other purpose than to tell us the characteristic marks of an object (1-4).

Function of the Intellect

When we say that a particular characteristic belongs to a particular object, it is because the matter has been considered by the intellect (5).

Memory and Dreams

Memory arises as a result of the union of the mind and the soul with the impressions of acts previously done. Dreams arise in the same manner; but they belong to a state that is near to sleep (6-9).

Ignorance and Knowledge

Ignorance arises from a defect of the senses, of education, or of training; and it may be said to be defective knowledge. When knowledge ceases to be defective, it is called knowledge (10-12).

Knowledge of the Sacred Books

A proper understanding of the sacred books, composed by the *Ṛṣis*, arises from a knowledge of the laws of life (13).

CHAPTER - X

GUṆAS OR THE ATTRIBUTES OF THINGS

PART- I

(Continued)

We can understand the difference between pleasure and pain, and doubt, certainty, and suspended judgement in the same manner (1-6).

We see that the different parts of the body gave a fixed place in the body, but the soul is different from all of them (7).

Pleasure and Pain

Pleasure and pain are the opposite of each other, because of the difference in the motive of desirable and undesirable things: the one is excellent, the other bad (1).

Doubt, Certainty, and Suspended Judgement

The state between doubt and certainty is one of suspended judgement, and it is different from knowledge. Doubt arises because of dependence on sense-perception; while certainty arises because of dependence on evidence. That which relates to the past may also give rise to doubt, specially when we do not perceive its effect. There is doubt also when we see the same object in a number of causes (2-6).

Body and the Soul

The different parts of the body have a fixed place in it. But there is something different from all these, and it has its own special characteristics: that is the soul (7).

PART - II

We can have knowledge of the cause of a thing in the same manner (1-3); and so also of its form (4-7); and understand the idea of what is meant for the benefit of all (8-9).

Knowledge of a Cause

The knowledge of a cause arises from its effect. It may also arise from some other combinations of things, which are the result of action (1-3).

Knowledge of Form, Touch, etc.

In the same manner we have knowledge of form, when we see how an object is subjected to action, as a result of which it acquires a certain form. We have perception of touch, etc. in the same manner (4-7).

Action Meant for the Benefit of All

When in the case of well-known objects we are unable to say for what purpose they are being used, we should take it that they are meant for the benefit of all (8-9).

VIII

THE MĪMĀNSĀ

The Mīmāṁsā: its Basis and Subject-Matter

The word *Mīmāṁsā* means 'profound thought or reflection', and the whole work is indeed so in the strictest sense of the term. The word is derived from the root 'man', which means 'to think, know, understand', from which we get the word *manas* or mind—on which, as we have observed, the main idea of the *Vaiśeṣika* is based; and this gives us the connection between the two systems. Indeed, the subject-matter of both is said to be Dharma, referred to the opening *Sūtras* of each; but, as the *Vaiśeṣika* has told us so little about it, the gap is filled by the *Mīmāṁsā*; so that the *Vaiśeṣika* is followed by it in a strict sequence of ideas.

Again, as we have seen, the *Nyāya* and the *Vaiśeṣika* deal primarily with the problem of knowledge; and though the latter refers to action too, its treatment of the problem is by no means adequate. This is provided by the *Mīmāṁsā* now, more specially as it links up the idea of Dharma with that of Action.

Further, as we have seen, there is a broad mention of the correct method of interpretation of the sacred books in *Nyāya*, and the *Vaiśeṣika* makes a passing reference to it too. But the whole idea needs to be properly elaborated and explained; and that is done by the *Mīmāṁsā*.

The four principal questions dealt with by the *Mīmāṁsā* are accordingly (i) Dharma; (ii) Action and its relation to Dharma; (iii) the subject-matter of the Vedas, with special reference to the idea of Dharma and Action; and (iv) the method of interpretation of the Vedas, with illustrations, by means of which we can understand them aright.

We have observed in an earlier place that the main idea of the *Mīmāṁsā* is based on the character of *ahaṅkāra* or the I-as an-actor; and it is indeed corresponding to this that Action, conceived in its widest significance as Dharma or the Law of Life, is the subject-matter of this system. It may be said to be a 'profound reflection' on the problem of Action, with special reference to the character of the mind as well as *ahaṅkāra*; and, as the special attribute of the one is desire, and of the other action, this gives us the connection between desire and action, and their corresponding systems of thought,—*Vaiśeṣika* and the *Mīmāṁsā*.

We have also seen how *ahaṅkāra* and the soul are closely connected too; and *ahaṅkāra*, in the original sense of the term, is nothing but the soul when it is conceived to be an actor. As we shall presently see, *Vedānta* is based on the pure character of the soul; and this gives us the connection between *Mīmāṁsā* and that system too; and this will explain why they are called *Pūrva-Mīmāṁsā* and *Uttara-Mīmāṁsā* respectively: for the line of thought commenced by the *Mīmāṁsā* is completed by *Vedānta*, which constitutes the last word on the problem of the soul with reference to both knowledge and action.

The Plan of the Mīmāṁsā

The plan of the work, though simple like that of the previous systems, is somewhat different. It is the longest of all systems of Hindu Philosophy, and is divided into twelve chapters which, with the exception of three, each of which has eight parts, consist of four parts each; and each part of a chapter deals with different aspects of the four questions which constitute the subject-matter of this system. Thus, the author begins by proposing to inquire into the nature of Dharma, and tells us what it means. He then goes on to state that the subject-matter of the Vedas is the same, and that we can understand them in this light if we adopt the correct method of interpreting them; and this concludes all the four parts of the first chapter.

The second chapter deals with the same problem again—with a fuller account of the Vedas and their contents, and a fuller explanation of the method of interpreting them, by means of which their hymns of praise addressed to the gods can be transformed into statements of the laws of Nature.

This process is followed throughout the work; and so each chapter contains an exposition of the idea of Dharma, conceived in its widest significance as action performed in a spirit of sacrifice—that is, as good, intelligent and joyful action, meant for the benefit of all—together with a reference to the Vedas as dealing with this question, the method of interpreting them in this light, and a number of examples to illustrate this method. Indeed, as the whole system is based on the character and function of *ahaṅkāra* or the I-as-an-actor, it gives us a detailed account of the Law of Action—its character and scope, origin and effect, the manner in which it takes place, its instruments, and relation to knowledge, and bearing on the final goal of life; and it concludes with a description of the act of creation as being of the essence and end of all that is in the world.

Treatment of the System

As a summary of each part of a chapter of the *Mīmāṁsā* has been given in the body of the work, it is not necessary to repeat it here. It would perhaps be more convenient to put together its main ideas, spread all over the text—relating to Dharma, Action, the Vedas, and their method of interpretation, together with illustrative examples—as that will enable the reader not only to have a clear idea of the character and scope of the system, but also to understand the basic idea of the Vedas as well as of the wonderful 'stories' of the Epics and the *Purāṇas*, which have been constructed on the same model as the Vedas, and can be analysed into accounts of the different systems of philosophy and religion in the same manner.

I. DHARMA

Dharma

Dharma, says the *Mīmāṁsā*, may be defined as the highest good; but its idea is not limited to sense-perception. It arises from action, which is the law of life. Action may be divided into natural (or spontaneous) action, and deliberate action, which requires an exercise of the intellect; and Dharma refers to the latter kind of action; for action arising from impulse is not Dharma. It may be said to be action conceived as a great sacrifice, and requires knowledge to understand it. So long as there is life, all things must conform to the Dharma of action; and the highest of such action is sacrifice.[1]

II. ACTION

The Character of Action

Action[2] is a part of our nature, and cannot be renounced. It is eternal and universal, and involves a material contact between an object and a place. It is characterised by purpose, and consists of parts. It means drawing something near to one's self, and requires the use of an organ or limb of the body. It is of many kinds, and includes the process of thinking and acquisition of knowledge; and we may conceive of it as a whole or in parts.

Two Classes of Actions

There are two main classes of actions—natural and deliberate action—and the latter involves the function of the intellect. There can be only one deliberate action at a time, and that is the best action that can be performed by a person at the time.

The Cause of Action

The cause of action is some purpose, a desire to obtain some satisfaction. It is only the living that can have this purpose, while the inanimate can but serve the purpose of the animate, and impel them to action.

Purpose

Purpose implies dependence as well as attachment, and

arises because of a connection between the actor and the objects of life. There are many kinds of purposes and actions in life which, however, are mingled together in accordance with a law. The final purpose of all deliberate action is improvement or purification, and so it is linked up with the idea of sacrifice.

Men as well as animals have a purpose in action; and there is reason to believe that there is purpose in the working of the great forces of Nature too; and it expresses itself through conflict. There is purpose even in actionlessness.

Action, purpose, and result are all connected together like the limbs of the body.

Desire

Desire is the basis of all action, and it is associated with knowledge. The notion that all desire is evil is a popular heresy. Desire is connected with action in various ways, and activity arises from association with desire and the *Guṇas* or the attributes of the objects of Nature.

Desire is an attribute of the mind; and once it begins, it goes on without end, expressing itself in newer and newer forms. It is necessary to control desires, and we should not act under their urge. But it is a law of action that if we suspend one action, we must begin another; and the desires of those who make sacrifices should be satisfied. It is not possible to renounce all desires; and we can renounce only those which constitute a dangerous obstacle in our path. But good as well evil desires can be associated with an intelligent action. All desires undergo a change through lapse of time.

The Instruments of Action

Action involves the function of all the faculties of man—his senses, mind, *ahaṅkāra*, and the intellect. The soul too has its own share in it.

Action involves the use of a limb of the body or an organ of sense. But in all action the mind comes first because of its attribute, desire. At the same time the main factor of action is *ahaṅkāra* or the I-as-an-actor; and in all deliberate action the decision to act belongs to the intellect. In every case, however, the fruit of action always belongs to the soul.

All these are closely connected together: for instance, when the intellect is associated with desire, it acts like the mind. Again, the function of the intellect involves the idea of Time, which enables us to understand the idea of the soul. On the other hand, *ahaṅkāra* is said to be an aspect of the soul when the latter engages in action; and the function or the mind implies that of *ahaṅkāra*, and is linked up with that of the senses.

Action and the Forces of Nature

The forces of Nature are characterised by action; and there can be no great human action without their association.

Necessity of Knowledge

It is necessary to have knowledge to be able to understand the law of action. For instance, we need to understand how it is related to Time, and how the latter enables us to have knowledge of the soul. The consecration of knowledge means intelligent action. But the principle of action should not be deduced from the manner of performing it or from the place where it occurs.

Effort

Action implies effort, which is of three kinds—primary, secondary, and neutral—the last signifying effort without any desire for the fruit of action.

All are entitled to act, but the manner of the action of each is different; nor are they entitled to the fruit of action. But the fruit always belongs to the soul.

Success in life is due to action. But if we do our best and yet fail, we may ascribe the failure to Time.

Energy

Action and effort imply energy, which means activity pervading every part of an organism. We can divide energy into parts, but not a unit of action characterised by a single purpose. All actions, however, are inter-dependent.

Change: Improvement: Time

Action implies improvement as well as change, but not the creation of a new substance. Progress is the result of various kinds of actions, and it is possible to trace it to its source. There is also an element of Time in action, but there is no fixed time or place for it.

All action begins with desire, and the idea of perfection arises later. Perfection, purification and sacrifice are synonymous terms, and imply the function of the intellect, whose chief role is to decide. Intellect accordingly plays a most important part in action; and it is progressive,—for in a series of intelligent actions, performed in a particular place, the last is likely to be the best.

Option

There is always an option before a deliberate action is undertaken. An option is determined by singleness of aim, and the decision to exercise it rests with the intellect.

Habit

Habit arises from a deliberate repetition of an action for some considerable length of time; and the innate disposition of a person is an important factor in its formation.

Action of the Whole Body

When a person acts, he does so as a whole entity, and all his faculties take part in action in greater or less degree. The body is accordingly compared to a chariot, which moves but as a single unit.

Satisfaction, Pleasure, Joy

All action gives some kind of satisfaction to the mind and the soul. Indeed, all other instruments of action,—the senses as well as the intellect—have their share of satisfaction in it too.

Pleasure arises because of the action of the mind and the

intellect; but an interval of time is necessary for its recurrence. Pleasure or enjoyment has power to impel a person to action; and the motive of pleasure is strong enough to lead to the attainment of an object; but it should not cause any pain.

Those who believe that Nature is the supreme creator of life maintain that there is no joy in action; but such persons really deviate from the norm.

Sacrifice

The highest kind of action is sacrifice, and it arises from an inner urge. An act of charity, and dying in the defence of some one are acts of sacrifice.

Animals and Men

Animals too, like men, have a purpose in action, and they are all governed by a common law. They also have a mind, but have only natural desires; and they lack the idea of perfection or purification, which belongs only to men.

Offspring

The instinct to have offspring is obvious. It is often stronger than reason, and implies action, and not its renunciation.

None but the living have a desire to procreate, and it serves the purpose of Nature; and, in its highest form, it is an act of sacrifice. It is a creative act, and there is always harm in indulgence.

Renunciation of Action

There can be no total extinction of action, for some part of it will always remain. We can refrain from action only at the end of our life, when all our tasks are done. Indeed, actions meant for the sake of Dharma should always be performed.

Freedom of the Soul

We can escape from the evil effects of action or the bondage of life only by discriminating between different kinds of actions; and so one form of activity is changed into another and a higher one in this way. Indeed, the union of goodness with intelligence makes for the best kind of action as well as freedom from the bondage of life.

III. THE VEDAS AND THEIR SUBJECT-MATTER

Number of Vedas

The Vedas[3] are three in number,—*Ṛk*, *Sāma* and *Yajur*. A fourth, called *Nigada*, is sometimes added; but it should really be included in the *Yajur*.

Ṛg Veda and Sāma Veda

Apart from certain improvements, the text of the *Ṛg Veda* is the same as that of *Sāma Veda* and the repetition of certain parts is meant to complete the chain of reflection. The name *Sāma* refers to active life and so we have an account of all that relates to living creatures in the *Sāma Veda*. However, in its absence, we may refer to the *Ṛg Veda*.

Mantras and Brahmanas

The Vedas consist of *Mantras* and *Brāhmaṇas*—hymns of praise addressed to the gods, and laws of life together with their explanation, respectively.

Subject-matter of the Vedas

There are some who believe that the *Mantras* are nothing but hymns of praise addressed to the gods, and should be understood to refer to the offering of sacrifices made with material objects—for that is the simple meaning of words used in the text. But we are unable to accept this view, because we find that the text, construed even as hymns of praise, makes little sense; and, in certain cases, casts reflections on those who are otherwise highly esteemed. On the other hand if we construe it in a different manner, and associate it with the idea of action, we find that it gives us complete satisfaction throughout; and the idea of hymns of praise is transformed into one of laws of life. Where, however, a *Mantra* does not refer to action, it would be found to refer to the soul.

The Problem of the Soul and Action

According to some, the Vedas deal with the problem of the soul as their principal subject-matter. But this is not correct, for we find that they deal with the whole world of Nature, and the problem of action, and tell us what actions to perform and how to perform them.

Action and Dharma

The real subject-matter of the Vedas is action, and Dharma is founded on their word; and it would be meaningless to interpret them in any other light. They are an exposition of the *Guṇas* or the inherent attributes of the objects of Nature, and refer to the laws of knowledge as well as action, which constitute the fundamental problem of life; and we can understand them in this light if we interpret their text correctly.

Ths *Aṅgas* of the *Mantras* of the Vedas are called 'limbs', because purpose, action and result are connected together like the limbs of the body; and that is their real subject-matter.

Action and Prohibition against Action

The Vedas enjoin action, but do not promise their fruit. They contain prohibition against action too; but that does not mean inaction. It only means prohibition against such actions as ought not to be performed by a good man.

The Text of the Vedas

All prescribed texts are an integral part of the Vedas, and the difference between them is due to the difference in the manner in which their ideas have been expressed. Their text is authoritative, and no unauthorised additions should be made. Their language is perfect, and we should not venture to alter it. It is difficult to understand, but it is possible to grasp it by means of devotion and proper study. All these things were taught long ago, and we have forgotten them; but we can understand them again: only we should use the proper method of interpretation, and consider them in the light of action; and then we shall find that they make good sense, and are consistent throughout.

IV. THE METHOD OF INTERPRETATION

Need of a New Interpretation[4]

We cannot have a single method of interpretation of the Vedas; but whatever method we adopt, it should have a regular plan, and be governed by definite rules. Indeed, if the Vedas have any real value, they cannot have the meaning commonly assigned to them; and so it is necessary to have a different method of interpretation. We are led to the same conclusion by the use of certain special terms in the text, such as those in connection with the god *Indra*. But it is necessary to have a regular method of interpretation, and we find that it exists—only it requires skill to use it—for different words have to be handled in different ways.

Three Ways of Explanation

There are three ways of explaining the meaning of words used in the Vedas. We may take their common meaning if it is suitable; but, if the meaning of a word has been specially defined, we should take it in that sense. On the other hand, if the common meaning does not make sense, or if there is no special definition of a word, we should divide it into parts, and take the meaning of each part to make up the meaning of the whole.

The Use of Words

The whole idea of the composition of the Vedas and the method of their interpretation is based on the use of words, and it is necessary to understand it.

Conflicting Opinions

But different people have different ideas about the use of words. There are some who believe that if a word refers to *Guṇas* or the attributes of the objects of Nature, there should be a clear reference to these attributes. But this is not always possible, for a word may have more than one meaning, and refer to more than one idea or object. Others believe that a word and its attributes should go together, and it should not be divided into parts to give its meaning, and that the rules in regard to all words should be the same. But this too is not possible; for if a word and its attributes should go together, so should a word and the object to which it refers. But we know that this is not possible.

The Test of Correctness

Thus we see that we cannot lay down any hard and fast rules to get the correct meaning of words, and their only test is that they should suit the context. This means that an attribute should be in its proper place with reference to its object, and nothing should be meaningless, and nothing should be left out. Indeed, the real test of correctness is the result that can be achieved.

The Use of Language : Verbs and Nouns

Life means action, and it has two parts—its performance, and the doer of the deed; and corresponding to this there are two principal kinds of words in a language—verbs and nouns; and the rest are all associated with them. Of these, nouns precede verbs, for verbs cannot be used without reference to nouns; and verbs are of two kinds—transitive and intransitive.

The Best Form of Expression

We have to express our ideas by means of language; and the best form of expression would be that in which a single word has a single meaning, and a single idea can be expressed by means of a single word. But if an expression has more than one meaning, it should consist of more than one part. If there are equal ideas to express, there should be separate statements for each; and the close connection of word with word should make for perfection of statement, and there should be no gaps anywhere. Where, however, an idea is intricate, and is likely to cause confusion, it should be described by means of a number of statements—specially where there are a number of parts of an action. These statements should normally be separate, and it is not necessary that they should be placed in close proximity to one another. Words, the origin of which can be traced, are the best.

The Language of the Vedas

It is in the light of this that we have to understand the language of the Vedas. Different words have been used to express different ideas in different ways; and in a number of cases the text has two meanings—the apparent and the real—both of which are consistent in themselves throughout. But the real meaning contains a reference to the law of action; and the whole composition is of this kind. But it does not appear to be in harmony with the objects described; and so it is necessary to reject the apparent meaning of words. But we should do so only if it does not refer to the laws of life.

The Principle of Method of Interpretation

The new method of interpretation of the Vedas depends primarily on changing the form of words used in the text, by dividing them into parts; and there is a principle underlying this idea Thus, we know that action implies change as well as improvement; and corresponding to this the form of words has to be changed to make for improvement of the whole idea. Similarly, the idea of Time is obtained by means of an orderly arrangement of things; and so it is necessary to rearrange the text in an orderly manner to get the idea of Time Again, action is associated with desire, and is divisible into parts, while desire changes from time to time and corresponding to this the form of words, expressive of these ideas, has to be changed, and they are divided into parts.

The reason for dividing a word into parts is that the different ingredients of an object can be clearly specified in this manner. Again, each part of a word is separate because it corresponds to each part of an action; and it has a bearing on the idea of the principal word, except in the case of a reference to the great forces of Nature, which are described in a different manner.

An Exact Description

The main reason for dividing a word into parts is that the author has himself formed it in this manner, in order to describe in the briefest and the best manner the constituents of an object. When we give a particular name to an object, there is generally a good reason for doing so; that is to say, certain qualities are intended to be described by the name. This can best be done when each part of a word refers to a quality; and that is what has been done in the words used in the Vedas. This, however, is possible only when words are newly coined for the purpose; and such is indeed the character of a number of wouds used in the text. When words are arranged in this manner, they can cover the entire range of subject-matter of Dharma of the law of life, and their meanings can be fixed; and that is what we find in the Vedas. There are also certain instructions in connection with these words to enable us to understand them. For instance, when a name is repeated, we should understand that it is for the sake of further explanation.

The purpose of this form of composition is that the properties of objects, which are closely connected with one another, should be properly described; and so, if there are any examples, they too should be in the same form. There is thus no similarity between the original and the new meaning of a word; and, as there is an exact correspondence between an idea and its form of expression—if a thing is not suitable for teaching, of is deemed to be contrary to Dharma, it is found to be expressed in a form which cannot be understood.

Meaning of Parts of Words

Each part of a word accordingly signifies a *dravya* or a substance in the philosophical sense of the term,[5] for it refers to a separate object, action, result, or the character of the doer of the deed. Thus, we can express the idea of a single action by means of a single note, and that is the best mode of expression.[6] This is based on the principle that there is only one exercise of the intellect at a time; and it also prevents repetition.

Thus, each part of a word is separate because it corresponds to each part of an object or action, and has a bearing on the idea of the principal word.

There is, thus, a theory in connection with the idea of the division of words into parts, and it enables us to understand the text in a new light. The chief merit of this form of composition is that it is based on an intelligent plan formed by the author himself. It is intentional, because we find that it is complete; for when, in accordance with this theory, we put words in their proper place, and nothing is left out, it transforms the idea of *Mantras* or hymns of praise addressed to the gods into that of laws of life.

The Krama Method of Recitation

When we divide a word into parts in accordance with this method, we are required to see that it remains altogether intact, and the position of its parts is not changed. Corresponding to this we are required to read the text in accordance with *Krama*,[7] which enables us to understand its new meaning in terms of action.

It may be argued that this is not possible. But there is a reference to the *Krama* method of recitation in the sacred books; and we find that a *Mantra* or a hymn of praise addressed to the gods is transformed into *Vidhi* or a law of life by its means. The text of the Vedas—wherever it is found that it does not make sense—should accordingly be interpreted in accordance with the *Krama* method of its reading.

In a number of cases the meaning of the principal word can be understood by means of *Krama*, and that of others by reference to the principal word. When we pronounce a word according to *Krama*, the whole word should remain intact; and if we have to break up its form, it should be done immediately, when it would give us the required meaning.

The *Krama* method of recitation is not intended to regulate time; and the reason for changing the form of a word is that it does not make sense otherwise. There are certain words which express their own idea completely; but even they need to be divided into parts when read in accordance with *Krama*, though there should be no change in their meaning.

There is good reason for following the *Krama* method of recitation, for the design of division into parts is indicated by its means. But the meaning of words is not obtained by adding up their parts. We should read the text properly according to *Krama*, and analyse words according to correct grammatical rules, when we shall be able to get their real meaning. But the same word should have the same meaning throughout.

The Principal Word

The principal word used in the text has a special significance, and without it the text itself would become meaningless. On the other hand, if the principal cause of action is not clear, or is not expressed by the principal word, the explanation should be contained in the text itself, and it should not be necessary to divide the principal word into parts, although a number of other words may have to be divided.

The method of division of words into parts applies, as a rule, to the principal or the most important words; and if there are a number of such words in a sentence, they should be regarded as synonyms. The meaning of the principal word is obtained by dividing it into parts, while that of its synonyms without it. With regard to the rest, we should change their form if their meaning does not appeal to reason. But it is necessary to have knowledge to be able to understand the meaning of some synonyms; while in certain cases we have to 'negotiate' their meaning, though not in the case of the best synonyms.

It is important to understand the meaning of principal words, as that enables us to understand the rest—and it can be done by means of the *Krama* method of reciting the text, while that of others by reference to the principal word. But we should adhere to the order of words used in the text.

In the case of principal words the parts which have the same meaning should be in close proximity to one another; and if a single note expresses the idea of an important thing, such notes should all be found together, and the things themselves should have the same maker.

All things are connected together in accordance with a law; and even so the meaning of all expressions is connected with the principal word. This, however, does not apply to the meaning of parts of words where the great forces of Nature are concerned. In other cases it should be possible to have this connection, which should enable us to understand the meaning of the text. On the other hand, if the principal word is removed, we cannot understand the text at all.

A Disguise

Thus we see that it is the law of life that has been described in the Vedas in this 'veiled' manner. The secret of this method consists in dividing words into parts; and that is the meaning of seeing through their 'disguise'. The common meaning of a word is its meaning without this 'disguise' or division into parts; and so a 'disguise' may be said to be a collection of qualities, which can be understood by means of inference; and seeing through this 'disguise' consists in our ability to know how things are connected with one another. We know that there is a 'disguise', because we can pierce through it, and find out the correct meaning of the text. But it requires knowledge, deep concentration, devotion of a lifetime, and a measure of good fortune to succeed.

How to Understand the Text

We can understand the real meaning of the text of the Vedas in the same manner as we understand the laws of life relating to animals—that is, by means of inference.

Three Ways of Recitation

There are instructions in regard to the manner of reading the text, each of which has a bearing on the method of interpreting it. In some cases we are required to sing aloud, in others to recite silently, while yet in others to read in a normal tone. The first implies that we have to change the form of words even as we do in singing; the second that no change should be made—for no words are uttered; and the third that we may do as circumstances require, and the meaning would, in any case, be the same.

Narrative Form

It is natural for a person to narrate action—of some person or past time; and this enables us to understand that there is a description of action in narrative form in the Vedas.

Meaning of Contradictions

We sometimes find that the latter part of a statement contradicts an earlier one; and we should take it that this is intentional, and meant to indicate that we have to divide words into parts to understand their meaning. Similarly, if we find that the text contains something that is incongruous, or casts reflection on some one otherwise held in high esteem, we should conclude that it requires a new interpretation; but the latter should be consistent throughout.

Utility and Beauty

Again, if we find that the description of an object is inconsistent, we should attach more importance to the object than to its description; and if there is an inconsistency between an object and its use, we should attach more importance to its use. Indeed, meaning is more important than elegance of expression; but language, like a garment, should have both utility and beauty—though utility or meaning comes first. But there should be a method in our work, and we should be able to combine parts with the whole, and select the best meaning, when we shall find that there is both beauty and utility in the contents of the text.

Predominant Thought

There can be only one predominant thought at a time, and it must produce its own effect or result; and we should bear this in mind in our attempt to understand the text. In certain cases, however, we can understand the meaning without any difficulty from the context or the effect that is produced; and where there is a doubt about an occurrence, it can be understood from its description—for there is nothing that cannot be described in words.

How to Discover a New Meaning

As when we discover an error in a course of action, we adopt some other means to remove the defect, we should do the same in connection with the text—that is, find out some other means of getting the correct meaning. In some cases we have to repeat the same process, while in others we have to find out where the weakness lies. But we should be satisfied only when we find that the whole thing is both intelligent and good.

The Best Meaning

We can accept the meaning of words in their natural form only if it is the very best; but it should not be derived from some detached or casual remark, except in special cases. It should not be obtained by breaking up the unity of idea, or by mixing up words. The best result is obtained by dividing words into parts; but we should take care to see that the whole text is connected together, and has an unbroken unity throughout.

A Substitute Expression

A substitute expression can be used only if it has the same meaning as the original word. But it is not always easy to find an exact substitute; and to that extent the language of the text, which is otherwise perfect, may be said to be imperfect.

Two Meanings : Need of Selection

When we get two meanings of a word, we must make up our minds as to which of the two we should accept; and we may find that the one we do has little connection with the ordinary meaning of the word. But the new meaning can transform the whole idea of the text, and the words retain their new character throughout.

Two Series

In this method of interpretation there are two series of words--the original one, and that formed by means of division into parts; and we should see that they correspond each to each in an exact order. It is based on the substitution of one form of a word for another, and is like an exchange, a strictly equal one. It means a new approach to the Vedas, and throws a new light on their value; but we cannot understand them properly unless we consider them in the light of action, and believe that they regard it as necessary.

Need of Knowledge

In case of difficulty or doubt there are suggestions in the text itself to guide us. But it is necessary to have knowledge to be able to understand the idea in this manner. The design of composition is such that each part is connected with the other, and there is no lack of words to complete the sense.

Newly Coined Words

We can get only the main idea by changing the form of words, while the subsidiary ones are obtained by means of words which lie in close proximity. There is, however, no difficulty in understanding the real meaning of the text in this manner. A number of words have been newly coined to fit into this scheme, and each succeeding idea is connected with the preceding one. Indeed, it is possible to have this system because a number of new words have been coined in this way. But all words are not of this kind; and a number of existing words, where suitable, have also been used. A single word can describe a composite action in this manner; and when we change its form, all that is required is that the new meaning should be formed out of the meaning of its parts. But we have to use our intelligence to fix upon the meaning.

Meaning of Purification

Indeed, it is necessary to use our intelligence in interpreting the text, specially if there is a conflict of opinion. Certain ideas have been expressed by means of similes; and the 'purification' or correct formation of a word really means that it is being expressed more exactly than before—that is, by means of its division into parts. When the form of a word is changed, there is an implication that it has not been clearly expressed in its original form. This, however, may not always be so; and we may change its form because it has been stated that we should do so.

Difficult Expressions

It is not always easy to describe an action in words; and so, if we find that a certain expression is unsuitable, we must not suppose that it is meaningless; and we may have to divide it into parts to understand it.

Condition of a New Meaning

We must not make any alteration in the language of the text; and if a word has a bearing on the idea of action, we should accept its meaning without changing its form. When we change the form of a word, the meaning may appear to be unusual; but we will not err, because certain technical terms have been used to guide us. The real meaning of a word is often very different from its common one, and we can understand it by dividing it into parts, or by referring it to its origin or root, In case of doubt, we may take its common meaning, though it may not be its Vedic sense—for the latter is usually obtained by dividing it into parts. There is nothing irregular in this method of division, for the whole word remains intact, and at the same time we are able to get the correct meaning of the text. However, roots of words should not be divided into parts; and the roots and parts of the same word should, as far as possible, not be mixed together.

How to Divide a Word into Parts

When we divide a word into parts, we may commence with the first part and go on step by step to the last, or we may begin with the last and go back step by step to the first—as suits us best; and when the plan of the most important part has been fixed, the rest will be found to fit into the whole scheme. This applies to single words as well as to compounds.

Miscellaneous Rules

This method of interpretation is not governed by any hard and fast rules; but there are certain directions to guide us, and they may be summed up as follows:—

When to Divide a Word into Parts

It is not necessary to divide all words into parts to understand their meaning. We should do so when the text does not make sense otherwise.

Effect of Division into Parts

When the form of a word is changed in this manner, it becomes an entirely new word, with no connection with its original form.

Uniformity of Meaning

The same word should have the same meaning throughout; and the meaning of a fundamental word cannot be obtained from some other word.

Selection of Meaning

If a word can be interpreted in two ways, which are equally balanced, we should divide it into parts only if it serves some special purpose. We should select the meaning that suits the context best, and has a bearing on the idea of action or a law of life.

Words Connoting Action

The form of words connoting action should, as far as possible, not be changed.

Cause and Effect

If there is mention of a result, we should see that we get a reference to its cause as well.

Fitness of Meaning

When we get a new meaning of a word by dividing it into

parts, it should fit into the whole context, and not stand in isolation by itself.

Authority of the Śruti

The meaning of the entire text should be in accordance with the teachings of the śruti, and that will convince us of its correctness. We shall find that the description of ideas and objects is so accurate, that they appear to be like living creatures.

No Arbitrary Meaning

We cannot give any meaning we like to a word, for there is often a good reason for the meaning that is assigned to it. We should bear in mind that each action is meant to secure an object, and requires that necessary means should be provided for the purpose. There must also be a sequence of cause and effect. We must bear all this in mind when we attempt to find out the meaning of an obscure word by reducing it to its rudimentary form. Indeed, the meaning can be regarded as properly fixed only when it yields a proper result; and, in any case, it must arise from the word itself, with all its parts intact.

The Idea of a God

We can understand the idea of a large number of gods by dividing their names into parts, The planets too are a kind of gods. There are also a large number of other names the real meaning of which can be obtained in the same manner.

Confirmation of Meaning

When we divide a word into parts, the meaning should be obtained from the parts of the word itself, and there should be a confirmation of it as we proceed with the text.

Rules of Grammar

We should divide words into parts in strict accordance with the rules of grammar, and follow the best grammarians. We should bear in mind that there is unity of idea underlying the whole text, and we must not omit any part. In case of doubt we should consult competent teachers, though there may be a difference of opinion among them too.

Result of Bad Arrangement

If words or their parts are badly arranged, we cannot get the correct meaning.

New Expressions

If an expression has never before been used, its form should not be changed, unless there are directions in the text itself requiring us to do so.

Definition of Meanings

If the meaning of a word has not been defined in the text, we cannot define it ourselves We may divide it into parts to get its meaning; but it cannot come to possess any new properties by reason of this division.

A Single Action

Words which express the idea of a single action should not be divided into parts.

Dropping of Parts

When we divide a word into parts some parts which have the same meaning may be dropped.

Parts with the Same Meaning

The parts of words which have the same meaning should be in close proximity to one another; and this rule applies to all principal words.

Variations

All words should have the same meaning throughout; and if there are any variations, they should be specified.

Interpretation of Vedic Hymns: Ṛg Veda

In the *Ṛg Veda* we usually get the correct meaning of words by dividing them into parts. In a number of cases, however, there is no conflict between the new and the original meaning of words. But it would, as a rule, be advisable to divide words into parts, and then we can always check up whether the meaning is correct or not.

The *Gāyatrī* verses and certain other hymns have to be interpreted by means of division of words into parts There are, however, a number of words which have to be interpreted in a different way. But we must not mix up words, or omit any part of the text, and need to use our intelligence to interpret it.

In the hymns of the *Ṛg Veda*, beginning with the word *Manota*, the form of words should not be changed. We can understand their meaning in different ways; and, in certain cascs, from thc cffcct thcy produce.

In the *Pavamāna* hymns, sung at the *Jyotiṣṭoma* sacrifice, it is necessary to change the form of words. We are also permitted to make a change in the text at our discretion. The words used are quite new, and the method of interpretation depends on the nature of the text; and the only test is that we should be able to understand it properly.

Sāma Veda

The different *Sāman* hymns constitute a single whole, and can be understood by dividing words into parts. But this need not be done in all cases—specially in connection with words which refer to action. In the *Bṛhat-sāman* and *Rathantara-sāman* hymns it is necessary to divide words into parts.

Special Cases

There are also some special cases which need to be dealt with in a special manner.

Numbers

For instance, there are certain special ideas attaching to numbers, and we have to use our intelligence to understand them. We may take these numbers as a whole or in parts, and they may also be compared to certain things. But we should accept what the sacred books say about them; and the idea of their totals is important.

Phenomena of Nature

The idea of the great phenomena of Nature has been dealt with in a special manner. The new and the full moon belong to this class, for they are governed by their own laws.

Desires of Animals

The idea of the attributes of animals cannot be obtained, by means of division of words into parts, for they have their own characteristics; and the theory of the division of words into parts does not apply to them because the nature of their impelling force is different. But we can represent the function of their mind and its relation to desire by means of division of words into partsthough even this is not possible in all cases. The desires of animals are accordingly described in a special manner, which may appear to be new, but is significant, and would be found to be appropriate too. The language of the text in connection with matters of sex is sometimes plain, and sometimes ornate, as occasion requires; but we can understand the idea by piercing through the 'disguise' of words.

The Test of Correctness

The test of correctness is the result that is achieved. But if we divide a word into parts and find that the meaning of one part fits into that of the following two, we may take it that it is correct; and then we can arrange our ideas of action by means of inference This method of interpretation involves a complete substitution of one meaning for another, with a new natural order of connection between words which would itself be a test of its correctness; and, according to Jaimini[8] it would be stupid to ask for more.

The Value of this Method

This method of interpretation means a new approach to the Vedas, and throws a new light on their value. The special character of this explanation is that it enables us to understand the working of the laws of Nature and the great forces associated with them, which are otherwise unintelligible. In this manner we can understand the nature of desire and its relation to action, and several other things. Indeed, the very idea of the *Mantras* or hymns of praise addressed to the gods is transformed into that of an account of the great laws of Nature, thus making for the glory and greatness of the Vedas.

ILLUSTRATIONS

The Subject-matter of the Vedas

The Vedas, as the *Mīmāṁsā* has explained, deal with the many problems of Nature and Man in a number of ways, and with great precision, beauty and wealth of description. Nature consists of an infinite variety of objects, and is governed by a number of laws; but, in spite of apparent conflict, it is characterised by a fundamental unity. Man consists of his body and soul; and the body is said to consist of intellect, *ahaṅkāra* or the I-as-an-actor (where the soul is conceived to be a non-actor), mind, and the senses of knowledge and action. We cannot conceive of the soul by itself, and so can think of it only in terms of these faculties of man; and man is associated with the objects of Nature through desire, purpose or aim; and seeks, by their means, some satisfaction, pleasure, or good—with perfection or purification as his final goal. All life is characterised by action; and action—deliberate action— conceived as Dharma or sacrifice, is the subject-matter of the Vedas; and all that is included in it has been described in a variety of forms, and can be understood by means of the method of interpretation explained by the *Mīmāṁsā*.

Three Ways of Explanation

The *Mīmāṁsā* then goes on to give us a number of illustrations to explain its idea.[9] It tells us that there are three ways of understanding the text of the Vedas: by means of (i) the common meaning of words, (ii) special definitions given in the text itself, and (iii) division of words into parts. It also tells us that, though all these are different from one another and there is often little in common between them, the common meaning of words is not, sometimes, without a connection with their meaning obtained by means of division into parts; and this has been rendered possible because a number of words used in the text have been newly coined for the purpose—though old existing words have also been used. It then gives us a number of illustrations to explain the different methods of interpreting the text—with special reference to the problems dealt with by the sacred books.

The Common Meaning

The first method, based on the common meaning of words, does not require any special illustration; but the *Mīmāṁsā* tells us that certain words—specially those bearing on the idea of action, should not be divided into parts. Indeed, it has been laid down as a fundamental principle of this method of interpretation, that we should at first take the common, current meaning of words; and it is only when they do not make sense, or are otherwise unsatisfactory, that we should divide them into parts to understand their real meaning.

Special Definitions

The *Mīmāṁsā* contains a number of names the meaning of which has been specially defined—and they relate to both Nature and Man; and we are required to accept this meaning in preference to any other.

Division of Words into Parts

The largest number of names, however, are those the meaning of which can be obtained by means of their division into parts. But, as special definitions and meanings obtained in this manner are often connected together, we have combined illustrations for both.

Nature and the Gods

There are a number of expressions of this kind that refer specially to Nature. The gods, for instance, are said to represent the great forms and forces of Nature, which, as the *Sāṅkhya* tells us, include the Intellect, *Ahaṅkāra*, Mind, the ten senses, the five great 'elements' and their respective properties; and so the principal gods of the Vedas refer to all of these. Some of them refer also to the soul; and so the *Mīmāṁsā* refers to a number of them—*Agni*, *Indra*, and *Soma*, *Vāyu* and *Viṣṇu*, *Mitra* and *Varuṇa*, *Heaven* and *Earth* and *Viśvedevas* (All-gods), and explains the meaning of many of them, and tells us how to understand the rest by dividing their names into parts. The planets too are said to be a kind of gods, and we are told how to understand their idea.

Nature and Sacrifice: The Vedi

Nature is also represented in a number of other ways, by means of its objects as well as other forms—grass, herbs, and trees—curd, milk, and water—animals, *śūdra*, or a 'woman'; while 'sweet' water means Nature 'sweetened' into the idea of God by means of sacrifice or good, intelligent and joyful action. Indeed, the whole world of Nature has been conceived in terms of action or a great sacrifice, in which Man too has an important place; and so we have a picture of this great Sacrifice, with its *Vedi* or great platform, in the midst of measured ground, made of bricks of different kinds, each in its proper place, sprinkled with holy water and covered with grass. Then there are the materials of sacrifice—fragrance and flowers, fruits and medicinal plants, and grains of all kinds, with rice above the rest; and all these refer to the world of Nature in the midst of which we live. Then there is the 'sacrificer', and the "priests" who help him to make the sacrifice; and they refer respectively to the soul and the faculties of man—his intellect, *ahaṅkāra*, mind and the senses—by means of which he acts.

Sacrificial Posts and Animals

Then there are a number of sacrificial posts, and animals tied to them with ropes; and these are meant to illustrate the inborn tendencies of man, and the different kinds of actions he performs.

Fire and Clarified Butter

The fire is then kindled, the gods invoked in due form, and clarified butter and a number of things mixed with it poured into the flames; and all this is meant to illustrate the idea and character and scope of intelligent action, and its association with goodness in the life of man.

Explanation of Terms

All these terms have been explained at considerable length and with great wealth of detail in the *Mīmāṁsā*. Thus 'measuring the sacrificial ground' means 'using the mind' in an intelligent action in the world; *Vedi* or the raised platform refers to Nature; the 'bricks' used in constructing it are desires of different kinds—and those placed in the middle are neutral or disinterested desires. Similarly, water, grass, flowers, fruits, grains, and medicinal plants symbolise the life-sustaining, gracious, and healing powers of Nature. Fire, as the *Mīmāṁsā* tells us, refers to the intellect; and so all that is done in connection with it signifies action and its purification, in which the gods or the great forces of Nature play a most important part. The "sacrificer" is the soul; and the four *Ṛtvij* priests are the four faculties of man—his intellect, *ahaṅkāra*, mind, and the senses respectively. The sacrificial posts, *yūpa* and *svaru*, refer to disinterested action and action with a purpose respectively; while the rope tied round an animal refers to the innate characteristics and tendencies with which a creature is born.

Other Illustrations

There are a large number of other expressions with a similar explanation. For instance, the hand represents the idea of action; so does the term *pṛṣtha*; while 'conquest of everything' signifies intelligent action. Early morning work means the best work; *Sāman* is 'active life'; *kapāla* (the alms-bowl) and life in the forest refer to renunciation of action; while *japa* (silent repetition of a sacred name) and an oblation offered to deceased ancestors signify action that is free from desire for fruit.

The Sun and Moon

The *Mīmāṁsā* tells us that Agni or fire refers to the intellect; and the idea of the Sun is the same. The Moon, on the other hand, refers to the mind, which has desire for its special attribute; and so all that relates to *Soma* or the Moon, for the idea of the two is the same—refers to the mind or to desire. Thus no-moon signifies the merger of the mind in the intellect, for the Moon is said to dwell with the Sun on the no-moon night; the new-moon refers to the birth of the mind in the form of desire; the changes of the moon to the changes of the mind and its desires; while the full-moon signifies the fulfilment of desire through action, or the union of the mind with the intellect, for the full-moon is said to be like the Sun.

Desire and its Satisfaction

The idea of desire and its satisfaction is also expressed in many other ways. The 'bricks' used in the construction of Vedi or the sacrificial platform, refer to desire, signifying that Nature (*Vedi*) consists of innumerable objects of desire. The idea of different kinds of desire is expressed in the same manner: for instance, the idea of desire with a purpose, and neutral desires, without any particular object—and so meant for the benefit of all—is expressed by means of certain specified 'bricks' used in the construction of the *Vedi*. Similarly, the word *chanda* (which has a number of meanings, including 'pleasure') signifies desire regarded as an obstacle in our path. Sweetmeats and cakes as well as other articles of food and drink and dress refer to desires and their satisfaction. The mass of people refers to different kinds of desires—some good, some bad—like the people themselves; and there are similar ideas associated with common things, like acts of buying and selling, eating cooked and uncooked food, wearing clothes, giving in charity, and offering sacrifices. Indeed, the whole world is conceived to be full of objects of desire—for the very basis of life, specially family-life, is desire, and so the birth of a son symbolises the satisfaction of desire.

Man and Woman

These illustrations have a great bearing on the ancient idea of human life and its relations. For instance, Man refers to the whole human race, and includes Woman too. But Woman, conceived as a special instrument of creation, is said to symbolise the idea of Nature or *Prakṛti*; and so, as the latter is said to be characterised by unconsciousness, 'woman', we are told, can neither have knowledge nor property. But we have to understand the sense in which the term is used—for all the disabilities associated with a 'woman' refer to her idea as a symbol of the creative power of *Prakṛti*. But woman, conceived as a living creature, is a co-partner of man in everything—knowledge, property, and deeds of sacrifice—even as the *Mīmāṁsā* tells us.

The Four Castes

We have to understand the idea of the four castes in the

same manner. They are said to be *Brāhmaṇa*, *Kṣatriya*, *Vaiśya*, and *Śūdra*; and the *Mīmāṁsā* tells us that the *Brāhmaṇa* refers to the intellect, while the *śūdra* to the objects of Nature; and then, if we obtain the meaning of the remaining two names in accordance with the method explained in the *Mīmāṁsā*, we find that the *Kṣatriya* refers to *ahaṅkāra* and the mind, while the *Vaiśya* to the senses of knowledge and action. Thus it is only the first three 'castes' that can be included in the idea of a living creature or Man, and all the characteristics of a human being can be applied to them; while the *śūdra*, referring as he does to the objects of Nature, can only be described in terms of the character of *Prakṛti*—that is, unconscious, and incapable of acquiring knowledge or property. Indeed, the *śūdra* is like a 'woman' in the sense in which the latter is symbolic of the idea of *Prakṛti*; and, as the latter, even as the *Sāṅkhya* tells us—exists for the sake of *puruṣa* or the soul, so is a 'woman' said to live for her puruṣa or "man." There is, - however, a small difference between the idea of a 'woman' and a *śūdra*. A woman is, indeed, an instrument of creation; but she can also be conceived as a supporter of life, for she gives milk to her young; and both are characteristic of *Prakṛti,* conceived as the original source of life. But the primary emphasis is on the creative power of a woman when she is conceived to be symbolic of the idea of Nature or *Prakṛti*. But we çan conceive of the objects of Nature as supporting the life of creatures too; and so it is possible to conceive of them independently of the idea of a 'woman', when she is regarded as a supporter of life. As the *śūdra* refers to the objects of Nature, he is accordingly the supporter or 'servant' of the living or the first three 'castes'. It is in this manner that the character of the *śūdra* and a 'woman' has been described in the sacred books; and we need to understand the exact meaning of these terms and the sense in which they are used to be able to grasp their original idea.

The Four Stages of Life

The *Mīmāṁsā* also contains a reference to the four stages of human life—that of a student, a householder, a dweller in the forest, and a renouncer of all actions. It tells us that the first is not meant for pleasure, but for acquiring knowledge. We have an experience of desire and its satisfaction at the next stage, and it also enables us to understand the idea of action performed as a sacrifice—for the head of the family thinks of the family in preference to himself, and all his actions are meant for the benefit of all its members. The third stage is one where the idea of family is extended to the whole world, and a person acts for the benefit of all creatures; and the last stage is that when he must pass away, and so renounce everything.

Sacrifice

The idea of sacrifice has a special significance in the Mīmāṁsā, for it deals with the problem of Dharma, which is nothing but action performed as a sacrifice. It tells us that sacrifice means good as well as intelligent action, which purifies both the doer of the deed and the materials used in connection with action; and then we have a number of references to *homa*, *rājasūya*, *jyotiṣṭoma*, a preliminary sacrifice, supplementary sacrifice, bone-sacrifice, renewal of sacrifice, consecration of animals, offering of five cups, and dying in the midst of a sacrifice—together with the names of a number of ceremonies and articles used in connection with them. All this is meant to explain the idea of action, conceived in the widest sense of the term, including all that is in Nature and Man, working in accordance with a law that is both intelligent and good, and preserves and sustains the universe.

Animals and Men

We have observed that an animal refers to the objects of Nature, and man to living creatures, specially the human race. But certain special ideas have also been associated with certain animals: for instance, the cow refers to the senses of knowledge, the horse to the senses of action, and the goat to action.

Figures of Speech

There are also a number of figures of speech in the text. For instance, certain objects have been personified: *Sarasvatī* is the name of a woman as well as a river; and a 'woman' and 'water' both refer to Nature or *Prakṛti*. Hence *Sarasvatī* refers to Nature or *Prakṛti*, and is represented as a goddess. Similarly, desire is personified as a god; but not so Time, for it is an unfailing cause of decay. The human body is described as a chariot, for the latter moves as a single unit, and the body acts in the same manner too; while words once uttered are compared to the action of a sword, because they are beyond recall.

Significance of Numbers

There is a special significance attaching to certain numbers: for instance, the numbers three, six, eleven, and sixteen all refer to the mind in its different aspects: three, where the mind may, for practical purposes, be identified with the intellect; six, when it is associated with only the senses of knowledge; eleven where it is associated with both the senses of knowledge and action; and sixteen where it is associated with the ten senses of knowledge and action, and the five properties of the five great 'elements'. There is no reference to the number twenty-one in the *Mīmāṁsā*; but it occurs in later literature, where it refers to the mind in association with the ten senses and their ten objects—the great 'elements' and their properties.

Similarly, the number five refers to the five senses of knowledge or of action; and ten to the ten senses of knowledge and action combined. The number ten also refers to the idea of multiplication, and one-tenth to that of division.

There are also a number of other ideas associated with numbers: for instance, the numbers 8, 12, 33, 34, 112, and 1200 all refer to Nature or *Prakṛti*—its divisions, variety, or vastness, as the case may be. The number twelve refers also to Time and the intellect; thirteen and four signifiy completeness, and thirteen may also refer to the soul; fifteen implies a sudden retirement from active life; seventeen refers to the 'subtle body' as well as the intellect or the soul, as should suit the context; twenty-six refers to God; while a thousand signifies something indefinitely large, or a long duration of time during which the laws of Nature operate.

The Original Idea of the Vedas

These and several other illustrations are scattered throughout the *Mīmāṁsā*, and they give us a new idea of the Vedas as dealing with the great laws of Nature, with special reference to the life of Man. They have been described in a new form—clear, concise, exact, and accurate—and yet full of life, colour and variety, which can be understood by means of the method of interpretation it has explained. It tells us that the same principle has also been applied to later works, called *smṛti*, for they too deal with the same problems of life, only they lay special emphasis on the character of the soul and the place of God in the scheme of the universe.

The Importance of the Mīmāṁsā

The *Mīmāṁsā* accordingly occupies a most important place, not only among the six systems of Hindu Philosophy, but all ancient and sacred literature. It covers the principal range of the subject-matter of the Vedas; and, as the same ideas have been repeated in later literature in different forms, by enabling us to understand the Vedas, it enables us to understand the central idea of all sacred books—the *śruti* as well as the *smṛti*—or they are all governed by the same method of interpretation, and have the same forms of expression, the difference between them being one of degree rather than kind. Indeed, it contains the substance of some of the most important ideas of ancient science, philosophy, and religion, and gives us a picture of the customs, manners, and ways of life of the people of the times; and so it is possible to reconstruct the ancient edifice of thought and life by its means. A number of ancient ideas, specially those relating to the 'caste-system' and the *śūdra*, the four stages of life, the status of 'woman', the conception of sacrifice and the renunciation of action—may not be the same as those of later times or our own; but that would only show how many changes have taken place during the intervening years.

REFERENCES

1. References to Dharma are contained in MS. I, i, 1-5, 24-26; I, iii, 1-14; II, i, 9-12; iv, 1-2, 14; and IX, i, 1-4.

   Sacrifice means good, intelligent, and joyful action, meant for the benefit of all. Such action can transform the idea of Nature into that of God; that is, if we believe that the action of Nature is good, intelligent, and makes for joy, we believe in God as *Sat-cit-ānanda*.

2. References to Action are to be found in almost every part of the *Mīmāṁsā*.
3. References to the Vedas are to be found throughout the *Mīmāṁsā*. References to their contents are contained particularly in I, i, 27-33; ii, 1-53; iii, I, 15-16, 26-35; II, i, 13-49; III, viii, 15-18; IV, iii, 17-27; ; VI, i, 33-43; ii, 17-30; iii, 13-17; VII, 1-2, 11-12; iii, 12-15; X, v, 26-58.
4. References to the method of interpretation are to be found in almost every part of the *Mīmāṁsā*, and only a brief summary is attempted here.
5. The *Nyāya* system mentions nine *dravyas*—the five great 'elements', Time, Space, mind, and the Soul.
6. The manner in which each part of a word, or a letter of the alphaber, represents an idea or action may be illustrated by words like UNO, UNESCO, etc., current in these days, where each letter, U, N, E, S, C, and O represents an idea or an object. The ancients, however, went much further than this, for they distributed all the *dravyas* or concepts of philosophy among the letters of the *Sanskṛt* alphabet, so that it was possible to give a fixed meaning to each letter, and coin fresh words without difficulty. The modern word-maker works from the opposite side, and forms a new word from the first letters of the names of certain objects; and the result often is that a letter may have as many meanings as there are words beginning with it. For instance, the letter A occurs in A.I.R. as well as F.A.O.; but it refers to *all* in the one (All-India-Radio), and *agriculture* (Food and Agriculture Organization) in the other case. This is not possible in the ancient system.
7. *Krama* is a peculiar method of reading the Vedic text, according to which the reading proceeds from the first member—word, syllable or letter—to the second; then the second is repeated and connected with the third; and then the third is repeated and connected with the fourth, an so on. This ensures that words are properly divided into parts, and no part is left out. Thus, when we read the word *Prakṛti* according to *Krama*, it has to be Pra-kṛ, kṛ-ti, so that the whole is clearly divided into Prakṛti, and its correct meaning is "(*iti*, an older form of) that is to say (*kṛ*, 'to act') action, (*pra*, 'great' or 'going forth') which is great or is going forth." *Prakṛti* accordingly means "great action about to begin or to go forth"; and this fits into the idea of the *Sāṅkhya*, which tells us that Prakṛti is a state of equilibrium of the three *Guṇas*, and is followed by action or evolution into different forms of life (SS. I, 60-66).
8. The celebrated author of the *Mīmāṁsā*, *Sūtras*.
9. These illustrations are to be found scattered throughout the *Mīmāṁsā*, and the reader may consult the Glossary and Index to the *Mīmāṁsā*.

IX

THE YOGA SYSTEM

From Mīmāṁsā to Yoga: Meaning of Yoga

After the *Mīmāṁsā* comes *Yoga*, based on the character of the intellect.

The word *Yoga* has a number of meanings in *Sanskṛt*; but it has been specially defined by the author of this system as consisting in the control of the activities of the mind; and its object is said to be to produce wholeness or harmony of life, and to reduce pain to a minimum.

The reference to the control of the activities of the mind is significant, for it can be exercised only by what is higher than the mind—namely, the intellect, which is the basis of this system. We have observed that the *Mīmāṁsā* is based on the character of *ahaṅkāra* or the I-as-an-actor; but its last chapter deals with the problem of sex life, as a part of creative action; and that is specially associated with desire or the activity of the mind, and needs to be properly regulated and controlled. As the intellect is higher than both mind and *ahaṅkāra*, we are thus able to make an easy transition from *Mīmāṁsā* to *Yoga*.

The Problem of Yoga

We have seen that *Nyāya* and *Vaiśeṣika* deal chiefly with the problem of knowledge, while the *Mīmāṁsā* is concerned with that of action. *Yoga* attempts to integrate both knowledge and action, and to give us an idea of wholeness or harmony of life, by means of which all pain can be reduced to a minimum.

Sāṅkhya and Yoga

The removal of pain is the chief problem of the *Sāṅkhya*

too, and it examines the relation of knowledge to action at considerable length—for it too partakes of the character of the intellect, and lays special emphasis on discrimination, an attribute of the intellect, as a means of securing freedom from pain. But its object is more to amplify than to integrate the different points of view of knowledge and action; and so it comes to the conclusion that there is no joy in life, and a man can attain his end only by means of renunciation of all actions. It admits, however, that a person must act so long as he lives; but he should do so sparingly, till gradually all action comes to an end, and he is made free. Action, according to the *Sāṅkhya*, is thus a necessary evil, and not a necessary good.

The point of view of *Yoga* is not exactly the same. As it attempts to integrate knowledge with action, it lays equal emphasis on both, and stresses the importance of knowledge as well as action. It points out that there is a measure of joy in life, and explains how great and good things can be achieved in the world by means of this integration. But it also believes that a time must come at last when all action comes to an end; and so a total cessation of action must still be regarded as the ultimate end of life.

The Idea of God

Yoga also takes us a step further towards the idea of God. The *Sāṅkhya*, as we have seen, dispenses with His necessity; but it has no objection to the existence of a God who is like a liberated soul, having nothing whatever to do with the world: only such a God can be of little use to man.

The *Nyāya* makes a passing reference to *Iśvara* or God, but regards Him more as a spectator of things—unable to provide or to prevent the result of actions.

The *Vaiśeṣika* refers, not to God, but to an Unseen Power, which plays an important part in the manifestation of extraordinary things; while the *Mīmāṁsā* tells us of gods or the great forms and forces of Nature, which are both seen and unseen, and without which no great action can ever take place.

Yoga takes up the *Sāṅkhya* idea of God, as corresponding

to that of a liberated soul, but points out that He has an important place in our life, and we can attain our goal by devotion to Him. Thus we have in *Yoga* what may be called a personal God; but it does not say that He is a creator in any real sense of the term.

Evolution of Ideas

Yoga is thus a further stage in this scheme of thought, but has a great deal in common with the *Sāṅkhya*. Indeed, as the *Bhagavad Gītā* tells us, there is little difference between the two systems; but their conclusions are not identical, for their points of view are not the same. *Yoga* recognises the importance of action, though it gives an equal or perhaps even a higher place to knowledge; and so paves the way for the final conclusion of *Vedānta*. That system, as we shall see, attempts to evolve a perfect harmony between knowledge and action; and includes all ideas of creation,— by *Prakṛti* or an Unseen Power or the great forces of Nature—as well as a personal God—in its conception of *Brahma*, who is both personal and impersonal, and combines *Puruṣa* and *Prakṛti* into one. Indeed, as we have observed, *Prakṛti* itself is transformed into God by being associated with the idea of Sacrifice, and so becomes *Sat-cit-ānanda*—goodness, intelligence, and joy.

The Plan of the Work

The *Yoga* system is divided into four chapters; and the whole work follows an integrated plan, being of the nature of a discussion.

In the first chapter the author gives us the meaning of *Yoga* and its implications, and goes on to discuss each of them separately. This is continued in the second chapter, where we are also told of the eight means of attaining to Yoga, five of which are examined in this chapter. The remaining three are examined in the third chapter, which also tells us of the many powers that can be acquired by means of *Yoga*. In the last and fourth chapter the author explains how the soul can attain to freedom from the bondage of life.

The text may now be summarised as follows :

CHAPTER - I

YOGA AND THE PROBLEMS OF LIFE

Yoga consists in the control of the activities of the mind (1-3). There are five such activities, some of which cause pain and some do not (4-6); and it is necessary to understand them (7-11). It is also necessary to understand the idea of restraint (12-14), freedom from desires (15-16), soul (17-18), life and its purpose (19-23), and God (24-29); and that will enable us to remove the obstacles that distract the intellect (30-32), and attain to calmness of mind (33-34) by understanding the behaviour of the mind itself (35-40). That will make for wisdom and a state of *samādhi*, where knowledge leads to righteous action (41-50),—and even beyond this, where there is no action at all (51).

The Meaning of Yoga

Yoga consists in the control of the activities of the mind; and it is only when a person is able to see things in their proper light, that he may be said to have been established in his real nature, and to understand himself (1-3).

Different Kinds of Activities

Activities are of five kinds, which cause pain as well as do not cause pain. They are (i) means of acquiring knowledge; (ii) misapprehension; (iii) doubt; (iv) slumber; and (v) memory (4-6).

The means of acquiring knowledge are sense-perception, inference, and the sacred books; misapprehension is false knowledge; doubt arises from following the meaning of words without understanding their real idea; slumber is a state of unconsciousness, when there is no sensation of any kind; and memory is the power of retaining a thing that has been perceived (7-11).

Restraint

A person can restrain his activities by means of repeated practice and freedom from worldly desires. Repeated practice is secured by means of effort; and when it is put forth assiduously, gently, without interruption, and for a long time, a person becomes firm in his restraint (12-14).

Freedom from Worldly Desires

A person becomes free from worldly desires, when he becomes conscious of his power to control all kinds of desires. But higher than the freedom from desires for objects is the freedom from desires for their attributes; and that is attained when a person perceives his own soul (15-16).

The Soul

The nature of the soul can be understood by means of reasoning, reflection, joy, and the idea of consciousness. One means of the knowledge of the soul is the cessation of all kinds of effort; and another is the residue of impressions of previous actions (17-18).

Life and its Purpose

Those who believe in *Prakṛti* maintain that all things will be dead in the end. But there are others who believe that, before that happens, there are many things to achieve—faith, heroism, memory, harmony of things, and wisdom; and all these can be attained by all kinds of persons,—only if they desire to be free from the violence of passion; and all can do so by means of devotion to God (19-23).

God

God is a special kind of *Puruṣa* or Soul who is untouched

by thought of pain, action, and its result. He is omniscient, and there is no one like Him. He is not limited by Time. His idea is expressed by means of the sacred syllable *Om*, and can be understood by means of its silent repetition. After that a person can understand his own soul, and all obstacle in his path disappear (24-29).

Obstacles and their Removal

The obstacles which distract the intellect are disease, idleness, doubt, negligence, want of energy, incontinence, perception of false ideas, instability, and looseness of conduct. Pain, despair, trembling of the body, and breathing in and out are linked up with these distractions; and the remedy against them is the constant practice of Truth (30-32).

Calmness or joy of mind is obtained by means of universal friendliness, compassion, sympathy in joy, and indifference to the objects of pleasure and pain, good as well as evil; and also by means of regulating the in-coming and out-going breath (33-34).

The manner in which the mind behaves depends on the nature of its activity as directed towards the objects of the senses; but the pure activity of the mind is without any sorrow; and the mind that is free from desire for its objects is free from sorrow too. Or this state may be attained by means of the knowledge of dreams and sound sleep; or it may arise from meditation; and the power of such a person extends to the infinitesimally small and the infinitely great (35-40).

Wisdom and the Vision of Reality

When a wise man is established in this state, and his worldly desires come to an end, his mind shines like a jewel, and is unaffected by anything. But when a man is perplexed by doubt, he falls into a state of confusion and uncertainty. But all uncertainty disappears when the memory is purified, when the form of a thing drops, as it were, and only the reality is seen (41-43).

It is in this manner that we can understand the real nature

of all things. But this state of *samādhi* or intense contemplation contains the seed of future actions. The soul attains to a state of serenity when it has experience of that which lies beyond the range of thought; and in such a state knowledge leads to righteous action; and its impressions can blot out all other impressions (44-50).

But when even this is destroyed, there arises—because everything has been destroyed—a state of contemplation which is without the seed of any future action (51).

CHAPTER - II

YOGA AND THE MEANS OF ATTAINING IT

The first state of *Yoga* is one of action, action performed as a sacrifice. It is of three kinds, and makes for wholeness or harmony of life (1-2).

There are a number of causes of pain (3), and it is necessary to understand all of them (4-11). That will enable us to understand that the root of pain lies in action (12-15); and it is possible to prevent it by not allowing impulses, which have not yet arisen, to arise (16-17), and by understanding the character of the soul and the objects with which it associates itself (18-20).

This association is caused by want of knowledge; and when the latter disappears, so does the bond between the soul and its objects, and it becomes free. This knowledge is acquired by different means of attaining to *Yoga* (21-28).

There are eight means of attaining to *Yoga* (29), and it is necessary to understand them. Of these the first five are (i) self-control (30-31), (ii) restraint (32-34), and we should understand the result of self-control (35-39) as well as restraint (40-45), (iii) posture of meditation (46-48), (iv) breath-control (49-53), and (v) the withdrawal of the senses from their objects (54-55).

Yoga of Action

The *Yoga* of action performed as a sacrifice consists in austerity or severe meditation *(tapas)*, study of the Vedas, and devotion to God; and its object is to produce wholeness or harmony of life, and to reduce pain to a minimum (1-2).

Causes of Pain

The causes of pain are absence of knowledge, egoism, desire, aversion, and intentness on securing an object (3).

Absence of knowledge can be in respect of things that are dormant or asleep, are minute, incoherent, or very large; and it consists in regarding that which is transient, impure, painful and not concerned with the soul as the very opposite of all this. Egoism consists in identifying the powers of the senses with those of contemplation; desire in thinking that pleasure will follow as a result of action; aversion in believing that there will be pain as a result of action; while intentness on securing an object is a natural characteristic of even a wise man. All these should be avoided at their very inception; and that is always possible by means of meditation (4-11).

The Root of Pain

The root of pain lies in action; and so long as this root lasts, there will always be pain. Actions have pleasure and pain for their result because of good and evil cause. But life is full of pain even to a wise man, because of the troubles of change, sorrow, impressions made on the mind, as well as opposition of the objects of Nature (12-15).

Prevention of Pain

But it is possible to prevent pain, for an impulse that has not yet arisen can be avoided; and the association of the seer with the objects seen is the cause of impulse (16-17).

Objects: Attributes: the Seer

A visible object is characterised by form, activity, and location in a place. It consists of the 'elements', it can be referred to the senses, and can be enjoyed or given away as a gift. The attributes of objects may be special, general, possessed of characteristic marks, and not possessed of characteristic marks. The seer is one who can see; and when pure, has perception of consciousness; and the seer is the soul, because it has perception of consciousness (18-20).

Bondage and Freedom of the Soul

The union of the soul with the objects of Nature enables it to understand the real nature of its own powers and theirs. But the cause of this union is *a-vidyā* or absence of knowledge; and when that disappears, the union also comes to an end. When the soul ceases to look at the objects of Nature—that is its frèedom from birth; and the means of this cessation are the faculty of discrimination and freedom from confusion; and the wisdom of such a person becomes sevenfold at the last stage. That is secured by means of acting in conformity with the means of attaining to *Yoga*; and when all impurity is destroyed, the light of knowledge enables a man to attain to discrimination (21-28).

Eight Means of Attaining to Yoga

There are eight means of attaining to *Yoga*—self-control, restraint, posture for meditation, breath-control, withdrawal of the senses from their objects, concentration of mind, meditation, and *samādhi* or intense contemplation, when the contemplator and the object contemplated become identified (29).

Self-control consists in non-injury, truth, non-stealing, continence, and renunciation. These are universal and required of all in all circumstances (30-31).

Restraint is not so universal, and consists in cleanliness or purity of mind, contentment, austerity, study of the Vedas, and contemplation of God. In this connection if one has a doubt, he should think of the opposite side of the question, and that will resolve his doubt (32-34).

Result of Self-Control

Non-injury means abandonment of all enmity. When a person is established in truth, he understands the interdependence of cause and effect,—of action and its fruit. Non-stealing means contentment and absence of covetousness of anything; and he who is established in it is wealthier than the wealthiest man in the world. When a man is established in continence, he gains manly power or energy. When a person renounces what he should renounce, he knows how to live in the world and be happy (35-39)

Result of Restraint

When a man becomes clean or pure in mind, he feels disinclined towards the organs of his own body, and does not associate with others. When the nature of his mind is purified, he is filled with gladness, becomes one-pointed, has control over his senses, and understands his soul. When he is contented, he becomes exceedingly happy. *Tapas* or austerity destroys his impurities, and makes for perfection of the body and the senses. The study of the Vedas makes for a proper understanding of the great forms and forces of Nature. A person can attain to *samādhi*, when he can identify himself with the object of his contemplation, by means of devotion to God (40-45).

Posture

The posture for meditation should be steady with ease. It should be followed by relaxation of effort, when there will be communion with the Infinite, and all differences between things will disappear (46-48).

Breath-Control

When a person is in that posture, and controls the motion of his in-coming and out-going breath, that is called breath-control. It is of three kinds—external, internal, and relating to the suspension of breath. There is also a fourth kind of breath-control, which goes beyond the external and internal; and it is at this stage that the veil drops, and a person sees the Light of Life. These acts of holding the breath make a man fit for *Yoga* (49-53).

Withdrawal of the Senses from their Objects

The senses are said to be withdrawn from their objects when there is no contact between them and their objects, and they are centred, as it were, in the mind (54-55).

CHAPTER - III

THE MEANS OF ATTAINING TO YOGA : THE POWERS OF YOGA

We can understand the idea of the remaining three means of attaining to *Yoga*—concentration (*dhāraṇā*), meditation (*dhyāna*), and *samādhi*, when the contemplator and the object contemplated become identified—in the same manner (1-3). These three can be taken together, and are called *saṁyama* or deep concentration (4-6); and, as compared with the preceding three, refer to the inner organ of man, beyond which there is a state called *nirbīja*, where there is no action and no result (7-8).

Restraint can achieve many things, and makes for one-pointedness (9-13); but a really pious man follows the law of life, and is not affected by the changing conditions of things (14-15). But *saṁyama* can achieve even more—leading ultimately to perfect knowledge, born of discrimination, which makes a person free (16-54).

Dhāraṇā or Concentration

Dhāraṇā or concentration consists in the fixation of the mind in one place (1).

Dhyāna or Meditation

Dhyāna or meditation arises when, in a state of concentration, a person fixes his attention on one and one object only (2).

Samādhi

Samādhi is said to be a state when the object of contemplation alone appears to exist, and one's own self, as it were, ceases to be (3).

Saṁyama

These three,—*dhāraṇā*, *dhyāna*, and *samādhi* constitute what is called *saṁyama* or deep concentration of the mind; and when that is attained, a person becomes supremely wise; and this *saṁyama* can be made use of in various ways (4-6).

These three, as compared with the five preceding means of attaining to *Yoga*, refer to the interior of the body; but even these belong to a state which is outside the range of what is called *nirbīja*, or that which is not followed by any result or action (7-8).

Powers of Restraint

A person is said to have developed his powers of restraint when, though his consciousness has been fully awakened, he is able to control himself; when he permits his powers to express themselves and even to prevail, but knows the suitable time for exercising restraint and can control his mind, which, having been purified, functions with calmness. When he attains to this state, all search after objects of the senses comes to an end, and he becomes one-pointed; and that is called oneness of the mind and the objects it seeks (9-13).

A pious person is he who follows the law of life irrespective of whether an object is calm or full of excitement; but the development of different persons is different, and that is the cause of the different methods they adopt (14-15).

Powers of Saṁyama

The powers of *saṁyama* or the combination of *dhāraṇā*, *dhyāna*, and *samādhi* are of various kinds. It enables a person to have knowledge of the past and future, the proper meaning of words, his own previous state of birth, and the approach of death, as well as of what is minute, concealed, or remote—and of his body, and the whole world. A person can, by its means, put an end to hunger and thirst, become steady, have knowledge of the mind and soul, and attain to perfection. He can penetrate into the minds of others, make his body light, hear wonderful sounds, pass through space, and remove the veil and see the light. He can have knowledge of the 'elements', and control his senses, leading to perfect knowledge and freedom from the bondage of life. It is this knowledge born of the faculty of discrimination that can make him free (16-54).

CHAPTER - IV

FREEDOM FROM BONDAGE

The different objects of life can be attained by means of various kinds of actions (1-3); but all actions, consciously performed by the mind, are characterised by a purpose (4-6). These actions produce their own results which, in their turn, are the cause of future actions, which again produce their own results; and so the chain of action goes on from birth to birth (7-11).

We know that Time exists (12-13); and need to distinguish between mind and matter (14-17), and the mind and the soul (18-21).

It is also necessary to understand the character of the functions of the intellect (22), and the mind (23-24); and that will enable us to attain to discrimination and put an end to all attachment (25-28). That will be the end of all affliction (29-33), and the soul will be for ever free (34).

Attainment of Objects

Objects can be attained in various ways—conditions of birth, medicines, application of the mind, exercise of the intellect, and *samādhi*. But when the original stage of a substance is completely developed, it changes into another in its natural course. Nevertheless, we cannot know the purpose of the first action in the first substance in Nature (1-3).

The Mind

But the human mind acts with a purpose, which arises

from a state of consciousness when it acts. A person has only one mind, though it prompts a number of senses to action; but when it is associated with the intellect, it becomes free from all vice (4-6).

Actions and their Results

The actions of a *Yogī* are neither good nor bad; while those of others are of three kinds—good, bad, and a mixture of the two. As a result of these actions, a number of impressions are made on the minds of those who are susceptible to them, so that there is an immediate store of future actions and their results, even though this may be in different births, places, and times; and that is so because memory and these impressions mean one and the same thing. But we cannot know the beginning of these actions, because desire, which is their cause, is eternal, and has no beginning. But, as all actions are governed by motive, result, attachment, and the interdependence of things, they come to an end when the latter disappear (7-11).

Time

The past and future exist as real because their course has different characteristics. The difference between them is subtle, but clear; and it is of the nature of the *Guṇas* or the attributes of Prakṛti itself (12-13).

Mind and Matter

We can understand the real state of a substance from the unity of its development. But its idea is also affected by the mind; for even if the substance be the same, if it is associated with different minds, the idea of any two of them may be different (14-17).

Mind and the Soul

The actions of the mind are always known to its 'master' or the soul, because it is always subject to change, while the soul is not. The mind is not self-illuminated, because it cannot see itself (18-21).

Intellect

We can form an idea of the function of our intellect when we see how thought-impressions are formed, and try to grasp the disposition of the mind from the expression of the face (22).

Mind as a Suitable Instrument

As the mind is coloured by both the seer (soul) and the object seen, it is suitable for all purposes. But even that mind, with its innumerable desires, acts for the sake of the soul (23-24).

Discrimination

So far as the soul or the seer is concerned, there comes a time when all thought of attachment must come to an end; and then the mind is inclined towards discrimination, and is not far from freedom from the bondage of life. So long as it is weak, it has desires arising from the impressions of previous actions; but all affliction ends with the end of these impressions (25-28).

End of Affliction

When a person has no interest even in reflection or meditation, he attains to a state of discrimination, and rises to a state of *samādhi*; and after that pain and action both come to an end. Then the perfectly pure one knows how infinite is knowledge, and how small the objects of Nature in the world. Then, as the *Guṇas* or the attributes of Nature have done their work, and displayed all that they had to display, the succession of changes, connected with the moments of Time and lasting till the extreme end of change is grasped, comes to an end (29-33).

Freedom of the Soul

This is the state of freedom of the soul. It means a return of the *Guṇas* or the attributes of the subjects of Nature—which have no further concern with the soul—to their original state of association with *prakṛti*, dissociated from the soul. Or we might say that the Mental Power is established in its own true nature (34).

X

THE VEDĀNTA SYSTEM

The Place of Vedānta

After *Yoga* comes *Vedānta*, the last of the six systems of Hindu Philosophy, based on the character of the soul.

We have seen how we begin with the *Sāṅkhya*, with its idea of *Prakṛti* as the supreme creator of things—all except the soul—and rise by clear gradations of thought to the idea of the importance of God in *Yoga*. But all that has been stated so far is implied in the *Sāṅkhya* itself, and all that the other systems have done is to explain or amplify its ideas; and, even as the *Bhagavad* Gītā tells us, there is no essential difference between *Sāṅkhya* and *Yoga*[1]. The *Sāṅkhya* is frankly dualistic in its conception of *Prakṛti* and *puruṣa* (or the individual soul) as two separate entities; and, while it has no objection to the existence of God in terms of a liberated soul who has nothing whatever to do with anything in the world, and can neither create nor cause anything to be done, it points out that such a God can be of little use to man; and maintains that the freedom of the soul from the bondage of life can be achieved only by means of self-knowledge and renunciation of action. It believes that there is no joy in life—for what is called joy is, according to it, but a form of pain; and this pain is caused by action, which is a characteristic of all things in the world. It tries to explain how we can put an end to action, stating that when a person does not engage in any new actions, the impressions of previous actions, which are the cause of further action—become fainter and fainter, till at last they totally disappear, and the soul becomes for ever free. But it does not succeed in establishing its theory, because, even as the *Mīmāṁsā* tells us, there can be no total extinction of action, and something of it will always remain.

In addition to this there are a number of other gaps of thought in the *Sāṅkhya*, and so the other systems do not hesitate to take a somewhat different point of view: for instance, the *Nyāya* and the *Vaiśeṣika* refer to the soul as an actor, while the *Mīmāṁsā* explains that it is both an actor and a non-actor—acting so long as it dwells in the body, and ceasing to act when it departs; and so their answer to the question of freedom from the bondage of life is not the same as that of the *Sāṅkhya*. *Yoga*, however, while differing from the *Sāṅkhya* in holding that there is joy in life, and many great things can be achieved by means of concentration of thought and effort, is at one with that system in maintaining that our ultimate goal—however far off—is a total renunciation of action. Also, like the *Sāṅkhya*, it makes an attempt to explain how there can be an absolute cessation of action. It, however, gives an important place to God, whom it conceives to be a special kind of *puruṣa* (or the individual soul), in the same manner as is suggested by the *Sāṅkhya* itself—for it does not conceive of Him as a creator in any real sense of the term; but it believes that devotion to this God makes for concentration of thought and effort and success in everything. *Yoga* accordingly gives us the idea of a personal God, but does not essentially take us any further in our quest.

There are thus a number of gaps of thought in these systems; and though a number of points have been amplified or explained, the essential problem still remains, and needs to be tackled from an entirely new point of view; and the solution, so far as it is humanly possible to solve such a problem—is provided by *Vedānta*.

The Meaning of Vedānta

It is commonly believed that the word *Vedānta* (*Veda-anta*) means "complete knowledge of the Veda"; but the opening Sūtra of this system which, as in the case of the other systems, describes its principal subject-matter, tells us that it is an inquiry into the nature of *Brahmā* or God; and that, as the *Mīmāṁsā* has told us, is not the subject-matter of the Vedas. The Vedas, we are told, deal not with the problem of God or even the soul— though there may be stray references to them too—but chiefly with the great laws of Nature and their application to the life of man. This is what the *Bhagavad Gītā* says too; for it tells us that the Vedas deal with the three *Guṇas* or attributes of the objects of Nature, and so it is necessary to go beyond them, and to understand the soul.[2] Hence, as the idea of God corresponds to that of the human soul, for there appears to be no other equally satisfactory way of understanding it—*Vedānta*, dealing as it does with the nature of *Brahmā* or God, cannot be restricted even to a complete knowledge of the Vedas, the subject-matter of which is so different.

It would accordingly be more correct to interpret the word (*Veda-anta*) as "(*anta*, 'end, out-skirt') that which is the end (or is at the end) of the Vedas"; and so would correspond to the idea of the *smṛti*, which refers to post-Vedic literature, and is distinguished from the *śruti*, which refers to the Vedas and all that relates directly to them. Indeed, the subject-matter of the *smṛti*, as distinguished from the *śruti*, is the nature of God and the soul; and, as it is said to follow the latter, so may Vedānta be said to come at the end of the Vedas; and it may be of interest to observe that there are a number of references to the *smṛtis* in the *Sūtras*. Thus, as *Vedānta* is based on the character of the soul, it comes after *Yoga*, based on the character of the intellect.

A New Aspect of Yoga

We have observed that it is not possible to conceive of the soul as pure soul, and so it is necessary to understand its idea in terms of the different faculties of man; and, as the highest of these is the intellect, it is often considered in its light, and the two are, for practical purposes, identified. Now, as *Vedānta* is based on the character of the soul, and *Yoga* on that of the intellect, it means that there should be a great deal in common between them, and the two may even be identified. But we find that their essential conclusions are very different. Hence, if what has been stated here be correct, there should be another way of looking at *Yoga*, different from what has been given in the *Sūtras*.

The Character of the Bhagavad Gītā

The colophon or inscription at the end of each chapter of the *Bhagavad Gītā* describes it as a "knowledge of *Brahma* in the *śāstra* (or sacred book) of Yoga"; and we find that it really deals with *Brahmā*, and at the same time each of its chapters is said to have a bearing on Yoga. Indeed, *Kṛṣṇa* has been described as Supreme *Brahmā*[3] as well as the God of *Yoga*[4] (*Yogeśvara*), and yet his idea is not the same as that of *Iśvara* or God as given in the *Yoga-Sūtras*; for though the latter conceives of a personal God, He is not spoken of as a creator anywhere, whereas *Kṛṣṇa* is referred to as such again and again.[5] He is a personal as well as an impersonal deity,—the knowable and the unknowable united together into one.[6] He is the Supreme Intelligence identified with the Supreme Soul, and can be understood only by the soul of man when it realises the highest Truth;[7] and it is for this reason that he is spoken of as the author of *Vedānta*, the knower of the Vedas,[8] greater than *Brahmā* himself,[9] nay, his very abode,[10] for it is by means of the intellect alone that we can understand the idea of the soul and of God in his manifest form—that is, as characterised by certain attributes. There is thus another way of looking at *Yoga*, different from the system described in the *Sūtras*; and there are a number of references to it in the *Mahābhārata*. It gives us a personal idea of God, as distinguished from his impersonal conception as *Brahmā* in the *Vedānta Sūtras*; and, as the whole idea is based essentially on the intellect, it is called by the name of *Yoga*: only we should remember that the intellect in this case is for practical purposes identified with the soul, whereas in the case of the *Yoga-Sūtras* it is intellect conceived in its own character as such. There are undoubted points of contact between the two conceptions, and to that extent the idea of the *Yoga-Sūtras* would coincide with that of the Vedānta-*Sūtras*, or the idea of *Yoga* in the *Mahābhārata*: otherwise they would be different. On the other hand, the *Kṛṣṇa*-idea. of God would include the personal idea of God in *Yoga-Sūtras* as well as the idea of *Brahmā* in *Vedānta*.

This is indeed, the idea of *Kṛṣṇa* in the *Bhagavad Gītā*; but, as the whole work is a synthesis of all the great systems of philosophy, it contains certain apparent points of conflict too, which can be resolved only when we look at the problem in the light of these systems.

Vedānta and the Mīmāṁsā

We have observed that the *Mīmāṁsā* is based on the character of *ahaṅkāra* or the I-as-an-actor; but that can be conceived to be a separate entity only when the soul is regarded as a non-actor. When, however, we think of the soul as an actor itself, the idea of *ahaṅkāra* can only be merged into it; and it can retain its separate character only in its secondary sense as *abhimāna* or egoism, which must disappear before the soul can understand its true character as soul.[11] The idea of *ahaṅkāra* in this secondary sense still continues to be used in literature.

Thus *ahaṅkāra*, in its original sense as the I-as-an-actor, is only an aspect of the soul; and, as the *Mīmāṁsā* is based on the character of the former, and *Vedānta* on that of the latter, the former is also called *Pūrva-Mīmāṁsā*, and the latter *Uttara-Mīmāṁsā*, or the first and latter part of philosophy. We also find that the *Mīmāṁsā* deals with the subject-matter of the Vedas and the method of their interpretation, while *Vedānta* deals with the problem of God and the soul, or what comes "at the end of the Vedas"; and it is for this reason that the one refers widely to the *śruti*, and the other to the *smṛti*. Again, the *Mīmāṁsā* tells us that the gods of the Vedas are nothing but the great forms and forces of Nature; and it is the idea of these powers, working in accordance with a law that is conceived to be good, intelligent, as well as conducive to joy of life, that has been evolved into that of *Brahmā* or the God of *Vedānta*.

Vedānta and the Other Systems:

An Alternative Solution—We have seen how the chief ideas of the *Sāṅkhya* have been explained or expanded by the other systems, so that the *Yoga* solution of the eternal problem of life—namely, freedom from the bondage of the world—is practically the same as that of the *Sāṅkhya*. We have also seen the main idea of this system in regard to the character of the soul and the manner of its obtaining freedom; and the reason why it fails to carry conviction is that it is impossible to agree that there can be a total annihilation of action, so that the soul cannot at any time divest itself of its 'subtle body', made up of the constituents of *Prakṛti*, and become its own self as pure soul again.

It is at this points that *Vedānta* directs its chief criticism. It maintains that if, as it is generally agreed, the soul cannot, at any stage, be separated from its 'subtle body', it cannot be regarded as altogether different from all that is in *Prakṛti* or Nature—for the 'subtle body' is said to be composed of seventeen parts—the essence of the intellect, mind, the ten senses, and the five properties of the five 'elements'. It is there when the soul abides in a body on earth and is said to live, and it accompanies it also after death; and the only difference between the two states of life, on earth and after death, is that the 'subtle body' comes to be associated with the five great 'elements' of Earth, Water, Fire, Air, and Ether in the one case, and is without them in the other. In the latter case it is also without *ahaṅkāra* or the I-as-an-actor, for no action, in the sense in which we understand the term, takes place.

The conclusion of *Vedānta* accordingly is that the soul and Nature belong essentially to the same class; and, if it is possible to hold—as the *Sāṅkhya* and the other systems do—that matter (the senses and the 'elements' and their properties) is formed out of the mind; we can conceive of *Prakṛti* itself as emanating from *Brahma*. Indeed, *Vedānta* conceives of *Brahmā* as *Prakṛti* and soul taken together as one, for the two are for ever inseparable both in a state of rest and action; and when life evolves or there is action emerging out of a state of rest—the great forces of Nature, from the intellect down to the 'elements', issue forth; but each of them contains within itself an essence of the energy of the soul as well. The latter has power to permeate everything, but is associated with them in various degrees: for instance, we cannot associate it so clearly with the 'elements' as with the mind and the intellect. It cannot be separated from its 'subtle body', and is said to live when it comes to abide in the midst of the 'elements' which constitute the basis of its physical body; and it passes away when it leaves these behind, and goes to dwell in some other world beyond; and is finally merged in *Brahmā*,—the fountain source from which all things arise, and into which they enter at the end.

Brahma

This *Brahmā* too is of the same character as the soul—the highest *Puruṣa* (soul) and *Prakṛti* (Nature) united together into one; and so *Vedānta*, unlike the *Sāṅkhya* and its allied systems, gives us a purely monistic conception of life. Thus we see that we begin with Nature as the supreme creator of things and think of the soul as different from all of them, and end with *Brahma*, where Nature and the soul are united together into one; and that is the ultimate Reality, which is both personal and impersonal, manifest as well as unmanifest. This is the final conclusion of *Vedānta*, and this the 'knowledge of *Brahmā*' in the *Bhagavad Gītā*, as expressed in the conception of *Kṛṣṇa*.

It is by no means difficult to understand this idea. Indeed, as we have seen, the very idea of Nature can be transformed into that of God by means of the idea of Sacrifice. The *Mīmāṁsā* tells us that sacrifice or good and intelligent action, performed in accordance with its law, and meant for the benefit of all, transforms and purifies not only the doer of the deed, but also sanctifies the materials of the sacrifice. It is this idea that is amplified by *Vedānta*, for the idea of *Prakṛti* itself is transformed into that of *Brahmā* or God by means of the idea of Sacrifice.

This really means that if we believe that the whole universe is governed by a law which is essentially intelligent and good, and makes for the preservation and continuance of life; and that despite all changes, including sorrow and death, there is joy in life when we take it as a whole—we believe that there is God in the universe, who creates, supports, and continues life without end, and that death itself is but a door to another life. It is in this manner that we can transform Nature itself into *Brahmā* by means of the idea of Sacrifice, and believe that the universe is full of life and joy without end; and this is the essential truth of *Vedānta*. It does not deny the reality of pain, but maintains that we are for ever acting to change it into pleasure or joy, so that freedom from the bondage of life consists not in the renunciation of action, but a state of equanimity in the midst of action and the experience of pleasure and pain.

The Conclusion of Vedānta

Thus we see that the conclusion of *Vedānta* is altogether different from that of the *Sāṅkhya*; but, while maintaining that life is synonymous with action, and action as a sacrifice is of the essence of the idea of God, it believes that knowledge and action are but counterparts of the same energy of the soul, and that with every breath we draw, we know and act at the same time; and so it includes all that the other systems have to say on the subjéct of freedom from the bondage of life.

The Plan of the Work

The 'work is divided into four chapters, and each chapter conists of four parts. As in the case of the other systems, the opening *Sūtra* tells us that its subject-matter is inquiry into the nature of *Brahmā*; and, as the idea of *Brahmā* is associated with that of the soul, and the latter is conceived to be characterised by desire as well as joy, and is regarded as a creator, we have a discussion of all these questions with reference to both *Brahmā* and the soul in the four parts of the first chapter.

In the second chapter the author examines the consequence of regarding *Prakṛti* as the supreme creator of things, and then goes on to consider the character of the soul as an actor, and of *Brahmā* with reference to *Prakṛti*.

In the third chapter we are told of the relation of the soul to the body, how a new birth takes place, and how the soul, after death, is said to live is the world beyond. The author also deals with the problems of knowledge, action, and pain; explains the process of creation in this world, and points out that creation by the Infinite must be of the same kind. He also tells us how we can understand the idea of God, and explains his idea of *Brahmā*, with special reference to the character of the soul.

In the last chapter the author considers the question of re-birth and transmigration of the soul, and explains the limitations of the idea of freedom of the soul from the bondage of life, as it is understood by the *Sāṅkhya* and the other systems; and points out that real freedom can consist only in a state of equilibrium in the midst of action and the experience of pleasure and pain. He who attains to this may be said to be free from the revolutions of birth.

The *Sūtras* may now be summarised as follows:—

REFERENCES

1. BhG. V, 4-5.
2. BhG. II, 45. This would explain why the references to the Vedas in the *Bhagavad Gītā* are not very eulogistic. The discourse of the *Gītā* takes us beyond the Vedas to the idea of God and the soul.
3. BhG. x, 12.
4. BhG. XI, 9; XVIII, 78.
5. BhG. VII, 6; VIII, 18-21; IX, 4, 7-8; X, 8, 39-42; etc., etc.
6. BhG. XII, 3-7.
7. BhG. XI, 52-55.
8. BhG. XV, 15.
9. BhG. XI, 37.
10. BhG. XIV, 27.
11. This is the idea of *Abhimanyu*, the son of *Arjuna*, in the story of the *Mahābhārata*. He personifies *abhimāna*, while *Arjuna* is the human soul; and the whole story of the life and character of each centres round these ideas. This has already been explained (MM. III-V).

CHAPTER - I

BRAHMA AND THE SOUL

PART - I

Let us now inquire into the nature of *Brahmā*, who may be described as the origin of the universe (1-11).

Freedom means joy, and joy is not opposed to desire (12-20). The soul is different from a number of things, like Ether or light, but is still characterised by joy (21-31).

Brahma

Let us now inquire into the nature of *Brahmā*. *Brahmā* is that which is the origin of the universe; but He has also been described as a spectator of things in the sacred books (1-5).

When we say that *Brahmā* is the origin of the universe, it does not mean that He should be associated with *Guṇas* or the attributes of the objects of Nature. We can conceive of Him independently of the *Guṇas* in the same manner as we are able to do of the soul (6-11).

The Character of the Soul

The state of freedom is one of joy; and we say so because the soul itself is full of joy (12-17).

There is no real contradiction between desire and joy, for desire can be in consonance with Dharma (18-20).

The soul is different from a number of things—for instance, Ether, vital breath, and light (21-24). It is possible to argue that if it is characterised by desire, it cannot be very different from them. But this is not a valid objection, for desires can be controlled; and we say that the soul is different from the 'elements' because they are divisible into parts, while the soul is not (25-26). Indeed, we cannot deny that the soul is different from these things (27-31).

PART - II

THE CHARACTER OF THE SOUL

We can prove that the soul exists, and is an actor and a propagator of the species; and, as there is joy in the act of creation, joy is a characteristic of the soul (1-18).

We cannot think of the soul as it is, and the best way is to think of it in terms of the intellect -(19-32).

The Character of the Soul

We can prove the existence of the soul; and it is generally agreed that it is different from *Guṇas* or the attributes of the objects of Nature; and, in any case, is conceived to be without a body. But it is an actor and, though small in size, can fill the whole body in the same manner as Ether (1-8).

The soul is an eater of food, and a propagator of the species. The act of creation is a secret act, corresponding to the nature of the soul. There is also joy in a proper act of creation, and joy is a characteristic of the soul (9-18).

This may appear to be a new conception of the soul, but is none the less true. The soul is an actor, because it is the original thinker; but, as it is unmanifest, we cannot conceive of it as it is, and have to clothe it in some form to grasp its idea. That form is the intellect, which is said to be a common characteristic of all men. We cannot deny that the intellect is the only form in which we can think of the soul; and there is general agreement of learned men on the subject (19-32).

PART - III

BRAHMA AND THE SOUL

We can understand the idea of *Brahmā* from the character of the soul (1-3). The soul is associated with the vital breath, but is different from it: so is *Brahmā* (4-9). The soul has other characteristics too, and the idea of *Brahmā* corresponds to them as well (10-43).

The Idea of Brahma

Brahmā is the resting place of Heaven and Earth and all ther things, and we can understand His idea from the character of the soul (1-3).

The Character of the Soul

The soul is the supporter of *prāṇa* or vital breath, but the two are different. It is associated with the vital breath in accordance with a law, so that it may live in the world and act and create (4-9).

It is imperishable because it abides in Ether, and that too is so in accordance with a law (10-12).

It is small in size but great in action, and can make itself manifest only through the body in which it abides, and by means of which it acts. But we cannot define it by means of words (13-24).

So far as the body is concerned, it fills the whole of it, but abides more spicially in the heart (25-26).

We cannot deny that the soul is an actor, or that it has a form—it is always known by its 'subtle body', which is its form, and by means of which it acts. It is eternal because this 'subtle body' of its is eternal too. The actions of the soul are of various kinds; and they arise from its own natural activity (27-43).

PART - IV

THE CHARACTER OF THE SOUL

The soul is an actor, and the body is its form (1-3); but no language can describe it truly as it is. It is sometimes described in terms of *prāṇa* or vital breath (4-12): but the two cannot be identified (13-28).

The Character of the Soul

The soul is an actor, and the body is its form. It is minute but all-pervading, because of its special characteristics; and it is because it depends on the body for its manifestation, that it desires to have different objects of Nature (1-3).

No language can describe the soul as it is, but its best description is that it is like the intellect. At the same time we cannot deny that it is an actor; and the original idea of the science of Astrology is based on its conception as such. It is for this reason that it is also described in terms of *prāṇa* or the vital breath, which is its chief instrument of action (4-12).

There are some who would identify the soul with the vital breath; but the logical consequence of this would be that we should regard *Prakṛti* or Nature as the sole supreme creator of the universe, including the soul (13-28).

CHAPTER II

THE LOGIC OF IDEAS

PART I

If we identify the soul with the vital breath, we must regard *Prakṛti* as the sole supreme creator of everything, and accept the logic of this idea (1-3); and it must mean that the soul cannot make itself free from the bondage of life. But if we believe that the very goal of its life is this freedom, we must come to a very different conclusion (4-37).

Logic of Ideas

We cannot deny that, if we identify the soul with the vital breath, the logical consequence is that we must regard *Prakṛti* as the sole supreme creator of all things; and this has the advantage of giving us a simple monistic conception of life (1-3).

The Issue

But the real point at issue is not this, but rather that the soul is not an actor, and only imagines that it is so, whereas the real actor is *ahaṅkāra*. It is said that the soul is able to imagine itself to be an actor because it imitates *ahaṅkāra*, and has the power of doing so. But this argument involves an inherent contradiction; for we cannot explain why, if the soul is really not an actor, it should imagine that it is so. Again, it would be impossible to show how, if it imitates *ahaṅkāra*, it can cease to do so; and in such a case there can be no possibility of its freedom from the bondage of life (4-25).

A Different View

But the very conception of the soul as a non-actor arises from this desire for freedom; and if that is not possible on this assumption, the assumption itself must break down. Hence we must agree that the soul is an actor. But this does not mean that it is subject to change: it only means that our idea of freedom has been changed, and life itself becomes like sport. It eliminates the idea of harshness or evil from things; for, if we look at the beginning of life, we find that there can be no harshness or evil in the first action of a creature; and it is this first action that makes for the continuance of action without end (26-37).

PART - II

THE SOUL AS AN ACTOR

We cannot know the origin of creation or action; but we know that each action is distinct from the other, and has a purpose to serve (1-7).

We cannot deny that the soul is an actor, and *ahaṅkāra* is only its form when it engages in action (8-21). The real actor is the soul, and it is the soul that perceives all things (22-33): but it cannot function without the assistance of the body (34-45).

The Nature of Action

We cannot know the origin of creation or action, and can only say that it is of the nature of life itself (1-3). But each action is distinct from the other, and has a purpose to serve (4-7).

The Soul is an Actor

We cannot deny the importance of the soul; nor can we divest it of its intellectual powers, or say that it is not an actor (8-12).

The Soul and Ahaṅkāra

The real actor is the soul; but, as it is without a form, it is necessary to give it a form to understand it; and *ahaṅkāra* is its form when it engages in action. This is proved by the fact that the two are not separate entities and cannot exist side by side; for we find from experience that when the higher one or the soul appears, the other disappears (13-21).

How the Soul Acts

The real actor is the soul, because there is continuity in action; and that is possible because there is a permanent factor of action—namely, the soul. We can understand this if we exercise our memory, and memory is an attribute of the soul (22-29).

There can be no existence without perception; and the real perceiver is the soul (30-33).

It is in this manner that the soul acts. But it is not the whole actor, for it cannot act without the assistance of the body. Thus we might say that there is no fundamental difference between the soul and the body because of their eternal co-existence. Indeed, we cannot even say which of the two is master or lord, and they are best described as friends (34-39).

At the same time we cannot say that the soul is like an organ of sense; but from a purely scientific point of view, there is no real contradiction between the soul and the body (40-45).

PART - III

GOD, NATURE, AND THE SOUL

Ether can be regarded as a creator only when it is identified with *Prakṛti* (1-8).

Prakṛti is said to be without origin, and we can understand the idea of God only by meditating on it (9-20).

The soul is minute like an atom; and it is an actor and experiencer of joy (21-36).

The idea of evil arises from absence of order, or impropriety of conduct (37-39). The actions of the soul can be said to be both good and bad; but at the moment when it acts, they are the best it can perform (40-42).

The soul is minute, and is like the light; it cannot be destroyed; but we cannot explain its real idea as it is (43-53).

Ether

Ether is not the original creator of things; but it may be said to be so in a secondary sense, when it is identified with *Prakṛti* or Nature, as it sometimes is in the sacred books (1-8).

Prakṛti and God

But *Prakṛti* is without any origin; and all vital energy is said to arise out of it. Indeed, we can understand the idea of God only by meditating on it and its characteristic marks, and not by means of our intellect or mind, as is sometimes imagined (9-15).

God is said to be the refuge of all that move and do not move. But this does not prove His existence. Nor can His existence be proved from the existence of the soul. It can only be proved by meditating on the character of Nature or *Prakṛti* (16-20).

The Soul

The soul is minute like an atom, and abides in the heart of man. In common parlance we might say that we get this idea from its association with the *Guṇas*, for the statement that it is minute like an atom is its *Guṇa*, attribute, or distinctive mark. Indeed, it is because it constitutes the core of the *Guṇas*, that it is said to be characterised by intelligence. But so long as we understand it as soul, there can be no defect in its idea merely because of looking at it in a particular way (21-32).

The soul is an actor, because it is admitted by all that it is an experiencer of joy, because it clings to life, and because we are required to perform certain actions as obligatory. Were the soul not an actor, there should be none of these (33-36).

Good and Evil

The idea of evil arises from absence of order, or impropriety of conduct, and it is based on our own perception of things. Impropriety of conduct arises from a perverse exercise of power, or a lack of proper adjustment of things (37-39).

The soul is really like a carpenter, who acts in both ways—that is, good and ill. But at the moment when it acts, it acts from the best motives, so far as its own self is concerned (40-42).

The Character of the Soul

The soul is minute, but can fill the body in which it abides. It is like light, and there is nothing higher than the soul (43-47).

The soul acts or refrains from action because of its bond with the body. As it is without mass, it cannot be destroyed. Indeed, it is beyond the grasp of the mind, and is superior to the intellect. We cannot explain its real nature by referring it to something else, for it is what it is by means of its own inner nature (48-53).

PART IV

THE SOUL AND THE VITAL ORGANS

The *prāṇas* or vital organs exist like the soul (1-7); but the soul is the best among them all (8-16). Nevertheless, the two are different (17-19); and the soul is characterised by both knowledge and action (20-22).

The Prāṇas

The *prāṇas* or vital organs exist like the soul, and they are possessed of *Guṇas* or the attributes of Nature from their very birth (1-7).

The Soul

But the soul is the best among all of them. It is said to have five functions like the mind, and is said to be seated in the intellect, and functions by means of the vital breath (8-16).

But the sense-organs are different from the soul, and the soul is superior to all of them (17-19).

Although the soul is said to be a personification of consciousness or knowledge, it is really a threefold actor. Never theless it is different from flesh and other constituents of the body (20-22).

CHAPTER - III

THE PROBLEM OF THE SOUL

PART - I

The soul dwells in the body in order to act and attain to perfection (1-3); and it does so by means of the function of the intellect (4-7).

The departed soul is re-born because of its previous actions (8-16); and its real problem is one of knowledge or action as its end (17-20). It is also concerned with the problem of pain (21-27).

The Object of Life

The soul is united with a body in order to engage in action attain to perfection (1-3). It does so by means of the intelect, which has an important place in action, and comes next after the soul itself (4-7).

Re-birth

The departed soul is born again as a result of its previous actions—both good and bad—and this takes place in accordance with a law (8-12).

The souls of creatures ascend and descend after dwelling for some time in the city of the god of Death; and we say so from the observation of their course of life (13-16).

The Problem of the Soul

The real problem of the soul relates to knowledge or action as the goal of life—for that is the problem under discussion here (17-20). There is a third problem too—that of pain;

and we say so because the occurrence of calamity is so common. But there are other things too besides pain, which are a source of joy in life (21-27).

PART - II

THE SOUL AND GOD

The act of procreation is an act of the soul (1-25), and it gives us an idea of creation by the Infinite (26-30), which may be called the Supreme Soul (31-32). We can understand the idea of God in a number of ways (33-41).

Procreation and the Soul

The act of procreation is an act of the soul, for after it the soul becomes self-conscious in a very special way (1-13).

The sex-instinct is indeed most powerful, and serves the purpose of Nature. But it is necessary to exercise restraint, and that too is done by the soul (14-25).

Creation and the Supreme Soul

This creation of the soul gives us an idea of creation by the Infinite, provided we agree that the Infinite creates (26-30); and so we may conclude that there is a Supreme Soul, for the idea of the individual and the Supreme Soul is identical (31-32).

An Intellectual Conception of God

We can have an intellectual conception of God by regarding the universe in a special way—that is, in terms of the idea of Sacrifice. There is also another idea of God, in terms of negatives ("not this, not that"); and both these enable us to understand His vastness and omnipresence; and then we realise that it is He who bestows the fruit of actions. Indeed, it is this that gives us the idea of Dharma too (33-41).

PART - III

THE FUNDAMENTAL IDEA OF VEDĀNTA

It is this that gives us the fundamental idea of *Vedānta* (1-10), for we cannot deny that there is joy in Nature (11-13). This also enables us to understand that all souls are alike (14-34).

The soul abides in the body, and does not sin through action (35-44); and it is an error to believe that it is *ahankāra* and not the soul that acts (45-49). We can understand how this error arises and how it can be removed; and then we can realise that all souls are the same (50-66).

The Fundamental Idea of Vedānta

This is the fundamental idea of *Vedānta*, based on the existence of a universal impelling force of life. There is complete agreement on the point among thinkers, and all works on the subject say so (1-10).

Indeed, we cannot deny that there is joy in Nature, and all sacred books are agreed that there is (11-13).

Identity of Souls

When there is absence of motive in action, it leads to meditation, which is the voice of our own soul. But the perception (or meditation) of each soul is different, as we see from subsequent results. We could regard all acts of perception as alike, if there were no difference between souls (14-19).

We can regard souls as alike when there is some other relation between them too—a relationship that is not due to some special cause; and we find that such a relationship exists. For instance, all of us can understand certain common ideas—like the fullness and omnipresence of light; and that is so because of this relationship between souls (20-24).

The sacred books say so too; but we do not know it because we do not understand them. There are many ways of understanding the text of the sacred books; but it requires knowledge to be able to succeed. If we do so, we shall find that there is no real contradiction among them (25-34).

The Nature of the Soul

The soul abides in the body, and there is a reciprocity between the two. At the same time we can distinguish between them. The soul is verily Truth; but while it abides in the body, it has its own desires too (35-39).

But the soul does not sin through action, though there is a separate result of each action (40-44).

It is an error to believe that it is *ahaṅkāra* and not the soul that acts; for when we get knowledge, we find that it is the soul that does so (45-49).

This error arises from the fact that attachment exists, and we believe that it cannot come to an end even when the soul comes to regard all things as equal or the same (50-51).

But it is possible for the soul to attain to this state, and it is honoured as supreme because it can act without attachment. This also enables us to understand that all souls are the same; because if the soul can regard all things as alike, it can make'no difference to it whether it abides in a body or not; and we believe that the souls are different because the bodies in which they abide are different (52-54).

Indeed, we might say that the limbs of the body are attached to the soul, but the soul is not attached to them; and the superiority of the soul consists in the fact that its actions are a sacrifice (55-57).

The souls appear to be different because of the difference in the use of words. But it is an error to suppose that they are different, because we find that the result of an action is not different in the case of different souls (58-60).

It is the nature of the soul to be united with the limbs of the body, and that is so because of the assistance it receives from them in performing its actions. Indeed, the connection of the soul with the body has never been regarded as contrary to reason (61-66).

PART - IV

THE SOUL AND THE DIFFERENT STAGES OF LIFE

This is the correct idea of the soul; but there are other ways of understanding it too (1-8).

Each system of philosophy has its own conception of the

soul; but they are all parts of one great whole, and need to be understood in that light (9-27).

There are different actions for different stages of life, and they are the result of the characteristics of both body and soul (28-40).

Fitness is not a necessary condition of success in life (41-43; and the fruit of action belongs not only to the soul, but to all the organs that take part in it (44-47). Indeed, there are different actions suited to different states and stages of life (48-52).

Idea of the Soul

This is the correct idea of the soul; but there are some who believe that the soul is that which remains after everything else in the body has undergone a change or disappeared. But this is an indirect way of getting at the idea of the soul, though there is no error in it (1-8).

The Soul and the Systems of Philosophy

Each system of philosophy has its own idea of the soul. But all systems are alike in their own way, and each is part of a great whole. There is a division of thought among them, just as we may divide a large number like a hundred. But it is not difficult to understand these systems, because we can know their meaning from the language of their text, and there are no symbolic expressions like 'kindling the fire' in them. Their whole idea of action as a sacrifice is based on reason; but even so it is necessary to have calmness and self-control to be able to understand their text (9-27).

Actions and Stages of Life

There are different actions for different stages of life: for instance, when a person is at the point of death, he is permitted to eat anything, but is unable to do so. Thus, a person can perform only certain actions at a certain stage of life, and that is so because he needs the assistance of different organs of the body at different times. In any case, these actions are the result of the characteristics of both body and soul; and we know that it is not always possible to overcome obstacles that lie in the way, and succeed (28-40).

Conditions of Success

But fitness is not a necessary condition of success in action—for it may be destroyed, or a person may not be able to make use of it. This statement may appear to be an extraordinary one, but is none the less true and easy to understand. At the same time we must not deprecate fitness as a means of success in action (41-43).

The Fruit of Action

The fruit of action belongs not only to the soul, but to all the organs that take part in it. Indeed, there are three factors of action—the actor, the instruments or organs that take part in action, and the object of action; and the fruit or result belongs to all of them (44-47).

Actions and Stages of Life

There are different actions for different states and stages of life; but the most comprehensive idea of it is to be found in that of the householder. The life of a *Muni* gives us another equally comprehensive, but that relates to a conception of a world that is believed to be full of obstacles. This leads us to believe that there can be no fixed rule in regard to the attainment of freedom from the bondage of life (48-52).

CHAPTER - IV

PART - I

RE-BIRTH AND REMOVAL OF SIN

The same soul is born again and again, and it alone can comprehend *Brahma* (1-5).

We can understand the idea of the soul in several ways: and when a person attains to knowledge of the soul, all his sins are removed (6-16).

According to some the highest action is that which is characterised by knowledge; and they believe that the highest goal can be attained by means of renunciation of all actions (17-19).

Re-birth

The revolution of birth takes place again and again; and we say so because of the characteristics of creatures; and it is the same soul that is born again and again (1-3).

Essential Character of the Soul

The soul does not consist in its outward form or the body; and it may be described as the faculty of seeing or understanding *Brahma* (4-5).

How to Understand the Soul

We can understand the idea of the soul in several ways. A person is said to exist because of the existence of the soul. We can grasp its idea by means of contemplation too. It is the one thing within the body that does not change; and we can grasp its idea in a state of one-pointedness, for then there is no difference between the seer (the soul) and the object seen. We also see that it abides in the body up to the time of death (6-12).

Removal of Sin

When a person attains to knowledge of the soul, all his sins are removed. Death also puts an end to sin; but that applies to actions not yet begun; and so far as previous actions are concerned, their sin is removed only when their effect comes to an end (13-16).

The Highest Action and the Highest End

According to some there is also another class of actions besides those that are good or bad—and they are actions characterised by knowledge. They also believe that it is only when a person destroys both good and evil actions by means of *Yoga*, that he can attain to the highest goal (17-19).

PART - II

THE SOUL AND ITS GOAL

It is a law that the lower abides in the higher; and so all things abide in the soul (1-5).

Real immortality consists in doing heroic deeds without injury to any one; but there are some who believe that it consists in being merged in the Supreme (6-16); and that the soul follows the path of light in the world beyond (17-21).

All Things abide in the Soul

It is a law that the lower abides in the higher; and so speech and the other sense-organs abide in the mind, the mind in *prāṇa* or vital breath, and that again in the soul (1-5).

Real Immortality

The soul cannot be seen; but all souls are essentially alike. Real immortality consists in doing heroic deeds without injury to any one; but there are some who have another idea of immortality—that is, when the soul, after passing through a number of births, is merged in the Supreme (6-8).

The soul is minute, but, at the same time, full of ardour and glow, which arise not from self-denial or prohibition, but rather from its association with the body (9-14).

We are told that all souls are at last merged in the Highest; and the Highest is without any division, as the sacred books declare (15-16).

It is said that when the soul attains to perfection, it is filled with light, realises its own self, and becomes full of joy. All its sense-organs are illuminated because of the strength of knowledge; and the remainder of its course on earth becomes sweet; and it values its own purity more than anything else. And when it passes away from this earth, it follows the path of light into the world beyond (17-21).

PART - III

THE HIGHEST END OF THE SOUL

Those who believe in this idea of immortality of the soul maintain that the soul passes through light, and comes into the presence of the Deity; and, as all its actions have come to an end, it is merged in the Highest, and thereafter has no desire for further action (1-16).

The End of the Soul

Those who believe in this idea of immortality of the soul tell us that it goes on and on through light—from cloud to air, and then into lightning that is above the sky, accompanied by its 'subtle body'; and then it is led by something that is of the nature of lightning itself, and comes into the presence of the Deity. All its actions having come to an end, the soul, together with the 'subtle body', is merged in the Highest; and after this it can have no intention of gaining anything through further actions (1-14).

This is what we are told, and the excellence of the idea is obvious (15-16).

PART - IV

REAL FREEDOM

It is said that when the soul arrives there;, it becomes free for ever afterwards (1-5).

But we are unable to think of the soul except in terms of the intellect; and so we must think of the problem of freedom too in its light. If we do so, we find that real freedom consists in a state of equilibrium in the midst of all actions, or the experience of pleasure and pain (6-22).

Into the Highest

It is said that when the soul arrives there, it becomes free, and lives on for evermore in the Highest; and this, we are told, is due to the fact that its own nature is like that of the Highest (1-5).

A Rational View

But we are unable to think of the soul except in terms of the intellect; for even when we try to think of it as soul, it appears to be full of reflection (6-15).

We have accordingly to think of the problem of freedom of the soul in terms of the intellect. There are some who believe that this can be achieved by means of renunciation of all actions in the world. But we find that there can be absence of action only if things were not connected with one another. But we find that they are all connected with the soul, though the soul itself is not subject to change. Hence the soul cannot refrain from all kinds of actions. On the other hand, it can be proved that it can attain to a state of evenness or equilibrium in the midst of all actions, or the experience of pleasure and pain. And this, according to the Scriptures, is the state of one who is said to be free from all revolutions of birth (16-22).

XI

SCIENCE, PHILOSOPHY, RELIGION

From Sāṅkhya to Vedānta

This substance of the great systems of Hindu Philosophy is enough to show that, even as *Vedānta* tells us, they are but parts of a magnificent whole, and deal with the many problems of life from different points of view. We begin with certain assumptions, and then, by a gradual process of thought, criticise, correct, or confirm them. For instance, we begin with the idea that *Prakṛti* or Nature is the supreme creator of life, and there is no place for God in the scheme of things; that the soul is altogether different from all that is in the world or the body in which it abides; that there is no joy in life, and pleasure itself is but a form of pain; that all desire is essentially evil; that there is an inherent opposition between knowledge and action; and that we can attain to freedom from the bondage of life only by means of a total renunciation of action and withdrawal from the world. Then, slowly and gradually, we understand the implications of the ideas of Nature and God, the real character of the soul and its relation to the body and the world, the nature of knowledge and action, good and evil, pleasure and pain, desire and its result—and come to the conclusion that there is no inherent opposition between the idea of Nature and of God, and that if we believe, as we must, that the working of the great forces of Nature is characterised by both goodness and intelligence, we transform the idea of Nature itself into that of God; that the soul, though different from many things in the world, cannot be dissociated from them, nor can its idea be separated from that of the intellect, which is said to be an expression of Nature itself; that there is joy in each true act of creation, and it is this joy that sustains the world; that the motive of each action is positive—the attainment of some satisfaction, pleasure, or good, besides the avoidance of their opposites; that there is an element of goodness in each desire, so far at least as the person who possesses it is concerned, and it can be in conformtiy with Dharma too; that the difference between pleasure and pain, and good and evil is one of degree, not kind; that there is no essential opposition between knowledge and action, and there can be no action without knowledge and no knowledge without action; and that freedom from the bondage of life is attained by living in the world, doing heroic deeds without injury to any one, attaining the highest that is in it, understanding the true nature of the soul and all that is called life, and living in a state of equilibrium in the midst of all actions and the experience of pleasure and pain. The whole process is rational or intellectual, and is illuminated by a wealth of ideas and imagery, and embodied in a form which, when we understand it, is as clear as it is coherent and concise, and is without a parallel in the history of human thought. At the same time there is an attempt to transcend the limitations of human reason too, and we are led into the realms of the Unknowable—the city of the god of Death, as well as the kingdom of eternal life and light, the abode of the Supreme. Thus, physical science and logic and ethics,—the laws of life and the theories of knowledge and action—together with psychology and metaphysics, the origin and essence of things, the nature of the soul, and the idea of God—are all integrated together to make a great whole which, when perceived from different points of view, gives us a number of *Darśanas* or clear visions of life, and constitutes the end of all our quest of Truth.

Indeed, it is no exaggeration to say that to understand these systems of philosophy is to understand the foundations of ancient thought and the essence of what is described in the sacred books. They all claim to derive their origin from the Vedas and the *Upaniṣads*; and the *Mīmāṁsā* tells us that the subject-matter of the Vedas is nothing less than the laws of Nature and the life of man—or Dharma that sustains the universe. It also explains the method by means of which we can understand them in this light.

The *Upaniṣads* are said to be an exposition of the secret doctrine of the Vedas, and we can now understand that they are really so. A great deal of what they contain is pure thought; and the same ideas have been expressed in the Vedas in a different form. But a considerable portion of the *Upaniṣads* too has been composed in symbolic form, and would need to be interpreted in the same manner as the Vedas, and in accordance with the method described in the *Mīmāṁsā*. The great Epic of the *Rāmāyaṇa* is said to be a Veda; while the *Mahābhārata*, the greatest of all, has been described as the fifth and last of the Vedas; and we are told that what "is in it is elsewhere too; and what does not occur in it, occurs nowhere else;"—for it includes the entire range of human thought from *Sāṅkhya* to *Vedānta*, when interpreted in accordance with the method explained in the *Mīmāṁsā*. The same is true of the *Purāṇas* too; and it is for this reason that the *Mahābhārata* is spoken of as "*itihāsa* or history of the *Purāṇas*"; but we need to understand them also in the same manner.

From Science to Philosophy

An examination of the different systems of philosophy will show that the whole process is purely rational or scientific; and the ancients must have known a great deal of physical sciences, in a strictly modern sense of the term, to be able to describe them in this form. Their conception of the 'elements' was indeed different from our own—for they conceived of them as great elemental forms and forces of Nature—Earth, Water, Fire, Air, and Ether—out of which all material objects are formed. The *Mīmāṁsā* tells us that the Vedas deal with the great laws of Nature and their bearing on the life of man; and what great truths a proper study of their text will disclose would be difficult to say. But the *Sāṅkhya* tells us that all matter is formed out of the mind; and the *Nyāya* and the *Vaiśeṣika* discuss the nature of the atom, refer to its division, and tell us how, though invisible, it can yet be perceived. They also define Ether and sound, describe the character of mass and action, and examine the properties of the 'elements'. The *Mīmāṁsā* deals with the conception of Time as something purely intellectual, speaks of its connection with action, and tells us how it can be described. It also gives us a scientific division of animals into vertebratc and invertebrate, and refers to Jyotiṣṭoma or the rays of light. There is also a reference to the many great things that can be achieved by means of *Yoga*; but if we understand the text correctly, we find that the principal idea is purely sceintific, for we are told that a body can be made to become light as cotton by means of its adjustment to motion; and we can hear wonderful sounds by concentrating on the essential character of sound.

Indeed, the great attempt of the ancients was not only to understand the laws of Nature, but also to integrate them into the life of man; and when they conceived of man as a microcosm, they fused science into psychology, and conceived of the six systems of philosophy: the *Sāṅkhya* based on a broad survey of Nature, and the rest on the five faculties of man—his senses, mind, *ahaṅkāra*, intellect, and the soul. Thus they transformed science into philosophy through the medium of psychology.

From Philosophy to Religion

The same process of thought enabled them to transform philosophy into religion; for we find that it is these systems of philosophy which constitute the bases of the different systems of Hindu religion, and exhibit the same unity of thought as the systems of philosophy themselves. It is sometimes believed that philosophy and religion are two different things—the one based on reason, and the other on faith—and the two have little in common with each other. While this is true of some great systems of religion, like Christianity and Islam, the essential idea of what are called the Hindu systems of religion is purely philosophical, even as the basis of their philosophy is a knowledge of the laws of Nature and their application to the life of man. Indeed, the ancients conceived of religion as the highest art of life—an attempt to live in the light of the highest Truth as we understand it. Dharma, the term commonly used for religion—was, accordingly, conceived to be action performed as a sacrifice, even as the *Mīmāṁsā* tells us; and that means nothing but good, intelligent, and joyous action, meant for the benefit of all; and it is this that sustains all life, both of the individual and the world, even as the word literally signifies. Religion is thus but a realization of the highest. Truth, an experience of an ideal conception of life, necessitating a harmony of both knowledge and action, reason and emotion—when the head and the heart act in unison, and meet in the awakening of the soul and the presence of God—the eternal principle of Goodness, Intelligence, and Joy (*Sat-cit-ānanda*) that fills the universe. The ancients believed that, as the ultimate object of all action is perfection, all life ministers to this end: and so all the fine arts—architecture, sculpture, painting, music and poetry—the most magnificent temples, the finest carving and statues, the most delicate painting and effects of light and shade, the deepest notes of music, and the most beautiful poetry—were pressed into the service of this idea of Dharma or religion. It has, indeed, drifted far away from its original conception.; but its basic ideas still remain, and it is yet possible to trace them to their source.

XII

THE SYSTEMS OF RELIGION

The Systems of Religion

As the different systems of philosophy constitute the bases of the different systems of religion, it would be of interest to correlate their fundamental ideas and theories.

Fundamental Ideas of Systems of Philosophy

As we have seen, the fundamental ideas of the different systems of philosophy may be resolved into the conception of knowledge or action as the final goal of human life; and we can understand their essential idea of the soul as well as God in their terms. For instance, the *Sāṅkhya* believes that action is the cause of all our sorrow and pain; that Nature is self-created and there is no place for God in the scheme of life; that the soul is different from all that is in Nature; and that it can make itself happy and free only by means of perfect knowledge and renunciation of all action. The other systems deal with the same problem from different points of view, and the conclusion of *Vedānta* is the very opposite of that of the *Sāṅkhya*.

The Idea of God and Systems of Philosophy

Now, if we conceive of God as *Sat-cit-ānanda* or the principle of good, intelligent and joyous action made manifest in the universe, the opposition between soul, Nature, and God disappears, and we can harmonise them into one great Whole. We can, therefore, examine the different systems of philosophy in the light of the measure of their belief in God as the supreme creator of the universe. We have seen that the *Sāṅkhya* has no place for Him in its scheme, while *Vedānta* conceives of Nature itself but as a form of God; and, between these extremes, the remaining systems have their own ideas of God.

Three Groups of Ideas

These may be divided into three groups. We may believe that Nature is the supreme creator of the universe, or that God is the supreme creator, or that the two together jointly create the world.

Now, if we believe that Nature is the supreme creator of life, it is possible to have three points of views: that Nature is the *sole* supreme creator; or, if there is God, He is but a spectator of Nature's work; or has, at best, but a small share in it. We cannot, in any case, agree that God is equal or superior to Nature, or the sole creator of the universe.

If, again, we believe that God and Nature are joint creators of life, we can have three points of view: that the share of Nature is more than that of God; that the two are equal; or that the share of God is more than that of Nature.

If, on the other hand, we believe that God is the supreme creator of the universe, there are again three points of view: that God is the *sole* supreme creator; or, if there is Nature, it is but a spectator of His work; or has, at best, a small share in it. This is the exact opposite of the first group of ideas based on the conception of Nature as the supreme creator of the universe, and the two exclude each other. Between them lies the second group, which has a point of view in common with each, and so may be said to be their connecting link. Thus, if, starting with the idea that there is no place for God in the scheme of things, we come to believe that He is a spectator of the work of Nature, and then that He is a small creator too, we not only rise to the top of the first group of ideas in this system of thought, but also find ourselves at the bottom of the second; and similarly, when we rise to the top of our second group, we are at the bottom of the third; and in this manner can ascend from the lowest to the highest point of thought in this scale.

The Trimūrti

It is this that gives us the *Trimūrti* or the threefold form of the Deity—*Brahmā*,[1] *Śiva*, and *Viṣṇu*, to which there are innumerable references in the sacred books. When we desire to live in accordance with the scheme of thought based on the first group of ideas, we get the system of religion called after the name of *Brahmā*; the second gives us the system of *Śiva* or *Mahādeva*; while the third that of *Viṣṇu*.

Jainism and Buddhism

We notice, however, that the system of *Brahmā*, based on the idea that Nature is the supreme creator of the universe, leads to the conclusion of the *Sāṅkhya* and its allied systems—namely, that the ultimate goal of human life is knowledge and renunciation of action. Action is a necessary evil so long as we have to live; but happiness or freedom from sorrow can be attained only by means of knowledge and the renunciation of action. But a total renunciation of action, as the *Mīmāṁsā* has taught us, belongs only to the last stage of human life, when the spirit departs. The course of life based on the system of *Brahmā* may, accordingly, be divided into two parts—the beginnings of life, when we learn to live, and so must have more of knowledge than action—and, the end, when we are about to die, when all action, however important, must come to an end; and corresponding to this the system of *Brahmā* was divided into two parts—*Jainism* and *Buddhism*—the one emphasising the role of knowledge at the beginning, and the other at the end, of life.

Śaivism and Vaiṣṇavism

Between these extremes lies the great work of life, which sustains and preserves the race, and demands the application of knowledge to action designed to that end. But here again we can have two points of view: we may believe that action is indeed necessary, but knowledge, coupled with renunciation, is still our final goal; or we may hold that knowledge and action are but two aspects of the same thing—life; and that there is an essential harmony between the two, and that life goes on for ever; and corresponding to this we have the two systems, of religion associated with the names of *Śiva* and *Viṣṇu*. The latter believes that not only is life not evil or characterised by constant sorrow and pain, but that it is based essentially on the principle of goodness, intelligence and joy; and so God himself is born from age to age in the world. It is this that gives us the idea of the 'incarnations' of *Viṣṇu*; and the systems of *Śiva* and *Viṣṇu* constitute the bulk of what is known by the name of Hinduism. They embrace the whole range of human life from the time a child grows into a boy and is able to think for himself and act; and so we go on through experience of family-life to a bond with the whole race and the world, and to the attainment of perfection through harmony of knowledge and action, when we realise that happiness or freedom from sorrow consists not in running away from life, but in its fulfilment, and the attainment of a state of equilibrium in the midst of all that may happen in the world. And so, if a person live in this manner—all his life becomes a sacrifice—full of goodness, intelligence, and joy—and death may come when it will, and he is not disturbed.

Jainism, Śaivism, and Vaiṣṇavism

We have observed that *Jainism* corresponds to the beginnings of human life, when there is an emphasis on knowledge more than on action; while *Śaivism* and *Vaiṣṇavism* refer to the rest, with a new conception of what belongs to active life and to its end; and, as this covers the entire range of human existence, these three systems still survive in India.

Buddhism

The system of *Buddha*, which too had its origin in this country, has, however, disappeared; and that, in spite of the fact that *Buddha* is said to be an *avatār* or 'incarnation' of

Viṣṇu. In this connection we have observed that *Buddhism*, as a system of religion or a scheme of life, corresponds to the end of a man's existence on earth, when all action must come to an end; and so it may be said to be a perfect plan of life in the path of death. But this is included also in the system of *Śiva*, according to which knowledge, together with renunciation of action, is said to be the ultimate goal of life; and so all that is of real value in *Buddhism* is included in the system of *Śiva*, and the existence of the two side by side can only cause confusion. Indeed, the existence of *Buddhism* as a separate system of religion would imply that it is in harmony with the main course of human life, whereas its principles apply largely to its end in death, when a man has completed his tasks and fulfilled his mission in life;[2] and an active practice of its philosophy of negation of action, by men in their youth and nations in their prime, can only lead to decadence; and this would appear to be the reason why it was 'driven out' of India as a separate system, and the best in it included in *Śaivism*.[3]

Systems of Philosophy and Religion

We have observed that these systems of religion are founded on the different systems of philosophy; and it is now possible to bring out their connection more clearly.

As we have seen, the *Sāṅkhya* has no place for God in its scheme of life; and it comes to the conclusion that the highest end can be attained only by means of knowledge and a total renunciation of action. Corresponding to this we have the first form of the system of *Brahmā* or the *Digambara* school of *Jainism*, which holds identical views.

Nyāya tells us that God does not grant the fruit or result of action, which accrues largely through our own effort. This may be taken to imply that God exists, but only as a spectator of the work of Nature or *Prakṛti*, which alone creates; or, if He may be regarded as a creator in any sense of the term—His creation is limited to the first act, after which all things work out in accordance with a universal law, without any direction or interference on His part. *Nyāya* accordingly believes in a limited scope of action, emphasises the role of knowledge, and explains the different means of acquiring it. As this attitude to life belongs to the stage of its beginning or the end,when we do not know how to act, or, being at the point of death, cannot do so—corresponding to this we have the *Śvetāmbara* school of *Jainism* and the *Hīnayāna* school of *Buddhism* respectively; and the latter also corresponds to the first form of the school of *Śaivism*.

After this we have the *Vaiśeṣika*, which refers not to God, but to an Unseen or Unknown Power, which has its own share in creation and shaping results; but we are not told exactly what it is. We are accordingly free to conclude that, if this Unknown Power may be identified with God, He would be deemed to act in conjunction with Nature or *Prakṛti*, and His share may be less than, equal to, or greater than that of the latter; and corresponding to this we have the whole range of the system of *Śiva*, which would also include the *Mahāyāna* school of *Buddhism*, and the first or dualistic form of the system of *Viṣṇu*.

The *Vaiśeṣika* is followed by the *Mīmāṁsā*, which, like the former, contains no reference to God, but tells us instead of a large number of gods, who represent the great forms and forces of Nature. We may, therefore, assume that its idea of God would be similar to that of the *Vaiśeṣika*, though wider in range. We have also explained that the *Mīmāṁsā* is but a first step to the philosophy of *Vedānta*; and so, in so far as the systems of religion are concerned, has little contribution of its own to make. This is due primarily to the fact that it is based on the character of *ahaṅkāra* or the I-as-an-actor; for, if we regard the soul itself to be an actor, as a number of systems—and more specially *Vedānta*—believe, there can be no separate place for *ahaṅkāra* as an actor; and, as the great systems of religion regard the soul as such, there is no Separate place for the *Mīmāṁsā* in their construction.

Yoga, as we have seen, assigns a special place to God for the attainment of perfection. We have also explained that there is another aspect of *Yoga*, where it is, for practical purposes, identified with *Vedānta*; and that is the point of view of the *Bhagavad Gītā* which, while giving a separate place to *Prakṛti*, tells us that the real creator is only *Kṛṣṇa* or God. There are thus two ways of looking at *Yoga*, so far as the relation of *Puruṣa* and *Prakṛti* or God and Nature is concerned: God is the chief creator of the universe, and so far as *Prakṛti* is concerned, it is either a spectator of His work, or is at best but a small co-sharer with Him. *Yoga* may, accordingly, be said to be the opposite of *Nyāya*; and, corresponding to its two aspects, we have the highest point of the system of *Śiva* or *Mahādeva*, and the qualified monistic school of the system of *Viṣṇu*. *Vedānta*, the culmination of all ancient thought, tells us that God is the *sole* supreme creator of the universe, and Nature itself is but His form. It is thus the exact opposite of the *Sāṅkhya*; and corresponding to it we have the pure monistic school of the system of *Viṣṇu*.

Integration of Ancient Thought

We thus see that the nine points of view of the three groups of ideas, which give us the three great systems of religion—of *Brahmā*, *Śiva*, and *Viṣṇu*—with three forms of each—are all dis-tributed among the five systems of philosophy; for the sixth, the *Mīmāṁsā*, as we have explained, has no place in the construction of the systems of religion. Of these the *Sāṅkhya* and *Vedānta*, at the two extreme ends of thought, have but a single point of view—the one holding that it is *Prakṛti*, and the other that it is *Brahma*, who is the supreme creator of life. The *Sāṅkhya*, indeed, gives a separate place to the soul, but does not explain its origin.

Similarly, *Nyāya* and *Yoga* have two points of view each, and are opposed to each other. The one holds that the chief creator is *Prakṛti*; and God, if He exists, is either a spectator of its work, or has, at best, but a small share in it. *Yoga*, on the other hand, maintains that the chief creator is God, and *Prakṛti* is either a spectator of His work, or has, at best, but a small share in it.

Between these two groups of opposites lies the *Vaiśeṣika*, which serves as a connecting link between them. It is based on the character of the mind, which, as we have explained, is characterised by electric energy and has its positive and negative charges. As these may be said to correspond to the idea of *Puruṣa* and *Prakṛti*, the *Vaiśeṣika* may be said to be based on the idea that God and Nature are joint creators of life, but we cannot say who is the greater of the two. We may, therefore, consider their relation from three points of view—the share of God being more than that of Nature, or the share of Nature being more than that of God, or the two being equal. These are the three aspects of the *Vaiśeṣika*, corresponding to the three forms of electric energy that we know—one static, and two dynamic—with their direct and alternating currents of electricity.

Special Character of the Vaiśeṣika

The *Vaiśeṣika* accordingly serves as a connecting link between the great systems of religion. We find that the two great systems of *Brahmā* and *Viṣṇu* exclude each other—the one holding that *Prakṛti*, and the other that *Puruṣa*, is the sole, chief, or major creator of life; and there is no point of contact between them. Between them lies the system of *Śiva* or *Mahādeva*, which maintains that *Puruṣa* and *Prakṛti* are joint and equal or almost equal creators of the universe; and this is the point of view of the *Vaiśeṣika* too; and it is this that gives it its special position—signified by its own name— in the ancient scheme of thought.

Systems of Philosophy and Religion

We can now correlate the main ideas of the great systems of religion with those of the corresponding systems of philosophy.

There are three aspects of the system of *Brahmā*, based on the character of Nature as the supreme, chief, or major creator of things; and these correspond to the basic conception of the *Sāṅkhya*, the first aspect of *Nyāya*, and the first aspect of the *Vaiśeṣika* respectively,—the first aspect of *Nyāya* being that God is but a spectator of the work of *Prakṛti*, and that of the *Vaiśeṣika* that He creates, but has a smaller role to play.

Similarly, there are three aspects of the system of *Mahādeva*, based on the idea of God and Nature being joint creators of life—and the share of the God may be more than that of Nature, or the two may be equal, or the share of Nature may be more than that of God; and these correspond to the second point of view of *Nyāya*, the second point of view of the *Vaiśeṣika*, and the first point of view of *Yoga*.

In the same manner there are three aspects of the system of *Viṣṇu*—the opposite of the system of *Brahmā*—based on the idea of God as the supreme, chief, or major creator of the universe—the monistic, qualified monistic, and dualistic schools of this system; and corresponding to these we have the basic conception of *Vedānta*, the second point of view of *Yoga*, and the third point of view of the *Vaiśeṣika*.

Thus we see how the points of view of the *Vaiśeṣika* extend to *Nyāya* on the one hand and to *Yoga* on the other, and connect together the two opposing groups of ideas and their corresponding systems of religion—those of *Brahmā* and *Viṣṇu*. The position of the system of *Mahādeva* is identical, for it is based essentially on the idea of *Puruṣa* and *Prakṛti* as joint creators of life, and that is also the basic conception of the *Vaiśeṣika* in its relation to the character of the mind.

Ascending Scale of Thought

This enables us to understand how all the great systems of philosophy and religion are connected together and are but parts of one great whole. We have already explained how that is true of the systems of philosophy; and it is not difficult to see that there is the same attempt at integration in the systems of religion too.

We have seen how we can rise from the *Sāṅkhya* to *Vedānta* by means of a gradual process of thought and the idea of sacrifice, or action characterised by goodness, intelligence and joy, and meant for the benefit of all. But, even as we find in the concluding portions of *Vedānta*—we can conceive of the soul and its problem of freedom only in the light of our intellect; and, as it is *Yoga* that is based on the character of the intellect, *Vedānta* and *Yoga*, conceived in this special light—may, like the soul and the intellect, be, for practical purposes, identified. We find that the same line of thought applies to the systems of religion too.

We have to begin with the system of *Brahmā*, extending from the *Sāṅkhya* to *Nyāya* and the *Vaiśeṣika*. We begin with the *Sāṅkhya*, and find that its theory of a total renunciation of action is an impossible one, for it means that we cannot live; and so we pass on to the next system, *Nyāya*. But even that does not satisfy us—for it lays special stress on the necessity of controlling all desires, and permits us only just to exist. We, on the other hand, wish not only to exist, but also to propagate the species; and so we pass on to the next system, the *Vaiśeṣika*; and this concludes the range of this system of religion. It is in this manner that we pass from the *Sāṅkhya* to *Nyāya* and thence to the *Vaiśeṣika*, and rise correspondingly to their respective ideas of God—as one who has no place in the scheme of existence, as one who is a mere spectator of life, and as one who has a minor part in the creation of things.

But when we reach the topmost point in the system of *Brahmā*, we find that we are at the bottom of the system of *Mahādeva*, with its range extending from *Nyāya* to *Vaiśeṣika* and thence to *Yoga*. We begin with the idea that God has but a small part to play in the world; and, as the idea of God is co-extensive with that of sacrifice—it means that there is but a small measure of goodness, intelligence and joy in life. But this does not satisfy us, and so we pass on to the next system, *Vaiśeṣika*, which tells us that the share of God and Nature can be equal too; that is to say, there is an equal measure of good and evil, or joy and sorrow in the world. But even this does not satisfy us, and so we pass on to the next system, *Yoga*, which tells us that the share of God is more than that of Nature, or that there is more of goodness and joy than evil and sorrow in life; and this completes the whole range of this system of religion.

When again we reach the topmost point in the system of *Mahādeva*, we find that we are at the bottom of the system of *Viṣṇu*, with its range extending from the *Vaiśeṣika* to *Yoga* and *Vedānta*. We begin with the idea that there is more of goodness and joy than evil and sorrow in life,— for that is the point of view of the *Vaiśeṣika* in this system. But we find, on further reflection, that it gives us more satisfaction to believe that good and evil, joy and sorrow are relative terms, and evil itself can be changed to good, and sorrow to joy; and so we pass on to the next system, *Yoga*. After this the next stage in our evolution is that there is nothing but goodness, intelligence and joy in the world,—and that is the real meaning of God as the sole supreme creator of the universe in *Vedānta*. And so we rise to the topmost point of human thought in *Vedānta* in the system of *Viṣṇu*. But we find that it is difficult to understand the idea of universal goodness, intelligence and joy in life; and so are content to drop down to the earlier point of view of *Yoga*—namely, that good and evil, joy and sorrow are relative terms, and that evil can be changed to good, and sorrow to joy.

Thus we see that, as intellect and soul and *Yoga* and *Vedānta* may, for practical purposes, be identified, the pure monistic conception of the system of *Viṣṇu* may, in the same manner, be identified with its qualified monistic view; and this is as far as it is possible for the human mind to go.

Descending Scale of Thought

This is how man can rise from the lowest to the highest conception of life in the ascending scale of thought; and when he does so, he may be said to have attained to perfection. This is what is possible for him to achieve in life; but there is also the fact of death, for there is no one who can live for ever. And so, after achieving the height of perfection in the world of life, man must also prepare for death; and so he comes down from his *Yoga* conception of life to that of the *Vaiśeṣika*, and then to

Nyāya,—believes that it is *Prakṛti* that rules below, and leaving his body behind to be reduced to its elemental form, lets his soul depart, to live in some unknown world, till its time comes again to renew its course of existence on earth.

The *Sāṅkhya*, as we have seen, is based on its own conception of Nature; and the real quest of man, having a bearing on the actual facts of his life, begins with *Nyāya*; but, having attained to perfection through *Yoga* or *Vedānta*, he comes down to *Nyāya* again. He begins with an attempt to control the activities of his senses; and, having completed the whole cycle of human thought and experience, finds that he is unable to use them—and so ends where he begins. This is the story of human life on earth; but there are other worlds too, and they have also their own stories to tell.

Original and Existing Ideas

This, in brief, is the main idea of the great systems of Hindu religion, as they are to be found in the sacred books, and they have the same relation to one another as the corresponding systems of philosophy. Their modern forms and practices, however, appear to be very different; but it is not difficult to understand how their original idea, along with that of the corresponding systems of philosophy, has been lost through the passage of Time. But the sacred books still remain; and their text, when properly interpreted, tells us what their ancient conception really was. Indeed, even in the midst of this great wreckage of Time, it is still possible—through the many forms, observances, laws, customs, and traditions that yet survive—to discover traces of their original idea, and re-construct the ancient fabric again, But this demands a separate treatment, and is outside the scope of the present work.[4]

REFERENCES

1. The word *Brahmā* is not the same as *Brahma*, although they are closely allied, and both are derived from *Brahman*. *Brahmā* is the nominative

masculine, while *Brahma* the nominative neuter form of this word; and the former refers to a personal, and the latter to an impersonal form of the Supreme Spirit—the sense in which it is used in the *Vedānta-Sūtras*.

2. The founder of *Buddhism* is called *Siddhārtha* (*Siddha-artha*), which means "he all whose objects have been attained"; and so it is only when a person has fulfilled his mission in life and attained to all he seeks, that he can awaken into the final truth (or become a *Buddha*—for that is the meaning of the word), that all action must ultimately be renounced. This is also the point of view of *Śaivism* or *Yoga*, but not of *Vaiṣṇavism* or *Vedānta*; for according to the latter, there is no end to life or action, and God himself is born from age to age.

3. The essential idea of the different systems of religion and their relation to the corresponding systems of philosophy has been dealt with elsewhere (MM. II); and it would be examined again in connection with the "story" of the *avatāras* or 'incarnations' of *Viṣṇu*. We shall then understand why Buddha, though an 'incarnation' of the Deity, is said to have been silent when questioned about the existence of God.

4. A fuller examination of the systems of Hindu Philosophy and Religion is contained in the Author's work, *The Mystery of the Mahābhārata*, VoL II.

XIII

THE ESSENTIAL IDEA OF THE SACRED BOOKS

The Sacred Books

We are now in a position to understand the essential idea of the sacred books of the Hindus.

The Vedas

The Vedas, as the *Mīmāṁsā* has told us, deal with the laws of Nature and the problem of action, with special reference to the life of man; and we can understand them in this light if we interpret them in accordance with the method it has explained. The *Mīmāṁsā* mentions three Vedas—Ṛk, *Sāma* and *Yajur*, and refers to a fourth, *Nigada*, but observes that it should be included in the *Yajur*. The real fourth Veda, which would appear to be of later origin, is *Atharva*; and it too should belong to the same class as the previous three.

Mantras and Brāhmaṇas

The Vedas consist of two principal parts—*Mantras*, believed to be hymns of praise addressed to the gods, and *Brāhmaṇas*, consisting of *Vidhi* and *Artha-vāda*—believed to be directions in regard to the ceremonies at which the *Mantras* are to be recited, and explanation of legends etc. connected with the *Mantras*. But the *Mīmāṁsā* tells us that, if we interpret the *Mantras* properly, we shall find that they deal with the laws of Nature and the problem of action, while the gods will be transformed into personifications of the great forms and forces of Nature. Similarly, as the word *Vidhi* also means a law, the *Brāhmaṇas* deal really with the same laws of Nature, and *Artha-vāda* is but an explanation of these laws, even as the word literally signifies.

But they too would need to be interpreted in accord-ance with the method explained in the *Mīmāṁsā*, to be understood in this light.

Ṛg Veda

The *Mīmāṁsā* tells us that the *Ṛg-Veda* deals with the problem of action, conceived in its widest significance, that is, with reference to all that the ancients knew of the world of Nature, including man.

Sāma Veda

The *Sāma-Veda*, we are told, deals with the problem of all living creatures; and so a considerable portion of the text of the *Ṛg-Veda* is repeated in the *Sāma-Veda*.

Yajur-Veda

The *Yajur-Veda*, even as is signified by the name, would accordingly deal with the law of sacrifice or good, intelligent and joyous action, with reference to both Nature and man.

Atharva Veda

The *Atharva-Veda* is said to have been composed by *Atharvan*, and is believed to consist chiefly of spells, incantations and formulas intended to prevent or cast out disease and counteract calamities. *Atharvan*, however, is said to be a priest who is associated with *Agni* and *Soma*; and we have seen that the one refers to the intellect, and the other to the mind. Hence, as the *Veda* is called after his name, it means that it deals with the problem of intellect and the mind, with special reference to the life of man; and if we understand their laws, we can avoid evil and disease. We can, however, understand all this only in accordance with the method of interpretation explained in the *Mīmāṁsā*.

The Upaniṣads

It is said that out of the *Brāhmaṇa* part of the Vedas arose the *Upaniṣads* and the *Sūtras*; and the *Upaniṣads* are said to describe the secret doctrine of the Vedas. As we can now understand the 'secret' form of the Vedic text, and know that they deal with the laws of life, we can understand that the Upaniṣads are really an exposition of the secret doctrine of the Vedas, for a great body of their text is composed in a form which is easy to understand, and it is not necessary to divide words into parts to get their meaning. But a considerable portion of even their text is symbolic and written in the form of stories, which need to be understood in the manner explained in the *Mīmāṁsā*.

The Sūtras

The *Sūtras* are said to be short, pithy sentences, or aphoristic rules, believed to hang loosely together like threads; and the *Vedāṅgas* and the systems of philosophy are composed in this form. These *Sūtras* have commonly been regarded as unintelligible in themselves, and our present-day knowledge of what they contain is based on certain commentaries of learned men, which are taken to be authoritative. But we have seen that the *Sūtras* of the six systems of philosophy are not only not unintelligible, but describe the different problems of life in a brief, direct, connected, and coherent manner. If the *Sūtras* of the *Vedāṅgas* are of the same kind—and they appear to be so indeed—they too should yield similar results.

Śruti and Smṛti

The Vedas and Vedic literature are called śruti, which means literally 'what is heard'; and they are believed to contain sacred knowledge orally transmitted from generation to generation. This is followed by what is called *smṛti*, meaning 'memory'; for it is believed to have been remembered by heart; and, in its widest application, it includes the *Sūtras*, the law-books of *Manu*, the Epics of the *Rāmāyaṇa* and the *Mahābhārata*, and the *Purāṇas*. But the terms *śruti* and *smṛti* can also refer to what is objective and subjective respectively—for what is heard is largely objective; while memory, being a special characteristic of the soul, is largely subjective. Taken in this sense, the Vedas and all Vedic literature, dealing as they do with Nature and its laws, and being objective in their approach, would be spoken of as *śruti* or what is possible orally to explain. On the other hand, post-Vedic literature, dealing as it does with the problem of soul and God, would be largely subjective, and refer to spiritual experiences, which are not so easy to explain, and can best be remembered. This division between Vedic and post-Vedic literature enables us to understand their division of thought and different points of view, as well as the connection between them.

The Rāmāyaṇa

The *Rāmāyaṇa* deals with the story of the life of *Rāma*, said to be a prince, and is called a Veda. *Rāma* is also said to be a great *avatāra* or 'incarnation' of *Viṣṇu*, the highest of the three great deities of the Hindus. Now we know that the Vedas deal with the great problems of Nature and man; and, if the *Rāmāyaṇa* is said to be a Veda, its subject-matter would be the same. The 'story', however, appears to be very different; but if we interpret it in the light of the method explained in the *Mīmāṁsā*, we find that it is transformed into an account of some of the great systems of philosophy and religion; and the 'fights' between *Rāma* and the *Rākṣasas*,—more specially *Rāvaṇa*— are but an exposition of their apparently conflicting points of view.[1] The idea of *Rāma* as an 'incarnation' of God is similar too.[2]

Purāṇas

The *Purāṇas* are believed to be a collection of ancient tales and legends, and are said to be eighteen in number. They are grouped together in different ways, but more generally in three divisions of six each, and associated with the three principal deities—*Brahmā*, *Śiva*, and *Viṣṇu*; and there are also separate *Purāṇas* dealing with each one of them. A number of them deal with the 'stories' of some of the 'incarnations' of *Viṣṇu*—*Matsya* (Fish), *Kūrma* (Tortoise), *Varāha* (Boar), and *Vāmana* (Dwarf); and there are also some in the name of *Agni* and *Vāyu* and a number of other gods and sages.

We have seen that the three principal deities—*Brahmā*, *Śiva*, and *Viṣṇu*—are associated with the great systems of religion which bear their names; and their accounts, as given in these works, will be found to correspond to what has been stated about them here. *Agni*, as we have seen, refers to the intellect; and *Vāyu* or Air to vital breath, the vehicle of the soul; and the two *Purāṇas* deal with their special problems; and the same would be true of other gods and sages, when we understand what they really signify.

The 'incarnations' of *Viṣṇu* have a special place in all post-Vedic literature—for there is a reference to them in all the principal *Purāṇas*; and it would be found on examination that they give us the different ideas of God in all the great systems of philosophy and religion. This will explain why they are regarded as so important.

The Mahābhārata

The *Mahābhārata* is perhaps the greatest, as indeed it is the longest, of all the sacred books of the Hindus. It is said to be the fifth and last of the Vedas, and is called 'the history of the *Purāṇas*'; and we are told in all seriousness that that which is in it, occurs elsewhere too; while that which is not in it occurs nowhere else. There is also a detailed description of the contents of the Epic in its opening chapter; and the claim made for it is so vast that, if true, it would appear to be nothing short of an encyclopaedia of all ancient knowledge.

But the 'story' of the Epic—the conflicts and rivalries of the heroes of the *Kaurava* and *Pāṇḍava* groups of families—does not appear to have anything to do with any great schemes of thought, or moral and spiritual values of life; and even the life of *Kṛṣṇa*, said to be a perfect 'incarnation' of of *Viṣṇu*, does not seem to be free from criticism or blame. The *Mahābhārata* contains the *Bhagavad Gītā* indeed; but the teachings of the latter appear to be so far removed from the idea of the main 'story', that there are not a few who believe that it is an interpolation, and has nothing whatever to do with the Epic as such.

There is thus an obvious contradiction between the 'story' of the Epic as it is, and the claim that is made for it; and so it is a fit subject for the application of the method of inter-pretation explained in the *Mīmāṁsā*. If we do so, and get a new meaning of the principal words used in the text by dividing them into parts, we shall find that what is claimed for the Epic is in effect true, and that it is the story of the life of man in terms of all the great systems of philosophy and religion—including the ascending and descending scales of thought—that is, from birth to perfection, and thence to death. We shall then understand that, since it is not possible to go beyond the range of thought of the six systems of philosophy, and the three great systems of religion—all that is written in it is also contained in the other sacred books, and what is not written in it, is contained nowhere else. It is thus an all-inclusive 'story' of the sacred books; and it is in this sense that we have to understand its idea as a "history of all the *Purāṇas*".

There is, however, a difference in the form of presentation of ideas in these works. While the *Rāmāyaṇa* and the *Purāṇas* deal with the problem of life in terms of wars and conflicts between gods and demons—who represent different aspects of the great forms and forces of life, and different ways of looking at them—the *Mahābhārata* presents the same conflict in terms of the life of human beings—with *Kṛṣṇa* or God to help each side in proportion to their faith in Him. Indeed, the personification of ideas and systems of thought in the *Mahābhārata* as well as the *Rāmāyaṇa*, is so perfect, that the 'characters', as in the case of the Vedas—to which there is a special reference in the *Mīmāṁsā*, appear to be like living creatures; and it is for this reason that they have so long been regarded as such.[3]

The *Bhagavad Gītā*—The *Bhagavad Gītā* occupies an important place not only in the 'story' of the *Mahābhārata*, but also all the principal sacred books of the Hindus. When we understand the 'story' of the Epic in terms of an account of the great systems of philosophy and religion, we shall find that the central idea of the *Bhagavad Gītā* is also the same; and each of its eighteen chapters has a bearing on the corresponding *Parva* (or section) of the Epic or a day of battle between the contending hosts.[4] It may accordingly be said to be the quintessence of all the sacred books classified as *smṛti*; and it is for this reason that it is possible to illustrate the ideas of all the systems of philosophy by its means.[5]

A Common Pattern

Thus we see how the whole body of sacred literature, from the Vedas to the Epics and the *Purāṇas*, presents the same essential pattern of thought and expression. The Vedas tell us of the great gods, who are but personifications of the great forms and forces of life; and if we understand that *Indra* refers to the soul, *Agni* to the intellect, *Soma* to the mind, and the two *Aśvins* to the senses of knowledge and action—and if we realise that they are believed to have their counterparts in the sun and the moon, and the planets and the stars—we can understand how we can make up a 'story' of the life of man in the midst of the great objects of Nature. We notice a tendency in this direction in the novelists of modern times, attempting to work out a 'story' with a scientific bias or background. But the whole form of ancient thought and mode of expression is unique, and must have called forth all the powers of invention and the genius of man. It is a vast body of literature, produced over hundreds of years—but all along the same lines of thought—a synthesis of science, philosophy and religion, worked out in the life of man, and expressed in the same form throughout. And the secret of the sacred books lies in the method of interpretation explained in the *Mīmāṁsā*.

REFERENCES

1. This will be explained in detail in a later work.
2. A brief explanation of the ten principal 'incarnations' of *Viṣṇu* follows in the next section of this work.
3. The whole story of the *Mahābhārata* has been explained in terms of all the great systems of philosophy and religion (MM. III-V).
4. The idea of the *Bhagavad Gītā* as an epitome of all sacred books has already been explained (MM. V, 463-545).
5. This will explain how a number of *Sūtras* of all systems of philosophy can be explained by means of references to the *Bhagavad Gītā*.

XIV

THE TEN INCARNATIONS OF VIṢṆU

The Ten Incarnations of Viṣṇu

Reference has been made to the ten principal 'incarnations" of *Viṣṇu*; and, as their idea is repeated in the Epics and the *Purāṇas*, and occupies an important place in the scheme of ancient thought, it would be of interest to explain what they mean. As in their existing form they do not appear to have any relation to any great moral or spiritual values of life, it would also show what can be achieved by means of the application of the method of interpretation explained in the *Mīmāṁsā*. However, only a very brief explanation can be offered here; but it would be enough to show that they follow the same pattern of thought as the systems of philosophy and religion, and explain the evolution of the idea of God in all of them.

The Idea of Incarnation

In this connection it is necessary to understand the idea of an 'incarnation' of *Viṣṇu*, as well as that of the deity. The *Mīmāṁsā* tells us that *Viṣṇu* refers to the intellect; and if we divide the word into parts, we shall find that he refers also to the mind and the objects of Nature. This means that he represents the idea of God such as we can obtain by reference to our intellect, mind, and the objects of Nature.

Now, *Vedānta* tells us that we can understand the idea of *Brahma* or God in three ways—by reference to the character of our own soul, by reference to Nature and its attributes, and by means of negative ideas, such as "not this, not that," the unknowable and the unmanifest. It also tells us that the best way of understanding Him is by reference to Nature, for, as we have seen, we can transform Nature itself into God by means of the idea of Sacrifice, and understand Him in terms of Goodness, Intelligence and Joy, or *Sat-cit-ānanda*. On the other hand, it is difficult to understand the true nature of the soul as soul, and the best way of grasping its idea too is to think of it in terms of the intellect. Similarly, 'negatives' can convey but little that gives us a definite idea of God, and only imply that He transcends all that the mind of man can think of or imagine. The simplest way of thinking of God is, therefore, to conceive of Him as Supreme Intelligence, if we think of Him in terms of intellect or the soul, and as Goodness, Intelligence and Joy or *Sat-cit-ānanda*, if we think of Him in terms of the attributes of *Prakṛti* or Nature. There is no contradiction between the two, for the intellect, as the '*Sāṅkhya* has told us, is part of *Prakṛti* itself; but in either case we attempt to associate certain attributes with Him, for otherwise we cannot form any definite idea of the Deity. This may be said to be an intellectual conception of God, having a bearing on the idea of goodness or the essential character of the mind, and also associated with the attributes or objects of Nature: and this, as we have seen, is the idea of *Viṣṇu*. As an 'incarnation' means an embodiment of an idea, the 'incarnations' of *Viṣṇu* would refer to different ways in which the idea of God can be represented in terms of the attributes and objects of Nature.

The *Sanskṛt* word for an 'incarnation' is an *avatāra*, which also means a saviour, or one who comes down to save those who are likely to be lost in error or the darkness of ignorance; and this really means that, if we understand the idea of God, as exemplified by an 'incarnation', we can be saved—from our own mental obscuration or evil in the world.[1]

Thus we see that there are two principal ways of thinking of God—as one without any attributes, and one with attributes; and the one is called *nir-guṇa*, and the other *sa-guṇa* conception of the Deity; and an 'incarnation' gives us the latter conception of God.

The Pattern

We have stated that the idea of the ten principal 'incarnations' of *Viṣṇu* follows the same pattern of thought as the great systems of philosophy and religion. We have seen the bases of the six great systems of philosophy, and noticed how the *Mīmāṁsā*, based on the character of *ahaṅkāra* or the I-as-an-actor, has no place in the construction of the three principal systems of religion, because they regard the soul as an actor, and, in the circumstances, there can be no place for *ahaṅkāra* also as such.

We have also seen how the range of thought of the system of *Brahmā* extends from *Sāṅkhya* to *Nyāya* and the *Vaiśeṣika*; of *Mahādeva* from *Nyāya* to *Vaiśeṣika* and *Yoga*; and of *Viṣṇu* from the *Vaiśeṣika* to *Yoga* and *Vedānta*. We have noticed that each of these has its own idea of the existence of God, so that, as there are nine points of view, we should have nine 'incarnations' of *Viṣṇu* to represent them. But, as we have observed, Vedānta is based on the character of the soul, and it is not possible to understand its true character as such, or without reference to the intellect; and so it is not possible to have an 'incarnation' of God in terms of His idea in pure *Vedānta*; and his highest 'incarnation' or conception in terms of any attributes corresponds to that of *Yoga*, where that system may, for practical purposes, be identified with *Vedānta*, even as intellect is with the soul. This, as we have stated, is the idea of *Yoga* in the *Bhagavad Gītā*, where *Kṛṣṇa* is called *Yogeśvara* or the God of *Yoga*. This gives us eight 'incarnations' of *Viṣṇu*, corresponding to the eight points of view of the different systems of philosophy, in so far as they are incorporated in the three great systems of religion; and this completes the whole ascending scale of thought from *Sāṅkhya* to *Yoga*, or the *Digambara* school of Jainism to the qualified monistic school of *Viṣṇu*.

We have seen that, after attaining to perfection, a man must prepare for death; and that is the descending scale of thought, represented by the ninth 'incarnation', *Buddha*.

We have now completed the whole cycle of human thought, and understood all ways of looking at Nature and God; and so, after this, whichever way we turn, we find nothing but the presence of God everywhere in the world: and this is signified by the tenth 'incarnation', *Kalki*.

This is the pattern of thought of the ten principal 'incarnations' of *Viṣṇu*; but it is necessary to understand what exactly they signify, and how this can be proved to be true.

Ten and Twenty-one Incarnations

We have referred to ten principal 'incarnations' of *Viṣṇu*; but the *Bhāgavat Purāṇa* mentions as many as twenty-one. In this connection it would be enough to observe that some of these additional 'incarnations' are meant to elucidate the idea of the ten principal ones, while others would refer to certain intermediate ideas of the different systems of religion. For instance, the first of the ten principal 'incarnations' is said to be *Matsya* or the *Fish*; while we are told that the first of the twenty-one is *Puruṣa*, which, as we notice in all systems of philosophy, refers to the individual soul; and we find that the idea of the two is identical. We shall accordingly limit our explanation to the ten principal 'incarnations' of *Viṣṇu*.

The Fish and the Sāṅkhya

We have to begin at the bottom of the scale—that is, with the *Sāṅkhya* in the system of *Brahmā*; and the first 'incarnation' is *Matsya* or the *Fish*. Let us see what is the connection between the two.

We have noticed that the *Sāṅkhya* has no place for God as a creator in its scheme; but it is prepared to concede that, if we conceive of Him as a liberated soul, altogether different from the world and having nothing in common with it—it would be possible to prove His existence. The crucial thing, therefore, is to understand the character of the soul, as it is conceived in this system; for it is this that is represented by *Matsya* or the *Fish* as the first 'incarnation' of *Viṣṇu*.

The story of this 'incarnation' is given in a separate Purāṇa, called by its name; and if we interpret the text in accordance with the method explained in the *Mīmāṁsā*, we shall find that the Fish refers to the soul, characterised by self-knowledge, and so may be regarded as the most perfect embodiment of the idea of God as conceived by the *Sāṅkhya*.[2]

The Tortoise and Nyāya

After the *Sāṅkhya* we pass on to *Nyāya*; and we have observed that it is based on the character of the senses; and, so far as the idea of God is concerned, it has two points of view—that He is but a spectator of the work of *Prakṛti*, or that He has but a small share in the work of creation. The first of these belongs to the system of *Brahmā*; and, as its main conclusion is that the soul should engage in the least little action it can, and remain as a spectator of things for the most part, this, it believes, can best be secured by means of a complete control of the organs of the senses. And it is this idea of control that is represented by the *Tortoise*, as the next 'incarnation' of *Viṣṇu*[3].

The Boar and the Vaiśeṣika

After *Nyāya* comes the *Vaiśeṣika*, based on the character of the mind, and constituting the topmost point of the system of *Brahmā*. We have observed that the attribute of the mind is desire, which contains an essential element of goodness, so far as the possessor of it is concerned. The 'incarnation' of God in this system would accordingly be one who, while doing good to himself, does good to others too; and it is this that is personified by the third 'incarnation', the *Boar*.[4]

Incarnations and the System of Brahmā

These are the three 'incarnations' of *Viṣṇu* in the system of *Brahmā*, which, as we have seen, is based on the character of *Prakṛti* or Nature as the supreme, chief, or major creator of the universe. They are all animals, for *Prakṛti*, as the *Mīmāṁsā* tells us, is represented largely by the animal world. They are also associated with water in more or less degree—the fish entirely so, the tortoise is amphibious, while the boar, though living on land, loves to wallow in the mire; and that is so because water is specially symbolic of the idea of Nature or *Prakṛti*, as land would be of God; and so the degree of association with water represents the measure of belief in the creative power of Nature or *Prakṛti*.

Incarnations and the System of Mahādeva

We have dealt with the idea of the 'incarnations' of God or the highest conception of the soul in the system of *Brahmā*, and now pass on to the system of *Mahādeva*, the range of whose thought extends from *Nyāya* to *Vaiśeṣika* and *Yoga*; and so it too has its three 'incarnations' corresponding to the idea of God and the soul in these systems. This system is based essentially on the idea of God and Nature as joint creators of the universe, and it is a matter for consideration whether the share of Nature is more than that of God, or the two are equal, or the share of God is more than that of Nature. Again, as the idea of God is represented by animals in the system of *Brahmā*, the 'incarnations' in the system of *Mahādeva* refer to human beings, for the idea of God and Nature, *Puruṣa* and *Prakṛti*, or man and woman—as joint creators of life—is best represented by the life of man.

The Meeting Place of the Systems of Brahmā and Mahādeva

But we have observed that when we attain to the topmost point of the system of *Brahmā*, we find ourselves at the bottom of the system of *Mahādeva*, and that is the connection between them. That is so because, though the topmost point of the former is *Vaiśeṣika* and of the latter *Nyāya*, their points of view are the same; for *Nyāya*, as we have explained, has two points of view in regard to the idea of God, as a mere spectator, and as a creator but having a smaller share than *Prakṛti*. We have seen that the *Vaiśeṣika* has three such points of view: the share of God being less than that of Nature, the two being equal, and the share of God being greater than that of Nature; and we notice that the first of these is the same as the second point of view of *Nyāya*.

Man-Lion and Nyāya

As we have observed, the system of *Mahādeva* begins with *Nyāya*, but with its second point of view—where God is conceived to be a creator, but has a smaller role to play than *Prakṛti*. This is the same as the first point of view of the *Vaiśeṣika*, the highest point of the system of *Brahmā*. But, as the idea of God in that system is represented by animals, and by man in the system of *Mahādeva*, and the two meet at this point,—its "incarnation" of God is a *Man-Lion*—a combination of a lion and a man—the highest of the animal world, and the lowest of the world of men.[5]

'There is also a similar correspondence between the idea of the *Boar* and the *Man-Lion*. We have seen that the former represents the highest conception of goodness in the world of

Nature, where individual good coincides with general good; while the latter represents the essence of joy in life without which it would not be possible to exist; and the idea of goodness is closely allied to that of joy. It is this substance of joy that is represented in the story in terms of the preservation of *Prahlāda*,[6] the demon-devotee of God.

The Dwarf and the *Vaiśeṣika*

After this we are concerned with the highest ideal of the life of man, and begin with the life of a boy at a stage where he is able to express his mind; for after *Nyāya* we come to the *Vaiśeṣika*, which is based on the character of the mind. This is represented by *Vāmana*, the *Dwarf*, an intelligent boy, six years of age,— and the number six represents the mind, as we know. He has his desires—the most elementary ones—for food, shelter, and clothes; but, because they are not opposed to Dharma, they need to be satisfied. And so this is our next idea of the character of the soul and the 'incarnation' of God.

Paraśurāma and Yoga

After the *Vaiśeṣika* we pass on to *Yoga*; and the next stage of life after that of a boy is that of an intelligent student, who acquires pure knowledge for its own sake, and is devoted to *Yoga*; and, as this is our idea of the soul, it represents also our idea of the 'incarnation' of God. That is the next 'incarnation' of *Viṣṇu*, *Paraśurāma*.

Incarnations and the System of Viṣṇu

After the system of *Mahādeva* comes the system of *Viṣṇu*, and its range of thought extends from *Vaiśeṣika* to *Yoga* and *Vedānta*. But we have seen that the idea of the *Vaiśeṣika* in this system—namely, that God and Nature are joint creators, but the share of God is greater than that of Nature—corresponds to that of *Yoga* in the system of *Mahādeva*; so that when we attain to the topmost point of the latter system, we find ourselves at the bottom of the system of *Viṣṇu*; and that is the connecting link between them.

We have also seen that the highest point of the system of *Viṣṇu*, *Vedānta*, based on the character of the soul, can have no 'incarnation', for it is impossible to understand the character of the soul in terms of the soul or as it really is; and so, even as we have to be satisfied with the idea of the soul in terms of the intellect, we have to be satisfied with the idea of 'incarnation', based on the character of *Yoga*, as the highest that the mind of man can conceive. The system of *Viṣṇu* has accordingly but two 'incarnations' of God, corresponding to His idea in the *Vaiśeṣika* and *Yoga*.

Rāma-Candra and the Vaiśeṣika

The system of *Viṣṇu* begins with the *Vaiśeṣika*; and, as it is but a continuation of the system of *Mahādeva*, we begin with the next stage of human life after that of a student—and that is that of the householder—the most perfect embodiment of which is *Rāma-candra*; and so he is the next 'incarnation' of *Viṣṇu*. We have seen that this point in the system of *Viṣṇu* is similar to that of the highest point in the system of *Mahādeva*; and the common link between them is represented by the word Rāma, which occurs in both *Paraśu-rāma* and *Rāma-chandra*.

Kṛṣṇa and Yoga

After the *Vaiśeṣika* we go on to *Yoga* in the system of Viṣṇu, and according to it God is the supreme creator of the universe, and Nature is but a spectator of His work. Corresponding to this the next stage of human life is one where a man extends the principle of his family to the whole world; and the highest conception of life in accordance with this idea is that of *Kṛṣṇa*, said to be the most perfect 'incarnation' of *Viṣṇu*. Indeed, the whole 'story' of his life, as described in the *Bhāgavat Purāṇa*; can be explained in this light in accordance with the method of interpretation explained in the *Mīmāṁsā*; and his sixteen thousand 'wives' express the idea of the whole world being of the family of God.

Buddha and the Descending Scale of Thought

We have traced the course of human thought in connection with the idea of God from *Sāṅkhya* to *Yoga*, and it is impossible for us to go any further. *Kṛṣṇa* is accordingly the most perfect 'incarnation' of God, because he represents the idea of the most perfect soul or the most perfect man, to whom the whole world is but one family. But even the most perfect of men must die, even as the most perfect idea of God disappears from the world, as, indeed, it has done. We have gone to the highest point in the ascending scale of thought, and must now go down, and prepare for death; and corresponding to this the next stage in human life is *sannyāsa* or renunciation of all action. And this is represented by the next 'incarnation', *Buddha*, who personifies a life of perfection in the path of death.

Kalki, the Last

We have traced the idea of perfection of the soul, that is God, from the beginnings of life to the highest point of human thought, and thence to death, and there is nothing more that it is possible to know. After this, wherever we turn, we shall find nothing but the essence of God—only we must remember that His basic conception arises through purity of life,—from the senses to the soul.[7]

The Incarnations of Viṣṇu and the Systems of Philosophy and Religion

We have seen how the systems of philosophy are linked up with those of religion, and both with the idea of the 'incarnations' of *Viṣṇu*; and the whole idea may now be represented as follows:—

I. SYSTEMS OF PHILOSOPHY

DIVISIONS OF OF LIFE	Nature		M		A	N
MEANS OF KNOWLEDGE	Nature	Senses	Mind	Ahaṅkāra	Intellect	Soul
SYSTEMS OF PHILOSOPHY	Sāṅkhya	Nyāya	Vaiśeṣika	Mīmāṁsā	Yoga	Vedānta

II. SYSTEMS OF RELIGION

DIVISIONS OF LIFE	NATURE	M		A		N
MEANS OF KNOWLEDGE	Nature	Senses	Mind	Intellect		Soul
SYSTEMS OF PHILOSOPHY	*Sāṅkhya*	*Nyāya*	*Vaiśe-ṣika*	Yoga	Vedānta	
SYSTEM OF RELIGION	System	of	Brahmā			

Jainism				
Digambara	Śvetāmbara			
	Buddhism			
	Hīnayāna	Mahāyāna		
	System	of	Mahādeva	
		System	of	Viṣṇu
Atheism	Agnosticism	Dualism	Qualified Monism	Monism

III. INCARNATIONS OF VIṢṆU

The Ascending Scale of Life

DIVISIONS OF LIFE	NATURE	M	A	N	
MEANS OF KNOWLEDGE	Nature	Senses	Mind	Intellect	Soul
SYSTEMS OF PHILOSOPHY	Sāṅkhya	Nyāya	Vaiśeṣika	Yoga	Vedānta
SYSTEM OF RELIGION	System	of	Brahmā		
INCARNATIONS	FISH (Soul)	TORTOISE (Control of Senses)	BOAR (Goodness of Life)		
SYSTEM OF RELIGION		System	of	Mahādeva	
INCARNATIONS		MAN-LION (Joy of Life)	DWARF (An intelligent Boy)	PARASURAMA (An inieligent Student)	
SYSTEM OF RELIGION			System	of	Viṣṇu
INCARNATIONS			RAMACANDRA (A perfect Householder)	KṚṢṆA (A perfect Man, having the World for his Family)	

The Descending Scale of Life

SYSTEM OF RELIGION	Buddhism
INCARNATIONS	BUDDHA (Perfection in Death)

A Universal Conception of God

KALKI

REFERENCES

1. Cf. BhG. IV. 7-8
2. As the 'fish' refers to the soul, and water,—even as the *Mīmāṁsā* tells us, refers to Nature, the relation between fish and water should, as far as possible, correspond to that between soul and Nature, as conceived by the *Sāṇkhya;* and that would illustrate the idea of an 'incarntion' more clearly still.

   The *Sāṅkhya* tells us that the soul is altogether different from all that is in the world, although it dwells in its midst; and corresponding to this we may conceive of the fish as altogether different from water, although it lives in it.

   The *Sāṅkhya* cannot explain the origin of the soul, and so it may be regarded as self-created. The fish belongs to the class of aquatic animals, some of which are characterised by parthenogenesis,—that is, that they can reproduce their species without any fertilization. The fish may, therefore, be said to represent this character of the soul.

   The fish may be said to move in water like the soul in the body. It is also believed to be characterised by memory, which is said to be a special attribute of the soul; and so it may be said to possess self-knowledge, the special characteristic of a liberated soul, according to the *Sāṅkhya*.

   As a total renunciation of action is a characteristic of the liberated soul according to the *Sāṅkhya,* the fish may be said to satisfy this condition too,—more than any other creature in the world: for like other animals, it needs no clothes to wear; but unlike many, needs no shelter too; and so far as food is concerned, it eats indeed, but becomes the food of others in its turn: and food, shelter and clothes are the essential causes of action, and the fish needs them the least.

   Thus, if we wish to describe the soul in terms of a living creature, we cannot do better than describe as a fish in water.

It may be of interest to point out that there is a reference to *Virāṭa* and the Kingdom of the fish in the story of the *Mahābhārata;* and there too the idea is exactly the same (MM. IV, 350-359).

3. As the *Bhagavad Gītā* tells us, the Tortoise represents the idea of a perfect withdrawal of the organs of the senses from their objects (BhG. II, 58).
4. See p. ccxxxiii n.
5. There are a number of references in the sacred books to creatures who are part human, part animal, *e.g. Gaṇeśa,*—and they all represent the same idea as *Nara-siṁha* or *Man-Lion.*
6. *Prahlāda (pra-hāda)* means '(*pra*) great (*hlāda*) joy' The idea of God preserves joy in the world of Nature, for God himself partakes of the character of joy. He is *Sat-cit-ānanda* or Goodness, Intelligence and Joy.
7. A detailed explanation of the ten principal 'incarnatio\ns' of *Viṣṇu,* after the manner set out here, will follow in a separate work, as soon as necessary arrangement can be made. The whole idea has been worked out in detail in accordance with the method of interpretation explained in the *Mīmāṁsā,* and only the barest outline has been given here. But it would serve to show what the original idea of the ancients was.

The real idea of these 'incarnations' can, in number of cases be obtained by dividing words into their parts, while in the rest, by means of other ways referred to n the *Mīmāṁsā*. For instance, the world *Matsya (Fish)* may be divided into *ma,t,s,ya,*—when its meaning would be "(*ya*) the intellect, (*s*) mind, (*t*) the senses of action and (*ma*) the senses of knowledge." It thus gives us an idea of the soul in terms of the different faculties of man, without which it would be impossible to understand it.

Similarly *Kūrma (Tortoise)* may be divided into *k,ū,r, ma,*—when its meaning would be (*ma*) the senses of knowledge and (r) the senses of senses being under the complete control of the intellect.

In the same manner the word *Varāha (Boar)* may be divided into *vara, ā,ha,*—when its meaning would be "*(ha)* the mind (*ā*) associated with (*vara, 'better, best'*) what is good or the very best". Another word for the *Boar* in the text is *Śūkara,—sū, kara—* meaning "*(kara)* doer of (*sū,* equal to *su* meaning 'good') what is good"; and so we see that both the idea of one who does good to others; and we know that a hog or pig serves as a natural scavenger. In living on filth or refuse it does good not only to itself, but to others too,—though unconsciously. It symbolises, therefore, the element of natural goodness in life, which, while serving its own ends, serves the purpose of something else as well.

All other names are like this, and would be explained in due course.

8. We have explained why there is no place for the *Mīmāṁsā* in the systems of religion. This systems is based on the character of *ahaṅkāra* or the I-as-an-actor; but, as all system of religion regard the soul as an actor, there can be no separate place for the *Mīmāṁsā* in this scheme. It has, however, a most important role in the systems of philosophy, as has already been explained.

XV

THE ESSENCE OF HINDUISM

The Essential Idea of Hinduism

It is now possible to understand the essential idea of Hinduism as a harmony of science, philosophy and religion, and the art of perfect life—as a rational system based on the knowledge of the laws of Nature and the fundamental needs of human life, expressing its ideal of perfection in terms of God, personal as well as impersonal, 'incarnate' as well as absolute. Its primary aim, like the quest of man, is freedom from the ills of life; and it conceives of God as one who creates the world, and is yet perfectly happy and free. The God of Hinduism is accordingly not a 'person' in the sense, in which the term is ordinarily used,—as a living being in human or some other tangible form, like the creatures we see—but rather as a personification of absolute reality or attributes of ideal life—*Sat-cit-ānanda*—real existence, characterised by goodness, intelligence and joy; and to the extent to which a living creature approaches this ideal, he comes nearer unto God. There is thus no contradiction between the conception of God and a perfect soul or a perfect Man, for the one is derived from the other; and so it is possible to conceive of a human being as a 'Son of God' in this sense. But all creatures, such as they really are, live under the limitations of their physical form and circumstances, and absolute perfection is impossible to find; and so no living creature can really embody the idea of God; and the idea of God in terms of a living creature is nothing but a personification of certain attributes of perfection. Hinduism is accordingly based essentially on reason and not faith, except where faith itself is but an extension of reason;[1] and so it is the religion of Man, even as Man is said to be a rational animal, as distinguished from the rest.

Sanātana Dharma

It is thus a universal religion, because it is based on the laws of life which are of universal application; and it is said to be *Sanātana Dharma* or eternal religion, because these laws are eternal and cannot change so long as there is life. Indeed, there is no form of opinion or belief, extending from atheism to pure monism of God, and no mode of life, extending from pursuit of knowledge and renunciation of action to the fulfilment of life through all forms of knowledge and all kinds of actions—that is not included in its range; and so all kinds of persons, at whatever stage of mental and spiritual development, can find comfort in its teachings, and understand the truth according to their view of life. *Jainism*, *Śaivism*, and *Vaiṣṇavism* are, accordingly, equally integral parts of Hinduism, —enabling us to rise from one stage of thought and life to another, and making the whole complete. *Buddhism* shows the path of perfection that ends in death; but, as it corresponds to the last stage of human life, and can be included in the other systems, it ceased to exist as a separate system, independently of the rest. It has its proper place as part of a whole scheme of life; but if we allow it to take the place of the whole, attempt to renounce action in the prime of life, before its tasks are done, it can only make for frustration and decay. It is for this reason that only a trace of it remains in the country of its birth, corresponding to its legitimate place in life.

Hinduism and Other Systems of Religion

Hinduism is the oldest of the world's great existing systems of religion, which include Buddhism, Christianity, and Islam. But it has its roots in the prehistoric past; and there is evidence of contact between Hindu thought and Greek civilization in the post-Buddhistic period. Indeed, if we understand the sacred books aright, we shall find that they throw a new light not only on the thought of Greece and Rome, but also solve some of the 'mysteries' of the Old and the New Testament,[2] and provide a rational explanation for the Islamic faith in "one and only one God, and nothing but God"—for that is the very idea of *Brahmā* in *Vedānta*. But, for obvious reasons, it is not possible to elaborate this idea here.

The Sacred Books of the Hindus

It is now possible to grasp more clearly the basic idea of Hinduism, as it is contained in the sacred books—the Vedas, the *Upaniṣads*, the six systems of philosophy, the Epics of the *Rāmāyaṇa* and the *Mahābhārata*, and the eighteen *Purāṇas*—all of which are believed to be sacred in their own way.

The Vedas, as the *Mīmāṁsā* tells us, contain an account of the laws of Nature—with special reference to the problems of different forms of life—specially Man; but we need to interpret them correctly to understand all this.

The *Upaniṣads* are said to be an exposition of the secret doctrine of the Vedas; and so they may be said to deal with the same problems more directly. Indeed, we find that they contain a great deal of pure philosophy; but some of their parts are not easy to understand, and would need to be interpreted in the same manner as the Vedas.

With regard to the six systems of philosophy, we have seen that they are closely connected systems of thought, and deal with the problems of life, with special reference to the laws of knowledge and action, and what belongs to Nature, Man, and God.

The different ideas of these systems—their apparent conflicts and the manner in which they can be reconciled, have been grouped together to form the different systems of religion, associated with the names of *Brahmā*, *Śiva*, and *Viṣṇu*, which include *Jainism* and *Buddhism* too; and the same have been rendered in story-form in the great Epics and *Purāṇas*, which can be understood as accounts of the different systems of philosophy and religion in accordance with the same method of interpretation as the Vedas.

A Hindu

A Hindu is said to be one who believes in all these sacred books; and as they, when properly interpreted, are found to deal with the fundamental problems of life—a Hindu is one who tries to understand the entire range of human thought extending from Nature to Man and God, and seeks to attain to perfection by attempting to live in accordance with their laws. Indeed, the different forms of rites and ceremonies, devotion and worship, as well as the 'castes' and the 'stages of life', together with the 'laws' relating to the family and other institutions, were intended to explain and illustrate this idea of perfection, and point the way to its achievement. But it is not possible to deal with this problem at length in this place.[3]

Hindu and Sindhu

There are some who believe that there is no such thing as a Hindu philosophy or religion, and that the term itself—which is a variant of Sindhu, signifying the great river of that name and so referring to the region around it—does not occur in the sacred books. They are of the opinion that the ancient Āryans lived at first in the region through which the Sindhu or the Indus passes, and subsequently migrated to the Gangetic valley in the east. The Hindus, according to them, are the people who took their name from the river Sindhu, and have little connection with any system of philosophy or religion—however their evolution took place.

We have already explained how closely connected are these systems of philosophy and religion; and, while there can be little doubt that the words Hindu and Sindhu are allied, they are also connected with ideas of philosophy, which give a special significance to them.

There are a number of references to the Sindhu in the Vedas, where it means not only a river, but also the sea or the ocean, and stands generally for a great flood of water. Now the *Mīmāṁsā* tells us that Water is symbolic of Nature or *Prakṛti*; and, as the Sindhu is the only river that is spoken of as masculine, whereas Prakṛti is conceived to be feminine—and Man and Woman represent the idea of God and Nature respectively,—it may be regarded as symbolic of the union of the two into one. Indeed, we have seen that it is the idea of Nature itself that is transformed into that of God by means of that of Sacrifice; and this would appear to be signified by the Sindhu, which is accordingly said to be a name of not only *Varuṇa*, but of *Viṣṇu* too.[4] Hence, as the word Hindu is a variant of Sindhu, it refers to one who, beginning with Nature, ends in the idea of God as the supreme creator of the universe, transforming Nature itself into God by means of the idea of Sacrifice. A Hindu is accordingly one who understands the essence of all the sacred books, and endeavours to live in conformity with what they teach; and Hinduism, as originally conceived, is a universal religion in this sense of the term, as we have explained.

Bhārata

The land of the Hindus is also called *Bhārata*, which has a bearing on the same idea. It means literally "descended from *Bhārata*", which is a name of *Agni*, "kept alive by the care of men";[5] and *Agni*, as the *Mīmāṁsā* tells us, refers to the intellect. *Bhārata* would accordingly mean "intellect which has been carefully preserved by human effort", or deliberate, as distinguished from natural, intelligence; and *Bhārata* or "what is descended from *Bhārata*" would refer to the final conclusion arrived at by means of the exercise of such intelligence.

Bhārata is also said to be the name of a number of princes, one of the more celebrated of whom is the youngest brother of *Rāma-candra*, the hero of the *Rāmāyaṇa*; and it has a bearing on the same idea. We have observed that *Rāma-candra* represents the dualistic school of the system of *Viṣṇu*, according to which God and Nature are conceived to be joint creators of the universe, but the share of God is greater than that of Nature; and we shall find, on a correct interpretation of the 'story' of the *Rāmāyaṇa*, that *Bhārata* represents that intellectual process by means of which we begin with belief in Nature as the supreme creator of life, and attempt to substitute it by God[6] Bhārata or "what is derived from *Bhārata*" is, accordingly, the final conclusion of this process of reasoning, by means of which we can transform the idea of Nature itself into that of God through the idea of Sacrifice, or good, intelligent and joyous action; and so the idea of *Sindhu*, *Hindu*, and *Bhārata* is the same.

An Ārya

A Hindu is also sometimes called an Ārya; and the word is said to mean "an inhabitant of *Aryāvarta* or India; one who is faithful to the religion of his country; a wise and highly esteemed person." With Buddhists an *Ārya* is one who has thought on the four chief truths of their faith, and lives accordingly.

The word *Ārya* is derived from the root *ṛ*; and if we divide it into *ār*, *ya*,—the meaning would be "(*ār*) attaining to (ya) intellect". An *Ārya* is accordingly an intelligent person who seeks to attain to truth, and lives in accordance with it; and that, as we have seen, is also the original idea of a Hindu.

A Hindu, in the original sense of the term, is accordingly one who is an earnest seeker after truth, and endeavours to live in accordance with it; and so he begins with a study of Nature and, understanding the real character of his soul and the purpose of human life, ends with devotion to God. In terms of ideas of philosophy and religion, he is one who begins with the *Sāṅkhya* and, having grasped the different points of view of all systems of philosophy, ends in *Vedānta*. He is also one who begins with *Jainism*, continues with the system of *Mahādeva*, and ends in that of *Viṣṇu*. That is the ascending scale of thought; and when his time comes to depart, prepares for death, lays down everything, and passes away. Thus, after attaining to the highest point of thought and life in the system of *Viṣṇu*, a person goes down to that of *Buddha* again; and that is why an *Ārya* has a special place in *Buddhism*—as one who lives in accordance with the teachings of that religion, which lays particular stress on the evil of desire, and the necessity of a total renunciation of action.

Hinduism

That is the ancient idea of Hinduism—a system of thought and life, aiming at the attainment of perfection through knowledge and experience, but with an eye to Truth. It has laid down a number of requisites for achieving this goal—knowledge of the sacred books, belief in *Karma* or action, transmigration of the soul, the four 'castes' and the different stages of life, and prescribed a number of forms and observances for the purpose; but all of them when properly understood, are found to bear on the same idea—the attainment of perfection in life. It is, as originally conceived, the religion of Man—a rational being who seeks to know and understand, and to live in accordance with the highest truth, and at the highest level of life.

REFERENCES

1. There is no necessary contradiction between reason and faith; and Hindu Philosophy recognises *śabda* or oral statement of a wise and trustworthy person, which is but a form of faith, as a proper means of acquiring certain knowledge. The *Bhagavad Gītā* tells us that faith is an integral part of a man (XVII, 2-3).
2. A brief reference to this is contained in MM. II, Chapter XV.
3. The *Mīmāṁsā* contains an explanation of a number of terms used in connection with ritual and sacrifice—sacrificial altar, fire, sacrificial posts, grass, priests, sacrificer, etc. etc. The four 'castes' refer to what is con tained in Man and Nature—the intellect, *ahaṅkāra* and the mind, the senses, and the objects of the senses respectively; while the four 'stages of life' are meant to deal with the different problems of life, with special reference to knowledge and action as its goal. All this has been dealt with in the present work, and considered elsewhere too (MM.I).
4. *Varuṇa* is the god of the ocean; and; as water is symbolic of *Prakṛti* or Nature, he refers to the latter as the supreme creator of the universe. *Viṣṇu*, on the other hand, refers to God as supreme creator; and *Sindhu*, as the name of both, signifies a fusion of the ideas of the two.
5. Cf. MWD. p. 747.
6. This will be explained more fully in connection with the 'story' of the *Rāmāyaṇa* in due course.

XVI

THE CHARACTER OF SANSKṚT

The Character of Sanskṛt

As will have been observed, all that has been stated in these pages can be understood by means of the method of interpretation explained in the *Mīmāṁsā*; and it is said to consist chiefly in the division of words into parts, and assigning suitable meanings to each, when the combined result would give us the real meaning of a word, and enable us to understand the text. Thus, the real meaning of the word *Agni*, commonly said to be the god of Fire, is intellect, as the *Mīmāṁsā* tells us; and it can be obtained by dividing the word into its parts,—*A*, *g*, *n*, *i*—and assigning suitable meanings to each part. This is necessary, for the dictionary gives a number of meanings to each letter of the alphabet, and we must make a proper selection which, as the *Mīmāṁsā* tells us, should have a bearing on the idea of action.

The *Mīmāṁsā* also tells us that a number of words used in the text have been newly coined to bring out the idea of action and the laws of Nature, with which the Vedas deal; and this, as well as the nature of the meanings of letters—for they are said to be the same throughout—raises the question of the character of the *Sanskṛt* language itself.

Most languages, we find, are associated with a people or a country; and so have 'a local habitation and a name'; but *Sanskṛt* is one of the few languages in the world which are without such limitations; and it would be found on examination that it is a really 'reformed" or "purified' language, as the word literally means. Indeed, if, as the *Mīmāṁsā* tells us, a number of words have been newly coined to fit into this scheme of composition, and they and their parts retain their meanings throughout, it implies that special meanings have deliberately been given to the letters of the alphabet to bring out the ideas sought to be expressed in the text; for without this it would clearly be impossible to frame so many words in this form. This conclusion is borne out by the statement made in the *Mīmāṁsā* itself that these letters signify *dravyas* or substances referred to in the systems of philosophy,—the five great 'elements', Space, Time, Mind, and the Soul.

Letters of the Alphabet and Centres of Sound

The whole structure of the *Sanskṛt* language, and the division of the letters of its alphabet into groups formed in accordance with the centres of sound from where they are produced— gutterals, palatals, linguals, dentals, and labials[1]—goes clearly to show that there is a deliberate design underlying its construction,—for it is possible only in a language that is either wholly new, or has been recast, 'reformed' or 'purified', as *Sanskṛt* is said to be. Indeed, it can only be the latter, for the *Mīmāṁsā* tells us that, in addition to a number of newly coined words, many old words have also been used in the text of the Vedas—only in a number of cases they have been made to conform to this scheme of composition.

A Language of the Gods

Sanskṛt is also sometimes spoken of as *Devanāgarī* or a language of the people of the city of the gods; and it is commonly believed that this is due to its extraordinary richness and sweetness of tone. But the expression has its own special significance too; for the *Mīmāṁsā* tells us that the gods refer to the great forms and forces of Nature; and what belongs to the people of their city can only refer to concrete ideas of life formed in accordance with them and their laws. And it is this that we might expect to be contained in the letters of the alphabet, by means of which we are able to understand the text in terms of these laws.

The Forms and Forces of Nature

We have seen what these forms and forces of Nature really are,—for they can refer only to what emerges out of *Prakṛti* when it evolves into life; and that, as the *Sāṅkhya* has told us, consists of the intellect, *ahaṅkāra*, mind, the ten senses of knowledge and action, and the five great 'elements' and their properties. It is these that constitute the *dravyas* or substances of the systems of philosophy, and have been distributed among the letters of the alphabet, so as to give us these meanings in turn.

The Voice of Nature

Conceived in this sense, *Sanskṛt* would be regarded as the voice of Nature itself. This is indeed true of all languages in more or less degree, for the object of human speech is to give expression to the thoughts of man in connection with all he can think of, imagine, or do; but it is so in the case of *Sanskṛt* in a very special sense.

The Theory of the Language

It is not necessary to discuss here the theory underlying the structure of the *Sanskṛt* language;[2] nor is it necessary to discuss the form of the older language, on which the existing language was based, a certain number of the words of which, as the *Mīmāṁsā* tells us, have been used in the text of the Vedas. It is possible, even as scholars believe, that there was a common stock of Indo-European languages, to which *Sanskṛt*, *Greek*, and a number of other languages belong; but *Sanskṛt*, in its present form, such as we find in the Vedas and later literature,—'purified' and 'reformed' out of the original tongue, as the word literally signifies--with special meanings attaching to the letters of the alphabet, which have retained their import throughout—could only have been devised in India, where it continues in its perfect form still.

The Idea of Vowels and Consonants

It may be of interest to observe that, though the letters of the alphabet of a language are usually divided among vowels and consonants, the consonants in *Sanskṛt* are separated from the vowels, and written in such a manner that they cannot be pronounced without their aid. At the same time, both vowels and consonants are referred to the same centres of sound from which they emanate: for instance, *a* belongs to the gutteral class, and *u* to the labial. This would appear to imply that, while both vowels and consonants refer to the great forms and forces of Nature, the vowels refer to some hidden power that moves them, while the consonants to something more objective and more easily grasped. It would thus be more convenient to consider the idea of the consonants first.

Consonants

We have observed that the consonants refer to the great forms and forces of Nature—from the intellect to the 'elements'. In this connection we have seen the idea of *ahaṅkāra*, or the I-as-an-actor—which too figures as one of the creations of *Prakṛti* or Nature—in the different systems of philosophy and religion, so that, if we regard the soul as an actor, there can be no place for *ahaṅkāra* as a separate entity. As the final conclusion of the systems of philosophy and religion is that it is the soul that acts, there is no place for the *Mīmāṁsā* or the system based on the character of *ahaṅkāra*, in the great systems of religion. Corresponding to this, it would be unnecessary to assign any separate role to *ahaṅkāra* among the letters of the alphabet, and its idea would be included in that of the mind on the one hand, and the soul on the other.

The idea of the consonants would accordingly be limited to the intellect, mind, the ten senses, and the 'elements' and their properties;—for, in addition to these, there is only the soul, which is unmanifest, and so its idea cannot be represented directly by the consonants.

The Principle of Distribution

It would be obvious that the principle of distribution of the forms and forces of Nature among the letters of the alphabet must be the same as is evidenced in the pattern of thought of the great systems of philosophy and religion and their prototype in the Vedas, for otherwise it would be impossible for these letters to represent the corresponding forms and forces, and with such consistency throughout; and it implies that this pattern was well-known from the very inception of the 'reform' which resulted in the formation of *Sanskṛt* and the composition of the Vedas, and was scrupulously followed by all who wrote on the same subject.

The Plan of Distribution

Let us see how it is possible to distribute the forms and forces of Nature among the letters of the alphabet, or *vice versa*. The *Sāṅkhya* tells us that the five great 'elements' are the last to arise out of *Prakṛti*—and they are Ether, Air, Fire, Water, and Earth. We are also told that the higher includes the lower, for the lower arises out of the higher in regular order. Thus, if we were to represent the 'element' Earth, which is at the bottom of the scale, by a single letter, it would be necessary to assign two to Water, three to Fire, and four to Air,— making a total of ten.

Above the Air there is Ether; and both *Nyāya* and *Vaiśeṣika* tell us that its place in this scheme of thought is a very special one. Its chief attribute is sound, which is a variant of motion; and the motion of Ether is said to fill all space, and so it permeates everything. The association of Ether with the senses of knowledge and action is, accordingly, a special one; for, as these senses are all characterised either by sound or motion, they partake of the character of Ether; and, as they are said to have been created simultaneously out of the Mind, and Ether also arises out of the same—the ten senses may be said to give us as clear an idea of Ether as it is possible for us to obtain; and their two groups—of knowledge and action—can represent its two characteristics—motion and sound. Thus, we may represent Ether as well as the ten senses of knowledge and action by means of ten more letters of the alphabet.

After Ether and the senses comes the Mind; and the *Mīmāṁsā* tells us that it is represented by the number six; and corresponding to this we may assign six letters to the Mind.

We have seen that it is not possible to assign any special place to *Ahaṅkāra* or the I-as-an-actor; and so after the Mind comes the Intellect; and it may be represented by seven letters of the alphabet.

Thirty-three Consonants

Thus we see that we need ten consonants to represent the 'elements' from Earth to Air; ten to represent Ether and the senses of knowledge and action; six for the Mind, and seven for the Intellect—making a total of thirty-three; and we find that that is the actual number of consonants in the *Sanskṛt* alphabet.

Vowels

We have observed that the vowels are connected with the consonants, and we find that they can be transformed into them in accordance with the rules of *Sanskṛt* grammar. Hence, they too must refer to the same forms and forces of Nature as the consonants. There are altogether seven vowels in this language, and so it is not possible to assign more than one vowel to each; and so *a* must refer to the Intellect; *i* to the Mind; *u* to the senses of knowledge; *ṛ* to the senses of action; *lṛ* to Air; *e* to Fire; and *o* to the 'element' Water*o* there is no reference to the 'element' Earth among the vowels of the *Sanskṛt* alphabet, and there is a very interesting idea behind it.[3]

Anusvāra and Visarga

The vowels include two more symbols—*anusvāra* and *visarga*; and they too partake of the character of the great forces of life, and represent the principles of attraction and repulsion in the world.[4]

The Soul and its Symbols

It sill be noticed that there is no symbol for the soul in this scheme. But, as we have observed, the soul,.in all systems except *Vedānta*, is conceived to be altogether different from all that is in Nature, and so cannot properly be represented by any symbol or letter of the alphabet. The same is also true of God, in His unmanimanifest or impersonal aspect.

But all systems of thought, including *Vedānta*, agree that the best way of representing the soul is in terms of the different faculties of man,—specially the intellect; and the same is true of God; and so we have to understand the idea of both God and the soul in terms of the symbols used for these faculties— specially the intellect.

Consonants and the Forms and Forces of Nature

We have assigned one vowel each to the different forms and forces of Nature, from the Intellect to the 'element' Water; and need to assign the consonants in the same manner now. This can be done in accordance with a certain regular plan, the principle of which has been examined elsewhere;[5] and here it would be enough to state that the following consonants refer to the following substances:

Intellect	*k ṇ d b ś sh y*
Mind	*c kh dh bh r s*
Senses of Knowledge (Ether)	*ṭ g ch n m*
Senses of Action (Ether)	*t gh j ṭh l*
Air	*p ṅ jh ḍ*
Fire	*ñ ḍh th*
Water	*ph v*
Earth	*h*

An Explanation

It would be found, on examination, that these meanings of the consonants correspond to a large number of meanings given to them in the dictionary. This has been examined elsewhere;[6] but it is necessary to understand the whole idea in its proper perspective. For instance, we have seven consonants to represent the character of the Intellect—conceived in its widest significance; and so it is necessary to understand its character. Now we know that the idea of the Intellect has a great bearing on that of Nature and God—for it is said to be the first manifest form of *Prakṛti* or Nature, and it is by means of it alone that we can understand the idea of God as supreme Goodness, Intelligence and Joy, or *Sat-cit-ānanda*. We have also seen that the intellect and soul may, for practical purposes, be identified; and that is true also of the intellect and the mind. At the same time we can associate it with the senses of knowledge and action too. It is also possible to think of it in its own character as intellect—as characterised by reflection, meditation, or pure thought. All these ideas have been associated with the seven consonants which refer to the intellect: for instance, *k* refers to its connection with Nature or God; *ṇ* where it may be identified with the soul; *d* expresses the idea of charity or sacrifice, which calls for a special exercise of the intellect; *b* refers to Nature, conceived as different from God; *ś* to the intellect with reference to the senses; ṣ as it may be identified with the mind; and *y* as pure intellect in itself.

The idea of other consonants is similar too: for instance, the letter *r* refers not only to the mind, to which group it belongs, but also to the intellect and the senses of action, because we can think of the mind in association with both. Similarly, the letter *s* refers to the mind as well as the soul, and for the same reason. In the same manner the letter *m*, which belongs to the group of the senses of knowledge, refers also to the mind—and for reasons easy to understand.

Dictionary Meanings of Letters

We have also to take into consideration a number of other factors in arriving at the meanings of the letters of the alphabet; but it is not necessary to consider the question here at any length.[7] It would be enough to observe that, in following the method of interpretation described in the *Mīmāṁsā*, that is, by means of division of words into parts—it would not, as a rule, be necessary to go beyond the meanings assigned to letters in a good dictionary; and that is stated in the *Mīmāṁsā* itself. But it is necessary to bear in mind that the sun and intellect, moon and mind are often identified in the sacred books; and sound and motion, the properties of Ether, may also be associated with the senses of knowledge and action in the same manner.

Thus, a dictionary meaning referring to the sun should be understood to refer to the intellect; that to the moon, to the mind; and that to motion or sound, to the senses; and that will enable us to interpret the text correctly.

This method of interpretation depends largely on the division of words into parts, and assigning suitable meanings to the letters which compose them; and this, with such further preparation and background as are necessary for the purpose, will enable us to arrive at the real meaning of the text. We shall then find that the gods of the Vedas really refer to the great forms and forces of Nature;[8] while all the sacred books, from the Vedas downwards, will be found to deal with the great laws of Nature and the problems of life in different ways. The story of the *Mahābhārata* has already been explained in this light;[9] the explanation of Vedic terms in the *Mīmāṁsā*, as given in the present work, follows the same principle; and the same method, applied to the *Rāmāyaṇa* and the *Bhāgavat Purāṇa*, is found to yield the same result.[10] We may accordingly conclude that it can be applied to all the sacred books of the Hindus.

Meanings of Letters

As we have observed, each letter of the *Sanskṛt* alphabet has a number of meanings; but, as those selected for purposes of interpretation of the text are strictly limited, it would be convenient to give them here.

VOWELS

a Intellect;[11] a particle denoting negation as well as comparison; a name of *Viṣṇu*.

ā Intellect;[12] a particle of comparison and assent; also implies diminution; leading to; a name of *Śiva*.

i Mind;[13] to arise from; to arrive at; a name of *Kāmadeva*, the god of Desire.

ī Mind;[14] to arise from; to arrive at; a name of *Kandarpa*, the god of Desire.

u Senses of knowledge;[15] a name of *Śiva*, of *Brahman*.

ū	Senses of knowledge[16]; moon; a name of *Śiva*; weaving.
ṛ	Senses of action[17]; to pierce through, reach, give.
ṛī	Senses of action[18]; to pierce through, reach, give.
lṛ, lṛī	These letters do not occur separately in the text; but they refer to the 'element' Air accord-ing to our theory of the alphabet.[19]
e, ai	These are a combination of *a* and *i*, and express the idea of these letters. According to our theory they refer to the 'element' Fire.[20]
o, au	These are a combination of *a* and *u*, and express the idea of these letters. According to our theory they refer to the "element" Water.[21]
Anusvāra	Following sound; the nasal sound, marked by a dot above a line or an arc (ँ), which cannot be separated from the preceding vowel. A symbol denoting union.[22]
Visarga	Emission, discharge, rejection, dismissal; a symbol (:) denoting repulsion.[23]

CONSONANTS

k	Intellect; sun, *Viṣṇu*; water[24]; the body.
kh	Mind;[25] sun; an organ of sense.
g	Senses of knowledge;[26] going, motion; singing.
gh	Senses of action;[27] striking, killing; a rattling, gurgling or tinkling sound.
ṅ	An object of the senses.[28]
c	Mind;[29] the moon; *Śiva*; and.
ch	Senses of knowledge;[30] tremulous; dividing.
j	Senses of action;[31] born, produced, connected with; enjoyment; poison.
jh	An object of sense;[32] wind accompanied by rain.
ṃ	Fire;[33] a singer.
ṭ	Senses of knowledge;[34] sound.
ṭh	Senses of action;[35] a loud noise.

ḍ	Air;[36] Prakṛti; submarine fire.
ḍh	Fire;[37] serpent.
ṇ	Intellect;[38] knowledge; certainty, ascertainment.
t	Senses of action;[39] the womb; that.
th	Fire;[40] an auspicious prayer; protection, preservation.
d	Intellect;[41] act of giving or gift.
dh	Mind;[42] name of *Brahmā* or *Kuvera*', wealth; sixth note of the gamut in music.
n	Senses of knowledge;[43] vacant, empty; a particle implying negation.
p	Air;[44] drinking; guarding.
ph	Water[45] flowing, bubbling boiling
b	Intellect[46] *Bhaga* or the sun; ocean.
bh	Mind;[47] light; *prakṛti*; name of Venus; resemblance.
m	Senses of knowledge;[48] the moon.
y	Intellect;[49] light; restraining; religious meditation.
r	Mind;[50] desire; giving; going.
l	Senses of action;[51] a technical term for the ten tenses and moods of verbs; cutting.
v	Water;[52] ocean.
ś	Intellect;[53] *Śiva*; abiding in.
ṣ	Intellect[54]; wisdom; final happiness; the number six.
s	Mind;[55] name of *Viṣṇu* or *Śiva*; knowledge.
h	Earth;[56] water; cipher; dying; knowledge, meditation; moon.

A Scientific Conception

These are the meanings of the letters of the *Sanskṛt* alphabet, within the range of which we can re-interpret the text of the sacred books in accordance with the method of interpretation explained in the *Mīmāṁsā*. It is possible that the correlation of the dictionary meanings of certain letters with human faculties and the objects of Nature may, to the uninitiated, appear to be somewhat remote; but it is necessary to remember that the ancients had their own conception of life, which they believed to be scientific in a modern sense of the term. Indeed, as the *Mīmāṁsā* tells us, these works were composed long ago, and need to be undertood in the light of the ideas of their own age, and we should not superimpose our own theories upon them. Thus, if there is a statement to the effect that the intellect, sun, and gold, of the mind, moon and silver may be identifled—we should, so far as the interpretation of the text is concerned, accept it as true; and then, if we like, try and find out if there is also any scientific or rational formation for such a view. But, so far as the interpretation of the text is concerned, the question whether or not we should understand the moon to refer to the mind, cannot arise.

The *Mīmāṁsā* is, however, careful to lay down certain conditions which must be satisfied before we can accept the correctness of this method of interpretation. We must see to it that the division of words into their component parts, as also our method of dealing with the language of the text, is in conformity with the rules of grammar, based on the authority of the best grammarians; further, that the letters retain their new meanings throughout; that so far as the gods and hymns of the Vedas are concerned, we transform them into personificateons of ideas and statements of laws of Nature by this means; and finally, that all this has a bearing on the idea and statements of laws of Nature by this means; and finally, that all this has a bearing on the idea of action, in the widest sense of the term. As the same method of interpretation is said to be applicable to both the *śruti* and *smṛti*, it means that the 'stories' of the Epics and Purāṇas can be transformed into accounts of the laws of Nature or systems of philosophy and religion, based on them, in the same manner.

It will be found on examination that, so far as the work of the present writer is concerned, all the conditions laid down in the *Mīmāṁsā* have been satisfied. The same letters of the alphabet have the same meanings throughout, from the Vedas to the Epics and the *Purāṇas*; and that is equally true of all characters—divine as well as human. The gods of the Vedas are transformed into great forms and forces of Nature, and the hymns, to the small extent to which they have been dealt with, into its laws;[57] the idea of these gods constitutes the basis of the different systems of philosophy, which, in their turn, are grouped together to form the different systems of religion;[58] and the same have been described in the form of stories in the great Epics and *Purāṇas*, and can be re-interpreted as accounts of the different systems of philosophy and religion in accordance with the method explained at such length in the *Mīmāṁsā*.[59]

The two principal tests of correctness of a theory, as the *Mīmāṁsā* tells us, are its consistency of plan in conformity with a rational system of thought, and more satisfactory results; and, so far as the sacred books are concerned, a new method of interpretation should be consistent throughout, and enable us to understand the text in a new light—of the laws of Nature and ideas of philosophy and religion; and it would be stupid, says *Jaimini*, to ask for more.[60] The theory of the *Sanskṛt* alphabet, with the meanings assigned to its letters, will be found to answer both these tests. It has been applied to the Vedas, the two great Epics of the *Rāmāyaṇa* and the *Mahābhārata*, and a number of *Purāṇas*; and the result is the same every time: they all deal with the same laws of Nature, and the same systems of thought, though in different forms and different ways.[61]

An Illustration

It would perhaps be of interest to illustrate this method of interpretation of the sacred text by means of an example. We have observed that the *Mahābhārata* is really an account of the different systems of philosophy and religion, but it is commonly believed to be a great store-house of wonderful and fascinating stories of various kinds; and one of them is that of *Kuntī* and *Karṇa*. *Kuntī* was the 'mother' of the *Pāṇḍava* brothers, who figure so prominently in the Epic; but, before her 'marriage' with *Pāṇḍu* she had a 'son', named *Karṇa*, by the heavenly Sun. The story, as given in the Epic, reads as follows:

KUNTI AND KARṆA

The Birth and up-bringing of Kunti

There was a chief among the *Yadus*, named *Sūra*, who was the father of *Vasudeva*. He had a daughter, named *Pṛthā*; but he gave her to his childless cousin *Kuntibhoja*, who brought her up, and so she was called *Kuntī*.

The Birth of Karṇa

While living in her adoptive father's house, she had been taught a *Mantra* by a *Brāhmaṇa*, by reciting which she could call any of the celestials to have children by him. *Kuntī*, curious to know the efficacy of the *Mantra*, invoked, while yet a maiden, the god *Arka* or the Sun; and of her union with him was born a hero, encased in a natural armour, and with a face brightened by earrings—known all over the world by the name of *Karṇa*. Then the Sun, after restoring her maidenhood to *Kuntī*, went away to heaven, and she threw her powerful son into water.

Karṇa was picked up by *Adhiratha*, the illustrious husband of *Rādhā*, and was brought up by them as their own son. He grew in strength, and became expert in the use of arms. He used to worship the Sun, until his back was scorched with its rays; and while he was engaged in his worship, there was nothing on earth that he would not give to the *Brāhmaṇas* (Ādi P. I, cxi).

Observations on the Story

This, in brief, is the story of the birth of *Karṇa*, one of the great heroes of the Epic, and a sworn enemy of his half-brothers—the *Pāṇḍavas*; and, like many other narratives of its kind, it is full of extraordinary incidents—strange, unnatural, and fantastic. There is indeed nothing extraordinary in the birth and parentage of *Kuntī*, as the daughter of *Sūra* and sister of *Vasudeva*, the father of *Kṛṣṇa*—the great 'incarnation' of *Viṣṇu*; but it is not a little uncommon for a childless Hindu to adopt a daughter rather than a son. But it is impossible to, think of any rational manner in which a woman can call a celestial to have children by him; nor is it easy to believe that the Sun can come down at the call of a maiden even by means of a *Mantra*, however powerful, in this way. It is equally extraordinary that the child born should be encased in a natural armour and have a face brightened by ear-rings; nor is it easy to imagine how the state of virginity can be restored to a mother. Again, it is only a most unnatural mother who can, without any compunction, throw her new-born babe into water; and there is not a word of disapproval in the text to show that the author regarded her action as wicked or inhuman.

With regard to *Karṇa*, while a cast-away child may be picked and brought up in the manner described, and he may grow up into a great hero too, and also worship the Sun, it would be a little difficult to understand how, when he had worshipped that deity and his back had been scorched with its rays, he was able to give to the *Brāhmaṇas* all that they demanded of him.

Thus we see that the story of *Kuntī* and *Karṇa*, as given in the Epic, raises a number of questions which cannot be answered in a rational way. The modern scholar has accordingly contented himself with the belief that the age itself, to which the Epic belongs, was most extraordinary; that the people, great in their own way, were made up of extremes—primitive and poetic, heroic and elemental, crude and refined, philosophic and unconventional, religious and superstitious—at the same time; and so they could mix up the actions of gods and great men, demons and the wicked ones; and, with their exuberant imagination, resort to any description, or give way to any conceit, however fantastic. He is, accordingly, not surprised at the extraordinary incidents in this or any other story in the *Mahābhārata*, for he finds similar accounts in other works of the same kind in India and elsewhere. These works have little more than antiquarian interest for him; and, though they may serve to inspire a poet and provide material for romantic tales, he finds nothing spiritual in them, or anything that can be construed into a systematic scheme of thought. Indeed, all attempts at finding a rational meaning in these stories, made from time to time—for the mind of man cannot reconcile itself to believe that they can be so fantastic—have yielded but little result, and been given up in despair.

Application of the New Method

But the *Mīmāṁsā* tells us that, whenever in our study of the Vedas, we find ourselves faced with such a difficulty, we should take it that the text needs to be interpreted in a different way; and the method of interpretation, as explained by the author, is said to apply to all sacred books, *śruti* as well as *smṛti*. We are told that there are three ways of understanding the meanings of words used in the text: we may accept their dictionary meanings, wherever suitable; or, if the meaning of certain expressions has been expressly defined, we should accept it in that form; or, in the absence of both these courses, we may divide words into their parts, and, assigning suitable dictionary meanings to the latter, construe the whole.

As the *Mahābhārata* is one of the *smṛtis*, and the story of *Kuntī* and *Karṇa* appears to be unnatural, it should be a fit case for the application of the method of interpretation explained in the *Mīmāṁsā*. But we must remember, even as the *Mīmāṁsā* itself is careful to remind us, that we have, by means of this method, to transform it completely into an account of the laws of Nature or systems of thought bearing on them, without omitting any important detail or part. The new explanation would need to be as full and continuous as the original story, and, at the same time, more simple and rational. Let us see what can be done.

Before, however, we can transform a story in this manner, it is necessary to understand that the different characters who take part in it can only be personifications of ideas and objects; and this is what the *Mīmāṁsā* tells us too. This personification can be effected in many ways, and there are a number of references to it in the *Upaniṣads*[62] and other sacred books. There may also be a personification of an idea, an object, a system of of thought, or of Nature or God. For instance, a Woman or the Vegetable Kingdom refers to Nature, as the *Mīmāṁsā* tells us, and it also gives us a number of similes and metaphors by means of which ideas and objects can be described.

As a story postulates different kinds of relationship between individuals—animals, men, demons, or gods,—they too can be used to personify ideas and objects in the same way. For instance, origin and end, cause and effect, action and its result, an idea and its logical conclusion, may be represented in terms of father and son, or other forms of relationship according to the degree of their affinity. Similarly, a variety of objects, making for a common or combined result, may be represented as friends; while those in opposition as foes; and the same terminology may be used in connection with the forces of attraction and repulsion, and the relation of the strong as against the weak.

The sacred books contain a number of references to terms of battle and weapons of war; and these have their own bearing on the idea of action—for a battle is a form of acute conflict of thought, expressing itself in terms of powerful action, and success lies on the side of those who can make the greatest sacrifice. A 'battle' in the story of the sacred books is, accordingly, an expression of an eternal conflict between knowledge and action, and the systems of thought corresponding to them; and as 'sacrifice' is conceived to be good, intelligent and selfless action, making for joy of life— and so ending in the idea of God in the universe—it is sacrifice that succeeds in their battles too.

Again, as the *Mīmāṁsā* tells us, this method of interpretation requires knowledge—of the laws of Nature, as well as the systems of philosophy and religion based on them; for it is only then that we can transform these stories into accounts of these systems.

Finally, the *Mīmāṁsā* tells us of the many different ways in which a word may be divided into parts—parts containing syllables, syllables and letters, or letters only. We are required to follow the rules of grammar and to accept the authority of the best grammarians; and in arriving at the meaning of a word divided into parts, we may commence from the beginning and go on to the end, or from the end and go back to the beginning, as may suit the case.

Let us now consider the story of *Kuntī* and *Karṇa*, and see if it can be transformed into something else.

Kuntī or Pṛthā

The first thing that strikes us in this story is the impossible things—on any rational scheme of thought—said in connection with *Kuntī*, and the unnatural course of her conduct; and so, following the principle laid down in the *Mīmāṁsā*, we may assume that she personifies an idea or an object of life, or else a law of Nature. But, as she is not said to be a goddess, she cannot refer to a law of Nature—for it is only a god (or a demon) who can do so. On the other hand, as she is a woman, who, as the *Mīmāṁsā* tells us, personifies Nature or its objects—she may be said to refer to an object of Nature. But the question is, what can that be?

We find that the dictionary does not help us; nor has the meaning of the word *Kuntī* been defined in a special manner anywhere. But the *Mīmāṁsā* also tells us that there are a number of suggestions in the text itself to point to the solution of the difficulty. Now *Kuntī* is also called *Pṛthā*, which has the same root (*Pṛth*) as *Pṛthvī*, meaning the Earth. This leads us to think that *Pṛthā* also may refer to the planet Earth. But, if that be so, the word *Kuntī* should also refer to the Earth; and we find that, if we divide it into parts, it signifies the Earth.[63] Hence we conclude that *Kuntī* or *Pṛthā* is our planet Earth.

The Father of Kuntī

But the idea of *Kuntī* as our planet Earth cannot stand alone. If it is a proper clue to the understanding of the real idea of the story, it must be supported by all the other statements regarding her. If she is the 'daughter' of *Sūra* of the *Yadu* race, and the 'sister' of *Vasudeva*, the 'father' of *Kṛṣṇa*—and if she also represents the Earth—the latter cannot be men, as we believe, but only symbols of great forms of life, like her.

We have observed that the relationship of father and son may be made to represent the connection between origin and end, or cause and effect; and similarly, brother and sister may represent ideas or objects arising from a common cause or source.

Yadu

We have to begin with *Yadu*, for the 'father' of *Kuntī* is said to belong to this 'race'.

As we are unable to understand what exactly it signifies, we may divide the word into parts; and, if we do so, we find that the meaning it conveys is that "the exercise of our intelligence makes for a proper function of the senses of knowledge".[64]

Sūra

This idea, however, appears to be incomplete, for a proper exercise of our intelligence makes for a proper function of the senses of action too; and so we are told of *Sūra* as "a chief of the *Yadus*", who refers to the association of the intellect with the senses of action, or action.[65]

The Descendants of Sūra

Now we have seen that, if we understand the idea of intelligence in its completeness, as making for both knowledge and action, we can, by a gradual evolution of thought and by associating the idea of 'sacrifice' with Nature, eliminate the difference between it and God, and so understand the most perfect idea of the Deity that is possible for man to know. As these ideas are derived from the original conception of *Yadu* and *śūra*, they may be said to be the 'descendants' of the latter.

Vasudeva and Kuntī

When we examine the problem of knowledge and action in the light of our intelligence, our attention is directed to Nature and all that is in it; and we find that it consists of a number of great and good objects; and one of them is our planet Earth. The idea of the great and good objects of Nature is expressed by *Vasudeva*,[66] and of the Earth by *Kuntī*;[67] and, as they are both derived from the same source, they are spoken of as brother and sister.

Kṛiṣṇa

Vasudeva is said to be the 'father' of *Kṛṣṇa*; and that would require some explanation too.

We are engaged in an examination of what Nature can create; and the sacred books tell us that it consists of eight divisions,—the five great 'elements' (Earth, Water, Fire, Air, and Ether), Mind, *Ahaṅkāra*, and the Intellect.[68] As the idea of the latter is derived from the former, it may be said to be 'descended' from it; and, as the former is *Vasudeva* (associated with *Devakī*), he should have eight children; and the last of them, *Kṛṣṇa* should refer to the intellect. We find, on an examination of his name and what is associated with him, that it is so.[69]

The Family of Kuntī

The whole idea may now be summed up as follows : There are a number of persons who believe that the exercise of intellect means the attainment of knowledge; and so the pursuit of pure knowledge, to the exclusion of everything else, is in accordance with an intelligent scheme of life (race of *Yadus*). But, if we pursue the idea to its logical end, we find that the intellect makes for action too; and so an intelligent scheme of life requires that knowledge should result in action (*śūra*).

The idea of intelligent action takes us to the source of all action—Nature or *Prakṛti*; and, if we understand the character of its different manifestations, we see that what arises from it is a number of great forms and forces of life, which are essentially good and governed by an intelligent plan (*Vasudeva*), and among them is our planet Earth (*Kuntī*). If now we wish to know what are the great objects of life that arise from Nature or *Prakṛti* (*Vasudeva* and *Devakī*), we find that they consist of eight things (eight children of *Vasudeva* and Devakī)—the five great 'elements' and all that belongs to them, Mind, *Ahaṅkāra* and Intellect. The idea of intellect is most important, for it is in its light that we can understand all things, including soul and God; and intellect and soul, and Supreme Intelligence and God may, for practical purposes, even be identified. Indeed, it is by means of intellect that we can, by associating the idea of sacrifice with Nature, transform it into God (*Kṛṣṇa*).

It follows from this that, if we understand the essential character of our planet Earth, we shall find that it is connected with the idea of God (*Kuntī* as the paternal aunt of *Kṛṣṇa*). And corresponding to this we are told that it is in this family that *Kuntī* or *Pṛthā* is born.

Kuntībhoja

But this is not a generally accepted view of Earth, for the people do not commonly believe that it belongs to the great family of God, and that we can understand the nature of His existence through it. They are rather content to think that it is a bountiful bestower of good things. But even this is allied to the process that leads to the idea of God, which is essentially based on the goodness of things that support life—though it does not by itself make for a proper conception of God.

Corresponding to this we are told that there was a childless cousin of *Sūra* named *Kuntībhoja*,[70] and *Pṛthā* was given to him to be brought up as his own daughter.

The Brāhmaṇa's Boon

We have to begin with the position that the Earth is a bountiful bestower of good things, without any direct reference to the idea of God (*Kuntī* is brought up by *Kuntibhoja*); and now we have to see what are those good things that it can bestow.

When we examine the character of Earth, we find that it is not possible for it to create anything by itself. But our intellect tells us that there are a number of great forces of Nature, and the Earth can create a number of things with their assistance.

This is the *Mantra* of the *Brāhmaṇa*, according to which *Kuntī* could call up any celestial to have children by—for a

Brāhmaṇa, as the *Mīmāṁsā* tells us, refers to the intellect, and a god or a celestial to a great form or force of Nature.

Kuntī and the Sun

If we make an intelligent use of our means of acquiring knowledge, we find that the creative power of the Earth is quickened by means of that of the Sun; and so the Sun may be said to be the great source of what the Earth creates.

Corresponding to this we are told that *Kuntī* made use of the *Brāhmaṇa's Mantra*[71] and invoked the Sun.[72]

The Birth of Karṇa

What is it that the Earth creates in association with the energy of the Sun? We find that the first form of creation on our planet Earth is the Vegetable Kingdom, the essence of which is seed or grain; and the ancients believed that all kinds of seed or grain arise in the bosom of the Earth as a result of the action of the rays of the Sun.[73]

Corresponding to this we are told that out of the union of *Kuntī* with the Sun was born a hero, called *Karṇa*; and he expresses the idea of seed or grain.[74]

Natural Armour and Ear-rings of Karṇa

If we examine the form of seed or grain (or fruit), we find that it is encased in a comparatively hard outer skin or rind. Similarly, there is bark on a tree; and they serve to protect the grain or plant. We also see that seed, grain, or fruit grows on the branch of a tree, and makes it look beautiful.

Corresponding to this *Karṇa* is said to have been born with a natural armour and ear-rings.[75]

Kuntī throws Karṇa into Water

Seed or grain has an element of moisture in it, and it cannot grow without it. That is so in accordance with a law of Nature.

Corresponding to this we are told that *Kuntī* threw her son into water as soon as he was born.[76]

Kuntī regains her Virginity

The essence of seed and the Earth is the same, and the two may even be identified.[77] The birth of seed or grain does not, accordingly, affect the structure of the Earth or its fecundity. It does indeed absorb the rays of the Sun, as a result of which grain or seed is born; but it can reflect back or radiate them again, and regain its original state.[78]

Corresponding to this we are told that the Sun restored her virginity to *Kuntī*, and went away.

Karṇa is Brought up by Adhiratha and Rādhā

It is food that supports the body, and makes all creatures live. Indeed, we might say that a person seeks to preserve grain because he is anxious for the preservation of his body; and this "anxiety for the body" is *Adhiratha*,[79] who is said to have picked up *Karṇa*, and brought him home to his 'wife'.

We have "anxiety for the body" (Adhiratha), because we have a desire to live, and desire is a special attribute of the mind. This is *Rādhā*, the 'wife' of *Adhiratha*. She refers to the mind and its attribute, desire—the desire to live;[80] and she is the 'wife' of *Adhiratha*, because this desire is intimately associated with "anxiety for the body".

The Arms of Karṇa

Seed or grain has a number of uses, and can be very effective. Corresponding to this we are told that *Karṇa* became an expert in the use of arms.[81]

Karṇa Worships the Sun

All seed or grain is ripened by the Sun, and the *Upaniṣads* say so too. Its energy may, therefore, be said to be due to the quiet manner in which it can submit to the action of the Sun. Corresponding to this *Karṇa* is said to worship the Sun.

Karṇa Satisfies the Brāhmaṇas

If we use our intelligence, we shall find that all our essential needs can be satisfied by the Vegetable Kingdom, when, under the action of the rays of the Sun, it becomes fully mature or ripe.[82]

Corresponding to this *Karṇa* is said to worship the Sun, and when his back was heated with its rays, there was nothing that he did not give to the *Brāhmaṇas*.

Two Meanings

This is the story of *Kuntī* and *Karṇa*, as given in the Epic, and we can see how it can be transformed into an account of laws of Nature, which, in their turn, constitute the bases of the different systems of philosophy and religion. It will have been noticed that the method of interpretation follows strictly the rules laid down in the *Mīmāṁsā*; and the two meanings, which are entirely different from each other, are equally complete, and no important idea or expression has been left out. This, as the *Mīmāṁsā* tells us, is necessary, if the new meaning is to substitute the old; and that is one of the excellences of the ancient art of composition. It is true of the Vedas, as the *Mīmāṁsā* says; it is true of the *Mahābhārata*, as has already been explained; and it is equally true of the *Rāmāyaṇa* and the *Bhāgavat Purāṇa*, as will be explained in due course. It would follow from this that it would be true of other sacred books as well.

It would perhaps be of interest to place the two versions of the story of *Kuntī* and *Karṇa* side by side.

Story	**Explanation**
There was a chief among the *Yadus*, named *Sūra*.	If we exercise our intelligence, we find that it leads to the idea of knowledge as an attribute of the intellect (*Yadu*). But if we make a further use of our intelligence, we find that the intellect is associated with action too (*śūra*). This leads us to the conclusion that the end of life is not only knowledge, but action too.
Sūra was the father of *Vasudeva*, and grand-father of *Kṛṣṇa*.	When we understand this law of life, and observe the universe in its light, we find that Nature consists of a great number of forms and forces, which work intelligently

Story	Explanation
	and for a good end (*Vasudeva*). Then, if we pursue the point further still we find that Nature may be divided into eight parts, the last of which is intelligence, which, when associated with the idea of sacrifice, gives us the idea of God as Supreme Intelligence immanent in the universe (*Kṛṣṇa*).
He had a daughter, named *Pṛthā*.	When we understand this law of life (*śūra*), we find that the Earth (*Pṛthā* or *Kuntī*) is a great form and force of Nature too, and that it belongs to this 'family of God'.
He had a childless cousin, *Kuntībhoja*, and he gave his daughter to him to adopt; and she came to be called *Kuntī*.	But all people do not believe that the Earth belongs to the great 'family of God'. They are satisfied with the view that it is a bountiful bestower of good things (*Kuntibhoja*), although this view is not, by itself, fruitful of any great results (childless). But if we pursue even this idea to its logical end, we find that it takes us to the idea of good action or action as a sacrifice, and so is allied to the idea of God—itself derived from that of sacrifice.
While residing in her adoptive father's house, *Kuntī* had been taught a *Mantra* by a *Brāhmaṇa*, by reciting which she could call any one of the celestials to have children by him.	But even if we agree that the Earth is a bountiful bestower of good things (*Kuntī* lives in her adoptive father's house), we cannot admit that it can create anything solely by itself. But if we exercise our intelligence (*Brāhmaṇa's Mantra)*, we shall find that the Earth can create with the assistance of the great forces of Nature. There are a number of such forces, and it can create a number of things by means of them (*Kuntī* can call up any celestial for purposes of creation).
Kuntī used the	If we exercise our intelligence

Story	**Explanation**
Brāhmaṇa's *Mantra*, and invoked the Sun; and, as a result of their union, was born a hero named *Karṇa*, encased in a natural armour, and a face brightened by ear-rings.	(*Brāhmaṇa*'s *Mantra*), we find that the Earth is closely associated with the Sun, and has power to attract and absorb its rays; and, as a result of this, there is formed within it the essence of seed or grain, the origin of the Vegetable Kingdom (*Karṇa*). The latter is encased in an outer cover of hard skin, rind or bark, and has a beautiful form, such as may be seen in fruit hanging on the branch of a tree.
The Sun, after restoring her virginity to *Kuntī*, went to heaven; and she threw her son into water.	The seed is of the same essence as the Earth itself, and its birth, at this stage, does not affect its constitution or powers; for it is not affected by the rays of the Sun that it absorbs, as it can radiate or reflect them back again (the Sun restores *Kuntī*'s virginity, and goes away). But the grain, even at this stage, contains an essence of moisture or water, like the nucleus of the cell (*Kuntī* threw her son into water).
Karṇa was picked up by *Adhiratha*, the husband of *Rādhā*, and brought up by them.	All creatures live by food, the origin of which is seed or grain. A creature accordingly picks up and preserves it, because of his anxiety to support his body in proper action (*Adhiratha*), and the desire to live (*Rādhā*).
Karṇa grew up and became an expert in the use of arms. He used to worship the Sun; and when his back	Seed or grain can grow into a tree, and the process of its development, and the uses to which it can be put, are wonderful (*Karṇa* becomes an expert in the use of arms). It absorbs the essence of the power of the Sun itself (*Karṇa* worships the Sun); and

Story	Explanation
was scorched with its rays, there was nothing on earth that he did not give to the *Brāhmaṇas*.	when it is fully mature or ripe (his back was heated with the rays of the Sun), there is no essential want of an intelligent person (*Brāhmaṇa*) that it cannot satisfy.

It is in this manner that the whole story can be transformed into a statement of facts and laws of Nature, each part cohering with the other, and making a new and complete whole. But it is necessary that the same 'character' should retain its own idea throughout the narrative; that is, *Kuntī* should always mean our 'mother' Earth, and *Karṇa* grain or seed, and the systems of thought associated with their ideas. Similarly, all other 'characters' in the Epic—for there must be uniformity of conception throughout—must represent different ideas and objects of life, and retain their own form everywhere. It is only then that, even as the *Mīmāṁsā* tells us, we can regard these works as sacred, as they are believed to be.

All this, so far as it relates to the *Mahābhārata*, has already been explained and need not be repeated here; and it would be found that the Epic is really an account of the clash and conflict of all the great systems of philosophy and religion, and shows how they can be reconciled in the end.

The idea of the *Rāmāyaṇa* and the *Bhāgavat Purāṇa* is similar too: only they deal with the problem in terms of the actions of gods and demons rather than of human beings, as the *Mahābhārata* does.[83] We may conclude from this that the idea of all other sacred books is also the same, and that they can be re-interpreted in the same manner.

Conclusion

This is the ancient, original idea of the sacred books of the Hindus, and of Hinduism—a rational system of thought and life, and a synthesis of science, philosophy, and religion. It has its share of emotion too—devotion, love, and faith—with all that the art of man can embellish—for there is no essential difference between the working of the head and the heart; and the two, like intellect and the soul, may even be identified.

But the ancient systems are not the same as we find them today. They are separated from us by three thousand years, during which many changes have taken place; but the traces of ancient thought yet survive in what remains, and can take us back to the past to re-construct it again.

At the same time, while this method of interpretation helps to solve a number of problems of the sacred books, and places the ancients and their thought in a new perspective—giving us a new idea of their standards of culture and civilization, their achievements in science and psychology, and the understanding of moral and spiritual values of life—it involves a re-orientation of a number of ideas bearing on science and psychology, ethics, history, metaphysics, and religion. But it is not possible, within the limits of the present work, to deal with even a fraction of these, and they must await consideration elsewhere.

REFERENCES

1. The letters of the *Sanskṛt* alphabet are usually arranged as follows:—

Vowels a. ā; i, ī; u, ū; ṛ, ṛī;lṛ, lṛī; e, ai; o, au, Anusvāra (.); Visarga (:).

Consonants

Gutturals	*k*	kh	g	gh	ṅ
Palatals	*c*	ch	j	jh	ñ
Linguals	*ṭ*	ṭh	ḍ,	ḍh	ṇ
Dentals	*t*	th	d	dh	n
Labials	*p*	ph	b	bh	m

Semi-vowels

Palatal y Lingual *r* Dental *l* Labial *v*

Sibilants

Palatal ś Lingual *ṣ* Dental *s*

Aspirate *h*

2. The theory of the *Sanskṛt* language has been discussed in MM. I, Chapter VI.

3. We have observed that there is a theory behind the structure of the *Sanskṛt*

alphabet, and it has been discussed at some length in a previous work (MM. I, Chapter VI). According to this theory the *Sanskṛt* alpha-bet represents all the great forms and forces of life in the world; and, according to the ancients, all that is in the universe is to be found in the organic cell (*Yathā piṇḍe tathā Brahmāṇḍe*). They accordingly conceived of the alphabet in terms of the organic cell, which consists of a nucleus and a cytoplasm—the vowels to represent the nucleus, and the conso-nants to represent the cytoplasm; and so, as there can be no change in the cyto-plasm without a previous change in the nucleus, it is not possible to pronounce a consonant without the assistance of a vowel. A number of grammatical rules have been framed to illustrate the connection between the nucleus and the cytoplasm, and the changes that they undergo. Similarly, as the nucleus consists of a fluid substance, the last vowel refers to the 'element' Water. This means that there is no essence of the 'element' Earth, or its property, smell, in it; and it is for this reason that the nucleus cannot disintegrate. The cytoplasm, on the other hand, contains all that is in Nature, including Earth and its attribute, smell; and so it is subject to decay. All this has already been explained, and need not be repeated here.

The vowels referred to here are all short; and, as the long vowels are but an elongated form of the short, they gave the same or closely allied meanings.

4. The *anusvāra* and *visarga* come after the vowels, and precede the conso-nants; and, as these refer to the nucleus and cytoplasm of the organic cell, the two symbols should also have a bearing on the idea of cell. It would be fund on examination that the form of *visarga* (:) corresponds exactly to that of the centrosome of the cell, which plays a most important part in its evolution; while the form of *anusvāra* (;) corresponds exactly to that of the combination of the centrosome with the chromosomes at the last stage of the development of the cell.
5. MM. I, Chapter VI.
6. Ibid
7. This has been dealt with in MM. I, Chapter VI.
8. Ibid, Chapter IX.
9. MM. III-V.
10. This has been worked out, and will be published in due course.
11. The letter *a* refers to the intellect because it is the name of *Viṣṇu*, who, as the *Mīmāṁsā* tells us, signifies intellect, specially where it may, for prac-tical purposes, be identified with the soul. Negation, assent, and comparison—all require an exercise of the intellect.
13. The range of the system of Śiva extends from the senses to the intellect; and *ā*, as a name of *Śiva*, would refer to this idea of the intellect—as associated with the senses and the mind, and as intellect in itself. Compari-son, assent, etc. require the function of the intellect.
13. *Kāma-deva* is the god of Desire, which is a special attribute of the mind. Hence *i*, as a name of *Kāma-deva*, refers to the mind.

14. *Kandarpa* is the name of *Kāma* or Desire, a special attribute of the mind. Hence ī, as the name of *Kandarpa*, refers to the mind.
15. The range of the system of Śiva extends from the senses to the mind and the intellect, and of *Brahman* or *Brahmā*, its masculine form, from Nature or its objects to the senses and the mind. The letter *u*, as a name of both *Śiva* and *Brahman*, refers to the senses of knowledge, in association with the mind on the one hand and the objects of the senses on the other.
16. The moon refers to the mind; and we have explained the range of the system of *Śiva*. The letter *ū* accordingly refers to the association of the senses of knowledge with the mind.
17. Piercing through, reaching etc. require the function of the senses of action; hence the meaning of *ṛ* as referring to the senses of action.
18. The meaning of *ṝ* is the same as that of *ṛ*, and so it refers to the senses of action, and for the same reason.
19. The dictionary meanings of these letters do not appear to refer to the 'element' Air. But if we understand the idea of Air with reference to its attribute, action, together with its implication, change—and therefore related to the character of *Prakṛti* or Nature—we shall be able to explain a number of its dictionary meanings in this light.
20. These letters, as defined in the dictionary, do not appear to refer to the 'element' Fire. But they are both interjections and particles of address; and Fire, as an 'element', is said to be closely connected with Speech. Hence their bearing on the idea of Fire.
21. The dictionary meaning of these letters does not appear to connect them with the 'element' Water; but Water is also symbolic of Nature or *Prakṛti*, on which the system of Brahmā is based; and the letter *o* is said to be a name of this god, and *au* is its elongated form.
22. The absence of separation signifies close union, which, as we have observed, is implied by this symbol.
23. Dismissal, rejection, discharge signify repulsion or division, which, as we have observed, is the idea of this symbol.
24. The sun refers to the intellect, and so does Viṣṇu hence the meaning of the letter as intellect.

    Water symbolises *Prakṛti*, as the *Mīmāṁsā* tells us; and its first manifest form, according to the *Sāṅkhya*, is *Mahat* or the Intellect: hence the meaning of the letter as water.
25. The dictionary meaning of the letter *kh* does not appear to refer to the mind; but, as we have seen, the mind can be conceived in terms of the organs of the senses on the one hand, and intellect on the other. Hence there is no contradiction in the meanings as given here.
26. Motion and sound are the characteristics of the 'element' Ether, to which the senses of knowledge as well as of action correspond. The senses of knowledge are associated specially with sound, while those of action with motion. The letter *g*, in its meaning as 'singing,' refers specially to the

senses of knowledge; while the reference to 'motion' implies that it may be used for the senses of action too; and the *Mīmāṁsā* tells us that this interchange is permissible.

27. The letter *gh* refers to the senses of action in our scheme, which again has a bearing on the idea of Ether, as we have explained; and Ether has sound for its attribute; hence the reference to sound. Killing or striking too has a bearing on the same idea, as this form of Ether, to which the senses of action correspond, is characterised by motion with change of place, as distinguished from elliptical motion, which too is a characteristic of Ether, and to which the senses of knowledge refer.
28. The letter *ṅ* refers to the 'element' Air in our scheme, which, after the senses of action, is the principal object of the senses.
29. The meaning of *c* as mind is supported by its other meanings as moon and *Śiva*, both of which refer to the mind.
30. The letter *ch* refers to the senses of knowledge in our scheme, which correspond to Ether with elliptical motion: hence the reference to 'tremulous.'
31. The letter *j* refers to the senses of action in our scheme, to which Ether, characterised by motion with a change of place, belongs. As the Mīmāṁsā tells us, all things are completed in the fourth stage of their existence, and it is for this reason that the number four is said to be important. Now the fourth stage in the order of development belongs to this aspect of Ether—the first three being the intellect, mind, and Ether characterised by elliptical motion or corresponding sound. Hence the meanings 'produced' etc. The reference to 'enjoyment' and 'poison' is significant; for these are the different ways in which we look at things produced, or manifest life.
32. The letter *jh* refers to Air in our scheme, and that is supported by 'wind' as its meaning.
33. The letter *ñ* signifies the 'element' Fire in our theory; and it has the tongue as an organ of speech corresponding to its character: hence the meaning 'singer'.
34. The letter *ṭ* refers to the senses of knowledge in our theory, to which Ether, with elliptical motion and sound for its characteristics, corresponds: hence the reference to 'sound' as its meaning.
35. The letter *ṭh* has a similar explanation. Its idea of senses of action in accordance with our scheme, is borne out by the reference to 'a loud sound', which is characteristic of Ether with motion involving change of place.
36. The letter *ḍ* in our scheme refers to the 'element' Air; and, as Air is associated with action, which is a characteristic of Nature or *Prakṛti*, it also refers to the latter, when we analyse words into their parts according to the method of interpretation explained in the *Mīmāṁsā*. There does not, however, appear to be any bearing on this idea in the dictionary meanings of

this letter. It is possible that 'submarine fire' may have some reference to *Prakṛti*.

37. The letter *ḍh* should refer to the 'element' Fire according to our theory; but there is no reference to it in the dictionary.

    It is possible that the meanings of *ḍ* and *ḍh* have, to a certain extent, been interchanged; and 'submarine fire', as one of the meanings of *ḍ*, is really that of *ḍh*; and 'serpent', as that of ḍh, is one of *ḍ*—for the 'serpent' often refers to Nature or *Prakṛti*, which, as we have observed, is specially characterised by action, and so connected with the 'element' Air.

38. The letter *ṇ* signifies intellect according to our theory, where it is, for practical purposes, identified with the soul. This is borne out by its dictionary meanings.

39. The letter *t* refers to the senses of action in our scheme; and the womb, as the chief organ of creation, would signify the same.

40. The letter *th* should signify the 'element' Fire, and that is supported by the dictionary meaning 'auspicious prayer', which may be said to be one of the highest expressions of the tongue, as an organ of speech, with which the 'element' Fire is closely associated.

41. The letter *d* should mean intellect; and a proper act of giving, or gift, requires an exercise of the intellect, as the *Mīmāṁsā* tells us. Hence the letter *d* is said to refer to sacrifice.

42. The letter *dh* should refer to the mind; and this is borne out by the reference to the number six, which, as has already been explained, refers to the mind. The range of the system of *Brahmā* also extends to the mind; and the idea of Kuvera, the god of wealth, is similar too.

43. The letter *n* should refer to the senses of knowledge, which are closely connected with Ether; and the latter makes for a vacuum in a scientific sense of the term. Hence the meanings "vacant, empty, a particle of negation".

44. The letter *p* should signify Air; and that is also one of its dictionary meanings.

45. The letter *ph* should signify Water; and the idea is expressed by its meanings "flowing, bubbling, noiling".

46. The letter *b* should refer to the intellect in our scheme; and we have observed that it also implies that intellect is the first manifest form of Nature or *Prakṛti*, even as the *Sāṅkhya* tells us. Hence its dictionary meaning, 'the sun', which symbolises the intellict. Hence also the reference to ocean or water, which symbolises Nature or *Prakṛti*.

47. The letter *bh* should refer to the mind according to our theory; and, as the mind is symbolised by the moon, we have one of its meanings as 'light'. It is the twenty-fourt consonant, and so refers to Prakṛti which, according to the *Sāṅkhya*, consists of twenty-four parts. Hence the reference to venus, the planet of the 'element' Water. *Śukra* or Venus also refers to *Soma*, which refers to the moon or the mind, signified by this letter.

49. The letter *m* refers to the senses of knowledge where they may be identified with the mind: hence the reference to the moon, which signifies the mind.
49. The letter *y* refers to the intellect in our theory; and that is also its meaning as given in the *mīmānsā*. Hence the dictionary meanings 'light,' etc., which are associated with the intellect or its symbol, the sun.
50. The letter *r* refers to the mnd in our theory; but the mind is conceived in a comprehesive sense, as associated with the intellect on the one hand, and the senses on the other. Hence the meaning desire, which is an attribute of the mind; while 'giving' or a girt repuires the function of the intellect, and "going" is associated with the senses.
51. The letter *l* refers to the senses of action in our scheme; and, as the latter make for action, this letter is associated with verb in a special manner. Cutting is an obvious form of action. This letter accordingly repers to the sorese of action and thier funtions.
52. The letter *v* should refer to water in our theory; and that fits in with its meaning as 'ocean'.
53. The letter *ś*, according to our theory, refers to the intellect, where the latter, in its turn, is associated with the senses of knowledge. Hence its other meaning *Śiva*, the range of whose thought extends from the senses to the intellect.
54. The letter ṣ should refer to the intellect in our scheme; hence its meaning "wisdom." As it is intellect or its special function, discrimination, that makes for final happiness according to the *Sāṅkhya*, this is also one of the meanings of this letter. As the intellect may also be identified with the mind, it means also the numbers six, which refers to the mind.
55. The letter *ś*, according to our theory, refers to the mind; but the mind in this case is associated with the soul. Hence the reference to *Śiva* and *Viṣṇu*, both of whom refer to the mind, while the idea of the latter extends to the soul.
56. The letter *h* refers to the 'element' Earth in our scheme; but there appears to be no reference to it in the meanings given to it. It is the last letter of the alphabet, and the meanings given to it correspond to the last or final analysis of things—*Puruṣa* or God, *Prakṛti* or Water, intellect (meditation) or the mind (moon). The idea of God is represented by a cipher; and that is also an expression of a particle of the 'element' Earth—which may be identified with a germ.
57. Cf. MM. I, Chapters VIII-IX.
59. Cf. MM. II.
59. Cf. MM. III-V. The present author had not studied the *Mīmāṁsā* at the time of writing *The Mystery of the Mahābhārata*; but the method of interpretation followed in that work is exactly the same as that explained in the *Mīmāṁsā*, though there is much greater wealth of detail in the latter.
    The *Rāmāyaṇa* and the *Bhāgavat Purāṇa*, as also the *Chāndogya Upaniṣad*, studied in the same manner, have yielded the same result; and the works will be published in due course.
60. MS. IX, ii, 39.

61. See p. cldxiii, n. 3.
62. SEB, I, 79; XV, 54-57.
63. The word *Kuntī* may be divided into.*Ku, n t, ī*, when its meaning would be "(*Ku*) the Earth, associated with (*n*) the senses of knowledge„ (*t*) the senses of action, and (*ī*) the mind"; or "the Earth as seen in the light of our knowledge of the senses and the mind."

As the senses and mind constitute the bases of the *Nyāya* and *Vaiśeṣika* systems of philosophy, *Kuntī* may be said to refer to the creative power of the Earth (or of *Prakṛti*, for the two are closely allied) according to these systems. This has a bearing on her character, as described in the Epic, where she is said to live sometimes with her 'sons', the *Pāṇḍava* brothers, and quite as often dwells in the household of their enemies. This can easily be explained if we understand what the *Pāṇḍavas* and their enemies, the *Kauravas*, really mean. The five *Pāṇḍava* brothers are but five parts of one Man, conceived as representing the whole Animal Kingdom; and their story is an account of the evolution of Man from the lowest to the highest point of thought, ending in *Vedānta*. Their opponents, on the other hand, believe that we must perform only necessary actions, for the ultimate goal of life is knowledge and not action; and so they adhere to the *Nyāya* and *Vaiśeṣika* systems. As Man has to understand these systems too before he can rise to higher forms of thought, *Kuntī* lives with her sons in the first part of their journey of life; but when he rises to higher systems of thought, she remains with the *Kauravas*, for she represents the ideas of their systems of thought. The whole story of the Epic is like that.

As the meaning of the word *Kuntī* depends on its first part, *Ku*, it is possible to vary the form of the remaining parts; but its essential meaning will remain unchanged. The word is sometimes written as *Kunti*, and may be divided intc *Kum*, (the letter m being changed to *n*, when followed by *o*, in accordance with rules of grammar), and *ti*; and the meaning would then be "(*Kum*, a form of *Ku*) the Earth, (*ti*, an older form of iti) that is to say". We have *Kuntī* or "that is to say, the Earth."

The idea of *Kuntī* as Earth with reference to the senses and the mind, can be extended further still. We have observed that, according to the ancients, the energy of the mind was electric, and that of the senses magnetic—the senses of knowledge referring to the one, and the senses of action to the other, magnetic pole. The energy of the mind and senses functioning together may, accordingly, be said to be electro-magnetic; and so the word *Kuntī* would signify that the ancients believed that there is a permanent electro-magnetic current of energy flowing through the Earth. The idea of *Kuntī* as Earth, and all that is connected with her, has already been explained (MM. IV-V).
64. The word *Yadu* may be divided into *ya, ḍ, u*, when its meaning would be "(*ya*) intellect associated with (*d*) sacrifice connected with (*u*) the 'senses of knowledge". It means that if we exercise our intellect, we understand

the nature of the sacrifice of the senses of knowledge; and, as 'sacrifice' means good, intelligent and joyous action, the idea is that the exercise of our intelligence enables us to understand all this with reference to our senses of knowledge. As there is no reference to the senses of action in the word, the idea is that the highest conception of life, in the light of our intellect, is that it is knowledge that makes for joy in the end.

As a proper understanding of the function of the intellect leads to the idea of action too, the latter is expressed in the idea of *Sūra*, who is said to belong to this race (or the body of those who hold this view).

65. The word śūra may be divided into *ś,ū,ra*, and its meaning would be "(*ś*) the intellect (*ū*) woven with (*ra*) the senses of action."

It accordingly means that the intellect is associated with the function of the senses of action.

The word *yadu* limits the intellect to the senses of knowledge, or to knowledge only; and it is necessary to conceive of it separately, because there are some who believe that, if we look at life in an intelligent manner, we can come to the conclusion that its end is knowledge and not action. But this idea is really incomplete, for we cannot separate knowledge from action; and the acquisition or attainment of knowledge itself is a form of action, as the *Mīmāṁsā* tells us. Hence the idea of *yadu* is followed by that of *śūra*, who refers to the intimate connection of intelligence (or an intelligent way of looking at things) with action.

66. The word *Vasudeva* may be divided into *Va, su, deva*, when its meaning would be "(*deva*) god or a great good object or force of Nature, (su) born of (va, 'water', symbolic of Nature, as the *Mīmāṁsā* tells us) Nature". *Vasudeva* accordingly refers to all that arises from Nature in terms of a god or the great good objects or forces of life. We have already seen that a god refers to these objects and forces.

Vasudeva in the story is said to have been married to *Devakī*, and they had eight children, the last of whom was Kṛṣṇa.

We have observed that 'marriage' implies an intimate union or relationship; and so we might say that the idea expressed by *Vasudeva* is now closely united with that expressed by *Devakī*; and the union of the two gives rise to eight objects.

Now *Devakī*, as a woman, refers to Nature; and if we divide the word into *Deva,kī*, the meaning would be "(*kī*) what is (*deva*) a god or a great good force or object of Nature?" Her union with *Vasudeva* signifies an intense desire to know what things arise from Nature; and they are its eight divisions, as the Bhagavad Gītā tells us (VII, 4). Hence *Vasudeva* and Devakī have eight 'children'.

67. The idea of *Kuntī* as Earth has already been explained.

68. We have a reference to this in the *Bhagavad Gītā* (VII, 4).

69. We can divide the word Kṛṣṇa into *K, ṛ, ṣ, ṇa*, when its meaning would be

"(*ṇa*) intellect associated with (*sh*) mind, (*r*) the senses of action, and (k) Nature or *Prakṛti*."

Kṛṣṇa accordingly refers to intelligence in its most perfect conception, as associated with the mind, action (or the senses of action) and the objects of Nature. That is to say, when we look at Nature, and see how it is associated with our intellect, mind, and the senses, and makes for action—we can get a complete idea of life; and if then we associate all this with the idea of 'sacrifice' or goodness, intelligence, and joy in action, we can transform Nature itself into *Brahmā* or God.

It is this that *Kṛṣṇa* represents; and the idea of sacrifice is expressed by means of his *Sudarśana Cakra*, which really means "(*Sudarsana*) good or beautiful (*cakra*, derived from '*kṛ*', meaning 'to act') action." This Cakra or action can never leave him, for he is always characterised by sacrifice.

The idea of *Kṛṣṇa*, as given in the *Mahābhārata*, has already been explained; and that, as given in the *Bhāgavat Purāṇa*, would be explained in due course. As we shall see, he represents the idea of God as Supreme Intelligence, immanent in the universe, and making itself manifest in acts of sacrifice. We might say that he represents the idea of God as it can be transformed out of that of Nature by means of the latter's association with sacrifice. It is for this reason that he is represented as being of dark colour, for that is said to be the colour of Nature or *Prakṛti*, as distinguished from that of God, which is said to be white. *Kṛṣṇa* is thus Nature transformed into God by means of sacrifice.

70. The word *Kuntī-bhoja* means "(*Kuntī*) the Earth as (*bhoja*) bountiful". *Kuntībhoja* may accordingly be said to be one who believes that the Earth is bountiful, or is a bestower of good things.

    He is said to be childless, because this conception of the Earth does not, by itself, produce any important result.

    He is the cousin of *Sūra* because even the idea of Earth as bountiful partakes of some intelligence. We have already explained that *śūra* refers to intelligence which is associated with action.

71. A *Mantra* means literally "an instrument of thought"; and so a *Brāhmaṇa*'s *Mantra* would mean "an instrument of thought based on an exercise of the intellect", for a *Brāhmaṇa* signifies intellect, as we have seen. Hence it may be interpreted as "an intelligent use of the means of thought or of acquiring knowledge".

72. Modern science tells us that the Earth derives a great deal of its energy from the Sun.

73. The Vegetable Kingdom is created on our planet Earth before the Animal Kingdom—for it constitutes the food of the latter, which could not exist without it. All creatures live by food, which consists ultimately of the Vegetable Kingdom, for even the carnivorous live on the herbivorous. The *Upaniṣads* also tell us- that the great Creator created first of all food, and then the eater of that food (SEE. I, 240; XV, 28).

The story of the birth of *Karṇa* shows that the ancients believed that seed or grain is created in the Earth by means of the action of the rays of the Sun. It may be of interest to point out that plants cannot grow properly, or at least yield fruit, without the action of sunlight.

74. The word *Karṇa* has a number of meanings in the dictionary, one of which is "grain furnished with chaff",—that is, grain fit for food as well as cultivation; and this is the appropriate meaning of the word throughout the *Mahābhārata*. The *Mīmāṁsā* tells us that it is not always necessary to divide words into parts to understand their meaning, and the dictionary meaning of a word may be quite suitable. It may also happen that the dictionary meaning of a word as well as that obtained by means of its division into parts, is the same. The word *Karṇa* belongs to this class; but, as its ordinary meaning is satisfactory, it is not necessary to divide it into parts here.

As *Karṇa* represents seed or grain, the story of the growth of the latter and the uses to which it may be put has been described in the Epic in terms of the growth of the hero and the use of his arms.

His "half-brothers", the Pāṇḍava brothers, and the remaining 'sons' of Kuntī, represent the Animal Kingdom, the highest form of which is Man; and the five 'brothers' represent the five parts of a man—his intellect, mind, breath or prāṇa as the vehicle of the soul, and arms and legs respectively. As the formation of arms and legs is different from that of the rest of the body, the last two 'brothers', *Nakula* and *Sahadeva*, are said to have a different 'mother', though they too are created at the instance of *Kuntī*; and, as arms and legs have a similar form, they are said to be 'twins'. As the five 'brothers' represent Man or the eater of food, and *Karṇa* is food or grain—and there is an apparent 'hostility' between food and the eater of food—*Karṇa* and his 'half-brothers' are 'enemies'. Arjuna is the arch-enemy of *Karṇa* for he represents breath that swallows food; and the 'combat' between the two is the process by means of which the eater of food eats food. The whole story of the Epic is like that.

As *Karṇa* represents food, the basis of all physical creative energy associated with Nature or *Prakṛti* in the *Sāṅkhya*—he also represents that system in the Epic. Man, on the other hand, rises from *Sāṅkhya* to *Nyāya* and *Vaiśeṣika*, and thence to *Yoga* and *Vedānta*. His opponents, the Kauravas, believe in *Nyāya* and *Vaiśeṣika*; and so the "battle of *Kurukṣetra*" is a contest between *Sāṅkhya*, *Nyāya* and *Vaiśeṣika* on the one hand, and *Yoga* and *Vedānta* on the other—the former represented by the *Kauravas* and their allies, and the latter by the *Pāṇḍavas* and their associates. It is in this manner that we have a conflict of systems of thought in the Epic. All this has already been explained.

75. The word for *armour* in the text is *kavaca*, which also means 'bark or rind', which is a natural 'armour' for all trees or seeds.

The word for an *ear-ring* in the text is *kuṇḍala*, which may be divided into two parts, *kuṇ*, *ḍala*. But, according to the practice of grammarians in framing compounds, *kuṇ* can be a substitutute for *kuṇa*, and *ḍala* for *ḍāla*; and so the meaning would now be "(*ḍāla*) a branch (*kuṇa*) bearing fruit." The idea of 'ear-rings' would thus be that of grain or seed on a branch which bears fruit. The point of this is that seed grows into seed again.

76. The real idea of this action of *Kuntī* would appear to be that there is an element of moisture in grain, and it makes its appearance as soon as it is formed by the action of the rays of the Sun on the Earth. This may be said to correspond to the existence of the nucleus of the cell, which is said to be a fluid substance.

The seed may thus be said to be composed of three 'elements',— Earth, Water, and Fire—the last corresponding to the heat or rays of the Sun. Or we might say that it partakes of the three attributes of these 'elements'—and has a colour or form, the property of Fire; taste, the property of Water; and smell, the property of Earth.

There is a reference to these three 'elements' in the systems of philo-sophy. (Cf. MM. I, 137).

77. Earth and food, the basis of which is seed or grain, are identified in the *Upaniṣads* (SBE. I, 96-97).

78. The story of the restoration of her virginity to *Kuntī* and the departure of the Sun implies that this is what the ancients believed—namely, that the birth of seed in the Earth does not affect its structure, and that it can radiate the rays of the Sun it has absorbed, and regain its original state.

79. The word *Adhiratha* may be divided into *Adhi-ratha*, when its meaning would be " (*adhi*) anxiety regarding (*ratha*, 'a chariot' which, as the *Mīmāṁsā* tells us, is symbolic of the action of the body) action of the body". *Adhiratha* accordingly signifies "anxiety in regard to the action of the body", which depends for its existence on food. He personifies this idea, and so picks up *Karṇa* (grain), and brings him home.

80. The word *Rādhā* has a number of meanings, one of which is 'lightning', which is the same as electric energy, and is identified with the energy of the mind. The mind, as we have seen, has desire for its attribute; and desire is at the root of all action—the most important of which is action for the preservation of the body. The idea of *Rādhā* is thus closely connected with that of *Adhiratha*: and so they are spoken of as 'husband' and 'wife'.

There is a reference to *Rādhā* in connection with *Kṛṣṇa* in the story of the *Bhāgavat Purāṇa*; and there too her idea is the same. This will be explained in due course.

81. The arm is an instrument of action; and 'arms' or 'weapons' used by it would accordingly refer to the manner in which instruments of action can be used. The 'arms' or 'weapons' of *Karṇa* would, accordingly, refer to the different ways in which grain can act—that is, the manner in which it can grow, and the uses to which it can be put. These are indeed many and

wonderful; and so *Karṇa* is said to be an expert in the use of arms.

The story in the Epic tells us that *Karṇa* showed his skill in the use of arms at the *Svayamvara* ceremony of *Draupadi*, when she selected her husband, and he was equal to *Arjuna*, the chief of the *Pāṇḍavas* in every way. But she rejected him because of his 'birth', and selected *Arjuna* instead. She afterwards became the 'wife' of all the five *Pāṇāava* brothers. We can understand the real idea of all this if we know what these characters signify. *Draupadi* is also called *Yajña-senī* or "mistress of sacrifice"; and so she represents the idea of sacrifice or good, intelligent and joyous action, as has already been explained.

The five *Pāṇḍava* brothers—*Yudhiṣṭhira, Bhīma, Arjuna, Nakula* and *Sahadeva*—represent five parts of a man—his intellect, mind, vital breath as the vehicle of the soul, and arms and legs respectively.

Karṇa is seed or grain, as has already been explained.

Karṇa is able to show the same skill as *Arjuna*, because there is little difference between the evolution and growth of the Vegetable and Animal Kingdoms, and their 'kinship' in this respect is now universally recognised.

Karṇa represents the Vegetable Kingdom, and *Arjuna*, as the soul of Man, the essence of the Animal Kingdom or Man. There is, however, one difference between them, while they are both alike so far as their natural actions are concerned: the Vegetable Kingdom is not capable of performing any deliberate action,—whereas Man is.

Draupadī represents sacrifice which, like Dharma—as the *Mīmāṁsā* tells us—refers to deliberate and not natural action. Hence she cannot have *Karṇa* for her 'husband' or one who can be intimately associated with the idea she represents. She selects *Arjuna*, because he represents the soul which, as all systems of philosophy, other than the *Sāṅkhya*, tell us, can engage in acts of sacrifice.

She becomes the 'wife' of all the five *Pāṇḍava* brothers, because it is possible to conceive of all the five parts of a man—his intellect, mind, soul having the vital breath for its vehicle, and arms and legs—as engaging in acts of sacrifice.

The story does indeed tell us later on that *Kṛṣṇa* himself made an offer to *Karṇa*, whereby he could 'share' *Draupadī* like the Pāṇḍava brothers, if he agreed to change sides and join them. This too is easily explained.

Karṇa represents food, and it is possible, as the Upaniṣads tell us, to conceive of food as a sacrifice offered to the soul; that is to say, it is good to eat food, and the soul partakes of it to be able to perform good and intelligent deeds. If we accept this idea, it follows that food can be intimately associated with the idea of sacrifice, and so *Karṇa* can 'shaie' *Draupadī* in the same manner as the five parts of a man.

But *Karṇa* also represents the *Sāṅkhya* system, as we have pointed out; and this system maintains that the soul is really not an actor at all. Hence, it cannot engage in any act of sacrifice. Indeed, the goal of life is said to be the renunciation of all action. Hence *Karṇa* cannot associate himself with the idea of sacrifice (or *Draupadī*), and so rejects the offer of *Kṛṣṇa*, as the story tells us.

82. The essential needs of an intelligent man are his food, shelter, and clothing; and all of them can be supplied by the Vegetable Kingdom.

 The action of the Sun on grain and its effect would appear to bear out the idea behind the modern theory of vitamins in different kinds of organic matter—for they are all believed to be connected with the Sun.

83. All this has been worked out, and will be published in due course.

INDEX

R

S

CHINA–PAKISTAN
STRATEGIC COOPERATION
INDIAN PERSPECTIVES

Centre de Sciences Humaines (Centre for Social Sciences and Humanities): Created in New Delhi in 1989 the CSH is part of the network of research centres of the French Ministry of Foreign Affairs. The Centre's research work is primarily oriented towards the study of issues concerning the contemporary dynamics of development in India and South Asia. The activities of the Centre are focused on four main themes, namely: Economic growth and sustainable development, International and regional relations, Institutional structures and political constructions of identity and Urban dynamics.

Centre de Sciences Humaines, 2, Aurangzeb Road, New Delhi- 110011, India, Tel: (91) 11 3041 00 70, Fax: (91) 11 3041 00 79
E-mail: public@csh-delhi.com
Website: http://www.csh-delhi.com

Institut Français de Pondichéry (French Institute of Pondicherry): Created in 1955, the IFP is a multidisciplinary research and advanced educational institute. Major research works are focusing on Sanskrit and Tamil Languages and literatures—in close collaboration with the Ecole Française d'Extrême-Orient—ecosystems, biodiversity and sustainability, dynamics of population and socio-economic development.

Institut Français de Pondichéry, 11, Saint Louis Street, PB 33
Pondicherry 605001, Tel: (91) 413 2334 168
Fax: (91) 413 2339 534
E-mail: ifpdir@ifpindia.org

China–Pakistan Strategic Cooperation *Indian Perspectives*

Edited by
SWARAN SINGH

MANOHAR

CENTRE DE SCIENCES HUMAINES
2007

First published 2007

ISBN 81-7304-761-8

Published by
Ajay Kumar Jain for
Manohar Publishers & Distributors
4753/23 Ansari Road, Daryaganj
New Delhi 110 002

Typeset by
Kohli Print
Delhi 110 051

Printed at
Lordson Publishers Pvt. Ltd.
New Delhi 110 007

for
Malti and Mini

Contents

PART III – FUNDAMENTALS OF STRATEGIC ENGAGEMENT

Preface

Understanding and then responding to the well-known 'time-tested', 'all-weather', 'defence-centric', 'special relationship' between China and Pakistan remains one of the most serious challenges for Indian intellectuals and policy makers. This is so because both China and Pakistan happen to be India's immediate neighbours and share a rather complicated history of violent wars and deep rooted conflicts that continue to persist and undermine their efforts at building peace and development. Reflections of India's concerns about China-Pakistan ties can be seen in the occasional hype in Indian media and strategic circles (even academia). They repeatedly flash, analyse, and debate these issues relying on occasional Western 'leaks' about such 'transfers' and 'promises' of transfers of sensitive and dangerous technologies and other relevant moral and material support from Beijing to Islamabad. Such hypes build up particularly during an exchange of high-level visits between China and Pakistan. This allows Islamabad to play up the 'China factor' in its interactions with New Delhi.

China-Pakistan ties, as a result, have come to be the staple food for India's post-Independence strategic debates feeding into foreign and security policies and diplomatic initiatives. To some extent, even the internal policies in India have been over-shadowed by New Delhi's perceptions about the motivations and implications of the China-Pakistan axis. More specifically, it is the 'strategic' nature of their cooperation in various sectors of defence production that promises to safeguard and strengthen their strategic cooperation in the long-run. Meanwhile, the China-Pakistan partnership has defied all challenges and earned the distinction of being the most enduring and only one of its kind. For a long time, North Korea was the only other country that had the distinction of continued friendship with Beijing but even Pyongyang has lost that distinction since the early 1990s when Beijing opened its diplomatic engagement with Seoul. This analogy is often cited to highlight China's growing bonhomie with New Delhi though this has hardly made any dent on the nature and magnitude of China–

Pakistan relations that continues to span across all sectors of their politico-strategic spectrum.

But there have been same changes that also indicate positive trends. The Pakistan–China strategic cooperation had been conventionally viewed by New Delhi as a zero-sum game, wherein any gains accrued by Pakistan or China through their partnership were seen as a direct detriment to the evolution of India–China or India–Pakistan relations. India has sure moved (though marginally) away from that fixation. While India–China relations have moved through tumultuous phases, they have since begun to underplay the Pakistan factor though the China–Pakistan axis still continues to haunt Indian experts and policy makers alike. Similarly, there has also been an improvement in India–Pakistan relations. Nevertheless, skepticism still continues to underwrite (read undermine) the bonhomie on the surface and various other diplomatic initiatives.

A part of the reason for this continued distrust is the lack of any regular Indian academic assessment or policy recommendations with regard to the apparently 'anti-India' China-Pakistan axis. Indian experts have also been unable to build a databank of information in respect to this perceived 'anti-India' China–Pakistan extente. In India, the China–Pakistan strategic cooperation has generally stayed in the realm of conjectures and speculation. These remain based (a) exclusively on sporadic media leakages from the United States and (b) highly emotive and biased extempore reflection by Indian leaders and intellectuals, all of which remain seasonal and short-lived.

Whether the China-Pakistan strategic cooperation has been guided by (a) China's desire to tie-down India to South Asia or (b) make inroads into the energy-rich Islamic Middle East or (c) ensure stability in its tumultuous Muslim-dominated border regions or (d) ensure an international stature and security for Pakistan against India (especially by assisting in its nuclear weapons programme) remains inconclusive. Recent revelation about Pakistan's nuclear proliferation record have once again brought the issue of China–Pakistan strategic cooperation to the centre-stage of strategic debates worldwide. Especially, the scourge of terrorism and its links with Islamic fundamentalism (and their increasing links with proliferation of weapons of mass destruction) has resulted in keeping these debates on the China–Pakistan axis alive and kicking.

It is commonplace knowledge today that China has supplied Pakistan with an abundance of relatively inexpensive conventional arms, as well as strategically vital nuclear weapon and ballistic missile know-how, training and technologies. Indeed, China has thus earned the distinction of being Pakistan's most enduring and most reliable supplier of moral (read political) and material support and the most important partner in defence production, especially in the most critical strategic sectors of nuclear and missile inventories. In reality, however, China has not fired a single shot in defence of Pakistan and yet managed to emerge as Pakistan's most trusted ally. Their defence cooperation today covers every sector of the defence establishment; from design and development to production and operational training and so on. The most important motivation for such an enduring axis has been their common adversarial relationship with New Delhi which has continued to strengthen their resolve for mutual cooperation.

In view of all this, apart from examining its impact on India as also likely options for Indian responses, this volume is an attempt to try and outline the extensive magnitude of the China–Pakistan strategic cooperation and to crystal-gaze its impact on the regional level as also on international non-proliferation norms and regimes. For example, does a continued China–Pakistan strategic cooperation augur well for China and Pakistan, both of whom are attempting to emerge as important players in the region? What impact will the strengthening of India–China ties have on the China–Pakistan strategic cooperation? Also, how does various sectors of China–Pakistan cooperation augur for their overall strategic cooperation. Analysts and diplomats also need to look at the options for reducing tensions in the region through evolving new alternative paradigms of international cooperation such as the Shanghai Cooperation Organisation and other cooperative arrangements that bring China–India–Pakistan closer as also ones that focus on strengthening their interdependence and cooperation?

This present volume, *China–Pakistan Strategic Cooperation: Indian Perspectives* is an attempt at brainstorming some of the aforesaid issues and make an assessment on its likely impact on India's national interests. In terms of contributing to policy, this volume examines options for policy makers to constructively engage in the understanding of this critical relationship between two of India's most immediate neighbours. Above all, what continues to intrigue most serious scholars is the vivid lack of reciprocity (even mutuality) in the China–Pakistan relationship which has otherwise thrived for over five decades of upheavals of all kind. The two perennial explanations have been (a) China's restive muslim separatism in bordering Xinjiang compelling it to befriend Muslim neighbouring states, and (b) this being part of China's encirclement of India strategy aimed at tying India to South Asia. This lack of visible reciprocity in China–Pakistan ties as also long history of Pakistani omissions and com-missions in annoying Beijing's leaders lends credence to this aforesaid hypothesis. Many experts therefore see it as virtually one-sided 'strategic' co-operation premised on China's singular indulgence of successive Pakistani leaderships. It is towards seeking answers to some of these questions that this volume tries to at least make a serious beginning.

Apart from making an effort to generate a serious debate around some of the aforesaid critical questions the publication of this volume also reinforces our belief that no such work can ever be possible without the encouragement and support of several well-wishers, friends and colleagues. First of all, I must thank the Centre de Sciences Humaines (New Delhi) and, its Director, Dr Veronique Dupont, for being such a support in making this project come through both as a workshop and in form of this publication. I also owe sincere thanks to several other friends at CSH for providing me a challenging environment and sustaining me through this enterprise.

My sincere thanks are also due to several people who had so graciously chaired various sessions of this two-day workshop and (more importantly) provided direction and critical inputs for revision of these papers. These include Ambassador C.V. Ranganathan, Professor Mira Sinha-Bhattacharjea, Dr K. Santhanam, Maj. Gen. Dipankar Banerjee and Professor Madhu Bhalla. I owe equally to the perseverance and patience of my contributors whose work has been such a learning experience for me. Most of these experts have been a constant support for my work in general and my thanks are especially due to all of them for displaying such great patience and understanding to my constant pestering which remains unavoidable with any endeavour to bring such a large and hyperactive team together and to achieve a quality product, all at the same time.

And finally, I must stand to own responsibility for all errors and omissions which may have eluded my eyes or my understanding.

New Delhi/July 2007 SWARAN SINGH

Contributors

SWARAN SINGH is Associate Professor, School of International Studies, Jawaharlal Nehru University, New Delhi.

ANINDYO J. MAJUMDAR is Senior Lecturer at the Department of International Relations, Jadavpur University, Kolkata.

SRIKANTH KONDAPALLI is Associate Professor, School of International Studies, Jawaharlal Nehru University, New Delhi.

SATYABRAT SINHA is Research Officer with Institute for Peace and Conflict Studies (IPCS), New Delhi.

M.V. RAPPAI is Fellow with Institute of Chinese Studies, Centre for Study of Developing Societies, New Delhi.

SONIKA GUPTA is Research Fellow with National Institute of Advanced Studies, Bangalore, India.

ARPIT RAJAIN is Senior Policy Analyst with Delhi Office of Centre for Global Studies, Mumbai.

SAVITA PANDE is Associate Professor, School of International Studies, Jawaharlal Nehru University, New Delhi.

RAJIV NAYAN is Research Fellow with Institutue for Defence Studies and Analysis (IDSA), New Delhi.

M. MATHESWARAN is a serving officer of the Indian Air Force.

VIJAY SAKHUJA [Commander IN Retd.] is Visiting Senior Fellow with Institute of South–East Asian Studies, Singapore.

W. LAWRENCE S. PRABHAKAR is Associate Professor with Madras Christian College, Chennai, Tamil Nadu.

MADHU BHALLA is Professor with Department of East Asian Studies, University of Delhi, Delhi.

D. VARAPRASAD SEKHAR is Assistant Professor, School of International Studies, Jawaharhal Nehru University, New Delhi.

ARVIND KUMAR is Research Fellow with National Institute of Advance Studies (NIAS), Bangalore, Karnataka.

APARNA KHER is Ph.D. Scholar with Department of Political Science, Binghamton University, New York, USA.

COLONEL (RETD) VIRENDRA SAHAI VERMA is formerly of the Indian Army.

ABANTI BHATTACHARYA is Research Fellow with Institute for Defence Studies and Analysis (IDSA), New Delhi.

PART I
Mutual Perceptions and Policies

CHAPTER 1

Introduction

SWARAN SINGH

China–Pakistan strategic cooperation is one subject that continues to intrigue several Indian experts and policy makers. Most of them find it 'extremely difficult to explain' its overwhelming impact on India's threat perceptions.[1] What particularly makes the China–Pakistan relationship an enigma is the divergence in their political systems, social cultures, overall size, level of development and the consequent absence of visible reciprocity in their interactions and mutuality in their interests and policies. All this clearly highlights China's marked indulgence towards Pakistan making it appear like a patron–client equation, that too one of its kind. If anything, it is the suspected secrecy about much of their agreements and initiatives that remains the hallmark of this 'special relationship' which is generally understood in India as being India-centric at least in its origins. As a result, China–Pakistan relations have remained both the driving force in India's relations with both Beijing and Islamabad and in turn their relationship remains driven mainly by their shared concerns and threat perceptions about India.

Conversely, this means that improving India–China and India–Pakistan relations in recent years seem to have eroded the *raison d'être* of this so-called China–Pakistan 'axis'. Several other factors have also contributed to this recent visible shift in the nature and significance of China–Pakistan relations. Some more prominent ones may include (a) rising China's need to be seen as 'acceptable and benign' and not one that supports problematic regimes, (b) Pakistan's inability, over the years, to fulfil its promises to Beijing of reining in the Taliban's abetment of China's Uighur violence in its Muslim-majority Xinjiang region, (c) Pakistan decision to 'go nuclear' thereby breaking out of a 'dependency' relationship with Beijing, (d) the recent A. Q. Khan nuclear and missile proliferation episode making Pakistan too notorious for Beijing to continue to display their proximity, (e) continued US and European pressures (and repeated sanctions) on both China and Pakistan against their alleged transfer of proscribed nuclear and missile technologies, and last but not least (f) the growing power profile of India and its concerted engagement with major players making both China and Pakistan circumspect and cautious in boasting the 'anti-India' element of their 'deep-rooted' and 'all-weather' friendship. Besides, given the post-Cold War context, the new flavour of multiple and multifaceted relationships has since replaced the rigid and lasting alliance systems of an earlier era.

While the visibility and significance of the China–Pakistan 'axis' may have been lately overcast by the above factors including India's rise, the reality of their expansive and time-tested strategic cooperation across all sectors has not disappeared (or even diminished) and it continues to underwrite regional dynamics across the whole politico-strategic spectrum. The Pakistani experts indeed believe that India's growing proximity to the US—aimed at the containment of China—today 'confers greater relevance to the deep-rooted and all-weather friendship developed by Pakistan and China'.[2] Therefore, it may be too misleading for us to begin reading too much into the shifting sands of their strategic focus and conclude an eclipse of a China–Pakistan strategic cooperation and thereby ignore its critical role and its potency in outlining the future course of India's foreign policy. Indeed, with much of the heat and dust having settled on India's emotionally charged perceptions about the China–Pakistan relationship, this may be the ideal time to evolve an objective understanding of the contours and implications of this 'axis' and to achieve a more balanced assessment of ground realities and thereby evolve more effective policy options. It is in this new context that this volume tries to initiate a serious academic debate in understanding various components of the China–Pakistan 'special relationship' that has remained such a major preoccupation of India's policy makers and academics.

Myths versus Reality

The genesis and evolution of China–Pakistan relations has been far more nuanced and complicated than what has been outlined by most commentaries that clearly betray their vulnerability to subjective emotions and political rhetoric that pushes analysis to populism. As a result, much of India's response has also remained simplistic and superficial adding to complications in our policies and perceptions. To deal with some of the popular myths about the initial period of China–Pakistan relations the following narratives could be indicative of the cross-currents that define the forces and factors that brought these two neighbours of India closer together into a relationship that was to become such an enduring influence in determining the nature of South Asian Security.

First, contrary to the general impression, the origins of China–Pakistan relations did not lie in Beijing's indulgence of Pakistan though this may have been far more decisive in the evolution of its later course and in highlighting their joint objectives. To begin with, Pakistan was the third non-communist, second Commonwealth and first Muslim country to extend official recognition to the beleaguered and completely isolated Communist China in January 1950; barely four months after China's liberation. That was the period when China really needed Pakistan more than the other way round and between 1947–53, Pakistan really warmed up to Chinese diplomacy.

Second, despite India's much celebrated bonhomie with China during the early 1950s and the two being seen as major Asian powers of the time, it was Pakistan–China trade that had hit $83.8 million for 1952—almost twice as much as the trade between China and India. It is important to note that this trade was not 'defence-centric' in nature as it was to become in later years. Though this situation lasted only a few years, yet it implies that the current India–China trade that is now several times more than the China–Pakistan trade must not be seen as something which is bound to resolve India–China political equations and thereby to undercut the significance of China–Pakistan 'axis'.[3]

Third, the initial years of China-Pakistan relations were not the period when Pakistan was part of US military alliances. Neither had the US opted for Pakistan as their military ally only after India had rejected US offers. During the first five years of Pakistan's independence—that is before it became member of SEATO and CENTO—it had been a vocal supporter of China's claim to its seat at the United Nations (UN).[4] Despite US–Pak parleys from early 1951, it was only from end-1953 that Pakistan was to begin its tilt towards the US.[5] As an US ally, it was to oppose China's membership of the UN till early 1960 when Pakistan was to revert once again to its supporting China's claims to its UN seat and this was, much before, the China–India war which is often cited as a catalyst for change in Pakistan's China policy.[6]

Four, after the first meeting of the two prime ministers—Zhou Enlai and Mohammad Ali of Bogra—during April 1955 at the Bandung conference of Afro–Asian nations, it was not Zhou Enlai but the Pakistani prime minister who would first visit China in October 1956. This was followed by a reciprocal visit by the Chinese premier in December the same year. What particularly displayed Pakistani commitment to building ties with China was the fact that Chaudhuri Mohammad Ali (who replaced Mohammad Ali Bogra) had twice planned to visit China and later his successor H.S. Suhrawardy undertook a 12-day visit to China barely weeks after his becoming prime minister.[7] All this, during a politically tumultuous period; and in spite of Suhrawardy being known for his strong pro-Western credentials.

Fifth, the China–Pakistan relationship is also generally understood as virtually 'one-sided' and 'defence-centric' in nature driven by China's motives of (a) tying India to South Asia and (b) befriending Muslim neighbours of its Muslim-dominated and turmoil-ridden Xinjiang region making Pakistan vital for Beijing.[8] Nevertheless, other than supplying weapons and contributing to infrastructure projects and other moral and material support, China has stayed clearly short of getting entangled in any of Pakistan's misadventures. This implies that China's current policy of neutrality in India–Pakistan relations is not as anomalous as it is often made out to appear.

Sixth, most analyses make it appear as if China has been the only force behind Pakistan's nuclear weapons and missile development programmes. In reality, the whole process had begun far earlier with President Eisenhower's 'Atoms for Peace' exhibition touring Pakistan during early 1950s followed by Pakistan setting up a 12-member Atomic Energy Commission in 1955. The thought of nuclear 'weapons' does not even occur in Pakistan before China's nuclear test of 1964 and serious efforts did not begin before India's nuclear test of 1974 or in wake of Pakistan's bifurcation in 1971. The first foreign contribution was to come from the Netherlands, in form of stealing of nuclear blueprints by A.Q. Khan who was to emerge as father of Pakistan nuclear bomb. Indirect support of Saudi Arabia, North Korea, Syria, the United States must also be acknowledged.[9]

Seventh, what remains equally overlooked is the fact that Pakistan has not been the only (or even most favoured) destination for China's nuclear and missile transfers. The most clearly established transfer of this nature were China's supplies of intermediate range ballistic missiles to Saudi Arabia in 1988. Similarly, more recent revelations about China's proliferations to other countries like Libya, North Korea, Iran, Iraq, Syria among other nations have often been insinuated by experts.[10] Amongst these, Pakistan may have been the one which has been the most sustained beneficiary as also the only beneficiary that emerged as a nuclear weapons state (and also one that further proliferated Chinese technologies and knowhow). Also, China has withstood censor and sanctions of the non-proliferation regimes to demonstrate its commitment to its strong relations with Pakistan.

Eighth, China–Pakistan relations have also not been confined to purely defence relations though during certain periods they did become excessively defence-cooperation oriented. Especially, in their initial years, it was their people-to-people contacts that clearly laid the foundations of their interactions. Indeed, much of the popular interactions had been between the elites of China and the erstwhile East Pakistan. It was only after the incision of Pakistan that West Pakistan was to seriously develop relations with China and it was this part that was to become overcast by Pakistan's security concerns leading to their relations becoming defence-centric. Even then, their popular contacts have not been completely absent and continue to make critical contributions to their mutual goodwill and trust.

And finally, irrespective of Pakistani claims during its wars with India, China has never ever fired even a single shot at India on Pakistan's behest. Yet, the China–Pakistan axis has always been a factor in India's threat perceptions and defence planning resulting in China having 'gained public recognition in both Indian and Pakistani assessments as the steadfast ally of Pakistan'.[11] Conversely, Indian debates have always underemphasized the significance of Pakistan in facilitating the August 1971 secret visit to China by Henry Kissinger that was to put both the US and China under an obligation to Pakistan and forever change the nature of international relations.[12] Recently, given the strong theories about the possible confrontation between the US and China such talk about Pakistan again playing the facilitator of US–China bonhomie have often been revived.

Current Dilemmas, Future Trends

Without doubt, Pakistani experts and policy makers continue to believe that their country remains central to China's vision of South Asia.[13] Indeed, many of them extend this logic to advocate that the recent trends in international terrorism and changing equations between India and the US provide added reasons for China and Pakistan coming further closer.[14] The recent period has also seen all three countries—China–India–Pakistan—not only taking steps toward improving their bilateral relations but also becoming joint partners at regional forums like the ASEAN Regional Forum, Shanghai Cooperation Organisation and South Asian Association for Regional Cooperation which seems to have deflected their focus from bilateral to regional problems. Yet they continue to face the pressures of their new regional level interface which remains all very new and fragile. As a result, despite this new flavour in their policies and perceptions, all three have continued to put greater faith in their well entrenched erstwhile equations. For example, inaugurating a two-day international conference on 'China and Emerging Asian Century' at Islamabad's Institute of Strategic Studies on 27 September 2005, Pakistan Prime Minister Shaukat Aziz was to describe China–Pakistan relations in the following manner:

> Pakistan and China enjoy all weather friendship based on complete trust and confidence. Our friendship is rooted in the psyche and ethos of our people. From Khunjrab to Gawadar, the symbols of Pakistan–China friendship dot the landscape. The mega projects that we have undertaken with China's help are like anchors that hold the two countries together in trusted friendship.[15]

Here, the mention of 'Khunjrab' and 'Gawadar' clearly had visible 'politico-strategic' connotations for being the first strategic land route and the future strategic sea port that symbolize the strength of China–Pakistan cooperation. Clearly, the focus was not on either social or economic contacts and their significance continues to be negated by Pakistani leaders. But, at the same time, leaders of both Pakistan and China have gradually begun to accept the reality of emerging India and become increasingly willing to positively reciprocate to India's engagement overtures.[16] Especially, Pakistan has overcome its initial fears about an India–China *rapprochement* and there is increasing talk about the three countries trying to stabilize their strategic equations. Sidhu and Yuan recommend that 'it is in interest of all parties—Beijing, Islamabad, and New Delhi—to work towards establishing a strategic restraint regime. Though unlikely to prevent confrontations, this should at least make them manageable when they do occur.'[17]

However, given the fact that their past had been tense for such a long time their future remains indefinite. Perhaps, given the virtual lowering of their inter-state threats the greater challenge today comes from their domestic constituencies and limitations. It is in this context that there is a strong need to revive debates in India on the nature and significance of China–Pakistan relations in order to evolve a better understanding and policy responses on these issues. Indeed, some of this can already be seen in some of the barely visible changing trends in India's perceptions (and policies) towards this whole issue of China–Pakistan 'strategic cooperation' which no longer seem to have as much impact on India's recent policy initiatives.

India's Changing Perceptions

First of all, the recent trade boom and expansion of China–India 'strategic partnership' has obtained New Delhi tremendous self-confidence and is gradually eroding the potency of the China–Pakistan relations as a factor in India–China or India-Pakistan interactions.[18] To cite Beijing's trade statistics, the proportion of India and Pakistan in China's trade with South Asia is instructive of these changing equations. In China's trade with South Asia between 1993 and 2003, while India's share has gone up from being only 35 per cent to 65 per cent, Pakistan's share has reduced from 44 per cent to 21 per cent.[19] This has strengthened the view that India should not let China–Pakistan relations distract New Delhi beyond a point. Partly, this view has also been facilitated by the India–Pakistan *rapprochement* in recent years. However, this is not to advocate complacency but to urge that we now need to evolve more appropriate and effective strategies to deal with the China–Pakistan 'axis' which continues to be the strongest pillar of their foreign relations. To give one example, with the growing focus of Beijing on investing abroad, China–Pakistan relations have also strengthened their economic content with China's investment in Pakistan now reaching over $4 billion with over 114 projects in the running at the end of year 2004.[20] This, of course, is much higher than China's total utilized investment in India.

Second, in the wake of India-Pakistan nuclear tests, China's policy towards India–Pakistan equations has also been guided by the sole consideration to 'prevent South Asia from any possibility of conflict escalation'[21] and the recent period has seen Beijing making overtures to offer its good offices for mediation between Islamabad and New Delhi. However, India as yet remains skeptical to such gestures.

Similarly, Pakistan has also lately displayed greater understanding and confidence about growing India-China relations and the recent upsurge in India–China *rapprochement* has not resulted in an equal upsurge (or even a desire for such an upsurge) in China–Pakistan counter-posturing. Indeed, it is for some time now that the Pakistani elite has described the China–India *rapprochement* as something that is expected to 'energize a restraining influence on India's ambitions in the region' which suits Pakistan.[22]

Third, closely related to the China-Pakistan axis has been this issue of Kashmir dispute. A complete transformation in China's Kashmir policy over the years has lent new confidence to India's ties with both Islamabad and Beijing. China has clearly moved far away from its 1960s position of 'staunch support to Pakistani claims as also to the Kashmiri Liberation struggle', to the 1990s posture of neutrality on India–Pakistan issues and, more recently, Beijing has been concerned about 'any escalation of conflicts over Kashmir . . . with horrifying consequences'.[23] Though China's policy shift on Kashmir can be traced as far back as to the late 1970s, it was particularly vivid during the India-Pakistan Kargil conflict during May–June 1999 when Premier Zhu Rongji was to describe Kashmir as an 'historical issue involving territorial, ethnic and religious elements' which, he said, need to 'be solved only through peaceful means' and bilateral consultations between Islamabad and New Delhi.[24] Similarly, China's Foreign Minister Tang Jiaxuan in his meeting with his Pakistani counterpart Sartaj Aziz during the latter's visit to Beijing on 11 June 1999 had said that:

> The Kashmir issue is a complicated affair with a long history and should be, and could only be, solved through peaceful means. . . . China hopes Pakistan and India will find an effective approach to bringing about a political solution to the Kashmir issue through negotiations and consultations.[25]

And finally, in the wake of the events following 9/11, Pakistan has faced tremendous pressure from various powers to rein in various terrorist outfits and proliferation networks believed to be in Pakistan. President Musharraf went on record to say that Pakistani nuclear scientist A.Q. Khan—who ran the world's largest nuclear proliferation ring—had exported 'probably a dozen' centrifuges to North Korea, critical in building Pyongyang's capability to produce nuclear weapons. However, he is reported to having said that after two years of interrogation it was still not clear whether Khan gave North Korea a Chinese-origin design to build a nuclear weapon.[26] All this has clearly been responsible for the whole transformation in China–India–Pakistan ties where these three are now beginning to evolve a far stronger understanding of mutual stakes and common objectives.

It is in this new context that each of these following chapters of this volume make an attempt to examine some of the generic issues as also specific sectors of China–Pakistan strategic cooperation. And each of these is an attempt to understand these issues from an Indian perspective as also to highlight India's options in dealing with this axis.

About this Volume

This volume is grouped into three main parts with each having six chapters moving from general to specific issues and sectors; all intend to evolve a general understanding of the China–Pakistan strategic cooperation. Part I begins with its focus on the evolution of their mutual policies and perceptions. It examines their mutual images, interests and attractions from the point of view of their popular perceptions but also examins the deep-rooted strategic and political cultures that underlie these mutual impressions and interactions. The two chapters particularly provide a detailed analysis about their place in each other's security perceptions which provides the necessary backdrop in the evolution of their strategic cooperation. While the first chapter is aimed at giving an overview of this section, it particularly tries to highlight the myths that have shrouded India's perceptions on China–Pakistan relations thereby contributing to its being either an enigma for India's policy makers or being spoken of in rather simplistic and rhetorical narratives.

Anindyo Majumdar in chapter two highlights the changing imperatives and the guiding principles that underlie the dynamics guiding China–Pakistan equations. He examines the evolution of China–Pakistan relations especially in the context of Cold War and the post-Cold War period. Special emphasis is laid on examining the new academic debates on nuclearism and micro-wars of the contemporary period as the new backdrop in which one has to evolve a fresh understanding of the China–Pakistan strategic cooperation. This is especially important to understand the emerging new trends of their relationship and its significance for the future of India's foreign and security policies. This chapter concludes that it is the politico-strategic consideration that has been and will continue to be the guiding force of China-Pakistan relations. The author stresses in his conclusion that it would be premature to ignore China–Pakistan relations as a factor in India's foreign and security policies.

Srikanth Kondapalli follows this by his counter-thesis on how, recently, some national and international security challenges have been denting into their 'all-weather' relations, though such policy shifts, according to him, have not been very sharp or completely explicit. Especially from the Chinese security point of view, 'opposing regional hegemonism' (which he calls as China's euphemism for India's rise) has been the regular refrain of China-Pakistan special relations. His conclusion is that both China and Pakistan have benefited by this axis and their anti-India premise has helped in raising their mutual trust and understanding. However, he highlights how this logic has eroded in recent years. He also outlines several other inherent limitations and difficulties that today characterize their axis as also vital to any crystal-gazing into its future.

Satyabrat Sinha tries to develop a mirror image of the Pakistani perceptions on China. He places their relationship in the Cold War context and sees their alignment as one guided by the Cold War logic. However, what remains baffling is the skewed perseverance and depth of their relations and yet the sheer uncertainty about its future. Especially, even in face of the recent blossoming China-India trade ties—that has clearly outstripped the bilateral China-Pakistan trade—most Pakistani writings and speeches continue to give an impression of an all abiding trust in the rising Asian giant (China) amongst the Pakistani elite.

M.V. Rappai's chapter tries to examine their mutual perception and policies from the standpoint of being only reflections of their strategic thinking and traditions. He stresses on a vital distinction when he says that while in the case of China there have been long traditions of strategic thinking since ancient times, in case of Pakistan, it remains much more short-lived tradition and it is a rather complicated exercise to decipher the continuation of any coherent strategic thinking and its influence on Pakistan's policies and perceptions about China. Indeed, he also problematizes the whole issue of Pakistan's national identity and inheritance as also China's isolation that remain equally integral to the evolution of their mutual perceptions and policies.

Sonika Gupta tries to extend Rappai's thesis further and highlight, the comparison between strategic culture and political culture. She explains how it is their political culture that remains overcast and which intertwines with their strategic culture to determine their contemporary policy options. For her, while bilateral ties between China and Pakistan remain driven mainly by strategic concerns and threat perceptions, it is their political culture that plays a rather pivotal role in strengthening their posturing and planning that underlie the success of their enduring relationship. Clearly, a different type of political culture (or systems) in either State, she says, would possibly have not resulted in enduring relationship as it today exists.

Part II of this volume has a set of six chapters that focus on the strategic and defence components, i.e. the core of China–Pakistan strategic cooperation. These six chapters flow from discussing the global and regional concerns about the proliferation of weapons from China in general to more specific sectors of their nuclear, missile and other defence production and sharing in aerospace, air and naval training and technologies. This outlines the general forces and factors that has been the driving force of their partnership in specific sectors.

Arpit Rajain, for example, outlines the general concerns about nuclear and missile non-proliferation regimes being flaunted by China–Pakistan cooperation. He highlights how the future of this relationship seems to be on the decline. For him, in the past Pakistan's importance in China's strategic calculations concerning South Asia made it difficult for Beijing to decline requests from Islamabad. Yet, providing such assistance seems to have increasingly aggravate Western suspicions and trigger sanctions. China still remains prisoner of its past promises and sees failure to respond to Pakistan's requests as something that can damage China's credibility with a prized ally, yet China fails to stand by such cooperation and continues to deny the existence of such programmes and to insist on the peaceful nature of their cooperation. This has allowed non-proliferation regimes to become far more effective in at least slowing down the pace of their sharing of sensitive technologies.

Savita Pande's chapter, on the other hand, focuses specifically on the problem of how the United States (and some other powers) have been directly responsible in undermining these non-proliferation norms and regimes. Like any other state, the US has always been guided by its national interest and, despite all the hype to the contrary, its proliferation concerns were often subordinated to it its national interests and other Cold War dynamics. It is therefore not surprising that in the context of bleeding the Soviet white in Afghanistan during 1980s, US needed both China and Pakistan to achieve its Cold War objectives. It is this context that marks the failure of non-proliferation norms and regimes with the US overlooking and China filling in the gaps on Pakistan's nuclear weapons programme making Pakistan a nuclear weapon state.[27]

Rajiv Nayan focuses on transfer of delivery systems—i.e. ballistic missile technologies—that have been the other most sensitive alleged technology transfers from Beijing. China is believed to having supplied full ballistic missile systems as also components and other technologies to refine or refurbish Pakistan's delivery systems. He portrays China as the frontline proliferator of missile technologies and cites how several countries—like Saudi Arabia, Iran, Iraq, Libya, North Korea and Pakistan—have been China's clients on strategic as well as commercial basis. Especially, the clandestine nature of China–Pakistan transactions has promoted a culture of disbelief and mistrust about Beijing which has repeatedly been subjected to economic sanctions in this regard.

M. Matheswaran talks about other delivery systems like aircrafts and other flying systems that support effective delivery of weapons. He outlines how China and Pakistan have established a whole range of collaborative arrangements for research and development in fields ranging from missiles to other air and aerospace technologies. Amongst other things, China has helped establish a considerable level of aerospace infrastructure in Pakistan. This includes aircraft overhaul factories, joint ventures in fighter aircraft and aero engine design and production. Besides, China has also supplied a variety of electronic warfare, radar, and unmanned platforms and has ensured collaborations and access to its space assets.

Vijay Sakhuja outlines the evolution and implications of China–Pakistan naval cooperation. What is most worrisome, according to him, is the fact that the PLA Navy has been keen to obtain oceanographic data of the Arabian Sea and Bay of Bengal. This is expected to enable China's submarines to potentially operate in India's coastal waters. Though his assessment of Chinese naval threat seems to rule out any naval confrontation between India and China yet the presence of Chinese submarines cannot be ruled out altogether. For the long run, however, Chinese maritime planners and strategists seem convinced that Pakistan offers them a favourable staging post in terms of regional influence and for ensuring security for their energy imports and sea lines of communication.

Lawrence Prabhakar expands this canvas further by examining not only the visible but also underlying forces that govern China–Pakistan maritime convergence. He shows how China rationalizes its extended presence around India on the premise that sea lines of communications for its oil imports from Persian Gulf and its merchandise trade with that region require that China has access to forward facilities in Pakistan. For Pakistan, in turn, this naval presence of China in South Asia signals assurance that China would be a countervailing force to deal with India's dominant influence. In specific terms, Gwadar port, for instance, provides Pakistan a dispersal port to berth Pakistani submarines and surface warships and perhaps could even be berthing point of the future PLA Navy fleet of the Indian Ocean. All this really makes China–Pakistan maritime convergence a subject of critical importance for India.

Part III of this volume focuses on elucidating what underlies their visible defence and strategic cooperation. These are sectors that promise to go far in supporting China–Pakistan currently military-centric strategic cooperation and enable them to deal with future challenges and other counter-currents. Though the focus on these areas of trade, investments and infrastructure building as also their critical linkages through the Karakoram and the Xinjiang factor have not been the focus of their official policies yet they remain the cushion that will ensure their continued close ties even when their defence ties become either circumscribed or less important component of their mutual engagement.

Madhu Bhalla's chapter opens this discussion on the strategic components in their economic relationship. She begins by highlighting how China's economic relations with Pakistan have moved beyond the geopolitical and strategic imperatives of the Cold War years. Now these are increasingly subject to the demands of China's modernization drive and the pressures of globalization which can not afford old-fashioned transactions on 'friendship prices' basis and so on. In light of these changing imperatives China–Pakistan economic relations are undergoing a kind of recasting of the geopolitics that underlies their overall economic engagement of recent years. Amongst others, this has led to a shift in China's aid policies which have moved their focus now towards financing joint ventures and where Beijing's interest have increasingly become the critical prerequisite.

D. Varaprasad Sekhar moves this debate to another critical level by examining how this economic engagement has been guided by the unfolding of new trends in Chinese and Pakistani economies and technologies. With its own rapid development in certain sectors, he says, China seems to have arrived at a position of being an exporter of technologies, at least to some of the developing countries. Pakistan being a strong ally for almost five decades has received various kinds of technology from China and this has played a critical role in improving Pakistani technological capabilities. Particularly, in the low and intermediate technology sectors and processes, both China and Pakistan can now stake claim to be emerging players with China gradually moving towards high-tech products and becoming globally competitive. This has strengthened China's ability to export various kinds of technologies to Pakistan which will go a long way in benefiting not only Pakistan but also China. This increasingly mutually beneficial as also ever evolving nature of their economic engagement promises to make it enduring as also a reliable basis for their strategic partnership.

Arvind Kumar's chapter then deals with one promising sector of their civilian technological cooperation, i.e. nuclear technologies. Cooperation in these has been evolving from 1970s though it was only as part of Deng Xiaoping's economic opening up that substantial partnership in civilian nuclear transfers developed from mid-1980s. Several other factors—like Soviet invasion of Afghanistan—had greatly facilitated this relationship and Arvind explores how this cooperation in civilian nuclear cooperation has had links with the nuclear weapons programme of Pakistan. Amongst some known examples of China's contributions to Pakistan in terms of civilian cooperation, Beijing is known to having helped it in building 300MW power reactor at Chashma as also assisted in building of an unsafeguarded 50–70 MW plutonium production reactor at Khushab plus another unsafeguarded plutonium reprocessing facility at Chashma. The interesting point to note here is that China had taken this decision to move into developing civilian nuclear cooperation with Pakistan after Japanese, German, and French firms refused to provide supporting systems and components to Pakistan.

Aparna Kher's chapter looks at Pakistan's weapons procurements from China. She tries to highlight the deeper logic of these transactions that has sustained this trend against all odds. Both China and Pakistan, she says, have several constituencies that have over time developed vested interests to ensure continuation of *status quo* in their defence relations. For her, despite the thaw in relations between China and India, the China–Pakistan strategic entente has not shown any major sign of stress. At least in this sector of weapons procurements the two remain interdependent—China for market and Pakistan for supplier—and these have been also the basis for their cooperation in more exotic nuclear and missile technologies. She concludes by saying that lately China also feels entangled with Pakistan given its restive Muslim population in Xinjiang and thus its need to assuage and engage moderate Muslim states especially on its borders.

Link with Xinjiang is further examined by the last two chapters one by Virendra Sahai Verma that elucidates various facets of the Karakoram highway and the other by Abanti Bhattacharya who dwells in the underlying logic of China's Xinjiang factor for its 'special relationship' with Pakistan. Colonel Verma's chapter exaplains how Islamabad considers the Karakoram highway to be their true gateway to both China and Central Asia. For Islamabad this represents the revival of the ancient Silk Route network through which Pakistan sees its expanding strategic depth and economic salvation. Similarly, China sees this as one of its alternative routes to South Asia and to the warm waters of the Indian Ocean. Though this route has had its share of difficulties and misunderstanding yet this strategic road link between the two have continued to be the umbilical cord between these two countries.

The last chapter on the Xinjiang factor deals with an issue that perhaps lies at the origins of this China–Pakistan axis. This is also perhaps the critical factor that continues to circumscribe their close relations. This chapter explains how this large region of China has come to be a critical barometer and the potent litmus test for the strength of China–Pakistan relations. Xinjiang demonstrates that friendship with Pakistan remains a vital factor in China's internal stability. This also shows how, in China's perceptions, Pakistan has potential to play a key role in minimizing Islamic militancy in this sensitive border region. As a result, despite Pakistan getting branded as a 'virtual terrorist state', China continues to gladly overlook these irritants in favour of long-standing friendship with Pakistan.

NOTES

1. Giri Deshingkar, in *Security and Science in China and India* [essays edited by Manoranjan Mohanty and Mira Sinha-Bhattacharjea], New Delhi: Samskriti, 2005, p. 59; also Swaran Singh (ed.), Omnibus Issue on 'Sino-Pakistani Strategic Cooperation', *Peace Initiatives*, vol. V, no. III-VI, May–December 1999, p. 216.
2. Maqbool Ahmad Bhatty, 'China and South Asia', *Strategic Studies* (Islamabad), vol. XXIII, no. 1 (Spring 2003), p. 81.
3. For details see Swaran Singh, *China-India Economic Engagement: Building Mutual Confidence*, Occasional Paper 10, New Delhi: Centre de Sciences Humaines, March 2005, p. 173.
4. Anwar Hussain Syed, *China & Pakistan: Diplomacy of an Entente Cordiale*, Karachi: Oxford University Press, 1974, p. 54.
5. William J. Barnds, *India, Pakistan and the Great Powers*, New York: Praeger, 1972, pp. 95, 323.
6. The first visible change in China–Pakistan relation was to come as part of July 1961 US visit by President Ayub Khan declaring to vote in favour of seating China at the UN and UNSC. Later, the fact that US had extended military help to India during China–India war was to further make Islamabad skeptical of US intentions and grow closer to China which also now had strong reasons to befriend India's archrival.
7. Anwar Syed, *China and Pakistan: Diplomacy of an Entente Condiale* London: Oxford University Press, 1974, p. 140; Mushtaq Ahmed, *Government and Politics in Pakistan*, Karachi: Pakistan Publishing House, 1963, p. 68; Syed Noor Ahmad, *Marshal La Se Marshal La* [From Martial Law to Martial Law], Lahore: Deen Mohammadi Press, 1965, p. 480; Shorish Kashmiri, *Husain Shaheed Suhrawardy*, Lahore: Chatan Publications, 1967.
8. M. Ehsan Ahrari, 'China, Pakistan and the "Taliban Syndrome"', *Asian Survey*, vol. 40, no. 4, July/August 2000, pp. 666–8.
9. Robert Einhorn, 'China and Non-Proliferation', *The National Interest*, vol. 2, issue 13, 2 April 2003, available online at http://www.inthenationalinterst.com/Articles/Vol2Issue13/Vol2Issue13einhorn.html
10. Dingli Shen, 'China and Nuclear Proliferation: General Policy with Application to South Asia', in Mukesh Kumar Kayathwal (ed.), *Security and Foreign Policy in South Asia*, Jaipur: Pointer Publishers, 1999, p. 82; Shirley A. Kan, 'Chinese Missile and Nuclear Proliferation: Issues for Congress', *CRS Issue Brief*, IB92056, 12 June 1992, p. CRS-4.
11. Sudarshan Bhutani, *A Clash of Political Cultures: Sino-Indian Relations, 1952–62*, New Delhi: Roli Books, 2004, p. 207; General

Mohammad Musa (Retd.), *My Version: India–Pakistan War 1965*, (Lahore: Wajidalis Ltd., 1983, pp. 11, 92.

12. B.R. Deepak, *India & China 1904–2004: A Century of Peace and Conflict*, New Delhi: Manak, 2005, p. 465.
13. Fazal-ur-Rahman, 'Pakistan's Relations with China', *Peace Initiatives* New Delhi, vol. 5, nos 3–6, May–December 1999, pp. 170–90; Ahmad Faruqui, 'The Sino-Pakistani Relationship: From Harmony to Disquiet', *Policy Forum Online* (02 January 2001) available at http://www.nautilus.organisation/fora/security/0101A_Faruqui.html
14. Apart from their continuing differences at the political level about Pakistan's role in rising violence in China's Xinjiang region (as outlined in China's November 2002 White Paper on National Defence blaming Taliban for training Uighur Muslims), the two militaries have also continued to evolve their anti-terrorism cooperation. The two, for instance, held their anti-terrorism military exercise name 'Friendship 2004' in China's Xinjiang during August 2004. Cited from Fazal-ur-Rahman, 'China–Pakistan Relations' (p. 7), a paper presented at the International Conference on 'China and Emerging Asian Century' held at Institute of Strategic Studies, Islamabad during 27–8 September 2005.
15. Prime Minister Shaukat Aziz's *Inaugural Speech* to the International Conference on 'China and the Emerging Asian Century' at Institute of Strategic Studies, Islamabad, on 27 September 2005.
16. 'Indo–US Relations Not a Cause of Concern: Aziz', *Dawn*, Karachi, 28 September 2005.
17. Waheguru Pal Singh Sidhu and Jing Dong Yuan, *China and India: Cooperation or Conflict?*, New Delhi: India Research Press, 2003, p. 67.
18. C. Raja Mohan, 'Sino-Indian Relations: Towards a Paradigm Shift', in C.V. Ranganathan (ed.), *Panchsheel and the Future: Perspectives on China-India Relations*, New Delhi: Samskriti, 2005, p. 223; 'Chindia Will Hold up Half the Sky', *The Hindustan Times*, New Delhi, 2 October 2005, p. 18; 'Strategic Cooperation Defines our Ties' [Chinese Ambassador to India, Sun Yuxi's interview to], M.K. Venu, *The Economic Times* New Delhi, 22 September 2005, p.12.
19. Swaran Singh, 'China–India Bilateral Trade: Strong Fundamentals, Bright Future', *China Perspectives*, Hong Kong, October–December 2005; also Swaran Singh, *China–India Economic Engagement: Building Mutual Confidence*, op.cit., p. 86. The data for this analysis are drawn from *China Statistical Yearbook*, Beijing: Office of the State Council, annual series.
20. Bahzad Alam Khan, 'China, Pakistan to Strengthen Defence Ties', *Dawn*, Karachi, 17 December 2004.
21. Zhang Guihong, 'US Security Policy Towards South Asia after Septem-

ber 11 and its Implications for China: A Chinese Perspective', *Strategic Analysis*, New Delhi, vol. 27, no. 2, April–June, 2003, pp. 145–71.

22. *Country Survey Pakistan*, *Jane's Defence Weekly*, vol. 18, no. 19, 7–11 November 1992, p. 31.
23. Jing-dong Yuan, 'China's Kashmir Policy', *China Brief* [The Jamestown Foundation], vol. 5, no. 19, 13 September 2005, p.13 also Swaran Singh, *China–South Asia: Issues, Equations, Policies*, New Delhi: Lancer Books, 2003, especially chapter on 'China's Kashmir Policy', pp. 71–99.
24. Shao Zongwei, 'Zhu Urges Quick Return to Stability in Kashmir', *China Daily*, Hong Kong, 29 June 1999, p. 1; also 'Li: Solve Kashmir Crisis Peacefully', *China Daily*, Hong Kong, 12 June 1999, p. 1.
25. 'China Hopes for Effective Solution in Kashmir', *China Daily*, Hong Kong, 12 June 1999, p. 1. For details see 'Pakistan Factor in Sino-Indian Ties: From Pokhran to Kargil', Anindyo J. Majumdar (ed.), *Nuclear Indian into the New Millennium*, New Delhi: Lancer's Books, 2000
26. David E Sanger, 'Yes, AQK Helped N. Korea Go Nuclear: Pervez', *The Times of India*, New Delhi, 14 September 2005, p. 27.
27. William Burr (ed.), *China, Pakistan, and the Bomb: The Declassified File on US Policy, 1977-1997*, National Security Archives Electronic Briefing Book No. 114, 5 March 2004, online at http://www.gwu.edu/~nsarchive/NSAEBB/NSAEBB114/index.htm

CHAPTER 2

The Changing Imperatives

ANINDYO J. MAJUMDAR

In pragmatic decision-making in international relations, tactical shifts attuned to ground realities are necessary components. Bilateral relations, therefore, are always unique and often defy attempts to formulate general categorizations. Irrespective of the state policy, that provides basic directions of state actions, bilateral relations are more susceptible to immediate needs, the elite's cognitive culture, leadership peculiarities and the evolving changes in the global or regional environment. Bilateral relations therefore, often reflect the tactical shifts of pragmatism. Consequently, fluctuations in relations do occur and nothing seems permanent—not even the all-weather and special relationships. In the face of this conventional understanding, relations between China and Pakistan appear astonishingly durable.

Indeed, some experts find 'China's cooperative relation with Pakistan is arguably *the most* stable and durable element of China's foreign relations'[1] and that very often, the military and strategic component in the relationship is duly highlighted. This explains that the cause lies not only in the inclinations of both the states to embrace each other but also in the surrounding milieu in which the parties operate and bilateral relations flourish. This relationship has been a product of certain historical developments and the depth, length and intensity of the relationship are vulnerable to changing equations among different actors. It is a different matter that changes in political behaviour of states in certain regions—mostly as a response and adaptation to radical, revolutionary changes in other regions—either require more time to take effect, or in the long run, fail to substantially alter the existing considerations.

The post-Cold War transitional phase manifests a situation where new power equations are being formed. No wonder, it is difficult to profess predictable patterns of state behaviour before the equations are somewhat crystallized to introduce a new and relatively stable arrangement. Nevertheless, the dominant streams can perhaps be ascertained, keeping in mind that logic itself has its limitations in international relations, individuals and events often move history to undesired directions and rationality itself is open to different interpretations. It is in this context that this paper makes an attempt at sketching out the evolution of China–Pakistan ties and see how the realist paradigms work, how the relationship adapts itself to the era of Terror War and the second nuclear age, and finally, how the triangular relations between China, India and Pakistan evolve and the possible responses to it in a changing world.

The Genesis & Growth

China–Pakistan relations may have been initiated by the normal considerations of improving and expanding the two-way interactions among states but it certainly developed and flourished on the simple strategic axiom: the enemy of my enemy is my friend. The usual line of analysis harps on interest complementarities: China and Pakistan need each other to neutralize India's growing military capabilities, and the proximity and geopolitical considerations cement their relations further. The relationship faithfully follows the paradigms of realism by forming a *de facto* alliance against India. One should presume that in such a relationship, intensity of bilateral cordiality would depend on the credibility of India as a potential or actual threat as perceived in Islamabad and in Beijing.

The initial years in the 1950s did not provide enough impetus for bilateral relations to grow, as the strategic considerations were not compatible for China and Pakistan. Roughly, Pakistan's considerations in the late 1940s-early 1950s were: (a) India was the primary threat, (b) Despite differences, India enjoyed a working relationship with China, (c) Soviet Union might extend its sphere of influence up to the Indian Ocean (in search of warm water ports) jeopardizing Pakistan's independence, and (d) China, as a communist state, would go along with the Soviet Union. On the other hand, China in the initial years was upbeat on the spread of Communist ideology and hence, was willing to cooperate with the then Soviet Union while resisting stiff US opposition. The developments were noteworthy: Pakistan did cultivate the US and joined SEATO and CENTO and China and Pakistan were on the opposite sides during the Korean War. This shows that the relationship did not flourish right from the beginning but adapted itself to changing needs.

As with time, China developed serious differences with India and the Soviet Union, equations changed too and the real association of China–Pakistan began. During the late 1950s-early 1960s and onward, Pakistan's considerations changed. In a general way, India remained the primary threat, and therefore, in view of a Sino–Indian rivalry, China needed to be cultivated. Further, in view of Sino–Soviet confrontations, and the evolving Indo–Soviet friendship, yet again, Pakistan needed to befriend China, with the understanding that the rivalry between China and the US was detrimental to Pakistan's interest. On the other hand, China considered that in view of new developments, friendship with Pakistan and the US would be beneficial and Pakistan would be handy in establishing links with the US, the West, and the Middle East.

Pakistan could also be used as a counter-balance to India. The resultant formulations crystallized in the early 1970s as the China–Pakistan–US axis was established and from now on China sought to establish a client relationship with Pakistan through military technology transfer. These considerations continued throughout the era of Cold War. Throughout this period the relations among the three gradually developed to encompass economic aspects as well, while minor frictions were overlooked in the greater interest of sustaining friendship. In the process, the US and Pakistan became important customers of Chinese goods. The Cold War, in spite of all its ideological trappings, was essentially an intense competition between the two most militarily powerful states, the US and the eastwhile USSR to find ways to outdo each other. The quest for a military balance is in effect a latent war and can end with the perceived superiority of either of the parties involved. As it happened, the Cold War ended with the fall of the Soviet Empire and the disintegration of the Union itself.

Apparently, in India, China and Pakistan found a common enemy. For Pakistan, the US (notwithstanding its 'us vs. them' mentality) seemed less reliable as an ally when India was concerned, and Pakistan increasingly veered towards China and thus began the special relationship between the two. Pakistan was also used as a conduit between China and the US and yet again, a special relationship between China and the US emerged against the common enemy: the Soviet Union. As if in response, India and the Soviet Union came closer and a treaty of friendship between them just fell short of a formal military alliance. The Cold War scenario was complete. There was a China–Pakistan–US axis to be balanced by the Indo–Soviet entente and the patterns of weapons procurement and trade largely reflected this arrangement. Within this broad framework of Cold War politics, the states had their own regional interests to cater to. India–China–Pakistan trilateral relations have therefore evolved in such a fashion that scholars often refer to them as constituting a strategic triangle. 'Security decision-making is *interdependent* between India, China and Pakistan in the sense that none of these countries can be oblivious to how the bilateral relationship between the other two is poised'[2]—observes a scholar.

However, of the three actors involved, Pakistan was the weakest militarily, and its passionate anti-India policies and a congenital urge to injure Indian interests, made it vulnerable to the amount of political, diplomatic, and military support it received from its friends in general and from China in particular. In the process, the significant special relationship that evolved was nothing but a subordinate-alliance relationship as China introduced—by supplying coveted weapons and technology—the dependency factor in the relationship.[3] However, it is to be noted that there was no formal undertaking that Pakistan would always be bailed out while in distress—the relationship fell short of a formal alliance.

On the other hand, towards the end of the Cold War, while Pakistan was mired in its self-created Indo-centric matrix, India and for that matter, the US, China, and the USSR moved out to each other, albeit intermittently. Eventually relations improved among them cutting across the Cold War considerations. Pakistan's friendship with China was directly proportionate to Pakistan's enmity with India. As the enmity was sustained, so also the friendship. Interestingly, India's rapprochement with China progressed while China continued to supply Pakistan with nuclear weapons and missiles.[4] In a way, this indicates that India had tried to come out of the trilateral 'interdependent' relations, as mentioned earlier, and opted for bilateral independent interactions while China responded favourably.

The end of the Cold War, however, introduced new elements for consideration. The US emerged as the sole superpower and started to view China as the future challenger to its global supremacy. Nevertheless, a policy of cooperative engagement appeared to be a better option than unnecessary confrontations. This relationship has been uneasy. Some American scholars lead us to believe that 'Engagement, the pursuit of a working relationship with a disagreeable regime, has rarely been attractive to Americans of any political persuasion.'[5] Apparently during the Cold War the US was compelled to develop relations with 'reprehensible regimes' to contain the Soviets but at the end of it there is no compelling justification to continue.[6] The Americans are also unsure whether a strong China is in the interest of the US.[7] Indeed, just after the end of the Cold War, the American search for a new enemy brought China to the forefront, and despite the asymmetry in terms of military strength, bestowed upon China a near-superpower status. China was viewed as the potential challenger and long-term adversary of the U.S. by some[8] and hence, preventing China from becoming a regional hegemon was outlined as the primary American objective.[9]

Even those who refused to view China from such alarming standpoints, nevertheless maintained that the US required a policy to contend 'with China's potential for destabilizing the region'[10] rather than a policy to deal with a future hegemon. China can become a respectable middle power within a decade, argues Kupchan, 'but it will not be America's principal challenger anytime soon'.[11] The debate came to an abrupt end and the focus swiftly shifted as with the 9/11 Al-Qaeda attacks on the World Trade Center and the Pentagon, the era of new terrorism began, inviting worldwide US response and the immediate China threat replaced the imaginary potential challenges. This in turn had its impact upon Pakistan and consequently on the *jihadi* activities in Kashmir and Xinxiang to an extent. In the meanwhile, in 1998, India and Pakistan had become nuclear powers minimizing chances of an all-out war between them and the lessons in nuclear manoeuvre were to be learnt by them in the subsequent years.

While it is to be remembered that the Sino–Indian thaw is not at the cost of Sino–Pakistan relations,[12] observers feel that China's efforts to balance its *entente cordiale* with Pakistan against its new rapprochement with India has made the Sino–Pakistan relations more nuanced and more complex.[13] Apparently, almost echoing the official line, a scholar has argued, 'China sincerely wishes that India and Pakistan can settle their disputes through peaceful consultations and negotiations, so that Sino–Indian relations, Sino–Pakistan relations and Indo–Pakistan relations can develop simultaneously and constitute a virtuous circle'.[14] With the normalization and improvement of Sino–

Indian relations, observes Ruisheng, the India factor, which had played an important role in the improvement of relations between China and Pakistan, has been removed and readjustments have been made.[15]

Indeed, a vast improvement in Sino–Indian relations in recent years is on record. Military confidence building measures, frequent bilateral official visits and summits, memoranda of understanding on border trades, cooperation in the judicial field and in education, renewable energy, ocean science and technology, cultural exchanges, simplifying visa procedures, and the willingness to refrain from toughening stands on the contentious border issues—all contributed to a steady growth in bilateral relations. Former Prime Minister A.B. Vajpayee addressing the audience in Peking University in June 2003 mentioned that Sino–Indian bilateral trade had shot up from around 200 million US dollars in the early 1990s to around five billion U.S. dollars. In November 2003 China and India had joint naval exercises in the East China Sea aimed at ensuring broad-based cooperation towards the safety of maritime trade and improving coordination in search and rescue at sea. In October, China had conducted similar naval exercises with Pakistan at the same venue. It appeared to be a new security concept of 'mutual trust, mutual benefit, equality and co-ordination'.

It is however easier said than done. Under the boundary agreement between them, Pakistan has ceded to China the occupied territory of the Indian State of Jammu and Kashmir and 'they jointly constructed the Karakoram Highway, which serves to strengthen their hold over the occupied territories'.[16] This highway provides China unhindered passage through Pakistan to the Persian Gulf. Unless India renounces its claims over the occupied territories and partition of Kashmir becomes a reality, the highway, in view of its strategic importance, would remain the vital cord of attachment between China and Pakistan. Moreover, as Garver maintains, 'A prudent Chinese policy would sustain Pakistan against India. . . . To sacrifice Pakistan would be tantamount to conceding South Asia as India's sphere of influence.'[17] Whether this observation is tenable in the contemporary changing world is a matter of further debate but it is for sure that a time-tested etente creates its own rationale for perpetuating the existing arrangements. Chinese Vice Minister of Foreign Affairs Wang Yi while referring to Pakistan said that it is the Chinese tradition to value an old friend.[18] Still, Sino–Indian relations have definitely progressed leading to the impression in some quarters that further developments

'. . . would gradually diminish the acuity and salience of Sino-Pakistan links'.[19]

Era of Nuclearism and Microwars

Nuclearism can be understood and explained as the belief in the necessity of nuclear weapons as the ultimate guarantee of security for a state, acting as a deterrent to an all-out war sparked by the adversary. During the Cold War period the ideology of nuclearism prevailed. As a result, it gave momentum to a debate regarding the proliferation of nuclear weapons beyond the big five. Kenneth Waltz line, that advocates more Nuclear Weapons States may be better for the balance and counterbalance of states and alliances, has become more convincing.[20] The cost of war *vis-à-vis* the gains, increases exorbitantly and therefore war becomes irrelevant in the long run. At the same time, there was a desperate attempt by the major powers to impose an arrangement of *status quo* that would prevent the revisionist powers to acquire nuclear weapons and thereby restrict the autonomy of action to the dominant few. In this essentially state-centric analysis, there was no place for non-state actors such as terrorist groups. In fact, in earlier studies, it has been pointed out that the organizations most likely to engage in nuclear terrorism would be national governments. Deterrence was viewed as nothing but 'passive terrorism on a grand scale'.[21]

The post-9/11 world community realized that terrorism and weapons of mass destruction made a deadly combination and with time, the threat became increasingly real. With repeated occurrence of average terror attacks the impact seems to wear off over time and the urge amongst terrorists to move towards catastrophic terrorism gains predominance.[22] According to Stern, terrorism is not a static phenomenon and new modes of terrorism have emerged with regularity. Ordinarily the terrorist groups are unlikely to resort to the weapons of mass destruction but counter-measures compel them to search for alternatives.[23] Moreover, if the agenda becomes vague, blurred and not so clearly discernible, the aims and goals become diffused and the terrorists then can use the weapons of mass destruction.[24] The international community is willy-nilly coming to terms with the understanding that nuclear weapons are best controlled—in the absence of disarmament—in a discriminatory arrangement. US-led coalition force's action in Iraq—ostensibly on the ground of alleged acquisition of the weapons of mass destruction by Saddam Hussain—failed to get overwhelming support from the world community but it has established a precedent. Force will be used to contain proliferation whether such an action contains a question of legitimacy or not.

Political terrorism has been generally understood as the systematic use of unpredictable violence against government and public to attain a political objective. Multi-faceted grievances—dissent, protest and resistance to dominant group or class—by an alienated group take the form of terrorism as the state tries to obfuscate the movement. Use of indiscriminate force may be viewed as more effective means than long-drawn never-ending futile negotiations. The era of Terror Wars has however changed the nature of terrorism as a political tool confined to a state; rather it becomes widespread and global. Today, terrorism, nuclearism and pre-emption as a response have emerged as the major security definers in the era of microwars that involve low-intensity conflicts and theoretically, surgical strikes.

Ikenberry has summarized the basic features of the pre-emption policy as propounded by the United States.[25] In the present unipolar world, there is no coalition of great powers and the absence of peer competition makes the US the global leader, protector, and enforcer. Terrorists are to be eliminated (as they cannot be deterred) and as they do not respect borders, neither can the United States (even if sovereignty principles are violated). This means that pre-emption operates without clear-cut norms for justifying force and results in general depreciation of abiding by international rules, treaties and security partnerships, which in turn presupposes that the US would have to work alone giving little value for international stability.

As a result, pre-emption risks a backlash. Apart from a search for multi-polarity, nuclearism takes a new form and the Chinese motives for proliferation can be viewed differently. As Indian intelligence agencies confirm, China had passed a weapon test design to Pakistan,[26] and also some equipments and materials.[27] It has been argued, 'Chinese WMD proliferation is likely part of a strategy to prevent US interference in East Asia by discouraging and undermining Yankee interventionism around the globe'.[28] In other words, 'China probably proliferates to make Asia's neighborhoods more dangerous and, thus, more uninviting to the United States, whose expanding presence there deeply troubles Beijing'.[29] It presupposes that the Chinese proliferation activities might continue—and whether it searches for new clients, remains to be seen. Following the same line of argument, one may surmise that the Sino–Pakistan relationship fits into the overall Chinese policy of strategic proxy. Here, ostensibly, the primary target is India (especially when India develops close ties with the US and a 'strategic partnership' takes shape).

China's export of missile systems or missile parts in contravention of the Missile Technology Control Regime has also been a matter of concern for the US. However, China made a strong commitment in November 2000 for not selling nuclear missile technology abroad and the outgoing Clinton Administration immediately waived sanctions against China for past missile technology transfers to Pakistan and Iran. The waiver came as China pledged to halt its exports of long-range missile technologies. In return, China gained the US promise regarding commercial space cooperation including the launching of US satellites by China.[30] The technology transfer issue was an irritant but not a crucial subject in Sino–US relations. Major states had generally showed a lack of concern towards these issues (many European firms operate in the nuclear black-market) till the spectre of worldwide catastrophic terrorism loomed large.

In May 2003, President Bush announced the Proliferation Security Initiative (PSI), which is an attempt to enhance and expand efforts to prevent the flow of WMD, their delivery systems and related materials to and from states and non-state actors of proliferation concern. The idea is to develop a broad range of legal, diplomatic, economic, military and other tools to interdict shipment of such items. PSI is essentially a series of action, it has not evolved into a formal regime yet and there is no formal mechanism for regular coordination with the United Nations.[31] Nevertheless, under the circumstances, nuclear weapons have truly become the weapons of last resort in the hands of a few 'responsible' powers. China as the emerging 'responsible' global power, will find it increasingly difficult to sustain a proxy nuclear arms race in the South Asian region by supporting Pakistan's programme especially after the official revelations of Pakistan's involvement in the nuclear arms bazaar which the A.Q. Khan episode thoroughly exposed. Reportedly, Khan had been peddling nuclear secrets to Iran, North Korea and Libya and nobody was sure whether in these clandestine sales, nuclear technology, designs and materials were sold to terrorist agents or not.[32] Pakistan's survival remains assured partly because the US needs it in its war against terror but the revelation is demoralizing for the international community.

Conventional weapons, meanwhile, remain the sole arbiter of conflicts. The presence or absence of nuclear weapons does not prevent microwars. War against terrorism is a long drawn struggle and incessant microwars are a reality. War at tactical or sub-tactical levels would require conventional arms cooperation and in this respect China-Pakistan cooperation would continue, even if China stops proliferating nuclear technology. China has emerged as the major, in fact, the most significant arms supplier to Pakistan and might remain so. China is annoyed with the *jihadi* activities from Pakistani soil but Pakistan takes special care so that the issue does not go out of control to seriously impair China–Pakistan relations.

Exploring the Guiding Principles

In an earlier work covering nuclear security relations between India and Pakistan,[33] I have argued that nuclear deterrence is essentially instinctive, and the survival instinct leads to a rational choice. Unless a party decides that suicide is better than survival, deterrence will work. This deterrence is achieved by the ability to deliver a few bombs on the enemy territory and therefore balancing tactical or strategic nuclear strength (and every component of it) of the adversary is useless in the long run. Nuclear deterrence is more commanding and potent for the neighbourhood enemies like India and Pakistan and remains the ultimate security guarantee against overwhelming aggression. Under the circumstances, at one point, it was felt that Pakistan would continue sub-tactical activities against India under a nuclear shield. But the futility of this approach too gradually became apparent. As the relations between the two reached a dead-end, leaders in both India and Pakistan chose to go down in history as peacemakers. The Islamabad SAARC Summit of 2004 gave the hints for the beginning of a new era. It appeared that the states had learnt the parameters of manoeuvre in the nuclearized milieu and the weapons (along with the related implications of an intense nuclear arms race) would exercise a sobering influence on the belligerent moods of the two neighbours. Under the circumstances, the Indo–Pakistan peace process—irrespective of frequent official meetings between the two parties at different levels and pious pronouncements—somewhat haltingly steps forward.

According to John Garver, China's perspective of constraining India includes fostering a strong, self-confident Pakistan on India's western flank and the policy has worked quite well. 'The more India is constrained, the less it will be willing and able to act in a hegemonistic fashion'.[34] India's un-hegemonic overtures—if one at all agrees that India has been un-hegemonic—however, have much to do with its own moral baggage that it has carried since Independence, and in no way constrained by Pakistan. But, contrary to Garver's observation, India has, managed to acquire the image of a bullying big brother in the South Asian region. Anyway, irrespective of the desired results, the same policy has perhaps been followed in making North Korea too a nuclear power, where Pakistan reportedly delivered the know-how, to constrain Japan. However, today, while the US is busy 'securing' the Pakistani warheads and Pakistan's programme is reportedly being 'squeezed',[35] China would have little role in continuing nuclear weapons cooperation with Pakistan.

Indeed, according to Ashok Kapur, the motivation for the May 1998 Indian nuclear tests was based on several calculations including the threat of the China–Pakistan nexus. He argues:

> The fact that almost 70 per cent of Pakistan's conventional armament is of PRC design and almost 90 per cent of its missile production is based on varied types of PRC aid makes Pakistan an extended arm of the PRC in the Indian subcontinent, in Indian estimation. . . . (The) series of nuclear tests in May 1998 was . . . to address direct Chinese military pressure against India through Tibet and the Himalayan border, as well as the indirect Chinese pressure through Pakistan and through Myanmar and the Bay of Bengal—the latter two function as India's strategic flanks and both play a role in China's India policy.[36]

Pakistan is China's land corridor to the Indian Ocean and the link to the Gulf and West Asia, which is also the emerging market for Chinese military exports.[37] As a Communist state, China found Pakistan useful in cultivating the oil-supplying West Asian Muslim states. According to a scholar, the US reclaiming of Pakistan after 9/11 has had no impact on China–Pakistan relations. For example, Pakistan has co-opted China in building a major naval base at Gwadar thereby permitting China's strategic intrusion on the Makran coast. Implications of such a development are serious for US strategic interests in the Gulf.[38] For instance, a $58.21 million preferential loan was provided by China to Pakistan for jointly building this strategic and multipurpose deep-water port.[39] Before we contest this argument, it is worthwhile to remember that the Indian media is concerned with China becoming the first country to have a broad based defence cooperation with Bangladesh,[40] and Myanmar is expanding its naval facilities on Great Coco Island—the site of a major signals intelligence facility near the Andaman and Nicobar Islands—with support from China.[41] If these developments appear as the Chinese attempt to encircle India, another line of argument presumes that India's improved relations with Japan, South Korea, ASEAN countries and especially the US, can send wrong signals to Beijing, and China might view these developments as the US attempt to make India a 'potential counterweight' against China.[42]

However, a velvet intervention into Pakistan by the United States is increasingly taking place either for searching and capturing Osama's men or for 'securing' nuclear weapons and material from falling into the hands of *jihadi* outfits—Pakistan has become too important for the United States to be ignored—and hence, the non-NATO ally status has been thrust upon Pakistan. The US–China–Pakistan alliance of the Cold War days is history now; in the changing world the US and the Chinese interests would compete in the region and Pakistan may find it increasingly difficult to balance such interests and exploit them to its benefit.

China, which has been the only steady ally of Pakistan *vis-à-vis* India, might lose its edge if India and Pakistan come to terms. Indeed, in a way, it is not entirely inconceivable that with increasing Chinese hegemonic assertion, strategic situations revert back to those of early 1950s, when Pakistan was interested in a joint South Asian defence against Chinese intentions as a member of the pro-US clubs. In other words, the possibilities are many, but one line of scenario building can proceed in accordance with the following possibilities: In view of the nuclear secrets sale by A.Q. Khan and consequent international pressure on China against nuclear technology/missile proliferation to Pakistan—China–Pakistan strategic relations may lose its momentum especially if the US oversees Pakistan's arsenals and provides necessary security systems as a non-NATO ally (which we have referred to as the 'velvet intrusion' of America into Pakistan). Again, between China and the US—Pakistan's ruling elite may be forced to choose the US for protection of Pakistan as a viable state-system and salvaging its crisis-prone economy. No less important is the consideration that the ruling elite in Pakistan require some sort of American support to survive a fundamentalist backlash. Further, because of the emergence of a commanding nuclear deterrence between the two hitherto adversaries (and also under the US pressure)—India and Pakistan might normalize bilateral relations making Pakistan free from its Indo-centric matrix of decision-making.

In view of the collapse of China's strategic proxy bargain and the consequent need for multi-polarity arrangements against the US domination of world affairs, and China's desire to emerge as a pole in the scheme, China will seek to follow a dual-track policy. On the one hand, incremental progress in bilateral relations between China and its neighbours would continue. On the other, to curtail India's ambitions (if Pakistan is no longer regarded as an 'extension of China in South Asia'), the focus will shift to India's north-east frontier. However, if China feels that Pakistan is becoming pro-US at the cost of China, its sense of being contained and encircled by the U.S. and its friends/allies (Japan–South Korea–Taiwan–South-East Asia–India–Pakistan) will be enhanced. It will continue to entice Pakistan, even with less return.

However, this is just one way of looking into the possibilities, and not necessarily the only one. Unanticipated events can change the approaches of the actors involved and the directions toward conflict or cooperation mode would consequently change too. It is to be noted that many prescriptions have been floated—albeit in different contexts—to resolve shimmering antagonisms among the neighbours in the region. For example, Kupchan writes:

> . . . Attaching India to an expanding zone of prosperity in Asia promises to help integrate the world's second-most-populous state into the global economy, perhaps bringing Pakistan along with it. Their troubled relationship would benefit, just as did that of Spain and Portugal when they joined the process of European integration.[43]

It is however, a matter of conjecture, how the states would respond to such ideas and take willful measures to materialize them.

Conclusion

It is the politico-strategic considerations that have been the prime mover behind a close China–Pakistan relationship throughout the last decades, and the same politico-strategic considerations would continue to affect the relationship. Whether or not the US decides to commit itself to diplomacy and international norms in the post-Cold War era, states are generally apprehensive of the emerging world order where the US not only enjoys preponderance of power, it also relegates other states to the backstage. There is no clear-cut alliance structure at present. China and India are two Asian powers—both continue to compete with each other—and under the circumstances, would seek to avoid direct confrontation. Both realize that the better course open for them is to try to engage each other through cooperative measures as a military confrontation to decide upon their respective supremacy and sphere of influence would be detrimental to their interests.

At the same time, both the states would take measures to protect their strategic interests and ally relations for two reasons: (1) if by any chance diplomacy fails, none of the two would want to be taken by surprise by the other, and (2) a legitimate force projection from both the sides would contribute to the necessity of maintaining a working relationship between the two. The apprehension that China's friendly overtures would change and Beijing would become more assertive with growing military and economic strength with time is not dismissed as baseless in India. In fact, both India and China would like to grow and both realize that such efforts would invite inevitable competitive response from the other side.

There is another angle to the problem. Examining the East Asian security scenario Ikenberry poses a question. He says,

> Economically most East Asian countries increasingly expect their future economic relations to be tied to China. In terms of security, most of these countries continue to expect to rely on American alliance protection. Indeed the rise of China makes this American security tie invaluable. The question is: can the region remain stable when its economic and security logics increasingly diverge?[44]

The divergence between economic and security logics is not only confined to East Asia. Beyond the East Asian region—more towards the Indian Ocean—countries like India too are confronted with the same challenge. Does this motivate India and like-minded countries in the Indian Ocean region to cooperate to ensure a multi-lateral security arrangement?

On the other hand, China–Pakistan relations will continue because of several mutually beneficial reasons and as mentioned earlier, in terms of the portions of Indian territory under their occupation, they are bound to maintain close links between themselves. We might fashion different possible scenarios suitable to our preferences and fancy that changing equations in the changing world would lead to an improvement in Sino–Indian relations that might in turn dilute the intensity of Sino–Pakistan relations. Such a development, however, would not be sufficient (and it is not necessary at all) to de-link Pakistan from China. Indeed, indications are that China and India might continue to engage each other and try to come out of the triangular relationship where Pakistan would be accorded increasingly lesser significance in the Sino–Indian bilateral economic and other functional considerations. But it is premature to completely set aside the Pakistan-factor till substantive settlements are achieved over the large expanses of disputed territory between Beijing and New Delhi. Indeed, as the Cold War Era predictabilities make way for simultaneous moves in different directions by the actors involved and where cooperation / dispute is essentially issue-based, shape of events might turn either way. Rather than following a coherent plan that would of necessity view the other actors in purely black and white, it is time for flexibility in response and cautious initiatives towards the neighbours.

NOTES

1. John W. Garver, *Protracted Contest: Sino-Indian Rivalry in the Twentieth Century*, New Delhi: Oxford University Press, 2001, p. 187. Emphasis in the original.
2. Kanti P. Bajpai, 'Managing a Strategic Triangle: India, China and Pakistan' in P. Sahadevan, ed., *Conflict and Peacemaking in South Asia*, New Delhi: Lancer's Books, 2001, p. 82. Emphasis in the original.
3. See also Swaran Singh, 'Pakistan Factor in Sino-Indian Ties: From Pokhran to Kargil' in Anindyo J. Majumdar, ed., *Nuclear India into the New Millennium*, New Delhi: Lancers Books, 2000, p. 194. For a comprehensive treatment of the evolution of China–Pakistan relations, see: Swaran Singh, *China-South Asia: Issues, Equations, Policies*, New Delhi: Lancers Books, 2003, especially Chapter 6: 'China-Pakistan: Special Relationship'. Also of interest: Shibashis Chatterjee, '50 Years of China's Pakistan Policy: A Partnership through Evolving World-Views' in Arun Kumar Banerji and Purusottam Bhattacharya, eds, *Peoples Republic of China at Fifty: Politics, Economy and Foreign Relations*, New Delhi: Lancers Books, 2001, pp. 95–128.
4. John Garver, *Protracted Contest*, p. 221.
5. Warren I. Cohen, *America's Response to China: A History of Sino–American Relations*, New York: Columbia University Press, 2000, p. 239.
6. Ibid.
7. Ibid. p. 242.

8. Richard Burnstein and Ross H. Munro, 'The Coming Conflict with America', *Foreign Affairs*, 76(2), March–April 1997, p. 73.
9. Ibid. p. 31.
10. Robert S. Ross, 'Beijing as a Conservative Power', *Foreign Affairs*, 76(2), March-April 1997, p. 34.
11. Charles A. Kupchan, *The End of the American Era*, New York: Alfred A. Knopf, 2003, p. 275.
12. P.L. Bhola, *The Spectrum of South Asian Relations*, Jaipur: RBSA Publishers, 2001, p. 100.
13. John Garver, *Protracted Contest*, p. 240.
14. Ma Jiali, 'India's China Policy after the Cold War' in Shen Qurong and Bhabani Sengupta, eds, *China Looks at the World*, Delhi: Konark, 1999, p. 263.
15. Cheng Ruisheng, 'China and India: Challenges and Opportunities for the Transformation of Ancient Relations in the Future', *China Report*, 35(1), 2002, p. 93.
16. P.L. Bhola, *The Spectrum of South Asian Relations*, pp. 82–3.
17. John Garver, *Protracted Contest*, p. 241.
18. *The Times of India*, 7 October 2002.
19. See C.V. Ranganathan, 'India and China: "Learning to Learn" ', *China Report*, 39(4), 2003, p. 551.
20. See Kenneth N. Waltz, 'More may be Better' in Scott D. Sagan and Kenneth N. Waltz, *The Spread of Nuclear Weapons: A Debate*, New York: W.W. Norton, 1995.
21. See Thomas C. Schelling, 'Who Will Have the Bomb?' in Augustus R. Norton and Martin H. Greenberg, eds, *Studies in Nuclear Terrorism*, Boston: G.K. Hall, 1979, p. 49.
22. For further elaboration, see Anindyo J. Majumdar, 'Nuclear Terror' in Omprakash Mishra and Sucheta Ghosh, eds, *Terrorism and Low Intensity Conflict in South Asian Region*, New Delhi: Manak Publications, 2003, pp. 46–57.
23. Jessica Stern, 'Terrorist Motivations and Unconventional Weapons' in Peter K. Lavoy, Scott D. Sagan and James J. Wirtz, eds, *Planning the Unthinkable*, Ithaca: Cornell University Press, 2000, pp. 202–29.
24. Dov Waxman, 'Terrorism: The War of the Future', *The Fletcher Forum of World Affairs*, 23(2), Fall 1999, pp. 202–3.
25. G. John Ikenberry, 'America's Imperial Ambition', *Foreign Affairs*, 81(5), September–October 2002, pp. 44–60.
26. *From Surprise to Reckoning: The Kargil Review Committee Report*, New Delhi: Sage Publications, 2000, p. 188.
27. Ibid. pp. 195–7.
28. Justin Bernier, 'China's Strategic Proxies', *Orbis*, Fall 2003, p. 633.
29. Ibid, p. 634.

30. 'China to Halt Missile Exports', *The Hindu*, 23 November 2000; *The Statesman*, Calcutta, 23 November 2000.
31. 'Proliferation Security Initiative: Frequently Asked Questions', Bureau of Non-Proliferation, US Department of State.
32. Raj Chengappa with Mohammed Shezad, 'Pakistan's Rogue Scientist', *India Today*, 16 February 2004, pp. 46–52.
33. See for elaboration, Anindyo J. Majumdar, *Lethal Games: Nuclear Security, Arms Control and Leadership in Indo-Pak Relations*, New Delhi: Lancers Books, 2004.
34. John Garver, *Protracted Contest*, p. 380.
35. Indrani Bagchi, 'Changing the Nuke Order', *India Today*, 15 March 2004, pp. 44–5.
36. Ashok Kapur, *Pokhran and Beyond: India's Nuclear Behaviour*, New Delhi: Oxford University Press, 2001, p. 4.
37. Bhola, *The Spectrum of South Asian Relations*, p. 100.
38. Subhash Kapila, *United States' Post September 11, 2001 Policy Impacts on South Asia: An Analysis*, Paper No. 454, South Asia Analysis Group, posted on 8 May 2002. http://www.saag.org/papers5/paper454.html
39. *The Indian Express*, 27 December 2002.
40. *The Indian Express*, 26 November 2002.
41. *The Asian Age*, 26 December 2002.
42. Faisal O Al-Rfouh, 'Sino-Indian Relations: From Confrontation to Accommodation (1988–2001)', *China Report*, 39(1), 2003, pp. 36–8.
43. Charles A. Kupchan, *The End of the American Era*, p. 283.
44. G. John Ikenberry, 'American hegemony and East Asian order', *Australian Journal of International Affairs*, vol.58, no.3, September 2004, p. 354.

CHAPTER 3

Pakistan in China's Security Perceptions

SRIKANTH KONDAPALLI

> Our two peoples have regarded each other as friends in need and brothers bound by common fate, always sympathizing with and supporting each other. The Chinese Government and people cherish profoundly the traditional friendship between our two countries and stand ready to join the Pakistani side in further solidifying this friendly and cooperative relationship.
>
> – PRESIDENT JIANG ZEMIN'S SPEECH TO THE PAKISTAN SENATE, 2 December 1996[1]

> . . . no matter what changes may take place in international situation and in each other's countries, the two peoples always support each other, sympathize with each other and help each other.
>
> – GENERAL YU YONGBO, MEMBER OF CENTRAL MILITARY COMMISSION, May 1997[2]

The People's Republic of China (PRC)'s interactions with Pakistan—since India and Pakistan detonated nuclear devices during May 1998—provide for a fascinating study of security policy continuities. To a large extent, while such interactions have provided for mutual cooperation in several fields such as political, economic, civil and military technical aspects, the broader security perspectives of the PRC at the global and regional levels have influenced its policy towards the region.

In the official and elite discourse on China's relations with Pakistan, one comes across several clichés like 'all-weather' relationship,[3] 'time-tested friendship'[4] that withstood the vagaries of international relations in the Cold and post-Cold War eras alike,[5] as based on 'solid foundation' and not on expediency,[6] 'enduring, multi-dimensional and comprehensive relationship'[7] or, as former Pakistan President Rafiq Tarar wrote in one of his poems, such 'friendship [is] higher than mountains, deeper than oceans, and sweeter than honey'.[8] To a large extent such discourse has roots in these bilateral security relations with perceived common interests and benefits for both countries. This hold even though recent events like the post-September 11 counter-terror campaigns, the United States' active military and diplomatic presence in the region following the Afghanistan war, improvement in India–China relations and so on may bring about changes in Sino-Pak interactions in the future.[9] This paper discusses in brief the context of the Sino–Pakistan security relations, and reflects on the Chinese security perceptions on Pakistan and related issues and draws certain broad conclusions.

Several Chinese scholars have analysed the PRC's security relations *vis-à-vis* its south-western neighbours.[10] To a great extent, China's policy towards Pakistan and other countries in the region have been influenced by its overall foreign policy objectives and, to an extent, its position towards the then superpowers and also by its emphasis on pursuing national interests [*guojia liyi*].[11] China's overall national goals may be located in its search for security. Given China's experiences of the United States' trade embargoes, friendship and then split with the Soviet Union, Third World solidarity, its independent foreign policy of peace and development has witnessed increasing emphases on the multipolar world or multilateralism. China's relations with the South Asian countries is rooted in history, though the current state-to-state relations have emphasized aspects of territorial boundaries, and sovereignty issues given the geographical proximity of most of these countries.

Another broad feature of this interaction is the return of aspects of the *Panchsheel* principles in Chinese foreign policy as a guiding philosophy, a long time after its birth in the mid-1950s and the 1955 resolve of PRC to build close links with its neighbours. An additional factor that influenced Chinese policy towards Southern Asia is the recently launched Western Development Campaign of China that aims to focus on development of its backward western regions. The success of this Campaign remains crucial not only to the balanced geographical development of the country and internal security but also in determining China's relations with the region. A stable environment across its western and south-western borders would not only lead to security in Xinjiang and other regions but also focus on economic development with its stress on infrastructure development which could also be used for military purposes. In the post-September 11 counter-terror global trends and given the festering of the Xinjiang Uighur 'separatist' movement, China is poised to take more than a cursory interest in this region.[12]

China's Perceptions of Pakistan

China's relations with Pakistan have been beneficial to the former given the latter's geographical proximity to the Islamic world in South-Western and West Asia,[13] as a counter to the growing economic and military power of India,[14] as a source of Western military technology, Pakistan's support to China in securing its United Nation's Security Council membership between 1961 and 1971,[15] and other factors. The secret visit of Henry Kissinger to China via Pakistan, that led to the normalization of relations between the US and China, has been acknowledged by several Chinese leaders.[16] Other aspects include the Chinese security concerns related to the Indian Ocean Zone of Peace as in the 1970s after the US bases in Diego Garcia came into being, and the 1974 South Asian Nuclear Free Zone proposals.[17]

The earlier shrill in the Chinese security outlook in the 1950s and 1960s against the United States is giving way to a more accommodative 'peaceful coexistence' in the recent period. In this context, with the US Secretary of State Colin Powell's announcement in March 2004 considering Pakistan as a major non-NATO ally, the region is poised to emerge once again in the Chinese security calculus after a similar agreement was arrived at by the US and Pakistan fifty years ago, though, while such contexts are different, China has shown remarkable flexibility in the recent period to the presence of the US forces in different regions of Asia.

In general, such Chinese security perceptions on Pakistan are related to efforts to build bridges with China's neighbours in the overall policy of 'good-neighbourliness' [*mulin zhengce*] and overcome the United States' trade embargoes and nullify the influence of encirclement of China by the Western powers through the SEATO/CENTO security treaties that came up in the 1950s; secure Tibet and Xinjiang portions from outside influence and intervention; create conditions in the international arena for the reunification process of the PRC with Taiwan and other regions; provide assistance to the Third World countries so as to maintain independence of these countries and keep at bay the 'hegemonic' influences in the region and the like. Building close relations with its neighbours will also contribute to forming allies and friends for China that may, in the short term create cushions for the security of the country as well as contribute to the global rise of China in the long term.

In the non-military fields, given the restive Xinjiang Uighur movement, efforts by China in persuading the concerned parties [such as the then Taliban-led Afghanistan and Pakistan] would be conducive to its national security. Another dimension is that, after the four modernization programmes were launched, energy requirements of China have increased, underlining the oil and gas supply routes security. Joint efforts with Pakistan in the Gwadar naval port construction comes in handy as it overlooks the Strait of Hormuz that roughly accounts for about 47 per cent of the Persian Gulf oil exports. Environmental considerations, drug and human trafficking, illegal financial flows are other areas China is also concerned about when we deal with such issues.

Surprisingly, China's perceptions about Pakistan have undergone a change from the worse, as in the late 1950s when the latter was a part of the US-led security apparatus, to the recent building of an 'all-weather' relationship that, as various leaders of these countries have noted, stood like a rock even in the fast-changing international relations.[18] In fact, from 1957 to 1960, Pakistan followed a policy of antagonism with China on the core issues of Taiwan, Tibet, PRC's United Nations membership and the like, though deterioration of the Sino–Indian relations quickly led to their coming together on the boundary issue that included portions of Pakistan-occupied Kashmir. Nevertheless, these relations survived without affecting their relations much despite Pakistan joining the US-led security arrangements.[19]

Credit, of course went partly to China in building relations with Pakistan in the 1950s, starting with the Bandung Conference sidelines.[20] During the first visit of the Pakistani Prime Minister H.S. Suhrawardy to Beijing in October 1956, the two sides 'expressed the desire of both the countries to further the friendly relations existing between China and Pakistan and to promote the great cause of world peace'.[21] In the discussions between the two sides during the ten-day visit by Premier Zhou Enlai to Karachi in December 1956, both sides

> . . . agreed that there has been an increase in tension and the situation requires constant vigilance and constructive action on the part of all peace-loving countries. It is absolutely essential that a climate of peace should be created. . . .

[T]he difference between the political systems of China and Pakistan and the divergence of views on many problems should not prevent the strengthening of friendship between their two countries. . . . They are happy to place on record that there is no real conflict of interests between the two countries.[22]

Ever since the 1960s, as tensions between India and China increased in the late 1950s, the Sino–Pak cooperation in several fields such as in the international arena, conventional, and later strategic, weapons programmes, industrial and science and technological aspects and trade have improved.[23] High-level political visits between the two countries are one indication of such growing relations as Table 3.1 depicts.[24] Indeed, such frequent visits were described by some Chinese as 'calling on relatives'.[25]

TABLE 3.1: MUTUAL HIGH LEVEL VISITS

Period	Visits and categorization
18–29 October 1956	Pakistan Prime Minister H.S. Suhrawardy's 'official friendly visit [*zhengshi yuohao fangwen*]'
20–30 December 1956	PRC Premier Zhou Enlai's first 'official friendly visit'
26 February–5 March 1963	Pakistan Foreign Minister's 'official friendly visit'
18–26 February 1964	Premier Zhou Enlai's 'official friendly visit'
30 October 1964	Vice Premier Chen Yi's 'stop over' [*jingting*] visit
December 1964	President Mohammad Ayub Khan visited
2–9 March 1965	Ayub Khan's 'state visit'
25–30 March 1965	Chen Yi's 'official friendly visit'
2 April 1965	Zhou Enlai 'transited' [*shunfang*] through Pakistan
2–3 June 1965	Zhou Enlai 'transited' through Pakistan
14 September 1965	Chen Yi 'transited' through Pakistan
26–31 March 1966	President Liu Shaoqi's 'state visit' [*guoshi fangwen*]
28–30 June 1966	Zhou Enlai's 'unofficial visit'
22–31 October 1966	Pakistan Foreign Minister's 'official friendly visit'
3–10 August 1968	Pakistan Foreign Minister's 'official friendly visit'
10–14 November 1970	President Yahya Khan's 'state visit'

Period	Visits and categorization
31 January–2 February 1972	PM Zulfikar Ali Bhutto's 'state visit'
17–19 June 1973	Foreign Minister Ji Pengfei's 'official friendly visit'
11–14 May 1974	Bhutto's 'official friendly visit'. In the same year China Airline opened Beijing–Karachi–Paris air route.
26–31 May 1976	Bhutto's 'official friendly visit'
14–19 December 1977	President Zia-ul-Haq's visit
6–8 September 1978	Pakistan Foreign Ministry Advisor's 'official friendly visit'
11–12 May 1979	Pakistan Foreign Ministry Advisor's 'official friendly visit'
18–23 January 1980	Foreign Minister Huang Hua's 'official friendly visit'
2–6 May 1980	Zia-ul-Haq's 'state visit'
6 June 1980	Foreign Minister Huang Hua's 'stop over' visit.
23–26 December 1980	Pakistan Foreign Minister's 'official friendly visit'
1–4 June 1981	Premier Zhao Ziyang's 'official friendly visit'
20 December 1981	Premier Zhao Ziyang's 'stop over' visit.
20–26 April 1982	Pakistan Foreign Minister's 'official friendly visit'
17–23 October 1982	Zia-ul-Haq's 'state visit'. In August the Protocol between China and Pakistan on opening Khunjerab Pass was signed.
15–16 May 1983	Pakistan Foreign Minister Yakub Khan's 'official friendly visit'
16 July 1983	Zia-ul-Haq's 'stop over' visit.
25–29 July 1983	Foreign Minister Wu Xueqian's 'official friendly visit'
5–8 March 1984	President Li Xiannian's 'state visit'
22–26 July 1984	Pakistan Foreign Minister Yakub Khan's 'official friendly visit'
17–23 November 1985	PM Mohammad Khan Junejo's 'official friendly visit'
27 March 1986	President Li Xiannian's 'stop over' visit.
24–29 December 1986	Pakistan Foreign Minister Yakub Khan's 'official friendly visit'

Period	Visits and categorization
21–24 June 1987	Premier Zhao Ziyang's 'official friendly visit'
22–23 May 1988	Prime Minister Junejo 'transited' through China
26–29 June 1988	Pakistan Foreign Minister Yakub Khan's 'official friendly visit'
11–13 February 1989	Prime Minister Benazir Bhutto's 'official friendly visit'
16 September 1989	Foreign Minister Qian Qichen's 'stop over' visit
14–17 November 1989	Premier Li Peng's 'official friendly visit'
2–6 May 1990	National People's Congress Chairman Wan Li's 'official friendly visit'
20–23 September 1990	President Ghulam Ishaq Khan's 'state visit'
14 November 1990	President Ghulam Ishaq Khan's 'stopover visit'
26 February–1 March 1991	PM Nawaz Sharif's 'official friendly visit'
26–30 October 1991	President Yang Shangkun's 'state visit'
6–10 October 1992	Nawaz Sahrif's 'official friendly visit'
4–9 December 1993	CPPCC Chairman Li Ruihan's 'official friendly visit'
27–29 December 1993	PM Benazir Bhutto's 'official friendly visit'
21–24 February 1994	Vice Premier and Foreign Minister Qian Qichen's 'official friendly visit'
2–8 December 1994	President Farooq Leghari's 'state visit'
31 August–1 September 1995	Foreign Minister Ali's 'official friendly visit'
4–8 November 1995	National People's Congress Chairman Qiao Shi's 'official friendly visit'
1–4 December 1996	President Jiang Zemin's 'state visit'
29–30 April 1997	President Farooq Leghari's 'working visit' [*gongzuo fangwen*]
2–5 September 1997	Foreign Minister Jauhar's 'working visit'
11–17 February 1998	Nawaz Sharif's 'official friendly visit'
April 1999	National People's Congress Chairman Li Peng's visit
June 1999	Nawaz Sharif's working visit against the backdrop of Kargil events
2000	CEO Musharraf's visit
3 January 2001	President Musharraf 'transited' through China to attend the SAARC summit in Kathmandu

Period	Visits and categorization
11–14 May 2001	Premier Zhu Rongji's official visit
20–21 December 2001	Musharraf's 'state visit'
14–15 May 2002	Foreign Minister Tang Jiaxuan's visit
2 August 2002	Musharraf's 'stopover' visit
24–26 March 2003	Pak PM's visit
3–5 November 2003	Musharraf's 'state visit'

Sources: Tang Jiaxuan, ed., *Zhongguo Waijiao Cidian* [Dictionary of China's Diplomacy], Beijing: World Knowledge Publications, 2000, pp. 552–3

On 2 March 1963 China and Pakistan signed a border agreement settling boundaries between China's Xinjiang and 'the contiguous areas the defence of which is under the actual control of Pakistan' which 'has never been formally delimited'. Article 6 of this agreement stated:

. . . after the settlement of the Kashmir dispute between Pakistan and India, the sovereign authority concerned will reopen negotiations with the Government of the People's Republic of China on the boundary . . . so as to sign a formal boundary treaty to replace the present agreement. . . .[26]

Two major incidents in this region contributed to the flowering of Sino-Pak security relations. The Indo-Pak wars of 1965 and 1971, as several Chinese authors contend, led to a 'common strategy' between the two countries, especially in the late 1970s that was further strengthened after the USSR's Afghan occupation.[27] In the 1965 Indo-Pak war, soon after India attacked Lahore on September 6, Premier Zhou Enlai reportedly advised Pakistan to wage a people's war of withdrawing from the territories and luring the adversary deep inside the country to be drowned later. As India had numerically superior strength, Pakistani forward postures would be detrimental to the latter.[28] On the occasion, Zhou said:

. . . the Indian reactionaries could not have engaged in such a serious military adventure without the consent and support of the United States. Everybody knows that for several months now U.S. imperialism has used every means in an attempt to compel Pakistan to give up its independent policy. The Indian reactionaries' armed attack on Pakistan was an inevitable result of this policy of the United States.[29]

During President Liu Shaoqi's visit to Pakistan in March 1966, a commentator, Anjam wrote in *Beijing Review* acknowledging Chinese support. He said: 'At the time of the Indian attack [in 1965], China boldly stood by Pakistan. . . . This will be remembered by all posterity in our country.' Another, an editorial of *Ta'Meer*, in the same issue of *Beijing Review* stated: 'No intrigue, threat or pressure can stand in the way of the ever-increasing mutual friendship and cooperation' between the two countries.[30] Liu Shaoqi himself outlined the Chinese security concerns during this visit. He stated, at the State Banquet on 1 April 1966:

> Last year, when Pakistan was subjected to India's armed attacks, its Government, people and army put up a heroic resistance and dealt a heavy blow at the aggressors. The Chinese Government and people *firmly* supported Pakistan in its righteous fight against aggression . . . [Sino-Pak] relations are in the fundamental interests of our two peoples. . . . The Pakistan people can rest assured that, when Pakistan resolutely fights against foreign aggression in defense of its national independence, sovereignty and territorial integrity, the 650 million Chinese people will stand *unswervingly* on their side and give them resolute support and assistance. . . . We have always held that the Kashmir dispute should be settled in accordance with the wishes of the Kashmir people.[31]

In the joint communiqué issued after the 1966 visit, the '[Pakistan] President expressed the deep gratitude . . . for the support they received from the Government and people of China in resisting aggression. . . .'[32]

The period 1970s was described by the Chinese as a common struggle with Pakistan against 'expansionism [*kuozhang zhuyi*] and hegemonism [*baquan zhuyi*]' in Southern Asia.[33] In the 1971 Indo-Pak war, Chinese reportedly advised Pakistan to make political settlement with the leaders of East Pakistan but in vain. In the event of the war, there was no concrete Chinese support to Pakistan's operations, even as some pressure was exerted by China on the India–China border areas. The Indo–Soviet Treaty and possible Soviet military build on the Chinese north-eastern and western borders were too unnerving to the Chinese to get militarily involved in the war.[34] Nevertheless, Chinese civilian and military aid to Pakistan increased by leaps and bounds from this period on.[35] For instance, Pakistan reportedly received nearly one-third of its arms from abroad from the PRC in 1966–80 period that is worth about US $1.5 billion. Subsequently Pakistan signed several agreements for further import of weapons from China.

Closer security cooperation between the two countries is visible from the 1970s. The joint communiqué issued during Prime Minster Bhutto's visit to Beijing in May 1974 mentioned 'the gratitude of the Government and people of Pakistan for China's steadfast and principled support on the question of withdrawal of forces from the territories occupied in the 1971 India–Pakistan war and the unconditional release and repatriation of the Pakistani POWs. . . .' In addition, 'the two sides emphasized the need for continued vigilance against tendencies towards hegemonism and expansionism and assertion of claims to positions of dominance or spheres of influence'.[36]

The 1980s and 1990s were a period of hectic activity between Beijing and Islamabad. The maximum number of high level political visits were made from either side during these two decades; more than any other previous period. It is perhaps no coincidence that the Chinese strategic and conventional weapons cooperation with Pakistan reached its peak in these two decades. A year before Indian Prime Minister Rajiv Gandhi's path-breaking visit to Beijing in 1988, Premier Zhao Ziyang, on a visit to Pakistan in June 1987, mentioned that 'the Chinese people will remain trustworthy friends of the Pakistani people no matter what the vicissitudes of the world'.[37] Nevertheless, the 1990s indicated to changes in the security perceptions of both the countries as issues of ethnic violence and terrorism emerged in this region as well as the rising expectations related to normalization of relations with India. It is no wonder that phrases like 'safeguarding peace and stability in South Asia' are being frequently used in the recent period by the Chinese leaders in their interactions with the Pakistani leaders, especially after cross-border terrorism incidents increased and spread to Xinjiang and the India and Pakistan became nuclear states.

Nevertheless, while high-level political visits increased between China and Pakistan, along with visits by military personnel of both the countries, China appears to have formulated a 'parallel' policy of engaging both Pakistan and India at different levels, instead of the previous policy of building closer relations with only Pakistan. The balance sheet in this regard appears to be hazy, dependent, as it were on the changing international strategic situation. To recount some of the significant statements, President Musharraf visited China between 20–24 December 2001 coinciding with the 50th anniversary of the establishment of diplomatic relations and to 'review' bilateral relations against the Afghan war backdrop. He said that the bilateral relations are 'based on a shared interest in peace, security and stability of South Asia' and 'opposed to international or regional hegemony'.[38] On 21 December 2001 while meeting the top brass of the Chinese leadership in Beijing, Musharraf promised that it would provide 'all-out support' to the Chinese in their fight against Uighur 'separatists' in Xinjiang region. As a *quid pro quo* Premier Zhu Rongji said China would further both countries' 'all-round co-operation to a new high in the new century'.[39] Meeting the Pakistan Chairman of the Joint Chiefs of Staff on 16 January 2002 at Beijing, Jiang Zemin, who worked in Pakistan in the 1970s,[40] stated that China would 'coordinate positions' with Pakistan in order to 'safeguard peace and stability in the region'.[41]

The new Chinese leadership installed in late 2002 appears to be re-working on its security relations with Pakistan, with Beiging focusing more on the non-military security challenges being faced in Xinjiang. When Musharraf met Hu Jintao, the latter made four-point proposal for furthering the bilateral relations in future. These include:

1. to continue frequent bilateral high-level contacts and promote bilateral exchanges between government and non-government institutions, especially between the youth of the two countries.
2. to strengthen bilateral cooperation for mutual benefit in such fields as economy, trade, science and technology, substantiate preferential trade arrangements, and encourage and support the expansion of cooperation between businesses of the two sides.
3. to deepen bilateral cooperation in the field of non-traditional security, and jointly combat drug trafficking, trans-national crimes and the 'three forces' which threatened regional peace.
4. to maintain bilateral communication and coordination in international and regional affairs.[42]

Even though Chinese official position on several issues have undergone some change including in areas close to the Pakistani positions like the Kashmir issue [on which its own problems related to the ethnic movements in its Xinjiang region and the occupation of Sakshgam valley may have contributed towards such change],[43] the 'all weather' special relationship between the two countries have stood the tests of changing times. Despite the 1996 tour of Jiang Zemin in which he reiterated the value of *all* South Asian countries to the Chinese in consolidating its socio-political and economic situation in to the twenty-first century,[44] the Kargil conflict in mid-1999 has indicated to the close relationship between China and

Pakistan and the Chinese resolve to open another possible armed front against India, bringing back to its position in 1971 Indo–Pak war.[45] That is, in other words, the Sino–Indian rapprochement of the late 1980s and 1990s have had their own limitations in the Chinese calculus, though Pakistani support to the Taliban in Afghanistan and through the latter to the Xinjiang Uighur Muslims could pose problems for the Sino–Pak relations, as was raised by the Chinese side during Musharraf's visit to Beijing in November 2003.

China's relations with Pakistan have been more beneficial, in concrete terms, in the military field. In fact, most of the Pakistani inventory is based either on the Western equipment or of those made in China. (See Annexure at the end of this chapter for conventional weapons.) More critical, of course, remain the strategic weapons transfers from China including its cooperation in the making of the nuclear weapons of Pakistan from the 1980s and transfers of short- and intermediate-range ballistic missile (M9 and M11) covering entire north Indian territories. Such close relations can also be seen in the fact that prior to launching of naval operations with India in November 2003, China conducted similar operations with Pakistan first.[46]

Conclusion

In the last five decades of interactions between China and Pakistan, the security dimension has remained predominant in the bilateral relations both during the Cold War and post-Cold War periods, though the nature of such relations have undergone certain changes. Whereas in the earlier period, China sided with Pakistan on several security related matters such as on the Kashmir issue, the 1965 and 1971 wars between India and Pakistan, and exported military items to Pakistan on concessional terms against India, certain national and international security challenges have been denting into this 'all-weather' relations, though such shifts have not been very sharp or completely explicit. From the Chinese security point of view, 'opposing regional hegemonism' [euphemism for India's rise] has been a crucial aspect in its relations with Pakistan. While both benefited by this relationship and were able to raise 'mutual trust', there have also been several limitations as well.

The post-9/11 events, recent Afghan War and the US presence in Pakistan and Central Asia and efforts to counter-terrorism, its non-proliferation agenda, and the like have added new dimensions to China–Pakistan equations. China has also been affected by the Uighur separatist movement some of which is reportedly trained by the Al Qaeda and other elements in Pakistan. The late 2003 Sino–Pak joint declaration mentioned the Pakistani need to curb such activities. Increasingly such high-level visits and joint declarations, from the late 1990s, include items more on further promoting economic relations or curbing terrorism. These security relations were also compounded by the inability of China to convince the other Shanghai Cooperation Organization members on the entry of Pakistan in the organization though, on the other hand, China has also joined the South Asian Association for Regional Cooperation.

Additional growing normalization efforts between India and China after Prime Minister Vajpayee's visit to Beijing in June 2003 have deflected attention from the Sino–Pak relations. In the economic security aspects, the balance of trade positions in favour of Beijing has been a major concern in Islamabad. Though the overall trade between the two countries is relatively low, with about US $ 2 billion, China has a surplus trade of nearly $ 700 million. In addition, some Pakistani writers allege that China has been swarming their market with dum-ping of goods, competition from cheap products, refusal to devaluate Chinese Yuan, smuggling, etc.[47] On the other hand, a growing two-way trade between India and China had hit an all time high of $24.9 bn for 2006 underlining the economic prospects in India–China relations.

With these changes in bilateral relations, there have been certain assertions on the need for Pakistan to re-evaluate relations with China. Growing anti-American and anti-Indian sentiments in Pakistani society have often led to calls for closer Sino–Pak relations—even to the extent of signing a defence agreement with China, though the latter reportedly rejected such proposals twice in the past. This clearly shows how Pakistan has not been as critical ally in China's policies and perceptions as has been China in Pakistani security calculus. Under these current circumstances, according to a well-known columnist, M.B. Naqvi, Pakistan needs to factor in several aspects in its relations with China. Apart from following the thrust of the recent Chinese foreign policies, Pakistan also need to realize the changes in the Chinese policies on some of the core Pakistani aims, i.e. on Kashmir issue, for

> There is the danger that the Chinese might not remain as steadfast and dependable an ally as they used to be in the past. Indeed various factors have in fact intervened and the Sino–Pakistan friendship, although it has survived in substance, has undergone imperceptible changes, beginning with 1974

when the Chinese Foreign Minister adumbrated anew China's Kashmir policy of all places in New Delhi. The old stance began to change from 1974 onward and by now it is no longer a blind support to Pakistan's stance on Kashmir.[48]

Changes in the Sino–Pakistan relations have proved to be conducive to the growth of India–China relations. Chinese stance on the Kashmir issue, cross-border terrorism, 'neutrality' between India and Pakistan and the like has been noted by several Indians as significant changes in such security relations. The growing understanding on the multi-polarity issues, expansion in the economic relations have been highlighted in the India–China relations. Nevertheless, on some of the core issues like the continuing Chinese proliferation of weapons of mass destruction to Pakistan, there appears to be little progress, despite certain Chinese declarative statements in this regard. Chinese nuclear transfers to Pakistan, Indian nuclear tests in May 1998 and Chinese efforts to roll back Indian nuclear capability through the United Nations Security Council Resolution No. 1172 are well known. Further, Chinese WMD technology transfers, despite an international outcry, have exposed the limitations in India–China relations.

NOTES

1. See Jiang Zemin, 'Carrying Forward Generations of Friendly and Good-neighborly Relations and Endeavoring Towards a Better Tomorrow for all' 2 December 1996 at http://www.fmprc.gov.cn/eng/4288.html.
2. Yu cited in 'Pakistan President meets Chinese Military Delegation' *Xinhua* 6 May 1997 in *FBIS-CHI-97-126* 7 May 1997.
3. For a recent reiteration of this see the Joint Declaration of Pakistan President Pervez Musharraf and People's Republic of China President Hu Jintao on 5 November 2003 at http://www.chinadaily.com.cn/en/doc/2003-11/05/content_278489.htm accessed on 2 December 2003.
4. See Chinese Ministry of Foreign Affairs, 'China and Pakistan' at http://www.fmprc.gov.cn/eng/4408.html
5. Cai Bingkui, the Vice Chairman of the Chinese People's Liberation Army (PLA)'s think-tank, China Institute of International Strategic Studies and a member of the newly formed (in March 2003) Sino-Pakistani Friendship Forum, argued that such relations withstood the test of times because of the 'mutual trust' evolved between the two countries based on 'common understanding and common interests'

and on 'broad consensus in understanding the international and *regional* issues'. The Friendship Forum, composed of the two countries 'celebrities' and specialists, met for the first time in September 2003. Its goal is 'to promote and *enhance* the friendly ties between the two nations'. See 'The Solid Foundation for Sino-Pakistani Friendship: High Level of Mutual Trust' *International Strategic Studies* (Beijing) No. 1 Serial 71 (January 2004) pp. 25–7 [emphasis added].

6. People's Daily editorial summarizing Chairman Liu Shaoqi's 1966 visit to Pakistan. See 'Successful Tour of West Pakistan' *Peking [Beijing] Review* no. 15, 8 April 1966, p. 3.
7. In addition, the Pakistan Ministry of Foreign Affairs terms such a relationship 'exemplary' and is based on 'mutuality of interest'. See 'Pakistan's Relations with China' at http://www.forisb.org/pak-majorpowers.html and 'Relations with Major Powers and Regional Blocs' at http://www.forisb.org/fpolicy.html.
8. See 'Pakistani President meets Premier Zhu Rongji' 13 May 2001 at http://www.fmprc.gov.cn/eng/10261.html.
9. In interpreting the enduring Sino–Pak relations, several scholars have viewed such relations from different prisms. Samina Yasmin, for instance, in her Doctoral dissertation on the subject, contends that such relations should be viewed from 'dominant-bilateral equation' which is 'characterized by differing strategic outlooks and responses. . .'. See Samina Yasmeen, 'China and Pakistan in a Changing World' in K. Santhanam and Srikanth Kondapalli, eds., *Asian Security and China 2000–10*, New Delhi: Shipra Publications & IDSA, 2004, pp. 309–19. One aspect of the neo-realist perspective is in forming security alliances as cushions against drastic and negative changes of the international relations. John W. Garver has argued that the fundamental rationale in such bilateral relations has not changed despite the changes in the international scenario but that the 'entente cordiale remained unchanged'. According to him, 'China's overriding strategic interest in South Asia is to maintain a balance of power favourable to itself. Most fundamentally, this entails the perpetuation of Pakistan's existence as a strong centre of power in South Asia, independent of Indian domination . . .' See 'Sino–Indian Rapprochement and the Sino–Pakistan Entente', *Political Science Quarterly*, vol. 111, no. 2, 1996, pp. 323–47 (cited on pp. 324 and 345). However, while several elements of neo-realist perspective are visible in the Sino-Pak security relations, one crucial variable- i.e., explicit security/defence alliance—is missing in such relations.
10. See Zhang Zhengwen, *Zhongguo yu zhoubian zhuyao guojia guanxi* [*Relations between China and its Important Neighbours*], Nanjing: Nanjing University Press, 1993, Chapter 7, pp. 222–54; Lin Liangguang, Ye Zhengjia and Han Hua, eds., *Dangdai Zhongguo yu Nanya guojia guanxi* [Contemporary China and South Asian countries relations],

Beijing, Social Sciences Reference Publications, 2001, and *South Asia–China Dialogue*, Colombo: Marga Institute, 1983.

11. Territorial integrity of the country, reunification of the 'lost' territories, nation building and the like being the major aspects of the national interests of China in the last five decades of the people's republic, one could see a subtle change in the successive leadership's perceptions on these aspects. To elaborate, while several ideological-socialist, anti-colonial, Third World identities and the like have influenced PRC's early history, one finds a certain 'de-ideolisation' [or to be more precise, re-ideolization] and a concurrent enhancement in the emphasis on pursuing national interests is visible in the recent phase of the country's external outlook. See, for instance, on China's renewed interest in its national interests concept, see Chu Shulong, '*Zhongguo de guojia liyi, guojia liliang he guojia zhanlue*' [The National Interest, National Power and National Strategy of China] *Zhanlue yu Guanli* [*Strategy & Management*] (Beijing) no. 4, Issue 35, 1999, pp. 13–18.
12. For an excellent account of the policy shifts of China towards this region and the factors behind them, see Han Hua, 'China and South Asia' in K. Santhanam and Srikanth Kondapalli, eds., *Asian Security and China 2000–2010*, New Delhi: Shipra Publications & IDSA, 2004, pp. 290–300. See also Cheng Ruisheng, 'Sino-Indian Relations after India's Nuclear Tests' May 1999 at http://lxmi.mi.infn.it/~landnet/NSA/cheng.pdf
13. Samina Yasmeen, 'Sino-Pakistan Relations and the Middle East', *China Report*, vol. 34, nos. 3 and 4, 1998 pp. 327–43. For the geo-political link with Pakistan see Lin Liangguang, et.al., 2001, p. 114.
14. See John W. Garver, *Protracted Contest: Sino-Indian Rivalry in the Twentieth Century*, New Delhi: Oxford University Press, 2001; Swaran Singh, *China-South Asia: Issues, Equations, Policies*, New Delhi: Lancers Books, 2003, pp. 172–5; Mohan Malik, 'The China Factor in the India-Pakistan Conflict' *Occasional Paper Series*, Asia-Pacific Center for Security Studies, Honolulu, November 2002; Shao Zhiyong, 'India's Big Power Dream', *Beijing Review*, 12 April 2001, p. 10.
15. See An Qiguang, '*Zhonghua renmin gongheguo yu Bajisitan guanxi*' [PRC and Pakistan Relations] in Tang Jiaxuan, ed., *Zhongguo Waijiao Cidian* [Dictionary of China's Diplomacy], Beijing: World Knowledge Publications, 2000, pp. 552–3 (p. 552).
16. Bei Monong, *Zhou Enlai yu xin Zhongguo waijiao* [Zhou Enlai and New China's Diplomacy], Beijing: Chinese Communist Party School Publication, 2002, pp. 475–8.
17. Sardar Aseff Ahmad Ali, 'A New Nuclear Doctrine', *The Nation*, Islamabad, 25 June 1998 in *FBIS-TAC-98-176*. 26 June 1998.
18. At one point of time the Pakistani establishment reportedly collaborated with the American agencies in covert operations in Tibet in the

1950s. See, for instance, 'Dhaka Airstrip used by CIA for Covert Operation' *Independent*, Dhaka, 23 April 1999.

19. In fact, Pakistan has voted against the PRC in the UN on issues related to Taiwan and Tibet uprisings, invited Republic of China's leaders in 1959, imposed ban on the Communist Party of Pakistan in 1954, proposed joint defence agreement with India to counter PRC-USSR southward march in 1960 and the like. See UD Bhatkoti, 'Sino-Pakistan Relations: A Chinese Perspective' Unpublished paper presented at IDSA Fellows Seminar, New Delhi, 21 December 2002. Nevertheless, despite periodic protests, China did not take any critical action on Pakistan and appeared to have taken a lenient attitude towards the latter. See Lin Liangguan, et al., pp. 116–32.
20. Premier Zhou Enlai met Prime Minster Mohammad Ali at this Conference in April 1955. See Han Nianlong's account, 'Solid Sino-Pak ties', *Beijing Review*, no. 10, 5 March 1984, pp. 16–17. Han, the first Chinese Ambassador to Pakistan in 1951, underscores here that in the past three decades of bilateral relations, 'there has never been any conflict of fundamental interests', ibid., p. 17.
21. See 'Joint Statement by Chinese Premier Chou En-lai [Zhou Enlai] and Pakistan Prime Minister Suhrawardy', 24 December 1956 in *China Today*, 1957, vol. 1, no. 1, p. 6 as reprinted in G.V. Ambedkar and V.D. Divekar, eds., *Documents on China's Relations with South and South-East Asia (1949-1962)*, Bombay: Allied Publishers, 1964, pp. 31–2.
22. See Ambedkar and Divekar, p. 32.
23. For a comprehensive account of the Sino–Pak relations, though dated, see Anwar Hussain Syed, *China and Pakistan: Diplomacy of an Entente Cordiale*, Amherst: University of Massachusetts Press, 1974 and Yakov Vertberger, *The Enduring Entente: Sino-Pakistani Relations, 1960–80*, New York: Praeger, 1982.
24. While there were 13 'official friendly visits' [*zhengshi yuohao fangwen*] from China to Pakistan by the late 1990s, Pakistani leaders paid 21 such visit to China and one 'non-official friendly visit' [*fei zhengshi yuohao fangwen*] was made by General Zia in 1977. On the other hand, while the Chinese leaders made four 'stop over' [*jingting*] visits in Pakistan, Pakistani leaders made only three such visits to China. Zhou Enlai and Chen Yi 'transited' [*shunfang*] through Pakistan thrice, though Pakistani leaders transited through China only twice. In the same period, Chinese presidents made four 'state visits' [*guoshi fangwen*] to Pakistan, their Pakistani counterparts made nine such visits to China. It may also be noted that while there were very few visits in the 1950s, more of these, about 13 visits, were forthcoming in the formative stages of bilateral relations in the 1960s when substantial foundation was laid to the special relationship. While there were only about eight visits in the 1970s, these would shoot up to 22 in the 1980s reflecting the close

cooperation in the backdrop of the Soviet occupation of Afghanistan. This tempo was maintained with about 18 visits mutually in the 1990s. These nuances are reflected in Tang Jiaxuan, ed., *Zhongguo Waijiao Cidian* [*Dictionary of China's Diplomacy*], Beijing: World Knowledge Publications, 2000, pp. 552–3.

25. See 'Pakistan Prime Minister 's "Homecoming to Beijing"', *Beijing Review*, no. 10, 11–17 March , 1991 p. 5.
26. 'Boundary Agreement between Pakistan and China' 2 March 1963 in New China News Agency, 2 March 1963 as reprinted in Ambedkar and Divekar pp. 218–21. See also Lin Liangguang, et al., pp. 136–7 and Li Baojun, *Dangdai Zhongguo waijiao gailun* [*Introduction to Contemporary Chinese Foreign Policy*], (Beijing: Chinese People's University Publication, 1999, pp. 56–7. Prime Minster Nehru, while making a statement in the Indian Parliament said that by this agreement, China 'is directly interfering in Indo-Pakistan relations'. See Ibid., p. 223. While PRC maintained by this agreement that it would be re-opened later, recently reports indicated to a hardening of the Chinese government's position on the issue.
27. See Lin Liangguang. et al., 2001. Another writer, Wang Taiping, writing for the Ministry of Foreign Affairs history during the 1970s, termed the Sino-Pak objective as 'Common Struggle' [*gongtong touzheng*]. See Wang Taiping, ed., *Zhonghua renmin gongheguo wiajiaoshi 1970-1978* [PRC's Diplomatic History 1970–8], (Beijing: World Knowledge Publications, 1999, p. 110.
28. Details about the Chinese advice in General Mohammad Musa, *My Version: India Pakistan War 1965*, Lahore: Wajidalis, 1983, as quoted in Ahmad Faruqui, 'China's Defence Policy and Its Implications for Pakistan' web address when accessed <http://www. defencejournal.com/ 2001/feb/china-defence.htm> Marshal Chen Yi reportedly advised Pakistan, during his visit to Karachi on 4 September, to occupy Aknoor Fort first and deny India the advantages in the war. Altaf Gauhar's account of this period as well recounts Zhou Enlai's and Chen Yi's advice to visiting President Ayub Khan in September 1965 on the need to wage a protracted warfare, raising people's militia, etc. See Gauhar cited in 'Chinese Wisdom for Pakistan's Benefit', *The Dawn* reprinted in *The Asian Age* 26 July 1999 [the author is grateful to Sreedhar for alerting him to this source].
29. 'Chinese Government Leaders Condemn Indian Expansionism and Aggression against Pakistan', *Beijing Review*, no. 38, 17 September 1965, pp. 10–11 (Zhou cited on p. 10).
30. 'Chairman Liu Shao-chi [Shaoqi] visits Pakistan', *Beijing Review*, no. 14, 1 April 1966, p. 3. During this occasion President Ayub acknowledged the Chinese support 'in that hour of trial', Ibid p. 4.

31. 'Chairman Liu Shao-chi's Speech', *Beijing Review*, no. 14, 1 April 1966, p. 5 [emphasis added].
32. 'China–Pakistan Joint Communiqué' 31 March 1966 in *Beijing Review* no. 15 8 April 1966 p. 6.
33. See Wang Taiping, 1999 op.cit., p. 110
34. See Faruqui, op. cit. During the secret conclave between US Secretary of State Henry Kissinger and Chinese Permanent representative to the UN Huang Hua on 10 December 1971 at New York, the latter, after listening to the imminent fall of West Pakistan in the 1971 War, asserted 'China would never stop fighting as long as it had a rifle in its armoury; it would surely increase its assistance to Pakistan'. However, no direct and active Chinese support to Pakistan was forthcoming. As explained by Zhou Enlai to Kissinger in Beijing during Nixon's visit, 'Of course we don't interfere in other's internal affairs but Yahya really did not lead his troops in East Pakistan. Even though we assisted with armaments, we didn't send single military personnel, who the Soviet Union calls military adviser. We only sent people to train in the use of the planes and guns we sent and afterwards brought those people back.' Zhou cited in 'Chinese Wisdom for Pakistan's Benefit', *The Dawn*, reprinted in *The Asian Age*, 26 July 1999.
35. See Tang Jiaxuan, ed., op.cit., 2000, p. 552.
36. 'Joint Communiqué', *Beijing Review*, no. 20, 17 May 1974, pp. 10–11.
37. 'China, Pakistan Good Neighbors', *Beijing Review*, no. 27, 6 July 1987, pp. 7–8.
38. Musharraf suggested that his visit would 'further intensify' Sino–Pak cooperation. See 'Sino–Pakistani Ties Prosper', *China Daily*, 19 December 2001, p. 11.
39. See Xiao Hu, 'Pakistan with China in War on Terrorism', *China Daily*, 22 December 2001, p. 1.
40. See for this revelation by Jiang himself, 'President Jiang Zemin met with Pakistan Chief Executive Officer Pervez Musharaf', 10 September 2000 at http://www.fmprc.gov.cn/eng/5116.html [downloaded on 10 August 2002]
41. 'Jiang Backs Pak Role in Afghan Peace Aims', *China Daily*, 17 January 2002, p. 1.
42. See 'China, Pakistan Highlight Cooperation', *Xinhua*, 3 November 2003 at http://www.chinadaily.com.cn/en/doc/2003-11/03/content_278040.htm. According to the Chinese Foreign Ministry 2004 Yearbook, such contacts between the two countries would be expanded into other fields as well. Indeed, during President Musharraf's visit to China in late 2003, a cultural agreement was signed to include for cooperation in the period 2004–6. See *Zhongguo Waijiao 2004* [China's Diplomacy, 2004], Beijing: World Knowledge Publications, 2003, p. 201.

43. On Kashmir issue, Chinese initial position on self-determination of the Kashmiris gave way to the recent position of peaceful settlement of the dispute by India and Pakistan, respect of the Line of Control between the two countries, and that it is a bilateral issue to be solved by these countries. See Garver, op.cit., 2001, pp. 227–34.
44. Jiang Zemin, 'Carrying forward generations of friendly and good-neighborly relations and endeavoring towards a better tomorrow for all' 2 December 1996 at http://www.fmprc.gov.cn/eng/4288.html. Except for the two initial paragraphs related to Pakistan, this speech emphasized more on the Chinese efforts to build relations with all the South Asian countries. Nevertheless, Jiang said on this occasion that China and Pakistan had 'closely coordinated' international affairs and the 'tree of our political, economic, cultural, scientific and technological cooperation has born rich fruit'. Jiang cited in 'Jiang Pledges to Forge Pakistan "Partnership"' *AFP*, 2 December 1996 in *South China Morning Post*, 3 December 1996.
45. Indeed during PM Sharif's visit to China amidst the Kargil events, Jiang not only indicated China's moral and political support to Pakistan but also reportedly decided to conduct military exercises in Tibet. See 'What is Meant by China's Military Exercises' *Ausaf*, 1 July 1999 in British Broadcasting Corporation, *Selected World Broadcasts Far East* section (hereafter *SWB FE) SWB FE/3577* A/5, 3 July 1999. During this visit, Sharif told Chinese news agency *Xinhua* that 'Pakistani–Chinese relations are not only mutually beneficial, but also conducive to strengthening this region's stability and security. . . '. See 'Prime minister discusses relations with China, Kargil fighting', *Xinhua*, 27 June 1999 in *SBB FE/3573 A/5-6*, 29 June 1999. The Pakistan Foreign Secretary Shamshad Ahmad said, after the meetings between the Pakistani and Chinese premiers, that the 'Chinese support and solidarity with Pakistan is a living reality, which has been a source of strength for Pakistan and cause of regional peace'. Ahmad cited by *Radio Pakistan*, 30 June 1999 in *SWB FE/3575 A/5*, 1 July 1999. Prior to these meetings, the Pakistan foreign minister Sartaz Aziz, who visited China in the first week of June 1999 stated that China has assured Islamabad of its deep and abiding interest in and support for sovereignty, territorial integrity, independence and security of Pakistan. See 'Foreign Minister says China Agrees on Need for Kashmir Settlement' *Radio Pakistan*, 12 June 1999 in *SWB FE/3560 A/7*, 14 June 1999. Such phrases have been euphemisms for more Chinese aid in offing to Pakistan, especially in the military field. See also 'Airborne Units Conduct Training Exercise in Tibet', *Xinhua*, 29 June 1999 in *SWB FE/3577 G/13*, 3 July 1999.
46. Zha Chunming, '*Zhongba haijun shouci haishang soujiu yanxi*' [Sino–Pak First Naval Search and Rescue Operation at Sea] *Bingqi Zhishi*, Beijing, Issue 194, December 2003, pp. 28–9. China reportedly did not

send its fleet to the Indian Fleet Review in 2001 citing the absence of Pakistan Navy in the event. Nevertheless, Chinese ships visited Mumbai subsequently. This has been a far cry from the 1986 Chinese naval visits to Chittagong, Colombo and Karachi skipping Indian ports.

47. See Shimaila Matri, 'From China with Love', *Newsline*, October 2003, pp. 76–80
48. M.B. Naqvi, 'The Role China is Playing' at http://www.defencejournal.com/2001/feb/role-china.htm. However, Cai Bingqui of the PLA think-tank has argued recently that 'regional disputes should be properly resolved' in South Asia. See Cai, 2004, op.cit., p. 26.

ANNEXURE: CHINESE CONVENTIONAL ARMS TRANSFERS TO PAKISTAN

Type	Designation	No.	Year	Delivery	Remarks
Fighter aircraft	F-6	100	1971	–	–
Fighter/ground attack	A-5- Fantan A	98	1991	–	With PAF Squadrons nos. 7 16 and 26
Fighter	F-7M Airguard	40	1991	1983	Include 20 trainer versions
Fighter	F-7P Skybolt	40	1992	–	–
Fighter	FC-1	150	1991	2005	Joint venture between China and Pakistan. Israeli avionics reportedly incorporated.
Fighter	Super 7	–	1999	–	Rechristened FC-1. To be produced for Pakistan from 2004. Deal struck during PM Nawaz Sharif's visit to China in June 1999
Fighter	F-7	75	1983	1986–90	–
Fighter	F-7MG	46	2001	2002	–
Fighter	F-7MG	11	2002	2002	–
Fighter/ground attack	Q-5 Fantan-A	100	1984	1986	For final assembly in Pakistan
Fighter trainer	FT-7P	15	–	–	With PAF squadrons no. 2 at Masroor; no. 2 at Masroor; nos. 18 and 20 at Rafique and no. 25 at Mianwali
Trainer aircraft	K-8	–	1999	–	PRC offered for export to Egypt the the Karakoram K-8 jets. Previously 75 of these were offered also to Pakistan from 1991
Transport	Y-12	–	–	–	–
Portable Surface-to-Air-Missile	Hong Ying-5	300	1988	–	Arming M-113 Armoured Personnel Carriers
Portable SAM	Anza	450	1988	–	–

Portable SAM	QW-1 Vanguard	560	(1993)	1994-2000	Licence manufacturing as Anza-2
Portable SAM	HN-5A	–	1988	–	Licence-production under way in Pakistan
Main Battle Tank-2000	Al-Khalid (P90)	–	1999	–	Original agreement date back to 1988. Chinese NORINCO and Pakistan Heavy Industries Taxila are partners
MBT	T-59	975	(1975)	1978–90	–
MBT	T-69 II	450	1989	1991–3	Deal worth $1.2 billion
MBT	T-85 II	12	1990	1993	–
Anti-tank missile	Red Arrow 8	200	1989	1990–2002	Nearly 9,600 to be licence manufactured on the whole as Bakhtar Shikan
Towed Gun 85 mm	Type 56	190	–	–	–
Submarine	Romeo	2	1988	–	For final assembly in Pakistan
Fast Attack Craft Patrol	Hainan class	3	1977	–	–
Hydrofoil	Huzhun	3	1971	–	–
FAC patrol	Huangfen	–	1971	–	–
FAC gun	Shanghai	12	–	–	–
FAC	Hegu	4	1981	–	–
FAC	Huangfen	4	1984	–	–
FAC patrol	Hainan	4	1976–80	–	–
FAC torpedo	Huzhuan	4	–	–	–
Ship-to-Ship Missile system	C-801/802	4	1996	1997	For the 4 Pakistani Jalatas
ShShM	C-802	32	1996	1997	For the 4 Pakistani Jalatas

Source: *SIPRI Yearbook*, Oxford: Oxford University Press, Annual Series.

CHAPTER 4

China in Pakistan's Security Perceptions

SATYABRAT SINHA

The Second World War brought about momentous changes in the world and set about a chain of events on the Asian landmass. The wave of decolonization gave rise to many new states and partition of Britain's Indian Empire led to the creation of Pakistan in 1947. Many of these newly independent states were truncated and moved to recover traditional areas of influence within their modern territorial incarnation. In addition some of these new divisions were colonial constructions with little consideration to their historical, geographical or for that matter their cultural contexts. The colonial empire in India had held sway over the entire subcontinent, i.e. from the Khyber Pass on the Pakistan–Afghanistan frontier to Burma. The division of the erstwhile British colonial empire divided this natural geo-political region into two major states with a congenital conflictual relationship that hovers like a spectre on the Indian subcontinent in a nuclear avatar. Here lies the beginning of the China–Pakistan special relationship which this chapter tries to survey in terms of Pakistani perceptions and perspectives.

The Historical Backdrop

The situation is set around the time, when the victory of the Mao Zedong-led Communist militia—over the Nationalist army and the Japanese—lead to the establishment of the People's Republic of China (PRC) in October 1949. China had risen like the proverbial phoenix after a century of colonial harrying by the imperialist powers. As first thing in reviving its old profile, in the early 1950s, the PRC incorporated Tibet to consolidate its south-western frontier bringing it in physical contact with the subcontinent. For the first time, this brought into direct contact, the two ancient Asian civilizations of India and China which was to change, the history of their ties as also those of the peripheral small states.

In the ancient and medieval era, the Indian and Chinese civilizations had deep religious and spiritual contacts with each other but mostly existed with their backs to each other. Tibet was a part of China only from the thirteenth century and after that intermittently independent, autonomous or at times under Chinese suzerainty, thereby performing the crucial function of a buffer. But in the 1950s, Chinese troops moved into Tibet to consolidate their hold, and the Dalai Lama with thousands of Tibetans escaped to India in April 1959. This was the first of a series of events that led to the short border war in 1962 between India and China and lay foundations of the China–Pakistan special relationship.

At the global level, this was the time when the cold war had divided global politics into two blocs, the US-led West separated from the Soviet-led Communist East by the Iron and then Bamboo Curtains. The United States employed regional military pacts to encircle the Communist countries by setting up NATO in Europe, CENTO in the West Asia and SEATO in South-East Asia. Pakistan was part of two of these three US-led pacts, the CENTO and SEATO. By the late 1950s, Sino–Soviet relations were plummeting and the break finally occurred after the river Ussuri crisis in 1969. This Sino–Soviet split was also to further reinforce China–Pakistan relations.

At the regional level, the newly colonized Afro–Asian states had emerged as a third group, overlapping with the Cold War blocs, better known as the Non-Alignment Movement or the NAM led by Asian leaders and notably Jawaharlal Nehru. The NAM was not very effective but at times this mass of newly emergent Asian and African nations managed to hold attention and carry their weight on a significant number of Third World issues. The NAM states participated in Afro–Asian conferences in the early 1950s to interact with each other and find a way to manoeuvre amidst the bitter cold war conflict. The PRC was an important participant at the first Afro–Asian conferences and this third front was a significant target of the Chinese strategy to open up its communication lines independent of the Soviet Union. It was at the Afro–Asian conference in Bandung 1955 that the support to have the Sino–Pakistan entente began. This chapter though traces the evolving Pakistani perceptions of China from much earlier.

Interface of Ideology & Islam

A basic understanding of Pakistan foreign relations begin with the formulation that Pakistan is an 'insecure small state' that perceives itself as disadvantaged. In such a strategic situation, Pakistan has to face a 'real and continuous threat' from a larger India, with its survival at stake. India is far more powerful than any combination of other states within this Asian sub-system and constructing a force within it to balance India was not feasible for Pakistan. Therefore, over the years, a central element of Pakistani policy has been to reach beyond South Asia to find support that might offset Indian dominance. This central element can be discerned in Pakistani efforts to avoid any bilateral arrangements that would put Pakistan in a one-on-one relationship with India. Pakistan foreign policy, in that context, was guided by a simple motive: to preserve national integrity.[1] The religious foundations of the state of Pakistan were expected to bring it friends among the Muslim countries. But as Javed Burki points out that,

> [I]n 1947, Islamic resurgence was still three decades into the future. Egypt, Turkey, and Indonesia all had their own problems. Afghanistan, the Muslim country with a long border with Pakistan, coveted some of its territory.[2]

The guideposts for a state's foreign policy are geographical compulsions and power realities, irrespective of ideological differences or social systems. However, given the context of cold war and especially so in Pakistan until 1962, ideology was an unusually important element. The ideological factor in foreign policy translated into practise meant preference for the Western countries and dislike of Communism.[3] Pakistan always regarded India as the greatest threat to itself but representative opinion in Pakistan for several years also regarded Communism as a serious threat to Islamic ideology. The poet Iqbal in a letter to the daily *Zamindar* of Lahore on 'Islam and Bolshevism' wrote: 'To hold Bolshevist views, in my opinion, is to place oneself outside the pale of Islam.'[4] Iqbal also took a dismal view of a nation that does not believe in God:

Denied celestial grace a nation goes
No further than electricity or steam;
Death to the heart, machines stand sovereign,
Engines that crush all sense of human kindness.[5]

Some opinions held by the Pakistan leadership with regard to communism are cited to illustrate the religious contempt on one hand and the fear of a large and looming communist bloc and ideology on the other. In 1950, for instance, Prime Minister Liaquat Ali Khan proposed that the US should encourage territorial guarantees to India and Pakistan, to 'keep out the potential menace of Communism'.[6] A member in the Constituent Assembly of Pakistan on a discussion on the Korean War stated that, 'Islam is against Communism and Pakistan cannot allow Communism to capture one country after another'.[7] On the Soviet Union's protest over American arms aid to Pakistan, *Dawn* formulated six charges against the 'Kremlin bosses', the fifth of which was that 'they have reduced the Russian people to a sub-human species because without complete freedom of thought man cannot remain man', material advantages are 'not adequate for the robbery of that divine spark called the soul which is the principal factor dividing man from beast' and, it added further that 'they do not believe in God and cannot therefore have any morals, because "religion"—whatever it may be—is the basis of all moral codes'.[8]

The then Prime Minister, Suhrawardy, is quoted as stating that the Cold War was a result of the Communist attempt to impose their ideology on the rest of the world and should Pakistan become a satellite of Russia 'we shall never be able to get out of the control of our master . . . we have seen . . . the manner in which East Germany suffered, and in which Hungary has suffered.'[9] Former President Ayub Khan went a step further and chalked out for special study on 'how can the offensive of Hinduism and Communism against the ideology of Islam be combated?'[10] Even after 'normalization' of relations with Communist countries, Ayub Khan in his autobiography calls Communism 'a panacea for an acutely diseased society'.[11] Such extreme opinions were a reflection of the confusion regarding Pakistan's strategic orientation that had merely the religious variable available. We also have evidence of Prime Minister Liaquat Ali seeking territorial guarantees from the United States to keep the communist menace out of both, India and Pakistan, in stark contrast to what President Ayub seeks.

Significantly, when Communism was reviled and abused during those early Cold War years, what was remarkable is the absence of any mention of China and it is the Soviet Union that lay at the end of all Pakistani criticism. There could be two explanations for this remarkable omission. The first and the simpler explanation is that

Communism during this time was identified with the Soviet Union, identical to a biological species type. The other explanation lies in geopolitics, with a resurgent China on their northern frontier, Pakistan was not willing to take any chances of any direct confrontation with the Asian giant.

BETRAYAL BY THE UNITED STATES

Soon after independence, when Pakistan stood virtually alone with its negligible military capabilities, the need for political backing and for modern military equipment led Pakistan to join the Central Treaty Organization (CENTO) and the South-East Asian Treaty Organization (SEATO). However, US–Pakistan ties utlimately were undermined, when Washington saw a chance to draw India closer to itself through economic assistance and support against the growing Chinese threat. This was also window of opportunity for Pakistan and young Zulfikar Ali Bhutto was the one to recognize it.[12] The deteriorating relations between India and China had already created an opening for Pakistan, and it strengthened those with perceptions about evolving a remarkable and durable political relationship with China.

Pakistan's strategic community in the years between the Chinese occupation of Tibet and the 1962 China–India war had also come to a realization that it was a mistake to put all eggs in one (American) basket. Khalid Bin Sayeed calls Chinese behaviour in the eyes of Pakistanis as 'politically impeccable', especially when seen in the light of American betrayal.[13] But Sayeed's formulation illustrates the Pakistani antipathy towards communism when he states that since Pakistan was surrounded by such hostile neighbours as India, Afghanistan and the USSR and 'with her friends like the United States and other members of the Commonwealth so far away, *what else could Pakistan do except to explore areas of understanding with the Communist Chinese*'? (emphasis added)[14]

Thus, it was the breaching of the *Hindi-Chini bhai bhai* bond that brought the dramatic turnabout in Pakistani perceptions. First, the Pakistani elite was unsure of US support in the event of an Indian invasion. Moreover, military aid to India after the war in 1962 forced Pakistan to reconsider its strategic choices. The events were swift and almost simultaneous and this is when the China–Pakistan border negotiations began. The border agreement negotiations received impetus after the 1962 war. As to the reasons for this momentum,

Khalid Bin Sayeed states that the, '. . . obvious answer was that since they (PRC) had been branded in the West as an aggressor in their border dispute with India, they were interested in changing this image and presenting themselves as a reasonable and friendly power'.[15] As to why the Pakistanis showed such urgency Sayeed says that:

> One could not say that it was merely out of spite for India that such an agreement was arrived at. An important consideration was that Pakistan might be subjected to a similar Chinese attack, particularly when the Chinese had good roads on their side, if a border agreement were not reached. Such Pakistani fears were also disclosed by Foreign Minister Bhutto in his speech in Dacca on April 8, 1963.[16]

The Sino–Pakistan border agreement had all the legitimacy of an upright accord but beneath the surface lingered the tectonics of the changing strategic situation that both China and Pakistan were keen to exploit. Pakistan took the view that the hot war between India and China would be of a short duration while their cold war had long-term prospects. Therefore, it was in Pakistan's interest to accord 'the right attitude of respect' to a power, which while capable of inflicting crushing and humiliating defeat on India, but was not likely to penetrate their country politically in the near future.[17] For the Chinese the border agreement was one part of a coherent Chinese policy to seek support through Pakistan among neighbouring Muslim countries in view of unrest among the Muslim tribes in Xinjiang and the Russian attempts to exploit it. China soon emerged as a friendly power in the eyes of the Pakistanis. And the *Dawn* turned into a powerful advocate of Pakistan's friendly policy towards China and agnostic communism was made palatable in its equal intolerance of all religions. The *Dawn* argued that, 'India always displayed implacable hatred for Muslims, whereas Red China at her worst was against all religions, but of all religions only one, namely Islam, is not singled out for degeneration'.[18]

The credit for taking the lead in changing Pakistani perceptions and for opening up to the PRC is given to Zulfikar Ali Bhutto. Stanley Wolpert in his biography of Bhutto states that Bhutto's incisive mind, discerned the changes in the Asian strategic environment while it was happening and moved early to gain maximum benefit out of it.[19] It was at the United Nations (UN) session in 1960 that Bhutto broke ranks with the US position on China, by abstaining rather than voting against China's membership in the world forum. On US dissatisfaction when the Foreign Minister, Qadir retracted Bhutto's discretionary powers on future UN votes, Bhutto wired home, 'I feel that the time has come for Pakistan to adopt an attitude in the United Nations more consistent with its recognition of the Peking regime than has been the case since 1954'.[20]

Bhutto bolstered his China argument by noting how important it was to 'strengthen our position' among the Third World Asians and Africans. He viewed Sino–Pakistani friendship not only as a counter to Indian hegemony but as one part of his blueprint for an Afro–Asian 'third force'.[21] Zulfikar Ali Bhutto was the foreign minister when the Sino–Pakistan boundary agreement was concluded on 2 March 1963 that was to become the cornerstone of Pakistan's strongest, most important Asian alliance.

Mapping Perceptions

After this general background of the settings amidst which the entente was negotiated we will now turn our attention to Pakistani writings on foreign and security policy that reflects their perceptions and interpretation. Khalid Bin Sayeed in an article, mentions that apart from idelogical, political and material factors, there is what he calls a 'ruling passion' in foreign policy. He further mentions that:

> Every country has a ruling passion in her foreign policy. When one calls it a passion, one is not suggesting that this is something entirely emotional or irrational. . . . Indeed very few countries were born in an atmosphere so surcharged with intense ill-will and mutual hatred as Pakistan was in 1947 as a result of the partition of the sub-continent. Almost every action of Pakistan can be interpreted as being motivated by fear of India.[22]

Former diplomat, M.A.H. Ispahani, in an article, begins with an early formulation of Jinnah to state how Pakistani Foreign Policy (PFP) was one of friendliness and goodwill towards all the nations of the world. Ispahani states that, Pakistan made every effort to keep its head above the water and maintain self-respect. Friendly cooperation from the more advanced countries in the task of development was welcome, but no pacts or alliances were envisaged.[23] Ispahani calls the change in policy after 1953, when Pakistan entered into a military alliance with the United States as 'American Penetration' and further states that, 'This was the thin end of the wedge which marked the penetration of alien influences into foreign policy. And with the passage of each month the wedge was driven farther and farther in.'[24] Ispahani is of the view that the military alliances worked against Pakistani interest. First SEATO, the first military pact that Pakistan entered into, envisaged aggression only from Communist countries and Pakistani efforts to include a provision to the effect that its signatories would stand up against aggression from whatever quarter it came—Communist or non-Communist (read India)—failed.[25] His conclusions are extremely illuminating:

> The sponsoring power (USA) was anxious not to incur the displeasure of India . . . Pakistan thus entered into an alliance to resist aggression from a quarter which, despite ideological differences, had posed no threat to its security. Neither the USSR nor China, the two leading Communist countries, had done anything, by word or deed, to make us fear that our freedom was in danger at their hands.[26]

The literature confirms that although Pakistan was not well disposed towards Communism, it welcomed the end of civil strife in China and the establishment of the PRC in 1949. But due to political instability at home and foreign domination, for almost a decade, Sino–Pakistan relations did not rise above the humdrum of routine diplomacy.[27] During this period, three main areas of tension in Sino–Pakistan have been identified: Pakistan's inability, from 1953 until 1961, to support China's admission to the United Nations; Pakistan's alliances with the United States the purpose of which was apparently to effect the containment of China; Pakistan's occasional endorsement of the American two-China policy.

In Anwar Syed's opinion, 'That in fact the Chinese were not annoyed quiet as much as they might have been must be attributed partly to their own policy of restraint and partly to the ingenuity of Pakistani diplomats.'[28] This points to the element of ambivalence that characterized Pakistan's China Policy until 1961 and proverbially speaking provided the fig leaf to mask the confusion in Pakistan's elite perceptions about China. Syed states that while Pakistan entertained no ill-will towards China, it was unable to support China on certain political questions due to the exigencies of their economic and military dependence on the United States. But despite this, the Chinese did not support India's position over the Kashmir dispute nor did they support Afghanistan over the Pakhtunistan issue.[29]

Most scholars point to Mohammed Ali Bogra's conversations with Zhou Enlai at the Bandung conference to illustrate early Pakistani position towards China. Bogra is stated to have told Zhou Enlai that Pakistan apprehended no aggression from China. The Bogra–Zhou talks infused warmth in the Sino–Pakistan relations and during 1955–6, numerous delegations exchanged visits. But according to Anwar Syed, the warmth did not last due to political instability in Pakistan and their dependence on US economic and military aid.[30] The Chinese actions in Tibet in 1959 and the events that followed evoked the fears of a Communist threat to the subcontinent. While India's relations with China suffered a serious setback, Pakistan too seemed pre-occupied with the growing Chinese Communist threat. It is in this fluid Asian geopolitical context which was 'transitional and exploratory' that Pakistani writers would like to judge Field Marshal Ayub Khan's proposals for a 'joint defence arrangement with India' against the threat from the North.[31]

In consequence, one cannot fail to read the apologetic tone in the Pakistani move towards China, which is reflected adequately in the early writings on the coming Sino–Pakistan entente. Ayub Khan's proposal for joint defence against the threat from the North is reflective of the general uncertainty in Pakistan's strategic orientation.

The Kashmir Question

In Pakistan's foreign and security policy, Kashmir has been and remains a 'core' issue, similar to the centrality that Taiwan commands in the China's. Kashmir involves ideological, identity, and territorial competition for both India and Pakistan. Kashmir has for the last sixty years been 'the touchstone by which friendship and animosity are tested'[32] in determining Pakistan's foreign and security policy and perceptions.

The PRC adopted a neutral stand on Kashmir in the years prior to the breakdown in Sino–Indian ties. A Mao Zedong statement of 1957 that China was neutral in its attitude to the rival claims to Kashmir was received with great jubilation in Pakistan, as it would not help India.[33] China's endorsement of Pakistan's *de facto* claim to Kashmir appears only during the border negotiations but, 'it never said or did anything—not even in the heyday of Sino–Indian friendship—that could even remotely be interpreted as betraying an anti-Pakistani disposition on the question of Kashmir'.[34] In fact, the importance of the 1963 Sino–Pakistan border agreement was the change from the earlier non-committal Chinese stand on Kashmir to a full support for

Pakistani claims.[35] After this the Chinese began to categorically support the 'Kashmiri people's right' to self-determination. It is important to note this change of position by the Chinese as it could have been cited to advocate a plebiscite solution of Taiwan, and this fact did not go unnoticed in Pakistan and was greatly appreciated.[36]

1965 India–Pakistan War

The war in 1965 permits a close examination of Pakistani perceptions of the Chinese role in India–Pakistan relations. The 1965 war is the first important crisis after the breakdown in Sino–Indian relations and the increased warmth in Sino–Pakistan ties. In the writings from Pakistan, this event is marked as a 'landmark'[37] in the development of Sino–Pakistan relations. Amongst the nations that 'condemned' India and supported Pakistan vigorously, China spoke the loudest. In particular, the Chinese during the war asserted that India's attack on Pakistan and 'intrusions' into Chinese territory were all a part of an Indian 'design of aggressive expansionism'. The frequency of Chinese complaints rose 'sharply' during the period of the war, which prompted notes to the Indian government as an ultimatum.[38] The Pakistani feeling that China alone was a reliable friend in any confrontation with India was confirmed during the war. In the words of Mohammed Ayoob,

> Even more important than the verbal support for Pakistan in the Indo-Pakistani war was the increased activity of the armed forces of China on the Sino–Indian border at that time with a view to obliging India to keep a large part of its army stationed on its border with Tibet and thus taking some of the pressure off Pakistan.[39]

A more cautious Pakistani reading of the situation was to suggest that while the

> Chinese were watching the situation closely, they would not risk for Pakistan what they had not risked for North Vietnam . . . China's impact on the conflict issued precisely from the uncertainty surrounding its intentions. . . . There can be no doubt that Chinese threats did influence Soviet and American behaviour. These two powers would have liked to support India. Had they been unencumbered by the Chinese factor, they would have felt free not only to aid India but also to put a great deal more pressure on Pakistan than they were actually able to do.[40]

Some of these writings also draw attention to the fact that the Chinese 'extended' ultimatum to India expired on 22 September and the ceasefire between India and Pakistan came into effect on 23 September.[41] With the acceptance of the ceasefire by Pakistan, the PRC climbed down from its provocative posture immediately. Such coordinated behaviour was read in Pakistan as based on a 'powerful community of interests between Pakistan and China'. But caveats were issued that this did not mean that Pakistan would become a satellite of China, even though it needed China as a counterpoise to India. Ayub Khan before accepting the UN ceasefire, made a short visit to China to evolve a common strategy.[42] The Chinese support during the war greatly increased Chinese popularity in Pakistan, especially in the attitude of the 'public', which was deeply appreciative:

> Karachi students, carrying huge portraits of Chou En-lai and Chen Yi, called on the Chinese ambassador to thank him. . . . Lawyers sent off a telegram to Chou . . . Poets wrote laudatory verses about China. . . . She (China) was represented as a mighty power devoted to the maintenance of peace and justice in Asia.[43]

But there also existed strong dissenting interpretations. Anwar Syed, notes that despite the popular euphoria, officialdom and major English-language newspapers in the country were cautious and underplayed popular sentiment.

> Rarely, if ever, did they (Officials and English newspapers) single out China when acknowledging help Pakistan received from abroad. They mentioned China along with Indonesia, Iran, Turkey and others. While China was referred to as 'our great neighbour', terms of affection such as 'fraternal' and 'brotherly' were reserved for Indonesia and other Muslim countries.[44]

Syed is probably the only scholar who maps such a strong dissenting note about the Chinese role in the war when he states that Rawalpindi 'ended up with an adverse, rather than a favourable, balance' on the Chinese role. In Anwar Syed's words,

> For obvious reasons of domestic and foreign politics, Pakistani officials would prefer not to acknowledge that they were in any measure disconcerted by the excessive vigor of the Chinese role during their conflict with India. However, some observers-reporting from Rawalpindi, London and Washington—suggested that policy makers in Pakistan were indeed annoyed and embarrassed. Chinese 'over-reaction' had encouraged the 'collusion'

theory and tended to damage what remained of Pakistan's good relations with the United States. . . . He (Ayub Khan) was making conciliatory gestures to India, and inviting the United States to play a vigorous role, not unlike that of a ward leader or a village elder, in the affairs of the subcontinent. Some commentators interpreted these sentiments as 'a virtual slap', which had all along endeavoured to expel American influence from Asia. . . . The Chinese did not secure their . . . objectives . . . neither has Pakistan been 'lured' away from the United States.[45]

Thus, the cleavage in the Pakistani perceptions that resulted from the Chinese role in the war is evident even during this golden period of China–Pakistan relations. The Chinese though, in a convergence of their global and regional strategy, saw Pakistan as an important ally. The increasing Chinese role in the subcontinent offered choices to Pakistan that did not exist before. Pakistan till then ensconced in the Western camp, was re-thinking its strategic choices till the 1965 war hastened the Sino–Pak flirtation into a lasting relationship.

The period from the 1962 border war to about the late 1970s was a low period in Sino–Indian ties. The visit by Foreign Minister Atal Bihari Vajpayee in 1979 and the change of guard in Beijing with Deng Xiaoping ushering in the new economic policies resulted in a strategic shift in China's international politics and also in China's Kashmir policy. References to self-determination in Kashmir were avoided and the Shimla agreement of 1971 and United Nations (UN) resolutions were the catch phrases. These developments occurred during the low intensity conflict against the Soviet occupation of Afghanistan that saw the peak of the US–China–Pak alignment. Pakistan showed 'understanding' of this shift and interpreted it as a 'tactical change' rather than a withdrawal of support.[46] But by the late 1990s, the diminishing support on the Kashmir issue had developed into an 'irritant' in Pak–China relations that had to be taken care of. In Fazal-ur-Rahman's words,

It was very disappointing for a majority of Pakistanis, when President Jiang Zemin, while addressing Pakistan's Senate in December 1996, made no reference to the Kashmir issue . . . and advised Pakistan to put the thorny issues aside and develop relations with India in less contentious sectors like trade and economic cooperation . . . indifference on the Kashmir issue was hurting for the Pakistanis.[47]

China's relations with Pakistan also have an important concern with regard to the role of foreign support to separatist elements in the

Xinjiang province, in what has been termed as the 'Taliban Syndrome' by Ehsan Ahrari.[48] After the Taliban captured power in Afghanistan, in the mid-1990s, it encouraged and abetted the rise in radical Islamist trend in the domestic and foreign policy of Pakistan and the contagious Central Asian states. The theological aspect of the Taliban made China apprehensive about it acting as a catalyst for Islamic revival in the disturbed province of Xinjiang. A PRC circular of late 1999 (same year as the Kargil war) believes that there is strong reason to suspect that Uighur separatists receive help from abroad. Moreover, explosives used in separatist activities in Xinjiang were of Chinese markings originally 'exported to Pakistan and then re-exported to Afghanistan' which found its way back to the Uighur separatists through the transnational jihadi link.[49] The Chinese then made discreet demands on Pakistan to control the jihadis and this also prompted maintenance of the special relationship as a means to be able to influence Pakistan.

It was the 'Taliban syndrome' that made the Chinese uncomfortable about the Kargil intrusions in 1999. In Pakistani perceptions, the neutral Chinese stand on Kashmir was further attenuated by fear of jehadi Islam during the Kargil war. In an article on the Kargil war, Farzana Shakoor, writes that

> . . . the Chinese response to Pakistan's appraisal of the situation could be best described as one of neutrality. The reasons are to be sought in the reservations that China always have had with regard to the insurgency in Kashmir. It feared that the movement might spill over into its Muslim dominated province of Xinjiang.[50]

1971 War: East Pakistan Secedes

The 1960s decade had seen the development of military relations through which the Sino–Pak bilateral ties acquired its depth. The United States banned all military supplies to India and Pakistan when the 1965 war broke out. For India, the Soviet Union was by this time a trusted partner and Pakistan found its military hardware support in China. By the time of the war and the emergence of Bangladesh in 1971, the contemporary great power interaction had altered and this in turn influenced the Chinese role in the 1971 war. The United States–PRC *rapprochement* mediated by Pakistan was imminent and Indira Gandhi prior to taking the East Pakistan gauntlet concluded a treaty of Peace and Friendship with the USSR.

Mohammad Habib Sidky in his article, 'Chinese World Strategy and South Asia: The China Factor in Indo–Pakistani Relations', writes that after a letter written by Zhou Enlai to Yahya Khan in April 1971 and until the outbreak of war in December, Chinese statements on the events were most notable for their absence.[51] The letter officially disclosed the Chinese government's stand towards the explosive situation brewing and assured Pakistan of full support. By December 1971 when war broke out, Chinese statements toned down rhetoric directed against 'American imperialism', which were also mirrored by a change in US attitude.[52] The Russian threat brought about a dramatic convergence of interests between the United States and the PRC.

Only in their final statement did the PRC, recognize for the first time the existence of a serious refugee problem in East Pakistan.[53] Pakistani writers are also puzzled by the rationale behind Peking's extension of moral and material support to Pakistan rather than to the Bangladesh movement, a national liberation movement. Sidky believes that the

> ... separatist movement (was) perpetrated by a small group of persons 'who want to sabotage the unification of Pakistan'.... Peking denounced the Bangladesh movement as a separatist uprising that was morally and materially encouraged and supported by an aggressive imperialist foreign power (India), which strived for the dismemberment of Pakistan. This in itself rendered any remote possibility for Peking's support of the secessionists in East Pakistan as inconceivable.[54]

One article specifically mentions that the Chinese support to Pakistan was based upon *specific* grounds. Naveed Ahmad, states that

> Peking did not identify itself with the Pakistan Government's policies and actions in East Pakistan, but it condemned outside interference in the crisis without reservation. A *People's Daily* commentary makes the scope of Peking's support to Pakistan quite clear. It stated that the 'Chinese Government and people will, as always, firmly support the Pakistan Government and people in their just struggle to safeguard state sovereignty and national independence....' *This statement avoided mentioning 'territorial integrity'*.[55]

Another striking feature was a Chinese statement at the UN that openly referred to the question of material assistance for Pakistan. Thus, China was moving beyond verbal declarations of support to Pakistan during war. This Chinese material assistance was of significant consequence, especially after the discontinuance of American military shipments yet again in March 1971. The military dependence of Pakistan had begun in the aftermath of the American arms embargo in the 1965 war.[56] Similar to the 1965 war the Chinese protested Indian border violations through two official notes. Sidky writes that however, the

> . . . warnings failed to bring any pressure on India and were not effective whatsoever. These protests were untimely and considerably milder than Peking's well-timed, harsh remonstration of 1965 which had threatened India with 'grave consequences'. Re-emerging upon the international arena of diplomacy after a period of self-withdrawal from global affairs during the Cultural Revolution, China in 1971 was determined to move cautiously and along sure grounds as it adjusted to a changed global environment. The support of the PRC for Pakistan in 1971, then, was of a somewhat limited nature.[57]

In Ahsen Chaudhri's view,

> . . . China could not act in 1971, the way it did in 1965, to relieve pressure on Pakistan as the Soviet troops equipped with nuclear weapons were concentrating along the Chinese border and the Soviet retaliatory attack could not be easily deterred.[58]

Remarkably, the constraints on Chinese role in the 1971 war were well appreciated by Pakistan. As another Pakistani writer puts it,

> China did what it could to support Pakistan in the United Nations, and after the war, it helped to pick up the pieces.[59]

Naveed Ahmad strikes another dissenting note with the general writings on the 1971 war from Pakistan in stating that support to Pakistan was passive also because China's interest mainly lay in the latter's western wing. Ahmad further states that Peking's central goal was not that Pakistan remains united, but that West Pakistan remains independent of India and friendly to China. And though China continued to supply arms to Pakistan, the government headed by Yahya Khan could not persuade Peking to promise active military support in case another Indo-Pakistan war broke out.[60]

The effort in this essay has been to examine the origin and the growth of this 'special relationship' between China and Pakistan from the point of view of the Pakistanis. This was necessary to lay bare the strategic imperatives that underlined it in order to examine the possible future development. The effort is also to provide insights into the nature of the relationship as it remains an impending block for India in its attempt to develop a beneficial and trustable partnership with China.

Sino–Pak Collusion and India

With the benefit of hindsight, it would be safe to assert that the Beijing–Islamabad entente evolved out of the convergence of China's South Asian strategy and its global strategy after the falling trust in Sino–Soviet relations. Some scholars are of the view that China's relations with Pakistan have to be understood within the context of South Asia's relevance to China's counter encirclement strategy.[61] Beijing saw its support for Pakistan as serving the double duty, since a stronger Pakistan could resist the erstwhile Soviet Union and also counter Indian pressure.[62] In the post-1962 phase a plethora of agreements were reached between China and Pakistan to buttress the entente on a variety of issues ranging with the December 1962 boundary agreement inclusive of trade, Most Favoured Nation (MFN) status and air travel in 1963.[63] The Sino–Pakistan strategic entente has also demonstrated remarkable tensile strength, considering the nature and sweep of changes in international politics since it was negotiated. Pakistan played an important role in the Sino–US *rapprochement*, as also in the Washington–Beijing alliance in opposing the Soviet occupation of Afghanistan.

The nature of this relationship while predominantly politico-military has persisting economic links. The terms of military transfers in the past were usually extremely liberal as loans and on credit, however of late these transfers have taken on a commercial aspect.[64] Fascinatingly there appears to be some evidence of the fact that Pakistan was not merely a buyer of Chinese military technology but also a junior partner in various defence projects and that the Pakistanis also provide technical inputs to Chinese defence projects.[65] During the Cold War years when the PRC had no access to Western technology, the Pakistani experience with American hardware exposed the Chinese to cutting edge technology and a number of reverse engineering projects.

The Sino–Pak equation assumed its notoriety when in the final decade of the twentieth century; American intelligence disclosed that the military transfers included nuclear devices, and ballistic missile technology. The motivation for the transfer by the Chinese was understood as an effort to maintain a balance of power in Indian subcontinent by preventing India from gaining an upper hand over Pakistan. The Chinese assistance to Pakistan's nuclear weapons and ballistic missile programmes was to counterbalance India's development of new weapons systems. Thus, India's preoccupation with Pakistan would box India to the South Asian region.

In the present context, while the Cold War rationale of the Sino–Pak special relationship remains a subject matter of historians, and though a rectification of sorts has taken place, yet some areas of concern persist. Unlike the immediate past, Sino–Indian relations are the key to China's South Asia strategy and Sino–Pak ties have assumed second position. But despite the change in China's India policy with the *rapprochement* in the early 1980s, the process has been slow and has traversed some low points. One of the key troughs in the relationship apart from the border conflict is China's special relationship with Pakistan and the continuing military transfers. The PRC asserts that the Sino–Pak relations are regular state to state interactions.

In the aftermath of the collapse of the Soviet Union and with the United States as the triumphant superpower both India and China had to examine their strategic orientation. For India, the trusted ally was gone and its successor, Russia, for various reasons could not play the assuring role. In case of the Chinese, the anti-Soviet, US–China alliance had lost its *raison d'être* while the decade old liberalized Chinese economy needed American cooperation to continue on its growth trajectory. The Indian state, hesitantly to begin with, followed the path of economic liberalization and a warming of relations with the United States took place over the 1990s. The new Chinese mantra has been to reduce tensions around its periphery in order to stabilize the 'peaceful international environment' for its ambitious four modernization programme.[66]

The opportunities and the competition for markets and investment ushered in by the liberalization processes in both China and India promoted and made them more open to economic interactions. Moreover, the presence of a single global power with which both the countries had more differences than similarities also necessitated political exchange even if there were tentative. The two sides interacted on issues of convergence like multi-polarity, opposing US unilateralism and common strategies on trade issues at the World Trade Organization (WTO).

This was the new reality that the old Sino–Pakistan ties had to face. It required a reinvention of the relationship in light of changing state to state relations which was dominantly driven by economic exchanges with politics taking second place. In such circumstances and given the chaos that Pakistan was during the decade after the collapse of the Soviet Union, India has been a better destination for Chinese products and collaboration. Over the first decade of the new century, the gap between the subcontinental rivals grew exponentially in India's favour driven by the services industry in general and the software engine in particular. The Chinese manufacturing economy prompted greater convergence with India.

The growing bonhomie in China–India ties and lately Beijing's attempts to distance itself from Islamabad has been favourable to India. However, even during this period China has not completely abandoned Pakistan and reports state that economic and military support to the crisis afflicted Pakistani state continued unabated.[67] During this period the Indian nuclear tests in 1998 was perhaps the most serious challenge to the even handed Chinese South Asian strategy. Owing to their complicity in Pakistan's nuclear development, China followed two approaches, the first was to go on a limited (so as not to damage the embryonic ties) verbal offensive against India and second to cooperate with the United States to capitalize on their common interests and deflect references to its own proliferation culpability. However, after the crisis caused by the nuclear tests had faded, the Chinese followed the even handed approach in India–Pakistan confrontations and specifically in the military stand off during 2001–2.

The second defining event after the end of the Cold War was the consequence of the 9/11 terrorist attacks which brought about unprecedented American presence in Central Asia and South Asia. Thus, while these developments had negative implications for the Chinese, the positives of its continued peaceful rise have served to increase Chinese influence in the region. The American presence was expected to shore up the Pakistani state, suppress Islamic militancy and also keep India and Pakistan out of war without any cost to China.[68]

Indo–US Nuclear Agreement and Sino–Pak Ties

The increased warmth in Indo–US relations owing to the convergence of interests brought about an unparalleled state of affairs between the two 'estranged democracies'.[69] In most discussions these commonality of interests[70] are centred on the containment of a rising China.[71] But, it would be self-defeating to categorize the warmth in Indo–US relations posited on the China threat theory and disregard the mutual benefits that both countries would harvest. The most important foreign policy imperative for all states in the world is to cooperate with the US given its politico-economic-military power. Strategic partnerships appear to be the order of the day and cut across the globe and these soft alliances are different from those that existed in the period prior to the great wars in Europe as a substantial amount of hedging of bets is present in the partnerships. Reflecting this, the three large Eurasian land powers, China, Russia and India have over the past few years been interacting with each other and deliberating over issues of common concern while at the same time maintaining close economic and political links to Washington.

In July 2005, India and the US, agreed to resume cooperation in the field of civilian nuclear energy and signed the US–India Framework Defence Agreement.[72] The agreement if implemented bestows *de facto* nuclear status to India. The nuclear deal can be expected to bring alive the dormant Sino–Pakistan relations given the past record of nuclear and missile transfers. However, it would be pertinent to mention the Dr A.Q. Khan episode in this context. Dr Khan the head of the Kahuta Research Laboratory in January 2004, confessed to selling nuclear technology to Iran, Libya and North Korea.[73] The father of Pakistan's bomb—as Dr Khan is known—in his televised testimony, incredulously asserted that the Pakistani state was not aware of such transfers. For China, which originally first proliferated the nuclear know-how to Pakistan, these developments could have been a source of acute embarrassment. The Chinese Foreign Ministry spokesperson urged Islamabad to undertake the investigations 'properly' and bring them to a conclusion 'quickly'.[74] The Libyan developments in the summer of 2004 once again highlighted Beijing's role in the nuclearization of the world's most volatile regions and also to Dr Khan's intimate links with China's nuclear establishment. In Mohan Malik's words,

> . . . China-watchers see no evidence of Beijing abandoning its national security strategy based on the principle of 'containment through surrogates' that requires proliferation to countries that can countervail its perceived rivals and enemies. Believing that proliferation is inevitable, the Chinese military has long practised what John Mearsheimer calls 'managed proliferation' it calls for providing nuclear or missile technology to China's friends and allies (Pakistan, Iran, North Korea) so as to contain its rivals through proxies

(India in South Asia, the United States in the Middle East and Japan in East Asia). Beijing has also engaged in proliferation to pressure Washington to curb its arms sales to Taiwan . . . also explains China's reluctance to sign on to the US-led Proliferation Security Initiative under which countries pledge to interdict shipments of weapons of mass destruction.[75]

Such embarrassments notwithstanding, there have been reports[76] that Pakistan is in talks to buy up to eight nuclear power reactors from China and construction on the plants could start by 2015 and end 10 years later. The message being that if Washington makes an exception for India, China will do so for Pakistan. Even given the past record of military transfers, interpretations, the intensity of China's engagement with Pakistan will increase dramatically as a result of the recent turn in Indo–US relations. The nuclear deal has the non-proliferation lobby up in arms as it would in the words of George Perkovich mean that, 'France, Russia and China [would] want to play by the same rules for Iran, Pakistan or Syria . . . and that [America] can't keep changing the rules. We tell the Russians not to sell to X, Y and Z, but we sell them to India.'[77] The first Chinese reaction on the issue came as late as early November when the *Renmin Ribao* accused the US of being soft on India and unsurprisingly said that if the US made an exception for India, other powers could do the same, thereby weakening the global non-proliferation regime.[78]

Changing Pakistani Perceptions

Thus, while the international context for Sino–Pak ties have altered dramatically, it remains for Beijing's modified strategy to emphasize the positives while, '. . . soft-pedaling the reality that Pakistan, as the weaker party, needed to continue to cater to China and rely on Chinese support. . .'[79] even while Beijing's support depended on positions and moves on the wider chessboard involving the United States and India. At the same time, it is important to state that these changing contours in the relationship have been perceived well by media commentators in Pakistan. In an opinion piece in the *Dawn*, Zubeida Mustafa, writes that Pakistan with an ambitious foreign policy has emerged as a more dependent partner to China.[80] Mustafa mentions:

> Although China has been signalling a shift in its policy for quite some time now, Pakistan has not responded to it and continues to proceed on the assumption that the China card is still available to it . . . China has been

> normalizing and expanding ties with India. . . . It is, however, important to take note of this development because of the fact that India is the country against which we have been using the China card. Does this not call for a modification in Pakistan's policy *vis-à-vis* New Delhi? [81]

Sultan Mohammad Khan, Foreign Secretary of Pakistan in the 1960s and 1970s and at one time Ambassador to Beijing, Washington and Tokyo in a special article states that,

> The old intimacy and warmth, which once were a hallmark of Sino-Pakistan friendship, is a part of history. I doubt if the Chinese premier will today visit the Pakistan ambassador's residence for lunch or dinner and stay for hours, as Zhou Enlai did, or spend ten hours over two days talking to Pakistan's foreign secretary about the situation in East Pakistan as Zhou Enlai did in 1971. China has some valid grounds for being wary concerning our policy in Afghanistan and Kashmir. It is up to us to remove these obstacles.[82]

Shahid Javed Burki, a regular opinion contributor to the *Dawn*, while concentrating on the economic challenges and opportunities to Sino–Pakistan trade ties with the then impending Chinese entry into the World Trade Organization (WTO) among other things believes that:

> In its quest for quasi superpower status, China has seriously revised its world-view. It no longer sees itself as the champion of the developing world as it did during the period of Mao Zedong and Zhou Enlai. Instead, it is now focused much more on pursuing its own strategic interests and on creating relations with other large powers—the United States in particular but also Russia, Japan, the European Union, India, and Brazil.[83]

Pakistani commentators have increasingly expressed concerns over the state of Pakistan's economic and trade relations with China, which to their disappointment have not matched the close political and diplomatic ties.[84] A consistent reference in this regard is the blossoming of trade ties between India and China which has outstripped the bilateral Sino–Pak trade by over five times and in a shorter duration. It is understood that Sino–Pakistan relations had their roots in the alignments dictated to by Cold War calculations. However, what remains baffling is the skewed depth of the ties and its sheer longevity. Pakistani writings give an impression of all abiding trust and belief in the Asian giant. The threat of 'survival' that makes Pakistan a perpetually 'insecure' state, continues to find its succour in China, giving it much needed confidence especially with regard to the unreliable United States. This psychological reflection is better illustrated in Ayaz Amir's words:

There is a material aspect to the relationship between Pakistan and China. But its essence is emotional and sentimental, fulfilling Pakistan's psychological need for an external anchor to shore up its position against India. To be honest, Pakistan with its constant and reiterative whining over Kashmir and other problems can test the forbearance of friend and foe alike. But China has conducted itself in exemplary fashion, much like a patient psychoanalyst, lending a sympathetic ear to Pakistan's often baffling troubles and proffering, when the occasion arises, calm and soothing advice.[85]

The survey of Pakistani writings on Sino–Pakistan relations to date, reflect the changing contours of Pakistani perceptions. Importantly for the Indian strategic community, it would be pertinent to focus on the evolving trajectory of the 'nexus', as this survey points to the changing alignments and re-alignments which were contingent on the evolving politics. Thus, while we can situate the special Sino–Pakistan relationship in the global context; Indian writings on the issue tend to entirely emphasize the containment of India. It would be efficacious to consider this as an over-simplification. Kanti Bajpai for one suggests that nuclear powers are extremely reluctant to share nuclear secrets, especially considering that in the 'game of nations';[86] there are no permanent enemies or friends. Bajpai, captures the crux of the issue in a comprehensive manner when he suggests that

. . . at least five factors caused Beijing to invest in Pakistan's nuclear weapons plans: maintaining a tested alliance relationship; limiting US influence in Pakistan; responding to Washington's military and political support of Taiwan; cultivating a 'moderate' and influential Muslim state; and gaining access to Pakistan's US-supplied advanced conventional weapon systems and possibly also to Pakistan's nuclear technology.[87]

Conclusion

While the rationale behind the robust Sino–Pak alliance has outlived its relevance, a remarkable section of the Pakistani strategic community has not lost their superlatives in describing the special relationship. While the majority of writings register the toning down of the Chinese support available in the past, analysis about the future is still caught in the Cold War furrow and adjectives are improvised to describe the ties. It is important to note the startling lack of economic depth between the two countries in this age of globalization but the writings do show a realism creeping in developing economic ties. The depth that Sino–Pak ties hold is largely the effort of the government interaction.

India and Pakistan have been in peace talks to solve all outstanding issues including Kashmir since 2002. The ceasefire on Kashmir continues to be respected and people to people communication links have been thrown open; the bus service from Srinagar to Muzzafarabad directly linked the two Kashmir's for the first time in 2005, rail links and even trade issues are being grappled with. While substantive development in key issues have not taken place, the composite dialogue is moving at an incremental pace and Confidence Building Measures (CBMs) in over six divergent areas have resulted in building positive opinion and trust.

To sum, the rising bonhomie of China–India relations seem to have lately become the most critical factor influencing Pakistani perceptions about China in recent years. With Premier Wen Jiabao's visit to India in April 2005, the two countries announced their 'strategic and cooperative partnership' for peace and prosperity, which put their equations in a rather positive realm. Also, the two have in the meantime signed an agreement on the political parameters and guiding principles for the settlement of the India–China border issue. The two countries have also been close in economic relations. Bilateral trade volume hit US $18.5 billion in 2005, an increase of over nine times compared to five years earlier. Meanwhile, they have also developed close and extensive exchange and cooperation in the fields of culture, military and science and technology. China is India's third largest bilateral trading partner and in the last SAARC Summit, China was given Observer status. India also has an Observer status in the Beijing dominated Shanghai Cooperation Organization (SCO). A buzzword 'Chindia', a combination of China and India, is in vogue in the global media symbolizing a sign that China and India will join hands to create a future. What is certain, at least for the present, is that the positives outweigh the negatives that seem to portend tiling of the regional balance in favour of India rather than Pakistan.

NOTES

1. Shahid Javed Burki, *Pakistan : Fifty Years of Nationhood*, Boulder: Westview, 1999, p. 191.
2. Ibid., p. 192.
3. S.M. Burke and Lawrence Ziring, *Pakistan's Foreign Policy: An Historical Analysis*, Karachi: Oxford University Press, 1990, p. 91.
4. Iqbal's letter (in Urdu) dated 23 June 1923 to the *Zamindar*, Lahore, reproduced in *Guftar-I-Iqbal*, p. 6.
5. V.G. Kiernan, *Poems From Iqbal*, Karachi, Oxford Univesity Press, 2005, p. 43.
6. *New York Times*, 13 April 1950.
7. Nur Ahmad, 11 October 1950.
8. *Dawn*, 31 March 1954.
9. Ibid.
10. Javid Iqbal, *The Ideology of Pakistan and its Implementation*, Karachi: Ferozsons, 1971, pp. xi, xii.
11. M. Ayub Khan, *Friends Not Masters: A Political Autobiography*, London: Oxford University Press, 1967, p. 166.
12. Stanley Wolpert, *Zulfi Bhutto of Pakistan: His Life and Times*, New York: Oxford University Press, 1993, p. 65.
13. Khalid Bin Sayeed, 'Pakistan's Foreign Policy: An Analysis of Pakistani Fears and Interest' in Hameed A.K. Rai, ed., *Readings in Pakistan's Foreign Policy*, vol. I, Lahore: Aziz Publishers, 1980, p. 53.
14. Ibid., p. 54.
15. Ibid., p. 55.
16. Ibid.
17. Ibid., p. 56.
18. Ibid., p. 58.
19. Stanley Wolpert, op. cit., n.18, p. 65.
20. Ibid.
21. Ibid.
22. Khalid Bin Sayeed, op. cit., n.13, p. 49.
23. M.A.H. Ispahani, 'The Ire of Pakistan', in Hameed A.K. Rai, ed., *Readings in Pakistan's Foreign Policy*, vol. I, Lahore: Aziz Publishers, 1980, pp. 80–1.
24. Ibid., p. 81
25. Ibid., p. 82.
26. Ibid.
27. Anwar Syed, 'Sino-Pakistan Relations–An Overview', *Pakistan Horizon*, vol. XXII, no. 2, 1969, p. 107.
28. Ibid., p.107.
29. Khalid Bin Sayeed, op.cit., n.13, p. 53.
30. Anwar Syed, op. cit., n. 29, p. 108.

31. Ibid., p. 109.
32. Mohammad Ayoob, 'India as a Factor in Sino–Pakistani Relations' in Hameed A.K. Rai, ed., *Readings in Pakistan's Foreign Policy*, vol. I, Lahore: Aziz Publishers, 1980, p. 606.
33. Ibid.
34. Ibid., pp. 605–6.
35. Pervaiz Iqbal Cheema, 'Significance of Pakistan–China Border Agreement of 1963', *Pakistan Horizon*, vol. 39, no. 4, p. 48.
36. Fazal-ur-Rahman, 'Pakistan's Relations with China', *Strategic Studies*, vol. XIX, no. 4, Winter 1998, p. 67. Also see Pervaiz Iqbal Cheema, 'Significance of Pakistan–China Border Agreement of 1963', *Pakistan Horizon*, vol. 39, no. 4, p. 49.
37. Anwar Syed, op. cit., n. 29, p. 115.
38. Ibid., p. 116. Also see Anwar Syed, 'China and the Indo–Pakistani war of 1965', in Hameed A.K. Rai, ed., *Readings in Pakistan's Foreign Policy*, vol. I, Lahore: Aziz Publishers, 1980, pp. 648–78.
39. Mohammad Ayoob, op. cit, n. 34, p. 619.
40. Anwar Syed, op. cit., n. 29, p. 117.
41. Mohammed Ayoob, op. cit., n. 34, p. 620.
42. Abdur Razzaq Khan Abbasi, 'Thirty Five Years of Pakistan–China Relations', *Strategic Studies*, vol. IX, Summer 1986, no. 4, p. 28.
43. Anwar Syed, 'China and the Indo–Pakistani War of 1965', in Hameed A.K. Rai, ed., *Readings in Pakistan's Foreign Policy*, vol. I, Lahore: Aziz Publishers, 1980, p. 669.
44. Anwar Syed, op. cit., n. 45, pp. 670–1.
45. Ibid., pp. 670–7.
46. Fazal-ur-Rahman, op. cit., n. 38, p. 73.
47. Ibid., pp. 85–6.
48. Ehsan M. Ahrari, 'China, Pakistan, and The "Taliban Syndrome"', *Asian Survey*, 40(4), 2000 (July–August), p. 662.
49. Ibid.
50. Farzana Shakoor, 'The Kargil Crisis: An Analysis', *Pakistan Horizon*, vol. 52, no. 3, July 1999, p. 61.
51. Mohammad Habib Sidky, 'Chinese World Strategy and South Asia: The China Factor in Indo–Pakistani Relations', in Hameed A.K. Rai, ed., *Readings in Pakistan's Foreign Policy*, vol. I, Lahore: Aziz Publishers, 1980, pp. 369–71.
52. Mohammed Ahsen Chaudhri, 'Strategic and Military Dimensions in Pakistan–China Relations', *Pakistan Horizon*, vol. 39, no. 4, Special Focus on Sino–Pakistan Relations, p. 22.
53. Mohammad Habib Sidky, op. cit., n. 53, p. 375.
54. Ibid., pp. 378–80.
55. Naveed Ahmad, 'Sino-Pakistan Relations (1971-81)', *Pakistan Horizon*, vol. 34, no.3, 1981, pp. 58–9.

56. Mohammad Habib Sidky, op. cit., n. 53, pp. 375–8.
57. Ibid., p. 381.
58. Mohammed Ahsen Chaudhri, op. cit., n. 54, p. 23.
59. Niloufer Mahdi, 'Sino-Pakistan Relations: Historical Background', *Pakistan Horizon*, vol. 39, no. 4, p. 68.
60. Naveed Ahmad, op. cit., n. 57, p. 59.
61. Samina Yasmeen, 'Sino-Pak Relations and the Middle East', *China Report*, 34 (3–4), July–December 1998, p. 327.
62. Stephen P. Cohen, *India: Emerging Power*, New Delhi: Oxford University Press, 2001, p. 209.
63. Sameena Yasmeen, op. cit., n. 63, p. 330.
64. V.P. Dutt, 'India–China: Promise and Limitation', in *Indian Foreign Policy: Agenda for the 21 Century*, vol. 2, New Delhi: Foreign Services Institute with Konark, 1998, p. 231.
65. Swaran Singh, 'Sino-Pakistan Defence Cooperation: Joint Ventures and Weapons Procurement', *Peace Initiatives*, vol. V, no. III-VI, May–December, 1999, p. 13.
66. Robert G. Sutter, *China's Rise in Asia: Promises and Perils*, Lanham: Rowman & Littlefield, 2005, p. 232.
67. Ibid., p. 233.
68. Ibid., p. 232.
69. The process had began in the 1980s when the Cold War was on its last leg. In the immediate context, the Jaswant Singh-Strobe Talbott talks after the nuclear tests in 1998 brought about a sea change in American perceptions to India's security concerns and was poignantly visible in President Clinton's visit to South Asia in March 2000. The second Bush Jr. administration took the relations to a higher level.
70. To quote Tellis, 'There is little doubt in my mind that today and in the foreseeable future both Washington and New Delhi will be bound by common interests in a diverse set of issue-areas, Preventing Asia from being dominated by any single power that has the capacity to crowd out others; Arresting the further spread of weapons of mass destruction and related technologies; Promoting the spread of democracy not only as an end in itself but also as a strategic means of preventing illiberal polities from exporting their internal struggles over power abroad; Protecting the global commons, especially the sea lanes of communications.' The commonality in interests are listed in Testimony by Ashley J. Tellis before the House Committee on International Relations, Ashley J. Tellis, 'The US–India "Global Partnership"': How Significant for American Interests?' available at http://www.carnegieendowment.org/publications/index.cfm?fa=view&id=17693&prog=zgp&proj=znpp,zsa,zusr
71. Ashley J. Tellis, 'Indo–US Relations Headed for a Grand Transformation? The Bush Administration's New South Asia Policy is no Longer a

Zero-sum Game', *YaleGlobal*, 14 July 2005, avialable at http://yaleglobal.yale.edu/display.article?id=5999. Also see, John Cherian, 'Deals and Doubts', *Frontline*, vol. 22, issue 16, 30 July–12 August 2005.

72. John Cherian, 'Deals and Doubts', *Frontline*, vol. 22, issue 16, 20 July–12 August 2005.
73. Wikipedia entry on Dr A.Q. Khan at http://en.wikipedia.org/wiki/Abdul_Qadeer_Khan
74. Mohan Malik, 'Nuclear Proliferation and A.Q. Khan's China Connection', 23 May 2004, available at http://english.epochtimes.com/news/4-5-23/21583.html
75. Ibid.
76. 'Pakistan May Buy Six Nuclear Reactors from China', *The News*, Pakistan, 4 January 2006 available at http://www.jang.com.pk/thenews/jan2006-daily/04-01-2006/main/main11.htm
77. Cherian, op.cit.
78. Siddharth Srivastava, 'Beijing Blusters over India's Nuclear Deal', *Asia Times*, 5 November 2005, available at http://www.atimes.com/atimes/South_Asia/GK05Df01.html cited in Arun Viswanathan, 'India, the NSG and the Indo-US Nuclear Agreement', Paper presented at the Pugwash National Seminar on 'Nuclear Power: Opportunities and Challenges' at the India International Centre, New Delhi, November 2005.
79. Sutter, op.cit., p. 238.
80. Zubeida Mustafa, 'How Effective is the China Card?' at http://www.dawn.com, 12 November 2003.
81. Ibid.
82. Sultan Mohammad Khan, 'The Warmth Cools By', at http://www.dawn.com/events/century/for3.htm.
83. Shahid Javed Burki, 'Among the Giants', at http://www.dawn.com, 5 February 2004. Also see Shahid Javed Burki, 'Should We Fear China?' at http://www.dawn.com, 30 December 2003.
84. Editorial, 'Economic Ties with China', at http://www.dawn.com, 26 November 2001. India–China bilateral trade in 2003 is $ 5 billion while Pakistan bilateral trade is at $1.8 billion. Trade figures from Zubeida Mustafa, 'How Effective is the China Card?' at http://www.dawn.com, 12 November 2003.
85. Ayaz Amir, 'Canker in an Ideal Relationship', at http://www.dawn.com, 18 May 2001.
86. Kanti P. Bajpai, 'Strategic Threats and Nuclear Weapons', in M.V. Ramana and C. Rammanohar Reddy, eds., *Prisoners of the Nuclear Dream*, New Delhi: Orient Longman, 2003, pp. 40–3.
87. Ibid., p. 44.

CHAPTER 5

Strategic Thinking and Traditions

M.V. RAPPAI

Under normal circumstances the behaviour of a nation state is determined by its historical experiences and ethos as also by its more immediate perceived short- and long-term interests and threat perceptions. Yet, the deeper and enduring behavioural pattern of a nation is, by and large, dictated by the historic experience and the prevalent strategic thinking and larger socio-political traditions that determine a nation's self-image and aspirations. Hence it will be very pertinent to explore the strategic thinking and traditions in both China and Pakistan in order to appreciate the mutual leverages and limitations that underwrite the tenor and logic of their special relations.

Further, the strategic thinking and socio-political traditions also reflect the core interests of the dominant social elite and their larger respective societies. However, one of the fundamental problems in studying the strategic thinking of a nation in an objective manner gets complicated due to elite interests. Many a times it may not be necessary that the core interest of the nation, or even the core interests of the dominant section of its masses, coincide with the articulated interest of the dominant social elite. This is particularly likely in cases where people's participation into decision-making has not been really institutionalized. It is this context that makes the case study of China and Pakistan particularly challenging and it is these all issues that this chapter will try to unravel in examining the underlying framework of China–Pakistan axis. By doing so, it will attempt to elucidate as to how far their mutual perceptions and policies reflect their respective strategic culture and traditions and to what extent this provides a stable basis for their 'special relationship' in coming years.

Sino–Pak Strategic traditions

In the case of China there has, of course, been long traditions of strategic thinking since ancient times. Only some of these however can be readily understood from the available knowledge on the subject. Many a study has been done on the nature and influence of military classics and other ancient texts available in China on this vast subject in its contemporary format. Further, China also has a long tradition of a selected bureaucratic system through which, part of this traditional —but ever evolving thinking—process has been preserved and enriched throughout the ages.

Pakistan's case by comparison remains a much more short-lived and complicated exercise of discovering inheritance and identity. This new nation state was formed as part of an imperial conspiracy and, surviving on the basis of a religion with a very narrow focus, was bound to have its share of difficulties. Further, this state still co-exists together with its larger neighbour, the erstwhile cultural and traditional entity in the form of a democratic federal republic that remains a constant reminder on the follies of the Pakistani leadership. Therefore, the elite thinking and behaviour in Pakistan needs closer scrutiny not only to understand its relations with its own people but more so with other states, especially a special friend like China. This is because the elite dominated institutions including the military have a direct stake in preserving the *status quo* and leaving few chances for questioning the official discourse on their strategic thinking and traditions.

Especially now, the ongoing process of globalization of economic decision-making is going to exacerbate their difficulties and pose more challenges for not only economy related decision-making processes but also in relation to national security in the near future. This brings us to the crucial question of the link between the overall national security concept and the role of the military as an institution in this ever changing kaleidoscope. As this chapter is not intended to deal with defence related issues in detail, some broad aspects may be touched upon to get a larger perspective of this complicated issue with regards to their strategic thinking.

Imperial Visions and Idea of Pakistan

Since a certain amount of work on China's strategic thinking process is available it will be useful to take a look at the strategic thinking and traditions in Pakistan first. Before starting to analyse this process, it will be useful to understand the evolution of the 'idea' of Pakistan as a nation state, which underpins its identity as a nation. And here, given the tumultuous history as a young nation, it is very difficult to categorize Pakistan into one particular model. Part of the problem lies in the historical evolution of India's freedom struggle and the subsequent partition of Indian subcontinent on a very artificial basis. British imperialist understanding of Islam was certainly tinged with its own understanding of a historical process in Europe and this only its analysis of Islam all the more complicated.

A typical result of this sort of convoluted thinking was, 'if India falls apart we may, I suppose, expect the Moslems to try and enlist British support by offering us all sorts of military and political facilities, to commit ourselves to what would be in effect the defence of one Indian State against another'. This clearly evinces the mindset of an imperial power, which wishes to keep its power directly or indirectly over its former colony for a long time to come. Further this presumption is also based on an utter lack of understanding about Islam as a religion and its adaptation to the Asian cultural and social milieu. At another level, the lessons learned by the British empire from India's first independence struggle in 1857 were neither fully comprehended nor were the issues analysed in its correct perspective. Being the colonial masters, a certain crop of British historians has always portrayed it as an insurrection by disgruntled members of the British forces—the 'Sepoy Mutiny'. Due to a variety of historical reasons and a very narrow understanding of Indian National Congress, this approach of 'peaceful protest' was not fully appreciated by the British and even Indian historians did not devote much energy to understand its significance.

The fundamental lesson learned by the British colonial masters was that they would never be able to comfortably subjugate an undivided India. Therefore, they crafted the devious policy of 'divide and rule'; after experimenting with various combinations they eventually concluded that a division of India, broadly based on religious beliefs was the best way to keep this region under British control for long time to come. The partition of India on the basis of religion in 1947 was the culmination of this strategy. However, history proved this to be a shortsighted analysis and the structure they built on the imagined religious enmity could not ignore other fundamentals like the strong cultural and linguistic affinities of groups of Indians following Islam as their faith. It will be wrong to assess that the people of present-day Bangladesh were made up of lesser Islamic faith just because their linguistic identity had evolved at least continuously from fourteenth century AD. The crux of the matter was their cultural and linguistic affinity was much larger than their perceived religious linkage which was politically 'expedient' to the then dominant Muslim leadership of the territory and society that was to continue to exist much beyond their day-to-day life.

In the 1940s Imperial Britain itself was passing through a very difficult period. Its over-stretched imperium was tottering under various internal and external pressures. While keeping a large colony like India was economically very tempting yet, in physical terms it was proving a tough task. Further, they assessed that a highly complex and dualistic religious and cultural entity like India would not be held under control as, relying largely on their historical understanding of European politics, they suspected that India was anyway bound to split and fragment sooner than later. Even in the case of Europe, this understanding was largely influenced by the developments of their history during a short period of the industrial revolution. Britain's shrinking colonial empire and its ever-expanding needs for markets and raw materials in larger quantity made its continued links with its ex-colonies critical. Moreover, the British decision makers believed that it will be prudent to maintain a strong link with a nation like Pakistan linked by a monotheist religious belief rather than highly diverse Hindu India.

This typical, Anglo–Saxon assessment made them assume that through this method they can carry forward their control over the subcontinent for a longer period of time to come. Not only the situation in India, but the emergence of a highly complicated bi-polar global structure in the post-World War II scenario was beyond their comprehension. India faced numerous trials and tribulations during this period. However, the consolidated leadership of an umbrella organization like the Indian National Congress (INC) with help from a strong and well entrenched bureaucratic machinery could hold this highly complex amalgam of linguistic and ethnic groups together way beyond the imagination of the British colonial masters.

New Pakistani Power Elite

On the other hand, in Pakistan the demise of Quaid-e-Azam Jinnah, the father figure of the nation, and the political instability that followed produced totally different results. The British Indian Army, basically trained to keep internal law and order and to support the imperial government as per their need, managing external security introduced an entirely new element in the complex post-colonial power structure of Pakistan. Especially, the perceived external linkages to Pakistan's internal turmoil was to really complicate Army's responsibilities in Pakistan. It is in this context that a power elite largely consisting of land owning Zamindars of erstwhile Punjab province of India was quick witted enough to understand this scenario and to incorporate the newly emerged armed forces firmly into their own fold. From then on the consolidated might of Pakistani Army was not only used for the integrity of a newly formed nation, rather its main interest was to protect the economic and class interest of this newly emerged elite in independent Pakistan.

The emerging global scenario was conducive for such a power elite to further their own self-interest. Immediately after Independence, the newly emerged dominions of India and Pakistan tried to create an independent foreign policy. This policy was to a large extent a by-product of the colonial struggle waged by the Indian National Congress and its leadership. If one were to look through India's freedom struggle, most of its leaders were educated in Europe in a liberal tradition and majority of them were ideologically more close to the left of centre, socialist groupings inspired by Fabian socialism of Britain. For them freedom and the capacity to act independently in the foreign policy arena was crucial. At the international level, the new post-colonial member-states of the British Commonwealth were to became exposed to a new bonding factor. Moral support for the freedom movements of other nations remained a very sentimental cause for these new leaders of independent India and Pakistan. In the case of Pakistan their linkages with the newly emerged or liberated Muslim dominant nations were a crucial factor.

New Security Parameters

Together with these ideational aspirations, practical issues like the consolidation and safeguarding of the fresh borders were to become a rather immediate task in hand. For the Pakistani leadership this was a real headache. If anyone were to take a look at the map of independent Pakistan, it will not be at all difficult to grasp this problem of two separate portions of one nation located far apart. Both West Pakistan and East Pakistan had their pockets of undemarcated and untamed border areas. In the case of the present-day Pakistan or the then West Pakistan this was all the more complicated and, even today this issue continues to haunt Pakistani leaders. Further, under British imperial rule the boundary between present-day Pakistan and Afghanistan was never clearly demarcated or settled and, this remains still a fluid mixture of warring fiefdoms controlled by powerful tribal chieftains.

Even inside its borders, independent Pakistan had inherited an ever boiling trouble spot on its western side. The fierce tribes, commonly grouped under the administrative control of the then North-Western Frontier Province (NWFP), were never totally under the control of British and later Pakistan's. This was further complicated by the historically nervous ties Pakistan enjoyed with its neighbour Afghanistan. Barring, probably for a short period under the Taliban, the Pakistani leadership has never had a friendly ruler in Kabul. This, together with the partially assumed and partially inherited apprehensions of a Communist Soviet Union complicated the Pakistani leadership's efforts to consolidate the border. The emergence of a newly liberated China in 1949 only compounded these complications.

On its eastern border Pakistan was faced with India. These two nations at their very birth were beset with a series of complicated relations. Starting from 1948, the question of accession of Kashmir further worsened their equations. For the Indian leadership the issue of Kashmir's accession was similar to that of any other erstwhile princely state. But, for the Pakistani leadership this suddenly became a question of national identity. For them all Muslim majority areas of India were their natural territory. The option of an area with a Muslim majority joining voluntarily with India put a question mark on their very legitimacy as a Muslim State. In many ways this quest for a national identity still haunts the Pakistani ruling elite.

This highly emotive Kashmir question still remains the 'core' problem in the relationship between India and Pakistan. The post-colonial period was further complicated by the attempt of Pakistani leadership to join Western-sponsored military alliances. For India, by comparison, non-alignment remained a fundamental principle of its foreign policy. Even today after the end of the Cold War and its vastly different leadership ethos this question remains an unresloved one. By the year 1953 its leadership decided to join the South-East Asia Treaty Organisation (SEATO) and Baghdad Pact. Then onwards Pakistan remained as a committed ally of one or the other power bloc. However, since 1953 it has developed special relationships with two powerful states—the United States of America and the People's Republic of China. It is not sure then how far Pakistani policies were guided by their strategic thinking and traditions. Since all those initiatives bore the personal stamp of individual leaders responding invariably with knee-jerk reactions, it has always seemed more like crisis-management rather than a strategic thinking driven by vision.

Shift from West to China

Apart from Pakistan's social elite, some specific institutions also need to be mentioned especially as they happen to be the creation of an imperial ethos and continue to carry that colonial culture of (a) divide and rule between the subject population and elite, and (b) of the militaristic jackboot instead of accountability. Given these turbulent ground realities, two institutions of Pakistan military—many a time either as a subordinate or closely linked organisation—the Inter Services Intelligence (ISI) agency and the nuclear establishment—deserves special mention in this context. The role of these two crucial agencies has contributed substantially to the strategic thinking process of the Pakistani elite. In some ways, Pakistan's anti-India policies and later its nuclear profile seem to have overshadowed Pakistan's strategic thinking and vison.

It is in this context that the nuclear linkage between China and Pakistan becomes the key component of this interlinkage between the strategic thinking and ethos of these two nations. First of all, this conclusion emanates from a fundamental appreciation in both nations about the nuclear weapon as a key strategic component in their national survival. Even though China is behaving like a *status quo* nuclear power in the global scenario, its obsession with nuclear weapons proliferation—as a key element in its struggle against imperial powers—still remains a powerful argument. For Pakistan, nuclear weapons and its usage as a potential currency of power to ensure its territorial integrity still remains basic to its strategic vision.

Chinese Strategic Thinking

If one were to take a broad look, China has had a unique historic development process. Even though she had various degrees of contact with the outside world, China has generally remained inward looking for much of its history. This may be partially true even today. At various phases of its history, this aloofness bordered on paranoia and total mistrust of outsiders. Even today the term generally used in Chinese for describing the foreigners can be divided into two broad categories, that is the overseas Chinese or compatriots (*tong bao*—literally means born of the same parents and the foreigners—*wai guo ren*). This strict categorization and the suspicious approach towards foreigners are embedded in their psyche. Take for example an old saying about the study of Chinese language:

Tian bu pa di bu pa, yinggai pa
Wai guixing shuo Zhong guo hua
Don't fear the heavens, don't fear the earth, but fear a foreign devil who speaks Chinese.

Apart from the long historical and cultural processes, one prominent ancient work on strategy still remains the bedrock of China's strategic thinking edifice. This is the classic text of military teaching in China, *Sun Zi Bing Fa* or Sun Zi's *The Art of War*. According to the traditional Chinese classification, there are seven military classics, which were a part of the study of almost all military and civil leaders. These include:

Sun Zi: The Art of War
Wu Zi
The Methods of the Ssu - ma (Su - ma Fa)
Questions and Answers Between T'ang T'ai-tsung and Li Wei Kung
Wei Liao-tzu
Three Strategies of Huang Shih-Kung
T'ai Kung's Six Secret Teachings.

Sun Zi's *The Art of War*

Apart from these, there were some other equally important treatises on strategy like 'Sun Bin: Art of War' and others which were also equally respected and studied traditionally by the Chinese mandarins. Especially, Sun Zi has lately emerged as a hero across disciplines and is taught across East Asia. One basic fact is, it presents us with an Eastern tradition of strategic thought that emphasizes outwitting one's opponent through speed, stealth, flexibility, and a minimum of force—an approach very different from that stressed in the West, where the advantages of brute strength have overshadowed more subtle methods.

The teachings found in these classics were practised by predominant Asian war heroes like China's Mao Zedong, Japan's Yamamoto and Vietnam's legendary hero General Giap. By applying these tactics, they were able to outwit their adversaries. In more recent times, these principles have been key to the achievements of many Asian cor-porations. Executives in Japan, Korea and Taiwan regularly study the Seven Military Classics. Unfortunately, even those far-sighted Western business leaders who have read Sun zi have glimpsed only a fraction of the knowledge their best Asian competitors use to plan corporate strategy—until now.

Apart from these fundamental works dealing with strategy and statecraft, a number of other popular works also came up in China. They supplemented the strategic culture of the Chinese. The popular works either written in the form of satire or a critique of the ruler, formed a repository of such knowledge. In ancient China, like in many other societies, the king was the 'heaven born' representative of the almighty on earth. He was unquestionable, and therefore, many an intelligent and influential author used literature as a medium for articulating his or her feelings toward the court.

Mao Zedong himself was heavily influenced by such literature during his formative years. He specially praised works like, *The Dream in the Red Chamber* and the *Romance of the Three Kingdoms. The Dream in the Red Chamber* (*Hong Lou Meng*) is the story of a great family in the early Ch'ing (the seventeenth century) period and its decline. Some of these works have formed an integral part of the strategic thinking process in the Communist era too. This sort of historic evolution and spreading of some of the works on strategic studies among the elite has helped China in nurturing a way of strategic thinking throughout its history. Another positive fallout for China from this traditional way of thinking is its integrated decision-making process.

Modern China's Strategic Culture

One notable feature of China's historic development process is the role played by popular uprisings, especially the uprisings involving its rural population. Here also one may come across a pattern wherein the overwhelming influence of literature and popular will inspired by traditional strategic thinking process played a role. In many way the success of the Chinese Communist Party (CCP) lay in making use of this strategic culture and integrating it in its historic struggle. This background is clearly reflected in the inception and development of People's Liberation Army (PLA), the modern military of China. The PLA was essentially a product of the revolution and the peasants' role in it. Such a developmental process provided China with a natural integration of military thinking with its overall national strategic thinking process.

How the whole process of strategic thinking helped China in its nation building may be a suitable subject for an academic debate. Yet there won't be many who will argue that this thinking process has not helped China in enhancing its interests to a great extend. One may argue that a country like India also made a lot of progress even in the absence of a codified strategic plan for the future. Nevertheless, the Chinese way of articulating its strategic goals well in advance and in clear terms have certain definite advantages.

Another significant aspect of this clearly articulated strategic goal is that it imposes a certain sense of responsibility on the ruling elite of the country to act in a definite way. Whereas, under a broader democratic process such as in India, the lack of a codified strategic structure allows the ruling elite a lot of scope for fudging and circumventing the ideals to meet their short time ends. Another major drawback for India is the total absence of a long-term perspective. Under a democratic system an average politician is only bothered about his next election. Issues like broader national interests as well as long-term perspectives naturally get reduced to the complexities and limits of his constituency or at the most to the concerns of the interest group he represents.

In the case of China this is entirely different. The overall hold of the CCP is a concept which cannot be challenged. Therefore, the ruling elite, by and large the senior Party cadres and mandarins are bound to protect this hold by resorting to more sophisticated constructs like highlighting linkages between their contemporary thinking and China's historic and strategic traditions.

However, it will not be correct to explain away all the achievements of China by raising the issue of China's strategic traditions. One significant factor in doing things, as they prefer to call, with Chinese Characteristics is that it assures a smooth transition of power and the clarity of goals. It will be useful to study this aspect in correlation with China's traditional way of clear strategic thinking. Under an authoritarian system like theirs they could ensure a smooth transition. Further, one advantage of this was that all such transitions were to a great extent smooth and they could manage the show without disturbing the social fabric much. Another significant factor in this transition process was that none of the heirs of Mao was nowhere near him in charisma and the grasp he had on the rustic rural China. Therefore, the way in which a set strategic goals helped them in achieving this so far peaceful transition into an altogether new entity (i.e. from revolutionary to a *status quo* power) is also worth studying.

China's Theory and Practice

This capacity to theorise about their operational objectives calls for a serious examination of the mechanics of how this strategic thinking and culture are applied to the process of nation building in both China and Pakistan. Military strategy forms only one component of this overall strategy though it remains a very central and defining component when it comes to the case of China and Pakistan. Hence, it may be useful to take a brief look at how Chinese military strategy has evolved in recent years.

At the very outset of any such analaysis of China's military strategy, China's use of force in the modern period cannot be easily explained within the ambit of accepted norms or traditions. Modern China used force against its neighbours irrespective of the fact that they were powerful or weak. Another peculiarity is that it used force at a time when China was undergoing serious domestic convulsions. One of the main aims of Chinese leadership in using this force was nothing more than strategic posturing. If we look back, in most of those acts of aggression they hardly added any fresh territory to China.

In recent times China has also realized the importance of its market potential and it has successfully integrated this factor into her strategic calculations. Its leaders at various levels always try to project the potential of its 1.2 billion people as a massive market for businesses. This integrated approach has helped China in attaining the desired goals in successful market bargains. In turn the Chinese leadership have no qualms in using these advantages in bargaining and gaining strategic concessions. The recent US Senate vote to discard a motion aimed at imposing sanctions against China is one example. The use of market potential in other fields also can be seen. Recently, to drive a point on democracy, President Jiang Zemin noted that, China has some 2,000 radio and television stations, some 2,000 newspapers, some 8,000 periodicals, some 100,000 new books published annually, 16 million Internet users, some 27,000 websites, some 70,000 Chinese domain names, and some 61 million mobile phone subscribers. The Chinese people have extensive and adequate information sources and channels to express their views.

Similarly, while examining the strategic culture and thinking of Pakistan one has to begin by first outlining the strategic thinking in India. This is partly becasue Pakistan as a successor State has inherited much of its history and strategic thinking from India. This is one key element that will serve the purpose given historical and geographical links that India has with both Pakistan and China. In view of the emerging geopolitical realities around India's neighbourhood the region consisting of Central Asia is going to remain as a focal point in the near future. These newly emerged nations straddle the oil rich Gulf and Caspian sea region on its sides. Some of these countries also have a large reserve of gas and other natural resources including uranium and other minerals. As some observers put it, apart from France, China is one country that studiously follows all developments in the field of revolution in military affairs (RMA) in the USA.

The second study came in the form a Year-end Report in the widely circulated *Renmin Ribao* (People's Daily). This report written by Xie Guang, vice-minister of the Commission on Science & Technology in National Defence (CONSTIND) and a Senior adviser to the China Association of International Strategy once again underscored the importance of nuclear weapons. He wrote,

> strategic nuclear weapons still have a long future as high technology warfare's defence umbrella. This argument is based on the premise that main nuclear nations will develop newer types of fourth-generation nuclear weapons. The struggle for and competition in nuclear technology advantage will be carried out mainly in the laboratory, but the possibility of major renewed ground testing cannot be ruled out. In the long term, nuclear weapons will develop into something used for threats, with the development of microelectronic technology, for example, the broad use of nano-technology. . . .

Future Trends

According to China's new concept of war in the age of technological integration and globalization has realigned the relationship of weapons to war. The appearance of new concepts of weapons, has gradually blurred the face of war. Does a single 'hacker' attack count as hostile act by state or not? Can using financial instruments to destroy a country's economy be seen as a battle? Did CNN's broadcast of an exposed corpse of a US soldier in the streets of Mogadishu shake the determination of the Americans to act as world's policeman, thereby altering the world's strategic situation? And should an assessment of wartime actions look at the means or results? Obviously, proceeding with the traditional definition of war in mind, there is no longer any way to answer the above questions. When we suddenly realize that all these non-war actions may be the new factors constituting future warfare, we have to come up with a new name for a new form of war: Warfare which transcends all boundaries and limits, in short the concept of unrestricted warfare propounded by China.

Ultimately the aim of all strategic thinking process must be the realization of a nation's long-term strategic goals. This thinking must make us aware what the future role of nuclear weapons will be very much part of the strategic calculation of China. And China's strong strategic thinking and traditions provide a strong basis for a modern nation. In the end, therefore, India has to keep the vigil to say the least.

blurred the face of war? Does a single hacker attack count as hostile act by state or not? Can using financial instruments to destroy a country's economy be seen as a battle? Did CNN's broadcast of an exposed corpse of a US soldier in the streets of Mogadishu shake the determination of the Americans to act as world's policeman, thereby altering the world's strategic situation? And should an assessment of wartime actions look at the means or results? Obviously, proceeding with the traditional definition of war in mind, there is no longer any way to answer the above questions. When we suddenly realize that all these non-war actions may be the new factors constituting future warfare, we have to come up with a new name for a new form of war: Warfare which transcends all boundaries and limits, in short the concept of unrestricted warfare propounded by China.

Ultimately the aim of all strategic thinking process must be the realization of a nation's long-term strategic goals. This thinking must make us aware that the future role of nuclear weapons will be very much part of the strategic calculation of China. And China's strong strategic thinking and traditions provide a strong basis for a modern nation. In the end, therefore, India has to keep the wind to say the least.

CHAPTER 6

Role of Political Culture

SONIKA GUPTA

Strong bilateral ties between China and Pakistan have been analysed in India mainly from the perspective of a security nexus against India. Different constituents of this relationship have been examined but the defence and security perspective has remained the dominant area of concern and investigation. This paper examines the role of political culture in shaping ties between the two countries. The argument here is that while bilateral ties between China and Pakistan are driven mainly by strategic concerns in South Asia, the political culture of both the countries plays a very important role in strengthening bilateral ties and in the successful conduct of relations. A different type of polity in either state would possibly have not resulted in an enduring relationship as exists today.

It is in this context that this chapter begins by outlining the basis of China–Pakistan ties and proceeds to situate them in the political culture of both the countries. A discussion of the linkages between political culture and strategic culture and their relationship with foreign policy-making provides the theoretical framework for the study. The evidence for the argument that Pakistan and China share similar attitudes towards the role of power is drawn mainly from the internal and external factors that enable the military to play such a dominant role in both these countries' politics. This follows the dominance of the military in foreign policy-making and their bilateral relationship clearly shows this inter-linkages. Finally, the role of the military in future Sino–Pak bilateral ties is briefly commented upon.

A Pragmatic Relationship

It is significant that the Chinese and the Pakistanis have built a deeply interdependent and mutually beneficial security relationship that is devoid of any common ideological agenda. In fact, even a sense of shared values, as between close allies, like the United States and Britain, does not exist between them. However, common strategic interests and similarities between their political cultures have allowed the two to build a strong strategic relationship in the absence of ideological unity. China and Pakistan share a realist understanding of the use of power and have provided a strong role for the military in nation-building. *This is the most significant shared trait in the political culture of the two countries.*

China and Pakistan have had dissimilar political development and consequently their political institutions are different. Pakistan inherited liberal-democratic political institutions and processes from the British and the People's Republic of China set-up a revolutionary political system guided by Marxist-Leninist thought. Over time, political institutions in both countries have undergone change. Pakistan's polity is dominated today by its military and China has moved away from revolutionary ideals to fashion a polity that supports its ambitious economic development agenda within a neo-realist framework. Despite the difference in political inheritance and later changes in polity, there are some similarities in the political culture of the two countries. A shared political understanding of a central role for the military in nation-building facilitated the building of a strong defence relationship between the two countries. Therefore, despite dissimilar paths of political development and even opposing ideological orientations, the two countries have been able to forge and sustain a mutually beneficial relationship through the years.

National security concerns born of their respective relationships with India and the attendant Cold War politics in South Asia brought the two together in the mid-1950s. From the mid-1950s through the 1960s, at a time when China operated within a stringently left wing revolutionary framework of interstate relations, its relations with Pakistan were an exception to the rule. Pakistan was a member of the 'imperialist' military alliances, the SEATO and the CENTO, led by the US. However, China chose not to use this to brand Pakistan an imperialist state or a 'running dog of the imperialists'. Further, Pakistan had a history of military rule that was ideologically against the revolutionary principle of people's power but the People's Republic of China (PRC) did not criticize this and considered it to be Pakistan's internal matter. While exigencies of great power politics in the subcontinent dictated China's acceptance of an ideologically untenable relationship with Pakistan, a common understanding of the role of power, as reflected in their defence relationship, cemented their extente.

On the other hand, Pakistan, despite being a part of US-led anti-Communist alliances, crafted a successful relationship with China. In fact, Pakistan's membership of these capitalist alliances was dictated by its security concerns *vis-à-vis* India. Therefore, as Pakistan improved its relations with China, its active participation in these alliances declined. After 1962, though Pakistan was a member of US-led alliances that sought to contain the spread of Communism, it did not work actively for this cause. And Pakistan's record of participation in these alliances provides evidence of this fact. Through the 1960s, American intelligence agencies documented the strengthening of Pakistan's relationship with China in violation of its treaty commitments to the US.[1] The Sino–Indian war in 1962 was responsible for the change in Pakistan's policies. Before 1962, Pakistan was forced by geo-strategic realities to adopt an alliance with the US. However, after the 1962 Sino–Indian war and US support to India during this crisis, both China and Pakistan revaluated their bilateral relationship. Both sides recognized the advantages of pursuing a cooperative political and military relationship to achieve their strategic objectives in South Asia. In consonance with this policy, the Pakistan government began distancing itself from the US and developing closer relations with China.

Pakistan's refusal to send troops to Laos and Islamabad's role in establishing diplomatic ties between China and Turkey between 1963–5, were considered by the US as breach of its SEATO and CENTO commitments respectively.[2] Pakistan did not also attend the SEATO ministerial conference in April 1963 and the CENTO ministerial conference in April 1965; withdrawing its offer to send troops to Laos in August 1964, and cancelling its joint naval exercises with the British Royal Navy in the same year.[3] In fact, there was speculation about a secret military understanding between China and Pakistan and US intelligence agencies reported the presence of Chinese military personnel in Pakistan as early as 1963. The latter points to the centrality of the military component in their bilateral relationship. This relationship was based on a common understanding of strategic objectives in South Asia and a shared understanding about the role of the military in achieving them. Further, a central role accorded to the military in domestic decision-making ensured that the bilateral relationship was prioritized in the foreign policy establishments of both countries.

The chronology of military cooperation between China and Pakistan is well documented and need not detain us here.[4] The role of the military in domestic political culture of the two countries and its linkages with bilateral relations is the point of departure here. Linkages between political culture and foreign policy formulation are crucial to understanding Sino–Pak relations. While studies of strategic culture do inform the study of foreign policy, the linkage between political culture and foreign policy needs to be established. For this an understanding of the evolution of the concept of political culture is required.

Political Culture and Foreign Policy

The concept of political culture evolved in the study of comparative politics and was greatly enriched by inputs from history. Glen Gendzel, in tracing the genealogy of political culture observed that Plato's concept of 'dispositions', Montesquieu's 'spirit of laws', Rousseau's 'mores', David Hume's 'manners', Tocqueville's 'habits of the heart', Durkheim's 'collective consciousness' and Weber's 'authority of systems' are predecessors to the concept of political culture.[5] The concept of political culture evolved in response to the need to deepen the analysis of politics from anthropological or psycho-cultural analyses of political behaviour. The study of political behaviour has evolved successively into studies of national character, study of political institutions, studies on values, attitudes and ideology. The link between politics, culture and power is, however, not recognized in these analyses. The following is an attempt to do this.

The recognition that politics is influenced by culture has always existed in the study of politics albeit without making the link between culture and politics the central concern of study or using it as an analytical tool. The concept of political culture is used in this study primarily to establish the linkages between strategic culture and domestic politics to argue that every country's foreign relations are formulated in a policy-making environment constituted by both these factors. Though strategic culture forms the basis of the analysis of the use of power of a state, however, the linkage between political culture and strategic culture is hitherto unexplored in studies of international politics.

When this linkage is established and Sino–Pak relations are examined within it, it becomes clear that in their existing political systems, the two countries share fundamental assumptions about the role of the military in perpetuating political authority. While there are differences in the practice of power between the two countries, the role of power in external relations is also significantly similar. Both the countries have institutionalized the role of force in domestic politics and external relations by evolving integrated structures of power between political governance, foreign policy-making and the military establishment. These similarities spring from shared notions of the nature and function of power in domestic and global politics. Thus, this shared understanding has facilitated the construction of close and mutually beneficial ties between two politically, culturally and ideologically disparate countries.

What constituents of a political culture define the relationship between political culture and foreign policy-making? Gabriel Almond and Sidney Verba defined political culture of a nation as 'the particular distribution of patterns of orientation towards political objects among the members of the nation'.[6] They called political culture the connecting link between micro and macro-politics and identified two variables that characterize a political culture. The first is called 'subculture' and is derived from the attitudes to authority within a political culture. According to them, a political culture may simultaneously have elements of parochial, subject and participant attitudes towards authority. Using Gabriel Almond and Sidney Verba's classification of attitudes to power, China and Pakistan can be said to share subject—participant attitudes to authority.[7] They define subject political culture as one characterized by an affective orientation towards governmental authority and an essentially passive relationship to it.[8] The participant culture is 'one in which the members of the society tend to be explicitly oriented towards the system' and 'tend to be oriented toward an 'activist' role of the self in the polity'.[9] In the mixture of the two that is the subject-participant culture,

> . . . a substantial part of the population has acquired specialized input orientations and an activist set of self-orientations, while most of the remainder of the population continue to be oriented towards an authoritarian governmental structure and have a relatively passive set of self-orientation.[10]

The second variable that characterizes political culture is 'role culture'. Almond and Verba, posit that the more complex political systems are characterized by specialized structures of roles that include the bureaucracy, the military, the political executive, party, interest groups and the media. The composition of each of these 'role cultures' as Almond and Verba define them, contributes to heterogeneity of the political culture. Role cultures are formed of specific institutional cultures and contribute to and take from the mainstream political culture. Both subculture and role culture constitute elements of a political culture. However, Almond and Verba did not explicitly identify or discuss the dialogical relationship of subculture and role culture to political culture. Political culture is as much altered by subculture and role culture as it is altered by it. Subcultures within a political culture shape, and are shaped, by prevalent attitudes to authority.

Similarly, role cultures formed of specific institutional cultures contribute to, and take from, the mainstream political culture. Stephen White argues that political culture both expresses *and* influences patterns of political belief and behaviour within a given political system. It is, hence, more than the sum total of political institutions and the attitudes towards it. According to White,

> (political culture) is a broader concept than 'operational code' or 'political style', terms which apply more properly to the actions or assumptions of a particular sub-group of a total population (and particularly to its political leadership); it is a narrower concept, at the same time, than more familiar notions such as 'national character' or 'public opinion', which have a frame of reference much larger than the political system.[11]

Therefore, all institutions in a state contribute to and are shaped by political culture. Almond and Verba categorized the political system into the 'nation' and the 'political systems' with the media, interest groups, political parties, legislatures and the executive as the inputs. The output objects are classified into the categories of the military, the police, civil authorities such as tax, education and welfare authorities. The political culture of a nation permeates and is created by above categories. The attitudes towards authority and power and their resultant structures and processes are part of every role culture within a political culture and this includes the military as well. Hence, while keeping in mind the specific role culture of the military, it is essential to probe the attitudes towards power within a culture.

Strategic Culture and Political Culture

The study of political culture was not informed by the link between culture and politics till the advent of post-modern critique of social sciences produced the insights of critical theory.[12] Both strategic and political culture deal with the notion of power. However, while the former deals only with the operational use of power, the latter explores only the concept of political power. The translation of political power into its operative component, that is, military power is an analytical gap that is not bridged by either concept. Part of the reason why this gap exists is compartmentalization of the concept of power into the disciplines of politics and strategic/security studies. The result is that the study of international politics, of which power is an integral and operative part, suffers from an analytical disunity between the concept of power and its use.

Foreign policy studies analysing a country's behaviour in international politics tend to concentrate on the operational use of power rather than a broader understanding of the nature of power. Culturally grounded notions of power determine leadership roles and political institutions; this includes the politicians, bureaucrats and the men in uniform. The choices made by leaders in the conduct of foreign policy are informed by their attitudes towards power and its use is guided by these attitudes in conjunction with the objective strategic conditions. In the case of Pakistan and China, an analysis of role culture of the military and the political elite and their relationship establishes similarities between the two political cultures. A discussion of the domestic and external reasons for the dominance of the military in Chinese and Pakistani political cultures establishing the similarity of attitudes towards power follows.

Attitudes towards power that shape domestic and foreign policy can be located by identifying the referents of security in a country. In both China and Pakistan, the military is both the referent and the provider of security. Referents of strategic culture may be identified as the entities that play a role in shaping strategic policy and are in turn shaped by it. This includes the state and 'nation' and the military and political elite.

In the PRC, the referents of security are the Party, the State, the armed forces and the People.[13] The role and position of the Party is sacrosanct and the State is the organized expression of the Party. The PLA as the military arm of the Party is the referent of *and* provider of security. Post-1949, the Party has used force within China to cement its position, notably during the Cultural Revolution and the Tiananmen Square incident and in Tibet. Similarly in Pakistan, a threat to the privileged position of the military is seen as threat to the internal stability of Pakistan that may invite threats to its external stability as well. The civil-military relationship in Pakistan clearly establishes the dominant role of the military both in external security as well as internal governance. The role of the military in maintaining internal stability in both the countries establishes the fact that strategic culture is not concerned solely with use or threat of use of force externally. In both these countries, the military is also a referent of security and thereby shapes the strategic culture.

As discussed above, strategic culture is a subset of political culture but the relationship between the two is dialogical. Existing studies of strategic culture are hampered by the fact that they do not investigate the nature of power concentrating instead exclusively on its use. In the case of China, the link between strategic culture and political culture is crucial as the army played a pivotal role in the creation of the PRC and continues to play a strong role in nation-building. In Chinese elite politics, the military plays an important role in state institutions and decision-making processes. The first and the second generation of Chinese leadership were composed predominantly of the veterans of China's revolutionary struggle. During the revolutionary struggle, there was no sharp distinction between political cadres and military cadres. The current institutional framework of political governance does have some differentiation but the political and the military role of the army are intertwined. The army is as much defender of 'socialism with Chinese characteristics' as it is a force to fight against external aggression. The army is also an important contributor to building a 'well off socialist society' and hence also plays an economic role in Chinese polity.

Similarly in Pakistan, the military has played a central role in defending Pakistan's national integrity and in providing it political stability. The recurrent military dictatorships in the country have resulted in institutions that draw heavily from the armed forces. Specifically during the Zia-ul-Haq regime, the practice of appointing high ranking serving or retired military officers to important posts in the bureaucracy including the Foreign Service, academia, and state funded commercial enterprises became prevalent. This practice has been continued in the present regime. This is in addition to institutions of political governance and the judiciary that are under the military's direct *de facto* control. Therefore, the role of the military is equally important in an analysis of Pakistan's political and strategic cultures and the linkages thereof. What factors have contributed to the military playing a dominant role in China and Pakistan?

Dominance of the Military-External Factors

Both China and Pakistan came into existence with heightened perception of external threat and this was a very major factor in the continued dominant role played by the military in their respective polities. Communist ideology pitted China against the rest of the 'imperialist' world wherein the United States and later the Soviet Union presented a physical threat to the People's Republic of China. Following the establishment of the PRC, the major concern of the state was to ensure the security of China's borders and protection from foreign aggression. Through the 1950s and 1960s, China was involved in a struggle to safeguard its borders and territory from 'great power hegemonism'. A *People's Daily* commentary succinctly mentions, 'the People's Republic of China was born in the campaign against imperialism, feudalism, and bureaucratic capitalism, suffered imperialist hostility, blockade and armed threats at the very beginning'.[14]

Setting up of the Nationalist government in Taiwan, US naval presence in Taiwan straits during the Korean War, deployment of Soviet troops along the Sino–Soviet and Sino–Mongolian border were major threats to China's territorial sovereignty. The Korean War in 1950, the prolonged border dispute with the USSR with the Ussuri river clashes in 1969, the Sino–Vietnam clashes were identified by China as imperialist aggression and part of the Great Power game being played out between the US and USSR. The resistance to French presence in Indo–China and support to Communist parties and forces in North Vietnam, Cambodia and Laos were also part of a larger Chinese intention to resist imperialist aggression close to Chinese borders. Mao advocated a policy of resisting these imperialist and expansionist wars by the use of maximum force at China's disposal. China's border had to be safeguarded if revolutionary goals were to be achieved. The PLA under the leadership of the CCP was to guide China in its quest for unity and territorial sovereignty.

Secondly, for China, to pursue an independent foreign policy was as important as protecting its territory in constructing a new identity of a powerful and resurgent China. In an address to the preparatory meeting of the new Political Consultative Conference in June 1949, Mao said, 'China must be independent, China must be liberated, Chinese affairs must be decided and run by Chinese people themselves, and no further interference, not even the slightest will be tolerated from any imperialist country'.[15] To achieve these two goals, the Chinese Communist Party outlined a central role for the PLA, which has continued to remain important till date. In fact, the US dominance of global politics backed by its military might has convinced China that a strong military is essential to pursue an independent foreign policy.

For Pakistan, the political, social and psychological dislocation of the Partition and its adversarial equation with India defined its external security environment. At the time of Partition, Pakistan was left with the challenge of defending the territorial integrity of a country, two halves of which were separated by a thousand miles of Indian territory. However, a more urgent security concern existed to the north where Pakistan claimed the princely state of Jammu and Kashmir on the basis of its Muslim majority population, a claim India refuted by arguing that the erstwhile Maharaja had chosen to accede to India. The Indo–Pak war over Kashmir in 1947 was only the first of three wars over this piece of territory and the Kashmir dispute continues to be the defining feature of Indo–Pak relations. The two sides again crossed swords in 1965 and 1999. The latter, i.e. the Kargil War, caused concern the world over as both sides were in possession of nuclear weapons.

Other than the Kashmir dispute, Pakistan faced a major security threat in its eastern territory which broke away from the Punjabi-Urdu dominated West Pakistan in 1971 and the independent state of Bangladesh came into being with the active help of the Indian Army. The massive military defeat and loss of territory suffered by Pakistan in 1971 has had an enduring impact on Pakistan's threat perception *vis-à-vis* India and convinced the Pakistani elite of the necessity of maintaining a strong military deterrent against India. This, in turn, has translated into a greater role for the army in policy-making and nation-building.

Internal Factors and Military Dominance

Other than the threat of external aggression, domestic factors have played a crucial role in determining the role of the military in the polities of the two countries. While in China the integrated nature of the state-party-military structure in China ensured a central place for the military in political governance, in Pakistan, there was no conscious attempt to build such integrated political structures in the immediate post-Independence period. In fact, the trend was to retain the institutions of executive, legislature and the judiciary as inherited from the British. The spearhead of the national freedom movement, the Muslim League, recast itself into a political party that assumed the responsibility for political governance of the country. But the political leadership was not equipped to handle the challenges of participatory politics. The transfer of the charismatic appeal of the popular leaders to independent institutions of political governance initially sustained the political process. However, as popular leaders left the political scene, a crisis of legitimacy developed in these institutions. As Hasan-Askari Rizvi argues:

> As they (the political leadership) did not appreciate the scale of task evolving participatory political institutions in the post-colonial societies, they faltered and adopted authoritarian approaches to political management, increasing their reliance on the state apparatus, the military being one of the state institutions availed of the opportunity to amass political clout.[16]

In other words, the task of political management of post-colonial crises proved overwhelming for the fledgling political system of Pakistan that was trying to create participatory institutions in the absence of a socio-economic revolution. While there was a popular movement to throw off the colonial yoke and to create a separate national identity for Pakistan, the much-needed social revolution to transform feudal structure and economic relations into post-colonial participatory practices and processes was not attempted. In absence of a truly participatory socio-political process, vested interests guided the nature and structure of institutions of state. In the absence of credible civilian institutions, the army with its ethos of discipline and commitment to the country emerged as the most attractive alternative. As Veena Kuckreja has observed:

> Thus the case of Pakistan represents an apt example of how an apolitical military could slowly be drawn into the political field due to the failure of political institutions and politicians, low political mobilization and external factors.[17]

In fact, in the 1950s, post-colonial social sciences literature identified the rise of the military as a positive phenomenon as the army was seen as an organized state institution that could provide the much-needed stability to politically weak post-colonial states.[18] However, this argument began to falter when the military dominated post-colonial states failed to evolve the kind of participatory institutions that had been envisaged and instead the military increased its influence in every aspect of political governance. Pakistan is a classic example of this process. Rizvi argues that by the mid-1970s, the 'developmental' and 'modernizing' role of the military was challenged and the military was beginning to be regarded as a major obstacle to development of democratic institutions in the post-colonial societies.[19] However, as evident in Pakistan's political history, loss of popular confidence in the sanctity and efficacy of civilian institutions has resulted in reluctant acceptance of guided democracy as opposed to political instability.

In China, since the institutional beginnings of the Party and the military were same, the state structure that evolved reflected this. After 1949, this translated into institutional structures of state where the role of the Party was supported by the PLA. Though the Party controlled the gun, the support of the PLA was crucial to maintaining the authority and the legitimacy of the Party. Each successive leader in China has realized this and consolidated the support of the PLA at the earliest.

Unlike Pakistan, the Chinese ruling elite accorded a central role to the military in construction of a revolutionary society. For Mao, military power was central to revolution and the subsequent construction of a Communist society. Mao acknowledged war as a necessary and sole instrument of capturing political power and professed, 'Every Communist must grasp the fact that political power grows of out the barrel of a gun: the army is the nucleus of the CPC ordered system in China.'[20] Mao accorded the military a central role in the perpetuation of political power when he argued

> Viewed from the Marxist theory of state, the army is the chief component of the political power of a state. Whoever wants to seize and hold on to political power must have a strong army.[21]

Mao did not consider fighting to be the sole function of the People's Liberation Army. The Army was the chief organization for waging class struggle and for capture of political power. The PLA, according to Mao, played an important role in 'agitating the masses, organizing them, arming them and helping them to set up revolutionary political power and even establishing organizations of Communist Party'.[22]

However, unlike Pakistan, the military is subordinated to the Party. In one of his most important writings Mao defined the relationship between the Party and the Army. 'To regard military work and political work as opposed to each other is to fail to recognize military work as only one of the means for accomplishing political tasks.'[23]

At the institutional level, the Central Military Commission (CMC) epitomises the integration between the political and the military apparatus. The highest leader in China is also the head of the CMC. Tai Ming Cheung has traced the evolution of the CMC from a revolutionary military organization to the present to establish the vertical and horizontal linkage between the Party and military in performing functions of political governance and domestic and foreign policy-making.[24] While the information about the actual functioning of the CMC is a closely guarded secret, the institutional linkages between the CMC, the State Council and the Standing Committee of the Politburo and the fact that the paramount leader is also the head of the CMC ensures that the military perspective is represented in major foreign policy decisions.

Future Role of the Military

What does the consistent involvement of the military in foreign policy making mean for Sino–Pak relations? The fact that within the broader bilateral relation, the defence relationship is the most enduring is, in part, owed to the fact that in both countries the military plays a very significant role in internal and foreign policy-making. In both countries, the role of the military is not confined to the defence of the country's borders but has a political and social role to play as well. To be specific, in both countries, political stability is directly linked to ability of the military to maintain internal cohesion. In effect, both countries acknowledge the role the military power plays in handling internal challenges to political stability and external security. Given this similarity in understanding the role of military power, China and Pakistan have never condemned each other's domestic use of force considering it a strictly internal matter. This has seen their relationship through in tough times like the aftermath of the Tiananmen Square incident for China or the coup by General Musharraf in Pakistan, to quote only one example each. This strong political relationship is in turn based upon a mutually beneficial defence relationship that is grounded in common strategic concerns in South Asia.

The depth and the nature of the defence relationship is exceptional. This relationship goes far beyond the buying and selling of weapons. The Chinese assistance for the Pakistani nuclear and missile programmes in the face of continued US displeasure, sanctions and international opprobrium indicates the mutuality of interests between the two sides over decades. China is not just a source of conventional and non-conventional arms for Pakistan, but has provided it with critical technologies that in turn have enabled Pakistan to develop indigenous nuclear and missile programmes.

Pakistan's nuclear facilities including the A.Q. Khan Research laboratories at Kahuta, the Kanupp pressurized heavy water reactor, the Khushab reactor, the Chashma pressurized reactor, the Chashma plutonium reprocessing facility and the Rawalpindi research reactor (PAAR-2) are all built with Chinese assistance.[25] Currently China is helping Pakistan develop a second nuclear plant at Chashma. In a capacity building exercise for Pakistani nuclear scientists, the Chinese allegedly involved them in a nuclear test at its Lop Nur test site in 1989.[26] With regard to missile technology, in addition to supplying Pakistan with the M-11 missile in the late 1980s, Pakistan also received missile technology in the early 1990s, which resulted in the US sanctions.[27] Pakistan's Shaheen missile is reportedly modelled on Chinese M-9 missiles for which China has supplied it with the technology.[28] In addition, China has clandestinely supplied Pakistan with critical chemical components for rocket fuel. The transfer of technology is also a part of China's conventional arms trade with Pakistan. The Chinese FGA aircraft and main battle tanks were produced under license in Pakistan. Pakistani Anza and Baktar Shikan are copies of Chinese SAM and Red Arrow missiles respectively.[29]

Conclusion

This close defence relationship forms the basis of the strong political ties between the two countries that is dictated by mutual strategic interests in the South Asian region. The political elite in both countries prioritises these strategic interests above other considerations. And given the fact that the military forms an integral part of the decision-making elite in both the countries, it has been possible to sustain their defence ties despite facing international criticism. A lesser involvement on the part of the top military brass in the decision-making process, would probably have seen a lesser commitment towards a strong defence relationship at least in China. In fact, the trend towards professionalization of the PLA has spelled some change in the way the PLA's interests are represented in national defence and foreign policy making.

David Lampton has argued that simultaneous effects of greater professionalization, corporate pluralization, decentralization and globalization have resulted in a 'thickening of the elite' in China.[30] This process was set in place by Deng Xiaoping and has continued at a gradual pace under Jiang Zemin and Hu Jintao. In contemporary China, the decision-making process is more varied with different constituencies within the Party, the PLA and government articulating their interest, often with competing demands for greater voice and resource allocation. While the broader principles of policy are still decided only at the very top, with competing institutional interests, policy difference have begun to emerge. Lu Ning adds to this saying that within the PLA different departmental interests of the intelligence community, the arms purchase/sale community and so on have emerged.[31] Therefore, it is no longer possible to speak of a monolithic PLA position on foreign relations.

However, given the long history of its relationship with Pakistan and its military, their defence relationship will continue to remain strong albeit with incorporation of emerging Chinese interest in improving relations with India. China's improving relationship with India and competing interests of the thickened elite in China might mean that China's policy might have to contend competing interests in its policy towards India and South Asia.

While the role of the military is being progressively redefined and a new 'thickened' ruling elite is emerging in China, in Pakistan, despite the presence of an elected government, the military stays firmly in control. Pakistan's external security atmosphere continues to be dominated by the issue of Kashmir creating a constant threat from India. After the nuclearization of South Asia, the management of the military threat from India has become more complex urging Pakistan to constantly develop its nuclear and missile capability. In this the Pakistan military would like to get continued support from its long-standing defence partner. However, the rise of extremism in Pakistan presents a challenge to the strong relationship between the two countries and could have implications for the defence relationship as well. The revelations of nuclear proliferation by Pakistan and the danger of Islamic extremists getting hold of WMDs is a cause for concern for China as well as it is facing a similar threat in Xinjiang.

Moreover, the proliferation of nuclear technology that China had supplied Pakistan and its global implications will cause a rethink about the defence relationship in Beijing. However, this does not mean that China is ready to dilute or snap its ties with Pakistan. The *raison d'être* of a defence partnership with Pakistan, i.e., to present a challenge to the India in South Asia, has not changed. In the post-Cold War global reordering, China will continue to seek to balance India's power and Pakistan is its best bet to do that. Unless there are radical changes in the strategic situation in the South Asia region accompanied by changes in the polities of the two countries that radically reduce the role of the military in political decision-making, the bilateral relationship will remain strong.

NOTES

1. Declassified internal CIA report dated 21 July 1995 detailing US policy problems with Pakistan. Available at http://www.gwu.edu/nasarchive/NSAEBB/NSAEBB114/chipak-1.pdf Accessed on 18 March 2004.
2. Ibid.
3. Ibid.
4. For Pakistan's conventional military imports from and joint weapons production with China see SIPRI database on arms transfer at http://projects.sipri.see/armstrade/PAK_MPTS_93-02.pdf For a detailed account of China's missile and nuclear assistance to Pakistan see the Center for Nonproliferation Studies, Monterey, California, database at www.cns.miis.edu/research/india/china/mpakchr.htm
5. Glen Gendzel, 'Political Culture: Genealogy of a Concept', *Journal of Interdisciplinary History*, vol. 28, no. 2, Autumn 1997, p. 226.
6. Ibid., p.15.
7. Gabriel Almond and Sidney Verba, *The Civic Culture: Political Attitudes and Democracy in Five Nations*, Princeton: Princeton University Press, 1963, pp. 14–29.
8. Ibid., p. 19.
9. Ibid., p. 19.
10. Ibid., p. 25.

11. Stephen White, *Political Culture and Soviet Politics*, London: Macmillan, 1979, p. 1.
12. For a representative exposition see Jim George, *A Critical (Re) Introduction to International Relations*, London: Macmillan, 1997.
13. The definition of the 'People' has undergone many changes with major political movements in China. The Hundred Flowers Movement, the Anti-Rightist Movement, the Great Leap Forward, the Cultural Revolution, the Movement against Spiritual Pollution and the economic liberalization of the PRC have all redefined the categories of the 'People'.
14. 'Historical Course in Diplomacy', Editorial, *People's Daily Online Edition*, 14 September 1999 http://english.peopledaily.com.cn/China/19990914A127.html
15. Mao Tse Tung, *Selected Works*, vol. IV, Beijing: Foreign Languages Press, 1961, p. 407.
16. Hasan-Aksari Rizvi, *Military, State and Society in Pakistan*, London: Macmillan, 2000, p. 17.
17. Veena Kukreja, 'Military Intervention in Politics: A Case Study of Pakistan', New Delhi: NBO Publishers, 1985, p. 50.
18. See for example Ayesha Jalal, *The State of Martial Rule*, Cambridge: Cambridge University Press, 1990, and *Democracy and Authoritarianism in South Asia*, Cambridge: Cambridge University Press, 1995
19. Hasan-Aksari Rizvi, *Military, State and Society in Pakistan*, p. 17.
20. Mao Zedong, 'The Role of the Chinese Communist Party in National War', October 1938 http://www.maoism.org/msw/mao_sw.htm accessed on 14 October 2002.
21. Mao Zedong, *Selected Works of Mao Zedong* http://www.maoism.org/msw/mao_sw.htm accessed on 14 October 2002.
22. Mao Zedong 'On the Rectification of Incorrect Ideas in the Party' 1929 http://www.maoism.org/msw/mao_sw.htm accessed on 14 October 2002.
23. Ibid.
24. Tai Ming Cheung, 'The Influence of the Gun: China's Central Military Commission and its Relationship with the Military, Party and State Decision-making Systems' in David M. Lampton (ed.), *The Making of Chinese Foreign and Security Policy in the Era of Reform*, Stanford: Stanford University Press, 2001.
25. 'China's Nuclear Exports and Assistance to Pakistan' Center for Nonproliferation Studies, Monterey Institute of International Studies, August 1999 available at http:/cns.miis.edu/research/India/china/npakpos.htm
26. Ibid.
27. 'China's Missile Exports and Assistance to Pakistan' Center for Nonproliferation Studies, Monterey Institute of International Studies, July 1999 available at http:/cns.miis.edu/research/India/china/mpakpos.htm

28. Ibid.
29. Stockholm International Peace Research Institute (SIPRI) *Data on Arms Transfers*. Available at http://projects.sipri.se/armstrade.PAK_MPT_93-02.pdf
30. David Lampton (ed.), *The Making of Chinese Foreign and Security Policy in the Era of Reform 1978–2000*, Stanford: Stanford University Press, 2001, p. 4.
31. Lu Ning, 'The Central Leadership, Supraministry Coordinating Bodies, State Council of Ministers' in David M. Lampton (ed.), *The Making of Chinese Foreign and Security Policy in the Era of Reform*, Stanford: Stanford University Press, 2001.

PART II

Defence and Strategic Cooperation

CHAPTER 7

Proliferation Concerns: An Overview

ARPIT RAJAIN

Diplomatic relations between Islamabad and Beijing began in the 1950s at the 1955 Afro-Asian Conference in Bandung when Premiers Zhou Enlai and Mohammad Ali Bogra initiated a series of high level contacts and visits. Pakistan had recognized the Peoples Republic of China on 4 January 1950 and the two countries established diplomatic relations a year later. The end of the 1950s also saw a downturn from the *Hindi–Chinni–Bhai–Bhai* days of Sino–Indian relations. After the 1962 Sino-Indian war, Pakistan realized that China could be an ideal friend against India. Earlier that year in a joint communiqué signed in February by Zulfikar Ali Bhutto and Marshal Chen Yi had urged that the Kashmir dispute should be solved according to the plebiscite that had been pledged by India.[1] Given the nature of their bonhomie, Pakistan was to claim during the 1965 war with India that it counted on China's support and that it had been promised to Pakistan.

It was as early as the mid-1960s that Zulfikar Ali Bhutto made strong overtures requesting the Chinese to help Pakistan develop nuclear weapon capabilities that could match the Indian programme. China did not oblige then, but in 1976, according to a subsequent intimation by Bhutto, the Beijing government had agreed to be more forthcoming. China reportedly supplied Pakistan with blueprints for a fission weapon around or before 1983.[2] Observers attribute this to the marked warmth and swing in Indian–Russian relations.[3] Pakistan also stood by China on all important issues especially those relating to the question of China's sovereignty, for instance in the case of Hong Kong, Taiwan and Tibet and other sensitive issues such as human rights at the UN Human Rights Commission. China often acknowledges that Pakistani support in the early 1970s helped break the international isolation of Beijing.

China kept insisting that the M-11 transfer which it had initially denied for many years were within the Missile Technology Control Regime (MTCR) guidelines. But a Congressional Research Service Report said 'transfers of Chinese M-11 short range ballistic missiles or related equipment exceed MTCR guidelines, because the missile has the inherent capability to deliver a 500 kg warhead to 300 km'.[4] In fact, there was so much evidence of Chinese assistance to the Pakistani nuclear programme that the US decided to impose sanctions on some Chinese companies that engaged in exports of super-computers, missile technology and satellites. These sanctions, effected in June 1991, were waived off in March 1993. On reports of missile transfer again in August 1993 sanctions were imposed and waived only after a Chinese commitment to stop missile transfers to Pakistan. A Joint Statement by Secretary of State Warren Christopher and Foreign Minister Qian Qichen on 4 October 1993 saw the lifting of the second set of sanctions.

In the mid- to late 1980s, China continued to criticize the Nuclear Non-proliferation Treaty (NPT) as being discriminatory, but also indicated that it accepted in principle the norm of nuclear non-proliferation. In 1991, shortly after France acceded to the NPT, China declared its intention to join, though it again expressed its reservations about the treaty's discriminatory nature. China formally acceded to the treaty in 1992 as a nuclear weapon state. Since its accession, China has praised the NPT's role in preventing the proliferation of nuclear weapons, and China supported the indefinite and unconditional extension of the NPT at the 1995 Review and Extension Conference at the UN in New York. However, China has continued to state that it does not view non-proliferation as an end in itself, but rather as a means to the ultimate objective of the complete prohibition and destruction of nuclear weapons.

Despite China's shift toward accepting the international norm of non-proliferation, significant concerns regarding China's nuclear trade with countries of proliferation concern continued into the 1990s which Pakistan emerging as one most visible example. And with the advantage of hindsight it is common place today that China's supplies of nuclear and missile technologies to Pakistan have led to their further proliferation to several other countries on both strategic and commercial terms (see Table 7.1).

TABLE 7.1: CHINA-PAKISTAN NUCLEAR AND MISSILE COOPERATION[5]

- Chinese transfer of M-11 (M-11/DF-11/CSS-7) test missile and launcher (1991).[6]
- Direct transfers of 34 complete M-11s (1992).[7]
- Chinese provision of M-11 components and technology (1992, 1995).[8]
- Chinese missile technicians visited Pakistan M-11 sites (1994).[9]
- Chinese training of Pakistani M-11 army units (1995).[10]
- Reports of Chinese assistance with indigenous Pakistani M-11 production (1996–7).[11]
- Continuing Chinese assistance, including blueprints and construction equipment Missile factory in Rawalpindi for manufacture of medium-range ballistic missiles, likely the M-11 or a similar missile (1996–7).[12]
- Hatf-1/1A Possibly developed with some Chinese assistance.[13]
- Hatf-2 Possibly developed with some Chinese assistance.[14]
- Shaheen Possibly similar to China's M-9.[15]
- Ammonium Perchlorate a Chemical used in rocket fuel Alleged illegal Chinese shipment of 10 tons to Pakistan (1996).[16]
- Anza Surface-to-air missile (SAM) Pakistani version of PRC-supplied SAM.[17]
- Arms Materials Special metals and electronics used in the production of Chinese-design anti-tank missiles (Pakistan's Baktar Shikhan is virtually identical to China's Red Arrow guided missile) Alleged Chinese shipment to Pakistan (1998).[18]
- Suspicion persists regarding China's continued missile cooperation with Pakistan. It has been speculation that the Shaheen-1 IRBM, which Pakistan tested in April 1999, is actually modelled on Chinese M-9 missiles. A 1999 CIA report stated that 'Chinese and North Korean entities continued to provide assistance to Pakistan's ballistic missile programme during the first half of 1998. Such assistance is critical for Islamabad's efforts to produce ballistic missiles . . . China's involvement with Pakistan will continue to be monitored closely.'

M-11 and Proliferation Debates

The alleged transfer of M-11 missiles had opened the proliferation debate in the early 1990s. Above all, this had led to greater tension between the US and China as it was against core US interests of pursuing non-proliferation. From a Pakistan point of view their relations with China had been rather fruitful. As Pakistan's Ministry of Foreign Affairs claims 'our ties with China constitute a cornerstone of our foreign policy and a fundamental element of our quest for regional peace and stability. . . . The vast spectrum of bilateral co-operation between our two countries ranges from political, economic and cultural spheres to the fields of defence and security. . . . The relations with China have served as a check on the hegemonistic tendencies of some other countries in the region.'[19] This broadly outlines the essence of Sino–Pak relations which is based on mutuality of interests, cooperation in fields of defence and security to serve as a check on possibly Indian hegemonic designs. China is following the Kautiliyan construction of assisting neighbour's neighbours. This is a low cost positive sum game for both Pakistan and China.

Chinese nuclear exports and assistance to Pakistan have been a major proliferation concern for many years. However, concerns have recently eased somewhat. Whereas most of China's other nuclear exports and cooperative projects have been for non-weapons purposes (though concerns still exist given the Chinese refusal to accept full-scope safeguards and the dual-use nature of much nuclear technology), China has allegedly provided direct assistance to Pakistan's nuclear weapons programme in the past. There have been reports that China supplied Pakistan with both the design and enough HEU (Highly Enriched Uranium) for at least two nuclear bombs. China has also provided assistance and transferred materials that could be applied in the development of nuclear weapons. Beijing insists, though, that China's assistance has mainly involved the provision of peaceful technical information rather than weapons-related technologies or materials. China claims it has adopted responsible nuclear export policies since joining the International Atomic Energy Agency (IAEA) in 1984 and acceding to the Non-proliferation Treaty (NPT) in 1992. Beijing has formally enunciated three principles governing its nuclear exports: (1) acceptance of IAEA safeguards; (2) peaceful use only; and (3) no re-transfers to a third country without China's prior consent. In recent years, China has also promulgated domestic laws regulating nuclear and dual-use exports.

China–Pakistan nuclear cooperation began in the early 1980s. The United States government has concluded that China assisted Pakistan in developing nuclear explosives prior to its accession to the NPT in 1992. In 1983, US intelligence agencies reported that China had transferred a complete nuclear weapon design to Pakistan, along with enough weapons-grade uranium for two nuclear weapons. China also reportedly was helping Pakistan operate its Kahuta uranium-enrichment plant.[20] US concerns at this time are summarized in a 1985 declassified State Department assessment of Sino–Pak nuclear cooperation. In 1986, China concluded a comprehensive nuclear cooperation agreement with Pakistan. That same year, Chinese scientists began assisting Pakistan with the enrichment of weapons-grade uranium, and China also reportedly transferred tritium gas to Pakistan that could be used achieve fusion in hydrogen bombs and boost the yield of atomic bombs. According to media reports the amount transferred was enough for making 10 nuclear weapons.[21] Since then, China has supplied Pakistan with a variety of nuclear products and services, ranging from uranium enrichment technology to research and power reactors.

The Sino–US controversy over Beijing's nuclear trade and co-operation with Islamabad stems from differences in Beijing and Washington's strategic, non-proliferation, and foreign policy considerations. US policy on the Pakistan issue has always aimed at preventing the latter from achieving nuclear weapons capability. Indeed, the US has introduced specific legislation aimed at dissuading Pakistan from continuing its nuclear weapons programmes by threatening to cut off economic and military aid and imposing sanctions. From China's perspective, Pakistan has long been a useful ally in its South Asia strategic calculations and Sino–Pak defence cooperation underlines this close relationship. The US is concerned about the impact of South Asian nuclear weapons programmes on the international non-proliferation regime; China, on the other hand, does not want to commit itself beyond its legal obligation to the NPT. At the same time, Beijing always insists on the legitimate peaceful use of nuclear energy and opposes restrictions on nuclear transfers and assistance under the name of non-proliferation. While China made a formal pledge in May 1996 not to provide assistance to unsafeguarded nuclear facilities, the fact that China has not adopted IAEA full-scope safeguards (FSS) contributes to US concerns about the potential of *indirect* Chinese transfers and assistance to Pakistan's nuclear weapons programmes.

Related to this issue is US concern over China's ability to enforce these commitments. While *direct* Chinese assistance in Pakistan's nuclear weapons programme has ended and the scope of nuclear technology transfers also narrowed, activities that could contribute *indirectly* to Pakistan's nuclear weapons programme have continued. China's refusal to adopt IAEA FSS means there is still potential for transferred items to end up in unsafeguarded facilities. The 5,000 ring magnets episode of 1995 also raises the issue of Chinese central government knowledge and ability to oversee activities of state-run companies with regard to effective export controls. For contextualizing Sino–Pak strategic relations it is crucial to situate it within the broad context of Sino–US relations.

Evolution of Sino–US Entente

Since 1949, for nearly twenty years no American politician dared to speak openly about the relations between Washington and the People's Republic of China.[22] The Korean War, McCarthyism, a Sino-Soviet alliance, China's development of an atomic bomb, the war in Vietnam, and the Cultural Revolution had all combined to make American leaders distrust their own country men who took a soft approach to China as well as the Chinese.[23]

Following the 1969 Sino–Soviet Ussuri river clashes followed by American presence in Vietnam the new context of US-Soviet détente was also to prompt a period of *rapprochement* with China during critical period of 1971–2.[24] As Henry Kissinger wrote about his secret visit to China, 'When we completed drafting the communiqué announcing my secret visit to China in July 1971, Chou Enlai remarked that the announcement would shake the world. He was right.'[25] However, US President, Richard Nixon's views on China had always been more pragmatic than ideological.[26] Nixon's views regarding China, much before his becoming the President can be gathered from one of the most quoted articles that he wrote in *Foreign Affairs* in 1967. In that article 'Asia after Vietnam', Nixon wrote

> Some counsel conceding to China a 'sphere of influence' embracing much of the Asian mainland and extending even to the island nations beyond; others urge that we eliminate the threat by pre-emptive war. Clearly, neither of these courses would be acceptable to the United States or to its Asian allies. . . For the short run, then this means a policy of firm restraint, of no reward, of a creative counter pressure designed to persuade Peking that its interests can be served only by accepting the basic rules of international civility. For the long run, it means pulling China back into the world community—but as a great and progressing nation, not as the epicenter of world revolution. In the long view, we can not afford to leave China forever outside the family of nations, there to nurture its fantasies, cherish its hates and threaten its neighbours.[27]

In the aftermath of the 1965 Indo–Pak War, the United States had decided to involve itself less in the South Asian region. Three factors were mainly responsible for this shift. First was the growing détente between the US and the former Soviet Union. The second was the deep American involvement in the Vietnam War. The third factor was the result of the first two factors—the US found none of its strategic interests at stake during this period in South Asia. Whether or not China desired but soon it came to be associated with a global power status.[28] In the early 1980s leading Chinese think-tanks and experts began suggesting the shift in China's strategic distance from the US.[29] After 1984, China started warming up to the US. As David Shambaugh noted, 'In the Chinese estimation, genuine superpower détente could contribute positively to a peaceful environment in East Asia which in turn was necessary for China, development during the Seventh Five-year Plan period.'[30] Both domestic factors—the Tiananmen Square and international factors—the break-up of the Soviet Union led to sharp down slide in China's relations with the Western world. More factors contributed to security challenges for China—the break-up of the Soviet Union, the Warsaw Treaty organization, the growing culture of Islamic fundamentalism in the Central Asian Republics and the Islamic world, a resurgent US post-Gulf War and a large US military presence in Central Asia following the Afghan campaign. Also at the systemic level was the process of globalization that was fast reducing economic borders between states.

In the 1990s yet again there were various discordant notes between the two countries. The US condemned China for violating arms limitation agreements, human rights and unfair trade practice. Policy makers in the US Congress in the 1990s have consistently focused on suspected Chinese transfer of sensitive technology to Pakistan and Iran. Since 1992 China, considering the change in world order that led to the emergence of the world's sole superpower, sought to change its image. In 1992 it agreed to abide by the Missile Technology Control Regime (MTCR); in March 1992 it acceded to the NPT, in January 1993 came the signing and subsequent ratification; in October 1994 statements on MTCR and fissile material production; in November, 1995 the White Paper on arms control and disarmament; in May 1996 the statement on making only safeguarded nuclear transfers; July 1996 came the announcement; on moratorium on nuclear testing; the CTBT signing followed this in 1996 September while in October 1997 China became a member of the Zangger Committee, in August–

October China released a series of export control regulations on NBC materials, and in November 2002 China released another White Paper on National Defence.

Much of the concern regarding China's nuclear exports has to do with the perceived inadequacy of China's nuclear safeguards and export control system. In 1991, China declared that it would report to the IAEA any export or import of nuclear materials and all exports of nuclear equipment, but, although China has placed all of its nuclear exports under IAEA safeguards, it still does not require full-scope safeguards. China is not a member of the Nuclear Suppliers Group (NSG), which establishes comprehensive export control guidelines to ensure that nuclear cooperation does not contribute to proliferation, nor has China adopted the group's export policies, which include requiring full-scope safeguards. In fact, China may be emerging as the predominant supplier of nuclear technology for developing countries because it is the only supplier that has the financing capabilities and does not require full-scope safeguards. Munir Ahmad Khan, former chairperson of the Pakistan Atomic Energy Commission (PAEC), supported this theory, saying that Pakistan is committed to developing nuclear power but could find no other suppliers besides China due to non-proliferation concerns. Many observers also doubted that China has sufficient capacity to monitor its exports, as illustrated by the 1996 controversy over the sale of ring magnets to Pakistan, which China insisted had taken place without the knowledge of the central government.

Since that episode the Chinese government has made a significant effort to improve its controls over nuclear exports. In May 1997 the State Council issued a Circular to government and non-government entities on what types of items could be exported.

US Sanctions Against China[31]

It is perhaps worthwhile to begin by citing a survey of the history and status of arms control/non-proliferation-related sanctions imposed against China and/or Chinese entities by the United States (see Table 7.2).

Meanwhile the US policy was turning from that of containment to engagement seeking to improve bilateral relations. While the US was trying to engage China, trying to increase interaction, the US was also aware that China was not adhering to various global non-

TABLE 7.2: US SANCTIONS ON CHINA

Date	Sanctions	Description	Status
21 May 1997	–Prohibition of US government procurement of goods or services from the sanctioned entities or persons —Prohibition of the importation into the United States of any products produced by the sanctioned entities	–Imposed pursuant to the Chemical and Biological Weapons Control and Warfare Elimination Act of 1991 –Imposed against five Chines individuals, tow Chinese companies, and one Hong Kong company for knowingly and materially contributing to Iran's chemical weapons programme –The entities and individuals were involved in the export of dual-use chemical precursors and/or chemical production equipment and technology –Imposed against: • Liao Minglong, Tian Yi, and Chen Qingchang (aka QC Chen), Pan Yongming, and Shao Xingsheng (all Chinese citizens) • Nanjing Chemical Industries Group (NCI) (Chinese company) • Jiangsu Yongli Chemical Engineering and Technology Import/Export Corp (Chinese company) • Cheong Yee Limited (Hong Kong company)	Duration of a minimum of one year

TABLE 7.2: CONTD.

Date	Sanctions	Description	Status
24 August 1993	–Prohibition of the export of Missile Technology Control Regime (MTCR) items and US government contracts; China criticized the sanctions on the grounds that they were based on inaccurate intelligence	–Imposed pursuant to the 1990 Missile Technology Control Act –The US Under Secretary of State for International Security Affairs determined that China's Ministry of Aerospace Industry and Pakistan's Ministry of Defence had engaged in missile technology proliferation activities –Imposed against the two entities and their subsidiaries, etc., denying export licenses for item in the MTCR Annex for two years, and denial of US govt. contracts relating to the same items –Also imposed against Chinese govt. organizations involved in development or production of electronics, space systems, or equipment and military aircraft –Imposed against (Chinese entities): • Chinese Ministry of Aerospace Industry (MAI) • MAI subsidiaries sanctioned: • China Precision Machinery Import-Export Corporation (CPMIEC) • China National Space Administration (CNSA) • China Aerospace Corporation (CASC) • China Great Wall Industry Corporation (CGWIC)	Waived 1 November 1994; Sanctions against Pakistani Ministry of Defence expired Agust 1995

		• Chinese Academy of Space Technology (CAST) • Beijing Wan Yuan Industry Corporation (BWYIC) • China Haiying Company • Shanghai Astronautics Industry Bureau (SHBOA) • China Chang Feng Group (Pakistani entities): • Ministry of Defence • On 1 November 1994, subsequent to the 4 October 1994 US–China joint statement on missile proliferation, the US State Department that in the interest of US national security, it was essential to waive the sanctions against the Chinese Ministry of Aerospace Industry and all its subsidiaries • Sanctions against the Pakistani Ministry of Defence remained in place	
25 June 1991	Prohibition of the export of missile-related computer technology and satellites	–Imposed pursuant to the 1990 Missile Technology Control Act –Restricting the export of missile technology, missle-related computers and satellites –No waivers on satellite export licenses –Imposed agaisnt (Chinese entities): • China Precision Machinery Importe-Export Corporation (CPMIEC) • China Great Wall Industry Corporation (CGWIC) (Pakistani entity): • Space and Upper Atmosphere Research Commission (SUPARCO) • The Bush administration announced on 21 February 1992 that the sanctions would be waived for national security reasons.	Waived 23 March 1992; Sanctions agaisnt Pakistan's SUPARCO expired

TABLE 7.2: CONTD.

Date	Sanctions	Description	Status
22 October 1997	Suspension of high-tech imports to China	The Reagan Administration, in response to the Chinese sales of anti-ship missile to Iran on 22 October 1987, suspended the process of gradual liberalization of the sophistication of high-tech items that were permitted to be sold to China –During Chinese Foreign Minister Wu Xueqian's March 1988 visit to Washington, DC, the US State Department announced that the Reagan Administration was lifting the suspension because it was satisfied that China was not selling Silkworm missile to Iran	Lifted 9 March 1988
16 December 1985	Prohibition of the export of nuclear materials, facilities, or components	–On 23 July 1985, China and the US signed a bilateral nuclear cooperation agreement –US Congress enacted an approval resolution (PL 99-183) that requires Presidential certification of certain conditions before export licenses may be issued for nuclear material, facilities or components covered by the agreement.	Active

Sources: Dianne E. Rennack, 'China: US Economic Sanctions', *CRS Report for Congress*, Congressional Research Service, The Library of Congress, 1 July 1996; *Risk Report*, October 1995, p. 8; 'US Imposes CW Sanctions Against Chinese Entities', US Department of State, Office of the Spokesman Press Statement, 22 May 1997, as cited in the online CNS database available at http://www.cns.miis.edu, accessed on 3 May 2000.

proliferation norms. In June 1997, the Director of Central Intelligence (DCI) submitted a report to Congress stating that during July–December 1996, 'China was the most significant supplier of WMD-related goods and technology to foreign countries . . . there is no question that China has contributed to WMD advances' in Pakistan and Iran.'[32] In early 1996 the Congress called for sanctions after there were reports of Chinese sale of 5000 ring magnets apparently in violation of the NPT and the US laws including the Arms export Control Act and the Export Import Bank Act (as amended by the Nuclear Proliferation Prevention Act of 1994).

The US imposed sanction on the China National Nuclear Corporation (CNNC). Sanctions continue to be a 'feel good' policy and are after toothless and have no effect. Clandestine help to Pakistan's nuclear and missile programme continued. The Defence Secretary's Report of November 1997, stated that 'China remains Pakistan principal supplier of missile related technology and assistance'.[33] The Defence Secretary's Report further stated that in April 1996 Iranians purchased an electro-magnetic isotope separation unit from China.[34] Citing the *International Herald Tribune* the CRS Report further adds that 'The CIA reportedly found that China delivered dozens or perhaps hundreds of missile guidelines systems and computerized machine tools to Iran some time between mid-1994 and 1995.'[35]

The core American interests of protecting the painstakingly crafted non-proliferation regime has been damaged to some extent by the Chinese indulgence with Pakistan. Yet economic sense dictates American access to Chinese markets. In the 1990s the US followed a policy of engaging China, trying to make it a member of as many international regimes from Kyoto Protocol to NPT to WTO. Besides, China also participated in regimes where the costs of a unilateral withdrawal remain rather high. The CTBT draft remains a case in point of China's support to US non-proliferation endeavours. The main contemporary issues that can cause friction between China and US include Taiwan, WTO, human rights and safeguarding against piracy and sea lanes of communications. The US often cites its commitments with Taiwan for an increased presence in the Asia Pacific region. But the question still remains. Will the US permit a use of force by China as method for the settlement of the Taiwan issue?

The US plans to extend Theatre Missile Defence to this region and this has upset China for a long time. Beijing considers these plans as threatening to its national interests. The main US motive behind these is defence for the whole US and its friends and allies against a small number of ICBM's that may be launched by a 'rogue' state.[36] However, such a system would also provide some residual capability against a small accidental or unauthorized launch of strategic missiles from China or Russia.[37] The Chinese contend that with the deployment of a NMD China will lose the very limited capacity to deter US from inflicting a first strike on it.

Especially upsetting have been the indications that US—along with Japan—may extent these facilities to Taiwan as well. This is clearly seen as an attempt by US to encroach on China's national sovereignty. The Chinese Foreign Minister Tang Jiaxuan told a press conference in March 1999 that 'China is very much concerned about it'.[38] China is also understood to having focused on building counter-measures to deal with TMD deployments in its region. In the end, it is in the interest of both, Beijing and Washington, to understand better what China thinks on nuclear security and regional stability of its region. It is also in the interest of Washington to undertake policies that promote regional stability rather than exacerbate regional tensions.

Strategic versus Commercial Concerns

The Chinese nuclear and missile assistance to Pakistan can be explained in a combination of commercial, strategic and foreign policy rationales. The steady supply of material and technology has helped the two countries forge a close partnership on key defence issues. Both these countries' had their respective defence needs, e.g. in China's case it was countering the Soviet threat and in the case of Pakistan the threat has been from India. The economic interests in this relationship were primarily Chinese. In the early 1980s the Chinese defence industries were under tremendous pressure to tap the international arms bazaar and this resulted in finding Pakistan as a lucrative market. Moreover, Beijing's assistance to Islamabad was fruitful in diplomatic terms as it became a bargaining chip in dealing against Washington's continued assistance to Taiwan & TMD deployment in East Asia.

China's special relationship with Pakistan has also been seen as one providing it with leverages when it comes to dealing with Washington DC. Chinese nuclear exports and assistance to Pakistan have remained a contentious issue in Sino–US relations over the years. There have been significant differences between Washington and

Beijing regarding nuclear non-proliferation and peaceful use of nuclear energy. US post-Cold War foreign policy has been premised on proliferation of WMD as a major threat to US interests and regional and global security and has undertaken specific measures, including strengthening the international nuclear non-proliferation regime and threatening/applying sanctions to punish/deter proliferation behaviour. While China supports the principles of nuclear non-proliferation, it has also emphasized the importance of promoting the peaceful use of nuclear energy.

China has been a strong critic of the policies of industrialized countries that restrict and deny the legitimate demands of developing countries for peaceful use of nuclear energy and technology transfers for economic development under the pretext of preventing nuclear proliferation. Therefore, for both political and commercial reasons, China does not require full-scope safeguards (FSS) as a condition of supply for its nuclear exports. Another major contention is that while the US looks at Pakistan mainly as a proliferation problem, China must consider the impact of its non-proliferation commitments on Sino–Pak strategic relations. Washington has imposed sanctions on both China and Pakistan to dissuade it from continuing the nuclear weapons programme. However, Chinese nuclear exports and assistance to Pakistan sometimes appear to have been offered or sustained out of a sense of obligation toward a valued ally.

Conclusion

In the end, Pakistan's importance in Chinese strategic calculations concerning South Asia seems to have made it difficult for Beijing to decline requests from Islamabad. Failure to respond to Pakistan's requests would damage Chinese credibility with a prized ally, especially when the requested nuclear technical assistance is not self-evidently useful in the development of nuclear weapons. On the other hand, providing such assistance could aggravate Western suspicion and concern, and possibly trigger sanctions. China has tended to deny the existence of such programmes (though this is increasingly difficult) or to insist the peaceful nature of the cooperation (which has become a long-standing Chinese practice).

The US objections to this centered primarily on the core US policy of non-proliferation which was being undermined. Also the assistance to Pakistan could trigger off a missile and arms race in South Asia.

The US has sought to compartmentalize the non-proliferation issues on their own merits failing to recognize and delink regional security issue from the larger policy objectives. Even though India made a hue and cry of the Sino–Pak relations, perhaps the US itself was not in a position to wield the kind of authority India wanted it to. Overall Sino–Pak relations have been mutually beneficial and have stood the test of time. Regional stability has thus been damaged. What matters in building up an arsenal is not the intent or the morality but the capability. China certainly has helped Pakistan to a great extend.

NOTES

1. See Rasul Baksh-Rais, *China and Pakistan: A Political Analysis of Mutual Relations*, Lahore: Progressive Publishers, 1977, p. 45.
2. State Department Briefing Paper: 'The Pakistani Nuclear Programme', 22 June 1983, in Joyce Battle, India and Pakistan: *On the Nuclear Threshold*, National Security Archive, Washington, DC, 2000, http://www.seas.gwu.edu/nsaarchive/NSAEBB/NSAEBB6/index.
3. Mujtaba Rizvi, *The Frontiers of Pakistan*, Karachi: National Publishing House, 1971, p. 192.
4. Shirley A. Kan, 'Chinese Proliferation of Weapons of Mass Destruction: Current Policy Issues', *Congressional Research Service Report*, 1 June 1998, available at http://www.fas.org/spp/starwars/crs/crs92056htm, accessed on 3 November 1999.
5. Adapted from the CNS database available at http://www.cns.miss.edu, accessed on 17 September 2002. The original sources have also been provided. Chart copyright CNS.
6. Jim Mann, 'China Said to Sell Pakistan Dangerous New Missiles', *Los Angeles Times*, 4 December 1992, p. A1, A18; Statement by Gordon Oehler, Former Special Assistant to the Director, CIA and Director DCI's Nonproliferation Center; Hearing of the Senate Foreign Relations Committee on Proliferation of Chinese Missiles; Gary Milhollin, Director; Wisconsin Project on Nuclear Arms Control; 11 June 1998. This was also the reason for US sanctions against China in 1991 and 1993.
7. Statement by Gordon Oehler, Former Special Assistant to the Director, CIA and Director DCI's Nonproliferation Center; Hearing of the Senate Foreign Relations Committee on Proliferation of Chinese Missiles; Gary Milhollin, Director; Wisconsin Project on Nuclear Arms Control; 11 June 1998; R. Jeffrey Smith, 'China Linked to Pakistani Missile Plant', *The Washington Post*, 25 August 1996, p. A1, A25.

8. Elaine Sciolino, 'CIA Report Says Chinese Sent Iran Arms Components', *New York Times*, 22 June 1995.
9. Bill Gertz, 'US, China Clash over Missile Deal: Beijing Argues Arms Sales to Pakistan Don't Violate Treaty', *Washington Times*, 4 October 1994, p. A8; Barbara Starr, 'US Links Chinese Ties to Missile Exports', *Jane's Defence Weekly*, 15 October 1994, p. 6; Bill Gertz, 'Pakistan-China Deal for Missiles Exposed: Nuclear Ambitions Spur US Concern', *The Washington Times*, 7 September 1994.
10. Bill Gertz, 'US, China Clash over Missile Deal: Beijing Argues Arms Sales to Pakistan Don't Violate Treaty', *Washington Times*, 4 October 1994, p. A8; Barbara Starr, 'US Links Chinese Ties to Missile Exports', *Jane's Defence Weekly*, 15 October 1994.
11. Statement by Gordon Oehler, Former Special Assistant to the Director, CIA and Director DCI's Nonproliferation Center; Hearing of the Senate Foreign Relations Committee on Proliferation of Chinese Missiles; Gary Milhollin, Director; Wisconsin Project on Nuclear Arms Control; 11 June 1998.
12. Office of the Secretary of Defense, Proliferation: Threat and Response, November 1997 (online version); US Department of State, Daily Press Briefing, 26 August 1996; R. Jeffrey Smith, 'China Linked to Pakistani Missile Plant', *The Washington Post*, 25 August 1996; Tim Weiner, 'US Suspects China is Giving Pakistan Help with Missiles', *New York Times*, 26 August 1996.
13. 'Pakistan's Ballistic-Missile Plans,' *Foreign Report*, 18 May 1995.
14. Ibid.
15. 'Pakistan Tests Chinese/North Korean-based Missiles', *Jane's Intelligence Review*, May 1999, p. 3.
16. *Jane's Intelligence Review*, 2 October 1996, p. 16.
17. Mushahid Hussain, 'Pakistan Missiles: First Pictures', *Jane's Defence Weekly*, 11 March 1989, p. 386.
18. Bill Gertz, 'US has Detected Metals, Electronics on the Way to Nuclear Weapons Lab', *The Washington Times*, 4 June 1998.
19. From the website of Pakistan's Ministry of Foreign Affairs http://www.forisb.org/Pak-majorpowers.htm, accessed on 6 June 2000.
20. Kathy Chen, 'Beijing Admits to Sale of Ring Magnets to Pakistan in Bid to Clear U.S. Tension', *Wall Street Journal*, 15 April 1996, p. B6.
21. Gerard White and Gary Milhollin, 'Bombs from Beijing: A Report on China's Nuclear and Missile Exports', Washington D.C., Wisconson Project on Nuclear Arms Control, May 1991, p. 17; See also in this context *The Risk Report*, May 1995, p. 8; and Gary Millhollin and Gerard White, 'A New China Syndrome: Beijing's Atomic Bazaar', *The Washington Post*, 12 May 1991, pp. C1, C4.
22. Robert D. Schulzinger, *Henry Kissinger: Doctor of Diplomacy*, New York: Columbia University Press, 1989, p. 79.

23. Nancy Bernkopf Tucker, 'Patterns in the Dust: Chinese–American Relations and the Recognition Controversy, 1949–50', pp.173–4, quoted in Robert D. Schulzinger, *Henry Kissinger: Doctor of Diplomacy*, New York: Columbia University Press, 1989, p. 79.
24. Besides the Nixon and Kissinger memories see in this context Jonathan Pollack, 'The Opening to America, 1968–82', in John K. Fairbank and Roderick MacFarquhar (eds.), *The Cambridge History of China*, Cambridge: Cambridge University Press, 1992, pp. 402–72.
25. Henry Kissinger, *My White House Years*, New Delhi: Vikas Publishing House, 1979, p. 163.
26. Seymour M. Hersh, *The Price of Power: Kissinger in the Nixon White House*, New York: Summit Books, 1983, p. 350.
27. Richard Nixon, 'Asia After Vietnam', *Foreign Affairs*, October 1967.
28. Jonathan D. Pollack, *China's Potential as a World Power*, Santa Monica: RAND Corporation, 1980.
29. Robert Ross, 'China Learns to Compromise: Change in US-China Relations, 1982–4', *The China Quarterly*, December 1991, p. 742–73.
30. David Shambaugh, 'Patterns of Interaction in Sino–American Relations' in Thomas W. Robinson and David Shambaugh (eds), *Chinese Foreign Policy: Theory and Practice*, Oxford: Clarendon Press, 1994, pp. 204–5.
31. Chart Copyright Center for Nonproliferation Studies, Monterey Institute of International Studies.
32. Shirlay A. Kan, 'Chinese Proliferation of weapons of Mass Destruction: Current Policy Issues' Congressional Research Service Reports 12056, June 1998, available at http://www.fas.org/spp/starwars/crs 92056.htm, accessed on 3 November 1999.
33. As cited in Shirley A. Kan, 'Chinese Proliferation of Weapons of Mass Destruction: Current Policy Issues', *Congressional Research Service Report*, 1 June 1998, available at http://www.fas.org/spp/starwars/crs/crs92056htm, accessed on 3 November 1999.
34. Ibid.
35. *International Herald Tribune*, 23 June 1995 cited in Shirley A. Kan, 'Chinese Proliferation of Weapons of Mass Destruction: Current Policy Issues', Congressional Research Service Report, 1 June 1998, available at http://www.fas.org/spp/starwars/crs/crs92056htm, accessed on 3 November 1999.
36. The US had officially dropped the use of the term 'rogue state' as according to a State Department spokesman the term had outlived its use. A new coinage 'states of concern' was used for a while in 2000 and 2001. However, George Bush used the term 'axis of evil' in his State of the Union Address in early 2002.
37. Lt. Gen. Lester L. Lyles the Director of the Ballistic Missile Defence

Organisation of Department of Defense on 24 February 1999, as cited in Zhu Mingguan 'US Plans on National Missile Defense (NMD) and Theatre Missile Defence (TMD): A Chinese Perspective' paper available on the website of the Centre for Non-Proliferation Studies at http://www.cns.miis.edu/db/Chinaengdocs/Zhu/1999.htm, accessed on 5 June 2000.

38. *Beijing Review*, vol. 42, no.12, 22–8 March 1999, p. 9.

CHAPTER 8

Nuclear Proliferation Concerns

SAVITA PANDE

As this chapter was nearing completion, the National Security Archive, an institute at George Washington University, released documents spread over three American Presidencies to further confirm the thesis of this chapter, that China has been helping Pakistan develop nuclear weapons, though the extent of this help 'remains conjectural'. New revelations, especially those confirming how US government officials repeatedly pressed the Chinese government to explain whether it was 'providing any assistance to Pakistan in the nuclear weapons field, but Chinese officials responded with denials and equivocation'.[1] Also, while 'exactly what the US government knew and when it knew it' remains 'highly secret in closed intelligence files' yet, new revelations also highlight the following—

- US unease over secret China–Pakistan security and military cooperation during the late 1960s.
- Chinese assistance to Pakistani nuclear-weapons related projects in 1977.
- the refusal by Chinese diplomats in 1982 to give an 'unequivocal answer' to queries about nuclear weapons aid to Pakistan.
- the conclusion reached by State Department analysts in 1983 that China was assisting with the production of fissile materials and possibly with the design of weapons.
- the George H.W. Bush administration's concern in 1989 over reports of Chinese assistance to Pakistan's nuclear weapons programme.
- denials by Chinese diplomats that same year of reports of Chinese nuclear aid to Pakistan.
- US pressure on China in 1992 to impose full-scope safeguards on the sale of a nuclear reactor to Pakistan because of proliferation concerns.
- more disquiet (late 1992) over China's continuing activities with Pakistan's nuclear weapons programmes.

- the Clinton administration's 1997 certification of improvements in Beijing's nuclear proliferation policies.[2]

The evidence may have come from Libya of Chinese-language material among the nuclear weapons-design documents supplied by Pakistan, but the timing of the revelation is equally important. It coincided with the decision on China joining the Nuclear Supplier Group in 2003. According to William Burr, director of the institute's nuclear documentation project, 'A decision by the Foreign Ministry to publicize the results of its investigation would be a great victory for transparency, although Beijing is more likely to sustain the secrecy surrounding its decisions on the Pakistani nuclear programme.'[3]

Secrecy in Sino-Pak Nuclear Ties

In the case of Sino–Pak nuclear relationship, two things need to be stated at the outset. One, everything related to nuclear trade, in general, and these two countries in particular, is shrouded in so much secrecy that it is very difficult to be exact about the details like the amount, the date or the manner of transaction. Second, the West still has the best intelligence reports and maximum vested commercial interests, most of the information on these issues is based on the Western sources.

The Chinese help to Pakistan ranges from transfer of weapon design information, assistance in setting up enrichment plant, supply of nuclear test data, conduct of nuclear test on Pakistan's behalf or provision of a test site, supply of heavy water and supply of reprocessing technology to transfer of nuclear weapon itself. Even after signing the Treaty on the Non-proliferation of Nuclear Arms (NPT), intelligence-based reports appeared in the American media about supply of 5,000 ring magnets by China to Pakistan for its A.Q. Khan Laboratories in Kahuta. Interestingly, the Americans, after initial bickering, have not been able to take action against the Chinese *vis-à-vis* the NPT otherwise held sacrosanct by them.

It is difficult to say when exactly the nuclear cooperation between the two began; the Chinese military may have decided to support it.[4] Although, to keep the record straight, Pakistan's quest for the nuclear bomb predated the Indian nuclear explosion of 1974, originating at the famous Multan meeting of 1972 addressed by Zulfiqar Ali Bhutto. Thus the assertions of scholars like Dennis Kux that when Pakistan decided to make the bomb only after India's Peaceful Nuclear Explosion (PNE) of May 1974 are not correct.

Chinese Claims

In its claim to have supported international non-proliferation, China's White Paper on National Defence lists the following steps taken by China: joining the International Atomic Energy Agency (IAEA) in 1984; voluntarily placing its civilian nuclear facilities under IAEA safeguards; acceding to the NPT in 1992; being among the first countries to sign CTBT in 1996; becoming a member of the Zangger Committee in 1997; signing Protocol Additional to the Agreement Between China and IAEA for the Application of Safeguards in China in 1998, and formally completing in early 2002, domestic legal procedures necessary for the entry into force of the Additional Protocol, thus becoming the first nuclear-weapon state to complete the relevant procedures.[5]

Regionally, China lays claim to have 'energetically backed up' its neighbouring countries efforts to set-up nuclear-weapon-free zones. China has also signed and ratified the protocols to the Treaty for the Prohibition of Nuclear Weapons in Latin America and the Caribbean (Treaty of Tlatelolco), the South Pacific Nuclear-Free Zone Treaty (Treaty of Rarotonga), and the African Nuclear-Weapon-Free Zone Treaty (Treaty of Pelindaba); 'expressly committing' itself to signing the protocol to the South-East Asia Nuclear-Weapon-Free Zone Treaty (Treaty of Bangkok) and supporting 'the initiative for the establishment' of a Central Asian nuclear-weapon-free zone.[6]

Global Perceptions

India is not the only country skeptical of Chinese behaviour, the United States has voiced equal concerns about proliferation behaviour of the Chinese. Paula A. DeSutter, the then US Assistant Secretary for Verification and Compliance, in a testimony in July 2003, said the United States continued to be 'deeply concerned about the Chinese government's often narrow interpretation of non-proliferation commitments and lack of enforcement of non-proliferation regulations. The government of China has not done enough to ensure that all Chinese entities abide by the non-proliferation commitments the Chinese government has made'. As Secretary Powell said last year,

'China's fulfilment of its non-proliferation commitments would be crucial to determining the quality of the United States–China relationship'.[7] Daniel Horner, Senior Policy Analyst, Nuclear Control Institute, says

> . . . even after acceding to the NPT—China has continued to assist illicit nuclear-weapons programmes, for instance in addition to supplying Algeria a plutonium-production reactor, China has supplied: Iraq with lithium hydride, an important material for making nuclear bombs (in 1990, in violation of the international embargo on Iraq); Iran with a research reactor and a calutron, a technology that can be used to enrich uranium to weapons-grade; and Pakistan with tritium (a material with applications to both basic and advanced nuclear weapons) and specialized ring magnets used in Pakistan's uranium-enrichment programme.[8] (discussed later) After this disclosure, China pledged, in May 1996, to send its nuclear goods only to safeguarded but in 1997 year, the CIA reported: '*During the last half of 1996*, China was the most significant supplier of WMD [weapons of mass destruction]-related goods and technology to foreign countries. The Chinese provided a tremendous variety of assistance to both Iran's and Pakistan's ballistic missile programmes. *China also was the primary source of nuclear-related equipment and technology to Pakistan, and a key supplier to Iran during this period*. . . . [Emphasis added][9]

Then there were reports in the 1980s of possible leaks from Los Alamos National Laboratory to the People's Republic of China whereby China acquired the designs of the W-88 warhead, some believe 'that the resulting warhead miniaturization (achieving similar yields at lower weights) could substantially aid its nuclear weapons modernization program'.[10] An unclassified report of 2003 to Congress said that China also made 'bilateral pledges to the United States that go beyond its 1992 NPT commitment not to assist any country in the acquisition or development of nuclear weapons.

For example, in May 1996, Beijing pledged that it would not provide assistance to unsafeguarded nuclear facilities, but as some unclassified reports of the US Congress suggest, it is not possible to rule out, 'some continued contacts subsequent to the pledge between Chinese entities and entities associated with Pakistan's nuclear weapons programme'.[11] The same is the case with Chinese behaviour regarding missile proliferation that was concluded in the US 2003 Noncompliance Report submitted to Congress, 'Chinese state-owned corporations have engaged in transfer activities with Pakistan, Iran, North Korea, and Libya that are clearly contrary to China's commitments to the

United States'.[12] The report further noted that these 'actions call into serious question China's stated commitment to controlling missile proliferation'.[13] It may be noted that China is not a member of the MTCR, but on several occasions has pledged not to sell MTCR Category I systems, more as an exigency measure. The unclassified report of 2003 cited above also said,

> The Unclassified report of 2003 also said that in November 2000, China 'committed not to assist, in any way, any country in the development of ballistic missiles that could be used to deliver nuclear weapons, and in August 2002, as part of its commitment, promulgated a comprehensive missile-related export control system, similar in scope to the Missile Technology Control Regime (MTCR) Annex. Although Beijing has taken some steps to educate firms and individuals on the new missile-related export regulations—offering its first national training course on Chinese export controls in February 2003—*Chinese entities continued to work with Pakistan and Iran on ballistic missile-related projects during the first half of 2003.*'[14] And '. . . in addition, firms in China provided dual-use missile-related items, raw materials, and/or assistance to several other countries of proliferation concern—such as Iran, Libya, and North Korea'.[15]

A CIA report said in 2003 that apart from Pakistan,

> firms in China provided dual-use missile-related items, raw materials and/or assistance to several other countries of proliferation concern—such as Iran, Libya and North Korea.[16]

The most interesting aspect of the codified norms of the arms control regime is the assured violation of its provisions. This is as true of the export control laws as it is of the Chinese behaviour. It must be stated at the outset that although the rules are supposed to be targeted at the exporters, it being an 'export' control regime, the sanctions are imposed on both exporter as well as importer. More often than not the latter is the victim.

The Issues and Instances

In a June 1997 report on spread of technologies related to weapons of mass destruction, the CIA said that, China was the 'primary source of nuclear related equipment and technology to Pakistan' (for the latter half of 1996). This was despite a pledge in May 1996 made in the context of the ring magnets controversy (discussed later) not to provide assistance to unsafeguarded facilities.[17] While it is difficult to trace the exact date of origin of China's collaboration with Pakistan, it is understood that agreement of June 1976 referred by the father of Pakistan's nuclear bomb Zulfiqar Ali Bhutto as 'his greatest achievement and contribution to survival of our people and nation' was the one concluded with China which came about as a result of eleven years of efforts. This puts 1965 as the year when the collaboration in principle began.[18]

The Chinese aid to Pakistan's nuclear programme is believed to be ranging from supply of design information, setting up of an enrichment plant, supply of nuclear test data, conducting nuclear tests on behalf of Pakistan or providing with the site, supply of heavy water and transfer of reprocessing technology.[19] The coming of General Zia-ul-Haq as Pakistan's new President following a military coup in 1977 did not affect this collaboration. In 1978 it was reported by an Iraqi news agency that a 'generous offer' of nuclear cooperation—to help build a reprocessing plant was made by China. According to this report, it was also meant to bring Pakistan on par with India in the nuclear field and to minimise India's influence as a nuclear power in the region. According to Chaudhari, in 1979 China pleaded on behalf of Pakistan when Vice Premier Deng held dis-cussions with the then US President Carter not to penalize Pakistan for an alleged nuclear weapon programme.[20]

The National Archive evidence now tells us that in 1979, assistant director of ACDA's Non-Proliferation Bureau, Charles Van Doren, providing a detailed briefing to the General Advisory Committee which met to discuss Symington Amendment and Israeli preemption plans. He is reported to having said that China was doing little to deal with Pakistan which headed the list of proliferation concerns. Instead, it was 'advising United States to help Pakistan against the "Soviet peril" and refrain from punitive action: "cutting off your nose to spite your face"'.[21] It is, of course a matter of regret that this is precisely what the United States did once the Soviets invaded Afghani-stan. Not only was the waiver to the Symington Amendment made, for the next ten years, year after year the American President continued to give a clean chit to Pakistan on its nuclear proliferation, despite its own evidence to the contrary.

In 1980 reports appeared in the media about China having responded positively to a Pakistani request to conduct a nuclear test on China's soil. In the early 1980s China also provided Pakistan with enriched uranium for one or two bombs.[22] In 1981 James Malone, US

Assistant Secretary of State said that China had supplied to Pakistan material other than fuel-related items which he declined to specify. A month later the *New York Times* reported that US officials were disturbed by intelligence reports that China had helped Pakistan in trying to develop a capacity to enrich uranium for weapon use.[23] In September 1982 the US suspended the talks with China for helping Pakistan in the latter's effort to help Pakistan acquire nuclear weapon capability. In June 1984 Senator Cranston told the Senate that 'Pakistan could make at least a dozen bombs. He based his report on a document prepared on Chinese assistance to Pakistan prepared by 90 experts. He said the State Department had been hiding this fact from Congress because it feared if Congress came to know this, it would stop $3.2 billion aid given to Pakistan in the wake of Soviet intervention in Afghanistan.[24]

A *New York Times* report in June 1984 reported that China was helping Pakistan operate its Kahuta uranium enrichment plant.[25] Interestingly, the US despite 'suspicions' that Beijing was providing 'weapons-related know-how' to Pakistan and the fact that China had provided assistance with the production of fissile materials and possibly in 'nuclear device design' continued to feel circumscribed by US commercial interests. The Chinese were going in for nuclear power in a big way, and as a consequence the United States decided to adopt cooperation with China 'that will encourage China to keep in close touch with us on nuclear issues'.[26]

In 1986 China and Pakistan signed an accord on nuclear energy.[27] China has agreed to extend financial and technical help to Pakistan for the second phase of the Chashma nuclear power plant for building another 300-megawatt nuclear power plant, likely to be completed within the next six years, and estimated to cost over $700 million.[28] *There is absolutely no change in Sino-Pak nuclear collaboration in the post cold war period if at all it has intensified* and there can be no denial that is the most serious security challenge to the countries of the region particularly. In 1989 China was reported to have designed a nuclear system for the Pakistani research reactor PARR_II which uses highly enriched uranium.[29] In 1991 a report in the *Washington Post* said Chinese scientists have been sighted at the Kahuta complex, and that in 1986 China sold tritium, an element used to boost the yield of fission weapons to Pakistan. China has also assisted Pakistan in construction of an unsafeguarded plutonium production reactor at Khushab[30] and possibly a reprocessing plant at Chashma.[31] China is also supplying Pakistan with an advanced computer control system.[32]

China also supplies heavy water to the safeguarded Kanupp reactor (originally supplied by Canada). According to a report by the Nuclear Control Institute, a shortage of heavy water is apparently the principal obstacle to the start-up of the nearly completed unsafeguarded Khushab reactor, which Pakistan has built with Chinese assistance. It says recent reports indicate that China is supplying heavy water to the safeguarded Kanupp reactor at a rate of two to four per cent a year to make up heavy water losses. Although the Kana reactor had large reported losses of heavy water in its initial years of operation, the facility was recently upgraded to bring the reactor into conformity with industrial standards, and reduce the heavy water loss rate to about one per cent annually. Thus, China may now be supplying Pakistan with up to four metric tonnes more heavy water per year than it needs for its safeguarded reactor. This leaves open the possibility of diversion of surplus heavy water to Khushab, which needs only 5 tonnes to operate at full power. 'These questions', it says, 'have yet to be resolved.'[33]

Much furore was raised when disclosures of China's ring magnets transfer to Pakistan were made in 1996. China's assistance to Pakistan's nuclear weapons programme was brought into public notice. It was first reported in the *Washington Times* on 5 February 1996, when intelligence reports on the transfer from China National Nuclear Corporation, a state-owned corporation, to the A.Q. Khan Research Laboratory in Kahuta were cited. According to the report, 'intelligence experts believed that the magnets provided to Pakistan are to be used in special suspension bearings at the top of rotating cylinders in the centrifuges'.[34] The custom built ring magnets made of an advanced samarium—cobalt alloy, would enable Pakistan to upgrade and replace its enrichment centrifuges at the rate of one thousand to two thousand machines a year. The ring magnets not on the trigger list, are an integral part of magnetic suspension bearings, which are controlled as dual use items by the Zangger Committee (which China joined recently). The ring magnets could enable Pakistan to double its capacity to enrich uranium for weapon purposes.[35]

The *New York Times* of 12 May 1996, reported that the shipment was made after June 1994 and was worth $70,000. The PRC company involved was China Nuclear Energy Industry Corporation, a subsidiary of the China National Nuclear Corporation.[36] Subsequently, the State Department's report on non-proliferation efforts in South Asia (21 January 1997) confirmed that 'between late 1994 and mid-

1995, a Chinese entity transferred a large number of ring magnets to Pakistan for use in its uranium enrichment program'.[37] In early 1996, some in Congress sought sanctions after reports of transfers made in gross violation of the NPT and contradiction of US laws, including the Arms Export Control Act and Export-Import Bank Act (as amended by the Nuclear Proliferation Prevention Act of 1994).[38]

The Clinton Administration's subsequent actions expose once again the myth of priority to non-proliferation. Clearly trade interests called the shot as a result of which differences cropped up among the decision makers. Even though US Secretary of State, Christopher instructed the Export-Import Bank to suspend financing for commercial deals in China for one month, he reportedly 'required time to try to get more information to determine if sanctions would be required'. Representative John Deutch reportedly said at a White House meeting that the Chinese officials may probably approve the deal at some stage, a view that was supported by the then Defence Secretary, William Perry though the Treasury and Commerce department officials disputed the claim as it 'lacked solid proof'.[39] On 10 May 1996, the State Department announced that China and Pakistan would not be sanctioned, citing a new agreement with China. It is another matter that in the interim the administration debated steps like imposing then waiving sanctions or focusing sanctions only on the China National Nuclear Corporation, rather than large-scale sanctions affecting the entire PRC government and US companies, such as Westinghouse Electric Corporation (which had deals pending with China National Nuclear Corporation) and Boeing Aircraft Company.

On 11 May 1996, China's Foreign Ministry issued a statement that 'China will not provide assistance to unsafeguarded nuclear facilities'.[40] While Pakistan denied any such transfer occurred, China said that its cooperation with Pakistan was solely for peaceful purposes. On 20 February 1996 the United States suspended the approval new Export Import Bank loan application to China. Following discussions between the then Secretary of State Warren Christopher and the Chinese Foreign Minister Qian Qichan at the Hague in April 1996 the US announced in May that no sanctions would be imposed on China subject to: (a) finding that senior level Chinese officials were not aware of the transactions, (b) China's public commitments not to provide assistance to unsfaeguarded nuclear facilities, (c) Chinese commitments to have a dialogue with the US on export controls.

As announced in Washington on 10 May China had promised not

to make such transfers in future or provide any other assistance to unsafeguarded nuclear facilities had confirmed its commitment to non-proliferation; and had agreed to consult with the US on export control policies and other non-proliferation issues. A public statement later by the Chinese same day, however, contained none of the pledges. The US Administration by way of explanation said that China did not wish to make this pledge publicly; the absence of denial from Beijing of the US statement should be taken as assent. The US Secretary of state subsequently also confirmed that he had accepted an oral pledge by China's foreign minister to that effect.[41]

In October 1996 CIA reported that China had provided Pakistan with dual-use furnaces and diagnostic equipment. It remains unclear whether these transfers took place before or after China's May 1996 pledge. On 8 April 1997, US Assistant Secretary of State Robert Einhorn said in a testimony before the Senate Foreign Relations Committee that China was continuing to aid Pakistan's nuclear weapon programme.[42] Interestingly, while the State Department said that it does not conclude that China has violated its statement that was issued on 11 May 1996 (see above) its statement did not 'address whether the reported transfers occurred before 11 May 1996, or violated the NPT or contradicted US laws (including the Arms Export Control Act, Export-Import Bank Act, and the Nuclear Proliferation Prevention Act of 1994), which may require sanctions'.[43]

Chinese help has also been reported in building Pakistan's nuclear power plant at Chashma and the unsafeguarded, plutonium-producing reactor at Khushab. The former is to have safeguards, but not full scope safeguards. In the latter case China may have provided some equipment for secret heavy water production plant at Khushab, reportedly generating weapons-grade plutonium.[44] The 300MW project, which is likely to be completed within the next six years, they said, would cost over $700 million.[45]

The CIA report in 2003 was reported to have said, 'We cannot rule out, however, some continued contacts subsequent to the pledge between Chinese entities and entities associated with Pakistan's nuclear weapons programme, and that while Beijing had taken some steps to educate individuals and firms on new missile-related export control regulations but, 'Chinese entities continued to work with Pakistan and Iran on ballistic-missile-related projects during the first half of 2003'.[46]

China is also believed to have provided Pakistan ballistic missiles and related components. On 20 June 1991, the Chinese Foreign Ministry said, 'China did supply some conventional weapons to Pakistan, including very small number of short-range tactical missiles', but did not specify if they were M-11 missiles.[47] In May 1991 and August 1993, the United States imposed limited sanctions on China for selling M-11 ballistic missiles to Pakistan. China officially agreed to observe the guidelines of the Missile Technology Control Regime, and not to export missiles inherently capable of exceeding the MTCR parameters. In exchange sanctions were lifted against China. China again supplied missile components to Pakistan again in 1996 and 1997.[48] According to CIA, China provided Pakistan with 30 ready-to-launch M-11 ballistic missiles, capable of delivering nuclear warheads to Pakistan. China also reportedly helped Pakistan build a missile production factory. And US intelligence has reported frequent trips by Chinese missile technicians to Pakistan.[49]

On 6 April 1998, Pakistan test fired surface-to-surface missile Ghauri with a range of 1500 km.[50] The missile is believed to be a variant of the Chinese Dong Feng class of missiles, although some think it may be North Korean Nodong variant. The latter, of course, seems improbable keeping in view the level of North Korean missile programme. According to Terence Taylor, deputy director of International Institute of Strategic Studies, there has been evidence of Chinese technology transfer of M-11 missiles to Pakistan and one can deduce that the new Pakistani missiles had large components of Chinese technology.[51] Paul Beaver, a missile expert at Jane's Group said that the 'whole missile system is based on Russian scud technology with improvements copied from M-9 and M-11 with a domestic launch capability'.[52] Pakistan disclosed plans to launch 2000 km range Ghazni. (Ghazni and Ghauri were both Afghan invaders of India).[53]

In September 2001, sanctions were imposed on Pakistan's National Defence Complex and a Chinese entity, China Metallurgical Equipment Corporation, on charges of collaborating on the transfer of sensitive missile technology under the MTCR guidelines.[54] According to a report in *The Dawn*, the curbs were imposed in the wake of leaked intelligence reports that a shipment of Chinese missile parts to Pakistan was detected by satellite on 1 May and inconclusive talks held in Beijing the week before between the US and Chinese officials.[55] The State Department said the new sanctions—which follow the ones imposed on the Pakistan Atomic Energy Commission and the space organization Suparco last year—are under Category 2 of the MTCR that refers to transfer of missile constituent parts and technology as opposed to transfer of whole missiles under Category 1.[56] As on previous occasions, Pakistan, who was informed of the move in advance by the State Department, described the sanctions as 'unwarranted and unjustified'. 'Our cooperation with China,' said the Pakistani Ambassador to the US, Maleeha Lodhi, 'does not violate MTCR guidelines, to which neither country is a party. But Pakistan abides by these guidelines, and there's nothing between China and Pakistan that violates the guidelines' and pointed out that both Pakistan and China had already 'denied the charges at the highest level.'[57]

Apart from the direct nexus between the two, there are reports of trilateral cooperation, say with North Korea. According to Parthasarthy reports indicate that in October 2000, China invited seven Pakistani and four North Korean nuclear and missile scientists to its nuclear test facilities in Lop Nor, to demonstrate, among other things, how to mate miniaturized nuclear warheads with missile systems.[58] Parthasarthy says encouraged by former Prime Minister Benazir Bhutto, Dr A.Q. Khan, paid a series of visits to North Korea, resulting in the sale of around 20 Nodong Missiles (christened 'Ghauri' by the Pakistanis) in return for supply of know-how for uranium enrichment to Pyongyang by Islamabad. And in 2001, during the visit of a three-member team of its nuclear scientists to North Korea in 2001, Islamabad shared data of its nuclear tests with Pyongyang.[59]

Parthasarthy also lists other instances of 'Trilateral Missile and Nuclear proliferation Axis' in recent years, these include: indications during the visit of a three-member team of its nuclear scientists to North Korea in 2001, of Islamabad sharing data of its nuclear tests with Pyongyang: US satellites picking up pictures of C 130 transport aircraft of the PAF picking up missile spares from North Korea in July 2002; a 'Shaheen Airlines' aircraft transporting 47 tonnes special aluminium (acquired by the Kahuta Research Laboratories established by Dr A.Q. Khan from the UK) to Pyongyang for its nuclear enrichment programme, adding, 'All this could not have happened without Chinese knowledge, acquiescence and encouragement.'[60]

Recently unclassified Report to Congress from the Director of Central Intelligence for the period July to December 2001 on acquisition of technology relating to weapons of mass destruction said Pakistan's ballistic missile programme continued to benefit from significant Chinese entity assistance during the reporting period. With Chinese entity assistance, Pakistan is moving toward serial production of solid-propellant SRBMs, such as the Shaheen-I and Haider-I.[61] The unclassified report of 2003 cited above says,

> Chinese entity assistance has helped Pakistan move toward domestic serial production of solid-propellant SRBMs and supported Pakistan's development of solid-propellant MRBMs.[62]

Conclusion

To conclude, therefore, the fact that India's peculiar position of having two nuclear neighbours—having a clear nuclear nexus, not only in terms of nuclear weapons but also in terms of their delivery systems—cannot but be a matter of utmost concern for India's policy-makers. One cannot but agree with the concern expressed in the letter written by Atal Behari Vajpayee to President Clinton on 13 May 1998 after Pokhran II, leaked in the press in the *New York Times*. It read:

> We have an overt nuclear weapon state on our borders, a state which committed armed aggression against India in 1962. Although our relations with that country have improved in the last decade or so, an atmosphere of distress persists mainly due to the unresolved border problem. To add to the distress that country has materially helped another neighbour of ours to become a covert nuclear weapons state. At the hands of this bitter neighbour we have suffered three aggressions in the last fifty years.[63]

As for the role of the United States, from the above-stated illustration, one draws the inference how every country in the world is guided by self-interest, proliferation being no exception. The so-called US proliferation concerns were subordinated both *vis-à-vis* Pakistan as well as China sometimes to protect security interests of the Cold War times (particularly Soviet intervention in Afghanistan till their withdrawal) and on others, commercial ventures (investment opportunities in China) have been equally compelling.

It is therefore, no mere coincidence that in the latest disclosures of Pakistan's export of nuclear and missile components and secrets to the nations designated by the United States the tip-off itself might have come from the United States. It is therefore not surprising that the United States has treated the issue as an internal matter of Pakistan. That the US needs Pakistan to achieve its objectives in the neighbouring Afghanistan as a 'frontline state' also remains another well-accepted and established explanation of such US behaviour.

To conclude, therefore, this history of continued collaboration between China and Pakistan in the field of nuclear technologies, and especially in the field of nuclear weapons designs and know-how continues to stare in the face of all the non-proliferation norms and regimes. This, in fact, particularly underlines the fraudulence of the NPT regime on the one hand and of the US export-control regulations on the other.

NOTES

1. 'Declassified Documents Show That, For Over Fifteen Years, Beijing Rebuffed U.S. Queries on Chinese Aid to Pakistani Nuclear Program' http://www.gwu.edu/~nsarchiv/NSAEBB/NSAEBB114/press.htm
2. Ibid.
3. Ibid.
4. Dennis Kux, *The United States and Pakistan 1947-2000: Disenchanted Allies*, Baltimore/Washington, D.C: Johns Hopkins University Press/ Woodrow Wilson Center Press, 2001, pp. 172 and 224.
5. Full text of white paper on China's non-proliferation policy and measures, http://www1.chinadaily.com.cn/en/doc/2003-12/03/ content_287062.htm. The paper also said, China actively participated in the work of the IAEA, the Preparatory Commission for the CTBTO and other related international organizations. It supported the IAEA's contribution to the prevention of potential nuclear terrorist activities, and took an active and constructive part in the revision of the Convention on the Physical Protection of Nuclear Materials.
6. Ibid.
7. Paula A. DeSutter, Assistant Secretary for Verification and Compliance, Testimony Before the US–China Commission, Washington, D.C. 24 July 2003, US Department of State, http://www.state.gov/t/vc/rls/rm/ 24518.htm
8. Daniel Horner, 'Past Transgressions and Current Concerns: Is Nuclear Cooperation with China in the National Interest?' *Congressional Research Service Briefing* 24 October 1997.
9. Ibid.
10. 'China Nuclear Controversy', *Proliferation Brief*, vol. 2, no. 6, Wednesday, 24 March 1999 (excerpts of briefing By Gary Samore, Special Assistant to the President and Senior Director for Non-proliferation and Export Controls at the National Security Council at the Carnegie Endowment on 17 March 1999), http://www.ceip.org/files/nonprolif/ templates/Publications.asp?p=8&PublicationID=96

11. Unclassified Report to Congress on the Acquisition of Technology Relating to Weapons of Mass Destruction and Advanced Conventional Munitions, 1 January Through 30 June 2003 http://www.cia.gov/cia/reports/721_reports/jan_jun2003.htm#17
12. Cited in Paula A. DeSutter, Assistant Secretary for Verification and Compliance, Testimony Before the US–China Commission, Washington, 24 July 2003, US Department of State, http://www.state.gov/t/vc/rls/rm/24518.htm
13. Ibid.
14. Unclassified Report to Congress on the Acquisition of Technology Relating to Weapons of Mass Destruction and Advanced Conventional Munitions, 1 January Through 30 June 2003 http://www.cia.gov/cia/reports/721_reports/jan_jun2003.htm#17
15. Ibid.
16. Sino–Pak N-ties can't be ruled out: CIA, *The News*, 15 November 2003, http://www.jang.com.pk/thenews/
17. Director of Central Intelligence, 'The Acquisition of Technology Relating to Weapons of Mass Destruction and Advanced Conventional Munitions, July–December1996', June 1997, Cited in Jennifer Weeks. 'Sino–US Nuclear Cooperation At a Crossroads', *Arms Control Today*, June/July 1997, p. 12.
18. Z.A. Bhutto, *If I am Assassinated*, New Delhi, Vikas Publishing House, 1979, p. 138. Also see Ashok Kapur, *Pakistan's Nuclear Development*, New York, Routledge & Kegan Paul 1987, p. 245.
19. P.K.S. Namboodiri, 'China–Pakistan Nuclear Axis', *Strategic Analyses*, vol. 6, no 7, October 1982, pp. 407–47.
20. G.W. Choudhury, *China in World Affairs: The Foreign Policy of China Since 1970*, Colorado, 1982, p. 262. According to him, 'Similar pleas have also been made by china to top-ranking policy makers who visited China in recent years.'
21. Created during the 1960s, its first chairman was the quintessential establishment figure John J. McCloy. During the Carter years Thomas Watson (Nixon's second ambassador to France) chaired the GAC; other members were McGeorge Bundy, Brent Scowcroft, Wolfgang Panofsky, and Paul Doty. See Document 6: Friday Morning Session, 14 September 1979, General Advisory Committee on Arms Control and Disarmament, Secret, Excised Copy, Excerpt Source: State Department FOIA Release Declassified Documents Show That, For Over Fifteen Years, Beijing Rebuffed U.S. Queries on Chinese Aid to Pakistani Nuclear Program http://www.gwu.edu/~nsarchiv/NSAEBB/NSAEBB114/press.htm
22. Leonard Spector et al., *Tracking Nuclear Proliferation*, Washington DC: Brookings Institution Press, 1995, p. 49.

23. *The New York Times*, 19 September 1982.
24. *The Times of India*, 22 June 1984.
25. *The New York Times*, 23 June 1984, 22 June 1984.
26. See Document 9: U.S. embassy China cable 17168 to State Department, 'US–PRC Nuclear Cooperation—Or the Lack of It', 18 December 1982, Secret Source: State Department FOIA Release; and Document 11: US State Department, 'The Pakistani Nuclear Program', 22 June 1983, Secret, excised copy Source: State Department FOIA release , 'Declassified Documents Show That, For Over Fifteen Years, Beijing Rebuffed US Queries on Chinese Aid to Pakistani Nuclear Program' http://www.gwu.edu/~nsarchiv/NSAEBB/NSAEBB114/press.htm
27. *The Hindustan Times*, 16 September 1986.
28. Beijing to help set up another N-power plant: Musharraf gets warm welcome in Boao, *The Dawn*, 2 November 2003, url=(0039)http://www.dawn.com/2003/11/02/top4.htm
29. *Nucleonics Week*, 9 August 1990.
30. Mark Hibbs, 'China May Continue D20 Reactor exports to Pakistan After U.S. Certification', *Nuclear Fuel*, 11 August 1997, p. 1.
31. Spector et al., n. 45, p. 97.
32. *Wall Street Journal*, 22 August, 1997, p. A10.
33. Steven Dolley, 'China's Record of Proliferation Behaviour', *Issue Brief*, Nuclear Control Institute, 29 September 1997, p. 5.
34. CRS Report: IB92056—China's Proliferation of Weapons of Mass Destruction: Current Policy Issues http://www.ncseonline.org/NLE/CRSreports/international/inter-73.cfm#_1_9 Shirley A. Kan, *CRS Issue Brief for Congress Foreign Affairs, Defense, and Trade Division*, 16 May 2001.
35. Tim Weiner, 'Atom Parts Sold to Pakistan by China, US Says', *New York Times*, 8 February 1996, p. A1.
36. CRS Report, op.cit.
37. Cited in Ibid.
38. CRS Report, op.cit.
39. Ibid.
40. Ibid.
41. Programme for Promoting Nuclear Non-proliferation (PPNN), *News brief*, no. 34, 2nd Quarter 1996, p. 13.
42. *Arms Control Reporter*, 1997, p. 454. B. 236.
43. CRS Report, op.cit.
44. *Nucleonics Week*, 23 March 2000; *Nuclear Fuel*, 12 June 2000.
45. 'Beijing to help set up another N-power plant: Musharraf gets warm welcome in Boao 'The Dawn, 2 November 2003, http://www.dawn.com
46. Sino–Pak N-ties can't be ruled out: CIA, *The News*, 15 November 2003, http://www.jang.com.pk/thenews/

47. Shirley A. Kan, 'Chinese Missile and Nuclear Proliferation: Issues for Congress', *CRS Issue Brief*, Congressional Research Service, 5 May 1992.
48. *Arms Control Reporter* 1998, p. 706, A.3.
49. Steven Dolley, n. 54, p. 5.
50. *The Times of India*, 7 April 1998.
51. *Arms Control Reporter* 1998, p. 706, B254.
52. Ibid.
53. *The Times of India*, 17 April 1998.
54. 'New Curbs on Missile Technology Transfer: Washington's Move Against Pakistan-China Cooperation', *The Dawn*, 2 September 2001.
55. Ibid.
56. Ibid.
57. The ambassador stressed that Pakistan was already facing several layers of sanctions, and the new measure against one particular entity would have no effect on the country's indigenous missile defence programme adding and pointed out that both Pakistan and China had already denied the charges at the highest level, ibid.
58. G Parthasarthy, 'China: An Axis to Grind', *The Pioneer*, 28 August 2003.
59. Ibid.
60. Ibid.
61. http://www.fas.org/irp/threat/bian_jan_2003.htm#10
62. Unclassified Report to Congress on the Acquisition of Technology Relating to Weapons of Mass Destruction and Advanced Conventional Munitions, 1 January through 30 June 2003, http://www.cia.gov/cia/reports/721_reports/jan_jun2003.htm#17
63. See text of the letter, http://www.indianembassy.org/indusrel/pmletter.htm

APPENDIX

TABLE 8.1: CHINESE NUCLEAR FORCES, 2002

Weapon System				Warheads				
Type	No. deployed	Year deployed	Range (km)	Stages	Payload (kg)	Warhead × yield	No. in stockpile	Comment
*Aircraft**								
Hong-6 (B-6)	100	1965	3,100	na	4,500	1-3 × bombs	100	Badger type
Qian-5 (A-5)	30	1970	400	na	1,500	1 × bombs	30	MiG-19 redesign
*Land-based missiles***								
Dong Feng-3A/CSS-2	40	May 1971	2,800	one	2,150	1 × 3.3 Mt	40	liquid/mobile
Dong Feng-4/CSS-3	20	Nov. 1980	4,750	two	2,200	1 × 3.3 Mt	20	liquid/caves/rollout
Dong Feng-5/CSS-4	20	Aug. 1981	13,000+	two	3,200	1 × 4-5 Mt	20	liquid/silo
Dong Feng-21A/CSS-5	48	1985–6	1,800	two	600	1 × 200-300 Kt	48	solid/mobile
Dong Feng-31/CSS-X-9	0	late-1990s	8,000	three	700	1 × 200-300 Kt	0	solid/silo-based

Submarine-based missiles								
Julang-1 (CSS-N-3)	12	1986	1,700	two	600	1 × 200-300 Kt	12	solid/one SSBN
Julang-2 (CSS-N-4)	0	2010?	8000	three	700	1 × 200-300 Kt	?	Solid
Tactical weapons								
Artillery/Rockets/ADMs	–	mid-1970s	–	–	–	low Kt	120	–

Dong Feng means East Wind; Julang means Giant Wave.

* Figures for bomber aircraft are for nuclear-configured versions only. Hundreds of aircraft are also deployed in non-nuclear versions. Aircraft range is equivalent to combat radius. Assumes 150 bombs for the force, with yields estimated between 10 Kt and 3 Mt.

** The Chinese define missile ranges as follows: short-range, less than 1000 km; medium-range, 1,000-3,000 km; long-range, 3,000-8,000 km; intercontinental range, over 8,000 km. The nuclear capability of the DF-16/CSS-6 (M-9)is unconfirmed and not included.

? Implies that there are multiple views/information on the name of the weapons system of the date of its transfer.

Source: http://www.nrdc.org/nuclear/nudb/datab17.asp

TABLE 8.2: SUMMARY OF PAKISTAN'S MISSILES

Name	Alternate Names	Range (km)	Payload (kg)	Test Firings	Developer	Status
Hatf-1		80	500	April 1989	KRL	In service since 1996
Hatf-1A		100	500	February 2000	KRL	
Hatf-2		260–300	500	April 1989	KRL	In service?
Hatf-3		800		3 July 1997?	KRL?	In service?
Hatf-4	Shaheen-1	750	1000	15 April 1999	NDC	Never deployed
Hatf-5	Ghauri-1	1100–1500	700	6 April 1998	KRL/DPRK	Deployed
Hatf-6?	Ghauri-2	2000	500–700?	14 April 1999	KRL/DPRK	September 2000
Hatf-7	Shaheen-2	2400–2500	1000	Declared ready for test Sept. 2000	NDC	
	Ghauri-3? (Ghaznavi?)	3000		15 August 2000??	KRL/DPRK?	
M-9	CSS-6/DF-15	600–650	500		China	Supplied?
M-11	CSS-7/DF-11	300	500–800		China	30–80 supplied

Notes:

1. NDC: National Defence Complex
2. KRL: A.Q. Khan Research Laboratories
3. DPRK: Democratic People's Republic of Korea (North Korea)
4. Hatf-2 may be a Pakistani manufactured M-11
5. Shaheen-1 believed to be based on Chinese M-9 technology and design
6. Shaheen-2 believed to be based on Chinese M-18 or DF-21 technology and design
7. Ghauri and Ghauri-2 are believed to be DPRK (North Korea) No-dong missiles or No-dong based designs

? Implies that there are multiple views/information on the name of the weapons system of the date of its transfer.

Source: http://nuclearweaponarchive.org/Pakistan/PakArsenal.html

CHAPTER 9

Ballistic Missile Technology Transfers

RAJIV NAYAN

The last five decades have been witness to Pakistan and China cooperating in a number of areas. However, in the beginning, Pakistan was closer to the Western military bloc and kept a distance from China even though the latter was among the first countries to extend official recognition to the new People's Republic of China. It was from the Bandung conference of April 1955 that China and Pakistan began coming closer, yet, their strategic cooperation was to take shape following the 1965 India–Pakistan war where improved Indo–US relations had resulted in putting a brake on the flow of military assistance from the US to Pakistan. Pakistan felt pressurized to look for alternative sources of military supplies and China filled the slot. And, given the backdrop of the China–India war of 1962 this was to lay the foundation of an enduring axis making their strategic cooperation the defining feature of peace and security in South Asia.

Just like their interest in nuclear technologies, the Pakistani establishment was also early to realized the strategic significance of ballistic missiles. The history of Pakistani missile development can be traced back to the formation of the Space and Upper Atmosphere Research Commission in 1961.[1] It initially worked for the indigenous missile development programme. On 5 February 1989, a few months before the first test firing of India's Agni, Pakistan's Chief of Army Staff, General Aslam Beg,[2] announced the testing of two types of missiles, called Hatf. This literally means 'deadly', and is the name used for the sword of the Holy Prophet. A section of the Western media believes that the work on these missiles was started in the early 1980s, but there is proof that it began in 1974,[3] when Zulfikar Ali Bhutto was Prime Minister of Pakistan.

However, the indigenous programme faced problems. Then, Pakistan looked outside. North Korea and China became the main suppliers of ballistic missiles to Pakistan, though officially, transactions were denied. Among the two countries China occupies pride of place as far as the transfer of nuclear weapons and ballistic missiles and their technologies are concerned. The paper will show areas of transactions and point out the area(s) where most of the transactions has/have taken place. The proposed study would explore the pattern of missile transactions between China and Pakistan. Finally, it would seek to find out whether sanctions and international pressure have brought forth any changes or not?

Pakistani Missile Programme

Officially, frequently, Pakistan has been announcing tests of a number of 'indigenous' missiles with many names. Hatf-I is a ballistic missile with a range of 80 km and its development in the 1970s was based on French technology. A report in 1992 suggested that the Hatf-IA, with a range of 100 km, was also being developed.[4] The missile can carry a payload of 500 kg. The Pakistani authorities describe the Hatf-II as a ballistic missile with a range of 300 km and payload capacity around 500 kg. Some Western reports mention that this particular missile is shorter in range. A Carnegie Endowment study sees its range around 180 km with the payload capacity of 500 kg,[5] whereas the Federation of American Scientists (FAS) in its report mentions its range around 280 km and payload 500 kg.[6] There was also a report of a missile programme called Shadoz, but it later turned out to be the Hatf-II. Sometimes, it is also called Abdali.

The Hatf-III is stated to be in the range of 600–800 km.[7] In December 1990, when the Pakistan Army chief stated that Pakistan had tested a long-range ballistic missile, it was widely believed that this was the Hatf-III.[8] In 1997, Pakistan claimed that it had tested the Hatf-III,[9] but many in the international strategic community voiced doubts that such a test had been successful. Some studies believe that this programme was abandoned.[10] Others believe that the Ghaznavi missile programme is nothing but old Hatf-III, although its range has been projected around 290 km and payload capacity about 500 kg[11]. Its first flight was stated to be on 27 May 2002 and is expected to be operational by 2004.[12] The FAS perceives that Shaheen is in fact Hatf-III. Its study also speculates the missile will be in the range of 300 km.

In July 1997, it is believed that Hatf-IV was test fired.[13] Some say, in fact, Hatf-IV was renamed Shaheen-1 and once again test fired in 1999. The range of this missile is stated to be between 600–800 km, is believed to have entered into service in March 2003. Hatf-V or Ghauri missile with a range of approximately 1500 km and a payload capacity of 700 kg was tested in 6 April 1998.[14] Some study indicates about Ghauri-2 or Hatf-VA with a range of 1600–1800 km and a payload capacity of 1500 kg test fired on 25 May 2002.[15] The Carnegie put the range of Ghauri-2 around 2000 km and the payload capacity about 700 kg. Centre for Defence Information lists Ghauri-2 missiles as Hatf-VI. The Centre informs that this missile is planned to have a range of 2300 km. Some find Hatf-VI is Shaheen-2.[16]

Generally, it is speculated that it has got a range of 2000–2500 km and a payload capacity of about 1000 kg. It was test fired on 9 March 2004. A report of test of engines of Ghauri-3 missiles came in 1999.[17] The studies done by Carnegie and Nuclear Threat Initiative state that the missile might be in the range of 2700-3500 km, whereas the FAS finds its range 2500 km. The FAS calls it Abdali missile. The Centre for Defence Information puts its range around 3000 km. On 11 May 1999, a Pakistani newspaper, the *Frontier Post*, reported that Pakistan would test a new missile named Tipu having a range of 4000 km on 28 May 1999. However, a confirmed report on its existence is still awaited.

Like its nuclear weapons, Pakistani ballistic missiles are also double-track. Scholars have been speculating reasons for this policy, although no satisfactory answer is still found. Two major explanations have come up. One is that Pakistan does not want to get bogged down, if any one system runs into problem for a variety of reasons. Another explanation is inter-institutional rivalry in Pakistan. It is already known that the Pakistan Atomic Energy Agency (PAEA) is assigned with the task of plutonium-based nuclear weapons, whereas the Khan/Kahuta Research Laboratory (KRL) is supposed to develop enriched uranium-based nuclear weapons. For ballistic missiles, two parallel organizations are KRL and National Defence Complex (NDC). Both are developing missiles of approximately the same range. All the Ghauri series of missiles is believed to be having liquid-fuel engine and developed with the help of North Korea. KRL is considered to be working on liquid engine, whereas NDC is supposed to work on solid fuel.

Nature of Missile Transfers

For decades, international media has been reporting China–Pakistan missile transactions. China has been giving all types of assistance to Pakistan. It ranges from training personnel to providing equipment and vital components to transfer of full-fledged missiles. Of late, American intelligence has been more forthcoming to admit how China's involvement in nuclear and missile proliferation is at least five times greater than what was estimated before.[18] In 1990, a report informed that Chinese scientists trained Pakistani scientists.[19] Again in 1991, the report about the Chinese training to Pakistan Air Force technicians was heard of.[20] Generally, it was suspected that the training was related to Pakistani missiles. In 1994, American intelligence agencies found that Chinese technicians were going to Pakistan to activate the transferred M-11 missiles.[21]

The Chinese had several important tasks left to undertake. These believed to be completion of the Sargodha missile facility to unbundle and assemble the M-11s, and even more importantly, training the armed forces of Pakistan to handle the M-11.[22] American spy satellites detected a few frames at Sargodha which looked similar to the frames at China's own M-11 production facilities.[23] In 1996, too, the presence of Chinese engineers was noted. This year, the construction of a ballistic missile production facility using pre-fabricated sheds in the Kala Chata mountain range near Fatehgunj, 40 km west of Islamabad, called the NDC was highlighted.[24] Later in 2002, reports came that a large-scale missile production had been started at the Fatehjung missile factory near Islamabad built with Chinese assistance.[25] That China is still providing technical expertise related to missile development to Pakistan is frequently reported in the Western media.

In 2001, *Washington Times* quoted American intelligence officials telling that 12 consignments for missile parts for Shaheen I and Shaheen II missiles had reached Pakistan either by ship or by truck.[26] The last of the consignment was reportedly detected by US reconnaissance satellite on 1 May 2001.[27] China initially encouraged Pakistan to develop its own guidance system for the Hatf-2,[28] though its standard was extremely poor, as has been admitted by General Aslam Beg.[29] In January 1992, guidance systems for M-11 missiles got transferred from China to Pakistan. Again in 1996, the media reported the import of navigation equipment such as gyroscopes and accelerometers.[30] The report about the transfer of guidance systems came in 2000[31] and

2002, too.[32] A report noted that the missile command system-CT-101 which was required for increasing better control and guidance for Ghauri-II and Shaheen-II missiles got transferred to Pakistan from China.[33]

In 1996, a shipment of ammonium perchlorate, used as a solid rocket propellant, was detected.[34] In 1995, the detection of some crates containing machine tools for rocket motors was reported.[35] Then, in 1998, a Chinese ship carrying special metals and electronics to the Pakistani Khan Research Laboratory was also spoken of.[36] In March 1999, the transfer of metal-working presses and a special furnace took place.[37] Again in 2000, the transfer of specialty steel was reported.[38] In 2000, the report about the transfer of fuel improvement ventilation system came into light. In 2002, the supply of solid fuel to Pakistan was also reported.[39] Besides, reports coming from time to time have informed that re-entry thermal protection materials, post-boost vehicles, missile computers and integration of warheads have also come to Pakistan from China.

In March 1991, *Time* reported Chinese supply of M-11 missile to Pakistan,[40] though later the same source claimed that the supplied items were mobile launchers and dummy missile frames.[41] A study[42] discovered that in the 1980s, Pakistan had entered into contract for the supply of 36 M-11s, as well as construction of a factory to produce missiles. Later, in 1988, a report referred to the sale of 84 M-11 missiles with 12 to 20 launchers.[43] It was reported that all the missiles had been transferred to the heavy missile brigade of Pakistan's army. In 1990, there was news about the Chinese willingness to sell its M-9 missiles, having a range of 600 km, to Pakistan. This news was based on a US Navy report.[44]

In May 1991, China agreed with the US Undersecretary of State, Robert M. Kimmit, that it had sold ballistic missiles to Pakistan.[45] On 20 June, Wu Jianmin, a spokesperson for the Chinese Foreign Ministry, admitted that a small number of short-range missiles had been transferred to Pakistan.[46] Also, Zhu Qizen, China's then ambassador to the US stated that China had dispatched a tiny number of short-range tactical missiles to Pakistan.[47] Again, on 5 July 1991, the press counsellor of the Chinese embassy, Chen Guoqing, said in an open letter to the editors of the *Washington Times* that it had sent very small quantities of short-range tactical missiles to Pakistan.[48] Throughout, China took the precaution of not stating that the missiles transferred to Pakistan had crossed the parameters laid down by the

MTCR. Through this technique, Pakistan tried to maintain the supply of M-11 without the American pressure.

In 1992, Western media reported that the training version of M-11 came to Pakistan.[49] This missile was accompanied with a transporter-erector-launcher vehicle.[50] Initially, American sources maintained that there only twelve M-11 missiles in Pakistan,[51] while another source reported that 24 M-11 ballistic missiles came to Pakistan. Indian sources put the figure at 60.[52] Another American Report later substantiated the Indian figure.[53] Besides, this report confirmed that Pakistan was working to increase the range of the missiles procured from China. In November 1992, US satellites located another shipment of M-11 missiles.[54]

However, some in the US believed that M-9s had also been transferred. Some Western writers speculated that the transactions involved licence or co-production of the system in Pakistan after proper training. In 1993, Mirza Aslam Beg stated that the M-11 could be the best carrier for Pakistani nuclear weapons.[55] In 1993, Pakistan got some equipment of M-11 missiles. Later on, reports came that the US had clinching evidence of the transfer of the complete M-11 system. In 1994, Zamir Akram, a political counsellor in the Pakistani embassy stated that the procurement of M-11 missiles was hardly a secret.[56]

In 1994, the then President of Pakistan, Farooq Leghari, officially confirmed that Pakistan had purchased missiles from China;[57] he also maintained that the procured missiles were within MTCR parameters. For the first time in May 1996, a US inter-agency report by the Weapons and Space Systems Intelligence Committee declared that the M-11 missiles were operational. The assessment was based on evidence provided by the CIA.[58] On 10 August 2000, Abdul Sattar, Pakistan's foreign minister, in an interview, once again stated that Pakistan and China have been cooperating on missile technology below the parameters set by the MTCR.[59] M-4X missile variants supplied by China made news in 2002.

An impression is being created that North Korea has replaced China as a supplier for missiles and missiles technology. Some even perceive that North Korea is nothing but a front for China for selling prohibited categories of ballistic missiles. North Korea is maligned for the act, whereas China is perceived as a responsible country of the comity of nations. The reality has not much changed, if one believes American intelligence agencies. A six monthly report of the CIA notes how Chinese entities continued to work with Pakistan and Iran on ballistic missile-related projects during the first half of 2003. Chinese entity assistance has helped Pakistan move toward domestic serial production of solid-propellant SRBMs and supported Pakistan's development of solid-propellant MRBMs.[60] After finding hurdles and roadblocks on the path of the indigenous ballistic missile development programme, the Pakistani ruling elite, realized the futility of chasing the mirage and went for the Chinses missiles. It is generally accepted that Hatf series of missiles failed. Hatf-1 to 4 were replaced with the Chinese M-series. Hatf-2 and -3 and Shaheen are considered M-11 missiles, Shaheen-1 is seen as M-9 missiles, and Shaheen-2 is stated to be the M-18 of China.

Their Strategic Significance

Pakistan has got ballistic missiles, which can be tipped with nuclear warheads. Pakistani rulers have been maintaining that ballistic missiles would be used for deterrence. On 10 June 1998, Raja Zafarul Haq, the leader of the House in the Senate and the Minister of Religious Affairs, informed the Pakistani Parliament that Pakistani missiles had been mounted with nuclear warheads.[61] The fact that Pakistan is acquiring ballistic missiles as delivery vehicles for its nuclear weapons is a foregone conclusion. Certainly, it will act as a nuclear deterrence against India. Pakistan wants to ensure its strategic symmetry in its arrangement with India. India is conceived to be a country enjoying superiority in conventional weapons. It seems that Pakistani rulers want to achieve both general and immediate deterrence in relation to India. General deterrence is conceptualized in terms of general military posture and an image emanating from it, whereas immediate deterrence is seen in terms of specific military capability and threats emanating from it.[62]

In the absence of ballistic missiles, Pakistan would have relied solely on its air force. A number of problems have been found with the sole reliance on aircraft-based nuclear deterrence. Seth Carus underlines two important functions of ballistic missiles.[63] The first is their role against strategically significant but relatively remote military installations from the frontline; precisely speaking, targets specified by him for this role are air bases, equipment storage depots, command posts, and air defence sites. The second is their role against hostile ground forces near the frontline. High speed and penetration in enemy territory are quite distinct features of ballistic missiles. Again, missiles hold an edge over aircraft in launching an attack at night and are found useful in counter-value strategy, operational flexibility in longer range, deceiving pre-emptive attack with its mobile-based capability.[64]

Moreover, a long period of sanctions has left the Pakistani aircraft industry quite crippled and truncated. It has been struggling with F-16 supplies for more than a decade. The indigenous or joint production of aircraft with China could not make its deterrence very attractive and effective. There are some other problems. A Western study points out,

> . . . the country's overall poor economic performance has prevented the Pakistan Air Force (PAF) from undertaking major fleet expansion and modernization efforts by making the switch from US to European and Russian suppliers. During the late 1990s, especially after India and Pakistan's May 1998 tests, US pressure combined with instability concerns in Pakistan prevented external suppliers from selling high-tech nuclear capable combat aircraft to Islamabad. Finally, the unfolding and proposed advances in India's air combat, air-defence, and long-range reconnaissance capabilities are channeling Pakistani investments into a ballistic missile-based capability for which India has no defense at present.[65]

Besides, all of the displayed or announced missiles of Pakistan are in either short-range or intermediate-range category. This gives India lesser time to react to a Pakistani offensive with ballistic missiles. Moreover, payload manipulation can also give Pakistan some manoeuverability in the battlefield.

In a classical sense, alliance is understood as a 'formal agreement between two or more nations to collaborate on national security issues'.[66] However, in history and in the contemporary period, a number of tacit and ad hoc alliances have been found to exist. Through the transactions of ballistic missiles and their technologies and goods China and Pakistan have acted as allies, but have not entered into any formal alliance. In the alliance, the status of Pakistan, by any established standards, appears as a secondary power.

The entry of China as a supplier has made Pakistani deterrence credible. Otherwise, the Pakistani claim of developing ballistic missiles on its own would have not been taken seriously by its adversary India. Pakistan has been enjoying extended deterrence of China, although there was no formal pact for this. Some may raise some fundamental questions related to the nature of this extended deterrence such as the need of much publicized statements to convey to the adversary that the Chinese nuclear weapons may be used to ensure defence of Pakistan. The media has solved some of these problems of communication for the credibility of China sponsored deterrence of Pakistan. Moreover, many writers on deterrence do not believe the necessity of over publicity for the credibility of such extended deterrence. Some wrote, 'It was also pursued *indirectly*, by acting in other situations so as to strongly suggest that if a situation you were concerned about ever arose you would do what you threatened to do.'[67]

It is stated that in the Cold War 'alliances and other linkages for extended deterrence often gave superpower clients resources for trying to settle neighbourhood and internal conflicts violently or refusing to settle or ease ones that might otherwise have been dropped'.[68] It may not be universally applicable in all cases, but it is definitely valid for Pakistan. It has been using its deterrence to blackmail India. Pakistan has been supporting terrorism in India and any corrective measure by India is threatened to turn into a nuclear battleground. Pakistani officials have been threatening to use nuclear weapons on more than one occasion. Munir Akram, the Pakistani ambassador to the United Nations, threatened to use nuclear weapons against India on 30 May 2002.[69] Generally, the concept of deterrence assumes that it would have indirect influence on the deterred. Any direct effect amounts to physical coercion.

Like any modern alliance arrangement and system, it is not restricted in its orientation and approach to the military. Its appearance and the *modus operandi* are military, but the target is political. It addresses the issue of balance of power. Although there is a debate whether China as transferred or is transferring missiles and their related technology to encircle India or not, still there is no doubt India has been put under tremendous pressure because of the transfers. It seems in this arrangement both the countries have two targets. Pakistan wants to deter India, and China, possibly, wants to deter US global hegemony and India's regional leadership or hegemony seen from a different perspective. The transactions between the two countries have brought into light the case of a clandestine alliance between the two countries to alter power equations not only at the regional level but also in world politics.

A report quoting US intelligence sources noted that the Chinese had developed the strategy of entering into covert military ties with Pakistan to blackmail the US into 'curbing US arms sales to Taiwan'.[70]

A number of experts in the US believe that China gives assurance of not supplying missile and related technology to Pakistan only after extracting concessions on a number of security and non-security issues. Therefore, China makes the ballistic missiles supply to Pakistan as a bargaining chip.

As in any clandestine arrangement, the number of parties to the alliance system is a matter of speculation. On the surface, it may appear a case of bilateral relationship. However, as events are unfolding, it looks there were more than two countries in this system. It may give an impression of a coalition of a few countries to pursue WMD. Gradually, the international community is realizing that the reach of this clandestine alliance is far away. As North Korea, Iran, Libya and Saudi Arabia to name the prominent, is involved security and strategic implications and ramifications of this alliance are at least in East Asia and the Middle East.

What has been the outcome of this alliance in the region and in the international system? The supporters of alliance systems of the Cold War system argued that alliances brought stability in the international system through a high degree of deterrence, an element of predictability and by restraining small powers' propensity to go nuclear. The Pakistan–China alliance, to an extent, may have contributed to deterrence. At the same time, the occasional threat of nuclear blackmail by Pakistan should not be ignored. There is total absence of predictability in the alliance system. There is total uncertainty. There is no sharing of risk in this arrangement, no arrangement of crisis management, and no visible scheme for redressal of grievances in this alliance. If we treat China as a major or primary power of the alliance system, so far, it has not demonstrated any evidence that it has willingness or intention to exercise restraint on Pakistan. As a self-fulfilling alliance, it is causing recurring tension and instability not only in the region, but also beyond it.

In the light of developments taking place in the past few years, some are asking a question: Will this alliance last? Is Pakistan an 'adversary partner' of China? Ken Booth has discussed this concept. He writes, 'Given their nuclear and other responsibilities, this means that the superpowers have common interests that are not shared by their allies: they have become "adversary partners".' The relationship between China and Pakistan is not performing all the traditional roles of an alliance. It is designed to promote national interests of both the countries. In history, there have been alliances between ideologically different countries, but it is argued that an alliance between countries of the same ideology is more stable and long lasting.[71]

It will be a completely different issue to examine in the future whether conflicting value systems will prevent or prolong mutually beneficial collaboration between China and Pakistan and among other networked countries. One may argue that no ideology is monolith, and it is on the basis of common points nations try to arrive at an agreement or a pact. In an age marked with clashing ideologies, all the countries had military understanding. The relationship among them was based on interests, not on ideology. It will be interesting to watch whether ideology will be a determining factor in the so-called age of end of ideology. Moreover, China and some of these countries have established authoritarian systems and Pakistan, too, has had quite fair share of military rule in its existence. Thus, together all may continue to build their relationship and alliance on the basis of ideology of authoritarianism and secrecy.

International Pressure

Although a number of countries have been expressing concern about missile proliferation in general and the proliferation between China and Pakistan in particular, still the US has been found the most active on this front. On a number of occasions, China and Pakistan were put under sanctions by the US for transactions in ballistic missiles. These sanctions were placed under the Missile Technology Control Regime provisions of the US export control laws. Apart from imposing sanctions, the US has also been using diplomacy to dissuade Pakistan and China from entering into missile deals. Many believe that it is because of the US pressure that China stopped supplying missiles and started refurbishing and strengthening its export control systems. In last two years, a number of initiatives have come from China to demonstrate to the international community that it was serious about non-proliferation. Certainly, the reality is quite elusive.

Both China and Pakistan have been deceiving the international community in general and the US in particular by frequently reiterating their commitment to non-proliferation. By promising to do so, both were able to get sanctions removed from them before the stipulated period. Both are still indulged into all types of proliferation between themselves and with other countries.

Conclusion

The strange alliance involving China and Pakistan is something more serious than diplomacy of coercion and violence. It formally denounces what it informally does. China has already supplied full ballistic missile systems to Pakistan. Now it is supplying technology to refine or refurbish the system. China has emerged as a frontline proliferator of nuclear and missile technology and goods. A number of countries procured technology from China. Reports about Saudi Arabia, Iran, Iraq, Libya, North Korea and Pakistan are well known by now. The entire episode has shown that a regional roguery is not restricted geographically, but has ramifications beyond a particular region. The entire transactions have proved the irrelevance of US sanctions as an instrument of foreign policy and non-proliferation. Western countries led by the US imposed some sanctions. Sanctions were lifted after and even before the completion of the legally specified period. However, transactions went uninterrupted; only methods for the task changed.

Sino–Pakistani collaboration has altered the balance of power in the region and the clandestine nature of Sino–Pakistani transactions has promoted a culture of disbelief and mistrust. Countries in the region will now be suspicious of signing any arms control or disarmament agreement. China is engaged in missile proliferation activities despite being an adherent country of the Missile Technology Control Regime. The report of its application for the full membership of the Regime will not build confidence. Nor will its projection through white Paper or its own missile control laws of 2002.

Before the May 1998 series of nuclear tests, there was mounting domestic pressure to build an appropriate combination of offensive and defensive missiles, which could counter the threat of the Pakistani missiles to Indian cities. Also, there are demands for anti-ballistic missile development. This pressure is going to grow, now that Pakistan has decided to become an overt nuclear weapon power, claiming that its missiles have been tipped with nuclear weapons.

NOTES

1. Cameron Binkley, 'Pakistan Ballistic Missile Development: The Sword of Islam?', in William C. Potter and Harlam W. Jencks, ed., *The International Missile Bazaar: The New Suppliers' Network*, Boulder: Westview Press, 1994, p. 76.
2. Duncan S. Lennox, ed., *Jane's Strategic Weapon Systems*, Issue 12, Jane'e Information Group, 1990.
3. Binkley, 'Pakistan Ballistic Missile Development'.
4. Lennox, *Jane's Strategic Weapon Systems.*
5. Carnegie Endowment for International Peace, World Missile Chart, http://www.ceip.org/files/projects/npp/resources/ballisticmissilechart.htm
6. Federation of American Scientists, Pakistan, http://www.fas.org/nuke/guide/pakistan/missile/index.html
7. Centre for Defence Information, Nuclear Weapons Database, Pakistani Nuclear Delivery Systems, http://www.cdi.org/issues/nukef&f/database/panukes.html
8. Lennox, *Jane's Strategic Weapon Systems.*
9. *The Indian Express*, New Delhi, 3 July 1997.
10. Center for Defence Information, Nuclear Weapons Database, Pakistani Nuclear Delivery Systems, http://www.cdi.org/issues/nukef&f/database/panukes.html
11. *SIPRI*, http://projects.sipri.se/nuclear/pakistan.pdf and Carnegie Endowment for International Peace, World Missile Chart, http://www.ceip.org/files/projects/npp/resources/ballisticmissilechart.htm
12. *SIPRI*, http://projects.sipri.se/nuclear/pakistan.pdf
13. *Pakistan's Deadly Arsenals: Tracking Weapons of Mass Destruction*, Washington: Carnegie Endowment for International Peace, 2002, pp. 214.
14. *The Indian Express*, New Delhi, 7 April 1998.
15. *SIPRI*, http://projects.sipri.se/nuclear/pakistan.pdf
16. *SIPRI*, http://projects.sipri.se/nuclear/pakistan.pdf, Federation of American Scientists, Pakistan, http://www.fas.org/nuke/guide/pakistan/missile/index.html, NTI, Pakistan Missile Overview, http://www.nti.org/e_research/profiles/Pakistan/Missile/index_3066.html
17. 'Pakistan Tests Ghauri III Engine', *Jane's Defence Weekly*, 13 October 1999, p. 6.
18. *Washington Times*, 22 June 2000.
19. *Defence & Foreign Affairs Weekly*, 30 April–6 May 1990, p. 3.
20. *The Arms Control Reporter*, 6–91, p. 706. B. 55.
21. *Wall Street Journal*, 14 September 1994.
22. *Washington Times*, 7 September 1994.
23. Ibid.

24. *The Asian Age*, New Delhi, 27 August 1996.
25. 'Pak Enhancing Nuke carrying Capacities', *Press Trust of India*, 12 January 2002.
26. *Military Procurement International*, vol. 11, no. 16, 15 August 2001.
27. Ibid.
28. *Jane's Defence Weekly*, 11 March 1989, p. 386.
29. Ibid., 14 September 1989, p. 779.
30. *The Asian Age*, New Delhi, 27 August 1996.
31. David E. Sanger and Eric Schmitt, Reports Say China is Aiding Pakistan On Missile Project, *New York Times*, 2 July 2000.
32. NTI, Pakistan: Missile Import/Export, http://www.nti.org/e_research/profiles/Pakistan/Missile3297_3299.html
33. Ibid.
34. *Far Eastern Economic Review*, 3 September 1996.
35. Elaine Sciolino, *New York Times*, 22 June 1995.
36. Bill Gertz, 'US Has Detected Metals, Electronics on the Way to Nuclear Weapons Lab', *The Washington Times*, 4 June 1998.
37. NTI, Pakistan: Missile Import/Export, http://www.nti.org/e_research/profiles/Pakistan/Missile3297_3299.html
38. David E. Sanger and Eric Schmitt, 'Reports Say China is Aiding Pakistan On Missile Project', *New York Times*, 2 July 2000.
39. 'Pak Enhancing Nuke carrying Capacities', *Press Trust of India*, 12 January 2002.
40. *Time*, 5 April 1991, p. 17.
41. *Time*, 22 April 1991, also the *New York Times*, 24 April 1991.
42. Andrew Koch, 'Pakistan Persists with Nuclear Disarmament', *Jane's Intelligence Review*, March 1997, pp. 131–3.
43. *The Arms Control Reporter*, 1998, p. 706.B.254, also see Gordon Jacobs and Tim McCarthy, 'China's Missile Sales—Few Changes For The Future', *Jane's Intelligence Review*, December 1992, p. 560.
44. *Defence & Foreign Affairs Weekly*, 16 April 1990, p. 1.
45. *Washington Post*, 16 May 1991.
46. *Xinhua*, Beijing, 20 June 1991, in *Nuclear Development*, 10 July 1991.
47. *Jane's Defence Weekly*, 6 July 1991.
48. Xin Hua Domestic Service (Beijing), 16 July 1991 in *Proliferation Issues*, 16 July 1991.
49. Gordon Jacobs and Tim McCarthy, 'China's Missile Sales—Few Changes For the Future', *Jane's Intelligence Review*, December 1992, p. 560.
50. Ibid.
51. *Los Angeles Times*, 4 December 1992.
52. *Milavnews*, August 1991, p. 19.
53. *Aviation Week & Space Technology*, 1 February 1993, pp. 26–7.
54. *Washington Post*, 11 November 1993.

55. *Pacific Research*, May 1994, p. 34.
56. R. Jeffrey Smith and Thomas W. Lippman, *Washington Post*, 8 September 1994.
57. *Reuters*, 5 December 1994.
58. *Jane's Intelligence Review*, March 1997, pp . 131–3.
59. *Kyodo News Service*, Tokyo, 10 August 2000.
60. Central Intelligence Agency, Attachment, A Unclassified Report to Congress on the Acquisition of Technology Relating to Weapons of Mass Destruction and Advanced Conventional Munitions, 1 January Through 30 June 2003, http://www.cia.gov/cia/reports/721_reports/jan_jun2003.htm#1
61. *The Hindu*, 11 June 1998.
62. Patrick M . M organ, *Deterrence: A Conceptual Analysis*, 2nd edn., Beverly Hills: Sage, pp. 42–4.
63. W. Seth Carus, *Ballistic Missiles in Modern Conflict*, New York: Praegar, 1991, p. 10
64. Steve Fetter, 'Ballistic Missiles and Weapons of Mass Destruction', *International Security*, vol. 16, no. 1, Summer 1991, pp. 5–42, and John R. Harvey, 'Regional Ballistic Missiles and Advanced Strike Aircraft: Comparing Military Effectiveness', *International Security*, vol. 17, no. 2, Fall 1992, pp. 41–83.
65. NTI, Pakistan Missile Overview, http://www.nti.org/e_research/profiles/Pakistan/Missile/index_3066.html
66. Ole R. Holsti, et. al., *Unity and Disintegration in International Alliances: Comparative Studies*, New York: John Wiley and Sons, 1973, p. 4.
67. Patrick M. Morgan, *Deterrence Now*, Cambridge: Cambridge University Press, 2003, p. 17.
68. Ibid., p. 49.
69. 'Defiant Pakistan Threatens to Use Nuke', *Press Trust of India*, 30 May 2002, http://in.news.yahoo.com/020530/20/1p549.html
70. *Washington Post*, 14 July 2000.
71. See for example, Harvey Starr, *War Coalitions*, Lexington: DC Heath, 1972, pp. 22–6.

55. *Pacific Research*, May 1995, p. 14.
56. R. Jeffrey Smith and Thomas W. Lippman, *Washington Post*, 4 September 1994.
57. *Reuters*, 5 December [illegible]
58. *Far Eastern Economic Review*, March 1997, pp. 22–24.
59. *Kyodo News Service*, Tokyo, 10 August 2004.
60. Central Intelligence Agency, "Unclassified Report to Congress on the Acquisition of Technology Relating to Weapons of Mass Destruction and Advanced Conventional Munitions, 1 January Through 30 June 2004", http://www.cia.gov/cia/reports/721_reports/jan_jun2004.htm.
61. *The Hindu*, 11 June 1998.
62. Patrick M. Morgan, *Deterrence: A Conceptual Analysis*, 2nd ed., Beverly Hills: Sage, [illegible]
63. W. Seth Carus, *Ballistic Missiles in Modern Conflict*, New York: Praeger, 1991, p. 19.
64. Steve Fetter, "Ballistic Missiles and Weapons of Mass Destruction", *International Security*, vol. 16, no. 1, Summer 1991, pp. 5–42; and John R. Harvey, "Regional Ballistic Missiles and Advanced Strike Aircraft: Comparing Military Effectiveness", *International Security*, vol. 17, no. 2, Fall 1992, pp. 41–83.
65. NTI, Pakistan Missile Overview, [illegible]
66. [illegible] *Comparative Studies*, New York: John Wiley and Sons, 1973, p. 4.
67. Patrick M. Morgan, *Deterrence Now*, Cambridge: Cambridge University Press, 2003, p. 17.
68. Ibid., p. 4.
69. "Defiant Pakistan [illegible]", *Times of India*, May 2002, [illegible]
70. *Washington Post*, 15 July 2001.
71. See, for example, [illegible] *War* [illegible], Lexington: D.C. Heath, [illegible] pp. 2–[illegible]

CHAPTER 10

Air and Aerospace Partnership

M. MATHESWARAN

The struggle for power amongst nations is the hard reality of international relations. This is because competition and conflict are inherent and inevitable characteristics of human nature. From the earliest historians and strategists such as Thucydides, Sun-Tzu, and Kautilya to the modern strategists, the reality of power politics remains the underlying *raison d'être* of any nation's grand strategy and international relations. Study of history, and modern history in particular, establishes the fact that the relations among nation states are inherently competitive. And, when it comes to competition amongst nation-states, this occurs most intensely in the realm of military security, though they also compete in other realms. The driving force in this competition remains their desire to sustain their power, and this concern is crucial in guiding their norms and behaviour. Strategic partnerships and military alliances are resorted to by nation states with a concern for their impact on relative power positions.

In Greece 2500 years ago, the city-state of Sparta, for example, had actively established alliances with the sole aim of restricting the growing power of its rival Athens. It resulted in a long-drawn out and disastrous conflict for both sides. Thucydides, in accounting for the catastrophic Greek war, assured his readers that 'human nature being what it is, these tragic events would be repeated in the future'. Father of Realism, Hans Morgenthau, 2,500 years later, was to define the nature of international relations in the same vein: 'International relations, like all politics, is a struggle for power. Whatever the ultimate aims of international politics, power is always the immediate aim.'[1] Little earlier, when Wilsonian idealism was the mood of the world, E.H. Carr had put the issue in a similar perspective: 'international relations is a blend of realism in large measure and idealism in a small and practical measure'.[2]

In an anarchic world characterized by power politics, nations with large resources and potential evolve competitive strategies for achieving or sustaining great power status. The international order is dictated and controlled by a few great powers, entirely Western. China has always been an important state in the international system, thanks to its great potential power, large territory, vast resources and a large population. Being one of the oldest civilizations and its long history as a major power, territorially, militarily and politically, China has set for itself the objective of achieving the status of a very powerful, wealthy, and technological state by the middle of the twenty-first century. From the time Chairman Mao's Communist party took power in 1949, China has openly displayed its readiness to seek immense strategic leverage through the use of military power. China has pursued a grand strategy conditioned substantially by its historical experience, its political interests and its geo-strategic environment, primarily to attain a significant geopolitical influence as a major, and perhaps primary, state. Frequent and at times intense application of coercive force along with diplomatic and military stratagems to isolate or pressurize its rivals has been a characteristic feature of the Chinese strategy. It is in this context that the China–Pakistan strategic partnership is of considerable importance to India.

India Factor in China–Pak ties

Since 1949, China's actions, policies, and its large presence in the world as a major military and economic power cast a significant shadow on the subcontinent, and on India in particular. Also, right from the beginning, Chinese leaders have viewed India as a rival and this has been the basis of its engagement with Pakistan. Beijing's strategies as a result have been focused on this singular objective. Although Nehru was, as Bharat Karnad calls him, 'that rare world leader whose understanding of history and historical trends was astonishing', he, unfortunately, failed to see through the ruthless strategy of the Chinese.[3] The Chinese began by swallowing up Tibet and thus, for the first time in their history the two nations became contiguous neighbours. India in 1954, surrendered all of its inherited rights in that country in exchange for nothing more than meaningless assurances of respect for principles of 'Panchsheel'.[4]

Steeped in Sun-Tzu's strategies, the Chinese generally follow a long-term game plan entrenched in realpolitik. This was to allow the PLA to make up its lack of sophisticated equipment and firepower through its large sized force structures and adoption of Mao's guerrilla warfare techniques. Paul Bracken calls this a perfection of the 'indirect approach' that is characteristic of the Eastern strategic culture. He sees the Chinese as masters of subtlety who take measured actions to manipulate an adversary without his knowledge.[5] Low-level violence often is the backdrop to a larger strategic campaign. In 1962, for example, China's war objective was not to occupy the disputed areas but humiliate India militarily and thus enhance its international standing.[6] It was also after 1962 that Pakistan became China's close friend and strategic partner. In the 1960s and 1970s this partnership enabled China to contain India so that it could focus on its territorial and ideological disputes with its more powerful foe, the erstwhile USSR. In addition, Pakistan's relationship with the US provided a reliable communication channel for dialogue between China and the United States.

Having surprised India militarily in 1962, China has evolved a fine tuned strategy of containing India to the subcontinent through its strategic partnership with Pakistan. This has enabled the achievement of three important objectives:

- Pakistan's role as a leading Muslim state and its proximity to the Central Asian states could be used gainfully to control insurgent tendencies in its Western province of Xinjiang.
- Pakistan's proxy war not only bleeds India, but more importantly it contains India's strategic influence.
- The Karakoram to Gwader highway corridor provides China an access to the Indian Ocean and, more importantly, the strategically vital Persian Gulf.

The value of these aspects to the China's strategic world-view remains considerable. This has also facilitated China strengthening its strategic partnership with Pakistan in the long-term. China's nuclear and ballistic missile assistance to Pakistan flows from this requirement. This has resulted in the following strategic parameters:

- Assure the survivability of Pakistan by enabling it to become a nuclear weapon state.
- A nuclear Pakistan was more emboldened to wage a proxy war against India without the fear of any major conventional response from India. It has met China's objective of containing India in a

perpetual India–Pakistan conflict syndrome for more than a decade.

- Especially, China's collaborations and joint research in several aerospace sectors has enhanced Pakistan and China's aviation and ballistic missile capabilities.

To achieve its objective of power and hegemony in Southern Asia, China has believed implicitly in the use of force directly or intensive application of coercive force and wide range of diplomatic stratagems of balance and manoeuvre, a strategy of 'indirect approach'. Throughout its history China has followed a combination of strategies to contain its rivals as well as enhance its security. Swaine and Tellis have determined that currently China follows a 'calculative security strategy'.[7] This is clearly evident in its strategy against India. While it advocates peace and tranquillity on the borders with focus on enhanced trade relations, it has quietly followed a strategy of encirclement of India through military and economic cooperation with Pakistan, Myanmar, Bangladesh, Sri Lanka, and Maldives. In short while in the near term the focus is on friendly relations involving economic cooperation, its long-term strategy is to contain and marginalize India's influence not only in Southern Asia but in the Indian Ocean region as well.

The oft-repeated statement that India is a South Asian power has served China's objective of removing India as its strategic competitor in world forums. As Stephen Cohen says, the term 'South Asia' is inappropriate and by boxing-in India in this dimension considerable damage has been done to India's strategic interests. India's strategic marginality was reinforced by the widespread view of Asia as a series of sub-regions, some more important than others. 'Seen merely as a state in South Asia'—says Cohen—'India jostled for attention in the foreign ministries of the world with other Cold War battlegrounds such as South-East and East Asia and the Middle East. These constructed sub-regions displaced the older, expanded notion of Asia.'[8] This South Asian concept has always suited China's strategy of containing India in an endless struggle with Pakistan.

For the emergent India, China not only poses a principal strategic challenge (in political-diplomatic, techno economic, and ultimately in military terms), but has the potential to cause serious damage to India's vital interests. And here, China assisting in the development of major Pakistani naval bases at Gwader and Ormara, which could provide docking and berthing facilities for the PLA Navy surely portends of things to come. This coupled with its creation of strategic assets in Myanmar and its encouragement of Bangladesh to interact and collaborate with the Pakistan Navy assumes great significance.

China's medium to long-term objective is to establish a significant presence in the Indian Ocean region in view of its growing dependence on the SLOCs of this area for trade and commerce. In addition, China looks at this region from the point of view of a large market for its products. In view of these economic considerations, China would like to limit India's influence as much as possible. To achieve this China will have to ensure its freedom for access to Straits of Malacca and the Gulf. A dominant presence in the Indian Ocean will enable it to achieve its aim for which it needs sufficient port facilities in Bay of Bengal and the Arabian Sea. In view of its objective of achieving global power status China is very conscious of the need to modernize its military power.

China's Aerospace Consciousness

Ever since Deng Xiaoping redefined China's grand strategy in 1978, China has pursued the development of 'Comprehensive National Power'. Modernization of its military is an important element of this objective. Chinese scholars have studied in great detail the impact of technology in the Gulf War of 1991. The result of these studies along with the events in the aftermath of the Cold War has convinced the Chinese that mastery over cutting edge technology is a mandatory requirement for great powers in the twenty-first century. Chinese assessment is that the world is currently in a transitional phase and that they are a major contributor in transforming the world into a multi-polar one. The Chinese believe that their evolution as major economic, technological and military power is a primary requirement to achieve that multi-polar world.

The post-World War II order has established a significant axiom for superpower status, which is the requirement of being a nuclear weapon state. China perceived this early and pursued this objective until it became a nuclear weapon state in 1964. However, economic power, technological prowess, and human resources are also mandatory attributes of national power. Deng Xiaoping's reformulation of China's grand strategy in 1984 as the requirement to achieve four modernizations is in tune with this fact. The world of twenty-first century is going to be dominated by powers that possess significant strength in economic, scientific, technological, human capital, and military power. In short comprehensive national power in the twenty-first century will depend largely on the ability of nations, and great powers in particular, to harness the cutting edge of technology for social, economic and military gains.

Throughout modern history, technology has played a major role in the effectiveness of and military capability in particular of the great powers. The leading powers were those who were also the leading military powers. Thus land power and sea power have dominated most of known history. Air power began in the twentieth century but its maturation as an aerospace power at the turn of twenty-first century has far greater implication for national power. The Chinese have come to understand this logic and seem focused on equipping themselves with the new knowledge. To begin with, aerospace Power stems from the fusion of the following four core technologies:

- *Aviation*
- *Space*
- *Computers*
- *Communications*

It becomes obvious that when viewed in a holistic manner, aerospace technologies provide the fundamental drivers for the 'third wave' of Heidi and Alvin Toffler or the knowledge revolution. The most visible capability of aerospace power is in military dimension, which was first demonstrated in the 1991 Gulf war which is where the Chinese began to take interest in aerospace and air technologies. Evolving as an synergetic application of aviation, space and information powers, aerospace power is bringing about a transformation in the nature of war through four major factors:

- Information (quality, quantity and timeliness)
- Command and Control (more effective prosecution of war through centralized planning and decentralized execution).
- Penetration (expansion of the theatre of war due to technologies such as stealth)
- Precision (precise application of force swift results)

While the impact of aerospace power on the military is revolutionary, it is no less significant on economic, technological and political dimensions. Aerospace industries form the most promising and emerging sources of economic power for major powers. Ray S. Cline's formula[9] for national power can be modified to reflect the impact of aerospace power on national power:

$Pp = (C+E+M) \times Ae \times np$
Where C= Critical Mass
E = Economic Power
M = Military Power
Ae = Aerospace Coefficient
and np = National Performance.

The pervasive impact of technology on the political, economic and military power of a nation is shown in this modified formula for calculation of its national power. This technology factor is the Aerospace Coefficient. Aerospace technology is generating applications in a variety of fields that have tremendous economic and military connotations. This fact is well recognized by the Chinese and hence their accent on military modernization is focused more on their space, aviation and nuclear capabilities. China has understood that aerospace dominance allows a state to achieve dominance in precise and decisive military force application, coercive ability as well as diplomatic advantage.

China Aerospace Capabilities

The strategic element of aerospace capability lies in nuclear deterrence which has become so much prominent in Southern Asian power equations. This includes ballistic missiles, satellite based early warning systems and extensive command and control systems which remain critical to make nuclear deterrence effective. Nuclear deterrence is almost entirely dependent on space capabilities in terms of early warning, command and control, communications and satellite based intelligence, surveillance and reconnaissance.

China has begun rapid modernization of its aerospace capabilities. It possesses the world's third largest nuclear weapons arsenal including more than 80 Intermediate Range Ballistic Missiles (IRBM) and more than 20 Inter Continental Ballistic Missiles (ICBM).[10] China's Air Force has 180 nuclear capable bombers, and its Navy deploys one nuclear submarine armed with 12 ballistic missiles. China is already converting its liquid fuelled missiles to accurate, mobile, solid-fuel ICBMs. Beijing is also expected to field ICBMs with multiple independently targeted warheads by 2010. China has deployed a variety of nuclear weapons including tactical nuclear weapons in Tibet. It has already fielded an ABM system using the Russian S-300 ABM, which according to Raja Menon, is essentially a destabilizing action.[11]

Recent years have witnessed China's space capabilities accelerating considerably. Its research and development in areas of satellite surveillance and reconnaissance, UAVs, command and control systems are maturing. Developments in commercial (profit oriented) aerospace programmes have had a positive effect on all levels of China's aerospace industry, including its military side. It has used extensive assistance from other countries, notably Russia, for its civilian space programme. This has resulted in its major achievement of manned flight this year. What is important for strategists is that the military spin-offs from its civilian space programme have been enormous. Reports indicate that the Chinese are working on considerable exploitation of space assets for military operations. Asymmetric strategies including ASAT weapon systems are being pursued for future operational doctrines. The Russians are said to have provided laser and missile interceptor technology that could be incorporated in the Chinese ASAT programmes. The Chinese have also started work on micro satellites and nano-satellites.

Having done an extensive analysis of the impact of technology, aerospace in particular, on future wars, China has gone in for extensive modernization of its air forces and its integration with space capabilities.[12] By 2010 China would have fielded more than 450 nuclear capable, long-range Su-27 aircraft. It has acquired force multipliers such as aerial refuellers and limited airborne control capability. Its national defence university has done considerable analysis of recent wars and has identified Information dominance as the most critical requirement in future wars. Its emphasis on RMA and aerospace technologies has increased considerably. Its modernization of its forces is focused on mechanization, rapid action forces and acquisition of modern weapons. The aim is to improve its capabilities in penetration, survivability, accuracy and mobility. A galloping Chinese technology in nuclear tipped ballistic missiles with MIRV, advanced nuclear powered and SLBM-armed submarines, a robust and modern command and control system, increasing number of satellites that provide extensive targeting data on India, and an ongoing aircraft carrier project; all together indicate that China will pose a considerably enhanced aerospace threat to India by 2010.

China–Pakistan Aerospace Collaborations

The rising aerospace capabilities of China has the potential to hasten China's metamorphosis into a great power. Chinese aerospace collaborations with countries like Pakistan are also transforming its war fighting capabilities and strategies from the traditional attrition model to the modern manoeuvre oriented model. Its thrust is now on fighting modern wars, on the lines of the Gulf War. Its long-term objective is to close the technological gap with the leader, the USA. As a result it is now shifting from a 'continental' strategy to 'ocean' strategy. This shift has important implications for India which must take appropriate measures to safeguard its interests. That lies in enhancing its aerospace capability and nuclear deterrence *vis-à-vis* China.

In consonance with China's larger strategy, Pakistan has played its role as an ideal foil to the larger ally. China and Pakistan have established a variety of collaborative arrangements for research and development ranging from nuclear weapons to aerospace technologies. China has helped establish a considerable level of aerospace infrastructure in Pakistan. It has set-up aircraft overhaul factories, set-up joint ventures in fighter aircraft and aero engine design and production, supplied a variety of electronic warfare, radar, and unmanned platforms and has ensured collaboration and access to its space assets. The recent successful flight test of a fourth generation fighter aircraft J-11 is indicative of the advanced level of collaboration between the two countries. China's support to Pakistan has enabled that country to play a role in South, South-West and Central Asia, larger than its population, economy, or domestic technological capacity would have allowed it to play.

China's assistance to Pakistan involves large-scale nuclear proliferation and sharing of space derived intelligence. The role of information is critical in warfare, particularly in the aerospace model warfare. Pakistan's ability to access Chinese aerospace information systems could prove critical in future conflict scenarios. The China–Pakistan partnership could enable both forces to model their war fighting strategies based on the achievement of information dominance and exploitation of the OODA principle. It also implies that Pakistan would be able to access force multipliers such as aerial refuellers and AWACS systems through China.

Implications for India

It is important for India to realize that the China–Pakistan strategic partnership is an enduring one that cannot be shaken easily. This is primarily because it serves to meet the national objectives of both: for China it meets its strategic objectives of containing or marginalizing a very capable rival from its global strategic landscape; for Pakistan it assures its survivability in the face of overwhelming economic, military and technological superiority posed by India. By 2025 India and China are likely to compete intensely in the realm of energy security. A guaranteed ally in Pakistan that provides access to the Gulf and the Arabian sea could, apart from securing China's vital energy supplies and sources, very well threaten India's very access to the region in the event of a conflict. The important considerations that emerge from the China–Pakistan strategic partnership are as follows:

- China has kept the vexed border problem with India unresolved. Its strategy is to keep the option open to activate hostilities at a point and time of its choosing. On the other hand China has compromised considerably to settle its border disputes amicably with smaller states. Its enhanced aerospace capabilities in the future could make it more aggressive.
- Its close partnership with Pakistan has primarily anti-India objective, apart from using this relationship for strategic gains in Central Asia and tranquillity in its Western provinces. In view of these considerations it has been instrumental in providing nuclear and missile assistance.[13]
- China has gone out of its way to woo countries on India's periphery like Myanmar, Bangladesh and Nepal with military and economic assistance.
- China follows a strategy of encirclement of India. For this it has developed close military and naval cooperation with Pakistan and Myanmar. China's involvement in Pakistan's missile and nuclear development programmes is well documented. It has not only

provided Islamabad with nuclear bombs, uranium and plants (all three Pakistani nuclear plants—Kahuta, Khushab and Chashma—have been built with Chinese assistance), but also their delivery systems; ready-to-launch M-9 (Ghaznavi/Hatf), M-11 (Shaheen), and a number of Dong Feng 21 (Ghauri) missiles.[14]

- Pakistan is not reconciled to the natural imbalance of power in favour of India. In this it has played into the hands of China, whose strategy is to use Pakistan to keep India contained within the subcontinent. Sino–Pak collusion is a serious strategic threat not only to India but Asia as well.
- Pakistan continues its obsession with Kashmir. The use of 'terrorism' as an instrument of policy forms an essential part of Pakistan's strategic doctrine, laying the basis for its threats to unleash nuclear weapons against a numerically stronger enemy.

In the light of these factors it becomes clear that the China–Pakistan strategic partnership poses a major security challenge for India. China's rapidly improving aerospace capabilities and its access to Pakistan could transform the nature of warfare in the region. The two allies could achieve capabilities of swift, precise and rapid operational deployments using aerospace capabilities.

Conclusion

Beginning with the First Gulf War of 1991, the world has been witnessing a paradigm shift in the conduct of warfare. If the Gulf War forms one end of the spectrum the other end is the 'Operation Enduring Freedom' in Afghanistan in 2001, with the Kosovo conflict of 1999 forming the middle. Unlike in earlier operations aerospace power has played the central role. The characteristics of information dominance, extensively networked command and control systems, precision attacks, and penetration to all levels of warfare simultaneously have been the essence of this aerospace model of future wars.

It is also a well-known axiom that Chinese have studied and researched these technologies extensively learning their lessons from the First Persian Gulf War of 1991. China's focus on developing war-fighting strategies emphasizing information dominance, asymmetric strategies, nuclear deterrence and aerospace capability are clearly evident. The advantages of this approach will certainly be reflected in the strategies of its closest ally, Pakistan. In any future conflict situation with India, it can be assumed with certainty that Pakistan stands to gain substantially from the emerging aerospace capabilities of China, particularly in areas of information and precision.

In addition to the military dimension, the impact of aerospace power on the economic, technological and political sectors of a country's national power will become increasingly apparent in the twenty-first century. Great powers of this century will necessarily have to be aerospace powers and China is an aerospace power. In any analysis of the impact that the China-Pakistan strategic partnership has on India, the aerospace dimension will necessarily form a significant dimension.

NOTES

1. Hans J. Morgenthau, *Politics Among Nations: The Struggle for Power and Peace*, New Delhi: Kalyani Publishers, 6th edn. Indian Reprint, 1991, p. 31.
2. E. H. Carr, *The Twenty Year Crisis: 1919–39*, London: Macmillan, 1939, 2nd ed. 1946, 15th Reprint, 1984, pp. 95–101.
3. Bharat Karnad, 'India's Weak Geopolitics and What to do about It?' in Bharat Karnad (ed.), *Future Imperilled*, New Delhi: Viking/Penguin, 1994, p. 34.
4. Ibid., p. 36.
5. Paul Bracken, *Fire in the East: Asian Military Power and the Second Nuclear Age*, New Delhi: Harper Collins, 1999, pp. 106–32.
6. In spite of vociferous propaganda of India–China friendship in the early 1950s, China attacked India in 1962. Given the Chinese Communist policy toward India since 1962, it seems likely that China wanted to prevent India from becoming a major world force. There was not going to be any 'Third Way (led by India) between Communism and the West. For more on China's aggressive strategy and historical analysis see Edward Timberlake and William C. Triplett II, *Red Dragon Rising*, Washington: Regnery Publishing, Inc., 1999, pp. 61–2.
7. The notion of 'calculative strategy' is defined in substantive terms as a pragmatic approach that emphasizes the primacy of internal economic growth and stability, the nurturing of amicable international relations, the relative restraint in the use of force combined with increasing efforts to create a more modern military, and the continued search for asym-

metric gains internationally. Primarily this implies buying time to acquire the requisite economic and military strength to play a more assertive role in the future. An assertive China could pose major security problems for India. For more see Michel D. Swaine and Ashley J. Tellis, *Interpreting China's Grand Strategy: Past, Present and Future* Santa Monica: RAND Publications, 2000, online, www.rand.org/publications/MR/MR1121, pp. 97–150.

8. Stephen P. Cohen, *India: Emerging Power*, New Delhi: Oxford University Press, 2001, p. 24.
9. Ray S. Cline, a former director of the CIA, evolved a widely accepted method for calculating the perceived power of nation states for rank ordering them during the peak of the Cold War period. In the light of the ongoing aerospace revolution this needs to be modified. The author has modified Cline's basic formula to factor in aerospace power in the twenty-first century environment. For more details on Cline's method see Ray S. Cline, *World Power Assessment 1977: A Calculus of Strategic Drift*, Boulder: Westview Press, 1977.
10. A 2002 CIA report predicts that 'the overall size of Chinese ballistic missile forces' over the next 15 years will increase to 75-100 warheads. In addition, it would field about 24 shorter-range DF-31 and DF-4 missiles. Shorter-range missiles are also deployed in Tibet. The new project 094 SSBN submarine is expected to carry 16 three-stage Julang II SLBMs with a range of up to 8000 km. Following allegations of Chinese theft of US nuclear warhead designs, the Cox Report of 1999 concluded that China, with 'aggressive development of a MIRV system', could deploy upwards of 1000 thermonuclear warheads on its missiles by 2015. See *SIPRI Year Book 2002: Armaments, Disarmament and International Security*, Appendix 10A.
11. Rear Admiral Raja Menon, *A Nuclear Strategy for India*, New Delhi: Sage Publications, 2000, p. 189.
12. Michael Pillsbury has done an in depth study of Chinese strategists' and scholars' views after extensive study of their work and interviews. There is a unanimous view on the need for integration of air and space capabilities for prosecution of future wars. Most Chinese scholars make a case that the current RMA will strengthen aerospace forces more than others. They emphasize the growing importance of precision strike capability, stealth, night vision, longer range attacks, lethality of smart munitions, increased C3I capability, and electronic warfare. They highlight the US capability in the 1991 Gulf war where aerospace dimension was exploited using 34 surveillance and reconnaissance satellites, 260 electronic reconnaissance planes and 40 EW aircraft. For detailed views see Michael Pillsbury, *China Debates the Future Security Environment*, Washington: NDU Press, January 2000.

13. John Woosey, former director of the CIA, stated in a testimony to US Senate Governmental Committee—'Beijing has consistently regarded nuclear armed Pakistan as a crucial regional ally and as a vital counterweight to India's growing military capabilities.'
14. China's assistance to Pakistan's nuclear capability is well described with official documents in a study carried out by the Center for Non-Proliferation Studies, Monterey Institute of International Studies, USA. Also see Mohan Malik, *The China Factor in the India–Pakistan Conflict*, Occasional Paper Series, Asia-Pacific Centre for Security Studies, November 2002.

CHAPTER 11

Naval Cooperation

VIJAY SAKHUJA

This chapter examines the evolution and impact of the China–Pakistan naval relations especially by examining the details of the Chinese component in Pakistan's naval inventory. It particularly explores the history of the reasons and initiatives of the Chinese interest in developing Pakistan's maritime infrastructure and its implications for Indian security. And finally, it also attempts to highlight Chinese strategic interests in building relations with countries that lie along the sea-lane from the Persian Gulf to the Malacca Strait and to crystal-gaze the future course of China–Pakistan naval cooperation.

Genesis and Evolution

Cooperation between the Pakistan Navy and Chinese Navy was established in 1970. But before that, in 1967, the Chinese Navy had sent a small group of painters to Pakistan to make paintings of ships at sea and in harbour. The painters also did some portraits of Pakistani Commanders-in-Chief that are now displayed at various messes and wardrooms of Pakistan's naval establishments.[1]

In September 1970, Vice Admiral Muzaffar Hasan, Commander-in-Chief, Pakistan Navy led a delegation to China.[2] This visit was the first ever by a Pakistani Naval Chief to China. During the visit, lasting ten days, the delegation visited Headquarters of North Sea Fleet at Qingdao, East Sea Fleet at Ningbo and South Sea Fleet at Zhanjinag. The discussions during these visits between the Pakistani and Chinese delegations were frank and manifest with trust and confidence. As a matter of fact, this visit resulted in a durable and long lasting impact on the bilateral naval relationship. The Pakistan delegation was conscious of the fact that the Chinese Navy was a coastal defence force and had a large number of small craft essentially for coastal defence. The Chinese Navy, however, had the modern missile fitted Soviet origin Osa and Komar class boats in large numbers.

Interestingly, a Pakistani delegation under General Yahya Khan had visited USSR in June/July 1968 and the Soviets had offered to sell Osa class missile boats to the Pakistan Navy.[3] The delegation also witnessed an impressive demonstration of a hydrofoil torpedo boat on the Yangtse River. The Chinese still possessed several old ships from the colonial era and these were well maintained and in good material state exhibiting the Chinese maintenance skills. Besides, the Chinese naval officers and sailors were knowledgeable about their equipment. The Pakistani naval delegation appears to have also visited a Chinese built Romeo class submarine. Like the missile boats, similar class submarine was on the Pakistan's naval purchase list from the USSR.

Vice Admiral Hasan also met Chairman Mao Zedong and Premier Zhou Enlai and held discussions on the regional security environment. What is of importance is the fact that Zhou Enlai expressed his concern over the situation in East Pakistan and cautioned that the slogan of autonomy could get out of hand and would affect security interests of both Pakistan and China. The premier advised the Chinese Navy Commander-in-Chief to let Pakistan take whatever could be supplied. He noted, 'Helping friends could not be measured in terms of money; in any case selling military equipment was an imperialist ploy abhorred by the People's Republic'.[4] However, Zhou Enlai did admit that Chinese naval hardware was not as sophisticated as those of Western origin.

It was agreed to transfer small patrol craft to strengthen the Pakistan Navy, ostensibly to counter the ongoing unrest in East Pakistan. An important aspect of this military transfer was that there were no clauses with regard to the cost or schedule of payments. But these vessels could not be delivered until after the 1971 India–Pakistan war and the creation of Bangladesh.

Naval Cooperation 1971–2003

Post-1971 India–Pakistan War and the emergence of Bangladesh, Zulfikar Ali Bhutto, prior to assuming the office of the President, led a joint military delegation to China.[5] The Pakistan Navy had then requested the Chinese for three submarines but plans were held in abeyance to be discussed in future military delegations. Also keeping in mind that the Pakistan Navy's responsibilities were limited to water in the Arabian Sea and smaller craft were no longer required, the Pakistan Navy placed orders for larger patrol craft and submarine chasers from China. These orders were followed by the acquisition of missile boats. The details of naval acquisitions during the 1970s[6] are as below:

No. Delivered	Platform/weapon	Description	Delivery
4	Hainan Class	PC	1976–80
4	Hegu Class	FAC	1981
4	Huangfen Class	FAC	1984
4	Huchuan Class	Hydrofoil FAC	1973
12	Shanghai Class	PC	1972–3

The 1980s marked the beginning of a more focused military cooperation that included military technology transfer and arms production but not 'free supply' of equipment. Apparently, this was due to the improvement in relations between New Delhi and Beijing and the resultant partial disengagement of troops from the border. Notwithstanding these developments, Pakistan still sought Chinese military hardware due to its relative availability and low price. The details of naval acquisitions during the 1980s are as below:

No. Delivered	Platform/weapon	Description	Delivery
8	Hia Ying-2	Missile	1981
4	Hia Ying-2	Launcher	1981
4	Hegu Class	FAC	1981
4	Huangfen Class	FAC	1984
16	Hia Ying-2	Missile	1984
4	Hia Ying-2	Launcher	1984
1	Fuqing Class	Support ship	1985
4	Type P58A	Patrol Craft	1989–90

In 1990, Pakistan and China signed a Memorandum of Understanding for a ten-year defence cooperation.[7] Pakistan Navy acquired the Fuquing class tanker from China. China also supplied Hola and Hegu class missile boats. Chinese C-802 SSMs are fitted on Jalalat class fast attack craft and the LY 60 (N) surface-to-air missiles of

Chinese origin are fitted on British-built Type 21 frigates. In 1985, the two sides began to explore the possible sale, including transfer of technology of F-22 frigates.[8] An earlier proposal for acquiring the South Korean HDF-2000 frigate was shelved and in 1992–3, Pakistan government sanctioned $US 700–800 million for Chinese origin vessels. Pakistan Navy has now finalized plans to acquire four Jiangwei-II frigates from China.[9] In June 2004, both countries formally signed the agreement for the supply of four Chinese F-22P frigates. One or two of these frigates would be built in China, while the rest in Pakistan. Pakistan Navy will also buy anti-submarine helicopters from China.[10]

The details of naval acquisitions during the 1990s and through the 2000–3 period are as below:

No. Delivered	Platform/weapon	Description	Delivery
6	LY-60	Launcher	1997
96	LY-60	Missile	1997
4	Type–347G	Fire control radar	1998
4	C-801/802	Missile system	1998
32	C-801/802	Missiles	1998
3	C-801/802	Missile system	1999
4	Type–347G	Fire control radar	1999
24	C-801/802	Missiles	1999
3	Type–347G	Fire control radar	2000
24	C-801/802	Missiles	2000
4	Jiangwei-II class	Frigates	2003–6

Towards Naval Nuclear Cooperation

Statements by senior Pakistani naval officers of a possible nuclear role for the Pakistan Navy have added a new dimension to the South Asian naval balance of power. In this context, Admiral Abdul Aziz Mirza, Chief of Naval Staff, noted that Pakistan had drawn up a long-term strategy for the three services and Pakistan navy was part of that plan.[11] It was also noted that Pakistan being a nuclear power, it was obvious that the government had to think of the means of delivery and a submarine offers the most credible delivery system. It was hinted that the navy was waiting for a go-ahead from the government to equip naval vessels (both surface and sub-surface platforms) with strategic weapons and develop a dedicated sea-launched missile capability or procuring a platform capable of handling nuclear weapons.

By 1990, Islamabad made enquiries with China for possible sale of Han class nuclear submarines.[12] Pakistan even had plans to train about two hundred personnel for operation and maintenance of the submarine. With regards to conventional submarines, Pakistan conducted negotiations with China, France (Agosta 90-B) and Sweden (Type–96) for purchase of submarines. The Chinese submarines were cheaper (US $180 million per vessel), as against the French (US $263 million per vessel) and Swedish offers of (US $333 million per vessel) but were not considered modern enough to challenge the Indian submarine force of Russian origin Kilo class. Besides, the Pakistan navy had rich experience in operating French and the US origin submarines.

Infrastructure Development

Gwadar is strategically located overlooking the Gulf of Oman and the entrance to the Persian Gulf region. It is 40 nautical miles to the east of Pakistan–Iran border and is 390 nautical miles from the Strait of Hormuz. The Strait of Hormuz is one of the world's most strategic choke points. It is fairly deep and vessels of 1,60,000 dwt (dead weight tonnage) can pass through this channel. About half of the world's traded oil passes through this strait. Interestingly, almost every operational tanker of the world transits through this strait some time or the other during the year. The maritime trade transiting the Hormuz represents nearly 17 per cent of the world's trade by volume and about 3 per cent by value. Gwadar's strategic geography therefore provides a good staging post for the Pakistan Navy to monitor the vital Gulf trade route, which accounts for a major part of the world oil traffic.[13]

In the past, several countries had shown interest in the development of Gwadar port. Initially, the Shah of Iran agreed to fund the development of the port since it was close to Iran and would provide a base for the Iranian Navy to control the entrance to the Gulf. Gwadar Port development was also included in Eighth Five-Year Plan (1993–4) of Pakistan. The Government of Pakistan undertook technical and financial feasibilities studies for the development of the port. In 1995, the Nawaz Sharif government cancelled the contract of an Omani firm (recruited by the Benazir Government) to develop the port. Later, the US-based Forbes and Company emerged on the scene and was entrusted with constructing and operating the port. Reportedly, the post-Chagai economic sanctions in 1998 took their toll on any US involvement in the construction.

In 1997, Pakistan sought Chinese assistance in developing and constructing the Gwadar port. The Pakistani initiative appears to have been driven partly by the Chinese successes in developing maritime infrastructure in Myanmar and from the Chinese side maritime strategic interests drove the interests. The project is an example of maritime strategic convergence. Reportedly, there were at least five companies in contention for the development of Gwadar Deep Sea Project (GDSP). These were (a) M/s Posford Duvivier–Gifford and Partners, UK (b) M/s Forbes & Co, USA (c) M/s STFA, Turkey and (d) one Belgian firm. The GDSP project was finally awarded to the Chinese firm M/s China Harbour Engineering Corporation (CHEC). The Pakistan government merely stated that the Chinese firm was the lowest in quotation, without disclosing the other firms tendering for the GDSP. The GDSP had been floated on a BOT (build, operate and transfer) basis.

In May 2001, the Chinese Prime Minister Zhu Rongji, during his state visit to Pakistan agreed to support Pakistan in the GDSP and the Coastal Highway Projects and by June 2001, the Chinese began to prepare a feasibility study of the Gwadar port and the coastal highway projects. On 22 March 2002, President Pervez Musharraf and the visiting Chinese Vice Premier Wu Bangguo laid the foundation stone of the GDSP. The first phase of the project would be completed in three years at a cost of US $ 248 million of which US $198 million would be contributed by China. The agreement to this effect was signed by the Government of China on 10 August 2001.

There are about one thousand Chinese and Pakistani personnel engaged in the project. The project involves construction of three berths of 200 metres each with 300 metres back-up area. On completion of the second phase, the port would be able to accept dry cargo vessels of 100,000 dwt and oil tankers of 200,000 dwt . The work has moved on a fast pace and will be completed by December 2004. Since January 2003, merchant ships have been able to offload hundreds of tonnes of cargo imported for the Project. Gwadar would eventually relieve the congestion at Karachi and provide facilities for sea borne trade and transhipment of cargo, including gas from/to Central Asian states, Xinjiang in China, Afghanistan and north-west India.

Pakistan has declared Gwadar as a special economic zone (SEZ) and the Project has been the special focus of the budget 2003–4. All imports coming through this zone would be exempted from customs duty and sales tax along with sufficient concessions on income tax. Pakistan's finance minister speaking at the post-budget press conference said the Gwadar Port Project being executed with the help of China was very important for Pakistan as well as for the development of Baluchistan. He declared that Rupees 12 billion would be spent on road sector development which would include the Gwadar–Karachi, Gwadar–Khuzdar–Quetta–Chaman, Gwadar–Khuzdar–Ratodero highways, opening route to Afghanistan and the Central Asian Republics (CAR). The port and the highway from Gwadar to Karachi, would be completed before December 2004 and Pakistan would build a road system linking the two ports and build a free trade zone.

In military strategic terms, Gwadar is being developed by Pakistan and China to monitor the sea-lanes from the Persian Gulf. As regards the Makaran coast highway, it offers an excellent staging area for launching missile attacks against enemy ships. Reportedly, a strategic directorate at Pakistan Naval Headquarters has been created that exercises direct command over the fixed and mobile missiles that would be based along the highway. Pakistan's current missile inventory includes the Hatf, Shaheen and the Ghauri series.

Missile	Range	Fuel	Pay Load
Hatf-1	80 km	Solid	500 kg
Hatf-2	280 km	Solid	500 kg
Hatf-3	600 km	Solid	500 kg
M-11	300 km	Solid	800 kg
M-9	600 km	Solid	950 kg
Shaheen-I	600-800	Solid	1000 kg
Shaheen-II	2500(?)	Solid	500 kg
Ghauri-I	1500 km	Liquid	700 Kg
Ghauri-II	2000 km	Liquid	700 Kg
Ghauri-II	3000 km	Liquid	NA

Shaheen missiles can be fired from mobile launchers, which could be placed onshore or aboard surface vessels. Islamabad plans to put weapons on the southern coast. Since most of these missiles have their origin in China/North Korea, it is quite possible that Chinese would provide Pakistan the required technology for advanced missile carriages as also help develop shore-based firing techniques.

Gwadar is of strategic importance to China. As noted, Gwadar lies astride the sea-lane originating from the strategic choke point of Hormuz. In 1994, China became a net importer of oil and about 60 per cent of its energy requirements come from the Persian Gulf and transit along this sea-lane. Notwithstanding the prospects of newer and attractive sources of energy, the Chinese reliance on Gulf oil will continue for quite some time and the bulk of this oil must transit through the Strait of Hormuz and the SLOCs of the Indian Ocean. From the Chinese perspective, the real importance of the region is that it continues to be a theatre of strategic interactions between major global, political and economic powers and the regional states.

The Chinese have been quick to deny that the joint project at Gwadar has any military dimensions. The Chinese foreign ministry spokesman Sun Yuxi has noted that Gwadar is a civil port and there is no (Chinese) naval involvement. It is fair to argue that Chinese interests in Gwadar development go beyond the safety of their energy related shipping from the Persian Gulf but the facility could provide the Chinese a forward base to monitor US naval activity in the Persian Gulf region as also Indian naval activity in the Arabian Sea. As a matter of fact, similar conditions prevail in the Bay of Bengal where the Chinese have established facilities at Coco Island in Myanmar to monitor Indian maritime activity and missile testing in Orissa.

The GDSP project award to the Chinese firm therefore is indicative of an extended Sino–Pak nexus with China having futuristic grand strategic designs in the Arabian Sea, after its exhibited presence in the Coco and Hangyi islands of Myanmar in the Bay of Bengal.

China–Pakistan–Myanmar Nexus

China has been actively engaged in building military infrastructure in Myanmar. It is believed that this infrastructure is for use by the Chinese Navy as and when it operates in the Indian Ocean. The Chinese build up in Myanmar did not take place till the 1990s when China's post-Cold War regional strategy began to take shape. The Myanmar military inventory today includes Chinese origin fighter aircraft, radar and radio equipment, surface-to-surface and surface-to-air missiles, rocket launchers and naval ships. China supplied six Huxian Class missile boats fitted with the YJ-1 (C801) surface-to-surface missiles. Myanmar is indigenously constructing the Myanmar Class missile boats that will be equipped with YJ-1 (C801) surface-to-surface missiles. Earlier, in 1995, the Myanmar Navy had acquired ten Hainan Class patrol boats from China.

China has been engaged in building a major naval base at Hangyi Island near the Irrawady river delta. Work on the project started in 1992, and by 1993, Chinese technicians were helping Myanmar to rebuild a naval base near Bassein. The Hangyi base is capable of providing facilities to much larger ships than the Mynanmar navy has and if the present pace continues it will soon be capable of hosting large PLA Navy vessels including SSBNs and SSNs. Meanwhile, the size of the Myanmar Navy has also grown and facilities for their support have been increasing. Since the bulk of the Myanmar Navy comprises ships of Chinese origin, these facilities will further augment the PLA Navy, as and when it starts to operate in the Bay of Bengal.

An important player in the Sino–Myanmar strategic calculus is Pakistan. In 2001, a Pakistani frigate, submarine and fleet tanker made a port call to Myanmar, a day before the arrival of Pakistani Chief Executive General Pervez Musharraf. What is more important is that Pakistan became the first foreign navy to pay a visit to Myanmar despite the fact that three other countries had sought permission for a port call by their naval ships. It is fair to argue that the Chinese had played a major role to facilitate the visit of Pakistan Navy ships to Myanmar notwithstanding the fact that no Chinese naval ship had made a port call since the takeover by the military junta. This initiative can offer a potential assistance to Pakistani naval vessels in case they operate in conjunction with the Chinese Navy on India's east coast, something New Delhi would be worried of. Besides, Chinese made tanks and some K8 trainer aircraft, co-produced by China and Pakistan are already available in Myanmar's military inventory.

An Emerging Relationship

The Chinese approach to maintaining and promoting diplomatic linkages with Bangladesh is also based on long-term maritime considerations. The geo-strategic location of Bangladesh provides a useful territorial over-bridge in reaching out to Myanmar, the Bay of Bengal and subsequently into the Indian Ocean. China has emerged as a major supplier of arms to the Bangladesh armed forces, particularly the Navy and the Air Force.[14] The importance of the PRC as a donor country to Bangladesh has been increasing steadily. The visit of General Yang Dezhi, Chief of General Staff, PLA, in 1987, called for an open commitment to military cooperation and enhancing military capability of Bangladesh. Admiral Zhang Lian Zhong, the erstwhile Commander of the PLA Navy, had reportedly assured his Bangladesh counterpart of cooperation in the sophisticated management of the Navy.[15]

It is fairly well known that China has emerged as a major supplier of arms to the Bangladesh armed forces particularly the Navy and the Air Force. During December 2003, while addressing the President's Parade at the Bangladesh Naval Academy at Patenga, marking the commissioning of mid-shipmen of Bangladesh Navy, Prime Minister Khaleda Zia pledged to turn the Bangladesh Navy into a three-dimensional force equipping it with modern equipment.[16] Though not related, Pakistan's Chief of the Naval Staff, Admiral Shahid Karimullah, after completion of a successful visit to China visited Bangladesh.

During the visit, Admiral Shahid Karimullah visited some of the units of Bangladesh Navy and attended a briefing on its operational capabilities. He also witnessed some of the naval construction projects and logistic facilities. There have been some unconfirmed reports that suggest that Bangladesh Navy was keen to undergo submarine training with the Pakistan Navy. There have also been some talks about the two sides negotiating a possible lease of a Agosta class submarine. If these initiative go ahead, there is a strong possibility of setting up a submarine facility in Bangladesh. This has to be viewed in the context of Chinese providing assistance to Bangladesh Navy in setting up infrastructure.

The Chinese motivation in coming militarily closer to Bangladesh stems from the perspective that Bangladesh could be used as one of the staging posts in its surge to the Malacca strait and the Indian Ocean. Further, Bangladesh offers a strategic listening post to Indian naval developments in the Bay of Bengal which might challenge Chinese interests in the region. At the same time, China is also interested in maintaining a favourable balance in terms of regional influence and security for its long SLOCs. China will not like to allow India to have a complete free hand in regional security matters and would like to influence events on its own terms as it did during the Indo–Nepal trade related conflicts. Bangladesh, on its part, perceive

India as a regional hegemon and looks up to China as a counter-veiling power to thwart any Indian influence. It has improved relations with Pakistan and such initiatives only support the Chinese overall perceptive of strategic encirclement of India.

Like Myanmar, it appears, that Bangladesh could provide facilities to the Chinese navy as and when it begins to operate in the Bay of Bengal or the Indian Ocean. The Chinese motivation in coming militarily closer to Bangladesh stems from the perspective that Bangladesh could be used as one of its staging/listening posts in its surge to the Malacca Strait and the Indian Ocean as is the case with the Coco Island. This would facilitate a strategic listening post on Indian naval developments in the Bay of Bengal. China and India: Conflicting Strategic Geography and Ambitions.

China has long understood the strategic importance of the Indian Ocean. The Indian Ocean figured in the strategic thinking of ancient mariners in China who sailed in these waters first for trade and then suzerainty.[17] The Chinese maritime planners and practitioners are convinced that the Indian Ocean dominates the commercial and economic lifelines of the Asia–Pacific region and this reality prompted, General Zhao Nanqi, Director of the General Logistic Department of the PLA, to issue a top-secret memorandum that explained in detail the PLA's strategic plans to consolidate control over the South China Sea and the Indian Ocean. He noted,'We can no longer accept the Indian Ocean as only an ocean of the Indians.'[18] Beijing has no doubt that India would oppose China's strategic surge and Zhao stated, 'We are taking armed conflicts in the region into account.'[19]

China has long been seeking an outlet into the Indian Ocean to safeguard its energy sea-lanes from the Persian Gulf and the markets of the region.[20] It is also well aware of the importance of choke points in maritime strategy.[21] Towards that end it has consolidated itself in Southern Asia and South–East Asia and has encircled the Malacca Strait by establishing a strategic staging/listening post to control the Western approaches of the Malacca Strait.[22] In the east, the Spratly Islands, currently under its control, offer a strategic location with respect to the sea-lanes.

China is interested in maintaining a favourable balance in terms of regional influence and security for its SLOCs.[23] China would not like to allow India to have a completely free hand in regional security matters. The Gulf countries have emerged as a major market for Chinese trade and military sales (Iraq, Iran, Saudi Arabia and Yemen).

In return, the Persian Gulf is a major source of Chinese energy requirements. China needs facilities for its navy as and when they operate in the Persian Gulf in support of Chinese strategic objectives.

As a part of its aggressive strategy to encircle India and safeguard its long and vulnerable energy sea-lane from Persian Gulf, China has taken economic and military initiatives in the Maldives as well. It is negotiating with the Maldivian government to construct a submarine base at Marao Island, a coral reef.[24] China already has had extensive experience of operating submarines in the shallow waters in the South China Sea. This initiative would enhance Chinese power projection capabilities as also challenge US naval activity at Diego Garcia. According to reports, China will lease Marao Island for 25 years and create jobs for locals by building infrastructure for tourism and fishing.[25]

Being a dominant power in South Asia, it is natural for India to consider the Indian Ocean as its own sphere of influence. In addition, New Delhi's strategic geography now extends far into the Pacific Ocean in the east and to the Red Sea in the west. Securing control/influence over this area is one of India's main strategic objectives. This strategic thinking is based on long-range naval operations and exercising influence around the strategic choke points of the Strait of Hormuz, the Strait of Malacca and the Sunda Strait. India's naval strategy can be thought of as a 'naval forward strategy'. As part of this strategy, the Indian Navy has been expanding its area of operations east into the South China Sea and the Pacific Rim, west towards the Strait of Hormuz, and, in the south, deep into the Indian Ocean towards the Cape of Good Hope. India's Minister of Defence, George Fernandes, confirmed India's shifting strategic geography and its naval areas of interests in April 2000 at the launching of the Indian warship *Brahmaputra*.[26]

The minister noted that India's 'area of interest . . . extends from the north of the Arabian Sea to the South China Sea'.[27] Soon after, the Indian Navy announced plans for naval exercises in the South China Sea.[28] The decision to conduct exercises was clearly aimed to project the extended operational areas of the navy's reach into the South China Sea.[29] Recent acquisitions, particularly the Delhi-class destroyers, Krivak-class frigates and TU-144 long range maritime patrol aircraft, point to the fact that the Indian Navy has the capability to undertake distant operations as far as South China Sea.

Another rationale for extending the naval strategic reach is in part to counter the growing threat of piracy in the Strait of Malacca. In November 1999, the Indian Navy and coast guard vessels captured a hijacked Japanese cargo ship *M.V. Alondra Rainbow*, after a 12-hour chase.[30] Frequent hijacking of Japanese merchant vessels prompted Japan to propose joint naval patrols in areas around the Malacca Strait.[31] It sought cooperation from China, India, Indonesia, Malaysia, Singapore and South Korea.[32] This proposal was not acceptable to Beijing who viewed it as yet another Japanese step towards extending the strategic reach of its naval operations. This in turn contributed to George Fernandes, former Indian defence minister, calling Japan and Vietnam key strategic partners in anti-piracy operations.[33]

Vietnam has a unique geographical and strategic location. Located on the east side of peninsular South–East Asia, in the north it lies at the southern border of China and in the south it forms the hypothetical choke point between Sabah (on the island of Borneo) and the southern tip of Vietnam.[34] Historically too, Vietnam has always been on the sea-route from China to South–East Asia and India. As far as India is concerned, Vietnam offers a window to monitor Chinese naval activity in the South China Sea and that serves as a strategic listening post for maritime activity east of the Malacca Strait.

New Delhi's policy toward Vietnam attempts to expand both economic and military ties. In April 2000, India signed a 14-article agreement for collaboration with Vietnam.[35] Much of the agreement concerned security issues and India offered military hardware and some training to the Vietnamese military and in return sought Vietnam army's jungle combat training experience to improve its ability to fight separatists in its north–east region.[36] According to the National Security Adviser to the Indian Prime Minister Brajesh Mishra, 'the programme will be strengthened with Indian officers being trained (in Vietnam) in jungle warfare'.[37]

In the broader strategic framework, maritime cooperation between New Delhi and Hanoi helps India to increase its area of influence in South–East Asia. Cooperation with Vietnam also enables India to position itself astride the South China Sea sea-lane. In the long run, India may get access to Cam Ranh Bay naval base.[38] Indian naval ships have on a regular basis visited Vietnamese ports on goodwill visits.[39] These visits were useful in showcasing Indian naval ship-building capability, and Hanoi has shown interest in purchasing naval vessels from India. In 2000, both Indian and Vietnamese navies carried out joint exercises.[40]

The growing relationship between India and Vietnam in part aims to contain Chinese influence throughout South–East Asia.[41] This is bound to generate increased tensions between India and China. China is the central geopolitical issue for both India and Vietnam. For India, China is both a potential competitor for regional hegemony and a potential threat to growing Chinese influence in South Asia. For Vietnam, Chinese assertiveness and forcible occupation of Vietnam's island territories are some of the security issues that present challenges to Hanoi. These mutual concerns are potential grounds for greater military cooperation between the two countries.

Since the mid-1990s, India and Japan have been discussing common security concerns that relate to nuclear policies and maritime security issues.[42] Japan is heavily dependent on Gulf oil for its energy requirements and its vessels have to transit the Andaman Sea-Malacca Straits and the Arabian Sea before setting course either to enter or exit the Strait of Malacca.[43] With regard to maritime cooperation, both Japanese and Indian warships have visited each other's ports and participated in the International Fleet Reviews. In 1995 and in 2000, Indian warships visited Tokyo and Sasebo, respectively.[44] This was in response to an earlier visit of the Japanese naval ship in 1995. Another area of mutual interest between the two maritime forces is search and rescue at sea.[45]

Both India and Japan have taken strategic initiatives to assert greater influence in the Asia–Pacific region. India held naval exercises in the South China Sea in 2000, while Japan has stretched its area of defence out to 4,000 nautical miles through the Malacca Strait, into the Arabian Sea. As of May 2004, thirty-six Japanese naval vessels had completed deployment in the Arabian Sea in support of US-led Operation Enduring Freedom and Operation Iraqi freedom. Because of their geographic locations, the two countries do not appear to compete with each other for influence. Instead, their strategic geographic areas overlap, covering a large proportion of the South China Sea. This clashes with Chinese interests in the same area, and from the Indian and Japanese perspectives they should contain Chinese influence in the region.

India is expanding its role in South–East Asia as part of its 'Look East' policy by building military and economic links with Indonesia and Vietnam, and Japan is expanding its influence from North–East Asia to South–East Asia by gaining access to Singapore's naval facilities for staging operations in the Malacca Strait to challenge any Chinese initiatives in the region.[46]

According to J. Mohan Malik of the Asia-Pacific Center of Security Studies, Honolulu, Hawaii, the main aim of China's Asia policy is to prevent the rise of a potential rival or a competitor.[47] Towards that end, Beijing's strategy is aimed at 'restraining Japan and containing India'. He notes that 'what distinguishes China from its near-rivals, Japan and India, is its permanent membership of the UN Security Council and declared nuclear weapon state (NWS) status, making it a far more important player in international fora and the sole Asian negotiating partner of the United States on global and regional security deliberations'.[48] In order to counter the influence of India, Beijing has developed close economic and military relations with Pakistan, Sri Lanka, Bangladesh and Myanmar.[49] As regards Japan, the Chinese strategy is aimed at propping up North Korea to challenge any Japanese regional ambitions.[50]

India's 'China threat' and the naming of China as the threat that prompted its 1998 nuclear tests has been an important factor in Sino–India relations. A series of verbal exchanges and the subsequent retraction of statements led to a better diplomatic atmosphere between the two nuclear weapon states. In March 2000, China's Foreign Minister Tang Jiaxuan grudgingly noted, 'Generally speaking China and India do not pose a threat to each other. . . .'[51] And in July 2000, President K.R. Narayanan noted that India and China were 'not necessarily rivals'.[52] Notwithstanding these initiatives, both India and China view each other as rivals and have engaged in aggressive geo-strategic initiatives to counter the other's influence.

Given the creeping Chinese assertiveness in the Indian Ocean based on its politico-military and economic initiatives, it is fair to argue that there could be a clash of interests between New Delhi and Beijing. In that context, in the naval realm the clash could occur under two scenarios. First, if India becomes part of the larger US-led coalition aimed at containing China then there could exist a possibility of the two navies being drawn into confrontation. The likely area could be on either side of the Malacca straits where the Chinese are currently in the process of extending influence. In the second scenario, the Indian Navy may come face to face with the Chinese Navy in the event of formation of a strategic alliance among China, Pakistan, Bangladesh and Myanmar. In recent times, the Chinese have been making frequent forays into the Indian Ocean. These visits, though labelled as goodwill, like any other navy, are aimed at testing the strategic reach. Since 2000, these have emerged as an annual feature.

YEAR	SHIPS	PORTS OF CALL
1985–6	Destroyer, Supply Ship	Karachi, Colombo, Chitagong
1993	Zhang He (Trg Ship)	Karachi, Mumbai, Chitagong
1999	Destroyer, Supply Ship	Lumut, Malaysia
2000	Destroyer, Supply Ship	Dar Es Salaam, Cape Town
2001	Destroyer, Supply Ship	Karachi
2002	Destroyer, Supply Ship	S'pore, Italy, France, Britain, Germany

It can be seen that the Chinese Navy ships have frequently made a port call at Karachi. This is a reflection of the relevance and importance of the relationship between Beijing and Islamabad. In 2001, despite an invitation for the International Fleet Review, Beijing 'backed out' and declined to participate. It is believed that Chinese protests over Indian naval manoeuvres in the South China Sea may have been one of the reasons. Besides, the Pakistan Navy had not been invited for the event. Interestingly, two months later, in May 2001, two Chinese naval ships *Harbin* and *Taicang* with Rear Admiral Zhang Yan, deputy commander of North Sea Fleet China, on board, visited Karachi in connection with the fiftieth anniversary celebrations of Pakistan–China relations. Rear Admiral Zhang noted that the two countries were close neighbours, shared common waters and mountains and their friendship enjoyed a long history and was time-tested.

Joint Naval Exercises

On 21 October 2003, the Chinese Navy engaged in a joint naval exercise with the Pakistan Navy off Shanghai. According to the Chinese, these exercises were the first with any foreign country and the Pakistani's described the event as another milestone in the long-standing bilateral cooperation of the two countries in the defence sector.[53] The exercise involved the Pakistan Naval Ships, *Babur*, a destroyer and the Chinese built ocean going tanker *Nasar*. Earlier, these Pakistani ships had visited Lakgkawai, Malaysia to participate in the LIMA2003 (Langkawi International Maritime and Air show).

In all about 1600 naval personnel from both sides participated in the exercises. The exercises included joint search and rescue and joint patrolling and search for suspected vessel.

According to Commodore Muhammad Shafi of the Pakistan Navy, 'We are going to have an intensive exercise. . . . The exercise will be tactical in nature and covers several dimensions of modern-time naval warfare. It also includes joint search and rescue, joint patrolling and search for suspected vessel. . . . It provides a platform for professional interaction between the two navies.'[54] The Commodore also noted that it [exercises] would enhance professional capability and understanding of each other's operating philosophy and the Pakistan Navy was expected to make tremendous gain from the joint exercise. The Chinese too were enthusiastic of the joint exercises and the Chinese Navy Admiral Xiu Ji Wen said that China is proud of participating in a joint maritime exercise with Pakistan, an old, traditional and trust-worthy friend. He said Pakistan was the first foreign country with whom, it [Chinese Navy] was conducting a joint exercise. He said, he was sure the exercise would be successful and help to strengthen their strategic partnership for peace and security.

Admiral Shahid Karimullah, Chief of Naval Staff, Pakistan Navy visited China in May 2004. During the visit, Admiral Karimullah called on General Cao Guangchuan, Defence Minister, Vice Admiral Zhang Dingfa, Commander People's Liberation Army Navy and Lieutenant General Li Jinai, Head of General Armament Department.[55] The two sides held detailed discussions and agreed to continue to hold joint naval exercises and cooperate in non-traditional security fields to strengthen their defence capability and enhance professional skill. It was agreed to have a long-term cooperation, through joint naval exercises, exchange of high level visits and bilateral training. Admiral Karimullah's visit to China is bound to bring the two navies closer. The Chinese Navy has been invited for a joint naval exercise in 2004–5.

What is more worrisome is the fact that the PLA Navy is keen to obtain oceanographic data of the Arabian Sea and Bay of Bengal to enable its submarines to operate in the region. Producing a full set of oceanographic data of these areas is a slow process since sea temperature and salinity levels vary according to the seasons. Besides, such data is built up over long periods by physical presence of ships or submarines. The Chinese are well aware of the limitations and thus believe that as part of their naval cooperation with Pakistan, such information could be availed. At the time of the 1962 Indo–China war, the Indian military leadership had taken note of the potential combined naval threat from China and Pakistan. The Chinese Navy had 25 submarines and twenty-one of these had the capability to operate in Bay of Bengal and Arabian Sea. A reassessment of the Chinese naval threat ruled out a naval conflict but presence of Chinese submarines had been confirmed.

Conclusion

After decades of evolving relations, Beijing and Islamabad have cemented their strategic links. Their cooperation now covers almost all facets of economy, energy, industry, and infrastructure, with nuclear and military cooperation at its core. The Chinese diplomatic and military efforts in Pakistan also exhibit a conspicuous policy of power projection against competitors like US and India. The Chinese strategists, maritime planners and practitioners are convinced that Pakistan offers them favourable staging post in terms of regional influence and security for its energy sea lines of communication.

The Sino–Pakistan cooperation has been both at the political and military levels with nearly forty percent of Pakistan's defence equipment of Chinese origin. Pakistan considers China as an 'all-weather friend' and Sino–Pakistan military relations as the 'corner stone' of Pakistan's foreign policy. Another aspect of the Sino–Pak relations is their shared perception of India, as both a competitor and a challenger. Although China played a limited role during the 1965 and 1971 India–Pakistan wars, Beijing gave full political support to Islamabad on the Kashmir issue. However, in recent times, China has been careful not to be drawn into India–Pakistan tensions and has emphasized restraint on both sides.

Today, the relationship has come to symbolize mutual trust and matured into a strategic partnership and the bilateral relations have shown an enduring consistency. The nature and scope of Sino–Pakistan military and nuclear proliferation has been an area of concern to India. Besides, China views Pakistan geo-strategically important as an outlet to the Indian Ocean and also as a land corridor to the Persian Gulf and West Asia.

NOTES

1. Pakistan Navy Historical Section, *Story of Pakistan Navy, 1947–72*, Islamabad: Elite Publishers, 1991, p. 253.
2. Ibid., pp. 301–2.
3. Ibid., p. 285.
4. Ibid., p. 301.
5. Ibid., p. 366.
6. See sections on Pakistan Navy in *Jane's Fighting Ships 1970–1 to 1979–80.*
7. Sujit Dutta, 'China and Pakistan: End of a Relationship', *China Report*, vol. 30, no. 2, p. 127.
8. Ayesha Siddiqa-Agha, *Pakistan's Arms Procurement and Military Buildup 1979–99*, New York: Palgrave, 2001, p. 165.
9. See Pakistan Navy section in *Jane's Fighting Ships 1999–2000.*
10. Pak Navy to acquire 4 warships from China: Naval Chief Friday 7 May 2004 at http://www.paktribune.com
11. 'Pakistan Navy All Set to go Nuclear', *Pakistan Observer*, 11 June 2001. Also see 'Pakistan Navy Waiting For Government Nod to go Nuclear', *Indian Express*, 11 June 2001.
12. Tai Ming Cheung,'Nuclear Deal On Han', *Far Eastern Economic Review*, 6 September 1990, pp. 20–1.
13. Gwadar is also flanked by two Pakistani naval bases, i.e. Jiwani, 30 nautical miles to the West and Pasni, 60 nautical miles to the East. The Jinnah Naval Base at Ormara is located about 120 nautical miles to the East.
14. *Jane's Fighting Ships, 2000–1*, pp. 42–9. Some frigates and a large number of patrol crafts of Bangladesh navy are of Chinese origin. Besides, the army's tanks and Air Force combat aircraft are all Chinese. In short, China has forged Bangladesh into a military-equipment client state like Pakistan.
15. R. Chakrabarti, 'China and Bangladesh', *China Report*, vol. 30, no. 2, 1994, p. 155.
16. Navy To Be made 3-Dimensional Force: Khaleda, *The Daily Star*, 29 December 2003.
17. C.P. Fitzgerald, *The Horizon History of China*, New York: American Heritage Publishing Co., 1969, pp. 239–42.
18. Yossef Bodansky, 'The PRC Surge for the Strait of Malacca and Spratly Confronts India and the US', *Defence & Foreign Affairs Strategic Policy*, Washington, 30 September 1995, pp. 6–13.
19. Ibid.
20. In 1990, China's oil demand was pegged at 2.1 million barrels/day and is expected to rise to 6.3 million barrels/day thus registering a growth of

nearly 2300 per cent. In the period 1993-99, China's imports doubled from 313,000 barrels/day to 600,000 barrels per/day. For more details, see Rahul Roy–Chaudhury, *India's Maritime Security*, New Delhi: Knowledge World, 2000). p. 99.

21. For more details on Chinese understanding of Sun Tzu's *The Art of War* see Vijay Sakhuja,' Sun Tzu's Art of War and Chinese Maritime Ambitions' at the website of *Peace Forum, Taiwan* at http://www.dsis.org.tw/peaceforum/papers/2003-05/MM0305001e.htm
22. The South China Sea in the east and India and Indonesia in the west dominate the approaches to the Malacca Strait. By virtue of its geography, Myanmar sits astride the sea-lane that transits the Malacca Strait from the Indian Ocean into the Pacific Ocean.
23. Subhash Kapila, 'Bangladesh–China Defence Co-operation Agreement's Strategic Implications: An Analysis', Paper No. 582, 14 January 2003 available at website of *South Asia Analyses Group* at http://www.saag.org.
24. A.B. Mahapatra, 'China Acquires a Base in Maldives Against India With Some Help From India', at the website of *News Insight.Net* at http://www.indiareacts.com.
25. Ibid.
26. See 'India Challenges China in South China Sea', at homepage of *Stratfor* at http://www.stratfor.com/ dated 26 April 2000.
27. Ibid.
28. Ibid.
29. Indian naval ships have, in the past, carried out exercises in the Asia–Pacific waters, but the important aspect of recent exercises was that long-range maritime patrol aircraft based in India were to fly that far and carry out exercises.
30. Vijay Sakhuja, 'Maritime Order and Piracy', *Strategic Analysis*, February 2001, p. 2007.
31. The Japanese concern over piracy has become more serious following the disappearance of 4,200 ton *M.V. Tenyu*, a Panama registered Japanese vessel owned by the Kobe-based Masumoto Kisen Shipping Co. The vessel was on its way from Kuala Tanjung, North Sumatra to South Korea with a cargo of aluminum ingots worth US$1.9 million. The ship apparently turned up under a new name and all fifteen crewmembers were reportedly missing or presumed killed or murdered. Unlike *Tenyu*, *M.V. Alondra Rainbow*, another Japanese owned vessel, was fortunately captured by Indian security forces in the Arabian Sea and subsequently handed over to its owners. These incidents have only added to Tokyo's concern about the vulnerability of Japanese owned shipping.
32. The Japanese government was keen to dispatch Maritime Safety Agency (Coast Guard) ships to the Malacca Strait for anti-piracy operations.

The vessels were expected to form part of the multi-national anti-piracy patrol comprising of coast guard and naval vessels of China, Republic of Korea, Malaysia, Singapore and Indonesia.

33. See 'India Challenges China in South China Sea', at homepage of *Stratfor* at http://www.stratfor.com/ dated 26 April 2000.
34. It is not a choke point per se but can be termed as a high seas strategic passageway. It is fairly wide and shipping traffic transit through this keeping well clear of the Spratly group of islands.
35. See 'India Aims for Influence in Southeast Asia' at homepage of *Stratfor* at http://www.stratfor.com/ dated 29 March 2000.
36. Ibid.
37. Ibid.
38. See 'Advantage: Hanoi in Intensifying Geo-strategic Game' at homepage of *Stratfor* at http://www.stratfor.com/ dated 14 February 2001.
39. The author has visited the port city of Ho Chi Minh on two different occasions in 1993 and 1995. During discussions with senior officers of the Vietnamese navy in 1995, it emerged that they were keen to collaborate with the Indian navy in building ships. Both navies have a large component of Russian naval hardware in their inventories. Besides, they were also keen on joint exercises particularly anti-piracy.
40. Julia MacDonald, 'South Asia and South East Asia in 2001', *National Strategy Forum Review*, Spring 2001 at website of *National Strategy Forum* at http://www.nationalstrategy.com/nsr/v10n3 Spring01/100313.htm
41. During author's discussions with Vietnamese CSCAP members at Beijing in December 2000, it emerged that Vietnam was concerned about Chinese naval activity in the South China Sea. Though part of ASEAN, Hanoi believes that it will not be possible for any ASEAN country to challenge China all by itself. Vietnamese officers cite the example of clashes between the Philippines and the Chinese navy in the South China Sea.
42. Arpita Mathur, 'Prospect for Indo-Japan Security and Political Cooperation: An Indian Perspective', Paper presented at the JIIA-IDSA Bilateral Dialogue, Tokyo, 14–15 May, 2002.
43. John H. Noer, *Choke Points: Maritime Economic Concerns in South East Asia*, Washington: NDU Press, 1996, p. 18. In 1993, half of the crude oil tankers entering the Malacca Strait were bound for Japan.
44. The author has visited Tokyo in 1995 and was present during the official briefings.
45. Discussions with Indian navy officials at New Delhi in December 2002. In 1995, the Indian Navy had provided navy assistance to a Japanese vessel for search and rescue in the Indian Ocean south of Sri Lanka.
46. Tokyo and Singapore concluded a bilateral military agreement in 2000 that permits Japanese patrol ships and aircraft to be stationed in Singa-

pore to evacuate Japanese nationals in disturbed areas as also to assist UN peacekeeping operations in South–East Asia. Earlier, during the Indonesian crisis leading to the fall of President Suharto, Tokyo had positioned aircraft and patrol vessels in Singapore on standby for evacuation duties. This agreement increase Japan's naval presence in the Malacca Strait and South China Sea, as far as two thousand miles from home. For more details see *Weekly Global Intelligence Update*, at homepage of *Stratfor* at http://www.stratfor.com. Dated, 3 May 2000.

47. Mohan Malik, 'China's Asia Policy: Implications for Japan and India' at the website of *Virtual Forum on Asian Security* at http://www.arts.monash.edu.au/mai/savirtualforum /PaperMalik1.htm
48. Ibid.
49. Ibid. Malik notes that China expert, Alastair Johnston, points out 'Chinese diplomatic strategy is to negotiate from a position of strength to an enemy who is militarily weak and/or tied down with multiple security concerns. The objective is to convince the enemy that the military situation has shifted to his disadvantage and thus to force him to concede.' By building up the military capabilities of allies such as North Korea *vis-à-vis* Japan and Pakistan's and Burma's *vis-à-vis* India, Beijing seeks to tie Japan and India down with multiple security concerns.
50. Ibid.
51. During the 3rd Session of the Ninth National People's Congress, Foreign Minister Tang Jiaxuan held a press conference in Beijing on 10 March 2000 and noted that there are some disagreements and even some outstanding issues between China and India. But generally speaking, China and India do not pose threat to each other.
52. Satu P. Limaye, 'India-East Asia Relations: India's Latest Asian Incarnation', Occasional Analysis, Pacific Forum, CSIS, 3rd Quarter 2000. During President K.R. Narayanan's May-June 2000 visit to China to mark the fiftieth anniversary of bilateral relations, Narayanan pressed for speedier progress on resolution of the border dispute. In response, Jiang Zemin, counselled patience, saying that the problem was 'left over *by* history'. Narayanan responded that it must not be 'left over *for* history'.
53. See 'Pak-China Joint Navel Exercises Begin' at http://www. Pakistani Defence.com
54. Ibid.
55. 'Pakistan, China To Extend Defence Ties, To Hold Regular Naval Exercises Strengthening Defense Capability', available at http://www. paknews.com dated 29 May 2004.

CHAPTER 12

The Maritime Convergence

W. LAWRENCE S. PRABHAKAR

The trilateral dynamics of India, China and Pakistan constitutes a quintessence in the international system. In terms of its geo-strategic significance, the dynamics features the overlapping of bilateral interests, tensions, rivalries, equations, issues and policies generating a unique framework for the regional system of Southern Asia and the Indian Ocean Region. The competitive and cooperative dimensions of the trilateral equations of the India, China and Pakistan rest on two permanent realities; one the geo-strategic, geopolitical and geo-economic imperatives of China as a Pan-Asian power and its ability to extend its domain and influence into Southern Asia and the Indian Ocean; two the assiduous Chinese diplomacy and grand strategy to nurture and sustain cordial bilateral relations with the states of South Asia and the Indian Ocean littoral.

The southern Asian and Indian Ocean strategic space offers China the plausible strategy of two land-based maritime access into the Indian Ocean. The near-western access is through Myanmar and the Kunming-Yunan 'Irrawaddy Corridor'. Given the strong, enduring Sino–Myanmarese links in the political, economic, military and technical infrastructure arena, China has gained commensurate maritime access and the possibility of its surge into the Bay of Bengal. Its land-sea interface is complete with the access to facilities in Myanmar with the possibilities of its rendezvous with its South China naval fleet that could transit through the Straits of Malacca.

Pakistan constitutes China's far-western access through the Sino-Pakistan Friendship 'Karakoram Highway'.[1] The China–Pakistan convergence is a dyadic reciprocal relationship that has been stable for over 50 years. In spatial and strategic significance, the China–Pakistan relationship provides for China's extension into southern Asia with a conduit to the Middle East. As a result, China's motivation to nurture special relationship with Pakistan emerges primarily from the strategic rationale to contain India, with the obvious intent to limit its influence in Central Asian Region and also in the Indian Ocean Region. China rationalizes its extended presence with the fact that Sea Lines of Communication (SLOCs) for its oil imports and other merchandize with the Middle East provide it the basis for building forward facilities in Pakistan, Myanmar and its probes to gain similar access in Maldives.

In these, the salience of the Sino–Pakistan strategic convergence is premised on three pillars of critical support: Diplomatic, Political, Economic with substantive technological and industrial assistance. It has sustained Pakistan on a non-reciprocal basis with the three pillars of support: Development and Infrastructure assistance; Conventional Weapons; and Nuclear/Missile transfers and its extended nuclear deterrence to Pakistan *vis-à-vis* India. In the canvas of these pertinent issues of collaboration, the context of the Sino–Pakistani maritime cooperation in its causal factors, linkages, the significance and scope of China's naval access and domain in the Northern Arabian Sea and the Middle East; its nuclear submarine deployments presents serious implications for India.

China's rationale to secure and monitor its critical oil jugular from the Straits of Hormuz to the Straits of Malacca is an apparent intent. China's real strategic intent would be the nurture of a long-term naval presence in the Indian Ocean to counter India's perceived domination of the Indian Ocean.[2] Quite often the naiveté prevalent in the Indian strategic community makes them dismissive of the real Chinese intent in the Indian Ocean region. It is in this context that the Sino–Pakistani maritime cooperation could be understood from the emergent context of the Indian Ocean maritime strategic dynamics.

Indian Ocean Security Alliances

The strategic significance of the Indian Ocean Region (IOR) in the twenty-first century has emerged with the spawning of new alliances; the increasing presence of extra-regional actors in alliance with regional powers. The scope of intensified extra-regional naval presence and the quest to seek naval access and bases emerges from the drive of the extra-regional players in their strategic and economic quest to seek and exploit resources and markets in the region primarily in the domain of on-shore and offshore sources with the pursuit to stake their geo-strategic interests and geo-economic interests and jockey for postures in the region to bolster their effective presence and in securing their SLOCs.

The prospective patterns of maritime balance in the IOR would be highly competitive in nature. The extra-regional navies are engaged in alliance formations with regional navies in the quest to seek a *comprehensive maritime security*[3] of the region as defined and projected to suit their interests. Such a pattern would result in the evolution of the following typologies:

First, extra-regional navies and their regional partners remain premised on the convergence of interests being termed as strategic partners. The nature of convergence would be premised on the strengths of the complimentary nature of interests and the autonomy of the regional naval interests, e.g. India–US naval interests in the region that are no longer viewed as threatening but has evolved certain complimentary areas of maritime cooperation.

Second, extra-regional navies in independent deployment of their naval assets posturing for active bilateral maritime partnerships premised on the evolution of multilateral maritime alliances with the regional actors in the quest to establish a regional power profile in challenge to regional balance of forces, e.g. Sino–Pakistan alliance and the Sino–Myanmarese naval alliance.

Third, regional navies in their maritime domains that would like to zealously preserve their maritime autonomy and would prefer to resist extra-regional maritime hegemony of the region, e.g. Iran

Fourth, regional navies developing modest yet optimal second-strike nuclear strategic capabilities to deter hostile powers with the premiums on nuclear tipped Cruise Missiles, e.g. India's Sagarika on board the ATV and Israel's Popeye Turbo Cruise Missiles on board its Dolphins.

Fifth, the submarine Order of Battle (ORBAT) of the IOR powers would be in the order of EKM 877 class Kilos in the Iranian, Indian and Chinese PLA-Navy, the Agosta class submarines with Pakistan Navy, the Dolphins with Israeli Navy constituting the conventional submarine forces. In the nuclear realm the Indian ATV would be in place (if sufficient breakthroughs are made) along with the Chinese Type 093, attack and Cruise missile platforms would be in place in the Indian Ocean along with the Type 094 nuclear powered Ballistic Missile Submarines SSBN with JL-2 SLBMs.

And finally, the extra-regional nuclear submarine forces of the

United States would be dominant with their SSN-688 Los Angeles Class and the SSN-21 Sea Wolf class in substantial numbers. Extra-regional submarines like the French Scorpene class submarines in service with the Indian and Pakistan navies would have Air Independent Propulsion (AIP) technologies giving them better endurance and optimal operational capability and would have attack and Cruise missile launch capabilities.

The second context of the extra-regional naval posture and influence in the Indian Ocean littoral would be the deployment of nuclear weapons on the surface and subsurface naval platforms in the maritime region. The deployment of nuclear weapons around the world had been comprehensive in form depth charges, ASROC munitions, nuclear tipped Cruise missiles launched from surface and surface platforms, free fall and guided munitions of the carrier based attack aircraft. Much of this has been integral part of the US Fifth Fleet under the aegis of the US CENTCOM, the Soviet Indian Ocean detachment that was a part of the Soviet Pacific Fleet, the French and the British Ballistic missile submarine forces (SSBNs) and their nuclear powered and tipped attack submarines. The new players in the region are the PLA Navy that had occasionally sent its Xia class SSBN into the region equipped with the JL-1 SLBM in the 1990s into the Arabian Sea.[4]

The third context of the nature and strategic salience of the Indian Ocean Region for India has been the access of extra-regional powers to several Indian Ocean littoral bases spurned by the demand to build capabilities for intervention in the regional conflicts, as also to facilitate optimal logistical support to arms transfusion into the region in peacetime.[5]

The role and posture of the regional and littoral powers offering bases and access facilities in the near future would be a vital factor which considering the nature of bases and access facilities. Two determinants would work in that regard: one would be the evolution of a regional coalition centered around the US on one hand and another probable coalition centred on China. The probable US coalition would provide access and basing facilities in Ethiopia, Eritrea, Kenya, Pakistan, Sri Lanka, Singapore, and Thailand in the arc of the region.

The probable Chinese, led coalition of powers could be Egypt, Saudi Arabia, Pakistan, Maldives, and Myanmar. It is not clear how will Pakistan choose between the United States and China if it really comes to making such a choice. The competing geo-energy and geo-economic interests in the Persian Gulf oil resources and Central Asia would motivate these two coalitions. The pursuit for bases and access facilities would be hectic as US and China would be converging on Pakistan for access to the same. Pakistan would thus emerge with a leverage value for the access facilities. Besides Pakistan, Maldives, Sri Lanka, Bangladesh and Myanmar would be convergent spots for the Chinese and US influences to access their facilities.

The fourth context would be the hostile resistance to the entire process of basing and access facilities in the region that would emerge from Iran. Iran would be keen to adopt an access denial and basing denial posture and would deploy its submarine forces and missile forces that would essentially target US facilities in the region. Iranian missile targeting of the US bases in the region would be increasingly possible and realistic in the future. While Iranian opposition would be against US facilities, it may view Chinese facilities with a benign approach. In an Iranian perspective, Chinese facilities would be viewed as an essential counterweight to the US facilities.

The fifth context is the role of countries like Sri Lanka, Maldives, Bangladesh *vis-à-vis* basing and access facilities to both US and China as it would serve them well for being equidistant in their relationships with the two extra-regional powers. The US would be able to significantly garner facilities in Sri Lanka in the Colombo, Trincomalee, and Ratnamala Air Station as they offer the US naval and air units' optimal access points. Bangladesh would be more in tune with China given its close proximity and the naval exercises of the Pakistani–Bangladesh naval units off the North Andaman Sea in April 2001 is a solid reminder of the emergent Pakistan–Bangladesh and Chinese axis.[6]

The analysis of the maritime dynamics of the IOR presents the matrix of diverse issues in contention and the possibilities of the emergent maritime alliances centering on the United States, China and India. Pakistan occupies the geo-strategic pivot in the Northern Arabian Sea-Straits of Hormuz and accrues considerable geo-strategic location and advantages. Its heartland access to Central Asia on one hand and its westward access to South-West Asia offer the competing extra-regional powers naval access and basing facilities to derive optimal economic and military aid.

Pakistan offers China a land-maritime access that could be China's springboard into Central Asia with the prospects of the

Central Asian hydrocarbon reserves as well as westward access into the Islamic World with access to energy reserves.

China–Pak Maritime Convergence

The Chinese have been quite consummate in their diplomatic efforts to ease their boundary confrontation with India without fully resolving the contention. The agreements of 1988 and 1996 had provided the basis to stabilize and create an atmosphere of peace and tranquillity even as it pursues its modernization and other strategic objectives. China has not completely ruled in favour of comprehensive pacific settlement given the persistence of rivalry and competition. The PLA Naval expansion in South Asia with the aid of its friendly states is essentially a strategic initiative of China to contain India in her region. To this extent China has gone out of its way to accommodate all contentious issues with the smaller states of South Asia if any, and thus has been able to focus on India.[7]

China's naval presence in South Asia is a signal assurance to Pakistan that its naval presence would be a countervailing one to India's dominant influence and naval power in the region and beyond. The specific dimensions of the PLA Naval strategy are analysed below:

(a) *Naval Diplomacy*: The PLA Navy has been keen on regular port visits and bilateral naval joint exercises that indicate its sustained maritime and naval presence in the region. The PLA Navy had sent one of its vessels named *Zheng He* in 1993 to the Bombay port reminiscent of the imperial Ming Navy admiral whose fleets sailed through the Indian Ocean. The PLA Naval port calls to Karachi, (Pakistan), Colombo (Sri Lanka) and Chittagong (Bangladesh) are a regular affair as these ports are in the perimeter pattern.[8] Naval diplomacy provides the PLA Navy a vital platform to sustain its presence and stake its posture in the region. It also provides the rationale for the PLA navy to secure its SLOCs in the Indian Ocean region and also a future possible opportunity to size up to the regional naval forces as well as the US Fifth Fleet, thus fulfilling its role in the Offshore Defense Concept that seeks to confront enemies at a safer distance rather than waiting for enemy within one's territorial waters or territories.

(b) *Naval Basing Facilities*: The PLA Navy in the second phase of its South Asian operations is seeking access to and is involved in the construction of naval bases. The development of Pakistan's Gwadar naval base as an independent naval station with its deep-water profile has been abundantly funded and constructed with Chinese expertise. In return the PLA Navy would be enjoying full access to dock and service with possible options to station a future flotilla in this base. Besides Gwadar, Pakistan is developing its second naval base Ormara in the Baluchistan province known as the Jinnah Naval Base.[9]

China's investment in infrastructure buildup in Pakistan is yet another dimension of its relentless bolstering of Pakistan to make the latter resilient against all odds. The visit of China's Premier Zhu Rongji in May 2001 was in relation to the support of China for the massive development project in Gwadar in Pakistan's western Baluchistan province. The visit was timed with the fiftieth anniversary of the establishment of Sino–Pakistani relations in May 1951. The Chinese support for the first phase of the project was pledged at $400 million in August 2001 with further commitments forthcoming. The Gwadar Development Project entails the construction of a major deep-water port.

The harbour is to be dredged and a construction of 23 deep-sea ship berths is envisaged. The complex would have new wharves, warehouses and other critical harbour facilities and support infrastructure. The port complex would feature container and petroleum loading and unloading facilities. Linking the port would be a network of new railroads connecting Gwadar to the main east-west rail link to Iran at Dalbandin. A highway is envisaged from Gwadar along the Makaran coast. The Makaran highway and the rail road to Dalbandin will link the Gwadar port to the existing road and rail networks of Pakistan. A new high–voltage electrical transmission line is envisaged from Turbat to Gwadar. Gwadar would thus emerge as the second hub to Karachi in Pakistan's seaborne trade.

The Gwadar port is also seen as a strategic convergent hub of the projected sea terminus of the oil pipelines proposed by Pakistan during the mid- and late-1990s emanating from the Caspian Sea region.[10] China's involvement in the Gwadar project has the objectives of aiding Pakistan in its infrastructure development, nurturing and building access to Central Asian oil with the pipeline projects.

From a military strategic perspective, Gwadar offers Pakistan the decongestion point to Karachi which hosts the dominant units of the Pakistan Navy (similar to Project Sea Bird in Karwar as an alternate port to Mumbai). Gwadar would be the second major seaport

450 km further from the border of India, providing Pakistan relative littoral depth than Karachi. Gwadar provides Pakistan with a dispersal port to berth Pakistani submarines and surface warships and perhaps could even be a berthing point of the future PLA-Navy fleet of the Indian Ocean. The Kargil War endgame off the seas in 1999 did witness the Indian Navy's ability to swiftly contain the Pakistan Navy and massed a formidable flotilla off the Karachi port. The Kargil War endgame was perhaps the decisive point for Pakistan to decide on the Gwadar port development.

The convergence of the oil pipelines into Gwadar signals the Pakistani intent to emerge as a pivotal link between Central Asia and the Arabian Sea attempting to scuttle the India–Iranian undersea pipelines that skirts Pakistani territorial control. Gwadar offers the geo-economic and geo-strategic pivot to China and Pakistan.

To China, Gwadar is an extremely ambitious project that opens up the maritime interface to its road linkage, the Sino–Pakistani Friendship 'Karakorum Highway' that opened China's access to Pakistan and southern Asia in the late 1960s. The Gwadar project could be regarded as the cornerstone of the emergent maritime strategic convergence of China and Pakistan. It acts the tacit pressure that China leverages on India even with its improvement of its relations with India; it assiduously cements its entente cordiale with Pakistan.[10]

(c) *Chinese arms transfers:* China has been pursuing its agenda of cultivating excellent bilateral relations with South Asian states through the policy of offering developmental assistance to low technology projects in agriculture, industry along with Chinese arms supplies in substantial quantities. The purpose of this arms transfer has been to engage the South Asian states within a security relationship, nurturing the idea that they should stay clear of India's influence and simultaneously secure access rights to their ports. Pakistan and Myanmar have been the most significant beneficiaries economically and in terms of receiving huge quantities of Chinese weaponry at special prices.[11]

These sales have come under the category of supply side with intents to improve good political relations and use the same to tilt the regional balance against India, China's regional rival. Pakistan has received Type 59 tanks, Type 531 armoured personnel carriers fast patrol naval craft, F-7P jet fighters, M-9, M-11 ballistic missiles, HJ-8 anti-tank missiles, HN-5A portable SAMs.[12]

(d) *Control of the sea gates:* China's efforts to broadbase its naval presence and posture necessitates it to gain free uninterrupted access to the sea straits in its maritime areas. The critical ones are the Taiwan Straits, the Straits of Malacca, Singapore Straits and the Straits of Hormuz. Beijing's objective would be to have a rapid access to these sea gates in peacetime (which is most probable) and equally possible during a crisis.[13] Its naval power projection through its surface fleet could be effective if it has the rapid ability to surge through the Straits to the open seas. Any attempt by the regional powers to block the Straits in anticipation of a hostile Chinese action or reaction either connected to the Taiwan Crisis or the South China disputes could spark off a swift local skirmish engaging the regional powers.

In the southern Asian context, the PLA Navy would have to surge through the Straits of Malacca to reach the Bay of Bengal the Andaman Sea to reach Myanmar or traverse further in the Indian Ocean to reach the Arabian Sea. In a crisis that would bring India and China into confrontation, the effective Indian naval counter-response would be the deterrence of the Chinese naval flotilla before the Straits of Malacca to prevent their rapid movement into the South Asian region or Indian Ocean. It is now evident that India has declared that its navy has a wide area of operation that spans from the Straits of Hormuz to the South China Sea past the Straits of Malacca. Indian Navy's Delhi Class destroyers, its accompanying frigates along with their naval logistics have been operating in the South China Sea and engaged in joint regional manoeuvres with the Philippines Navy, the South Korean Navy, the Vietnamese Navy and has participated in the Western Pacific Naval Symposium.[14]

Beijing is however determined to challenge the Indian dominion of the South Asian region since it asserts that the Indian Ocean does not belong to India. Thus the obvious intent is to surge through the Straits of Malacca and challenge the Indian dominion in South Asia. The approaches to the Straits of Malacca can be dominated from the Spratly Islands and the south-eastern tip of Myanmar in the Bay of Bengal. Any resistance to the assertive approach of the PLA Navy at the Straits of Malacca could be met by serious challenges from Malaysia, Singapore, Indonesia and this could possibly trigger local skirmishes.

The consequences of a possible Chinese control of the Straits of Malacca with a strike force of surface combatants and submarines could provide them with complete domination of the South China

Sea and the eastern Indian Ocean. This could mean that all Japanese, Australian, Malaysian, Indian SLOCs in the region could come under the hostile coverage of the PLA Navy which would be able to link well with its Myanmarese stations. Similarly a possible PLA Navy naval squadron of an assortment of surface combatants and attack submarines operating from the Pakistani port of Gwadar could stretch to the Straits of Hormuz with potential naval interdiction of Indian and other SLOCs emanating from the area. The PLA Navy could perhaps be using the China Ocean Shipping Company (COSCO) vessels as support ships in such operations.

The PLA Navy's articulation of the Offshore Defence Concept has the prime objectives of the control of the sea gates that are vital for Beijing's force projection. It is evident that Beijing's strategy to control the straits of Malacca is obvious and could be effective with its links with Myanmar and the inexorable logic would be to link Myanmar–Pakistan–Bangladesh into a regional alliance with Beijing.

(e) *Integrated Sea Control Strategy:* Beijing's naval doctrine and posture has been rapidly evolving from the initial defensive brown water capability to the green water island defense capability with the evolving blue water ambitions. The evolving PLA Navy battle order of high performance surface combatants features an impressive mission: the quest for a sea control capability through the procurement or construction of an aircraft carrier with its assorted escorts, the procurement and indigenous construction of attack, cruise missile, ballistic missile submarines provide the basis for a evolving integrated sea control capability in the near future. With much literature available on the PLA naval modernization updates, the implication is that an expanding PLA naval force structure would soon have an independent fleet for the Indian Ocean South Asian hub given the growing geo-strategic importance of Myanmar and Pakistan.

Regional Naval Development

The meticulous articulation of the PLA naval strategy in South Asia has a parallel unfolding in the South Asian regional naval relations. Pakistan and Bangladesh have conducted joint naval manoeuvres off the Andaman Sea in the last week of April 2001 preceding the visit of General Pervez Musharrf, Chief Executive of Pakistan (now the President of Pakistan) to Yangon on 1 May 2001. The Pakistani flotilla included three destroyers, an Agosta class submarine, a fleet tanker held the joint manoeuvres with Bangladesh naval units from 16–26 April and then proceeded to the Thilwa docks south of Yangon for a *courtesy call*, the first ever foreign naval flotilla visit apart from China.[15]

It should be mentioned here that this is the first time that the Pakistan Navy ventured into the Bay of Bengal after its fateful war with India in 1971 that lead to its dismemberment. The more curious development has been that Bangladesh that saw its origin and evolution as a result of its liberation through India's agency has joined the naval exercises in India's naval backyard the Eastern Naval Command.[16] The joint naval exercise with Bangladesh and the *courtesy visit* to Yangon preceding General Pervez Musharrf visit to Myanmar is a most interesting pointer for India, even as it pursues its naval diplomacy by naval manoeuvres with South Korea and Vietnam.[17]

The participation of the Bangladesh naval units with the Pakistani warships in joint exercises in 2003 had come as a surprise to the Indian naval establishment. Especially, it was important to note that these joint exercises had come soon after the fierce skirmishes in the Indo–Bangladesh border between the Bangladesh Rifles and the Indian Border Security Force.[18] Though the democratically elected civilian government of Sheikh Hasina condemned this skirmish between the BSF and the Bangladesh Rifles and ordered its retreat. Yet, the Bangladesh military establishment's new camaraderie joining with Pakistan was negatively viewed in India's military circles.

Indian defence sources view these developments as the naval encirclement of India actively abetted by China, which has kept a low profile but has stage-managed it very well. Indian defence sources point out that the naval manoeuvres have come in the aftermath of the visit of General Fu Quanyou, Chief of Army Staff of the PLA to Pakistan, which saw the consolidation of all China's military commitments with Pakistan.

The prospect of a Pakistani naval flotilla docking in the Andaman Sea is providing a new dimension to India's rapidly transforming naval security environment in the region. In fact, with the establishment of the Far Eastern Naval Command in the Andaman & Nicobar Islands, India's comprehensive naval operations of offshore patrol, maritime reconnaissance, anti-submarine patrols and its own submarine patrols have increased.[19] The Indian Far Eastern Naval Command is now acting in conjunction with the Indian Coast Guard in dealing with a wide variety of activities that range from anti-piracy missions to maritime security missions. Beijing's role in this naval strategic convergence is indirect, as it has usually been the case.

Pakistan's naval apprehensions have been in the light of the Indian Navy's absolute sea control of the Arabian Sea and the effective check on any Pakistani naval misadventures at the height of the recent War in Kargil in 1999. The Indian Navy's Western command effectively checked any Pakistani naval move and was battle ready to take the war into Pakistan's home waters. It also effectively checked and choked Pakistani SLOCs from the Straits of Hormuz. In the event of a future conflict Pakistan would probably be speeding out many of its warships across to the Bay of Bengal–Andaman Sea area to be within the access range of Myanmar's ports to avoid being quarantined by the Indian Navy. Pakistan is also pursuing its diplomatic relations with Vietnam and South Korea with whose navies India had recent naval exercises.

Beijing's primary motivation to promote this regional naval security architecture much to its own tune is the growing Indian strategic convergence with Japan and Australia besides the South-East Asian states.[20] The access and ultimately the control of the Straits of Malacca would matter for the Chinese surge into the Indian Ocean and South Asian region. But Japan and Australia have preferred the Indian collaboration for joint naval partnerships emanating from the common security concern of Beijing's surge toward the Strait of Malacca. Beijing's logic is if India were tied down in its own region through Beijing's allies then the Indian challenge to China in the South China Sea by its friendly naval manoeuvres would be limited.

China's Naval Force Projection

China's Indian Ocean Policy has been primarily conditioned by its imperative to contain India in the South Asia–IOR. Its sea-based nuclear deterrent and its nuclear-attack submarine force would be the lead elements in a future PLA-Navy presence in the IOR. In the historical evolution of the PLA-Navy's doctrine and technological capabilities, the period 2000–10 would be the culmination and attainment of its Integrated Sea-Based Nuclear Deterrence that would feature the technological evolution of its second generation SSBN expected by 2010.[21] Though the cross-straits crisis with Taiwan would draw the PLA-Navy's substantial naval forces in sea-denial and amphibious missions, the convergence on the Indian Ocean and the gradual evolution of surface platforms and nuclear attack and ballistic missile submarines would provide for power projection missions. The Type 094 SSBN would be the follow-on to the earlier Type 092 featuring greater survivability and endurance with its Submarine Launched Ballistic Missiles—the Julang II with an 8000 KM targeting range capability.

In terms of its nuclear attack missions, the PLA-Navy strategy would be to introduce its nuclear attack submarines of the Type 93 into the region. The Type 93 SSN is the equivalent of the ex-Soviet/ Russian Victor III that would deploy cruise missiles of the C-801 and the tactical land attack missiles.[22] The likely deployment of PLA-Navy submarines could be as follows:

The PLA-Navy's modern diesel-electric submarines of the indigenous Song and the Kilo Class Project 877 and 636 could enhance the PLA-Navy's sea denial capabilities closer home and in littoral operations for clandestine operations, offensive mining operations and blockade missions. In terms of the outer defence perimeter and the defence in-depth missions the PLA-Navy's SSN/SSGNs would be deployed beyond the second island chain. The submarines could also be used for interdiction of SLOCs in the South China Sea as well as in the Indian Ocean.

In tune with its naval deployment strategy, the PLA-Navy's Type 93 SSN/SSGN could be deployed in the Indian Ocean Region with contiguity of naval access at Gwadar and also in the Myanmarese bases thus providing the basis of flanking operations *vis-à-vis* India.

China's second strike capability with its Type 094 SSBN and its Julang II SLBMs would be deployed in the South China Sea and yet achieve targeting profiles in the Indian subcontinent. The deployment of its SSN/SSGN would be along with its SSBN units and the carrier task force *circa* 2020 in the Bay of Bengal or Arabian Sea would have portentous consequences of land attack missions in the region.

The deployment of the PLA-Navy Carrier Battle Group (CVBG) in the Indian Ocean *circa* 2020 in the Bay of Bengal in access to the Myanmarese bases would be supplemented by its SSN/SSGN squadrons in the Arabian Sea with access to Gwadar. China would justify its CVBG deployment to provide protection to its convoys transiting through the Straits of Malacca Strait and obtain a land route for its trade through Myanmar.[23]

The possibility of joint exercises and patrols of the Pakistani conventional submarines of the Agosta and Scorpene classes that have the Air-Independent Propulsion technologies with the PLA-Navy's

Type 93 SSN/SSGN in the Arabian Sea. This deployment would provide Pakistan its reassurance from China against any containing operations by the Indian Navy like the repeat of the 1999 Kargil War naval operations in the future. The prospect of the Type-93 SSN/SSGN in the Northern Arabian Sea operating in conjunction with the Pakistani Navy would have its restraint on the Indian Navy's Western Naval Command units unless India deploys its SSN to balance the PLA-Navy's nuclear attack squadron. Indian SLOCs could suffer possible interdiction during war times from the PLA-Navy's SSN forces.

China's nuclear posture and atomic diplomacy with India has been evident in the context of the India–Pakistan conflict spectrum. China had exercised the same with its nuclear deterrence bolstering Pakistan *vis-à-vis* India. The deployment of the PLA-Navy's SSBN force with its improved SLBM capability of the Julang II would have to be viewed in the context of the strategic convergence of China and Pakistan and in the contexts of the prevalent nuclear asymmetry between India and China with China enjoying nuclear superiority in deployed platforms, warheads and targeting strategy in its land-based missiles complemented with its sea-based nuclear deterrent of the Type 94 SSBN.

Implications for India

The China–Pakistan strategic convergence in its maritime dimension opens a new gambit against India. The implications are quite evident by the correlation of strategy and diplomacy. In terms of maritime threat that is vivid and manifest, the fact is that PLA-Navy warships can cruise and enjoy access to Gwadar in Pakistan and the Myanmarese bases in proximity to the Indian coast it has the following operational implications:

(a) Naval surveillance and reconnaissance of all Indian Navy operations in the Western, South-Western, Far Eastern and Eastern Naval operations, with prospects and scope to share such intelligence with Pakistan is very profound;

(b) The prospect of the Chinese and Pakistani naval forces to interfere with trade routes and intimidate India's coastline at will is very evident.[24] During a full-scale war, Chinese and Pakistani attack submarines can play havoc against Indian shipping, military installations, and oil rigs. The difficulties of detection beyond few thousand yards even with the advanced sonar are real;

(c) The prospects of a regular deployment of China's nuclear attack submarines of the Type 93 in Gwadar with nuclear-tipped land attack missiles in the Western sector has its apocalyptic consequences for India's industrial heartland;

(d) The sea-based threat from China to the Indian island territories lying across the SLOCs in the area could be the focus of attention, along with offshore assets in the Andaman Sea and the Lakshwadeep Islands in the Arabian Sea. An amphibious operation by a Chinese Carrier Battle Group and nuclear attack submarines in the South Asian region is an emerging possibility. The deployment of such a force would require an Indian Rapid Reaction force of surface warships and nuclear submarines. Indian retaliatory options require carrier based offensive strike power against Chinese naval ships and the naval bases that anchor PLA-Navy squadrons backed by Indian nuclear attack submarines and nuclear ballistic missile submarines.[25]

Conclusion

In conclusion, the maritime strategic convergence of China and Pakistan gains salience with serious implications for India. While the optimists of India–China bilateral relations echo sentiments of optimism and growing understanding, the pragmatists of the India–China relations would cautiously weigh the consequences of the emergent tangible China–Pakistan maritime strategic convergence manifest in infrastructural aid and support; China's extended nuclear deterrence through its sea-based nuclear deterrent and strike forces to Pakistan; the consistent support to Pakistan's defence-industrial sector; the unabated efforts to strengthen Pakistani resilience in maritime trade and security evident in the Gwadar Development Project; the convergent efforts in networking and harnessing the geo-energy lines of communications in the maritime interface from the Straits of Hormuz and through the land interface from the Central Asian Region with converging pipelines into Gwadar; the synchronization of the PLA-Navy's Offshore Defense Concept in terms of a evolving Blue Water—Third Island capability in the IOR that has regional pivots like Pakistan and Myanmar are all the certain signs of a decisive Chinese Maritime Grand Strategy and forays into the Southern Asian–IOR domain is a multifaceted gambit of strategy and diplomacy with the obvious intent to contain its peer rival India.

NOTES

1. The Sino–Pakistan Friendship Karakoram Highway which was constructed by Chinese and Pakistani engineers over disputed Kashmir territory was China's first land interface with Pakistan and its expanding domain into Southern Asia. For an articulate analysis see John Garvar 2002b, 'The Future of the Sino-Pakistani *Entente Cordiale*' in Michael R. Chambers (ed.), *South Asia in 2020: Future Strategic Balances and Alliances*, Carlisle: Strategic Studies Institute, U.S. Army War College, November 2002. Mohan Malik, *The China Factor in the India–Pakistan Conflict*, Occasional Paper Series, Honolulu, Asia Pacific Center for Security Studies, November 2002.
2. For a comprehensive analysis see Thomas Kane, *Chinese Grand Strategy and Maritime Power*, London: Frank Cass, 2002.
3. Comprehensive Maritime Security could be interpreted variously as the approaches to naval access, basing, posture, doctrine and alliances of extra-regional powers could develop with regional littoral powers.
4. Srikanth Kondapalli, 'Chinese Navy in the Indian Ocean', *Journal of Indian Ocean Studies*, New Delhi, vol. 8 nos. 1 and 2, August 2000.
5. See Swaran Singh, 'Myanmar: China's Gateway to the Indian Ocean' *Journal of Indian Ocean Studies*, vol. 3, no. 1, November 1995, pp. 80–5, and Rodney Tasker and Bertil Linter 'Kunming-Yangon Highway' *Far Eastern Economic Review*, 21 December 2000.
6. Subir Bhaumik, 'Bangladesh–Pakistan joint naval exercises; Musharraf's visit to Myanmar; India's encirclement begins' 28 April 2001, http://www.tehelka.com/currentaffairs/apr2001.htm
7. Swaran Singh, 'Sino–South Asian Ties: Problems and Prospects', *Strategic Analyses*, vol. XXIV, no.1, April 2000, pp. 31–49. A comprehensive analysis is in Swaran Singh, *China-South Asia: Issues, Equations, Policies*, New Delhi: Lancers Publishers, 2003.
8. Ibid.
9. Amrish Sahgal, 'The PLAN's Plan', *Indian Defence Review*, vol. 17, no. 4, October–December 2002, pp. 63–9; See 'Pak–China to discuss Gwadar port development', *Navy News*, 8 June 2001, Defence India http://www.defenceindia.com/test1.php3? filename=navy.htm. Also see B. Muralidhar Reddy 'China May Help Build Strategic Pak Port' *The Hindu*, 13 June 2001, *The Hindu* on the indiaserver.com http://www.the-hindu.com/stories/0313000.htm 'Pakistan's Ormara Naval base' *Strategic Affairs* http://www.stratmag.com/issue/july 15.2000.htm
10. John Garvar, 'The Gestalt of Sino-Indian Relationship' in Carolyn Pumphrey (ed.). *The Rise of China in Asia: Security Implications*, Carlisle: Strategic Studies Institute, U.S. Army War College, January 2002, p. 412.

11. Karl W. Eikenberry, 'Explaining and Influencing Chinese Arms Transfers', *McNair Paper* # 36 Washington: Institute for National Strategic Studies, National Defense University, 1995, pp. 5–15.
12. Ibid.
13. Yossef Bodansky, 'The PRC Surge for the Strait of Malacca and Spratly Confronts India and the US', *Defence & Foreign Affairs Strategic Policy*, Washington , 30 September 1995; Yosef Bodansky, 'Beijing Surges for the Strait of Malacca' http://www.freeman.org/m_online/bodansky/beijing/html
14. Amit Baruah, 'Navy Taking Part in Multilateral Exercises', *The Hindu* on indiaserver.com, 13 June 2001, http://www.the-hindu.com
15. Subir Bhaumik, 'Bangladesh–Pakistan Joint Naval Exercises: Mushrraf's Visit to Myanmar; India's Encirclement Begins', 28 April 2001, available at http://www.tehelka.com/currentaffairs/apr2001.htm
16. Atul Aneja, 'Pak Naval Ships in Myanmar on eve of Musharraf's Visit', http://www.the-hindu.com 1 May 2001.
17. Subir Bhaumik www.tehelka.com/currentaffairs/apr2000/ca04280/musharaff.html
18. Ibid.
19. Prakash Nanda, 'Strategic Significance of the Andamans', *Indian Defence Review*, vol. 17 (3), July–September 2002, pp. 12–25.
20. Amit Baruah, 'Australian Warships Confront the Chinese Navy', *The Hindu* on the indiaserver.com Monday 30 April 2001; also 'Australia and India Mend Ties' *Global Intelligence Update*, http://www.stratfor.com/SERVICES/giu2000/071100.ASP
21. Report to the U.S. Congress (2003) (Pursuant to the FY 2000, National Defense Authorization Act) *Annual Report of The Military Power of the People's Republic of China*, Washington: U.S. Congress, 28 July 2003.
22. See Wilfried A. Herrmann, 'Chinese Military Strategy and its Maritime Aspects', *USI Digest*, vol. II, no.3, September 99-February 2000.; Srikanth Kondapalli, 'China's Naval Equipment Acquisition', www.idsa-india.org
23. R.B. Suri, 'Maritime Dimension of India's Security', *Agni*, New Delhi, vol. I. no. 2, November 1995, p. 114.
24. *The Statesman*, 20 January 2000.
25. Rahul Roy-Chaudhury, *India's Maritime Security*, New Delhi: Knowledge World, 2000, p. 99; also Rahul Roy-Chaudhary, 'Indian Energy Security', *Journal of Indian Ocean Studies,* New Delhi, November 1998, pp. 14–21.

PART III

Fundamentals of Strategic Engagement

CHAPTER 13

Geopolitics of Economic Relations

MADHU BHALLA

Since the latter half of the 1990s China's economic relations with Pakistan has moved beyond the geopolitical and strategic imperatives of the Cold War years and are increasingly subject to the demands of China's modernization drive and the pressures of globalization. As with the rest of South Asia, China's trade and investment with Pakistan is increasingly linked to profits and access to markets. This has resulted in a decline in the close and fairly stable set of economic interactions between the two. However, the same long and stable history of Sino–Pakistani relations over the last half century has established a network of trade and institutional contacts that are of significance in China's currently dominant economic concerns even as the geo-strategic and geopolitical environment in Central and South Asia now ensures that strategic concerns no longer drive this economic interaction.

The Geopolitical Background

The People's Republic of China (PRC) established and nurtured its economic relations with Pakistan within the framework of military/strategic needs. A direct consequence of the deteriorating relations with India in South Asia and with the erstwhile Soviet Union in the 1950s, these relations with Pakistan served China's geopolitical concerns until the 1990s. Pakistan balanced India in South Asia and facilitated China's relations with the United States and the West Asian countries, all areas of critical concern for the PRC. Therefore, no other geographical area of China's external economic relations was so closely bound to its broader security and policy concerns as with Pakistan.

Pakistan, too, saw its close relations with China as reflecting and serving its security needs in South Asia.[1] The acceptance of military aid from the US and the Mutual Defense Agreement of 1954 between the United States and Pakistan laid the foundation of Pakistan's policy against the communist states during the 1950s. This affected policy in South Asia as well. However, this early alliance with the US was inherently unstable given Congressional conditions on military aid and the increasing American involvement in Vietnam in the 1960s. Therefore, soon after the Sino–Indian conflict in 1962, Pakistan's leaders sought out the Chinese for a closer strategic and military relationship.

The Chinese revived a 1959 Pakistani proposal to negotiate an agreement on outstanding differences over the boundary running between China's province of Xinjiang and contiguous areas to the south-west and an agreement was signed in 1963.[2] China's willingness to sign an agreement involving territory that was clearly in dispute between Pakistan and India indicated China's support for Pakistan's position on Kashmir. This became the bedrock of the subsequent relationship between the two especially since 'attain(ing) a bargaining position *vis-à-vis* India in the . . . dispute over Kashmir' was firmly entrenched as one of the three objectives of Pakistan's foreign policy.[3]

As the smaller of the two partners, and the more vulnerable economically and politically, Pakistan's economy gained from China's strategic concerns what it would not if the invisible hand of market forces was brought into play. By August 1963 the diplomatic success of the boundary agreement was translated into a series of economic agreements between the two on trade, shipping and commerce with calls for wider economic cooperation. Pakistan was accorded most-favoured-nation status on trade with China, it was offered an interest-free loan of US $50 million and its national airline was allowed to fly to selected Chinese cities.[4]

Significantly, economic relations with China served Pakistan's strategic needs as well. In fact, a large part of the 'trade' between the two was trade in military equipment from China to Pakistan and to China's investments for military production in Pakistan, affirming the central geopolitical concerns of the two countries.[5] Since the emergence of the Central Asian republics and in the wake of 9/11, China has clearly distanced itself from Pakistan's strategic concerns and no longer feels the need to use economic incentives to sustain the strategic relationship.

Economic Relations

China's economic relations with Pakistan have historically covered three broad areas: economic aid, trade in arms and military equipment and trade in goods and commodities including Chinese investments in Sino–Pakistani joint ventures. The three areas have not been evenly balanced and the pattern of imports and exports and emphasis on collaborative activity has varied with the political situation in the region. China's aid to Pakistan has remained low and the volume of civilian trade has not reflected the level of their partnership in the region.

ECONOMIC AID

Within the economic relationship, aid and soft loans to Pakistan have been driven by strategic concerns. Thus, early loans were a payoff for Pakistan's strategic usefulness in South Asia and later soft loans have been made available to for domestic budgetary crisis.

Despite the fact that China's aid to Pakistan has remained low in absolute terms, since the first offer of aid in 1963 the PRC's aid to China has increased overall. In 1970 China was eighth on the list of countries against which Pakistan had outstanding foreign aid loans, being listed only slightly behind France. By 1977 Pakistan, along with Cambodia and North Korea where China also had critical strategic interests, was one of the three largest recipients of aid from China. Of the US $3.8 billion that the PRC extended in aid to all Asian countries put together its three top donors including Pakistan received US $2.8 billion. While Pakistan's indebtedness to China increased at a much slower rate than to other donor countries, with the exception of Britain, it had still tripled by 1990.

Most of the increase in China's foreign aid loans to Pakistan came during the Afghan crisis when Pakistan became crucial as a frontline state in the opposition to Soviet presence in Afghanistan. In November 1985, for instance, Pakistan's Prime Minister Mohammad Khan Junejo received a new aid package to offset the country's expenses during the crisis.[6] Pakistan received a total of US $1billion in assistance for Afghan refugees to which Islamic countries and non-consortium countries contributed 8 per cent.[7]

However, from the late 1970s China did phase out its aid policy. This was a consequence partly of its own modernization and a recognition of its changed strategic needs after its rapprochement with the US. China's own position since its early modernization drive has been less that of a donor nation than a recipient of foreign aid, loans and preferential economic assistance from leading industrial countries such as Japan and international economic institutions.[8] Hence, thereafter aid to Pakistan came in the form of soft loans such as the more recent ones intended to allow Pakistan to tide over its foreign debt repayment crisis.

Between 1996 and 1997 China gave Pakistan US $30 million to enable Pakistan to boost its foreign exchange reserves to US $1 billion and tide over its immediate debt payments needs. But this was a small contribution considering that Pakistan was looking to pay back US $250 million on its foreign debt in May of 1997 and nearly US $600 million by June of the same year. Given the enormous pressure on Pakistan's own banks, which had already loaned the government Rs 270 billion (Pakistan) against a target of Rs 330 billion, China gave Pakistan an additional soft loan of US $150 million along with a US $6 million grant under the Chinese Technical Support Programme after Prime Minister Nawaz Sharif's visit in early 1998.[9] Most of China's interest free loans to Pakistan came with strings attached and were tied to specific projects and commodities as well as purchases from China.[10]

Between 1998 and 2000 China's aid policy was directed primarily to sectors in Pakistan that involved Chinese joint ventures, infrastructure and manufacturing activities and reflected China's outward investment policies. As a result there has been an increase in the absolute value of China's 'economic cooperation' with Pakistan at approximately US $1.12 billion since 1990. The assistance was made under the heads of interest-free loans, project/commodity loans, balance of payments support, technical cooperation and grants. Grants constituted 52.67 per cent of the total with the rest disbursed under the broad head of loans. Over half of this went to defence projects in the form of grants and loans.[11]

Significantly, while Pakistan's total foreign debt remained more or less constant between 1999 and 2003 during the period when it restructured its foreign debt repayments under IMF and World Bank supervision (between US $33.5 billion in 1999 to US $33.4 billion in 2002) China's loans fell drastically from US $72.356 million in 1998–9 to US $0.958 the following year and inched up to a mere US $11.932 in the first quarter of 2003. Much of this was on account of the uncertainty in the domestic situation in Pakistan before and after 9/11 but a great deal also had to do with China's domestic crisis regarding SARs, among other things.[12] During Pakistan's budgetary crisis China, like many other countries rescheduled part of Pakistan's payments on loans outstanding towards the PRC but did not, like many other Paris Club and Consortium countries cancel or defer any part of it.[13]

TRADE IN ARMS AND MILITARY EQUIPMENT

China's trade in arms and military equipment and technology to Pakistan has been the clearest manifestation in the past of the strategic objectives of Sino–Pakistani economic relations. Arms transfers to Pakistan increased during the 1980s given the Soviet presence in Afghanistan. Some of these were outright transfers while others were sales against grants and soft loans made to Pakistan during this period. During 1984–8 period, the value of all arms transfers into Pakistan equaled US $2010 million.

Of this, the US share of arms transfers was US $1200 million, France US $20 million, UK US $30 million, Czechoslovakia US $20 million, and Italy US $50 million. China's was second only to the US, its contribution amounting to US $330 million.[14] By the 1980s, China's policy on weapons assistance had changed and China became an active exporter rather than a supplier of arms. While China's major profits accrued from arms sales during the Iran-Iraq war, Pakistan became a long-term preferred customer. Between 1986 and 1990, the value of China's exports of conventional weapons to Pakistan amounted to US $1,202 million.[15]

By 1993 Pakistan's acquisitions list boasted of an impressive array of Chinese-manufactured weapons and equipment for all three arms of its military. Its defence budget went up by US $32 million between 1990 and 1991 alone.[16] By the mid-1990s, China had contracted to supply Pakistan with 25 K-8 Karakoram, 8 jet trainers and 282 T-85-IIAP main battle tanks (MBT) for an unspecified amount, and an additional 450 T-69-11 MBT's in a deal worth US $1.2 billion.[17] In overall world figures, China's military trade may seem insignificant. It has less than 3 per cent of the world military export market, yet it is the fifth largest supplier of military equipment and arms after the US, Russia, UK and France. Its principal recipient is Pakistan and some African countries.[18] Between 1966–79 alone, the value of

Chinese arms transfers to Pakistan amounted to more than US $630 million.[19]

What was equally significant was the Chinese assistance in developing Pakistan's indigenous defence production facilities after the Indo–Pakistan war of 1965. In fact, part of the interest-free loans given by China in 1963 (app. US $28 million) was intended for the supply of industrial commodities to be used in armaments production.

The post-1963 relationship enabled Pakistan not only to be self-sufficient in small arms, ammunition and infantry weapons, but also to export small arms to Greece, Turkey, the Middle East, South-East Asia, and Sri Lanka. China effectively transferred conventional weapons technology to Pakistan through its collaboration in the production of artillery rockets and the Karakoram-8 jet trainer, as well as by licensing the production of its older Type 54 machine gun and solid-propellant motors.[20]

By the time the Iran–Iraq war was at its height, Pakistan had built-up a small but profitable military-industrial complex with the assistance of China and on the basis of licensing and assembly agreements with the US, France, Germany, Belgium and Argentina.[21] Comparable figures for India, China and Pakistan indicate the significance of this development. Between 1978 and 1984, the year in which Pakistan's imports and exports reached their highest level, imports rose from the base year 1978 by 3.7 per cent of total imports, while exports increased by 9.2 per cent of total exports. The comparable figures for India are 3.1 per cent and 0 per cent, and for China, 5 per cent and 6.4 per cent.

The largest and most effective doses of financial help from China came after each military crisis in South Asia—after the 1962, 1965 and 1971 wars and during the Afghan crisis.[22] Subsequent technical aid packages were meant for Sino–Pakistani cooperation in the nuclear fields. These included Pakistan's purchase of a 330 MW nuclear power plant for Chashma near Islamabad in 1990, and the US $225 million given by China to build-up the Pakistani air force. The contrast between the aid packages for military and economic purposes is evident from the fact that a year before Pakistan received the aid for it air force, it got a mere US $84 million for a copper project in Baluchistan.

The strategic significance of Pakistan to China waned considerably after 1990 as China and India moved to normalize relations, the Soviet Union disintegrated and global politics changed rapidly after the first Gulf war. But the relationship has never really been in jeopardy until the post-9/11 period partly because the competitive aspect to India–China relations remains even if the hostility has waned, but more importantly because Pakistan continued to have economic and strategic value as a window to the Islamic world especially in Central Asia, Iran and Turkey even though China has since the mid-1990s institutionalized effective trade and strategic relations with the Central Asian republics. This is evident from the Chinese and Pakistani joint declarations in the 1980s and early 1990s which routinely called for an expansion in civilian trade and commerce while the arms trade and transfers of military technology remained the mainstay of Sino–Pakistani economic relations.

However, China's increasing socialization in the norms and conventions of global military security and disarmament and its decision to take its place as a responsible power on the world stage changed its position on arms transfers and nuclear technology transfers for military purposes in the 1990s. It began to regulate more stringently the export of arms and equipment by its domestic arms producers, primarily units of the People's Liberation Army without being quite able to end these. Since the Iraq war and the punitive implications of proliferation of weapons of mass destruction China has increasingly sought to distance itself from its practices in the past.[23]

REGIONAL ECONOMIC INTERACTION

Economic imperatives have gradually overtaken strategic considerations in regional economic collaboration as well. Regarding Central Asia, China and Pakistan's relations, since the end of the Cold War, are based more on economic considerations and less on security concerns. China's difficulty in creating a stable, strategic partnership with Russia in Central Asia in the early 1990s and the emergence of Muslim dominated Central Asian republics allowed Pakistan to play a useful and supportive role in the region initially.[24]

Overland trade between China and Pakistan was a fallout of the investment in roads and other infrastructure that supported China's strategic concerns in its western border regions. Pakistani assistance in preventing Islamic fundamentalist groups from entering China's predominantly Muslim province of Xinjiang has also been China's main strategic concern in the past but that function is now taken care of by US pressure on Pakistan to distance itself from the fundamentalist cause since 9/11, and by the American military presence in the region.

China is also aware that after 9/11 Pakistan is being seen more as the problem in the two most contentious issues—terrorism and proliferation of WMDs—than as a solution and a predominantly strategic partnership with Pakistan at the old level is untenable.

The American presence in Pakistan also limits the scope for any strategic cooperation in the present circumstances. Meanwhile China has established strategic partnerships with Russia and the Central Asian republics that expressly forbid the exportation of Islamic fundamentalism, put in place a series of CBMs that make the region less volatile and more conducive to business, and institutionalize a regional dialogue that emphasizes economic cooperation in infrastructure building, joint ventures and border trade.[25] On Kashmir, Pakistan's chief strategic concern in South Asia, China has distanced itself from the Pakistani position. Pakistan, therefore, can no longer ride China's strategic coat-tails in regional economic interactions in Central and West Asia although China has been more than willing to use Pakistan's goodwill in the Islamic world to facilitate its economic concerns in the area. In this region competitive economic considerations with regard to energy resources, transportation, border trade, and joint ventures in infrastructure and construction have become central to China's concerns.

Hence, both China and Pakistan, separately, for some time now have focused on regional economic agreements that would address the issues of energy, transportation and trade in the area. Pakistan had a head start because it was already part of an Islamic states' network, the OIC, as well as of the Economic Cooperation Organisation (ECO). The three initial members of the ECO—Pakistan, Turkey and Iran—quickly welcomed the newly independent Muslim Central Asian republics into the organization in 1992.[26] At a subsequent ECO meeting the following year, its members developed a 'comprehensive economic plan' to establish a communication and infrastructure network.[27] In 1992, the republics of Kyrgyzstan and Kazakhstan, together with China and Pakistan, set-up a working group to study the feasibility of a road network that would go through Xinjiang to the Karakoram, and then on to Karachi.

China has transformed its confidence building measures with the CIS states and Russia into a full-fledged organization that addresses economic as well as strategic issues within the framework of what the Chinese term as 'comprehensive security'. The bedrock of the economic aspect of this arrangement is China's booming border trade with the Central Asian republics and Russia. China already has a large volume of trade with Kazakhstan, which exported US $228 million worth of goods to China and imported US $204 million by 1992 and US $460 million by 1996. It is also in close cooperation with Kyrgyzstan. Its long borders with these two and Tajikistan, and the commonality of interest in opening up the Central Asian steppe for oil exploration, makes China and the Central Asian nations natural economic partners.[28]

Pakistan's efforts to implement any concrete collaborative economic projects have been hampered because of the war in Afghanistan, suspicion over its support to Islamic fundamentalists in Afghanistan and the region, and its own slower rate of economic growth.[29] Until recently, Pakistan made a contribution of approximately US $120 million to the Central Asian States, a pittance compared to the amount spent by other ECO states.[30] China's energy needs, directed to its national and western areas development policy has meant that China and Pakistan come together on common regional forums where Pakistan's position in the Islamic arc has often been beneficial to China.

Transportation

Both countries interact closely in global deliberations for a trans-Asian transport network. Pakistan's role in this is to become a part of the highway network over which Central Asia's oil and gas, and trade in commodities and goods could be sent to port outlets. The landlocked Central Asian republics are already looking to Caspian Sea outlets through Iran and Turkey. This is a tortuous route for China and Pakistan's port facilities, after upgradation, offer better opportunities.

Therefore, as part of the network China has invested in Pakistan's new port at Gwadar and in improving infrastructure at Karachi port which will aid Pakistan in transporting commodities through Iran to Central Asia and to West Asia by sea. This will also give China preferential use of the ports and tertiary services thus opening up alternative land and sea routes to West Asia and decreasing China's dependency on the sea route through the Malacca Straits and the Indian Ocean where Chinese shipping could be threatened in the event of conflict with its South-East Asian neighbours in the South China Sea or India around China's strategic listening posts in Myanmar.

The potential for collaboration between China and Pakistan on a transportation network is not just a pipe dream. An early major collaborative effort between the two was the agreement after the 1965 war to extend the Karakoram Highway, already under construction by Pakistan, up to the Chinese border. A few years later came the plan to extend it into an all-weather and dual carriage highway that would link Pakistan with the old silk route in Central Asia. China, on its part, linked the Tibet-Xinjiang Highway to the Karakoram Highway, thus opening up a transportation route for Xinjiang and Central Asian trade to the port of Karachi.

Pakistan too has made considerable efforts to become part of a transport grid that would link China, Central Asia, Pakistan, Iran and Turkey with ports in South Asia and the Caspian. It has formulated a plan to develop road networks at an estimated cost of US $5,000 million. These plans include the construction of bypass roads and flyovers in Karachi to connect the port to a superhighway via Mauripur. A part of the Asian Land Transport Infrastructure Development Plan (ALTID), Pakistan will link to the trans-Asian Railway, which will be part of the New Silk Railway from China via Central Asia to Iran, Turkey and Europe. It will also link to the trans-Asian highway by reactivating its earlier road projects.

Also, while the development of Karachi port leaves much to be desired and Pakistan's shipping fleet declined from 451 tons to 398 tons between 1985 and 1998, its tonnage increased by 6.1 per cent per annum between 1994–5, indicating that increased volumes of freight are to be expected in the near future.[31] Pakistan hopes to upgrade its commercial shipping in the future to take advantage of increases in the volume of freights that can be expected once the work on the ports is completed. The implications of this are that Pakistan can play the role of junior partner in the economic relationship with China, providing tertiary services when the northern passage through Afghanistan becomes safer.

Pakistan viewed the opening of the Karakoram Highway and the Gilgit–Skardu Road as an opportunity for the development of tourism and for the extension of border trade with China. Tourism has not been a great success, showing a dismal occupancy and spending record given the volatile military and political situation, as well as to the fact that tourist facilities in the area did not measure sufficiently up to world standards to attract the Western tourist.

Barter trade has done somewhat better, rising from Pakistani Rs 0.024 million in 1969 to Pakistani Rs 5,000 million in 1986 and makes up a considerable portion of Pakistan's total trade with China currently. Yet, China's primary focus on Central Asian markets limits the actual incidence of barter trade with Pakistan.[32] However, China's focus on western development and its concerted policy of encouraging border trade will make some difference if the political situation in Xinjiang and Central Asia becomes stable soon. With China's renewed support for barter trade in Central Asia and especially given economies that lack full currency convertibility and are strapped for foreign exchange the potential for barter trade to rise exists. Pakistan's State Bank has recently responded to this by implementing schemes to assist barter trade.

Energy

The significance of transportation and communications projects involving China and Pakistan in Central Asia is underscored by the need to have access to Central Asia's energy resources. Both countries suffer from a shortfall in energy supply. China's predicted shortfall by the year 2000 was equivalent to 1.36 to 1.58 billion tons of standard coal, with the bill for import of oil and natural gas accounting for a large part of import expenditures. As of 1994, Pakistan was already self-sufficient in electricity produced through its thermal, hydro and nuclear power plants, but had a considerable shortfall in coal and petroleum production.

Pakistan's needs for energy also far outstrip its production of coal, crude petroleum and electricity. In fact, one of the first interest-free loans from China in 1963 was used to transport coal to Pakistan. The increasing gap between production and consumption means higher levels of imports each year, an expenditure that the Pakistan economy can ill afford. Shortfalls in natural gas supply in 1997–8, for instance, affected production in vital industries like fertilizer.[33]

China sees itself as the energy gateway to Japan and the Far East, and Pakistan to South Asia although the US military presence in the CIS states has complicated the picture somewhat. However, an ambitious plan to lay a network of gas pipelines from Turkmenistan via Kazakhstan, Uzbekistan and China's Tarim Basim to Japan in the Far East, and another from Turkmenistan via Afghanistan to

Karachi and perhaps to India is already afoot. In fact, China has won the right to exploit two of Kazakstan's largest oil fields, estimated to have as much as 178 billion barrels of oil, second only to those in the Gulf.[34]

China and Pakistan have a cooperative rather than competitive attitude in the field of energy. This is not unique to China's relations with Pakistan. During 1988–98 period, Pakistan has been one of twenty countries with which the PRC has agreed to cooperate to develop nuclear energy and China has assisted Pakistan's fledging energy industry. The PRC's assistance in setting up nuclear energy and hydel plants in Chashma, near Islamabad and in the Northern Areas, respectively, could enable Pakistan to become part of an energy grid in the area.

Pakistan could export excess hydel and nuclear powered energy in exchange for scarce oil and natural gas. China exported its indigenously designed 300MW nuclear power plant to Pakistan in 1989. In April 1997, the two countries agreed to cooperate in the manufacture and production of hydel power machinery.[35] Pakistan Northern Areas are best suited for small-scale hydel electric generation. These are also the areas accessible by the road link to China in the north. By 1987, the Government of Pakistan had already included plans for 16 hydel power generation plants for the Northern Areas in its plans for the fiscal year 1986–7.[36]

China and Pakistan have also established collaborative ventures in the area of energy production. With one collaborative venture at Haripur already underway, Pakistan has also entered a memorandum of understanding with Hong Kong's Consolidated Electric Power Asia Limited to develop a power station, port and a special industrial zone at Keti Bandar. Pakistan's newly restructured energy policy, which has an emphasis on privatization of power plants and distribution, is meant to attract global investment. It will certainly be more attractive to China which is already active in this sector.

More important for the newly market-conscious Chinese is the fact that Pakistan promises to implement its hydel and thermal power plants on a Build-Own-Operate-Transfer (BOOT) and Build-Own-Operate (BOO) basis respectively.[37] However, the Pakistani power sector's record of unpaid electricity bills and uncertain labour and political conditions and Chinese experience of bad local management practices in collaborative ventures in other sectors are certain drawbacks.

Bilateral Trade

China's trade with Pakistan took a backseat to geopolitical considerations which have shaped the economic relationship between the two. Yet, as part of a long, stable and supportive relationship Chinese and Pakistani leaders from 1963 to 1998 have expressed a desire to extend trade between the two countries.[38] There are however, constraining factors for the low level of trade between the two.

First, despite the fact that China and Pakistan shared security concerns in the region, China's pre-1978 developmental path of import substitution policies left no room for increasing trade with the world, including Pakistan.

Second, after 1979 China's internal modernization and liberalization drive ensured that it would turn to the developed economies and to economies willing and able to invest in China rather than to the Third World for investment and trade.

Third, Pakistan's surplus of cotton and traditional goods did not fit the needs of the Chinese market which was itself the biggest exporter of cotton and cotton goods.

The direction of China's trade was heavily weighted in favour of the socialist countries. China's balance of payments position indicated a trade surplus with the Third World of US $282 million in 1960–4 with the surplus rising to US $2829 million by 1978. Before 1979 trade between the two countries, as has been pointed out above, was subsumed under the rubric of aid and interest-free loans for specific commodities such as the export from China of coal. The US was, and remains, its largest trading partner. Between 1978–85 China's imports with the Third World increased bringing down its surplus by half.[39] But this resulted from the fact that the commodity composition of China's exports and imports were affected by developments in Chinese agriculture and industrial development after 1978, and the fall in world oil prices in the 1980s.[40] Pakistan's economy, for its part, survived on large doses of foreign aid from the US until the end of the Afghan war.

Within the framework of China's current economic policy, trade with Pakistan is not likely to increase unless Pakistan can address the PRC's economic needs. Visible trade between China and Pakistan remained low and stagnant through the 1980s and 1990s. This is amply clear from the figures for China's trade with and investment in Pakistan and vice versa. Though recent period has seen rapid increase

TABLE 13.1 PAKISTAN'S EXPORTS AND IMPORTS BY REGION AND PRINCIPAL DESTINATION (%): 1980–93

Exports	1980	1985	1989	1990	1991	1992	1993
US	5.3	10.1	12.3	12.4	4.5	12.8	14.7
Americas	7.3	12.1	14.1	14.4	13.7	15.4	18.4
UAE	4.7	4.6	3.6	3.2	3.5	5.0	0.5
Saudi Arabia	5.5	6.7	2.3	2.9	4.0	4.3	4.3
Hong Kong	6.6	3.1	5.3	5.0	6.0	7.9	5.5
India	2.7	1.4	0.6	0.9	0.7	1.9	0.7
Imports	1980	1985	1989	1990	1991	1992	1993
US	14.1	14.0	15.3	12.8	11.1	10.4	9.3
Americas	16.8	16.4	17.5	15.1	14.0	13.1	11.5
Saudi Arabia	9.6	9.8	4.6	6.3	5.1	5.3	5.3
India	0.1	0.3	0.4	0.6	0.5	0.6	0.7
E. Asia	21.1	25.2	29.1	29.4	31.8	32.4	35.7
UAE	6.3	4.0	1.6	2.1	3.7	3.0	7.1

Source: *Gatt: Trade Review Policy: Pakistan*, p. 12.

in China–Pakistan bilateral trade—reaching US $4.266 billion for 2005—the direction of China's trade is weighted heavily towards North America with China's exports rising to US $22 billion for 1994 to $44 billion by 1999.

The US and Japan took the largest share in the two groups respectively at US $21421 and US $21490 millions.[41] Exports to Pakistan were valued at a mere US $606 million and imports from Pakistan even lower at US $162 million. Corresponding figures for Pakistan stood at US $54 and US $4421 million for 1994 and US $119 million and US $576 million for 1996 indicating both the slow pace of as well as the imbalance in trade.[42] If one were to include trade with Hong Kong as part of Pakistan's trade with China since Hong Kong has been for long a re-exporting centre for Chinese goods and for goods into China, the picture is not much happier.

Hong Kong's imports from Pakistan rose from US $98 million in 1985 to US $627 million with the total for SAARC at US $2643 of which India's share was US $1875 million. Exports from Hong Kong indicate even lower levels of trade beginning at US $30 million in 1985 when SAARC trade (exports) stood at US $300 million. It rose slowly to US $76 million when exports to SAARC stood at US $1825. Bangladesh's share of this was US $501 million, India's at US $803 and Sri Lanka's at US $364 million.[43]

China's foreign direct investments in Pakistan are limited as well. China has preferred to invest in cooperative ventures and joint venture entreprises in Pakistan. Some of its major investments have been in the area of energy production, both nuclear and hydel, and transport (the Karakoram Highway) as well as in mining as in the Saindak copper and gold mining plant in Baluchistan. China is the world's third largest exporter of mineral products and is keenly interested in tapping into the world market in this sector.[44]

China's ventures abroad, especially in Pakistan, have been constrained by its own lack of personnel and funds as well as by local problems related to bad management practices (as in Pakistan's Saindak gold and copper mines) or unstable political conditions where it cannot guarantee the safety of its personnel and technical staff.[45]

Until recently Pakistan's foreign investment policies were, as well, restrictive. Total direct investments in Pakistan rose from Pakistani Rs 186 million in 1988 to Rs 419 by 1994 but most of this went into portfolio investments by the latter year rather than in investment in industrial and manufacturing ventures. This reflected the volatility as well as the lack of opportunity in the Pakistani economy. Substantial investments from Hong Kong for the period 1991–3 went into portfolio investments amounting to US $ 83.7 million in 1991–2 (accounting for all of Hong Kong's investment in that year) and US $48.8 million of US $61.2 million for the fiscal year 1992–3.

However, the ailing Saindak project is being revived by an infusion of funds from domestic banks and under Chinese management and contract to install refinery technology. Much of the copper extracted at Saindak is exported to China. The total copper reserves at Saindak are estimated at 412 million tonnes. While China's National Non-ferrous Metals Industry Corporation has taken on the management of Saindak, its petroleum Engineering Construction Corporation has signed contracts with Pakistan for engineering and labour services. It has emphasized large engineering projects worth approximately US $30 million each involving the laying of oil pipelines, setting up oil refineries and oil collecting stations.[46]

Where China has invested in Pakistan in the past it has been careful to choose projects that were low risk and small scale in nature and that were aimed at natural resource development. This seems to be changing partly because of its current foray into mega oil projects in Central Asia which necessitate planning for refineries, pipelines and collection and storage centres in the region.

China's objective in making investments abroad has been to gain information from the international market that would not be otherwise available to it, to acquire advanced technology and equipment, and to be able to expose its personnel to new management techniques. None of these conditions are liable to be fulfilled in the present state of Pakistan's economy.[47] However, Pakistan's attempts to do away with restrictions in line with GATT requirements have been viewed positively by China. China also views Pakistan's economy at this stage in its development as fitting into China's needs for primary commodities.[48]

The Sino–Pakistan potential for economic cooperation in Central Asia is immense but for the moment it has been put on the back burner until the Afghan situation is resolved. Yet one sector in which China and Pakistan could possibly have a trading relationship is through intra-regional trade which allows for some movement of goods in the area. However, the evidence indicates that the increase in Sino–Pakistan trade at the regional level remains limited at best. This is partly because the Central Asian trade environment is still in transition from its socialist past and partly because its potential as a resource market is still to be tapped.

TABLE 13.2 NET FOREIGN INVESTMENT IN PAKISTAN BY COUNTRY OF ORIGIN (US$ MILLION)

Country	1988–9			1989–90			1990–1			1991–2			1992–3		
	D	P	T	D	P	T	D	P	T	D	P	T	D	P	T
US	94.7	1.7	96.1	93.9	-2.0	91.9	130.0	5.0	135.0	213.4	50.9	264.3	136.9	25.7	162.6
HK	6.3	0	6.3	0.9	0	0.9	3.3	0.1	3.4	0	83.7	83.7	12.4	48.8	61.2
Ger	10.0	1.6	11.6	11.2	0	11.2	12.5	2.3	14.8	21.4	0.5	21.9	36.2	–	36.2
Jap.	16.7	-4.9	11.8	+6.1	-4.2	11.9	26.2	-5.3	20.9	17.7	0	17.7	22.0	6.3	28.3
UAE	12.9	0.9	13.8	15.9	-2.8	13.1	9.0	1.6	10.6	10.5	47.6	58.1	9.5	0.4	10.4

Source: GATT: *Trade Policy Review, Pakistan, 1995*, p. 32. D=direct investment, P=portfolio investment; T=total of D+P.

TABLE 13.3 PAKISTAN'S REGIONAL BALANCE OF TRADE (IN PAK. RUPEES MILLION)

Name	Total Trade		Balance of Trade		% Change		% Share in Pakistan's global trade	
	1984–5	1985–6		1985–6			1984–5	1985–6
American Region	17,934.8	20,631.4	(-)	7,975.6	(+)	15.0	14.0	14.7
W. Europe	30,470.8	39,789.4	(-)	10,506.2	(+)	30.6	23.9	28.3
E. Europe	3,773.2	5,161.8	(+)	818.8	(+)	36.8	3.0	3.7
Middle East	30,994.8	27,460.0	(-)	9,759.2	(-)	11.4	24.3	19.5
Africa	4,462.2	4,419.3	(+)	1,252.1	(-)	1.0	3.5	3.1
Other Asia	37,094.2	39,541.1	(-)	12,845.6	(+)	6.6	29.0	28.1
Oceania	3,077.6	3,535.5	(-)	2,338.6	(+)	14.9	2.4	2.5
Grand Total	127,757.6	140,558.5	(-)	41,354.1	(+)	100.0	100.0	100.0

Source: *Pakistan 1988: An Official Handbook*, Government of Pakistan, 1989, p. 133.

TABLE 13.4 INTERSUBREGIONAL MERCHANDISE TRADE LOW MATRIX, 1995
(FIGS. IN MILLIONS OF US$. FIGS. IN PARENTHESIS INDICATE %)

From / To	ASEAN	SAARC	ECO	South Pacific Forum	East Asia PRC, HK, ROK, ROC	Total Asia and Pacific + Aus., NZ, Jap.	Total Exports
ASEAN	68470	6847	2431	397	48415	182054	311489
	(22.0)	(2.2)	(0.8)	(0.1)	(15.5)	(58.4)	(100)
SAARC	2728	2020	905	5	3945	13219	45739
	(6.0)	(4.4)	(2.0)	(0.01)	(8.6)	(28.9)	(100)
ECO	1703	1241	2525	1	3682	12584	56293
	(3.0)	(2.2)	(4.5)	(0.01)	(6.5)	(22.4)	(100)
S. Pacific Forum	218	9	1	12	357	2540	3494
	(6.2)	(0.3)	(0.03)	(0.32)	(10.2)	(72.7)	(100)
East Asia	50676	6692	3826	99	163473	305240	559325
	(9.1)	(1.2)	(0.7)	(0.03)	(29.2)	(54.6)	

Source: ECOSOC *Survey of Asia and the Pacific: 1997*, p. 102.

By the mid-1980s Asia (excluding the Middle East and including the ECO, the PRC, Hong Kong, North Korea and Taiwan) was Pakistan's second largest export market with a share of 29.0 per cent of all trade. For the same period its share of imports from the same region ranged from 26.1 per cent in 1984–5 to 20.5 per cent in 1985–6 with the share of ECO trade rising from 1.6 to 2.6 per cent.[49] Between 1984 to 1986, however, the total percentage of change was only 6.6 as compared to 30.6 for West Europe and 36.8 for East Europe.

For the ECO, East Asia (including China, Hong Kong, North Korea and Taiwan) was its second largest partner in trade by 1995. In comparative terms the ECO had the third largest volume of subregional trade lagging behind the ASEAN group and East Asia and staying somewhat ahead of SAARC and the South Pacific Forum. Yet, here again, the direction of trade was heavily weighed towards Asia and the Pacific as a whole (22.4 per cent), with East Asian trade amounting to 4.5 of the total ECO trade for 1995. The effects of interregional trade on the China's trade with Pakistan could, therefore, only be minimal at best.

Within the ECO, as well, Pakistan's total exposure to Central Asia is still quite limited in comparison to China and to the other ECO partners. In US dollor terms it amounts to only 120 million as opposed to Turkey's credits of up to US $150 million per annum in each of the Central Asian countries, and the PRC's rising levels of barter trade and oil contracts in the region.[50] However, early this year the EBRD granted official project financing to Pakistani firms to invest in Turkmenistan.[51] It remains to be seen how the European sanctions imposed after Pakistan's nuclear explosion this May will affect this funding. For now, however, the share of intra-ECO trade in the total share of world trade remains low at 5 per cent in 1994.[52]

Conclusion

Sino–Pakistan trade has been low over the years and has survived because the wider economic relationship has been stable and long lasting. However, while the regional situation may impact on trade between the two countries to some extent, in the final analysis the growth of trade will rest on whether the Pakistani economy can respond competitively to China's expanding market and on China's economic policies in relation to its modernizing needs.

NOTES

1. Yaacov Vertzberger, *The Enduring Entente: Sino-Pakistani Relations, 1960-1980*, Washington: Georgetown University, 1983.
2. Zulfikar Khalid, *Pakistan in the Pamir Knot*, Lahore: Vanguard Books, 1987 for text of the boundary agreement between China and Pakistan, pp. 220–5.
3. Tehmina Mehmood, 'Pakistan's Foreign Policy: Post Cold War Period', *Pakistan Horizon*, 50/3, 1997, p. 102.
4. Zulfikar Khalid, pp. 96–7.
5. The extent to which this is true is evident in the absence of secondary literature on economic relations between the two countries. See Anwar H. Syed, *China and Pakistan: Diplomacy of an Entente Cordiale*, Amherst: University of Massachusts Press, 1974), Yaacov Vertzberger, op. cit., Steven I. Levine, 'China in Asia: The PRC as a Regional Power', in Harry Harding, ed., *China's Foreign Relations in the 1980s*, New Haven: Yale University Press, 1984.
6. *Far Eastern Economic Review* (hereafter *FEER*), 12 December 1985, pp. 24–5.
7. *Pakistan 1988: An Official Handbook*, Ministry of Information and Broadcasting, Government of Pakistan, 1989, p. 143.
8. *The Aid Programme of China*, Paris: OECD, 1979, pp. 6–7.
9. *FEER*, 29 May 1997, p. 12; *Pakistan and Gulf Economist*, 23 February–1 March 1998, p. 36.
10. *Pakistan 1988*, p. 142.
11. According to Pakistan's Ministry of Foreign Affairs, total economic assistance amounted to RMBY 3.244 billion (US $1.7 billion) (a) Interest-Free Loans RMBY 0.833 billion (i) Project/ Commodity loans RMBY 0.278 billion (ii) Balance of Payments Support US$ 0.5 billion (b) Technical Cooperation RMBY 1.568 billion (c) Grants RMBY 1.077 billion Defence Projects total assistance RMBY 1.876 billion (a) Grants RMBY 1.077 billion (b) Loans RMBY 0.799 billion. There was also a goods procurement loan amounting to RMBY 0.391 billion and for the armed forces to the tune of RMBY 1.876 billion. Therefore the final figure is not USD 1.7 billion as ministry sources state but USD 1.12 billion. 'Foreign Economic Assistance', pp. 1–20.
12. *Economic Survey*, 'Foreign Economic Assistance', Pakistan Ministry of Finance, Government of Pakistan, March 2003, pp. 1–20. www.finance.gov.pk/survey/chapter10-fea.pdf ; Mohammed Uzair, 'Foreign Aid and Indebtedness in Pakistan', *Pakistan Horizon*, 46/1, 1993, p. 32.
13. *Economic Survey*, Table 10.2.
14. *World Military Expenditures and Arms Transfers, 1989*, Washington: US Arms Control and Disarmament Agency, 1990, p. 118.

15. *SIPRI Yearbook 1991.*
16. *The Military Balance, 1992–3*, London: IISS, 1994, pp. 135–7.
17. *SIPRI Yearbook* 1996, pp. 514–15.
18. Sydney James, 'Military Industry', in Gerald Segal and William T. Tow, eds., *Chinese Defence Policy*, Chicago: University of Illinois Press, p. 128; *The Military Balance*: *1996–7* (IISS).
19. *World Military Expenditures and Arms Transfers: 1966–7 and 1970–9*, pp. 78 and 130.
20. Ibid., p. 515; Roger Frost, 'Pakistan's Ordnance Factories: A Rising Crescent in Defense Production'. *Strategic Digest*, New Delhi: IDSA, xix, 10 October 1989, pp. 1317–30.
21. Roger Frost, pp. 1320–5, *SIPRI Yearbook 1996*, pp. 514–15.
22. Tanvir Ahmad Khan, 'Pakistan's Regional Policy with Special Reference to India and Afghanistan', *Pakistan Horizon*, 43/4, October 1990, pp. 9–28; Iqbal Akhund, 'National Security and Pakistan's Foreign Policy in a Changing World', *Pakistan Horizon*, 43/2, April 1990, pp. 13–22.
23. Chinese positions on arms transfers.
24. Zulfikar Khalid, *Pakistan in the Pamir Knot*, p. 159.
25. See treaties with Russia and Central Asian states, 1996, and the Shanghai Cooperation Organization communiqué.
26. *Pakistan Horizon*, 46/1, January 1993, pp. 160–6.
27. Ahmad Rashid, pp. 73–4.
28. Ibid., pp.121, 151, 155.
29. *Pakistan Horizon*, 50/3, July 1997, pp. 3–4, 47.
30. *Pakistan and Gulf Economist,* 11–17 May, 1998, p. 23.
31. *ECOSOC Survey of Asia and the Pacific, 1997*, Bangkok: ECOSOC Commission, 1997, pp. 189–90.
32. Jennifer Anderson, *The Limits of Sino-Russian Strategic Partnership*, Adelphi Paper 315, IISS 1997.
33. *Pakistan and Gulf Economist*, 12–8 January, 1998, p. 18.
34. *FEER,* 10 April, 1997, pp. 22–5; *Pakistan and Gulf Economist*, 27 April–3 May 1998, p. 10.
35. *Pakistan Horizon,* 50/3, July 1997, p. 4.
36. See *Pakistan 1988: A Handbook* and *Pakistan 2000: A Handbook*, Islamabad: Govt of Pakistan.
37. *Pakistan and Gulf Economist*, 12–18 January, 1998, p. 18.
38. *Pakistan and Gulf Economist*, 23 February–1 March 1998, p. 36.
39. Kevin B. Bucknall, *China and the Open Door*, New York: Allen and Unwin, 1989, pp. 58 and 94.
40. Hong Wang, *China's Exports Since 1979*, New York: St. Martin's Press, 1994, pp. 130–1.
41. *Statistical Yearbook for Asia and the Pacific: 1996*, Bangkok: U.N., 1997, p. 115.

42. *IMF: Direction of Trade Statistics Yearbook*, IMF, 1997, p. 304.
43. *Statistical Yearbook for Asia and the Pacific: 1996*, pp. 169–70.
44. *China Daily: Business Weekly*, 21–7 September , 1997, p. 2.
45. *Pakistan and Gulf Economist*, 1–7 December, 1997, p. 14.
46. Qian Hao and Xie Yangan, 'China's Foreign Direct Investment: Inflows and Outflows', in *Development Papers No. 10: Foreign Investment, Trade and Economic Cooperation in the Àsian and Pacific Region*, ECOSOC Commission for Asia and the Pacific, UN, 1992, pp. 171–92.
47. Ashfaque Khan, 'Trade Strategies in a Post-Uruguay Round Trading Environment: The Case of Pakistan', *Expansion of Trading Opportunities to the Year 2000 for Asia Pacific Developing Countries: Implications of the Uruguay Round and Adaptation of Export Strategies* UNCTAD, 1995, pp. 577–604; Li Cong, 'Developing Nations in the Surging Tide of Economic Globalization', *Journal of Foreign Affairs*, Beijing, no. 46, December 1997, pp. 7–15.
48. Qian Hao and Xie Yangan, 'China's Foreign direct Investment: Inflows and Outflows', in *Development Papers No. 10: Foreign Iinvestment, Trade and Economic Cooperation in the Asian and Pacific Region*, Ecosoc Commission for Asia and the Pacific, UN, 1992, pp. 171–92.
49. Ashfaque Khan, 'Trade Strategies in a Post-Uruguay Round Trading Environment: the Case of Pakistan', *Expansion of Trading Opportunities to the Year 2000 for Asia Pacific Developing Countries: Implications of the Uruguay Round and Adaptation of Export Strategies*, UNCTAD, 1995, pp. 577–604; Li Cong, 'Developing Nations in the Surging Tide of Economic Globalization', *Journal of Foreign Affairs*, Beijing, no. 46, December 1997, pp. 7–15.
50. *Pakistan, 1988: A Handbook*, pp. 131–7.
51. *China Daily: Business Weekly*, 26 April–2 May 1998, p. 2.
52. *Pakistan and Gulf Economist*, 11–17 May 1998, p. 23.

42. IMF, *Direction of Trade Statistics Yearbook* 1991, 1997, p. 104.
43. *Statistical* [illegible] 1996, pp. 167–70.
44. *China Daily, Business Weekly*, 21 September 1992, p. 2.
45. *Pakistan and Gulf Economist*, 25 December 1993, p. 16.
46. Guo Hai and Xie Yanxian, 'China's Foreign Direct Investment Inflows and Outflows', in *Development Papers No. 10, Foreign Direct Investment, Trade and Economic Cooperation in the Asian and Pacific Region*, ECOSOC Commission for Asia and the Pacific, UN, 1992, p. 101.

47. Ishtiaq Khan, 'Trade Strategies in a Post-Uruguay Round Trading Environment: The Case of Pakistan', *Expansion of Trading Opportunities to the Year 2000 for Asia Pacific Developing Countries: Implications of the Uruguay Round and Adaptation of Export Strategies*, UNCTAD, 1994, [illegible] Cong, 'Developing Nations in the Surging Tide of Economic Globalization', *Journal of Foreign Affairs*, Beijing, no. 45, December 1997, pp. 2–16.
48. Guo Hai and Xie Yanxian, 'China's Foreign Direct Investment Inflows and Outflows', in *Development Papers No. 10, Foreign Direct Investment, Trade and Economic Cooperation in the Asian and Pacific Region*, Economic Commission for Asia and the Pacific, UN, 1992, pp. 101–02.
49. Ishtiaq Khan, 'Trade Strategies in a Post-Uruguay Round Trading Environment: The Case of Pakistan', *Expansion of Trading Opportunities to the Year 2000 for Asia Pacific Developing Countries: Implications of the Uruguay Round and Adaptation of Export Strategies*, UNCTAD, 1995, pp. [illegible] Developing Nations in the Surging Tide of Economic Globalization', *Journal of Foreign Affairs*, Beijing, no. 45, December 1997, pp. [illegible]
50. *Pakistan* 1997 [illegible] Book, p. 131.
51. *China Daily, Business Weekly*, 18 April–1 May [illegible] p. 2.
52. [illegible] *Herald Tribune*, 11–12 [illegible] 1998 [illegible]

CHAPTER 14

Civilian Technology Transfers

D. VARAPRASAD SEKHAR*

The second half of the twentieth century was to witness the largest technology transfers that the world had ever seen—a process which was essentially led by the developed countries. Towards the end of the century the pace of this process had come to be redefined largely by two factors. Firstly, it was the rapid evolution and expansion of knowledge economies and information societies led by information and communication technology (ICT) revolution in the advanced countries.[1] Secondly, a slow and steady expansion of the same in the developing countries leading to a scenario of narrowing the 'digital divide' that exists between the advanced and advancing countries. As a result, at least some of the developing countries—such as China and India—are evolving their home-grown technologies, some of which are derived from their collaboration with and assistance from the advanced countries. However, they are now themselves in a position to export technologies to other countries and thereby changing the nature of technology transfers.[2] At the beginning of the twenty-first century, therefore, it is imperative to know the dynamics of technology flows from one country to another to understand the nature of these and their impact on the international, regional and bilateral relations.

China, with its own rapid technological development in certain areas seems to have finally arrived at a position where it can export technologies to some of the developing countries. Pakistan being a strong ally for almost four decades has received various kinds of technology from China which has played an important role in improving its own technological capabilities. It is in this broad context, that this chapter attempts an analysis of civilian technology transfer

*The author is thankful to Kalyan for his insightful comments on an earlier draft of this chapter.

between China and Pakistan—two close allies that have had one of the most consistent bilateral relations in the post-World War II period, despite some minor irritants, particularly in the 1950s. This chapter, however, does not touch upon nuclear technology transfers where there are contentious debates about China's role in the development of Pakistan's nuclear capabilities.[3]

Two preliminary facets are to be noted prior to delving into civilian technology transfers between China and Pakistan. Firstly, there has been very little research done in the area of civilian technology transfer from China to other countries in general and to Pakistan in particular.[4] Most of the literature relating to Chinese transfer of technology deals with importing advanced technologies from developed countries.[5] Secondly, the nature of relations between China and Pakistan needs to be kept in mind while delineating transfer of technology. The relations between the two are explained poetically as being 'higher than the Himalayas, deeper than the oceans and sweeter than honey' by Pakistani President Pervez Musharraf, while others call their bilateral relations as an 'all-weather friendship' oriented. All these epithets do emphasize the nature and the depth of bilateral relations between China and Pakistan.

While analysing the civilian technology transfer from China to Pakistan, the chapter will situate it in two broader contexts: (i) international and regional, with technological and political dimensions; (ii) the place and role of foreign economic ties and technology transfer in China's foreign relations. This forms part of section II. Section III, the main part of the chapter, details origins, evolution and trends in, along with various problems and future of, technical cooperation between China and Pakistan since 1950 till 2004. In section IV some lessons for India are highlighted. And the last section provides some conclusions.

The New Context

The international and regional contexts with technological and political components and the place of economic ties and technology transfer in Chinese foreign relations deserve detailing because of their role in determining and shaping the nature of civilian technology transfer between China and Pakistan.

The international-technological context for technical cooperation between China and Pakistan is also determined by the very nature and pace of the development of technology across the globe. As mentioned earlier, in the post-World War II period technology progressed at a rapid pace leading many developed countries to begin thinking of using technology for further development of their economies. The developed countries with a two hundred history of the development of science and technology behind them have been in a better position to use their technologies in their multilateral and bilateral trade and expand their influence in the developing world.[6]

Alongside the demand and commitment to using various kinds of technology among the developing countries has seen a rapid growth leading to a higher proportion of trade in various kinds of technologies with a strong focus on the capital-intensive technologies. Moreover, technology importing countries generally would like to acquire advanced technologies given their financial abilities but when these are not forthcoming for various reasons they look to the next-best. For instance, soon after the establishment of the People's Republic of China entertained the thought of importing technology from the US and Europe but it never occurred purely for ideological factors. But China imported one of the largest consignments of technology from the USSR when they had cordial relations in the 1950s.

The international political context where technology transfers take place is also vital because technology transfers occur in a political context of the nature of bilateral relations that countries forge based on their domestic political ideologies and compulsions. During the Cold War period the two superpowers played a major role in shaping the way countries are allied and grouped into different blocks which played a major role in the way that China and Pakistan came to forge strong bilateral relations with significant segment of technical cooperation. In the early 1950s the colonial experiences of China and Pakistan brought them together. Pakistan's quick recognition of communist China in 1950 further paved the way for strong relations between the two. The US with its strong opposition to the expansion of communist ideology led Pakistan into South-East Asian Treaty Organization (SEATO) in 1954 thus making the relations between China and Pakistan go sour for the first time in an otherwise friendly bilateral relationship since 1949.

Here one must not lose sight of Pakistan's interest, in joining SEATO, aiming at gaining the American support thereby in a better position to deal with a strong India. From 1954 till 1961 Pakistan supported the US in opposing PRC replacing Republic of China (ROC) at the United Nation's Security Council. This irritation was pacified at the 1955 Bandung Conference when Chinese Premier Zhou Enlai and Pakistani Prime Minister Mohammad Ali Bogra met and ironed out some of these differences. But the relations touched a low ebb between 1957 and continued till 1963 during which time Pakistan went through one of the most volatile domestic crises after its independence. The year 1963 saw China and Pakistan signing a major border and air travel agreement that set the relations between the two on a steady course that continues even today.

The year 1963 is significant in the sense that it was soon after the 1962 war between India and China. The war seemed to have confirmed to the Pakistani leadership the military might of China and its utility in contributing to its own national agenda. Though ideological differences had determined the groupings it had very little impact on the relations between the two. What brought them together was the need for each other in their calculations of promoting their national interests by being together despite the differences in their domestic political systems. In the 1970s Pakistan played a major role as a facilitator in Sino–American rapprochement, which was mainly hastened by the expansion of Soviet power[7] in Central Asia–Afghanistan, and thus gained their support. Pakistan arranged the 'secret' meeting between the American National Security Adviser Henry Kissinger and Mao Zedong which eventually paved the way for the 1972 rapprochement when the US president Richard Nixon visited China and signed Shanghai Communiqué.

In the 1990s the international political context began to see marked changes wherein the relations among powers, including superpowers and the rising powers found themselves in a completely new situation with the end of the Cold War. This changed scenario provided immense scope for the rising powers such as China to play an active role in international politics. During this time China's relations with the US and other major powers, despite some crises have been favourable.

The regional-technological context for forging civilian technology transfer is partly related to the development that countries like Japan, South Korea and Singapore have been making by importing advanced technologies and thereby achieving significant progress. Countries like Pakistan have been observing this process and would like to emulate. While the desire is laudable the social, political and economic conditions in these countries are not entirely conducive for technology to take deeper roots and make vital impact on the lives of the people.

The commitment to follow the Japanese and the East Asian Tigers' model is confined to those at the top echelons and not caught by those at the lower levels who play a considerable role in making or marring this desire a reality.

The regional political dimension, where India figures in a major way in bringing the two powers closer is also significant in understanding the context in which technical cooperation between the two has been taking place. It is only India that has had conflictual relations and a history of fighting wars with both of them. This antagonism with India brought them together. As Anwar Hussain Syed points out, 'Pakistan's fear of India and her resentment at American military aid to that country (India) were doubtless factors impelling her to seek China's goodwill.'[8] It was their mutual antagonism with India[9] that cemented the relations and further strengthened the scope for cooperation in civilian technology.

Technology Transfer and Foreign Relations

China's foreign relations with superpowers and other major powers since the establishment of the PRC along with some historical legacies has played a crucial role in enabling China to stand where it stands now in international politics. It is also instrumental in contributing to the fast pace with which it is rising in global politics. As Segal and Goodman argue 'there can be no more important issue for the international system than to understand China's rise'.[10] Its foreign policy, particularly foreign economic policy[11] is very much linked to its domestic economic reform programme perhaps much stronger than many developed and developing countries.

Though foreign trade or economic relations has emerged as an important variable which deserves focus on its right, it needs to be considered integral to foreign policy primarily because the way it is used in strengthening China's economy and thereby its place in international politics.[12] The Chinese leadership seems to be more inclined than ever to view economic development as a means to strengthen even national security as Denny Roy points out.[13] Peace and development came to be the two pillars of China's foreign policy since the middle of 1980s. The leadership believes that peace in the region would provide the much needed conducive environment for it to carry on with its economic development programme. Based on these two goals, China has, except with India and some of the South-

East Asian countries, resolved its border disputes and has been having active economic ties with them.

Economic cooperation with, and technology transfer from, the developed countries are considered by the Chinese political leaders as two most important engines of economic growth for China which had found itself in deep crisis in the late 1970s. The very open door policy *kai fang zhengce* that China has formulated after 1978 is aimed at using economic ties and technology in its developmental programme. It is to be noted here that economic ties and technology transfer have not been considered by the Chinese leaders as two important variables within Chinese foreign policy thinking in an explicit manner. But these two factors have been given an important place in an implicit manner in Chinese foreign policy. Economic ties and technology transfer do not figure in a major way as two critical components in the writings on China's foreign policy.[14] In some writings only economic ties are considered as a factor in Chinese foreign policy.[15] The component of technology transfer is either subsumed within foreign economic relations or completely left outside the purview of foreign policy. Therefore, civilian technology transfer is delineated as a vital input along with foreign economic ties in China's foreign policy.

A major focus of the diplomatic negotiations that China has had since early 1980s is on how to use economic ties and import technology from the advanced countries and thereby promote its domestic economic development. Every time a top Chinese leader visits a country a big delegation of experts relating to economy and technology would invariably be going to finalize various deals. For instance, in 1994 when Premier Li Peng visited several European countries he signed a number of deals with several European firms amounting to US $3 billion dollars.[16]

Chinese economic ties with both the developed and developing countries have taken a new dimension and expanded ever since China opened its economy to the outside world in 1978. This has transformed the Chinese economy in a major way.[17] For quite some time, say until 1980 China was exporting natural resources rather than finished products. Only after 1980 it slowly began to export manufactured products and now it is beginning to export high-tech products. This is one of the positive effects of the reform programme. Secondly, its bilateral trade with the US, Japan, and many European countries has not only grown but they have been in Chinese favour. At the beginning of the twenty-first-century China has emerged as the third largest economy and is poised to become the second largest in the next couple of decades.[18] It is the second largest recipient of FDI after the US with US $53.5 billions in 2003.

In terms of FDI Confidence Index, an annual survey of chief executive officers, chief financial officers, chief financial officers and top executives from the world's largest companies, China has replaced the US as the number one destination for the last three years.[19] The commendable factor in attracting such large amount of FDI is that China uses it as a source of acquiring advanced technology from countries like the US, Japan, France and Germany. This has paid rich dividends to China in the last two decades.

Technology transfer occurs in two distinct modes: Direct and Indirect Transfers.[20] The former includes sale of technology—whole plants and know-how, consultancy, project contracts and licensing along with partial licensing. Foreign direct investment, joint venture and subcontracting are part of the latter mode. Technology transfer 'is not as easy as the purchase of capital good or the acquisition of its blue print' as Rosenberg and Frischtak[21] argue, in fact, it is not only not easy but much more complex because there are two participants involved—one supplier and the other buyer. Invariably the supplier would supply to ensure that there are sufficient returns for the investment made while the buyer would see that the technology being bought is not only state-of-the-art but also cost-effective. Since 1980s Chinese technology imports have been more of the licensed technology rather than complete machinery. But what is most critical in reaping the benefits of technology imports is the process of assimilation and adaptation to the local conditions of demand and tastes.[22] China has a mixed record in this respect. While the State-Owned Enterprises (SOEs) are lagging behind it is the private sector and joint ventures that have been quite successful and are leading the success story of Chinese economic development.

After initiating the economic reform programme China took about a little more than two decades to improve its domestic technological capabilities and close the gap between its technology and the technology in the advanced countries.[23] In this process the Chinese government has introduced a number of institutional, managerial and personnel reforms in the field of technology besides some technology programmes such as '863', '973', Key Tasks Programme and 'Torch' to make China self-sufficient in its technological capabilities, particularly in the realm of high-technology[24] and thereafter be able to export to other countries. Government spending on research and development (R&D) has also increased substantially. Its R&D spending is the third highest in global R&D spending, after the US and Japan, and recently surpassed Germany.[25]

Apart from providing the much needed impetus on the domestic front, China has also embarked on participating in the international technology trade and international collaboration in technology development which is slowly taking Chinese technology development to higher levels. Chinese policy of 'import-led' export strategy[26] of importing advanced technologies from the developed countries and thereby export manufactured products not only to the developed countries but also to the developing countries seems to have been quite successful. The Chinese government spending on importing advanced technologies has been increasing over the last few years. In fact, from 1991 to 1997 there has been a three-fold increase from 900 million yuan (US $ 110 million) in 1991 to 2365 million yuan (US $ 300 million) in 1997 in purchase of foreign technologies.[27]

Though there are certain problems in the diffusion and the Chinese ability in adapting these technologies and the technological prowess that China boasts of is essentially owned by the MNCs as George Gilboy argues,[28] their overall impact on the development of domestic technologies cannot be underestimated. In fact, the very presence of the MNCs in China has provided a platform for the Chinese companies to know how they are functioning and doing their business. Moreover, Chinese firms are slowly enhancing their technological capabilities in several ways. Collaboration with foreign technology institutes and technologists has also been on the rise. About 32 laboratories had been established by foreign companies in China by 2000. In 2002 about 4683 Chinese scientists are involved in collaborative research in projects abroad and about 4060 are involved in foreign projects in China.[29]

All these measures have played a major role in building Chinese technological capabilities so much so that they have a major bearing on its export performance as Wall and Yin argue.[30] There is a strong correlation between the level of technological development and the kind of exports to other countries. As technology develops there will be greater share of the manufactured goods in the overall volume of exports. Chinese exports of manufactured goods have gone up from

36.3 per cent in 1985 to 87. 3 per cent in 1997.[31] As China's technology matures it is aiming to export technology intensive goods not only for strengthening ties but also for the growth of its domestic technology companies. In other words, China is now moving from being a net importer of technology to an exporter of technology to other developing countries.[32]

It is in fact, in the initial phase of emerging as a major player in exporting its various home grown technologies. These exports are slowly increasing by the year. The growth of technological development in China is also posing challenges to its developed neighbours such as South Korea and Singapore.[33] The share of high-tech products in the overall technology-intensive exports is one of the signs of a country's technological prowess. In this segment China's exports of high-tech products has been on the rise. For instance, in 2002 China exported high-tech products worth 602,000 million yuan—a 50 per cent increase over 2001.[34]

For some developing countries importing technology from the developed countries is more promising for their national developmental goals but it is exorbitantly expensive, though it is superior in terms of quality in comparison to that of the technology from the developing countries. As the quality of Chinese technology is reaching world standards in certain sectors, indigenously developed Chinese technology is becoming more attractive for the developing countries. Moreover, in terms of pricing it is quite competitive and thus the developing countries that do not have financial wherewithal are beginning to consider Chinese technology. In other words, China is emerging as one of the destinations for purchasing technology.[35]

It is in this context of domestic and international aspects of the rapid technology development in China one must situate the discussion on the transfer of civilian technologies from China to Pakistan. Moreover, geographical proximity also plays a role in facilitating the process of technology transfer. The closer a country is to another nation with a strong base of technology, the more the chances for closer ties in the export of technology provided they have stable and friendly bilateral relations. In this regard, China and Pakistan fit the bill. Trust is also vital in forming technology alliances as Daellenbach and Davenport (2004) argue.[36] Both China and Pakistan have a four-decade history of trust in each other which is reinforced by their mutual need for each other. This has further strengthened the scope for technology transfer from China to Pakistan.

Civilian Technology Transfers

The extent and depth of civilian technology transfer from China to Pakistan is determined by two factors: the requirement and demand in Pakistan[37] for capital-intensive goods and the deepening and expansion of their bilateral trade.[38] Pertaining to the first aspect, a glance at Pakistan's imports[39] of machinery, transport equipment and chemicals which constitute about 50 per cent of the total imports with $1.5 billion, $0.5 billion and $1.3 billion[40] respectively shows the extent of its domestic requirements where China can play a crucial role in meeting some of these needs. Moreover, as China is able to increase its technological sophistication it is in a better position to supply the technologies that Pakistan requires. This also depends on the pace of the growth of domestic technology in Pakistan.[41] Pakistan, given its slow rate of technology development, 'will continue to import basic technology design from abroad'.[42]

Relating to bilateral trade, the more the trade the more the scope for technology transfers. In 1997 the total volume of bilateral trade between China and Pakistan was less than US $1 billion dollars.[43] Since then it has been on the rise leading to better prospects for trade in technology-intensive goods. In 2002 China was the third largest exporting country to Pakistan with a share of 6.8 per cent of the total imports.[44] In 2003–4 China and Pakistan had $2.5 billion dollars worth trade, which is estimated to be 30 per cent more than 2002–3. Both countries hope to expand this in future.

In 1983 China and Pakistan established China-Pakistan Joint Economic, Trade, Scientific and Technological Cooperation Commission (CPJETSTCC) which is something similar to what China and US have between them—the Sino–US Joint Committee on Scientific and Technological Cooperation. And in 2000 they had their 11th session in Beijing wherein they have pledged their commitment to further economic and S&T cooperation in the twenty-first century.[45] Cooperation in civilian technology is part and parcel of one of the four point-proposals that underwrite the bilateral relations between China and Pakistan in the contemporary international context.[46] This proposal was later written into the China–Pakistan Joint Declaration signed on 4 November in 2003. Point four of the third section of the Declaration reads as follows: Guide and encourage their government departments scientific research institutes and universities and high-tech enterprises to conduct broad level technological cooperation in areas of mutual interest such as telecommunication, water conservancy, electric power, aviation, space technology, computer automation, metallurgy, IT, medicine and health, petrochemistry, biotechnology and peaceful utilization of nuclear power. The two parties will endeavour to transfer know-how and exchange of information. In this context the two parties will give full play to the guiding and coordinative role of the intergovernmental Joint Committee on Scientific and Technological Cooperation (JCSTC).[47]

EVOLVING NEW TRENDS

Following Cooper's broad framework of direct and indirect technology transfers, China's technology transfer to Pakistan is dominated by the direct mode. What China has been doing in its civilian technology transfers to Pakistan is what the erstwhile Soviet Union did to China in the 1950s in terms of building a number of industrial establishments in China. But the difference in Sino–Pak civilian technology transfers is that the scale is rather small in comparison primarily because of current limitations of the Chinese technological wherewithal.

There are three major trends in the civilian technology transfer between China and Pakistan. The first trend is that of economic aid wherein China gave Pakistan various amounts of aid from time to time to meet some of its economic imperatives. This was the pattern in the first decade after the establishment of bilateral relations. The second trend is that of building some major industrial complexes which started in the 1960s and carried out vigorously in the 1970s and 1980s. This trend is also in operation now in certain areas. The third trend is the rise of indirect technology transfer in the 1990s and in the twenty-first century. During this period the technical cooperation between China and Pakistan had taken a new dimension where the number of technologies transferred increased substantially. As part of the indirect technology transfer there are a number of Chinese technical experts who are working on various projects in Pakistan. This has provided a direct contact between the Pakistani experts and the Chinese thereby a source of enhancing their technical skills. It is not clear as to how many Chinese scientists, engineers and other professionals are in Pakistan training their counterparts. One estimation is that there are at least 500 of them. Given the Chinese potential, in September 2004 the Pakistani government sought Chinese assistance in boosting vocational training system and upgradation of manpower in various spheres.[48] There are about 200 Pakistani professionals being trained in different Chinese universities, academies and institutes such as Tsinghua University, Beijing Institute of Technology and Fudan University.

ORIGINS AND EVOLUTION

China and Pakistan have signed about 116 agreements and protocols pertaining to political, economic, technical and cultural components between 1951 and 1990.[49] During this period technical cooperation between the two had been an integral part of their economic cooperation at least until 1975. In other words, economic and technical cooperation went hand in hand. In all they had about 12 economic and technical agreements between them during 1965–76. The first ever economic and technical cooperation agreement signed between the two was in November 1965 when China agreed to build the Taxila heavy machine project. As Anwar Hussain Syed explains the most notable project built by the Chinese in Pakistan is 'heavy mechanical complex at Taxila, capable of producing machines that would make cement, sugar, textiles, boilers, road-building equipment, and railway engines'.[50]

Prior to that they had some sort of barter agreement in operation wherein, for instance, in 1963 they exchanged Chinese portland cement for Pakistani unprocessed jute. In the same year they also signed an agreement on the transmission of picture service between Beijing and Karachi. In 1971 China agreed to assist Pakistan in building a sugar mill. In 1973 it was agreed that China would help constructing the Tarbela-Wah transmission line and Tarbela cotton spinning mill. Setting up of a fertilizer company was agreed upon in 1974. In 1975 China supplied 41 diesel generating sets to Pakistan besides setting up a textile mill in Punjab province. Pakistan also supplied China 10 ships in 1978 for cash payment within five years. In 1979 China agreed to export steel billets, tools, workshop implements, sheet and glass plates, construction and road building machinery, agricultural implements and telecommunications equipment. In a 1980 protocol China concurred to provide assistance in chemical fertilizers industry, construction technology, and biogas.

Since 1976 scientific and technical cooperation came to emerge as an independent component in their bilateral agreements. For the first time in May 1976 they signed a specific scientific and technical cooperation agreement. There were 16 such agreements signed from May 1976 to July 1990. Before they finalized some of the agreements on scientific and technical cooperation they had four sessions on how to go about scientific and technical cooperation which eventually led to the agreement on the establishment of China–Pakistan Joint Committee for Economic, Trade Scientific and Technical Cooperation in 1983. With this comprehensive expansion of economic ties between the two they went about specifying the number of areas in which they would cooperate. For instance, in 1983, Pakistan agreed to cooperate in ten items on China's request and China offered to undertake 15 items for that year. A high-level Chinese military delegation held talks with senior officials of the water and power development authority in Lahore on 6 May 1985. The delegation was informed that China's engineers and technicians are now engaged in installing in Guddu a 210-MW unit which is now at the last stage of completion. It was told that in view of the shortage of electricity being faced by Pakistan, it is necessary to carry forward Pakistan's atomic energy programme without any hindrance.[51] Discussions were underway for a second 210-MW project in Jamshoro.[52]

In 1986 Pakistan agreed to cooperate in eight areas as proposed by China and China in turn took up seven new programmes as proposed by Pakistan. The number of areas of cooperation went up as the years passed by. In 1987 there were 16 areas and in 1989 about 24 areas had been identified for bilateral cooperation. This was a sure sign of expansion of scientific and technical cooperation. Some of the areas covered as part of the agreements are agriculture, energy, including renewable energy, health, railway technology, manufacturing of surgical appliances, mineral research, oil exploration, river delta survey, electronics, marine science, industrial development, food technology. China and Pakistan have signed 417 intergovernmental agreements in the field of science and technology since 1976.[53] This means that China and Pakistan had 401 agreements signed between them since 1990.

Transfer since 1990

The following section would detail civilian technology transfer from China to Pakistan in various fields of critical importance. Besides, there may also be several other areas which are not possible to ascertain (or have not been ascertained) due to certain problems such as secrecy involved in the whole process of technology transfer between them.

TRANSPORTATION

Cooperation in various modes of transportation has seen a rapid growth. Aviation industry is one of the three sub-segments. Yang Chunshu, President of China National Aero-Technology Import and Export Corporation (CATIC) highlighted the progress of Chinese exports of various airplanes such as Qing-5 and Qing-7P to Pakistan and expected that more will be exported in future.[54]

In 2003 China signed an agreement with Pakistan to supply about 1300 railway wagons, one of the biggest consignments that China has ever exported to any other country so far. Out of this, 420 are to be manufactured in China and exported to Pakistan and the rest to be manufactured in Pakistan as part of the Joint Venture package. This means that China will have manufacturing units in Pakistan which would involve more Chinese technical experts going to Pakistan and interacting with their Pakistani counterparts. The supply of these wagons will be carried out by two Chinese companies—Dongfang Electric Corporation and South China Locomotive and Rolling Stock Industry Corporation.[55]

Several Chinese engineers are working on a project to develop Gwadar[56] with an estimated cost of $ 114 million dollars as a deep-water port comparable to the one in Karachi which could serve as a major hub for many parts of Asia, particularly West Asia and South Asia. But the main issue which needs attention is China's goal of seeking 'sovereign rights' before investing such huge sum of money in the project. What is not clear as yet is what 'sovereign rights' mean for Pakistan and China. It perhaps means that China will have unhindered and full access to the port as it aims to expand its presence in Asia in its pursuit of competing with the US as one Chinese scholar pointed out.[57]

INFORMATION TECHNOLOGY

China and Pakistan are quite enthusiastic about strengthening cooperation in the IT sector. There have been a number of efforts at developing this into a full-fledged area of cooperation. IT is also viewed as a potential factor in forging stronger relations. Both countries feel that they can be mutually benefited. Cooperation in software industry between China and Pakistan began as early as 2002 and it is in its embryonic stage with immense potential and some problems for cooperation. China and Pakistan have signed a Memorandum of Understanding (MoU) in 2002 when China Software Industry Association (CSIA) visited its Pakistani counterpart Pakistan Software Export Board (PSEB) at the invitation of the Pakistani Minister of Science and Technology.[58] The MoU highlights the possibilities of joint development of their respective software industries. In fact, CSIA went to Pakistan to explore the potential of investing in the development of Pakistani software industry and found Pakistani software industry quite advanced and invited Pakistani software companies to come and work with them in their version of Silicon Valley-Zhong Guan Cun, very close to both Peking University and Qinghua, the two best universities in China trying to emulate Stanford university in establishing start-ups.[59]

Pakistan has three well-developed Software Technology Parks (STPs) in Islamabad, Lahore and Peshawar. The interesting factor, like in India, is that they are imbued with English language proficient IT professionals who are viewed by the Chinese as probable partners in the development of their IT industry in their efforts in developing software indigenously. Moreover, China has a fairly advanced hardware sector which is contemplating of setting up manufacturing units in Pakistan. And Pakistan is keen on this in exchange for their IT professionals to work and to set-up an educational institution in China.

A number of Chinese IT companies have visited Pakistan and similarly quite a few Pakistani IT companies have attended various international IT exhibitions in China. This has enabled both the parties to understand and estimate the strengths and weaknesses and accordingly formulate appropriate policies to do business in the IT sector. One important factor that could strengthen IT cooperation between China and Pakistan is the change of focus that came about in Pakistan in its software exports from the North American and European countries to China and other Asian and African countries.

ENERGY SECTOR

Energy has since come to be the buzzword in all rapidly developing countries like China and Pakistan and given India's own economic success this has special significance for New Delhi. Pakistan is hopeful of increasing cooperation with China in its efforts to be self-sufficient in its energy security, particularly in the electricity segment besides what it had received from China before given the meteoric rise in the demand for energy.

In March 2004 Pakistan and China signed an agreement for the construction of a second nuclear power plant at Mianwali, Chashma, on the banks of the Indus river in Punjab province. The power station would have a capacity of 300 megawatts and the project would include a loan of US $350 million from China.[60] This is the second plant that China will be constructing in Pakistan. The first one was completed in the same province in 1999 and began functioning in the same year.

China also exports some of its solar energy technologies to Pakistan. The irony is that while China exports its home grown solar energy technology to Pakistan,[61] it also imports advanced solar energy production technology from Germany.[62] Chinese solar energy technology is efficient in low temperature and it is trying to improve upon this and begin to move towards producing tubes that can withstand high temperatures which is why China is importing those technologies from the advanced countries. Jiangsu Solar Energy Research Institute has agreed to supply the needed technical assistance to Pakistan to produce solar collector tubes. China has also agreed to build two power plants that would generate 300 megawatts of electricity in the Sindh area of Thar.[63]

TELECOMMUNICATIONS

Capital Communication of China (CCC), a Chinese telecommunication company has recently shown keenness to manufacture telecommunication equipment such as hand sets, CDMA, and broadband infrastructure in Pakistan.[64] This has been welcomed by Awias Ahmad Khan, Minister for Information Technology because he believes that setting up of manufacturing units in Pakistan would provide an interface between the advanced technologies of other countries and the domestic technological potential and provide the much needed fillip to enhance their own capabilities.

FOOD SECURITY

Though Pakistan had its own Green Revolution[65] which had enabled it to be more or less self-sufficient it desires that its food security to be comprehensive. Moreover, as Burki and Laporte argue that 'Pakistan has a rich—and still largely untapped—agricultural potential.'[66] It is in this context that China's advancement in agricultural technology including biotechnology and genetic engineering can be of immense use for Pakistan. China has been helping Pakistan in its endeavours to improve its food security by transferring some of its hybrid varieties to Pakistan and trying to help Pakistan enhance its research capabilities in agricultural research particularly in areas such as genetic modification. In 2004 the Pakistani leaders wanted the Chinese to set-up joint ventures in Pakistan for formulation and production of pesticides besides learning from the Chinese experience of seed production.[67]

Problems and Prospects

There are certain problems that can slow the pace of civilian technology transfers between China and Pakistan. One of them is social in nature-terrorism in Pakistan. Terrorism is a major problem that could hamper the bilateral technical cooperation as it has demonstrated on 3 May 2004 when three Chinese engineers were killed and nine injured at Gwadar port in south-western part of Pakistan. In another incident on 14 October 2004 one of the two Chinese engineers held hostage was killed in the rescue operation.[68] These incidents have put enormous pressure on the Chinese engineers and technicians in going to Pakistan and work.

The other relates to the trajectory of technology development in Pakistan. One of the goals that Pakistan's Executive Committee on National Economic Council has recently set for the Pakistani economy is to be self-sufficient in all aspects of designing, installation, construction and operation through both product and process transfer of technology.[69] It remains to be seen how China would help Pakistan fulfil this significant goal which would go a long way in making Pakistan self-sufficient and less dependent on China in future.

Despite the problems enumerated above technology transfer between China and Pakistan is likely to continue in future given the history of their bilateral cooperation in political, cultural and other dimensions unless some major deadlock crops up. As Pakistani technology matures with the help of technology imports from the US, China and other countries, its dependence on China may decline in future.

The future dynamics of civilian technology transfer between China and Pakistan is also dependent on several factors including the way technology develops in India and China and the way they move forward in resolving the bilateral issues, especially the border dispute. Both China and Pakistan are watching India emerging as a dynamic technology power, particularly in the area of software technology which will also be an important player in supplying cheaper technologies not only to Pakistan but also to China. Moreover, the glacial pace with which India and Pakistan are moving in resolving their bilateral disputes will come to an end some time in future. The day they are resolved the utility of China may see a substantial change which in turn will redefine the relations between China and Pakistan in the realm of civilian technology transfers.

Lessons for India

Two lessons are particularly relevant for India. The first is with regard to the place and role given to economic ties and technology transfer in its foreign relations. India must make economic ties and technology transfer as two important variables in its foreign relations as the developed countries like the US and Japan have been doing for quite some time and China has started doing in the post-Mao period. The Indian leadership has to take up this vital responsibility of making these two as significant components of the Indian foreign policy and be able to accrue the benefits thereof in the much clichéd emerging information societies and knowledge economies. Security and military preparedness is vital for safeguarding India's national sovereignty and territorial integrity but the entire foreign policy cannot be reduced to these segments. While attaching importance to them it must improve the place and role of these two vital variables in its foreign policy. The way this can be done is to move away from predominant political content to making adequate space for economic ties and technology transfers in its relations with other countries.

Like China now and Japan in the 1950s and 1960s, India must import advanced technologies in large scale while allocating adequate funds for effective assimilation and later for promoting innovation of those imported technologies for sometime to come and stop importing technologies where India would have made substantial progress as Japan did in the 1970s.[70] This process would strengthen the Indian technological capabilities by leaps and bounds and India does not need to reinvent the wheel and not try to be too self-reliant. The private sector, particularly the IT segment in India seems to have learnt this and begun to implement appropriate measures and thereby leading the way in leapfrogging and trendsetting in the international context by importing some of the advanced technologies besides investing substantially in industrial R&D and thereby in a position to generate various home-grown technologies. But the majority of the industrial firms in India are under the management of the Indian government. Unless Indian government at the centre and state governments quickly restructure and not disinvest indiscriminately they will stand to lose.

The second lesson pertains to the specific context of civilian technology transfers from China to Pakistan. Civilian technologies if used properly will improve the lives of the millions of Pakistanis living below poverty line. India does not have to worry about civilian technology cooperation including even nuclear technology between China and Pakistan as long as it keeps its edge in technological sophistication by allocating more financial resources in research and development (R&D) and linking education with the development of science and technology. A confident India needs to take a mature approach towards this. Though China may be helping Pakistan with both military and civilian technology transfers India in no way needs to fret. Some[71] report India fretting whenever China and Pakistan further cement their relations by cooperating in several areas. The journalist community reports such sentiments because the government entertains and expresses them. The Indian government must eschew such fears and in fact, India must stop limiting its foreign policy always linked to Pakistan and SAARC countries and move forward to expand its reach and scope. India is not a nation-state, rather it is a civilizational-state and therefore it must formulate its foreign policy befitting its historical legacy despite some aberrations in between.

Conclusion

With a steady economic growth coupled with a deep integration of its economy in Asia and in the rest of the world China has slowly embarked on the path to becoming an important player in technology transfers particularly in the intermediate and low technology end products and processes and slowly emerging as a significant player in high-tech products despite some problems. This has strengthened its ability to export various kinds of technologies to Pakistan which will go a long way in benefiting not only Pakistan but also China in the long run. In helping Pakistan in its developmental process China facilitates the development of its firms at home. However, there are certain problems relating to the transfer of high-tech products wherein China's presence is behind some of the developed countries. It is in this realm that Pakistan will turn to other providers. It remains to be seen how both will cooperate in the future given the trajectory of 'demand pull' and 'technology push' factors.

NOTES

1. For more on knowledge economy and China's place in it see Carl J. Dalhman and Jean-Eric Aubert, ed., *China and the Knowledge Economy: Seizing the Twenty-first Century*, Washington: World Bank, 2001.
2. A number of studies have been done on technology transfer from the north to the south or from developed countries to the developing countries which detail various critical issues of technology transfer from the north to the south whether or not they are contributing to the development of the south. But few studies look at the nature and impact of technology transfers within and among the developing countries such as Sanjay Lall 'Trade in Technology by a Slowly Industrializing Country: India', in Nathan Rosenberg and C. Frischtak, ed., *International Technology Transfer: Concepts, Measures and Comparisons*, New York: Praeger, 1985.
3. While the US, Russia and India besides several other countries acknowledge Chinese supplies to Pakistan, the Chinese deny that they had supplied anything of that sort to Pakistan.
4. There are very few book length studies on China–Pakistan relations such as Anwar Hussain Syed, *China and Pakistan: Diplomacy of an Entente Cordiale*, London: Oxford University Press, 1974 and numerous research papers but most of them either deal with general bilateral relations with a strong focus on strategic and security considerations.
5. Charles Feinstein and Christopher Howe, eds., *Chinese Technology Transfer in the 1990s: Current Experience, Historical Problems and International Perspectives*, Cheltenham: Edward Elgar, 1997, Mark A. Cohen, A. Elizabeth Bang and Stephanie J. Mitchell, ed., *Chinese Intellectual Property Law and Practice*, The Hague: Kluwer Law International, 1999, Yizheng Shi, *Chinese Firms and Technology in the Reform Era*, London: Routledge, 1998, Samuel P. S. Ho, 'Technology Transfer to China During the 1980s—How Effective: Some Evidence

from Jiangsu', *Pacific Affairs*, Vancouver, vol. 70, no. 1, Spring 1997, pp. 85-106. Rustan Kosenko, and A.C. Samli, 'China's Four Modernizations and Technology Transfer', in A. Coskun Samli, ed., *Technology Transfer: Geographic, Economic, and Technical Dimensions*, Westport: Quorum Books, 1985 and many other writings focus only on Chinese acquisition of technologies and there is no book length study done on Chinese exports of its technologies to other countries.

6. It is to be noted that the developed countries were not prepared to supply the state-of-the-art technologies primarily to maintain the edge.
7. Both US and China were quite concerned about this and used Pakistan in coming together.
8. Syed, n. 4, p. 107.
9. Robert G. Wirsing, '"The Enemy of Enemy": Pakistan's China Debate', http://www.apcss.org/Publications/SAS/ChinaDebate/ChinaDebate_Wirsing.pdf
10. David S.G. Goodman and Gerald Segal, eds., *China Rising: Nationalism and Interdependence*, London: Routledge, 1997, p. 5.
11. Barry Naughton argues that the Chinese economic development strategy after 1978 was a main force behind the normalization of relations with other countries in 'Foreign Policy Implications of China's Economic Development Strategy', in Thomas Robinson and David Shambaugh, eds., *Chinese Foreign Policy: Theory and Practice*, New York: Oxford University Press, 1994.
12. There are a number of well researched books and articles on foreign trade but most of them look at it in the context of either bilateral or multilateral economic cooperation and domestic development of China's economy rather than as an important variable in China's foreign policy. See, for instance, Nicholas R. Lardy, *Foreign Trade and Economic Reform in China 1978–90*, Cambridge: Cambridge University Press, 1992, Nicholas R. Lardy, *China in the World Economy*, Washington: Institute for International Economics, 1994, Harold Jacobson and Michel Oksenberg, *China's Participation and in the IMF, the World Bank and GATT: Towards a Global Economic Order*, Ann Arbor: University of Michigan Press, 1990, Susan Shirk, *How China Opened its Door: The Political Success of the PRC's Foreign Trade and Investment Reforms*, Washington: Brookings Institution Press, 1994. But this paper tries to consider it as an important factor in China's foreign relations.
13. Denny Roy, *China's Foreign Relations*, Lanham: Rowman & Littlefield, 1998, p. 104.
14. Doak A. Barnett, *The Making of Foreign Policy in China: Structure and Process*, Boulder: Westview Press, 1985, Samuel S. Kim, *China and the World: China's Foreign Relations in the Post-Cold War World*, Boul-

der: Westview Press, 1994, Thomas Robinson and David Shambaugh, ed., *Chinese Foreign Policy: Theory and Practice*, New York: Oxford University Press, 1994, Andrew Nathan and Robert S. Ross, ed., *The Great Wall and the Empty Fortress: China's Search for Security*, New York: W. W. Norton and Company, 1998. Michael D. Swaine, *Domestic Change and Foreign Policy*, Santa Monica: CA Rand, 1995, Denny Roy, *China's Foreign Relations*, Lanham: Rowman & Littlefield, 1998, John W. Garver, *Foreign Relations of the People's Republic of China*, Englewood Cliffs: Prentice Hall, 1993, Lu Ning, *The Dynamics of Foreign Policy Decisionmaking in China*, Boulder: Westview Press, 1997, David Lampton, *The Making of Chinese Foreign and Security Policy*, Stanford: Stanford University Press, 2000, Department of Policy Planning, Ministry of Foreign Affairs, *China's Foreign Relations*, 2003 Edition, Beijing: World Affairs Press, 2003,Yang Fucheng, *Contemporary China and Its Foreign Policy*, Beijing: China Foreign Affairs University, 2002.

15. Bruce Cummings, 'The Political Economy of Chinese Foreign Policy', *Modern China*, October 1979, pp. 411–61.
16. David Bachman, 'China in 1994: Marking Time, Making Money', *Asian Survey*, vol. 35, no. 1, January 1995, p. 45.
17. Nicholas R. Lardy, 'The Role of Foreign Trade and Investment in the China's Economic Transformation,' in Andrew G. Walder, ed., *China's Transitional Economy*, Oxford: Oxford University Press, 1996, pp. 103–21.
18. Shang-Jin Wei, Guangzhong James Wen and Huizhong Zhou, *The Globalization of the Chinese Economy*, Cheltenham: Edward Elgar, 2002 and Nicholas R. Lardy, *Integrating China into the Global Economy*, Washington: Brookings Institution Press, 2002.
19. See http://biz.thestar.com.my/news/story.asp?file=/2004/10/20/business/9176201&sec=business
20. Charles Cooper, 'Relevance of Innovation to Developing Countries', in Charles Cooper, ed., *Technology and Innovation in the International Economy*, Cheltenham: Edward Elgar, 1994, p. 16.
21. Nathan Rosenberg and C. Frischtak, ed., *International Technology Transfer: Concepts, Measures and Comparisons*, New York: Praeger, 1985.
22. For more on this see Yizheng Shi's interesting work along with case studies, *Chinese Firms and Technology in the Reform Era*, London: Routledge, 1998, pp. 151–2.
23. See, for instance, 'China's Current Civilian Technology' http://www.rand.org/publications/MR/MR/1292.ch3.pdf
24. See Adam Segal's *Digital Dragon: High-Technology Enterprises in China*, Ithaca: Cornell University Press, 2003. Segal asserts that the success of high-tech enterprises, particularly those that fall in the cate-

gory of *minying*, non-governmental, is uneven largely because of the political and regional factors.

25. Richard Kraus, 'China in 2003: From SARS to Spaceships', *Asian Survey*, vol. 44, no. 1, 2004, 154.
26. Roy, n. 13, p. 89.
27. Ministry of Science and Technology, *China Science and Technology Indicators*, Beijing: Science and Technology Literature Publishing, 1998, p. 64.
28. George J. Gilboy, 'The Myth Behind China's Miracle', *Foreign Affairs*, vol. 83, no. 4, July–August 2004, pp. 33–48.
29. National Bureau of Statistics *China Statistical Yearbook on Science and Technology*, Beijing: China Statistics Press, 2003, p. 479.
30. David Wall and Yin Xiangshuo, 'Technology Development and Export Performance: Is China a Frog or a Goose?' in Charles Feinstein and Christopher Howe, eds., *Chinese Technology Transfer in the 1990s: Current Experience, Historical Problems and International Perspectives*, Cheltenham: Edward Elgar, 1997, pp. 169–92.
31. Dalhaman and Aubert, n. 7, p. 21.
32. This is more appropriate with regard to civilian technology and not so much in relation to non-civilian technology where China has been exporting to some of the developing countries for some time.
33. Nam Young-sook, 'China's Industrial Rise and the Challenges Facing Korea', *East Asian Review*, vol. 16, no. 2, Summer 2004, pp. 43–64.
34. National Bureau of Statistics, National Development and Reform Commission and Ministry of Science and Technology, *China Statistics Yearbook on High Technology Industry*, Beijing: China Statistics Press, 2003, p. 561.
35. Young-sook, n. 34, pp. 43–64.
36. Urs S. Daellenbach and Sally J. Davenport, 'Establishing Trust during the Formation of Technology Alliance', *Journal of Technology Transfer*, vol. 29, no. 2, 2004, pp. 187–202.
37. See S. Akbar Zaidi, *Issues in Pakistan's Economy*, Oxford: Oxford University Press, 1999; Robert E. Looney, *The Pakistani Economy: Economic Growth and Structural Reform*, London: Praeger, 1997; Anita Weiss, *Culture, Class, and Development in Pakistan: The Emergence of an Industrial Bourgeoisie in Punjab*, Boulder: Westview Press, 1991; Various articles on Pakistan's economy, along with articles on other South Asian countries, are put together in Prema-Chindra Athukorala, ed., *The Economic Development of South Asia*,vols. I-III, Cheltenham: Elgar Reference Collection, 2002.
38. Their bilateral trade depends on two factors of evolving trade environment in Pakistan and the global trading environment. For more on this see Asfaque H. Khan and Zafar Mahmood, ed., *Pakistan and Emerg-*

ing Global Trading Environment: Challenges and Opportunities, Lahore: Vanguard Books, 2000.

39. There are three major segments in Pakistan that import technology from other countries. The government imports, private capital goods imports and private consumer goods each with a certain quota of imports. See Stephen R. Lewis Jr., *Pakistan: Industrialization and Trade Policies*, London: Oxford University Press, 1970, p. 24.
40. The Economist Intelligence Unit, *Country Report*, February 2004, p. 5.
41. Shahjad A. Mufti, 'Science and Technology Funding System in Pakistan', in Proceedings from the International Forum on *Science Funding System Oriented to the Twenty-one Century*, Beijing, P. R. China, 1–3 August 2001, Beijing: Higher Education Press, 2002, pp. 199–205.
42. Ijaj Nabi, 'The Competitiveness of Pakistani Exports', in Sharukh Rafi Khan, ed., *Fifty Years of Pakistan's Economy: Traditional Topics and Contemporary Concerns*, Oxford: Oxford University Press, 1999, p. 196.
43. Statistics from China General Administration of Customs in 'Sino-Pakistan Relations', http://www.news.xinhuanet.com/english/2003-11/22/content/_1192925.htm
44. The Economist Intelligence Unit, *Country Report*, February 2004, p. 5.
45. http//:www.fpeng.peopledaily.com.cn/20005/15/eng/2000515_40854.html
46. This is part of the economic, trade, science and technology cooperation. The other three are continuing high-level exchanges, deepening non-traditional security relations and maintaining cooperation in the international and regional affairs.
47. See http://www.fmrc.gov.cn/eng/wjb/zzjg/wzs/gjlb/2757/2758/t40148.htm for the entire document.
48. 'Pakistan Seeks Chinese Assistance to Boost Vocational Training System', *PakTribune*, 17 September 2004, Web Edition.
49. Wolfgang Bartke gives very useful details of various agreements signed between China and Pakistan in *The Agreements of the People's Republic of China with Foreign Countries 1949–1990*, 2nd revised and enlarged edition, Munchen: K.G. Saur, 1992), pp. 137–42. The author is very grateful to Bartke for this compilation. This section is largely based on his compilation. Pakistan is just behind the US and Japan in the number of agreements that China had outside the Communist block.
50. Syed, n. 4, p. 142.
51. 'Chinese Army Told of Pakistan's Energy needs', SWB/FE/7948/A3/7.
52. 'Pakistan Prime Minister Leaves for China', SWB/FE/8070/A3/2.
53. 'Sino-Pakistan Relations', http://www.news.xinhuanet.com/english/200311/ 22/content/_ 1192925.htm
54. 'China-Pakistan Reaffirm Air-Links', *China Daily*, 10 September 2003.

55. http//:www.thehindubusinessline.com/bline/2003/02/24/stories/2003022400090601.htm
56. For more on this see Amy Waldman, 'City of Fishermen in Pakistan Becomes a Strategic Port', *New York Times*, September 2004, Web Edition.
57. Shen Dingli, Concluding Comments at a workshop on 'China-US-India Triangular Relations', Fudan University, 29 May 2004.
58. 'Delegation of China Software Industry Association (CSAI) to Pakistan' http://www.pseb.org.pk/ News/csai.cfm
59. See the Chinese, not English, websites of the said universities for more on how each university has started about 50 start-ups.
60. 'Chinese Engineers Killed by Bomb-Nuclear Contract with China', *Keesing's Record of World Events*, vol. 50, mo. 5, 2004, p. 46003.
61. 'China to Help Pakistan in Developing Solar Energy', *Pakistan Times*, 26 March 2004.
62. 'China Sets-Off the Biggest Solar Plant', *Pakistan Times*, 17 July 2004.
63. 'China to built(d) Two New Powerhouses in Thar', *Pak Tribune*, 19 June 2004, Web Edition.
64. 'China to Manufacture Mobile Sets in Pakistan', *Pakistan Times*, 7 July 2004.
65. Leslie Nulty, *The Green Revolution in West Pakistan: Implications for Technological Change*, New York: Praeger, 1972.
66. Shahid Javed Burki and Robert Laporte Jr., *Pakistan's Development Priorities: Choices for the Future*, Oxford: Oxford University Press, 1984. Though this has been said in the early 1980s it is still relevant given the slow development of Pakistan's agriculture.
67. 'Chinese Companies Interested in Investing in Pak's Chemical Sector', *Pak Tribune*, 26 May 2004, Web Edition.
68. 'One Chinese Killed and One Freed in Pakistan', *People's Daily*, 15 October 2004, Web Edition.
69. *Pakistan Times*, 29 July 2004.
70. Hioroyuki Odagiri Akira Goto, 'The Japanese System of Innovation: Past, Present, and Future', in Richard R. Nelson, ed., *National Innovation Systems: A Comparative Analysis*, New York: Oxford University Press, 1993, pp. 76–114.
71. See Sudha Ramachandran, 'India Frets as China and Pakistan Embrace', *Asia Times*, Web Edition, 23 November 2004.

CHAPTER 15

Civilian Nuclear Cooperation

ARVIND KUMAR

There have been a number of conflicting perspectives on the matters related to China–Pakistan civilian nuclear cooperation.[1] This chapter tries to make a modest attempt in addressing the various facets of Chinese cooperation with Pakistan on civilian uses of nuclear energy which is one area where their transactions remain far more established and transparent. However, in light of its implications for India, this chapter will also try and examine the level at which China has been cooperating with Pakistan and especially analyse China's motivations, goals and strategies in evolving this time tested civilian nuclear cooperation with Pakistan. The analysis on these issues may still have limitations in terms of resources as, despite this claim to transparency, several transactions related to Chinese cooperation with Pakistan on civilian uses of nuclear energy remain shrouded in secrecy or are so suspected by several experts. Hence, it is important to underline, at the very outset, that this chapter confesses to provide an analytical approach that remains rooted in Indian perspectives on the subject.

Genesis of Civilian Nuclear Cooperation

Historically, starting from the tour of American exhibitions under Eisenhower's Atoms for Peace programme, Pakistan had made several serious efforts in exploring possibilities of cooperation in nuclear technologies in the early years of its friendship with China during 1960s. China's response in the early years especially during early 1960s was not very forthcoming let alone favourable. China was still grappling with its own internal contradictions of Cultural Revolution and suspected Pakistani intentions. The Chinese nuclear programme was yet nascent in character and it wanted to maintain the secrecy given the sensitivities involved in its own nuclear programme. Especially, following the Sino-Soviet split, China was under tremendous pressure from outside powers with no major allies to depend on.

The first major reason for not being favourable to Pakistan's desire to procure nuclear technologies from China was Pakistan's strong support for Eisenhower's 'Atoms for Peace' statements. Indeed, until late 1950s, Pakistan had been a well-known ally of the US as part of US containment of China. The Chinese approach to the US 'Atoms for Peace' statements were absolutely opposite in character especially in comparison to Pakistan's optimism and enthusiasm. Despite the serious efforts made by President Ayub Khan for initiating the possibility of cooperation in nuclear technologies during the early years of China–Pakistan ties in 1960s, China had not shown any interest in the beginning.

Despite the fact that Pakistan got a lukewarm response from China on the matters related to civilian nuclear cooperation, Pakistan was very determined to pursue research in nuclear science and technologies on its own. As its first display of its official commitment in that direction, Pakistan had appointed a 12-member Atomic Energy Committee (AEC) under the Chairmanship of Dr Nazir Ahmad in 1955. The major task assigned to the Atomic Energy Committee was to focus on the civilian uses of nuclear energy. To an extent, the committee was able to neatly draw methodologies for the civilian uses of nuclear energy. However, not much was achieved till early 1970s and then India's nuclear tests of May 1974 was to provide a major stimulant to Pakistan's nuclear programme as also to its pursuit of China for nuclear cooperation.

In reality, therefore, the genesis of China–Pakistan civilian nuclear cooperation can be seen during the late years of seventies decade.[2] What also greatly facilitated China–Pakistan nuclear cooperation is that China had kept itself isolated during the decades of 1950s, 1960s and 1970s and was not part of the international regimes including International Atomic Energy Agency (IAEA), Nuclear Non-Proliferation Treaty (NPT) and more importantly from the nuclear export guidelines. The rationale behind keeping isolated from all these international regimes was to see that nothing could hamper the growth of Chinese industries more particularly the nuclear industry. The other plausible argument for China keeping isolated might be seen in the context of Chinese nuclear exports and it is now clear and many

Chinese have now confirmed how their nuclear exports have largely been driven by economic considerations. China preferred nuclear trade and cooperation to generate foreign currency it needed to revitalize its economy on the one hand and to develop civilian nuclear industry on the other.

The New Context

It is, however, true and obvious that China started cooperating with Pakistan on civilian nuclear industry intensely as part of its economic opening up from the mid-1980s which presented an altogether new context for their nuclear collaborations. Reform focused China of Deng Xiaoping was now beginning to initiate fundamental changes into China's nuclear policies and programmes. There are instances to prove that China did supply nuclear equipments and services even during the early and late 1970s[3] but the intense cooperation started after China signed nuclear cooperation agreement with Pakistan during 1985–6. It is suspected that China's assistance to Pakistan's civilian nuclear programme over the decades was crucial and pertinent to Pakistan's nuclear weapons development. The nuclear cooperation prior to 1984, the year China became a member of IAEA, there had been no strict guidelines for indulging itself in nuclear proliferation and trade.

After China became a member of IAEA, it devised some of the principles on which its future nuclear trade and cooperation could be based. For example, the following principles were adopted by China after joining IAEA which was to have a major impact on the nature of China's nuclear collaborations with Pakistan:

- China declared that its nuclear trade and exports should be used exclusively for civilian purposes;
- All nuclear exports should be subject to IAEA safeguards; and
- The recipient country should not transfer the nuclear technology to a third country without prior Chinese approval.

It was stated by China in strongest sense of the term that all nuclear trade with the countries with which it had signed nuclear cooperation agreement will be for peaceful uses of nuclear energy. However, the abiding rules and guidelines for nuclear exports and nuclear trade more particularly with Pakistan had sparked off a number of debates among analysts and the members of strategic community. There seems to be leniency on the part of China when matters related to nuclear trade were related with Pakistan. There are a number of secondary sources literature on the subject to prove Chinese leniency.[4] The reasons for China being liberal to Pakistan on the matters related to nuclear cooperation are obvious.

The New Imperatives

China's nuclear exports more particularly with Pakistan was driven by politico-strategic calculus and motivated by its security concerns. Pakistan might have been chosen for cooperation by China to establish a counterweight to India in the region. And this impetus to China might have come from the Sino–Indian war of 1962. It was argued between China and Pakistan during Bandung conference in 1955 itself that both the countries, China and India were emerging as rivals for leadership among Afro–Asian countries and hence the need was felt by China and Pakistan for cooperating and evolving a working relationship despite differences in their political systems and ideologies.

However, in this new context there were several new imperatives guiding and goading China's nuclear engagement of Pakistan. Pakistan was being now treated and categorized as a long time ally of China and as its bulwark in South Asia. Pakistan also constitutes the only exception where China has managed to have stable and friendly equations throughout the last five decades. Despite the fact that there is no formal or full-fledged military alliance between China and Pakistan, China–Pakistan ties have been clearly dominated by their defence cooperation and by China's alleged assistance and supplies of nuclear and missile technologies component and know how.[5]

The Sino–Pak civilian nuclear cooperation as stated earlier began during the mid-1980s. China has never asked the recipient countries more particularly Pakistan to abide by the provisions of full-scope safeguards enshrined in the IAEA. The provisions of full scope safeguards are intrusive in nature. Such steps on the part of China would have jeopardized China's nuclear trade with Pakistan. However, China had stated that in process of any nuclear export, the recipient government was suppose to provide an assurance in writing to the Chinese government that it would follow the principles on which

Chinese nuclear export was based. Hence, the onus was put on the recipient country.[6]

Links to Nuclear Weapons Programme

China's nuclear cooperation with Pakistan has always been a matter of debate among analysts. China's dealings with Pakistan on these matters have always been shrouded in secrecy. The academic debate on these matters has continued to be controversial. It can be seen that during the 1960s and 1970s, when the Chinese were publicly championing the cause of proliferation, their words were not matched by their deeds. There is considerable evidence to show that China exported nuclear technology contrary to the Nuclear Suppliers Group (NSG) guidelines. The NSG is a mature, effective, and widely accepted export control arrangement. Over the past one decade, the NSG has established a Dual-Use Regime (DUR), adopted full-scope safeguards as a condition for nuclear supply, created an effective Joint Information Exchange, and strengthened controls over technology and re-transfers. China has been the only major nuclear supplier among all the other nuclear weapon states.

China has been accepted into the NSG in May 2004. It can be said that China's membership in the NSG might be a tacit acknowledgement by the other members states including the United States, Britain, France and Russia—that China supposedly can be trusted with a bigger role in global nuclear trade.[7] It is anticipated that now as a member of the NSG and with the legitimacy that it carries, China might make plans to enter the commercial nuclear market in a substantial way. Just prior to becoming a member of the NSG (during first week of May 2004), China announced that it would build nuclear power plants for Pakistan, a major proliferator of nuclear and missile technologies.

The most controversial discussion on China–Pakistan nuclear weapons cooperation centers around a report during late 1995 regarding the transfer of 5,000 ring magnets from China Nuclear Energy Industry Corporation to an unsafeguarded Pakistani nuclear facility. While Pakistan denied that any such transfer occurred, China maintained that its nuclear cooperation with Pakistan was solely for peaceful purposes. China's sale of ring magnets to the unsafeguarded Kahuta facility had set-off a major controversy internationally. After this much publicized event, China was forced to make a promise to the members of international community in general and the US in particular that it will not provide assistance to Pakistan's unsafeguarded nuclear facilities. The real fear was that Chinese civilian nuclear cooperation with Pakistan might be misused. Many of these concerns regarding China's nuclear exports more particularly with Pakistan have to do with the lack of adequate export control guidelines on part of China.

Given its close association with the Soviet Union which, during those days, never insisted on 'safeguards' on its supplied nuclear reactors, China also never expected its recipient states to pledge for any inspections or reports. With the rising pressures to comply with international norms, China did gradually began to accept idea of monitoring and safeguards. However, despite the Chinese declaration that it would report to the IAEA with regard to any export or import of nuclear materials and put both import and export of nuclear materials under IAEA safeguards, there seem to be some slackness on the part of establishing a comprehensive export control guidelines. It is, therefore, clear that there was no guarantee to ensure that nuclear cooperation did not contribute to proliferation. The current trend suggests that China has been an emerging supplier of nuclear technology for developing countries because it is the only supplier that has financing capabilities.[8]

China promulgated nuclear export controls in September 1997 and based those controls on an itemized list that was substantively identical to the trigger list developed and used by the NSG. China had also committed publicly not to provide any assistance to unsafeguarded nuclear facilities and nuclear explosive programmes. All these actions were taken by China prior to becoming a member of Zangger committee. China strengthened dual use controls by the end of 1998. Those dual use controls use a control list substantively identical to the one used by the NSG.

In the current context, China should act in accordance with the NSG Guidelines (as contained in INFCIRC/254/Part 1 and Part 2, including Annexes, as amended) and duly exercise export control over nuclear and nuclear dual-use-items. The NSG rules, which require members to withhold nuclear transfers where there is a risk that materials could be diverted for use in weapons, will have the greatest impact on China's ties with Pakistan. China remains determined to supply nuclear power technologies to Pakistan. Even the NSG allows its members to fulfil the earlier obligations made prior to becoming a member of NSG.

The Real Extent of Cooperation

China, in terms of its civilian cooperation with Pakistan, had helped in building 300 MWe power reactor at Chashma. The interesting point to note here is that China took this decision after Japanese, German, and French firms refused to provide supporting systems and compo-nents for this power reactor to Pakistan. China was also believed to have assisted Pakistan with building an unsafeguarded 50–70 MW plutonium production reactor at Khushab and also helped in developing an unsafeguarded plutonium reprocessing facility at Chashma that was left unfinished when earlier French assistance was terminated in the late 1970s.[9]

As a part of real civilian cooperation, China signed a comprehensive nuclear cooperation agreement with Pakistan during 1986. It was also reported that by then Chinese scientists had begun assisting Pakistan with the enrichment of uranium. China had done sufficient research & development (R&D) on gas centrifuge technology for enriching the uranium. This R&D was done to find an alternate technology to replace the gaseous diffusion plants. The expertise attained during the conduction of R&D was being shared with Pakistan after formally signing the nuclear cooperation agreement.

Since the signing of nuclear cooperation agreement with Pakistan, China has been supplying Pakistan with a variety of nuclear products and services, ranging from uranium enrichment technology to research and power reactors. There seem to be a rigorous and intense civilian cooperation. It is estimated in terms of real China–Pakistan civilian nuclear cooperation that China has been the strongest source for nuclear power development in Pakistan. China has routinely supplied Pakistan with heavy water and to an extent it has insisted on providing it only to safeguarded facilities. China has clearly stated that the heavy water supplied to Pakistan is only meant for use at the safeguarded Kanupp facility and not to the unsafeguarded Khushab facility. The heavy water is needed during the operation of reactors and if it reaches unsafeguarded facility like Khushab then the concern will be more because it might be used to produce plutonium for nuclear weapons.

China also supplied special industrial furnace to Pakistan during mid-1990s as a part of civilian cooperation. However, the report appeared in media suggests otherwise. The special industrial furnace supplied by China to Pakistan was apparently for Khushab facility, which was an unsafeguarded one. In fact, Chinese scientists helped Pakistan in installing the furnace. The other important aspect of the cooperation was in the field of high-tech diagnostic equipment. The high-tech diagnostic equipment had dual uses and could have applied to both civilian and military projects. China also supplied auxiliary equipments including heaters, condensers, and water tanks. China has exported a power plant computer system to Pakistan in the year 1997. In a nutshell, China has been the primary source of nuclear-related equipment and technology to Pakistan.

The Khushab reactor of something between 50-70 MW was reportedly built with Chinese assistance under the shadow of civilian nuclear cooperation. The Kahuta laboratory of Pakistan is also unsafeguarded and it is generally believed that Chinese scientist assisted with the enrichment of uranium.

Most recently in March 2004, China and Pakistan have agreed on the technical details for the sale of a second nuclear power plant to Pakistan.[10] The 300 MW plant would be built at Chashma, next to the first Chinese supplied nuclear power plant, which became operational in 1999. The deal underlines the close cooperation between the two countries and comes after revelations that a group of Pakistani scientists led by Abdul Qadeer Khan, the Father of Pakistan's nuclear bomb project, sold nuclear know-how and technology to Iran, Libya and possibly North Korea. China will have to comply with the deal made even after it has become a member of NSG. However, this new reactor at Chashma called C-2 or Chashma-2 will have to be put under safeguards to make certain that they were used only for generating electricity.

Despite these reports where analysts have either speculated or conjectured on Sino–Pak collaboration, China has continued to insist that it does not encourage nuclear proliferation and that its nuclear cooperation with Pakistan is purely for peaceful purposes. Despite these claims made by China, it is pertinent to point out here that their nuclear trade and cooperation with Pakistán have caused significant concern for India. This concern is important for the simple reason that neither China nor Pakistan accepts the provisions of full scope safeguards. China has, however, completed the legal procedure for the entry into force of the Additional Protocol between China and the

IAEA, the first among five nuclear weapon states to do so. Most of the nuclear exports related item has dual uses and hence it ignites the concern on part of India in particular.

Evaluating the Research Perspective

There have always been a number of perspectives on the matters related to China–Pakistan cooperation in the field of civilian nuclear power. The research perspective will look into the various positions taken by China and Pakistan on related issues and then make a modest attempt in providing with an Indian perspective on the whole range of issues.

As regards China, it has always stated that 'all cooperation between China and Pakistan in the field of nuclear energy is under IAEA safeguards'. However, the Chinese position on the matters related to nuclear cooperation with Pakistan and its linkages with safeguards procedures is not very much clear. There is no doubt in the fact that during the year 1993, China and IAEA signed an agreement to apply IAEA safeguards to a Chinese nuclear power station sold to Pakistan. The applicability of IAEA safeguard is mentioned in the document INFCIRC/418. The point to note here is that INFCIRC/418 was outside the ambit of full scope safeguards and hence it was less intrusive.

India had shown special concern in this regard. All these Chinese policies and actions with regard to their export control policies came under sharp criticism on a global scale. It is obvious that with the notable exception of China, all the other members of the nuclear club strictly follow the rules in the sense that they do not sell nuclear technology to any nation that refuses to open all its facilities to IAEA inspections or adopt full scope safeguards. It is also argued among analysts that the dividing line between military and civilian nuclear programmes is too narrow to promote cooperation without an explicit understanding of the safeguards. And, hence, Chinese nuclear co-operation with other nations more particularly with Pakistan without abiding by the rules of IAEA comprehensive safeguards has undermined the efficacy and validity of the NPT.

Especially after ring magnet controversy during late 1995, China was pressurized by the members of international community in general and the US in particular to end its nuclear cooperation with Pakistan. It was suggested that it was not wise for China even to engage with Pakistan for civilian nuclear cooperation with safeguarded nuclear facilities. China and Pakistan have continued to argue that their nuclear cooperation is entirely for civilian use. However, it seemed that the pressure on China in reality never worked and it was insistent that it would continue such cooperation. Pakistan strongly objected to all those pressures made against it and opined that no international convention or law has been violated during the process of civilian cooperation with China. India, too, was having concern on all these related developments.

The other case in point to debate with a research perspective on China–Pakistan civilian nuclear cooperation could be the matters related to China's selling off a special industrial furnace and high technology diagnostic equipment to unsafeguarded facilities in Pakistan. India apparently saw it as a violation of Chinese pledge not to provide assistance to unsafeguarded facilities. The major concern on part of India was that the equipment was of a dual use nature. China, on the other hand, had always maintained that it only conducts normal international cooperation on the peaceful utilization of nuclear energy with Pakistan.

China also continued its earlier policies of encouraging proliferation even after it acceded to the NPT in the year 1992. It certainly assisted Pakistan's unsafeguarded nuclear programme under the guise of civilian cooperation. As stated earlier, China's nuclear assistance to Pakistan has been to prop up a military counterweight to tie down India's nuclear assets. The other factor, which cannot be overlooked is that China has not yet demonstrated its commitment to vigilantly follow up and monitor the end-use assurances on its nuclear and nuclear-related exports within recipient states and facilities. Most of the nuclear facilities in Pakistan are unsafeguarded and certainly not indigenous.[11] The nuclear facilities like Kahuta laboratory, where Chinese scientists assisted with the production of weapons-grade uranium and Khushab reactor reportedly built with Chinese assistance are case in point.

Challenge to Non-proliferation

By doing all this, China has posed formidable challenges to the international non-proliferation regime. The instances related to Sino–Pak nuclear cooperation discussed earlier did confirm China to be a major contributor to proliferation primarily because of the role of Chinese companies in supplying a wide range of materials, equipment and technologies that had in a way contributed to WMD proliferation. The recent disclosure regarding selling of atomic secrets and equipment around the world and Pakistan's involvement in it is a serious global concern.[12] China had also posed another challenge through the lack of transparency in its domestic nuclear safeguards and security measures. Since China became a member of Zangger Committee in October 1997, it has been able to streamline its export control guidelines and now it has been accepted as a member of NSG. It signals that China after becoming a member of Zangger Committee published its own 'nuclear exports control list' of controlled technologies and equipments, including nuclear-related, dual use equipment and technology.

China has been maintaining cooperation consistently since China signed nuclear cooperation agreement with Pakistan. In reality, China and Pakistan have been able to sustain a cosy, fruitful and all weather relationships. Pakistan–China friendship has always been like mother's milk and 'it was passed on from generation to generation, there was no need to "educate" anyone about it'.[13] The cosy relationship enjoyed by two of the world's nuclear powers, China and Pakistan, is well known and both the countries have described their cooperation as an indispensable factor in maintaining peace and stability in Asia. China's role in civilian cooperation with Pakistan has always been important and critical. China's role has been critical not only because of its economic strength and its performance, but also because of its geographic might in the region.

Conclusion

To conclude, therefore, China has helped its close ally Pakistan build the first stage of the Chashma nuclear power plant in Punjab province, despite the United States opposition to it. Concerned about the likelihood of Pakistan diverting China's technologies for nuclear weapons, the US has been asking China to halt nuclear cooperation with Pakistan at all levels. The main fear in this regard has always been that Chinese assistance in the second phase (the deal has already taken place) would allow Pakistan to obtain enriched uranium while being a non-signatory to the nuclear non-proliferation treaty.

Despite China's growing acceptance of international non-proliferation regimes and its verbal promises, the civilian cooperation between China and Pakistan has posed many questions than answers.

However, China–Pakistan civilian nuclear cooperation as of now has not received international acceptance. As a result, there remains the constant fear of diversion—from civilian to military purposes. Recently, China's decision to join the NSG suggests that it is moving towards full participation in the global non-proliferation regime.

However, the past experience of more than three decades and more particularly of the nature of the Sino–Pak cooperation suggests that it will take some time to arrive at a stage of full confidence on China's expressed intent for restraint. Especially, it will remain arduous to make any assessment on China's policies in the field of nuclear exports and nuclear cooperation. To what degree, China will disclose the background of its nuclear relationship with Pakistan remains to be seen in the years to come. However, the trend seems to be in favour of increasing transparency which gives hope of future assessments reaching greater accuracy as also coming years witnessing greater restraint on any 'diversions' in China–Pakistan nuclear cooperation.

NOTES

1. Scholars in China, Pakistan, India and the USA provide a different and alternate perspective altogether. There is a lack of unanimity on this vast subject.
2. On 29 January 1977, China signed a protocol with Pakistan on scientific and technical cooperation. Chinese assistance for development of nuclear energy was implicit in the protocol.
3. A very good analysis can be seen in the works of Richard W. Fischer and John T. Dori, 'The Strategic Implications of Pakistan's Nuclear Assistance to Pakistan', Asian Studies Center of the Heritage Foundation, *Backgrounder*, no. 532, 16 June 1998.
4. Many studies have been conducted by eminent think tanks located in the USA. The studies conducted more particularly by the Center for Non Proliferation Studies, Monterey and Carnegie Endowment for International Peace are noteworthy. Websites: http://cns.miis.edu/research/india/china/npakpos.htm and http://www.ceip.org/programs/npp/china.htm.
5. Swaran Singh, *China–South Asia: Issues, Equations and Policies*, New Delhi: Lancers Books, 2003, p. 171.
6. Statement by Ambassador Li Changhe of the Chinese Permanent Mission in Vienna at the meeting of the Zangger Committee, 16 October 1997.

7. 'Helping China Proliferate', *The Washington Times*, 1 June 2004. Website: www.washingtontimes.com
8. See, China's Nuclear Exports and Assistance, Website: http://www.nti.org/db/china/nexport.htm
9. On China, see 'Tracking Nuclear Proliferation 1998: China', Website: http://www.ceip.org/programs/npp/china.htm
10. 'Chinese Close to Sale of Second Nuclear Power Plant to Pakistan', *Financial Times*, London, 8 March 2004.
11. See, n. 8 and 9.
12. William J. Broad, David E. Sanger and Raymond Bonner', 'A Tale of Nuclear Proliferation: How Pakistani Built His Network', *New York Times*, 12 February 2004. Website: www.nytimes.com/2004/02/12/inter....../12NUKE.html
13. Pakistan's Information Minister, Sheikh Rashid recently made this statement during 19–20 July 2004 at the SAARC Foreign Minister's meet in Islamabad. It was quoted in China's *People's Daily* and Also see, Jyoti Malhotra, 'Mother's Milk', *Indian Express*, New Delhi, 22 July 2004.

CHAPTER 16

Pakistan in China's Arms Trade

APARNA KHER

This chapter attempts to examine the 'supply and demand side'[1] of the strategic motivations of China's arms transfers to Pakistan and to highlight its implications for India. More specifically, this chapter attempts to analyse: (a) trends in Chinese arms trade with Pakistan; (b) the profile of Chinese arms trade with Pakistan, and (c) the choices India faces in terms of coping with increased uncertainty in the regional security environment prompted by China supplying arms to Pakistan. The underlying purpose of this chapter is to explore what security and/ or military imperatives guide China's arms relationship with Pakistan and how that affects India.

The China–Pakistan entente has remained the one of the strongest cornerstones of South Asian security and strategic dynamics since the early 1960s. The relationship has displayed an incredible tenacity especially in the post-Cold War period. During the Cold War period, China–Pakistan relations had hinged on dual motives—containing Soviet Union and restricting increasing Indian influence in South Asia. In the post-Cold War era, the focus has primarily shifted to the latter.[2]

Prima facie, Pakistan has been a ready and a rich market for Chinese weapons, the returns of which have simultaneously fuelled China's defense modernization drive and provided the Chinese a testing ground for their weapons technologies. Pakistan has been a gateway to Western technologies for China. On the Pakistani front, these arms transfers have has proven to be a godsend in the face of frequent wavering of United States support. The relationship has also benefited the Pakistani defence industry, the single most important sector in the country by helping it in terms of its civilian spinoffs and to help Pakistan move towards an indigenous defense production capability.

Demand-side Factors

While demand-side rationales for importing Chinese weapons and related technologies have changed over time, three broad reasons can be discerned as the forces creating enduring motivations amongst their respective power elite:

FITTING THE POCKET—CHEAP TECHNOLOGIES

The primary motivation behind Pakistan's imports of Chinese weapons has been their relatively low prices.[3] Despite the inferior quality of the inventory, Chinese weapons have not only appropriately matched Pakistan's military requirements, but have also suited Pakistan's pockets in terms of their prices. In its attempt to build a large military, Pakistan in substituting volume for quantity, has combined a few sophisticated Western weapons systems with larger numbers of Chinese weapons.

NUTS AND BOLTS—EASE OF OPERATIONS AND MAINTENANCE

With limited levels of military professionalism and a low technological base, a vital motivation for Pakistan to continue its arms relationship with China has been the ease of operation and maintenance of Chinese weapons.[4] Military self-sufficiency, especially in face of its involvement in the protracted conflict with India over Kashmir has been a vital goal of the Pakistani political and defence establishment. The Sino–Pak arms relationship has also given Pakistan a bargaining chip in the international arms bazaar. China's arms supplies to Pakistan has also elicited interest from other weapon supplier countries, especially those that have an interest in containing China's growing sphere of influence in Pakistan.[5]

RELIABILITY IS THE KEY

Compared to its supplier counterparts in the international arms market, China has been a relatively reliable source of weapons to its clients, especially as a supplier of last resort. In the face of a US weapons embargo, a closed Russian market and expensive French Mirage fighters, China faithfully sold Pakistan F-7 fighter aircrafts.[6] Importing weapons from China have therefore helped Pakistan avoid depending on the United States and the West for military support. Moreover, Beijing's weapon exports carry few if any political strings. Indeed, 'Beijing is often willing to sell arms to countries when Western nations are not.'[7]

Supply-side Factors

Despite having a strong commercial interest in exporting its arms to most of its clients, China's relationship with Pakistan has specifically reflected its underlying security and foreign policy imperatives in the South Asian region—the containment of Soviet Union during the Cold War, and India in the post Cold War era.[8]

Arms transfers have also contributed to an expansion of Beijing's strategic reach.[9] The fact that China is now escalating its oil and energy needs has prompted it to look beyond its traditional sources of oil—most of which are US allies—to newer suppliers of oil. A Sino–Pak arms relationship has ensured China an entryway into the Middle East, not only giving China influence in this strategically vital region, but also allowing China and Middle Eastern and Central Asian countries to trade in oil, with Pakistan.

Even more to the advantage of China, its ongoing defence relationship with Pakistan has provided it with a strong bargaining chip in the international arena and especially with the United States. A case in point: a 1992 US decision to sell 150 F-16 fighters to Taiwan led China to withdraw from P-5 talks on conventional arms transfers.[10] Later that year, there were reports of the transfer of 34 complete Chinese M-11 systems to Pakistan.[11] This was followed by MTCR-related sanctions on China by the US[12]—a step that was denounced by China and prompted Beijing to threaten reneging from its promise to observe the MTCR.[13]

Genesis and Growth

Pakistan has been China's foremost recipient of weapons and military technology in South Asia, especially since their border settlement pact of March 1963. Between 1966–80 China accounted for over 1/3rd of Pakistan's arms imports, far ahead of its other major suppliers.[14] The history of China's relationship with Pakistan can be divided into three phases: from 1960s to 1979; 1979 till the end of , Cold War and the post-Cold War period. A fourth phase can also be discerned in the face of events post-9/11.

THE BEGINNING—PRE-1979

Throughout the first phase, Chinese arms exports to Pakistan, whose profile consisted fundamentally of small arms and light weapons, were predominantly given as free military aid,[15] initially as part of the Chinese attempt to emerge as a viable entity separate from Soviet Union, thanks to the zero-sum influence game played between Moscow and Beijing during the 1960s. Throughout the Cold War, Pakistan was an especially crucial Chinese ally against the Soviets. The two countries worked together with the US to arm the Afghan *mujahedeen* and to prevent Soviet expansion.[16]

Recurring arms embargoes by the United States against Pakistan, especially during the 1965 Indo–Pak war, prompted the Pakistani military and political elites to move towards a self-reliant and diverse defense production industry.[17] China's profile as a weapons trader in the international arms bazaar fits Pakistan's needs. Not only were their weapons cheap, and easy to operate and maintain (a prerequisite for the yet nascent and technologically unsophisticated Pakistani Armed Forces), the Chinese were proving to be highly reliable in their deliveries. For China, on the other hand, not only did Pakistan open up as a vast market for inferior quality Chinese weapons, it gave the Chinese a foothold into the Islamic world. The upsurge in Sino–Pak relations in this phase closely followed the deterioration of Sino–India relations. China had just fought a war with India, and Pakistan's longstanding rivalry with India, made the two countries come closer.

THE SOVIET FACTOR: FROM 1979 TILL END OF THE COLD WAR

By the late 1970s, Beijing's arms relations with Pakistan became hinged on offsetting the Soviet influence in South Asia. Elsewhere the PRC had adopted a more 'pragmatic' policy, with arms exports being largely commercially driven.[18] By the mid-1980s, China was the world's fourth largest arms supplier (after the Soviet Union, United States, and France) and by 1990, Chinese arms exports had thus, captured 8 per cent of the global market.[19]

Sino–Pakistan arms relations also underwent an adjustment at this time. While there was an underlying strategic rationale for China to supply arms to Pakistan—the restricting of Soviet influence in South

Asia—there were commercial strings attached to the arms exports as well. This transformation in Chinese attitudes could be discerned in the context of improving Chinese relations with the United States and India during the 1980s.

AFTER THE WALL: THE 1990s

The end of the Cold War denotes the beginning of the third phase of China's arms transfers to Pakistan. Both quality and quantity of Chinese arms deteriorated in this period. By 1996, China had dropped to the fifth largest exporter of conventional weapons to the developing world accruing $600 millions.[20] The entry of inexpensive, yet state-of-the-art Russian arms in the global arms bazaar, posed severe competition to the Chinese arms exports, which fell by a whopping 75 per cent between 1990 to 1998.[21]

With Pakistan, however, Chinese arms relations have been as strong as ever. Beijing's arms transfers during the 1990s, has been reflective of its desire to emerge as a regional power and as a viable global power alternative to the United States. The most telling sign of the former is Beijing's attempt to supply arms and strike defence co-operation deals with India's peripheral neighbours, prompting analysts to comment of the creation of a Chinese ring around India.

Beijing's arms trade with Pakistan in this period has however, been a little more than just commercially driven or hinged on offsetting India's influence in the region. Arms exports to Pakistan have been explained by many as an attempt by Beijing to award Islamabad for supplying the former with Western military technologies. The faithfulness of Pakistan as an arms partner fuelled China's defence modernization drive. Weapons and weapon technology transfers are being viewed by Beijing as a means to develop national techno-industrial bases and to rescue a defence industry that was in deep crisis.[22] The Pakistani military, particularly the Pakistani Air Force, had superior operational know-how, something that they had acquired from their close relations with the Americans. This operational know-how was effectively tapped by the Chinese to modify and upgrade their weapon system designs. Beijing's military assistance on the other hand was vital for developing Pakistan's poor defence industrial resources and technology.

Strategically, with the Soviet threat gone, the greatest benefit to both countries lied in offsetting an increasing Indian military power and influence in the region. Both China and Pakistan have fought wars with India, and India has supported Tibetan dissidents against Beijing. The May 1998 Indian nuclear tests were ostensibly directed against China, increasing Beijing's shared strategic concerns with Islamabad. By strengthening Pakistan's military capabilities, China forces India to devote more resources to its border with Pakistan and less to its border with China.[23] Pakistan has in turn become a critical strategic bulwark for China. Karachi is a regular refuelling point for Chinese aircraft flying to Europe, Africa, and the Middle East, and Pakistan acts as a mediator for China and various Islamic countries, helping facilitate China's relations with Iran, Saudi Arabia, and other Muslim nations.

Islamabad, for its part, increasingly needs Beijing as a strategic ally. Western nations, particularly the United States, have distanced themselves from Pakistan because of its nuclear programme. Other countries, such as Russia, may be hesitant to jeopardize lucrative ties to India in order to improve relations with Pakistan. Thus, China is the only major arms supplier consistently willing to work with Islamabad.

Owing to improvements in Sino–Indian relations prompted by the signing of the 1993 and 1996 agreements on confidence building measures (CBMs) between the two states, Beijing has attempted to moderate its policy towards Pakistan, projecting a more evenhanded diplomatic approach. It has thus, moved away from its backing for Pakistan's position on Kashmir and calls for self-determination to a position supporting a bilateral settlement. Nonetheless, its defence and strategic ties with Islamabad remain an important element of its strategic posture in the region.

9/11—NEW CHALLENGES

The initial period of the post-9/11 phase witnessed a certain chilling in China–Pakistan relations, especially with Pakistan becoming the frontline state against the Taliban in the war against terror by the United States, overnight. However, recent trends have shown that Pakistan's strategic military relations with China have largely remained unchanged in content.

In early 2002, Pakistan invited China to develop and construct a deep-sea port at Gwadar on the Makaran coast.[24] This project can have a wide reaching strategic significance inasmuch as it gives

China access and basing facilities in the Indian Ocean and a close proximity to the Straits of Hormuz. It also amounts to maritime encirclement of India in the sense that with the presence at Gwadar at one end and at Cocos at the other, the Chinese Navy can threaten India's security.[25]

According to a CIA report, 'The Acquisition of Technology Relating to Weapons of Mass Destruction', covering the period between 1 January to 30 June 2003, Chinese entity assistance has helped Pakistan move toward domestic serial production of solid-propellant short-range ballistic missiles (SRBMs) and supported Pakistan's development of solid-propellant medium range ballistic missiles (MRBMs).[26] In November 2003, the Joint Declaration between the People's Republic of China and the Islamic Republic of Pakistan on Direction of Bilateral Cooperation stated that:

> The two parties attach great importance to the role of the China–Pakistan Defence and Security Consultation Mechanism in promoting military-to-military exchanges and cooperation. In this regard, the efforts of the Sino–Pakistan Joint Committee on Cooperation in Defence Technology and Industry shall be supported to enhance defence industrial cooperation.[27]

In the post-9/11 period, yet another area of strong Sino-Pak cooperation has emerged—terrorism. Pre-9/11, China had virtually turned a blind eye to Pakistani sponsored Islamic extremism and Islamabad's resolute backing of the Taliban regime. 9/11 revealed to Beijing the ugly spectre of Islamic fundamentalism and extremism in its full force. China has been battling the Uighurs extremists in Xinjiang region. In January 2004, in what is seen as a significant move on the part of the Chinese, China forwarded a list of Chinese terrorists and outfits linked to Al-Qaeda to Pakistan and asked Islamabad to initiate action against these groups.[28]

For India, a China–Burma–Pakistan strategic triangle has also become a disconcerting reality. In December 2001, it was revealed that two Pakistani nuclear scientists (Suleiman Asad and Mohammed Ali Mukhtar) had moved to Myanmar in November 2001 when US intelligence officials were investigating their involvement with the Al-Qaeda network.[29] Pakistan has also been providing small conventional weapons and training to Myanmar's armed forces, and has joined China in concluding an intelligence sharing agreement with Myanmar regarding India's force deployments in north-east India and the Bay of Bengal.[30]

At the same time, there have been increasing concerns in Beijing about Pakistan's hand in supporting extremism in Xinjiang. The putting off of a 1995 Pakistan–China–Kazakhstan–Kyrgyztan transit trade agreement was attributed to Beijing's anxiety to restrict contacts between the Uighur nationalist elements and the Islamic parties of Pakistan.[31] In February 1998, the *Xinjiang Legal Daily* reported that there was evidence of drug and weapon trade over Xinjiang's borders with Pakistan-occupied Kashmir.[32] There have also been reports of Uighurs from Xinjiang undergoing religious education in Pakistani *madrasas.* Several Uighurs have been trained in guerrilla warfare in training camps at Jalalabad in Afghanistan and at Landi Kotal, in the Khyber Agency of Pakistan.[33]

While the manifestation of recent developments regarding the involvement of Pakistani scientist, A.Q. Khan, in the development of Libyan, North Korean and Iranian nuclear programmes haven't been apparent in Sino–Pakistan relations, the link-up might have proven to be embarrassing for the patron of the Pakistani nuclear programme—China. This could in the future lead to a certain modicum of volatility in Sino–Pak relations.

Profile of Chinese Arms Transfers

In the decades of China–Pakistan arms relationship, China has sold and even gifted away Type-59 tanks, Type-531 armoured personnel carriers, missile boats, F-7P jet fighters, and M-11 missiles[34] among other systems to Pakistan.[35] China has also assisted Pakistan with facilities to produce an array of conventional systems including jet trainers, the Type-69 tank, the HJ-8 anti-tank missile, and the HN-5A portable surface-to-air missile.[36] Between 1993-2000, China provided Pakistan with Al-Khalid battle tanks and F-7 jets.[37]

Beijing has played the role of a benefactor in Pakistan's nuclear programme, much to the consternation of the Indian Government and the rest of the global community. According to an August 1997 report by the US Arms Control and Disarmament Agency, 'Prior to China's [1992] accession [to the NPT], the United States concluded that China had assisted Pakistan in developing nuclear explosives. . . . Questions remain about contacts between Chinese entities and elements associated with Pakistan's nuclear weapons programme.'[38]

China has also apparently provided Pakistan with custom-built samarium-cobalt alloy magnets worth $70,000, for the Kahuta Research Laboratory in 1994–5, that would enable Pakistan to upgrade and replace its enrichment centrifuges at the rate of 1,000 to 2,000 machines a year.[39] Ring magnets find a place in the list of dual use items drawn by the Zangger Committee.[40]

It is alleged that China assisted Pakistan in building unsafeguarded 50-70-MWt plutonium production reactor at Khushab along with a unsafeguarded plutonium reprocessing facility at Chashma.[41] These allegations has far-reaching implications for India especially since these developments would give Pakistan the capacity to develop plutonium for use in nuclear weapons.[42]

China has actively involved itself in the Pakistani missile programme. In 1992 for instance, there was a transfer of M-11 short-range ballistic missile components between China and Pakistan, and in August of the next year, China shipped additional equipment related to the M-11 missiles. China's assistance to Pakistan with missile technology has prompted the United States to twice impose and then lift Category II sanctions in the early 1990s on the Chinese and Pakistani organizations related to these transfers.[43]

Several unofficial reports that have made the rounds of the media however indicate that the sanctions did not deter China from continuing its missile technology relationship with Pakistan. An April 1996 Pentagon report, stated, 'China remains Pakistan's most important supplier of missile-related technologies'.[44]

Pakistan's Ghauri, a 1,500-km-range ballistic missile, is speculated to be developed with Chinese assistance. It has also been alleged that the Shaheen-1 IRBM, which Pakistan tested in April 1999, is actually modelled on the Chinese M-9 missiles.[45] A February 1999 CIA report, stated, 'Chinese and North Korean entities continued to provide assistance to Pakistan's ballistic missile programme during the first half of 1998. Such assistance is critical for Islamabad's efforts to produce ballistic missiles. . . .'[46] A September 1999 National Intelligence Council (NIC) report confirmed this.[47] The report also referred to the transfer of 34 M-11 missiles delivered in November 1992.[48]

A 2001 report in the *Washington Times* revealed that a Chinese company had sent shipments of missile components to Pakistan. The report noted that the China National Machinery & Equipment Import & Export Corporation, known as CMEC, reportedly supplied the missile components for Pakistan's Shaheen-1 and Shaheen-2 missile programmes.[49]

Implications and Options for India

The China–Pakistan-India strategic triad remains the fulcrum of the South Asian security environment. In so far as China has kept up with its military relations with Pakistan, India has perceived China as constituting a grave threat to its security and strategic interests in the region. Indeed, the period in which Chinese arms transfers to Pakistan were at its peak—1980s—Sino–India relations were at its lowest. Surprisingly, though while Chinese arms relations with India's other peripheral states have considerably tapered off in recent years, the Sino–Pakistani strategic entente has displayed incredible tenacity over the years.

India is—geographically, politically and strategically—at the heart of South Asia. Despite sharing a troubled past—India and China fought a territorial war in 1962 and have ever since quarrelled over contested territory and China has not taken India's acceptance of Tibetan refugees lightly—both the countries have recognized the necessity to forge cordial relationships. For India, having stronger relations with its powerful neighbour is essential for its security and strategic interests as the most powerful state in the region.[50] More specifically, India's long standing dispute with Pakistan over Kashmir and strong Sino–Pak relations, make the strategy of friendship with China a prudent policy to follow. More so, if it allows China to untie some of its links with Pakistan.

In fact, the recent thaw in Sino–Indian relations has best reflected in Chinese neutrality during Kargil and the growing trade relationship between the two countries. Trade figures are even more encouraging. Between 1993 and 1997, while Pakistan's share in South Asia's bilateral trade with China declined from 44 per cent to 26 per cent, India's share increased from 35 per cent to 46 per cent. [51] In 1998, following the nuclear explosions in India and Pakistan, Pakistan's annual trade with China registered a negative growth of nearly nine per cent.[52] Despite this, India's trade remained positive showing a 5.02 per cent increase.[53] These trends clearly show that there is growing economic interdependence between the two coun-tries—a fact that confirms the idea that both countries require each other as economic partners in order to develop into the regional and global powers they want to be.

While it does take *two to tango*, and China also requires India, both for strategic, security and economic reasons, this paper only concerns itself with the options that India has in order to engage China as a strategic and economic partner.

A state that faces threats from another state generally has three options available to it in terms of countering the threat. The state can reallocate resources under its control, therefore making itself more powerful compared to the threatening state; negotiate with the threatening state; or form alliances with other states in order to balance with the threatening state.[54] India's options in countering the Chinese threat in South Asia, especially with respect to its strategic relationship with Pakistan, can suitably fall within the above three categories.

First of India's triad of options in countering China's growing influence in South Asia and its relationship with Pakistan, could be to modernize its defence industry in order to offset the increasing disparity in the relative military capabilities of the two countries. The early 1990s witnessed a de-acceleration in India's defence production and military R&D owing to several reasons: budget cuts, collapse of ally Soviet Union and economic restructuring.[55] Almost simultaneously, China's defence industry embarked on a defence reform process: official defence budget for the military grew 5 billion RMB to 64.8 billion RMB between 1990 and 2003.[56] For the same period, the official funding for military equipment increased 153 per cent.[57] Although clearly ineffective,[58] these reforms have helped create techno-military asymmetry between the two countries.[59] This asymmetry has contributed to a large extent to the insecure environment in South Asia.

India can counter the growing Chinese military influence in the region, by allocating more of its internal resources to military and defence development. By doing so, India will also be able forge arms relations with its South Asian neighbours, who had in the face of the dearth of a viable arms supplier moved towards China. Indeed, creating a indigenous Indian arms exports industry could be a way of containing China's increasing power in the region.

Yet another option for India would be to negotiate and cooperate with China. One of the ways that India can exercise this option is by expounding confidence and security building measures (CSBMs) that help maintain long-term peace along the Line of Control. The 1993 India–China agreement forms the basis for this.[60] India should also encourage economic and cultural relations both with China and with Pakistan. Increasing cross-border trade would give China a stake in

India's development and growth and will link the prosperity of China's southern provinces to India's well-being. China is something of a blind spot for most Indians. This can be attributed to very low levels of people-to-people exchanges and the relative isolation of the two countries from each other. Trade and investment relations too remain at low levels. China has not encouraged greater interaction and is even wary about opening more trade points along the Indo–Tibet border. Since the two sides officially resumed their border trade in December 1991, the monetary value of border trade between the two countries has stayed less than $1 million per annum. This remains far lower compared to India's border trade with either Bangladesh or Myanmar.[61]

The third option available to India *vis-à-vis* China and Pakistan would be to create bilateral and multilateral alliances with states in South Asia and with other major powers including the United States, Russia, Japan and the EU in order to balance against the growing influence of China in the region. Moreover, China can be encapsulated in the alliance.

Conclusion

Despite the thawing of relations between India and China and India and Pakistan in the recent years, the Sino–Pakistan strategic entente has not shown any major sign of stress. The two countries are highly interdependent, especially in terms of their defence cooperation and have several constituencies that have overtime developed vested interest to ensure continuation of *status quo* of interdependence. As a result, even when their supplies of sensitive nuclear and missile technologies may have been slowed during recent years yet, China continues to supplies nearly one-third of Pakistan's conventional weapons and the trend seems to remain as strong at least for the short and even medium terms into the future.

NOTES

1. Karl W. Eikenberry, 'Explaining and Influencing Chinese Arms Transfers', *McNair Paper 36*, Institute for National Strategic Studies, National Defense University, Washington DC, 1995.

2. 'China's Missile Exports and Assistance to Pakistan', Center for Nonproliferation Studies. Available at http://cns.miis.edu/research/india/china/mpakpos.htm.
3. Karl W. Eikenberry, 'Explaining and Influencing Chinese Arms Transfers', *McNair Paper 36*, Institute for National Strategic Studies, National Defense University, Washington DC, 1995. http://www.ndu.edu/inss/McNair/mcnair36/36dem.html.
4. Daniel Sneider, 'China's Arms Bazaar', *Far Eastern Economic Review*, 18 December 1986, p. 23.
   Karl W. Eikenberry, 'Explaining and Influencing Chinese Arms Transfers', *McNair Paper 36*, Institute for National Strategic Studies, National Defense University, Washington DC, 1995. http://www.ndu.edu/inss/McNair/mcnair36/36dem.html.
5. Swaran Singh 'Pakistan–China Defence Cooperation', *Sapra India Bulletin*, May 1996.
6. 'Weapons Proliferation and the Military-Industrial Complex of the PRC', *Commentary*, no. 84, 27 August 2003.
7. Richard A. Bitzinger, 'Arms to Go: Chinese Arms Sales to the Third World', *International Security*, vol. 17, no. 2, Fall 1992, pp. 91–2.
8. Ibid.
   Karl W. Eikenberry, 'Explaining and Influencing Chinese Arms Transfers', *McNair Paper 36*, Institute for National Strategic Studies, National Defense University, Washington DC, 1995, p. 6.
9. Daniel Byman, Roger Cliff, *China's Arms Sales: Motivations and Implications*, Santa Monica: Rand Corporation. Available at http://www.rand.org/pubs/monograph_reports/MR1119/.
10. Testimony of Gordon Oehler, Hearing on the Proliferation of Chinese Missiles, Senate Foreign Relations Committee, US Senate, 11 June 1998. Quoted in Center for Nonproliferation Studies. 'China's Missile Exports and Assistance to Pakistan'. Avaialble at http://cns.miis.edu/research/india/china/mpakpos.htm.
11. Ibid.
12. Daniel Williams, 'U.S. Punishes China Over Missile Sales', *The Washington Post*, 26 April 1993, p.A1.
13. 'China's Missile Exports and Assistance to Pakistan', Center for Nonproliferation Studies. Available at http://cns.miis.edu/research/india/china/mpakpos.htm
14. Swaran Singh, 'Pakistan-China Defence Cooperation', *Sapra India Bul*-*le*tin, May 1996.
15. In 1964, China had offered Pakistan an interest free loan of $ 60 million.
16. Richard A. Bitzinger, 'Arms to Go: Chinese Arms Sales to the Third World', *International Security*, vol. 17, no. 2, Fall 1992, p. 85.

17. Swaran Singh, 'Pakistan-China Defence Cooperation', *Sapra India Bulletin*, May 1996.
18. This trend coincided with Mao's moving out of the Chinese political scene.
19. 'China and Conventional Weapons Nonproliferation', Available at http://www.nti.org/db/china/conpos.htm.
20. Ibid.
21. Ibid.
22. Bates Gill, 'Chinese Military Modernization and Arms Proliferation in the Asia-Pacific' in Jonathan D. Pollack and Richard H. Yang, eds., *In China's Shadow: Regional Perspectives on Chinese Foreign Policy and Military Development*, Santa Monica: Rand Corporation, 1998, p. 16.
23. Robert E. Mullins, 'The Dynamics of Chinese Missile Proliferation', *The Pacific Review*, vol. 8, no. 1, 1995, p. 142.
24. See report available at http://www.rebound88.net/02/oct/10.html. (Accessed on 11 February 2004).
25. Ibid.
26. Jessica Altschul, 'China & Pakistan Move Closer on "Official" Nuclear Cooperation', The Jewish Institute for National Security Affairs. Avaialble at http://www.jinsa.org/articles/view.html?documentid=2309. (Accessed on 31 January 2004.)
27, Joint Declaration Between the People's Republic of China and the Islamic Republic of Pakistan on Direction of Bilateral Cooperation. Beijing. 3 November 2003. Available at http://www.nti.org/db/china/engdocs/China_Pak_1103.htm.
28. 'Now China Hands Over List of Terrorists to Pakistan', *Hindustan Times*, 17 January 2004.
29. C.S. Kuppuswamy, 'China-Pakistan-Myanmar: The Triangular Relationship Needs Careful Watch', SAAG Paper 401, January 2002.
30. J. Mohan Malik, 'Pakistani Connection', *The Pioneer*, Oped 19 December 2001.
31. B. Raman, 'Continuing Unrest in Xinjiang', South Asia Analysis Group. 14 March 1999 Available at www.saag.org/papers/paper41.html. (Accessed on 1 February 2004.)
32. Ibid.
33. Ibid.
34. Center for Nonproliferation Studies. 'China's Missile Exports and Assistance to Pakistan'. Available at http://cns.miis.edu/research/india/china/mpakpos.htm. (Accessed on 1 February 2004.)
35. Eric Hyer, 'China's Arms Merchants: Profits in Command', *China Quarterly*, no. 132, December 1992, p. 1105.
36. Karl W. Eikenberry, 'Explaining and Influencing Chinese Arms Transfers'

McNair Paper 36, Institute for National Strategic Studies, National Defense University, Washington DC, 1995.

37. Richard Bingley, 'India *v.* Pakistan: What Exactly is the UK Doing to Stave Off Military Tension Over Kashmir?' Available at http://www.caat.org.uk/information/magazine/0202/kashmir.php. (Accessed on 1 February 2004.)
38. 'Tracking Nuclear Proliferation—China', 1998, Carnegie Endowment for International Peace. Available at http://www.ceip.org/files/Publications/TrackingChina.asp?p=8. (Accessed on 5 February 2004.)
39. Ibid.
40. Ibid.
41. Bill Gertz, 'China aids Pakistani Plutonium Plant', *Washington Times*, 3 April 1996.
42. Tracking Nuclear Proliferation—China, 1998, Carnegie Endowment for International Peace. Available at http://www.ceip.org/files/Publications/TrackingChina.asp?p=8. (Accessed on 5 February 2004.)
43. Ibid.
44. Office of the Secretary of Defence quoted in Tracking Nuclear Proliferation, 1998, China, Carnegie Endowment for International Peace. Available at http://www.ceip.org/files/Publications/Tracking China.asp?p=8.
45. Byman L. Daniel and Roger Cliff, *China's Arms Sales: Motivations and Implications*, p. 23.
46. Ibid. p. 23.
47. China's Missile Exports and Assistance to Pakistan. Available at http://www.nti.org/db/china/conpos.htm.
48. Ibid.
49. Bill Gertz, 'Beijing Arms Pakistan', *The Washington Times*, 6 August 2001.
50. Sujit Dutta, 'China's Emerging Power and Military Role: Implications for South Asia,' Santa Monica: Rand Corporation, p. 107. Available at http://www.rand.org/pubs/conf_proceedings/CF137/CF137.cha p5.pdf. p. 110.
51. Swaran Singh, 2000, 'China–India: Expanding Economic Engagement', *Strategic Analysis*, vol. XXIV no. 10.
52. Ibid.
53. Ibid.
54. Robert Powell, *Shadow of Power: States and Strategies in International Politics*, Princeton: Princeton University Press, 1999.
55. Sujit Dutta, 'China's Emerging Power and Military Role: Implications for South Asia', Santa Monica: Rand Corporation, p. 107. Available at http://www.rand.org/pubs/conf_proceedings/CF137/CF137.chap5. pdf.
56. Evan S. Medeiros, Roger Cliff, Keith Crane and James C. Mulvenon,

A New Direction for China's Defense Industry, Rand Corporation, available at http://www.rand.org/pubs/monographs/2005/RAND_MG334. pdf.

57. Ibid.
58. Ibid.
59. Ibid.
60. Ibid.
61. Swaran Singh, 'China-India: Expanding Economic Engagement', *Strategic Analysis*, vol. XXIV, no. 10.

CHAPTER 17

The Karakoram Highway

VIRENDRA SAHAI VERMA

One of the central features of geopolitics of South Asia has been the enduring strategic relationship between China and Pakistan. As in all international relations, the robust and lasting relationship is based on material exchanges, connectivity, communications facilities, all premised on principles of mutual benefit. And here, while Karakoram highway represents a kind of umbilical cord of China–Pakistan ties, several ups and downs of China–India equations and India–Pakistan hostility have played an important part in nursing their friendship. China looks at Pakistan as a gateway to the Islamic world and an easy access to the warm waters of Arabian Sea for trade. Besides, it also facilitates China's economic interactions with and access to Central Asian Republics.

Karakoram Highway and now Gwadar Port Project, which are on either end of Pakistan's geographical limits, are the two foundations for a long-term vision of Sino–Pakistan relations. The Gwadar Sea port is strategically located to pave the way for strengthening Pakistan's economic relations with China and Central Asian Republics providing access to warm waters of Arabian Sea through land access via Karakoram pass. Gwadar project whose foundation was laid on 23 March 2002 has been totally designed by Chinese engineers. Out of $248 million package, $198 million is being financed by China. The rest will be the share of Pakistan. The first phase is likely to be completed by 2005. Similarly, Karakoram Highway has also been another historic gift from China to Pakistan though it has been equally (perhaps more beneficial) to China as well.

Geo-Strategic Location

The main Karakoram (in Turki; black loose shale) range creates a watershed between Tarim Basin in Xinjiang Autonomous Region of

China and Indus river systems flowing through northern areas of Pakistan. In the West, this range bifurcates to join the Pamirs in the Tajikistan and Hindukush in Afghanistan. In the East, beyond Karakoram pass, which is in its extremity, range dissipates itself into high plateau of Western Tibet. 'Geographically, the area involved forms the apex of the great divide between the drainage of Central Asia and the Indian Ocean. Here we find the sources of Yarkand flowing northwards and of the tributaries flowing southwards to the Indus.'[1] The Karakoram region known as northern areas of Pakistan is an important strategic outpost of Pakistan where boundaries of Central Asia, Afghanistan, China and India meet.

Ancient Routes

The Silk Route along which passed Chinese merchandise including silk to Rome is actually a set of primary axes of transportation though the heart of Asia. The principal axes runs in parallel between the eastern coast of Mediterranean and the heart of China—roughly from east to west and vice versa. A set of auxiliary axes roughly perpendicular to the principle axes feed into the silk route from the heart of Asia or from the shores of the Indian Ocean. Kashi (traditional name Kashgar) and Yarkand both in Xinjiang in People's Republic of China are the strategic cities on this route. One of the important feeder axes to this route is through lower Himalayas—Indian and Pakistan-Occupied Kashmir.

The Mintaka pass, which was eastern-most on this axes was on the direct route from Hunza via Sarikol into Xinjiang. The British safeguarded these routes by close supervision through agents in Kafiristan, Gilgit and Hunza from time to time and by subsidies and treaties with Jammu and Kashmir State in respect of these states. In 1876, the Viceroy Lord Lytton signed an agreement with the Maharaja of Kashmir at Madhopur regarding Gilgit and obtained his agreement to the posting of an agent at Gilgit. The Russians controlled these routes from Pamir end except the Mintaka pass, which was accessible from Xinjiang. 'The country of the glacier and peaks in between the ranges and the Indus is sparsely inhabited by the Burushos, Chitrali, Dards, Balti and the Ladakhis (from west to east), who survive by canalization of the glacial waters for the irrigation and by herding livestock in the narrow pastures.'[2]

Historical Background

The Pamir was important as a meeting point of frontiers of Gilgit, Hunza, Chitral, Badakhshan, Wakhan, Kokand and Sarikol. It has been the focal point of the Great Game between Russia and the Britain since 1870. The British were successful in creating a buffer between Russia and British Empire interjecting a Afghanistan corridor known as Wakhan under the Pamir boundary agreement of 1895. This shifted rivalry to Sarikol and Taghdumbash Pamir. In 1760, Salim Khan, Chief of Hunza had defeated Kirgyzs and this feat was awarded by Chinese by giving cultivation, grazing and taxation rights to Hunza in Raskam and Taghumbash Pamirs on the other side of the water-shed of the Karakoram range. 'The existence of Hunza forts in Azghar and the signs of cultivation at other places in this area indicated that Hunza was in actual possession of Raskam for considerable period.'[3]

In 1897, Mir of Hunza sent some of his men to resume cultivation in Raskam valley. Humza was under the British suzerainty since 1891 and had British support. Russia viewed it as part of British design to extend their authority in their bid to outflank Russian influence. It was only after British assurance that they sought only cultivation rights and not territorial rights that Russians finally agreed to drop their objections to its lease to Hunza. In 1898, Government of India proposed to the Chinese through a note presented by Sir Claude Macdonald the exchange of Hunza's claims across Kara-koram to Chinese claims over Hunza. This is also seen as an attempt for abandonment of claims to Shahidullah, Suget and Aksai Chin. Alastair Lamb claims 'it is an extremely important document with some bearing on the alignment of Sino–Indian Border when it became subject of Chinese challenge in the fifties. . . . It is the only formal proposal on a boundary between India and China in Karakoram that is to say from Wakhan to Lanak Pass.'[4] China, however, did not acknowledge or make any commitment in answer to these package proposals.

By 1900 Lord Curzon who assumed change as Viceroy of India did not favour abandoning trans-Karakoram rights and revived, in 1912, Sir John Ardagh's proposal of 1 January 1877 under which British boundary was to run North of Tagdumbash Pamir and Raskam to include Suget and Shahidullah and further to the Kunlun mountains north-east of the Aksai Chin plains which is a bone of contention between India and China. However, the British government did not accept these proposals. The settlement of Raskam issue was now relegated to secondary position because British attached primary importance to the conclusion of Anglo–Chinese Convention of Tibet. However, British did not severe their claim in Raskam and Taghdumbash Pamirs. Mir of Hunza continued to levy annual grain taxes from Kirgyzs.

From 1899 to 1914, due to Russian influence in Kashgar, Hunza did not enforce its rights in Raskam. 'From 1914 onwards, when Russian influence was on decline and Chinese authorities had much reduced, Hunza resumed to the practice of deputing its men to cultivate these lands, brushing aside the Chinese objections. In doing so Hunza had received official concurrence from British-Indian Government'.[5] British fully understood the strategic importance of using Hunza rights in Taghdumbash and Raskam. Due to preoccupation with other issues, British did not apply pressure upon China for solving this issue and with the result Indo–China Border in Hunza and Aksai Chin sectors remained un-delimited even when British rule ended in 1947.

Northern Areas

Pakistan bifurcated the Pakistan occupied part of Kashmir into two zones: Northern Areas and Azad Kashmir. The five districts of Gilgit, Skardu, Dianir, Ghizer and Ghanche covering an area of 72495 sq km and a population of 15 lakh is known as Northern Areas. The sectarian break up in the Northern Areas consist of 8 major ethnic groups, which are the Baltees, Shins, Yashkuns, Mughals, Kashmiris, Pathans, Ladakhis and Turks who speak dialects of Balti, Shina, Brushaki, Khawer, Wakhi, Turki, Tibetan, Pushto, Urdu and Persian. The Northern Areas despite a very small population presents a very diverse sectarian picture, with the presence of four Muslim sects—Shia, Sunni, Ismails and Nurbakshis. The POK Act of 1968, POK Government Act of 1970 and new interim constitution of 1974 do not cover these Northern Areas, which come directly under Department of Kashmir Affairs of Central Government (of Pakistan) and are administered by a Civil Official. Federal Minister for Kashmir Affairs is the Chief Executive of Northern Areas. Northern Areas Council with 24 elected seats exists but over centralization of decision-making has ensured denial of powers to the Council. According to Western experts, 'The people of Northern Areas have existed without civil rights, a constitution status and a political identity.'[6]

A writ petition was instituted on 16 October 1990 in the High Court of Azad Kashmir by various political parties in Azad Kashmir, which sought to bring Northern Areas under the administrative control of Azad Kashmir Government. After a long drawn case, the High Court has given judgement in favour of Azad Kashmir, i.e. 'Azad Kashmir to assume administrative control of Northern Areas.' The Central Government of Pakistan has filed an appeal in the Supreme Court. JKLF chief, Amanullah Khan who is leading a movement to merge Northern Areas under Azad Kashmir talks of torture meted out to him and his workers in his autobiography 'Jehd-e-Musalsal (continuous struggle) (pages 198 to 222). The Northern Areas languish at literary rate of 14 per cent below Pak average of 31 per cent. Here 50 per cent of the population is Shia. In sectarian violence in 1989, it was reported entire villages around Gilgit were wiped out. Pakistan has been controlling the majority Shias by settling Sunnis from main land and NWFP. 'The resentment is growing, Pakistan never trusted the people of Gilgit and Baltistan though they have been exploiting the areas time & again.'[7]

Origins of Political Bonhomie

It was at 1955 Bandung Non Aligned Nations Conference, Zhou Enlai established first contact with Pakistan. He had assured Field Marshal Ayub Khan that Pakistan should not have any fear from China and that China would not permit any aggression against her, (although China had been showing certain parts of Pakistan as part of China in 300 miles long undefined border between Xinjiang and occupied Kashmir). This followed mutual visits between both countries. However, the shooting incident at Longju between Indian and Chinese troops in 1959 had revealed inherent dangers of Chinese designs in the territories of both of India and Pakistan. In 1960, President Ayub Khan had offered a joint defence of the Indian subcontinent. President Ayub had stated in a public meeting at Dacca, then East Pakistan, in early 1960. 'The crux of the whole matter was that the armies of both countries were continuing to face each other when they could have been released to defend their respective territories. . . . The need to have a joint defence originated from the basic fact that India and Pakistan lived in the same region, which had to be defended after an understanding between the people of two countries.'[8]

Beginning with April 1959, border violations by China on Pakistan held Kashmir Front had become a routine affair. There were also border skirmishes on Hunza border. In July 1960, Ayub Khan again stated as follows:

As a student of war and strategy, I can see quite clearly the inexorable push of north in the direction of the warm waters of the Indian Ocean. This push is bound to increase if India and Pakistan go on squabbling with each other. If on the other hand, we resolve our problems and disengage our armed forces from facing inwards, as they do today, and face them outwards, I feel we should have a good chance of preventing a recurrence of the history of the past, which was that whenever this subcontinent was divided—often it was divided—someone or the other invited the outsider to step in.[9]

In India, the proposal of Field Marshal Ayub Khan was linked with the Kashmir issue and was not considered adequately. However, India's unwillingness to discuss a joint defence policy with Pakistan was unquestionably a factor in the development of relations between China and Pakistan.[10] Swaran Singh–Zulfiqar Bhutto, foreign ministers level talks, did not make any headway. It was expected that resolution of Kashmir dispute on LOC is round the corner. However, the failure of talks turned Pakistan towards China. Ayub Khan's first step then was to send a formal note to Beijing on 28 March 1961, suggesting a boundary settlement. Chinese replied after a year suggesting a provisional agreement pending settlement of Kashmir issue. Finally, talks began in Beijing on 12 October 1962.

Sino–Pak Agreement 1963

Up to 1959, Pakistan as well as the Kashmir nationalists saw the Aksai Chin question in a similar light. There were moments indeed as during Zhou Enlai Indian visit in 1956 when Pakistan statesmen, anticipating a possible Sino-Indian Border Agreement, warned India not to surrender Kashmir territory in the Aksai Chin area of Ladakh. After 1959, the Pakistanis began their journey along the road to rapprochement with Beijing. In the process, they abandoned not only 'Aksai Chin, which in any case lay well beyond their grasp, but also all other extreme Ardagh type claims north of main Karakoram watershed. In this frame of mind, they were able without too much difficulty to come to a border agreement with China in March 1963, which was little more than a confirmation of the Western part of the 1899 line as it was unilaterally modified by Lord Curzon's Government of India in 1905. Thus, 1899 line made a more 'positive contribution to international relations. It is one of the foundations of Sino-Pakistan friendship'.[11]

The agreement based on the MacDonald proposal of 1899 abandoned Hunza claims of approx 4000 sq km over Taghdumbush and Raskam. 'It is prodigious Pakistan herself had warned India during Zhou Enlai Indian visit in 1956 not to surrender Kashmir territory in Aksai Chin whereas the basis of Pak Agreement is in MacDonald proposal which gave away to China not only Shaksgam valley but also lands across Karakoram.'

The agreement signed on 2 March 1963 between Zhou Enlai and Z.A. Bhutto, has formally delimited and demarcated the boundary between China's Xinjiang and contiguous areas 'defence of which is under the actual control of Pakistan'. The Article I explains that the agreement is based on 'traditional customary boundary line including natural features. The article VI makes the agreement provisional' as after the settlement of Kashmir dispute between Pakistan and India, the Sovereign Authority concerned will reopen negotiation with the Government of the people of China on the boundary. The Government of India had sent 'emphatic protest' to Pakistan on 10 May 1962 saying Government of Pakistan is not entitled to negotiate with China about territory which is not their own.

It also explained that the boundary alignment west of the Karakoram pass follows well-known natural features and does not require fresh delimitation. The protest note warned Government of Pakistan 'of the grave consequences of their action'. The reply of the Government of Pakistan dated 9 August 1962 justified that 'agreement of a provisional nature embodying an agreed understanding of the common border between Pakistan and China would be a positive contribution to the strengthening of peace in Asia'. Beijing in reply to an Indian note challenged 'as totally untenable the assumptions that Kashmir is under Indian sovereignty, that there is no common boundary between India and Pakistan'. Their reply stated, 'Why is it that the Indian Government cannot negotiate and settle its boundary question with the Chinese Government.'[12]

Sino–Pakistan treaty alignment followed the main Karakoram watershed. Shaksgam valley, which Pakistan has given to China is on southern slopes of Aghil range. According to K. Mason, who surveyed the Shaksgam valley in 1926, the Shaksgam (Oprang) river drains the plains (which seem like Lingzi Tang) between Karakoram and Aghil ranges and proceeds north-west to join Yarkand river.[13] Thus Shaksgam river appears to be on the other side of watershed and a well defined natural feature. As per *The Times* about 3400 square miles of border were overlapping on Pakistan and China's maps. 'The compromise border now agreed upon leaves about two thirds of it (2050 sq miles) on China's side, but while Pakistan has given up only claims on maps, China will be withdrawing their frontier forces and administration from about 750 sq. miles.'[14] The network of Karakoram highway and Aksai Chin Road, the latter built in the 1950s, passing through Aksai Chin is a bone of contention between India and China, and is strategically very important to China. This is a lifeline for Western Tibet. China has built a network of roads in the area and has interconnected them. The importance of Shaksgam is in providing strategic depth and an elbowroom for this network.

The boundary treaty was diplomatic reverse for India. The boundary treaty earned Beijing's open support for Pakistan's Policy on Kashmir (which was changed in 1980). In 1963, trade and barter agreement helped Pakistan's economy. Air service was opened between Dacca, Canton and Shanghai. China took sides with Pakistan during the 1965 war. Increased communication by air was followed by construction of the modern highways on both sides of Sino–Pakistan border 'where camels were the only transport since Marco Polo passed that way, roads were now built'.[15]

Karakoram Highway

The present highway has been the focus of military and strategic analysts. It is the pioneering venture of Pakistan Army Engineers in 1959 when work started on what was known as the Indus Valley road. After the Sino–Pak Border Agreement of 1963, Pakistan concluded an agreement to extend the road to the Chinese border. In 1967, it was decided to transform the road into an all weather and dual carriage highway over the Karakoram. Approximately 10 thousand Chinese and 15 thousand Pakistani engineers and army jawans completed the road in 1969. The highway was finally inaugurated in June 1978. It has 80 bridges, 300 Pakistani and 160 Chinese lost their lives.

'The highway starts with Havelian, 90 km north of Islamabad and propels itself through Abbottabad, Mansehra, Thakot, Chilas, Gilgit,

Hunza Valley and crosses Karakoram range through 16000 ft. Khunjerab pass into Chinese province of Xinjiang.'[16] Similarly, 'Gilgit is a central point for routes from North-West Route via Dorah Pass through Chitral as well as via Darkot Pass through Yasin, both are dominated by Gilgit. Gilgit is also strategically located to dominate Hunza Valley to the east, with Irshad, Wakhjar Kilik and Mintaka passes.'[17] The new alignment of Karokaram Highway has given up Mintaka pass, which was closer to Russian border, and it is now via Khunjerab Pass which is closer to and strengthens Aksai Chin–Tibet road and both are now interconnected, a considerable strategic significance.

At Urumqui, capital of Xinjiang in a square outside the Kaderia Hotel trucks bound for Pakistan 3000 km away assemble. The container includes assortment of items and textiles. Approx dozen such lorries leave everyday. The first major halt after four days of travel and 1400 km is at legendary Kashgar, the cultural capital of Uighurs who form the largest group of people in Xinjiang province. From Kashgar, trucks head for high mountains, which have woven together the civilization of China, South Asia, and Central Asia and Europe. The convoys finally cross Khunjerab Pass and reach 88 km away Tashergan a customs check point where containers are off-loaded from Chinese trucks to Pakistani vehicles. Next halts are at Sust in Hunza Region and Gilgit.

The onward journey from Gilgit is along river Indus passing through picturesque Hazara Valley passing through Abbottabad and Attock and finally Islamabad. The cargo from Urumqui to Pakistani capital takes around 15 days on an average. The land route between Xinjiang and Pakistan has several spin off benefits, which go far beyond trade. The road connecting the two countries is central to the strategic-relationship established between Beijing and Islamabad.[18] Karakoram road has become the important lifeline between Pakistan and China and helping in the economic and social emancipation of hitherto backward region. It is facilitating development of natural resources in the vicinity of highway. The distance between various cities of Xinjiang has been reduced with building of subsidiary tracts linking Tibet–Xinjiang road and Gilgit–Xinjiang road. The Tibet–Xinjiang road through Aksai Chin has also been linked with Karakoram Highway. London-based *Financial Times* highlighted a report with Karakoram Highways as 'China's new trade outlet to Africa and Middle East' in Pak Himalayas via 'modernized ancient silk route'.[19]

Vehicles from Karachi seaport reach China border in about 15–20 days. Exports to China through this route include cotton; cotton textiles and imports are coal, cement, iron, glassware, cutlery, chemicals, silk, etc. 'Mr Abdul Latif Khan, Chief Secretary of Northern Areas (CEO) had told Mr. Yuan Hanmin in May 1998, senior official from Khunjerab Dry port of China's Xinjiang Uighur Autonomous Region that trade volume across the border has arisen from the initial Rs 2,40,000 (US $5500) to about 200 million (US $4.5 million). He expressed satisfaction with the sound development of bilateral economic co-operation between Pakistan and China especially between Xinjiang and Northern Areas.'[20] According to study by the Geneva-based Center for International and Strategic Studies, Chinese nuclear and military equipment including MH missiles for Pak went through Karakoram Highway.[21]

In current strategic jargon, the Karakoram Highway is termed 'A Chinese window' opening towards Southern Asia. China is buying US weapons for Southern Xinjiang region. 'China also supplied weapons to Afghan Mujahideens via this route to keep Soviet troops engaged in 1980s.'[22] The increased trans-border movement has its fallout, as well, which have alarmed central leadership of China and reports had appeared in 1997 of Chinese erecting fencing on the Chinese side of Karakoram border. The Xinjiang Uighur Autonomous Region of China is the only region in China where Muslims are in majority and the religious sentiments are deep rooted. There is large concentration of Muslim Uighurs in southern part of Xinjiang. Xinjiang has been traditionally politically sensitive. It was at the heart of competition for influence among great powers in the past in the last century and beyond, because for the access it provided to India, which was very important to British. Now it is a vital link to oil rich Central Asian republics.

The threat of separatism comes mainly from a section of 70 lakh Uighurs who comprise the largest, single ethnic group in Xinjiang province. The Uighurs population is roughly 38 per cent out of total population of 1.5 crore in Xinjiang. China is settling large number of people in Xinjiang from main land. The race relations between Hans (main land Chinese) and Turkic people of Xinjiang have been marked by distrust and hatred. Young Uighurs would prefer to learn Urdu than Chinese, as it would facilitate trading with Pakistan 'Increased trans-border trade and traffic between Xinjiang and adjoining region of Kazakhstan, Kyrgyzstan and Pakistan (via Karakoram Highway) has resulted in greater interaction between Turkic people which are working to achieve goal of separation of Xinjiang from China.'[23] The activities of stock piling of weapons and arming young recruits have increased after 1990.

Any separatist movement can threat to delink China from Central Asia and large parts of South Asia and Western Tibet. Therefore, 'China can hardly be expected to sit back and accept the unlikely possibility of Xinjiang's emergence as a buffer state between itself and Central Asia in future.'[24] 'China has designated Xinjiang as a gateway for bringing in oil from Central Asia into the country. It has built strategic rail link between Xinjiang's capital Urumqui to Kazakhstan. Border trade with Kyrgyzstan across the Turgurt Pass, which breaches the Tien Shan mountain range, is also being encouraged.'[25]

President Musharraf during his November 3 visit to China pledged to never allow any separatist forces including then 'East Turkistan' terrorist campaigners to use Pakistan territory for anti China activities.[26] In another significant development reported by *Daily Times* (Islamabad), China has asked Pakistan to investigate a list on terrorists operating in Xinjiang to make an independent Eastern Turkistan. The list concerns two militant outfits, Eastern Turkistan Islamic Movement and Eastern Turkistan Liberation Organization which are reported to be connected to Osama Bin Laden and have intensified their activities after 11 September 2001.[27]

Future Prospects

Developing strategic relationship between Pakistan and China began as a counter strategy against India and in that boundary agreement of 1963, which facilitated Karakoram Highway, was first gigantic step and 'opened a new era in the tangled international relationship in Asia'. Pakistan has taken a lead to build bridges with five Central Asian Republics of Turkmenistan, Kazakhstan, Uzbekistan, Kyrgyzstan and Tajikistan, which hold oil reserves of an estimated 20 million barrels and seven trillion, cubic of meters of gas. 'Pakistan is again trying to sell its geo-strategic location in Western Himalayas by becoming 'Gateway' for Western businessmen to Central Asia.

Islamabad considers Karakoram Road as the true gateway to People's Republic of China and into Central Asia—the path of new Silk Road. And there lies the future and strategic salvation of

Pakistan'.[28] Islamabad sees that road system in the Western approaches to the silk road and thus people's Republic of China will enable it to enjoy economic and political benefits beyond it hoped to gain on the basis of country's economic scientific and population posture. Karakoram Highway and Gwadar will enable Pakistan to provide access to China and Central Asia to warm waters of Indian Ocean. This is key to its future and fortunes.

NOTES

1. Rohit Vohra, 'An Old Route Across Karakoram Mountains—From Khabalu in Baltistan to Yarkand', *USI Journal*, New Delhi, July–Sept 1987, quoting Surveyor General Brigadier E.A. Tendy.
2. Sachdev Vohra, 'The Karakoram-Hindukush: Routes from China and Russia', *USI Journal*, New Delhi, July–September 1992, p. 339.
3. K. Warikoo and Dawa Norbu, *Ethnicity and Politics in Central Asia*, New Delhi: Allied Publishers, 1992, p. 165.
4. Alastair Lamb, *Sino–Indian Border in Ladakh*, Canberra, 1972, p. 50.
5. K. Warikoo and Dawa Norbu, *Ethnicity and Politics in Central Asia*, New Delhi: Konark, 1992, p. 171.
6. Jasjit Singh, ed., *Pak Occupied Kashmir under the Jackboot*, New Delhi: Knowledge World, 1995.
7. Wajahat Hassan Chairman Gilgit Baltistan Thinkers Forum During his Visit to India', *The Hindu*, New Delhi, 10 September 1999.
8. Dorothy Woodman, *Himalayan Frontier*, London, 1969, p. 306, quoted from 'Ayub Khan's Foreign Affairs' 1960.
9. Ibid., p 306.
10. Alastair Lamb, *Sino-Indian Border in Ladakh*, Canberra, 1972, p. 74.
11. Dorothy Woodman, *Himalayan Frontier*, London, 1969, p. 307.
12. *White Paper VI*, MEA, Beijing to Indian Embassy in Beijing, 31 May 1962, p. 99.
13. K. Mason, *The Exploration of the Shaksgam Valley and Aghil Ranges*, (1926) quoted by Sachdev Vohra, 'The Karakoram Hindkush: Routes from China and Russia', *USI Journal*, New Delhi, July–September, 1992, p. 340.
14. Dorothy Woodman, p. 309, Quoting, *The Times*, London, 21 June 1965.
15. Khalid Zullfiqar, *Pakistan in the Pamir Knot-Geo-Strategic Imperatives*, Lahore, 1987.
16. Dorothy Woodman, p. 310.
17. Sachdev Vohra, 'Routes and Tracks from Central Asia to Kashmir', *USI Journal*, New Delhi, July–September 1989, p. 295.

18. Atul Aneja, 'Sino–Pak Trade Flourishes Through the High Ranges', *The Hindu*, 13 September 1999.
19. *Dawn*, Karachi, 30 April 1971 quoting *Financial Times*, London.
20. *China Daily*, Hong Kong Edition, dated 4 May 1998.
21. *The Hindu*, New Delhi, 10 December 1999.
22. K. Warikoo, *Ethnic-Religious Resurgence in Xinjiang*, op. cit., p. 16.
23. Ibid, p. 17.
24. Siwei Mao, 'China and Kashmir Issue' *Strategic Analysis*, March 1995, p. 1579.
25. Atul Aneja, 'China Working Towards Consolidation of Xinjiang', *The Hindu*, 10 September 2000.
26. *The Hindu*, New Delhi, 5 November 2003.
27. 'China Gives Pak Terrorist, Seeks Action', *Asian Age*, New Delhi, 18 January 2004.
28. Yossef Bodansky, 'Pakistan, Kashmir & Trans Asian Axis' Freeman Centre for Strategic Studies, Houston Texas, Research Paper, 1995, p. 9.

CHAPTER 18

The Xinjiang Factor

ABANTI BHATTACHARYA

This is commonplace that the military and strategic contents of Sino–Pakistan partnership remain predominant in defining the essential nature of China–Pakistan relations. However, in the post-9/11 world, the element of terrorism has injected a new flavour in determining their equations. It is in this new context that turmoil ridden Muslim majority Xinjiang province of China has come to be a critical barometer and the best litmus test for the so-called time-tested Sino–Pakistan relations. China's major security concern today emanates not from across its borders but from within its own internal dynamics of domestic discontent. In the wake of post-9/11 and American war on terrorism, China has also became far more vocal about its terrorist threats and Uighur insurgents in Xinjiang Autonomous Region have since been branded as terrorists posing a security threat to China's territorial integrity. China suspects the hand of Islamic fundamentalists from across its borders and blames their continued aiding and fomenting of these elements of separatism in Xinjiang. It is this context that makes the Xinjiang factor critical to the future of China–Pakistan relations.

To find answers to some of these questions, this chapter attempts to first understand Xinjiang's historical position looking particularly into the various influences that shaped the distinct historical evolution. Following this it will highlights political and economic importance of Xinjiang, which informed China's concerns in the region and explained the region's significance to China's national and security interests. Then it will try and situates Xinjiang in Sino–Pakistan relation and highlight how Xinjiang has since come to be a diplomatic, political, economic and military tool in circumscribing the nature of Sino–Pakistan relations. This chapter argues that the Xinjiang factor instead of driving a wedge between China and Pakistan, has acted as a diplomatic and economic tool in sustaining the traditional ties between the two countries.

Genesis and Evolution

Xinjiang has emerged as a factor in Sino–Pakistan relations due to its complex historical evolution. This complexity is informed due to its peculiar geo-strategic location on the crossroads of several cultures and histories—Central Asia, China and Russia.

> The record of the Chinese in Central Asia is by no means continuous; in fact, their effective control has been estimated at only about 425 out of about 2000 years, divided into a number of periods, of which the present Chinese rule in the province of Sinkiang is the fifth major period.[1]

The above lines from Owen Lattimore's classic study of the Central Asian region of China provide a perspective on the current Xinjiang problem. A rather intermittent rule by the Chinese accentuated the Uighur identity that historically enjoyed a separate political identity and existence. The Xinjiang region was the homeland of various branches of Turkic tribes such as the Uighur, Kazak, Kyrgyz, Tatars and Uzbeks. The Uighurs comprised the single largest ethnic group in Xinjiang based on common Turkic ancestry and rich Uighur language. Located on the famous Silk Road network, Uighurs played an important role in cultural exchanges between the East and the West, and developed a unique culture and civilization of their own.[2] The Uighurs set-up the kingdom of Karakhoja or Qocho in present-day Turpan (southern Xinjiang) that lasted for four centuries (AD 850–1250).[3]

Clearly, in history the Uighurs were known as a Central Asian power and Uighur scholar Makhmud Qashqari has documented this in the eleventh-century encyclopedia *Diwan Lughatit Turk*.[4] The existence of such a rich civilization of the Uighurs gave them a distinct political identity. Following Max Weber's notion on ethnicity, even after the Uighur kingdom disintegrated the belief in common ethnicity persisted implying that the pulls of political identity are deep.[5] Historically, Xinjiang was never an integral part of China. Due to its peculiar geopolitical location and kinship-based oasis societies it became vulnerable to the influence of several powers from time to time—Greeks, Bactrians, Huns, Kushans, Mongols, Chinese and Russians.[6]

In the nineteenth century Xinjiang region turned into a bone of contention among the British, the Russian and the Chinese. The Chinese incorporation of Xinjiang took place only in the nineteenth century and consequently the region's history was hijacked and projected distortedly as a Chinese frontier province since the Han period. Though from the eighth century onwards the Chinese incursion to this region took place with their building of the Great Wall in order to ward off the nomadic invasion from China's west, it was never brought under the direct Chinese rule. Apart from resisting the nomadic incursions, the Chinese imperial state took added interest in the region having discovered the profitable trade route through Central Asia. The interest in horses induced the Chinese to latch on to the Silk Route trade and, therefore, the western region of China turned important both strategically and economically. But China had no control over Xinjiang until the last Qing dynasty, which were non-Han, non-Chinese rulers.

Geographically, Xinjiang region consisted of two distinct parts separated from one another by the Tien Shan range. North of the Tien Shan laid the Jungaria belt and on the south of the Tien Shan laid Kashgaria. Geography, in fact, rendered these two regions to follow two different historical courses.[7] Jungaria was more associated with the Mongols in the east and on the eve of Manchu conquests, it was inhabited mainly by the western Mongols. Kashgaria was, on the other hand, predominantly populated by Turkic people, mainly the Uighurs and their cultural and political affiliations were more closely tied to the Central Asian region.

However, both these regions remained outside the Chinese empire till the Ming dynasty. It was only during the last Qing dynasty that the Manchu rulers could no longer ignore the evolution of Central Asian politics and officially incorporated the region into Qing territory[8] and gave the new name *Xinjiang* that meant new border or new territory. It is this peculiar history of the region, which as Doak Barnett wrote, 'more associated with Central Asia than with China'[9] was the source of the problem for China and this problem persisted throughout the later period of Chinese direct rule. Xinjiang from time to time witnessed series of rebellion against the Chinese state. There were in fact, two attempts at establishment of brief statehood; one from 1931 to 1934 called the Turkish-Islamic Republic of East Turkestan and another from 1944 to 1949 called the East Turkestan Republic.

In 1955, the People's Republic of China (PRC) gave Xinjiang the formal status of 'autonomous region' and assigned the Uighurs a minority nationality status. However, the region remained turbulent given its strong Islamic and Turkic identity and historical aspirations for establishing an independent state. After 1960 in the face of growing Sino–Soviet confrontation, large garrisons of the People's Liberation Army (PLA) were deployed in the region and the border with the Soviet Union was closed. With the Soviet invasion of Afghanistan a fresh security problem erupted in China's backyard. China believed that Soviet invasion of Afghanistan was part of Russia's historical southward expansionism.[10] An article in *Renmin Ribao* on Soviet occupation of Afghanistan said,

> The Chinese people cannot but pay close attention to this and hope that the Soviet Union will take concrete actions to remove this threat in order to enhance the improvement of Sino–Soviet relations. It has been the Chinese people's consistent and unshakable stand to resolutely support the Afghan people in their just struggle and to demand that the Soviet Union withdraw its troops unconditionally so that the Afghan people can solve their own problems without external interference and restore the country's independence, sovereignty, and nonaligned status.[11]

Xinjiang was then turned into a base for Chinese operations in Afghanistan and Xinjiang emerged as the main element in China's Afghanistan policy.[12] John K. Cooley wrote that in the 1980s a Sino–Pakistani–American axis based on mutual aid to the anti-Soviet holy warriors in Afghanistan was 'well and truly launched'.[13] This development, in fact, took a logical conclusion in the aftermath of China's rapprochement with the United States in the 1970s. But the emergence of this grand coalition against the Soviets was kept secret. In fact, the US accomplished the construction of two important US electronic intelligence posts in Xinjiang.[14]

China trained and dispatched Uighurs to fight against the Russians in Afghanistan, fearing that the old silk route along the Karakoram highway could come under Moscow's domination if the Soviet Union was not dislodged from Kabul.[15] Lilian Craig Harris mentions that Beijing's supply of weapons to the Mujahideens was estimated at US $400 million between 1980–5.[16] In opposing Soviet Union, Pakistan emerged as the frontline state both for the US and China. China showered Pakistan with military hardware at subsidized prices.[17] It has been reported that in 1981 Mujahideens used Chinese mortars and rocket launchers. In subsequent years more sophisticated Chinese weapons were used such as 82 mm recoilless rifles and anti-tank cannons.[18]

However, China's own strategy of supporting the Mujahideens in Afghanistan boomeranged when the Uighurs trained by the Taliban unleashed militant activities in Xinjiang. There is considerable debate among scholars whether Karakoram highway was used for sending war material from China to Pakistan and thence to the hands of the *jihadis*. However, there is consensus on the fact that militant Islam did enter through this route to Xinjiang to revolt against the Chinese state during the final years of the twentieth century.[19] In fact, the opening of the Karakoram Highway coincided with the 1978 war in Afghanistan.

From the 1990s onwards, there was a perceptible shift in the nature of the Uighur movement in Xinjiang. Although, the separatist tendency in Xinjiang is part of the region's history, the element of violence in the movement does not predate 1986 when Uighurs from the southern Kashgar area of the province first joined the anti-communist *jihad* in Afghanistan.[20] In 1989, limited quantities of weapons were first smuggled into western Xinjiang.[21] This showed the foreign involvement in the region bringing in guns, money and ideas to the hitherto silent protest of the Uighurs. With this, the activities of ethnic separatism within China entered a new active stage.[22] A more potent factor that strengthened the separatist activities in Xinjiang was the collapse of the Soviet Union that unleashed new hope among the Muslim populace of the region in gaining freedom similiar to their brethren in adjacent Central Asia. The decade of 1990s, thus, witnessed a series of unrests and disturbances throughout Xinjiang; the most significant of them were the 1990 Baren uprising and the 1996 Yinning uprising.

Erkin Elptekin, a German-based spokesman of the Uighurs, claimed that 45 uprisings took place in Xinjiang during April and May 1996 alone, in which 65,000 people participated and over 1,000 killed.[23] In June 1997, Chinese officials in Xinjiang seized tons of explosives, arms and ammunitions from the Uighur separatists. The Uighur Chairman of the province revealed that the 'Party of Allah', a fundamentalist Muslim party with about 1600 members, was in existence.[24] The *Public Opinion Trend* (*POT*) reports that Chinese officials were of the opinion that these militants were trained in Afghanistan and used Afghan heroin to fund their activities.

From 1990s onwards the Chinese government gave up their hitherto secretive position about Xinjiang's unrest and more and more reports came out urging Xinjiang's stability. *Xinjiang Ribao* from Urumqui stated, 'unity among the nationalities is a prerequisite and guarantor for success in all fields of work in Xinjiang. Religion is closely related to stability and unity in the autonomous region. The major danger in Xinjiang comes from domestic and international separatists of nationalities who usually stir up separatism and disturbances under the banners of nationalities and religion.'[25]

After the 9/11 terrorist attacks on the US a new dimension of terrorism to the Xinjiang region could be discerned. The Chinese government sought to link the crackdown on the Uighur movement as part of the global war on terrorism. The Chinese State Council in January 2002 issued a detailed report *East Turkestan' Terrorist Forces Cannot Get Away With Impunity* that detailed the extent of terrorist activities since 1990. The report listed more than 200 incidents that resulted in 162 deaths and 440 injuries, and included bombings, assassinations, armed assaults on government organizations, establishing training bases and plotting riots.[26] The Report also mentioned the names of about nine internal terrorist organizations operating in Xinjiang. Given this volatile situation in Xinjiang, question arises why Xinjiang is important to China.

Importance of Xinjiang to China

The importance of Xinjiang is both due to security and economic factors. First of all, Xinjiang, bordering eight nations, constitutes a security problem for China. Particularly, Xinjiang's nine million Muslims deeply influenced by nine hundred years of Islamic culture, pose a threat to its integration with China. This threat is exacerbated with the demise of the former USSR and the establishment of Central Asian states which has triggered off an awakening among the Muslims of Xinjiang about their Islamic and pan-Islamic identity. In fact, a large number of Uighurs, as many as 500,000, are spread across the Central Asian states.[27] Further, increased trans-border trade and traffic between Xinjiang and Kazakhstan, Kyrgyzstan, Afghanistan and Pakistan has resulted in greater interaction among the Xinjiang people and their counterparts in Central Asia, Turkey, Pakistan and Saudi Arabia. The 9/11 factor has further enhanced China's security threat to its 'western backyard'. This geopolitical location of Xinjiang coupled with its turbulent history presents Xinjiang, as a politically volatile region of China. Therefore, Xinjiang's ancient role as a buffer zone to China proper is still a significant determinant in China's security policy.

Economically, Xinjiang is a region of vast mineral resources and agricultural potential. Xinjiang contains approximately two-fifths of China's oil, 40 per cent of its wool and is a rich source of gold and copper. The region is also rich in resources like thermal power and natural gas. Its reserves of mineral resources, namely beryllium, copper and mica, are the highest in China.[28] The oil reserves in Xinjiang are believed to be thrice as much as those in Saudi Arabia and exploiting them could make China independent of imports from the Middle East. Xinhua news reports that forty oil and gas field have been discovered in the region with proven reserves of two billion tons of oil and 160 billion cubic meters of natural gas.[29] Xinjiang is also China's largest producer of cotton. The yield per hectare is also the highest in China. It is now the country's biggest production base for food industry-use tomatoes and Chinese wolfberries. The fabled silk route passes through the resource-rich region of Xinjiang and China is all set out to revitalize the ancient economic land route to contemporary modernization drive. Xinjiang is therefore, an important strategic region to China both in terms of its geopolitical location and its resource potential.

Further, the Chinese government has started investing heavily in the Xinjiang region with the launching of the Western Development Project in 1999. The programme comprises several key projects including building the Qinghai–Tibet railway; transmitting electricity and natural gas from western areas to the east; protecting natural forests, grasslands and rivers; promoting elementary, occupational and higher education; fostering specialized farming; setting up mining bases; building tourist facilities with local characteristics; improving infrastructure in large cities; and expanding the wide-band digital transmission network.[30] China has already injected 300bn Yuan in 2002 in this western development. China's western ambitions do not end here. At present, there are five new airports under construction. The roads in use total 57,700 km in length.[31] Apart from developing the Chinese West, China eyes the Central Asian region to secure its energy supplies. Its new ventures include building of oil pipelines from Kazakhstan to China. The new gas and oil pipeline to be built by China and Kazakhstan, starts from the Caspian Sea continental shelf, via Atasu, to Alataw Pass in Xinjiang of China with a total length of 3,088 km.[32] All these ventures, in effect, indicate that China has enormous economic stake in the region and this has considerably raised China's security interests in Xinjiang.

Factoring Xinjiang in Sino–Pakistan Relations

XINJIANG AS A POLITICAL FACTOR

Having analysed the geopolitical importance of Xinjiang and its resource potential, the Xinjiang factor renders a significant twist to Sino–Pakistan relations in numerous ways. Politically, Xinjiang acquires importance in Sino–Pakistan relation due to the Kashmir factor. China acquired 5180 sq km of land, which was ceded by Pakistan under the Border Agreement of 1963. Also it has occupied some 33,000 sq km of India's province of Jammu and Kashmir. Occupation of the part of Kashmir has become an important reason for China's interest in Kashmir.[33] This has 'created both geographical and Islamic connection linking China's internal security to that of India and Pakistan'.[34]

It may be pointed out that China may not want the solution of Kashmir issue for then it would have to settle the fate of 5180 sq km of land, which is subject to the final resolution of Kashmir dispute according to the Border Agreement of 1963. Therefore, China adopted the Pakistan card to keep India embroiled in a conflict and in effect, drain and divert India's economic resources. In other words, by keeping India–Pakistan hostility alive China sought to maintain a balance of power in the South Asian region. Pakistan, on the other hand, gained valuable diplomatic support from China in its wars with India and also received much-needed military support in terms of nuclear technology, conventional weaponry and missile systems. Therefore, India emerged as 'essential glue' in the Beijing–Islamabad entente.[35] The edifice of this relationship that was shaped by the Cold War politics remained relevant even in the post-Cold War era.

XINJIANG AS AN IDEOLOGICAL FACTOR

The Cold War politics created much insecurity for China as it faced a hostile US while its alliance with the Soviet Union tied the PRC in an uneasy dependence.[36] In fact, it was China's insecurity in the western border, particularly its uneasy relationship with the Soviet Union that prompted China to look toward Pakistan. In the 1950s, having emerged from the throes of semi-colonialism and civil war, China's primary concern was maintenance of its territorial integrity and sovereignty. China soon realized that the boundary and the territorial question plagued its relationship with most of its neighbours.

It may be recalled that even after the communist takeover in 1949, Xinjiang remained for some time under the influence of the Soviet Union.[37] In Xinjiang the Soviets had a satellite army and joint Russian-Chinese state enterprises. Also there were three large Soviet Consulates in Kuldja, Urumqui and Kashgar. This made China's position in Xinjiang very vulnerable. The region already had the history of Soviet aid to the ethnic disturbances. The short-lived East Turkestan Republic (1944–9) in fact, came about with Soviet assistance. More importantly, Soviet and Chinese nuclear testing sites, as well as, nuclear bases, faced each other across the Xinjiang-Kazakhstan border.[38] Therefore, the security of Xinjiang was uppermost priority in the Chinese calculus of security.

On the external front, China's relation with the other superpower—the US was already soured in the aftermath of the latter's support to Guomindang regime in Taiwan. The Korean War generated further bitterness between China and the US. Therefore, the China–Pakistan partnership should be traced to these vulnerabilities posing China's security in the Cold War era. Zhang Chengli wrote, 'Pakistan served as channel for China to link it up with the outside world when China was blocked and contained by certain superpowers in 1950s and 1960s.'[39] It is important to note here that though initially there were suspicions on both sides due to the contrasting ideology, culture and ethnicity, essentially there was no major conflict of interests between China and Pakistan.

In the 1960s in the aftermath of the Sino–Indian War and growing differences with both USA and USSR, China feared political encirclement. China came to realize the importance of Pakistan as the only reliable partner in South Asia region.[40] Pakistan also realized that in spite of its military pacts with the US, the US displayed pro-India bias during the 1962 India–China War.[41] Pakistan's (often) dis-enchantment with the US made it realize the need for its partnership with China. Already the Bandung Conference of 1955 ushered in Sino–Pakistan understanding where in Pakistan's Prime Minister Mohammad Ali Bogra had assured that in spite of its membership in SEATO and CENTO, it was not against China. This mutual under-standing laid the ground for subsequent Sino–Pakistan entente cordiale.

While China demanded nothing from Pakistan, Pakistan achieved two significant gains: One, support on Kashmir and two, substantial military aid from China at a time when military aid from America virtually dried up.[42] In fact, in 1963 both the countries signed three major agreements: the Trade Agreement, the Civil Aviation Agreement and the Border Agreement. It was the Border Agreement which was highly significant for it facilitated Beijing to legitimize Pakistan's claim that Kashmir was not an integral part of India.[43] The agreement defined China's posture over Kashmir dispute and China called for the right of self-determination in Kashmir.

In the post-Cold War era the scenario changed substantially. China was freed from its triangular politics with the US and the USSR. It adopted essentially an independent foreign policy of peace. It could concentrate on economic development. This development-oriented foreign policy got added rationale in the post-Cold War era when peace and stability and 'Good-Neighbourly' relationships acquired prominence in the face of US dominated world order. This bore direct impact on China's relationship with India when China and India both proceeded for rapprochement

The Pakistan card was however, a contradiction in Sino–Indian relationship in the post-Cold War era. But China diffused this contradiction by adopting the *Policy of Readjustment* that called for maintaining a balance of power in South Asia. In fact, it was only Pakistan that could constrain and balance India in any serious way.[44] Thus, constraining India still remained a fundamental geopolitical consideration in Sino–Pakistan relationship. Nevertheless, the significant policy shift in Chinese foreign policy toward South Asia in general and India in particular was evident in China's position on Kashmir. It no longer pledged to support Pakistan on Kashmir dispute. In June 1980 Deng Xiaoping first stated that the Kashmir issue was a bilateral dispute between India and Pakistan that should be solved peacefully.[45]

However, from time to time China also added that Kashmir dispute to be solved in accord with 'relevant UN resolutions'. John W. Garver has indicated in a table form how China's position on Kashmir evolved from pro-Pakistan to a somewhat neutral position. China's stand during the Kargil war of 1999 completed the shift. In fact, Kargil also proved that China emerged as a crucial balancer in India–Pakistan relations.[46] As Chinese scholar Wang Jisi said, China plays a fine balance between India and Pakistan so that Pakistan is checked from being too reckless a power and India is not encouraged to the extent that it poses a challenge to China. But a deeper analysis would show that more than balancing, it was China's domestic compulsions that brought a change in China's Kashmir policy.

The demand for self-determination in Xinjiang made the Chinese leadership totally averse to the idea of self-determination. China feared that sticking to 'self-determination' idea as a resolution to the Kashmir dispute could have led to similar demands in Xinjiang or for that matter Tibet or Taiwan. The same logic also led China reject third-party interference in the Kashmir issue. China was apprehensive that in case it advocates third-party mediation in Kashmir, it could be setting a trap for itself by offering the West an analogical case to apply the same principles in Xinjiang, Tibet or Taiwan.[47] Xinjiang, thus, emerged as a precipitator in China's policy of readjustment.

XINJIANG AS A DIPLOMATIC FACTOR

Xinjiang emerged as a factor in China–Pakistan war against terrorism. In the post-9/11 scenario when terrorism emerged as a global threat, Pakistan and Afghanistan came to focus as epicentres of religious extremism and global terrorism. China believed Pakistan had a hand in Xinjiang's unrest. China did express its dismay over Pakistan's role in Xinjiang. However, China avoided turning this into a major issue in its relationship with Islamabad. In fact, China used Pakistan's help to control the Uighur separatists operating from Pakistan and Afghanistan. In fact, much before the 9/11 episode China asked Pakistan to pressurize the Taliban to stop the export of militancy to Xinjiang.[48] China realized its prime need of establishing peace in Afghanistan and it knew very well that such a peace required the cooperation of Pakistan, as Islamabad would not abandon its interests in Afghanistan unless, it had China to guarantee them.[49]

Terrorism in Xinjiang though did not create a wedge between Pakistan and China, there is certainly no pro-Pakistan tilt in China's foreign policy. In fact, what China wants today is to *manage* Pakistan. Professor Dingli Shen says that in the post-9/11 world order China and India jointly need to maintain peace in the South Asian continent.[50] This implies that China today views the support of India as crucial to its security in the north-west border. Therefore, Xinjiang has added a new dimension in Sino–Pakistan relations. It has strengthened Sino–Pakistan relation but not at the cost of Sino-Indian relations. In fact, more than the fact of Pakistan as a strategic counterweight against

India, it is the survival of Pakistan that is crucial to China's security in its north-west border.[51]

Given Beijing's belief that limiting the Taliban's effectiveness was the key way to minimize Islamic militancy in the Xinjiang region and that only Islamabad had influence to realize this objective, Pakistan emerged as a frontline state in China's war against terrorism. There were reports that General Musharraf visited Afghanistan in January 2000 to pressurize the Taliban regime to stop exporting terrorism in Xinjiang.[52] In December 2001, on a visit to China, Musharraf met the Imam of the Grand Mosque of Xian and said, 'Islam is a religion of peace and we don't believe in any violence and therefore, you, being a part of China, have to be very patriotic and for the good of China, all Muslims in China should work for the good of China.'[53]

In November 2003, China and Pakistan pledged to fight the '3 evils'—extremism, ethnic separatism and terrorism. Musharraf said, 'Pakistan stands resolutely against terrorism and will never allow anti-China forces—including ethnic Uighurs seeking independence for the north-western Xinjiang region—to use Pakistan as a base'.[54] Jamaat-i-Islami and jihadi organizations say that China has always supported Muslims on a number of issues, including those of Kashmir and Palestine. Therefore, all the jihadi and religious organizations should help China in solving its internal problems. These organizations have decided to help China in internal issues, including that of Xinjiang.[55] These steps greatly assuaged China's fears on Xinjiang and buttressed China's friendship with Pakistan.

Second, US presence in the border of Xinjiang has further impacted on Sino–Pakistan relations. The US has established an air base in Kyrgyzstan, only 200 miles from the Chinese border. It has entered into a series of military and economic alliances with Uzbekistan. Also China is highly uncomfortable with the extended US military presence in four Pakistani bases to execute the Afghan campaign.[56] Due to the US presence, China needs to strengthen its relation with Pakistan in order to counter the US influence in the region. Therefore, W. P. S. Sidhu and Jing-dong Yuan write, 'Although it can be argued that Beijing's support of Musharraf lies in a desire to maintain stability against rising Islamic fundamentalism, it is likely that China is more interested in keeping Islamabad under its influence at a time of encroaching US presence without encouraging its ally to embark on reckless adventures.'[57]

Moreover, Pakistan is important to China to secure its energy sources. Beijing needs to ensure its continued access to Central Asia's oil resources. China has deficits in its energy requirements and it is looking westward to supply the shortfall. It is investing heavily in Kazakhstan's oilfields and planning a pipeline into Xinjiang. The US presence in Central Asia is a serious blow to China's interest. To China therefore, primary interest would be to maintain peace in Afghanistan so that the influence of the US is reduced from the Central Asian region.

Third, Xinjiang is an important diplomatic factor in China's relations with Pakistan for it provides a gateway to the Islamic world for China.[58] China has made considerable efforts to maintain good relations with the Islamic World. This is because China has dual interests toward the Islamic world. One, China has interests in securing oil from Central Asia and Middle East. Second, it needs to control Muslim separatism in China. Beijing's closest friend in the Muslim world is Pakistan; therefore, it provides the Muslim dominated autonomous region of Xinjiang a significant link in building China's ties with the Middle East and Central Asia. As John W. Garver wrote, 'there is far more to the Pakistan–China relationship than common hostility toward India. There are distinct Muslim and Middle Eastern aspects to that relationship.'[59]

Karachi was the first airport outside the Soviet bloc opened to China in the early 1960s. It served as a transit point for Chinese air traffic to the Middle East, Africa and Europe. China also benefited by having Pakistan host Chinese Muslims making the Haj to Mecca. James Piscatori in his monograph wrote, 'The regime in Beijing believes that the use of Islam can help to legitimate it in the eyes of the Arab regimes.'[60] China is also eyeing for membership in Organization of the Islamic Conference (OIC). Partnership with Pakistan would facilitate China to enter it. Pakistan actively participates in the activities and programmes of the OIC. The OIC continues to extend valuable support to Pakistan on the issues of vital importance and the fight against international terrorism.[61] In October 2001, the then Foreign Minister Tang Jiaxuan told Foreign Minister Sheikh Ahmad of Qatar, concurrently chair of the OIC, that China desired to improve 'con-sultation and cooperation with Islamic countries in fighting terrorism'. He also explained that China recognized 'Islamic countries are also the victims of terrorism' and stressed that China 'opposed . . . associating terrorism with any religion, nationality, or religion'.[62]

XINJIANG AS AN ECONOMIC FACTOR

The importance of Xinjiang is heightened due to China's energy needs and here Pakistan is vitally important by providing access to and bases in the Persian Gulf.[63] China's Gross Domestic Product rose at a rate of 9.1 per cent in 2003, and surpassed Japan to become the world's second-largest oil importer after the United States. Domestic energy production is rapidly expanding, but China continues to rely on imported fuel to keep its economy growing. China is vulnerable to a blockade of sea-lanes either in the Malacca Straits or in the South and East China Seas.[64] Therefore, an underlying strategy in China's energy security policy is to seek domestic energy resources and pipelines from adjacent Asian countries to reduce its vulnerability.[65] Pakistan is also eying for Central Asian oil. But Pakistan faces two distinct disadvantages. One, Pakistan does not share a land border with any of the Central Asian states. Two, all its major routes to Central Asia pass through Afghanistan which is politically unstable. Therefore, to Pakistan Xinjiang emerges as a possible window for future energy supplies from the Central Asian region.

China's programme of Western Development in Xinjiang is yet another cementing factor in Sino–Pakistan relations. Hu Shisheng, a researcher from a Beijing Think-tank, read a paper entitled 'The Great Western Development and Sino–Pakistan Relations' in a seminar organized by the Institute of Strategic Studies to mark the 50th anniversary of Sino–Pakistan relations. In it he highlighted the prospects of Western Development project as furthering ties between China and Pakistan.[66] This assumption is based on various factors. Geographically, the Xinjiang region is close to Pakistan's northern borders. The southern part of Xinjiang is only 2500 km from Karachi and Gwadar. Therefore, as the industrial and economic production of Xinjiang expands, there would be substantial economies in using Pakistan's ports by China.[67] Second, Pakistan and Xinjiang that have distinction of enjoying land route communication link through Khunjerab Pass have bright prospects to further develop their economic ties.[68]

In June 2004 China signed an agreement on transit transportation that will allow Pakistani vehicles to go to Kyrgyzstan and Kazakhstan through Xinjiang.[69] Also the Preferential Trade Agreement (PTA) that came into effect in January 2004 would help strengthen Sino–Pak bilateral economic trade through the Karakoram Highway. The PTA would open greater opportunities for Pakistani products to access the Chinese market. According to the agreement, China allows tariff concessions to Pakistan on more than 800 items, whereas the Pakistani side will give concessions to China on about 200 items.[70] Third, Xinjiang has huge oil and gas deposits close to the border of Pakistan. It is also rich in other minerals and has built up a sizeable industrial base. Therefore, there is enormous scope to develop economic and trade relations between China and Pakistan. In this context, China has offered new trade opportunities to Pakistani businessmen to undertake joint ventures in its western region, Xinjiang.[71]

The *Dawn* reports that, Xinjiang a Muslim majority province, may emerge as a hub of Sino–Pak economic cooperation, with new opening establishing joint ventures in the fields of agriculture, light industry, foodstuff, textile, medicines and petrochemical industry. Also a report from Beijing mentions that Pakistan and China being close allies and neighbours enjoy much better prospects to set-up a free trade zone to promote their export to Central Asia and Middle East.[72] It can be argued that widening cooperation in the economic field would in turn reinforce the political ties between the two countries. In fact, the deeper economic relations would provide incentive for combating terrorism and promote peace and security in the region. Therefore, Xinjiang's economic prospects and the Great Western Development project present the scope for strengthening bilateral ties between the two countries.

XINJIANG AS A MILITARY FACTOR

From the military angle, Xinjiang has proximity to Pakistan's Gwadar port. China pledged to build a seaport at Gwadar at an estimated cost of US$1 billion. Gwadar would provide an outlet to exports coming by road from Central Asian Republics and China.[73] Gwadar, strategically located at the mouth of the Persian Gulf, could serve as a naval base for Chinese submarines.[74] This would also enable China to exercise considerable control over the Indian Navy, which is supposed to be seeking to develop a blue water force projection capability.[75] Economically, for the industries located in Xinjiang, Gwadar will be the shortest and most viable access to warm waters via the Karakoram Highway.[76] For Pakistan the need for Gwadar port is first, to reduce dependence on the Karachi port which handles 80 per cent of Pakistan's international trade; second, to find an alternate outlet for external trade if Karachi is blockaded by the Indian Navy in the event of war; third, for an outlet for the trade of the Central Asian Republics. Xinjiang, thus, provides the outlet for promoting Sino–Pakistan relation on the Gwadar project.

9/11 and Remapping of Xinjiang Factor

In the post-9/11 era Xinjiang has diluted the strength of Sino–Pakistan relations from mainly two aspects: Central Asia and India.[77] In both the aspects it is the element of terrorism that caused the dilution and redefinition of China–Pakistan relations.

China's interaction with Central Asian countries got a major fillip only in the post-Cold War era and particularly with the emergence of the Commonwealth of Independent States in Central Asia. The emergence of Central Asian States was both an opportunity and a threat for China. While the presence of Central Asian countries reduced the Russian threat to China, it enhanced security threats to China's western border, particularly to its politically volatile Xinjiang region. Three of the five Central Asian Republics created after the collapse of the Soviet Union—Kazakhstan, Kyrgyzstan and Tajikistan—share borders with Xinjiang.

Lillian Craig Harris has argued that China's West Asia focus has shifted from the Middle East to Central Asia after the fall of the Soviet Union.[78] These Central Asian bordering countries are also the countries which share common ethnicity and Islamic religion with Xinjiang. Their presence on the western border of Xinjiang reopened the issue of China's right to sovereignty over Xinjiang as Craig Harris pointed out. China in the post-Cold War era took effective policy decisions to turn Central Asia into a land of opportunity. In tandem with China's broader policy of 'Good Neighbouring Policy' and peaceful peripheral environment, China reached crucial agreements on the border issue with Russia, Kazakhstan, Tajikistan and Kyrgyzstan. This dialogue on issues of border and territory led to the foundation of 'Shanghai Five'.

By June 2001, with the inclusion of Uzbekistan, Shanghai Five got the new name of Shanghai Cooperation Organization (SCO) for the purpose of 'cracking down on terrorism, separatism and extremism' and maintain 'regional security'.[79] Bishkek also emerged as a new counter-terrorism centre before the 9/11 attacks. This significantly points to the place of Xinjiang in Chinese foreign policy where in

China looked toward Central Asia than to Pakistan for effective solution of ethnic separatism in Xinjiang. (China did not term separatism in Xinjiang as terrorism before 9/11.) Post-9/11 era significantly enhanced China's security in Xinjiang and here Central Asia plays a far greater role in counter-terrorism mechanism than Pakistan. In fact, Pakistan's clandestine support to the Uighurs was the primary element in redefining China's Asia policy.

This new focus of China on Central Asia is also buttressed by its deepening economic relation. For instance Kazakhstan is China's biggest trade partner in Central Asia. Bilateral trade volume registered 2 billion US dollars in 2002, ten times more than that with China's second largest trade partner in Central Asia, Kyrgyzstan.[80] In contrast China's trade relation with Pakistan is rather minimal. In fact, as late as this year China has proposed Pakistan to explore its trade and economic relations in Xinjiang.[81] Chinese official point out that Pakistan's trade with Xinjiang is being carried out at low-business level. Moreover, huge quantities of Chinese goods travel to Pakistan through illegal means.[82]

Further, looking at the significance of Karakoram Highway one may question how far it really served as a bridge between the two countries. Though it is the only land route connecting the two, it has been underutilized. The climate of the region does not allow full utilization of the highway that remains closed for nearly seven to nine months due to heavy snowfall and landslides. Second, unlike the ancient Silk Route that promoted cultural exchanges between the east and the west, Karakoram does not have such cultural importance to Pakistan. Pakistan is not interested in Sinic culture.[83] Third, in the late 1980s and early 1990s this highway became an exporter of Islamic militancy in the Xinjiang region. That explained China's need to close down the highway for some time. Though in recent years China called for upgradation of the highway, it is going slow with its policy for fears of Taliban inroads and terrorism through this highway.

Similarly with regard to China's relation with India, Xinjiang has precipitated the rapprochement between China–India relations. It has been earlier indicated in the chapter and need not be elaborated again, how China's domestic compulsions on Xinjiang's growing separatism brought a change in China's Kashmir policy and China has increasingly emphasized a balanced foreign policy approach towards India and Pakistan. This has obvious impact on China's traditional relationship with Pakistan.

Conclusion

If the issue of terrorism in Xinjiang did not create a wedge between China–Pakistan relations, it is because there are diplomatic, political, economic and military considerations about Xinjiang that bring China and Pakistan together. Xinjiang is the bridge between China and Pakistan. Xinjiang demonstrates that Pakistan remains a vital factor in China's internal stability. Pakistan could play a key factor in minimizing Islamic militancy in China. Second, despite Pakistan getting branded as a 'virtual terrorist state', it offers China excellent opportunities for diplomatic shopping, particularly in the Islamic world. China would, therefore, gladly overlook minor irritants in favour of long standing friendship with Pakistan. Third, due to the increased US presence in China's north-west border, the importance of Pakistan is heightened in China's foreign policy. Therefore, China is unlikely to reduce its support to Pakistan lest the latter 'is forced to align itself completely with Washington without any reference to Beijing's views'.[84] Fourth, Xinjiang became a factor in China's 'policy of readjustment'. It facilitated China to adopt a neutral position on Kashmir and created an environment for further improvement in Sino–Indian relations in the coming decades. Finally, Xinjiang also provides the enormous scope to develop trade relations between the two countries. In particular, the Western Development Project has opened new vistas for Pakistan's economy to grow.

Looking at the future of Xinjiang in Sino–Pakistan relations, it may be argued that Xinjiang will remain a linchpin in Sino–Pakistan relations. The statements of Pakistan leaders indicate that Pakistan will remain a guarantor of peace and stability in Xinjiang. As a logical corollary to this, China is unlikely to give up its special relationship with Pakistan. Nevertheless, owing to Xinjiang, China's relationship with India has shown signs of improvement. This has diluted Pakistan's strategy of counterbalancing China against India and brought about a perceptible shift in China's policy toward South Asia. In fact, in the post-9/11-world era, China is talking about India and China's joint efforts to maintain peace in the South Asian subcontinent. It basically implies that China aims at India–China's joint effort to 'manage' Pakistan. Post-9/11 also heightened the importance of Xinjiang in China–Central Asian relations and this has in some ways caused redefinition of China's ties with Pakistan.

The Shanghai Cooperation Organization (SCO), a multilateral

forum comprising the six nations—Russia, China and four Central Asian countries—address the common concerns of fighting radical Islamic fundamentalism and thwart separatism in the region. SCO has enabled to not only secure energy supplies to this region but also sought to act as a bulwark against the US interference in the region. Thus, Xinjiang today has more relevance in China's Central Asian politics than with regard to Pakistan. There are signs of emerging redefinition of China's relationship with Pakistan where Xinjiang is less a factor in their bilateral ties. More so, Xinjiang being more tilted toward Central Asian politics since historical times, its relevance to Pakistan gains significance in the context of Afghanistan factor. Nevertheless, the importance of Xinjiang would heighten with the deepening of economic relations between China and Pakistan. In future, the economic aspect of Sino–Pak trade, which was far subservient to military aspect, could become an important factor, courtesy Xinjiang.

NOTES

1. Owen Lattimore, *Inner Asian Frontiers of China*, Oxford: Oxford University Press, 1940, 1988. The four other periods that Lattimore talks about is first, the Han dynasty (206 BC–AD 220); second, the Tang dynasty (AD 618–906); third, the Mongol Yuan dynasty (1260-1368) and fourth, the Manchu Qing dynasty (1644–1911).
2. See Linda Benson, 'Introduction: Text and Turpan: The Historiography of Place in Inner Asia', *Central Asian Survey*, vol. 18, no. 3, 1999, pp. 277–9.
3. For a detailed account of the early Uighur history see, Svat Soucek, *A History of Inner Asia*, Cambridge: Cambridge University Press, 2000. Chapter 4 of the book describes in detail the Uighur civilization and cultural achievements under the Qocho.
4. Dolkun Kamberi, 'A Survey of Uighur documents from Turpan and their importance for Asian and Central Eurasian history', *Central Asian Survey*, vol. 18, no. 3, 1999, p. 283.
5. See John Rex and Montserrat Guibernau, eds., *The Ethnicity Reader: Nationalism, Multiculturalism and Migration*, Cambridge: Polity Press, 1997, p. 3.
6. For a lucid account of the history of the region in ancient, medieval and modern times see, Ahmed Rashid, *Jihad: The Rise of Militant Islam in Central Asia*, Lahore: Vanguard Books, 2002.

7. Gavin Hambly, et al., *Central Asia*, New York: Dell Publishing Co., 1969, p. 294.
8. Ibid.
9. Doak Barnett, *China's Far West: Four Decades of Change*, Boulder: Westview Press, 1993, p. 343.
10. Andrew J. Nathan and Robert S. Ross, *The Great Wall and the Empty Fortress: China's Search for Security*, New York: Norton, 1997, p. 49.
11. Commentator's article, 'Troop Withdrawal Is the Key to a Political Settlement of the Afghan Problem', *Renmin Ribao*, 26 December 1985 p.2, in the United States Department of Commerce, Foreign Broadcast Information Service: *China Daily Report* (hereafter *FBIS-CHI*) *FBIS-CHI*-85-248.
12. Quoted in Ross Terrill, *The New Chinese Empire*, New York: Basic Books, 2003, p. 234.
13. John K. Cooley, *Unholy Wars: Afghanistan, America and International Terrorism*, London: Pluto Press, 2000, p. 67.
14. Ibid.
15. Rahul Bedi, 'Will the USA Find a Foothold in Kashmir?', *Jane's Intelligence Review*, February 2002, p. 34.
16. Quoted in Ahmad Lutfi, 'Blowback: China and the Afghan Arabs', *Issues and Studies*, vol. 37, no. 1, January/February, 2001, p. 205.
17. Ahmad Faruqui, 'China card could yet trump Musharraf', *Asia Times* online, http://www.atimes.com/ind-pak/DE25Df02.html , 25 May 2002.
18. Cited in Mohammed Ahsen Chaudhri, 'Strategic and Military Dimensions in Pakistan-China Relations', *Pakistan Horizon*, vol. 39, no. 4, Fourth Quarter 1986, p. 27.
19. John K. Cooley, p. 72.
20. 'The Chinese Connection', *POT Afghanistan*, vol. XXV, no. 2, 3 February 2000, p. 17.
21. Anthony Davis, 'Xinjiang Learns to Live With Resurgent Islam,' *Jane's Intelligence Review*, vol. 8, no. 9, September 1996, p. 419.
22. 'Commentary on Ethnic Separatism, Religious Activities', *Xinjiang Ribao*, 7 May 1996, *FBIS-CHI-96-100*, 22 May 1996, p. 75.
23. 'The Chinese Connection', *POT (Afghanistan)*, vol. XXV, no. 1, 6 January 2000, p. 17.
24. *POT Afghanistan*, 6 January 2000, p. 17.
25. Editorial on Stability, *Xinjiang Ribao*, 11 October 1990, *FBIS-CHI-90-216*, 7 November 1990, p. 50.
26. 'East Turkistan Terrorist Forces Cannot Get Away With Impunity', *Beijing Review*, vol. 45, no. 5, 31 January 2002, pp. 14–23.
27. 'Uighur militants committee for Eastern Turkistan', http://www.fas.org/irp/world/para/uighur.htm , 5 December 1999.
28. 'Xinjiang Bridges China, Central Asia', *Xinhua*, http://english.

peopledaily.com.cn/200310/02/eng20031002_125317.shtml , 3 October 2003.

29. 'PRC Xinjiang Records Economic Growth', *Xinhua*, 22 March 1996, *FBIS-CHI-96-060*, 27 March 1996.
30. 'China Eyes Breakthroughs in Western Development', *Xinhua* 8 August 2001, http://www.hartford-hwp.com/archives/55/263.html , 12 August 2001.
31. 'Xinjiang Bridges China, Central Asia', *Xinhua*, 3 October 2003, http://english.peopledaily.com.cn/200310/02/eng20031002_125317.shtml , 9 October 2003.
32. 'Ancient Silk Road Becomes Oil Route', http://news3.xinhuanet.com/english/2004-05/19/content_1477138.htm , 19 April 2004.
33. Swaran Singh, *China-South Asia: Issues, Equations, Policies*, New Delhi: Lancers Book, 2003.
34. Ibid., p. 72.
35. See, ibid.
36. See Michael Yahuda, *The International Politics of the Asia-Pacific, 1945–95*, London: Routledge, 1996, p. 193.
37. S.C.M. Paine, *Imperial Rivals: China, Russia and their Disputed Frontier*, New York: M.E. Sharpe, 1996.
38. Peter Ferdinand, 'Xinjiang: Relations with China and Abroad', in David S.G. Goodman and Gerald Segal, eds, *China Deconstructs: Politics, Trade and Regionalism*, London: Routledge, 1994, p. 276.
39. Zhang Chengli, 'China-Pakistan Relations and Situation in South Asia', *Pakistan Horizon*, vol. 49, no. 3, July 1996, p. 11.
40. Samina Yasmeen, 'China and Pakistan in a Changing World', in K. Santhanam and Srikanth Kondapalli, eds, *Asian Security and China 2000–10*, New Delhi: Shipra Publications, 2004, p. 310.
41. See Niloufer Mahdi, 'Sino-Pakistan Relations: Historical Background', *Pakistan Horizon*, vol. 39, no. 4, 1986, pp. 60–8.
42. M. B. Naqvi, 'Pakistan's Place in Chinese Calculations', *Pakistan Horizon*, vol. 39, no. 4, 1986, p. 31.
43. See Anwar Hussain Syed, *China and Pakistan: Diplomacy of an Entente Cordiale*, London: Oxford University Press, 1974, p. 480. Also see, Devin T. Hagerty, 'China and Pakistan: Strains in the Relationship', *Current History*, vol. 10, no. 656, September 2002, p. 286.
44. John W. Garver, *Protracted Contest: Sino-Indian Rwalry in the Twentieth Century*, New Delhi: Oxford University Press, 2001, p. 217.
45. Ibid., p. 228.
46. See Table on p. 239, ibid.
47. Bhartendu Kumar Singh and Satyajit Mohanty, 'Contexualizing Kargil within China's security paradigm', in Maj. Gen. Ashok Krishna and P.R. Chari, eds., *Kargil: The Tables Turned*, New Delhi: Manohar, 2001, p. 229.

48. 'Comments: Angry China Forces Musharraf To Rein Taliban', *POT* (*Afghanistan*), vol. XXV, no. 16 January 2000, pp. 37–9.
49. Opinion of a European Union diplomat, p. 38, ibid.
50. Dingli Shen gave this view during a Round Table discussion in Jawaharlal Nehru University, School of International Studies, New Delhi, on 23 February 2004.
51. Waheguru Pal Singh Sidhu and Jing-dong Yuan, *China and India: Cooperation or Conflict?* New Delhi: India Research Press, 2003, p. 66.
52. 'Comments: China's Concern Over Taliban Activities', *POT* (*Afghanistan*), 6 January 2000, p. 40.
53. Quoted from Ahmad Faruqui, 'China Card Could yet Trump Musharraf', *Asia Times* online, http://www.atimes.com/ind-pak/DE25Df02.html , 25 May 2002.
54. Jiang Zhuqing, 'Sino-Pakistan Pledge to Fight the 3 Evils', *China Daily*, 4 November 2003.
55. Muzammil Suhrawardi, 'Internal Disturbances in China: Religious Organizations Assure Cooperation', *FBIS-CHI-2001-0515*, Rawalpindi Nawa-i-Waqt, Tuesday, 15 May 2001.
56. Rahul Bedi, 'Will the USA find a foothold in Kashmir?', p. 34.
57. Waheguru Pal Singh Sidhu and Jing-dong Yuan, *China And India: Cooperation or Conflict?*, p. 66.
58. C. Raja Mohan, 'India and Sino-Pak Ties', *The Hindu*, Delhi, 6 November, 2003. Also see, Andrew Scobell, 'Chinese Foreign Policy and the War on Terror', http://www.asiamedia.ucla.edu/article.asp?parentid=7205, 30 January 2004.
59. John W. Garver, *Protracted Contest*, p. 189.
60. James P. Piscatori, 'Asian Islam: International Linkages and their Impact on International Relations', in John L. Esposito, ed., *Islam in Asia*, New York: Oxford University Press, 1887, p. 247.
61. 'Foreign Policy of Pakistan', http://www.embassyofpakistan.org/pb1.php
62. Andrew Scobell, 'Chinese Foreign Policy and the War on Terror' http://www.asiamedia.ucla.edu/article.asp?parentid=7205, 30 January 2004.
63. Mohan Malik, 'India's Dragon Delusions', http://www.atimes.com/atimes/South_Asia/EJ17Df03.html
64. Philip Andrews-Speed, Xuanli Liao and Roland Dannreuther, 'The Strategic Implications of China's Energy Needs,' *Adelphi Paper*, 346, Oxford University Press, 2002, p. 25.
65. Ibid.
66. Quoted in Maqbool Ahmad Bhatty, http://www.dawn.com/2001/08/06/op.htm
67. Ibid.

68. 'China Offers Joint Trade Ventures to Pakistan', *The Dawn*, 26 May 2002.
69. 'Pakistan–China Border to Reopen Next Week', 2 June 2004, http://www.dailytimes.com.pk/default.asp?page=story_1-5-2004_pg7_34
70. Ibid.
71. Ibid.
72. 'Sri Lanka, China for FTA, Good Trade ties with Pakistan', http://pakistantimes.net/2004/02/27/business1.htm, 27 February 2004.
73. Ahmad Faruqui, 'Op-ed: The Impact of 9/11 on Sino-Pakistan Ties', http://www.dailytimes.com.pk/default.asp?page=story_18-6-2002_pg3_2, 16 June 2004.
74. See Ibid.
75. Ahmad Faruqui, 'China Card Yet Trump Musharraf', http://www.atimes. com/ind-pak/DE25Df02.html, 25 May 2002.
76. 'Brief on Gwader Deep water Port Project', Board of Investment, Government of Pakistan, http://www.pakboi.gov.pk/html/Gawadar_Waterport_project.html, No date.
77. View shared by Madhu Bhalla, Associate Professor, Centre for East Asian Studies, Jawaharlal Nehru University, New Delhi.
78. See Lillian Craig Harris, 'Xinjiang, Central Asia and the Implications for China's Policy in the Islamic World', *The China Quarterly*, no. 133, March 1993.
79. Xia Yishan, 'Significance of the SCO Foreign Ministers Meeting', *Beijing Review*, vol. 45, no. 5, 31 January 2002.
80. 'Hu Jintao Seeks to Cement Cooperation Between China, Kazakhstan', CCTV.COM, http://www.cctv.com/english/news/TVNews/NoonNews/20030603/100603.html, 3 June 2003.
81. 'China-Pakistan Joint Declaration', Foreign Ministry of People's Republic of China, http://www.fmprc.gov.cn/eng/zxxx/t40148.htm, 4 November 2003.
82. 'Xinjiang acts as a bridge to promote China, Pakistan trade', *Pakistan Times* Business and Commerce Desk, http://www.pakistantimes.net/2004/03/03/business2.htmlbid., 3 March 2004.
83. Based on discussion with Professor P. Stobdon, Director, Centre for Strategic and Regional Studies, Jammu University, Jammu.
84. Samina Yasmeen, *China and Pakistan in a Changing World*, op.cit., p. 318.

Bibliography

PRIMARY SOURCES

Central Intelligence Agency, *Unclassified Report to Congress on the Acquisition of Technology Relating to Weapons of Mass Destruction and Advanced Conventional Munitions*, 1 January through 30 June 2003, at http://www.cia.gov/cia/reports/721_reports/jan_jun2003.htm#1

Department of Policy Planning, Ministry of Foreign Affairs, *China's Foreign Relations*, 2003 edition, Beijing: World Affairs Press, 2003.

DeSutter, Paula A., Assistant Secretary for Verification and Compliance, Testimony Before the U.S.-China Commission, Washington, D.C. 24 July 2003, US Department of State, available at http://www.state.gov/t/vc/rls/rm/24518.htm

From Surprise to Reckoning: The Kargil Review Committee Report, New Delhi: Sage Publications, 2000.

Full text of white paper on China's non-proliferation policy and measures, http://www1.chinadaily.com.cn/en/doc/2003-12/03/content_287062.htm

Hearing of the Senate Foreign Relations Committee on Proliferation of Chinese Missiles; Gary Milhollin, Director; Wisconsin Project on Nuclear Arms Control; 11 June 1998.

Horner, Daniel, 'Past Transgressions and Current Concerns: Is Nuclear Cooperation with China in the National Interest?', *Congressional Research Service Briefing*, 24 October 1997.

'Joint Statement by Chinese Premier Chou En-lai [Zhou Enlai] and Pakistan Prime Minister Suhrawardy' 24 December 1956 in *China Today*, 1957, vol. 1, no. 1, reprinted in G.V. Ambedkar and V.D. Divekar, eds., *Documents on China's Relations with South and South-East Asia (1949–62)*, Bombay: Allied Publishers, 1964.

Kan, Shirley, 'Chinese Missile and Nuclear Proliferation: Issues for Congress', *Congressional Research Service Issue Brief*, Congressional Research Service, 5 May 1992.

Ministry of Science and Technology, *China Science and Technology Indicators*, Beijing: Science and Technology Literature Publishing, 1998.

National Bureau of Statistics, *China Statistical Yearbook on Science and Technology*, Beijing: China Statistics Press, annual series.

National Bureau of Statistics, National Development and Reform Commission and Ministry of Science and Technology, *China Statistics Yearbook on High Technology Industry*, Beijing: China Statistics Press, 2003.

Office of the Secretary of Defense, *Proliferation: Threat and Response*, November 1997 *Pakistan 1988: An Official Handbook*, Ministry of Information and Broadcasting, Government of Pakistan, 1989.

Statement by Gordon Oehler, Former Special Assistant to the Director, CIA and Director DCI's Nonproliferation Center; Hearing of the Senate Foreign Relations Committee on Proliferation of Chinese Missiles; Gary Milhollin, Director; Wisconsin Project on Nuclear Arms Control; 11 June 1998.

The Joint Declaration of Pakistan President Pervez Musharraf and People's Republic of China President Hu Jintao, on 5 November 2003 available at http://www.chinadaily.com.cn/en/doc/2003-11/05/content_278489.htm

Unclassified Report to Congress on the Acquisition of Technology Relating to Weapons of Mass Destruction and Advanced Conventional Munitions, 1 January through 30 June 2003 available at http://www.cia.gov/cia/reports/721_reports/jan_jun2003.htm#17

Unclassified Report to Congress on the Acquisition of Technology Relating to Weapons of Mass Destruction and Advanced Conventional Munitions, 1 January through 30 June 2003 available at http://www.cia.gov/cia/reports/721_reports/jan_jun2003.htm#17

US Department of State, *Daily Press Briefing*, 26 August 1996.

Zhongguo Waijiao 2004 [China's Diplomacy, 2004], Beijing: World Knowledge Publications, 2003.

BOOKS

Almond, Gabriel and Sidney Verba, *The Civic Culture: Political Attitudes and Democracy in Five Nations*, Princeton NJ: Princeton University Press, 1963.

Athukorala, Prema-Chindra, ed., *The Economic Development of South Asia Vols. I-III*, Cheltenham: Elgar Reference Collection, 2002.

Bajpai, Shiva Chandra, *The Northern Frontiers of India*, Bombay: Allied Publishers, 1971.

Baksh-Rais, Rasul, *China and Pakistan: A Political Analysis of Mutual Relations*, Lahore: Progressive Publishers, 1977.

Banerji, Arun Kumar, and Purusottam Bhattacharya, eds., *Peoples Republic of China at Fifty: Politics, Economy and Foreign Relations*, New Delhi: Lancers Books, 2001.

Baojun, Li, *Dangdai Zhongguo waijiao gailun [Introduction to Contem-*

porary Chinese Foreign Policy], Beijing: Chinese People's University Publication, 1999.

Barnett, Doak A., *The Making of Foreign Policy in China: Structure and Process*, Boulder: Westview Press, 1985.

———, *China's Far West: Four Decades of Change*, Boulder: Westview Press, 1993.

Bartke, Wolfgang, *The Agreements of the People's Republic of China with Foreign Countries 1949–90*, 2nd, revised and enlarged edn., Munchen: K.G. Saur, 1992.

Bhola, P.L., *The Spectrum of South Asian Relations*, Jaipur: RBSA Publishers, 2001.

Bhutto, Zulfiqar Ali, *If I am Assassinated*, New Delhi: Vikas Publishing House, 1979.

Bracken, Paul, *Fire in the East: Asian Military Power and the Second Nuclear Age*, New Delhi: HarperCollins, 1999.

Bucknall, Kevin B., *China and the Open Door*, New York: Allen and Unwin, 1989.

Burke, S.M. and Lawrence Ziring, *Pakistan's Foreign Policy: An Historical Analysis*, Karachi: Oxford University Press, 1990.

Burki, Shahid Javed, *Pakistan: Fifty Years of Nationhood*, Boulder: Westview Press, 1999.

Burki, Shahid Javed and Robert Laporte Jr., *Pakistan's Development Priorities: Choices for the Future*, Oxford: Oxford University Press, 1984.

Carr, E. H., *The Twenty Year Crisis: 1919–39*, London: Macmillan and Co., 15th Reprint, 1984.

Chambers, Michael R., ed., *South Asia in 2020: Future Strategic Balances and Alliances*, Carlisle: Strategic Studies Institute, U.S.Army War College, November 2002.

Chaudhury, Rahul Roy, *India's Maritime Security*, New Delhi: Knowledge World, 2000.

Choudhury, G.W., *China in World Affairs: The Foreign Policy of China Since 1970*, Boulder: Westview Press, 1982.

Cline, Ray S., *World Power Assessment 1977: A Calculus of Strategic Drift*, Boulder: Westview Press, 1977.

Cohen, Mark A., A. Elizabeth Bang and Stephanie J. Mitchell, eds., *Chinese Intellectual Property Law and Practice*, The Hague: Kluwer Law International, 1999.

Cohen, Stephen P., *India: Emerging Power*, New Delhi: Oxford University Press, 2001.

Cohen, Warren I., *America's Response to China: A History of Sino-American Relations*, New York: Columbia University Press, 2000.

Cooley, John K., *Unholy Wars: Afghanistan, America and International Terrorism*, London: Pluto Press, 2000.

Cooper, Charles, ed., *Technology and Innovation in the International Economy*, Cheltenham: Edward Elgar, 1994.

Dalhman, J. and Jean-Eric Aubert, eds., *China and the Knowledge Economy: Seizing the 21st Century*, Washington: World Bank, 2001.

Eikenberry, Karl W., *Explaining and Influencing Chinese Arms Transfers*, McNair Paper 36, Washington: Institute for National Strategic Studies, National Defense University, 1995.

Esposito, John L., ed., *Islam in Asia*, New York: Oxford University Press, 1887.

Fairbank, John K. and Roderick MacFarquhar, eds., *The Cambridge History of China*, Cambridge: Cambridge University Press, 1992.

Feinstein, Charles and Christopher Howe, eds., *Chinese Technology Transfer in the 1990s: Current Experience, Historical Problems and International Perspectives*, Cheltenham: Edward Elgar, 1997.

Fitzgerald, C.P., *The Horizon History of China*, New York: American Heritage Publishing Co., 1969.

Fucheng, Yang, *Contemporary China and Its Foreign Policy*, Beijing: China Foreign Affairs University 2002.

Garver, John W., *Foreign Relations of the People's Republic of China*, Englewood Cliffs: Prentice Hall, 1993.

———, *Protracted Contest: Sino–Indian Rivalry in the Twentieth Century*, New Delhi: Oxford University Press, 2001.

George, Jim, *A Critical (Re) Introduction to International Relations*, London: MacMillan, 1997.

Gill, Bates, 'Chinese Military Modernization and Arms Proliferation in the Asia-Pacific' in Jonathan D. Pollack and Richard H. Yang, eds., *In China's Shadow: Regional Perspectives on Chinese Foreign Policy and Military Development*, Santa Monica: RAND Corporation, 1998.

Goodman, S.G. David and Gerald Segal, eds., *China Deconstructs: Politics, Trade and Regionalism*, London: Routledge, 1994.

———, eds., *China Rising: Nationalism and Interdependence*, London: Routledge, 1997.

Goto, Hioroyuki Odagiri Akira, 'The Japanese System of Innovation: Past, Present, and Future', in Richard R. Nelson, ed., *National Innovation Systems: A Comparative Analysis*, New York: Oxford University Press, 1993.

Hambly, Gavin, et al., *Central Asia*, New York: Dell Publishing Co., 1969.

Harding, Harry, ed., *China's Foreign Relations in the 1980s*, New Haven: Yale University Press, 1984.

Hersh, Seymour M., *The Price of Power: Kissinger in the Nixon White House*, New York: Summit Books, 1983.

Holsti, Ole R. et al., *Unity and Disintegration in International Alliances: Comparative Studies*, New York: John Wiley and Sons, 1973.

Hussain, Syed Anwar, *China and Pakistan: Diplomacy of an Entente Cordiale*, London: Oxford University Press, 1974.

Indian Foreign Policy: Agenda for the 21st Century, vol. 2, New Delhi: Foreign Services Institute with Konark, 1998.

Jacobson, Harold and Michel Oksenberg, *China's Participation and in the IMF, the World Bank and GATT: Towards a Global Economic Order*, Ann Arbor: University of Michigan Press, 1990.

Jalal, Ayesha, *Democracy and Authoritarianism in South Asia*, Cambridge: Cambridge University Press, 1995.

———, *The State of Martial Rule*, Cambridge: Cambridge University Press, 1990.

Jiaxuan, Tang, ed., *Zhongguo Waijiao Cidian* [Dictionary of China's Diplomacy], Beijing: World Knowledge Publications, 2000.

John Rex and Montserrat Guibernau, eds., *The Ethnicity Reader: Nationalism, Multiculturalism and Migration*, Cambridge: Polity Press, 1997.

Kane, Thomas, *Chinese Grand Strategy and Maritime Power*, London: Frank Cass, 2002.

Kapur, Ashok, *Pakistan's Nuclear Development*, New York: Croom Helm, 1987.

———, *Pokhran and Beyond: India's Nuclear Behaviour*, New Delhi: Oxford University Press, 2001.

Karnad, Bharat, ed., *Future Imperilled*, New Delhi: Viking/Penguin, 1994.

Khalid, Zullfiqar, *Pakistan in the Pamir Knot-Geo-strategic Imperatives*, Lahore: Vanguard Books, 1987.

Khan, H. and Zafar Mahmood, eds., *Pakistan and Emerging Global Trading Environment: Challenges and Opportunities*, Lahore: Vanguard Books, 2000.

Khan, M. Ayub, *Friends Not Masters: A Political Autobiography*, London: Oxford University Press, 1967, p.166.

Khan, Sharukh Rafi, ed., *Fifty Years of Pakistan's Economy: Traditional Topics and Contemporary Concerns* , Oxford: Oxford University Press, 1999.

Kim, Samuel S., *China and the World: China's Foreign Relations in the Post-Cold War World*, Boulder: Westview Press, 1994.

Kissinger, Henry, *My White House Years*, New Delhi: Vikas Publishing House, 1979.

Krishna, Maj. Gen. Ashok and P. R. Chari, eds, *Kargil: The Tables Turned*, New Delhi: Manohar, 2001.

Kukreja, Veena, *Military Intervention in Politics: A Case Study of Pakistan* New Delhi: NBO Publishers, 1985.

Kupchan, Charles A., *The End of the American Era*, New York: Alfred A. Knopf, 2003.

Kuppuswamy, C.S., *China–Pakistan–Myanmar: The Triangular Relationship Needs Careful Watch*, SAAG Paper 401, January 2002.

Kux, Dennis, *The United States and Pakistan 1947–2000: Disenchanted Allies*, Baltimore/Washington: Johns Hopkins University Press/ Woodrow Wilson Center Press, 2001.

Lamb, Alastair, *Sino-Indian Border in Ladakh*, Canberra: Australian National University Press, 1973.

Lampton, David, ed., *The Making of Chinese Foreign and Security Policy in the Era of Reform 1978–2000*, Stanford: Stanford University Press, 2001.

Lardy, Nicholas R., *China in the World Economy*, Washington: Institute for International Economics, 1994.

———, *Foreign Trade and Economic Reform in China 1978–90*, Cambridge: Cambridge University Press, 1992.

———, *Integrating China into the Global Economy*, Washington, D.C.: Brookings Institution Press, 2002.

Lattimore, Owen, *Inner Asian Frontiers of China*, Oxford: Oxford University Press, 1940, 1988.

Lavoy, Peter K., Scott D. Sagan and James J. Wirtz, eds., *Planning the Unthinkable*, Ithaca: Cornell University Press, 2000.

Lewis Jr., Stephen R., *Pakistan: Industrialization and Trade Policies*, London: Oxford University Press, 1970.

Liangguang, Lin, Ye Zhengjia and Han Hua, eds., *South Asia–China Dialogue*, Colombo: Marga Institute, 1983.

Looney, Robert E., *The Pakistani Economy: Economic Growth and Structural Reform*, London: Praeger, 1997.

Majumdar, Anindyo J., *Lethal Games: Nuclear Security, Arms Control and Leadership in Indo–Pak Relations*, New Delhi: Lancers Books, 2004.

Mishra, Omprakash and Sucheta Ghosh, eds., *Terrorism and Low Intensity Conflict in South Asian Region*, New Delhi: Manak Publications, 2003.

Monong, Bei, *Zhou Enlai yu xin Zhongguo waijiao* [Zhou Enlai and New China's Diplomacy], Beijing: Chinese Communist Party School Publication, 2002.

Morgan, Patrick M., *Deterrence Now*, Cambridge: Cambridge University Press, 2003.

Morgenthau, Hans J., *Politics Among Nations: The Struggle for Power and Peace*, New Delhi: Kalyani Publishers, 6th edn., Indian Reprint, 1991.

Musa, General Mohammad, *My Version: India Pakistan War 1965*, Lahore: Wajidalis, 1983.

Nathan, Andrew J. and Robert S. Ross, eds., *The Great Wall and the Empty Fortress: China's Search for Security*, New York: W.W. Norton 1998.

Ning, Lu, *The Dynamics of Foreign Policy Decision-Making in China*, Boulder: Westview Press, 1997.

Noer, John H., *Choke Points: Maritime Economic Concerns in South East Asia*, Washington: NDU Press, 1996.

Nulty, Leslie, *The Green Revolution in West Pakistan: Implications for Technological Change*, New York: Praeger, 1972.

Paine, S.C.M., *Imperial Rivals: China, Russia and their Disputed Frontier*, New York: M.E. Sharpe, 1996.

Pakistan Navy Historical Section, *Story of Pakistan Navy, 1947–72*, Islamabad: Elite Publishers, 1991.

Pakistan, *Deadly Arsenals: Tracking Weapons of Mass Destruction*, Washington: Carnegie Endowment for International Peace, 2002.

Pillsbury, Michael, *China Debates the Future Security Environment*, Washington: NDU Press, January 2000.

Pollack, Jonathan D., *China's Potential as a World Power*, Santa Monica: RAND Corporation, 1980.

Potter, William C. and Harlam W. Jencks, eds., *The International Missile Bazaar: The New Suppliers' Network*, Boulder: Westview Press, 1994.

Pumphrey, Carolyn, ed., *The Rise of China in Asia: Security Implications*, Carlisle: Strategic Studies Institute, U.S.Army War College, January 2002.

Qurong, Shen and Bhabani Sengupta, eds., *China Looks at the World*, Delhi: Konark, 1999.

Rai, Hameed A.K., ed., *Readings in Pakistan's Foreign Policy*, vol. I, Lahore: Aziz Publisher, 1980.

Raja Menon, *A Nuclear Strategy for India*, New Delhi: Sage Publications, 2000.

Ramana, M.V. and C. Rammanohar Reddy, eds., *Prisoners of the Nuclear Dream*, New Delhi: Orient Longman, 2003.

Rashid, Ahmed, *Jihad: The Rise of Militant Islam in Central Asia*, New Haven: Yale University Press, 2002.

Rizvi, Hasan-Aksari, *Military, State and Society in Pakistan*, London: Macmillan, 2000.

Rizvi, Mujtaba, *The Frontiers of Pakistan*, Karachi: National Publishing House, 1971.

Robinson, Thomas and David Shambaugh, eds., *Chinese Foreign Policy: Theory and Practice*, New York: Oxford University Press, 1994.

Rosenberg Nathan and C. Frischtak, eds., *International Technology Transfer: Concepts, Measures and Comparisons*, New York: Praeger, 1985.

Rosenberg, Nathan and C. Frischtak, eds., *International Technology Transfer: Concepts, Measures and Comparisons*, New York: Praeger, 1985.

Roy, Denny, *China's Foreign Relations*, Lanham: Rowman & Littlefield, 1998.

Roy-Chaudhury, Rahul, *India's Maritime Security*, New Delhi: Knowledge World, 2000.

Sagan, Scott D. and Kenneth N. Waltz, *The Spread of Nuclear Weapons: A Debate*, New York: W.W. Norton, 1995.

Sahadevan, P., ed., *Conflict and Peacemaking in South Asia*, New Delhi: Lancers Books, 2001.

Samli, A. Coskun, ed., *Technology Transfer: Geographic, Economic, and Technical Dimensions*, Westport: Quorum Books, 1985.

Santhanam, K. and Srikanth Kondapalli, eds., *Asian Security and China 2000–10*, New Delhi: Shipra Publications & IDSA, 2004.

Schulzinger, Robert D., *Henry Kissinger: Doctor of Diplomacy*, New York: Columbia University Press, 1989.

Segal, Adam, *Digital Dragon: High-Technology Enterprises in China*, Ithaca: Cornell University Press, 2003.

Shi, Yizheng, *Chinese Firms and Technology in the Reform Era*, London: Routledge, 1998.

Shirk, Susan, *How China Opened its Door: The Political Success of the PRC's Foreign Trade and Investment Reforms*, Washington: Brookings, Institution Press, 1994.

Siddiqa-Agha, Ayesha, *Pakistan's Arms Procurement and Military Buildup 1979–99*, New York: Palgrave, 2001.

Sidhu, Waheguru Pal Singh and Jing-dong Yuan, *China and India: Cooperation or Conflict?*, New Delhi: India Research Press, 2003.

Singh, Jasjit, ed., *Pak Occupied Kashmir Under the Jackboot*, New Delhi: Knowledge World, 1995.

Singh, Swaran, *China–South Asia: Issues, Equations, Policies*, New Delhi: Lancers Books, 2003.

Soucek, Svat, *A History of Inner Asia*, Cambridge: Cambridge University Press, 2000.

Spector, Leonard et al., *Tracking Nuclear Proliferation*, Carnegie Endowment for International Peace, 1995.

Starr, Harvey, *War Coalitions*, Lexington: DC Heath, 1972.

Swaine, Michael D., *Domestic Change and Foreign Policy*, Santa Monica: RAND Corporation, 1995.

Syed, Anwar Hussain, *China and Pakistan: Diplomacy of an Entente Cordiale*, London: Oxford University Press, 1974.

Taiping, Wang, ed., *Zhonghua renmin gongheguo wiajiaoshi 1970–8* [PRC's Diplomatic History 1970–8], Beijing: World Knowledge Publications, 1999.

Terrill, Ross, *The New Chinese Empire*, New York: Basic Books, 2003.

Timberlake, Edward and William C. Triplett II, *Red Dragon Rising*, Washington: Regnery Publishing, 1999.

Tow, William T., ed., *Chinese Defence Policy*, London: Macmillan, 1984.

Trivedi, Ram Naresh, *Sino-Indian Border Dispute and its Impact on Indo-Pak Relations*, New Delhi: Allied Publishers, 1977.

Tung, Mao Tse, *Selected Works*, vol. IV, Beijing: Foreign Languages Press, 1961.

Vertberger, Yaacov, *The Enduring Entente: Sino-Pakistani Relations, 1960–80*, New York: Praeger, 1982.

Walder, Andrew G., ed., *China's Transitional Economy*, Oxford: Oxford University Press, 1996.

Wang, Hong, *China's Exports Since 1979*, New York: St. Martin's Press, 1994.

Warikoo, K. and Dawa Norbu, *Ethnicity and Politics in Central Asia*, New Delhi: South Asian Publishers, 1992.

Wei, Shang-Jin, Guangzhong James Wen and Huizhong Zhou, *The Globalization of the Chinese Economy*, Cheltenham: Edward Elgar, 2002.

Weiss, Anita, *Culture, Class, and Development in Pakistan: The Emergence of an Industrial Bourgeoisie in Punjab*, Boulder: Westview Press, 1991.

White, Stephen, *Political Culture and Soviet Politics*, London: Macmillan, 1979.

Wolpert, Stanley, *Zulfi Bhutto of Pakistan: His Life and Times*, New York: Oxford University Press, 1993.

Woodman, Dorothy, *Himalayan Frontier: A Political Review of British, Chinese, Indina and Russian Rivalries*, London: Barrie and Rockliff, 1969.

World Military Expenditures and Arms Transfers, 1989, Washington: US Arms Control and Disarmament Agency, 1990.

Yahuda, Michael, *The International Politics of the Asia-Pacific, 1945–95*, London: Routledge, 1996.

Zaidi, S. Akbar, *Issues in Pakistan's Economy*, Oxford: Oxford University Press, 1999.

Zhengwen, Zhang, *Zhongguo yu zhoubian zhuyao guojia guanxi* [*Relations Between China and its Important Neighbours*], Nanjing: Nanjing University Press, 1993.

MONOGRAPHS/OCCASIONAL PAPERS

Anderson, Jennifer, 'The Limits of Sino–Russian Strategic Partnership, *Adelphi Paper*, 315, London: International Institute of Strategic Studies 1997.

Andrews-Speed, Philip, Xuanli Liao and Roland Dannreuther, 'The Strategic Implications of China's Energy Needs', *Adelphi Paper*, 346, Oxford University Press, 2002.

Eikenberry, Karl W., 'Explaining and Influencing Chinese Arms Transfers', *McNair Paper*, # 36, Washington: Institute for National Strategic Studies, National Defense University: 1995.

Fischer, Richard W. and John T. Dori, 'The Strategic Implications of Pakistan's

Nuclear Assistance to Pakistan', Asian Studies Centre of the Heritage Foundation, *Backgrounder*, no. 532, 16 June 1998.

Limaye, Satu P., *India–East Asia Relations: India's Latest Asian Incarnation*, Occasional Analysis, Pacific Forum, CSIS, 3rd Quarter 2000.

Malik, Mohan, 'The China Factor in the India-Pakistan Conflict', *Occasional Paper Series*, Asia–Pacific Center for Security Studies, Honolulu, November 2002.

Malik, Mohan, 'The China Factor in the India-Pakistan Conflict', *Occasional Paper Series*, Honolulu, Asia–Pacific Center for Security Studies, November 2002.

Mathur, Arpita, 'Prospect for Indo–Japan Security and Political Cooperation: An Indian Perspective', Paper presented at the JIIA-IDSA Bilateral Dialogue, Tokyo, 14–15 May 2002.

Singh, Swaran, 'China's Changing National Security Doctrines', *Delhi Paper* 9, New Delhi: Institute for Defence Studies and Analysis, 1999.

——, 'China-India Economic Engagement: Building Mutual Confidence', CSH Occasional Paper 10, March 2005.

Yossef, Bodansky, Research Paper, *Pakistan, Kashmir & Trans Asian Axis*, Houston: Freeman Centre for Strategic Studies, 1995.

CHAPTERS IN BOOKS

Ayoob, Mohammad, 'India as a Factor in Sino–Pakistani Relations' in Hameed A.K. Rai, ed., *Readings in Pakistan's Foreign Policy*, vol. I, Lahore : Aziz Publisher, 1980.

Bajpai, Kanti P., 'Managing a Strategic Triangle: India, China and Pakistan', in P. Sahadevan, eds., *Conflict and Peacemaking in South Asia*, New Delhi: Lancers Books, 2001.

———, 'Strategic Threats and Nuclear Weapons', in M.V. Ramana and C. Rammanohar Reddy, eds., *Prisoners of the Nuclear Dream*, New Delhi: Orient Longman, 2003.

Binkley, Cameron, 'Pakistan Ballistic Missile Development: The Sword of Islam?', in William C. Potter and Harlam W. Jencks, eds., *The International Missile Bazaar: The New Suppliers' Network*, Boulder: Westview Press, 1994.

Chatterjee, Shibashis, '50 Years of China's Pakistan Policy: A Partnership through Evolving World Views', in Arun Kumar Banerji and Purusottam Bhattacharya, eds., *Peoples Republic of China at Fifty: Politics, Economy and Foreign Relations*, New Delhi: Lancers Books, 2001.

Cheung, Tai Ming, 'The Influence of the Gun: China's Central Military Commission and its Relationship with the Military, Party and State Decision-making Systems', in David M. Lampton, ed., *The Making of*

Chinese Foreign and Security Policy in the Era of Reform, Stanford: Stanford University Press, 2001.

Cooper, Charles, 'Relevance of Innovation to Developing Countries', in Charles Cooper, ed., *Technology and Innovation in the International Economy*, Cheltenham: Edward Elgar, 1994.

Dutt, V.P., 'India-China: Promise and Limitation', in *Indian Foreign Policy: Agenda for the 21st Century*, vol. 2 , New Delhi: Foreign Services Institute with Konark, 1998.

Ferdinand, Peter, 'Xinjiang: Relations with China and Abroad', in David S. G. Goodman and Gerald Segal, eds., *China Deconstructs: Politics, Trade and Regionalism*, London: Routledge, 1994.

Garver, John 'The Future of the Sino-Pakistani *Entente Cordiale*', in Michael R. Chambers, ed., *South Asia in 2020: Future Strategic Balances and Alliances*, Carlisle: Strategic Studies Institute, U.S. Army War College, November 2002.

———, 'The Gestalt of Sino–Indian Relationship', in Carolyn Pumphrey, ed., *The Rise of China in Asia: Security Implications*, Carlisle: Strategic Studies Institute, U.S. Army War College, January 2002.

Hao, Qian and Xie Yangan, 'China's Foreign Direct Investment: Inflows and Outflows', in *Foreign Investment, Trade and Economic Cooperation in the Asian and Pacific Region*, Development Papers No. 10, ECOSOC Commission for Asia and the Pacific, UN, 1992.

Hua, Han, 'China and South Asia', in K. Santhanam and Srikanth Kondapalli, eds., *Asian Security and China 2000–10*, New Delhi: Shipra Publications & IDSA, 2004.

Ispahani, M.A.H., 'The Ire of Pakistan', in Hameed A.K. Rai, ed., *Readings in Pakistan's Foreign Policy*, vol. I, Lahore: Aziz Publishers, 1980.

James, Sydney, 'Military Industry', in Gerald Segal and William T. Tow, eds., *Chinese Defence Policy*, Chicago: University of Illinois Press.

Jiali, Ma, 'India's China Policy after the Cold War' in Shen Qurong and Bhabani Sengupta, eds., *China Looks at the World*, Delhi: Konark, 1999.

Karnad, Bharat, 'India's weak Geopolitics and What to do about It?', in Bharat Karnad, ed., *Future Imperilled*, New Delhi: Viking/Penguin, 1994.

Kosenko, Rustan, and A.C. Samli, 'China's Four Modernizations and Technology Transfer', in A. Coskun Samli, ed., *Technology Transfer: Geographic, Economic, and Technical Dimensions*, Westport: Quorum Books, 1985.

Lall, Sanjay, 'Trade in Technology by a Slowly Industrializing Country: India', in Nathan Rosenberg and C. Frischtak, eds., *International Technology Transfer: Concepts, Measures and Comparisons*, New York: Praeger, 1985.

Lardy, Nicholas R., 'The Role of Foreign Trade and Investment in the China's Economic Transformation', in Andrew G. Walder, ed., *China's Transitional Economy*, Oxford: Oxford University Press, 1996.

Levine, Steven I, 'China in Asia: The PRC as a Regional Power', in Harry Harding, ed., *China's Foreign Relations in the 1980s*, New Haven: Yale Univeristy Press, 1984.

Liangguang, Lin, Ye Zhengjia and Han Hua, eds., *Dangdai Zhongguo yu Nanya guojia guanxi* [Contemporary China and South Asian countries relations], Beijing: Social Sciences Reference Publications, 2001.

Lu, Ning, 'The Central Leadership, Supraministry Coordinating Bodies, State Council of Ministers', in David M. Lampton, ed., *The Making of Chinese Foreign and Security Policy in the Era of Reform 1978–2000*, Stanford: Stanford University Press, 2001.

Majumdar, Anindyo J., 'Nuclear Terror', in Omprakash Mishra and Sucheta Ghosh, eds., *Terrorism and Low Intensity Conflict in South Asian Region*, New Delhi: Manak Publications, 2003.

Nabi, Ijaj, 'The Competitiveness of Pakistani Exports', in Sharukh Rafi Khan, ed., *Fifty Years of Pakistan's Economy: Traditional Topics and Contemporary Concerns*, Oxford: Oxford University Press, 1999.

Piscatori, James P., 'Asian Islam: International Linkages and their Impact on International Relations', in John L. Esposito, ed., *Islam in Asia*, New York: Oxford University Press, 1887.

Qiguang, An, 'Zhonghua renmin gongheguo yu Bajisitan guanxi' [PRC and Pakistan Relations], in Tang Jiaxuan, ed., *Zhongguo Waijiao Cidian* [Dictionary of China's Diplomacy], Beijing: World Knowledge Publications, 2000.

Sayeed, Khalid Bin, 'Pakistan's Foreign Policy : An Analysis of Pakistani Fears and Interest', in Hameed A.K. Rai, ed., *Readings in Pakistan's Foreign Policy*, vol. I, Lahore : Aziz Publishers, 1980.

Schelling, Thomas C., 'Who Will Have the Bomb?' in Augustus R. Norton and Martin H. Greenberg, eds., *Studies in Nuclear Terroris,* Boston: G.K. Hall, 1979.

Shambaugh, David, 'Patterns of Interaction in Sino–American Relations', in Thomas W. Robinson and David Shambaugh, eds., *Chinese Foreign Policy: Theory and Practice*, Oxford: Clarendon Press, 1994.

Sidky, Mohammad Habib, 'Chinese World Strategy and South Asia: The China Factor in Indo-Pakistani Relations', in Hameed A.K. Rai, ed., *Readings in Pakistan's Foreign Policy*, vol. I, Lahore: Aziz Publishers, 1980.

Singh, Bhartendu Kumar and Satyajit Mohanty, 'Contexualizing Kargil within China's Security Paradigm', in Major General Ashok Krishna and P.R. Chari, eds., *Kargil: the Tables Turned*, New Delhi: Manohar, 2001.

Singh, Swaran, 'Pakistan Factor in Sino-Indian Ties: From Pokhran to Kargil', in Anindyo J. Majumdar, ed., *Nuclear India into the New Millennium*, New Delhi: Lancers Books, 2000.

———, 'China–India Border Trade: A Tool for Building Mutual Confidence', in Isabelle Saint-Mezard and James K. Chin, eds., *China and India: Political and Strategic Perspectives*, Hong Kong: Center for Asian Studies, 2005.

———, 'Peace Prospects in Sri Lanka: A Theoretical Perspective', in V.R. Raghavan and Karl Fischer, eds., *Conflict Resolution and Peace Building in Sri Lanka*, New Delhi: Tata McGraw-Hill, 2005, pp. 119–34.

———, 'China's Expanding Energy Deficit: Security Implications for Indian Ocean Region', in Dennis Rumbley and Sanjay Chaturvedi, eds., *Energy Security and the Indian Ocean Region*, New Delhi: South Asian Publishers, 2005, pp. 166–88.

———, 'Taiwan Factor in India's Look East Policy', K. Raja Reddy, ed., *India and Southeast Asia*, New Delhi: Century Publications, 2004.

———, 'The Efficacy of Sanctions Regimes: Experience from Asia', in Greg Mills and Elizabeth Sidiropoulos, eds., *New Tools for Reform and Stability: Sanctions, Conditionalities and Conflict Resolution*, Johannesburg: The South African Institute of International Affairs, 2004, pp. 37–62.

———, 'China's South Asia Policy', in Mahavir Singh and Victor Krassilchtchikov, eds., *Eurasian Vision*, New Delhi: Anamika Publishers, 2003.

———, 'China and South Asian Security Complex', in V.T. Patil and Nalini Kant Jha, eds., *India in a Turbulent World: Perspectives in Foreign and Security Policies*, New Delhi: South Asian Publishers, 2003.

———, 'China's Afghan Policy: Limitations and Leverages', in K. Warikoo, ed., *Afghanistan Crisis: Issues and Perspectives*, New Delhi: Bhavana Books, 2003.

———, 'Strategic Triangle and the Ballistic Missile Defence', in Gilles Boquerat and Frederic Grare, eds., *India, China, Russia: Intricacies of an Asian Triangle*, New Delhi: India Research Press, 2003.

Stern, Jessica, 'Terrorist Motivations and Unconventional Weapons', in Peter K. Lavoy, Scott D. Sagan and James J. Wirtz, eds., *Planning the Unthinkable*, Ithaca: Cornell University Press, 2000.

Syed, Anwar, 'China and the Indo–Pakistani war of 1965', in Hameed A.K. Rai, ed., *Readings in Pakistan's Foreign Policy*, vol. I, Lahore: Aziz Publishers, 1980.

Wall, David and Yin Xiangshuo, 'Technology Development and Export Performance: Is China a Frog or a Goose?', in Charles Feinstein and Christopher Howe, eds., *Chinese Technology Transfer in the 1990s: Current Experience, Historical Problems and International Perspectives*, Cheltenham: Edward Elgar, 1997.

Waltz, Kenneth N., 'More May be Better', in Scott D. Sagan and Kenneth N. Waltz, eds., *The Spread of Nuclear Weapons: A Debate*, New York: W.W. Norton, 1995.

Yasmeen, Samina, 'China and Pakistan in a Changing World', in K. Santhanam and Srikanth Kondapalli, eds., *Asian Security and China 2000–10*, New Delhi: Shipra Publications, 2004.

———, 'China and Pakistan in a Changing World', in K. Santhanam and Srikanth Kondapalli, eds., *Asian Security and China 2000–10*, New Delhi: Shipra Publications & IDSA, 2004.

RESEARCH ARTICLES/REPORTS

Abbasi, Abdur Razzaq Khan, 'Thirty Five Years of Pakistan-China Relations', *Strategic Studies*, vol. IX, Summer 1986, no. 4.

Ahmad, Naveed, 'Sino-Pakistan Relations (1971–81)', *Pakistan Horizon*, vol. 34, no. 3, 1981.

Ahrari, Ehsan M., 'China, Pakistan, and The "Taliban Syndrome" ', *Asian Survey*, 40(4), 2000 (July–August).

Akhund, Iqbal, 'National Security and Pakistan's Foreign Policy in a Changing World', *Pakistan Horizon*, vol. 43, no. 2, April 1990.

Al-Rfouh, Faisal O, 'Sino-Indian Relations: From Confrontation to Accommodation (1988–2001)', *China Report*, vol. 39, no. 1, 2003.

Ashok Kapur, 'China and Proliferation: Implications for India', *China Report*, vol. 34, no. 3 and 4, 1998.

Beijing Review, vol. 42, no.12, 22–28 March 1999.

Benson, Linda, 'Introduction: Text and Turpan: The Historiography of Place in Inner Asia', *Central Asian Survey*, vol. 18, no. 3, 1999.

Bernier, Justin, 'China's Strategic Proxies', *Orbis*, Fall 2003.

Bingkui, Cai, 'The Solid Foundation for Sino-Pakistani Friendship: High Level of Mutual Trust', *International Strategic Studies*, Beijing, no. 1, Serial 71, January 2004.

Bitzinger, Richard A., 'Arms to Go: Chinese Arms Sales to the Third World', *International Security*, vol. 17, no. 2, Fall 1992.

Bodansky, Yossef, 'The PRC Surge for the Strait of Malacca and Spratly Confronts India and the US', *Defence & Foreign Affairs Strategic Policy*, Washington, 30 September 1995.

Burnstein, Richard and Ross H. Munro, 'The Coming Conflict with America', *Foreign Affairs*, 76(2), March–April 1997.

Carus, W. Seth, *Ballistic Missiles in Modern Conflict*, New York: Praegar, 1991.

Chakrabarti, R., 'China and Bangladesh', *China Report*, vol. 30, no. 2, 1994.

Chaudhri, Mohammed Ahsen, 'Strategic and Military Dimensions in Pakistan–China Relations', *Pakistan Horizon*, vol. 39, no. 4, 1986.

Chaudhri, Mohammed Ahsen, 'Strategic and Military Dimensions in Pakistan–China Relations', *Pakistan Horizon*, vol. 39, no. 4 (Special Focus on Sino–Pakistan Relations).

Cheema, Pervaiz Iqbal, 'Significance of Pakistan–China Border Agreement of 1963', *Pakistan Horizon*, vol. 39, no. 4.

Chen, Kathy, 'Beijing Admits to Sale of Ring Magnets to Pakistan in Bid to Clear U.S. Tension', *Wall Street Journal*, 15 April 1996.

Cheng Ruisheng, 'China and India: Challenges and Opportunities for the Transformation of Ancient Relations in the Future', *China Report*, 35(1), 2002.

Chengli, Zhang, 'China-Pakistan Relations and Situation in South Asia', *Pakistan Horizon*, vol. 49, no. 3, July 1996.

'China Nuclear Controversy', *Proliferation Brief*, vol. 2, no. 6, Wednesday, 24 March 1999.

Cong, Li, 'Developing Nations in the Surging Tide of Economic Globalization', *Journal of Foreign Affairs*, Beijing, no. 46, December 1997.

Cummings, Bruce, 'The Political Economy of Chinese Foreign Policy', *Modern China*, October 1979.

Daellenbach, Urs S. and Sally J. Davenport, 'Establishing Trust during the Formation of Technology Alliance', *Journal of Technology Transfer*, vol. 29, no. 2, 2004.

David Bachman, 'China in 1994: Marking Time, Making Money,' *Asian Survey*, vol. 35, no. 1, January 1995.

Dolley, Steven, 'China's Record of Proliferation Behaviour', *Issue Brief*, Nuclear Control Institute, 29 September 1997.

Dutta, Sujit', China and Pakistan: End of a Relationship', *China Report*, vol. 30, no. 2, 1994.

Fazal-ur-Rahman, 'Pakistan's Relations with China', *Strategic Studies*, vol. XIX, no. 4, Winter 1998.

Fetter, Steve, 'Ballistic Missiles and Weapons of Mass Destruction', *International Security*, vol. 16, no. 1, Summer 1991.

Frost, Roger, 'Pakistan's Ordnance Factories: A Rising Crescent in Defense Production', ' *Strategic Digest*, New Delhi: IDSA, xix. 10 October 1989.

Garver, John W., 'Sino-Indian Rapprochement and the Sino-Pakistan Entente', *Political Science Quarterly*, New York, vol. 111, no. 2 (1996).

Gendzel, Glen, 'Political Culture: Genealogy of a Concept', *Journal of Interdisciplinary History*, vol. 28, no. 2, Autumn, 1997.

Gertz. Bill, 'US has Detected Metals, Electronics on the Way to Nuclear Weapons Lab', *The Washington Times*, 4 June 1998.

Gilboy, George J., 'The Myth Behind China's Miracle', *Foreign Affairs*, vol. 83, no. 4, July–August 2004.

Hagerty, Devin T., 'China and Pakistan: Strains in the Relationship', *Current History*, vol. 10, no. 656, September 2002.

Harris, Lillian Craig, 'Xinjiang, Central Asia and the Implications for China's Policy in the Islamic World', *The China Quarterly*, no. 133, March 1993.

Harvey, John R., 'Regional Ballistic Missiles and Advanced Strike Aircraft: Comparing Military Effectiveness', *International Security*, vol. 17, no. 2, Fall 1992.

Herrmann, Wilfried A., 'Chinese Military Strategy and its Maritime Aspects', USI Digest, vol. II, no. 3, September 1999–February 2000.

Hibbs, Mark, 'China May Continue D20 Reactor exports to Pakistan After U.S. Certification', *Nuclear Fuel*, 11 August 1997.

Hussain, Mushahid, 'Pakistan Missiles: First Pictures', *Jane's Defense Weekly*, 11 March 1989.

Hyer, Eric, 'China's Arms Merchants: Profits in Command', *China Quarterly*, no. 132, December 1992.

Ikenberry, G. John, 'America's Imperial Ambition', *Foreign Affairs*, 81(5), September–October 2002.

Kamberi, Dolkun, 'A Survey of Uighur Documents from Turpan and their Importance for Asian and Central Eurasian History', *Central Asian Survey*, vol. 18, no. 3, 1999.

Khan, Tanvir Ahmad, 'Pakistan's Regional Policy with Special Reference to India and Afghanistan', *Pakistan Horizon*, vol. 43, no. 4, October 1990.

Kondapalli, Srikanth, 'Chinese Navy in the Indian Ocean', *Journal of Indian Ocean Studies*, vol. 8, nos. 1 and 2 August 2000.

Kraus, Richard, 'China in 2003: From SARS to Spaceships', *Asian Survey*, vol. 44, no. 1, 2004.

Lutfi, Ahmad, 'Blowback: China and the Afghan Arabs', *Issues and Studies*, vol. 37, no. 1, January/February, 2001.

Mahdi, Niloufer, 'Sino-Pakistan Relations: Historical Background', *Pakistan Horizon*, vol. 39, no. 4, 1986.

Mao, Siwei, 'China and Kashmir Issue', *Strategic Analysis*, March 1995.

Mehmood, Tehmina, 'Pakistan's Foreign Policy: Post Cold War Period', *Pakistan Horizon*, 50/3 1997.

Mohammed Uzair, 'Foreign Aid and Indebtedness in Pakistan', *Pakistan Horizon*, vol. 46, no. 1, 1993.

Namboodiri, P.K. S., 'China–Pakistan Nuclear Axis', *Strategic Analyses*, vol. 6, no 7, October 1982.

Nanda, Prakash, 'Strategic Significance of the Andamans', *Indian Defence Review*, vol. 17, no. 3, July–September 2002.

Naqvi, M. B., 'Pakistan's Place in Chinese Calculations', *Pakistan Horizon*, vol. 39, no. 4, 1986.

Nixon, Richard, 'Asia after Vietnam', *Foreign Affairs*, October 1967.

'Pakistan Tests Chinese/North Korean-Based Missiles', *Jane's Intelligence Review*, May 1999.

'Pakistan's Ballistic-Missile Plans', *Foreign Report*, 18 May 1995.

'Programme for Promoting Nuclear Non-proliferation (PPNN)', *News brief*, no. 34, 1996.

Ranganathan, C.V., 'India and China: "Learning to Learn"', *China Report*, 39(4), 2003.

Robert E. Mullins, 'The Dynamics of Chinese Missile Proliferation', *The Pacific Review*, vol. 8, no. 1, 1995.

Ross, Robert S., 'Beijing as a Conservative Power', *Foreign Affairs*, 76(2), March–April 1997.

Ross, Robert, 'China Learns to Compromise: Change in US-China Relations, 1982–4', *The China Quarterly*, December 1991.

Sahgal, Amrish, 'The Plan's Plan', *Indian Defence Review*, vol. 17 (4) October–December 2002 .

Sakhuja, Vijay, 'Maritime Order and Piracy', *Strategic Analysis*, February 2001, p. 2007.

Samina Yasmeen, 'Sino-Pak Relations and the Middle East', *China Report*, 34 (3–4), 1998 (July–December).

'Successful Tour of West Pakistan', *Peking* [*Beijing*] *Review*, no. 15, 8 April 1966.

Shakoor, Farzana, 'The Kargil Crisis: An Analysis', *Pakistan Horizon*, vol. 52, no. 3, July 1999.

Shulong, Chu, '*Zhongguo de guojia liyi, guojia liliang he guojia zhanlue*' [The national interest, national power and national strategy of China], *Zhanlue yu Guanli* [Strategy & Management] (Beijing) no. 4 Issue 35 1999.

Singh, Swaran, 'China-India: Expanding Economic Engagement', *Strategic Analysis*, vol. XXIV, no. 10, January 2000.

———, 'China's Indian Ocean Policy—Indian's Security Options', in *Journal of Indian Ocean Studies*, vol. 13 no. 1 (April 2005).

———, 'China-India: Expanding Economic Engagement', *Strategic Analysis*, New Delhi: IDSA, vol. XXIV, no. 10, January 2001.

———, 'China and India—Building Trust', in *Asian Studies Journal*, Kunming, Yunnan, China, vol. 20, September 2004.

———, 'China's Internal Defence Strategy: Problems and Prospects', *Strategic Analysis*, New Delhi: IDSA, vol. XXIV, no. 12 (March 2001).

———, 'Hu Jintao and the Future of Tibet' in *Defence & Technology*, New Delhi, July 2003.

———,'Myanmar: China's Gateway to the Indian Ocean', *Journal of Indian Ocean Studies*, vol. 3 no. 1, November 1995.

———, 'Sino-Pakistan Defence Cooperation: Joint Ventures and Weapons Procurement', *Peace Initiatives*, vol. V, no. III-VI, May–December, 1999.

———, 'Tibet Factor in the Evolution of Sino-Indian Strategic Ties', *Journal of Peace Studies*, New Delhi, vol. 8, Issue 1, January–February 2001.

Suri, R.B., 'Maritime Dimension of India's Security', *Agni,* vol. I. no. 2, November 1995.

Tasker, Rodney and Bertil Linter on the Kunming-Yangon Highway in *Far Eastern Economic Review* 21 December 2000.

Vohra, Rohit, 'An Old Route Across Karakoram Mountains—From Khabalu in Balistan to Yarkand', *USI Journal,* July–Sept, 1987.

Vohra, Sachdev, 'Routes and Tracks from Central Asia to Kashmir', *USI Journal*, July–September 1989.

———, 'The Karakorum-Hindukush: Routes from China and Russia', *US Journal*, July–September, 1992.

Warikoo, K., 'British Policy Towards Kashmir Claims Across Karakoram', *Strategic Analysis*, December 1993.

Warikoo, K., 'The Shahidulla Affair: British Policy Towards Kashmir's Claims Across the Karakoram', *Strategic Analysis*, December 1993.

Waxman, Dov, 'Terrorism: The War of the Future', *The Fletcher Forum of World Affairs*, 23(2), Fall 1999.

Weeks, Jennifer, 'Sino–US Nuclear Cooperation At a Crossroads', *Arms Control Today*, June/July 1997,

White, Gerard and Gary Milhollin, 'Bombs from Beijing: A Report on China's Nuclear and Missile Exports', Washington: Wisconsin Project on Nuclear Arms Control, May 1991.

Weapons Proliferation and the Military-Industrial Complex of the PRC', *Commentary*, no. 84, 27 August 2003.

Yasmeen, Samina, 'Sino-Pakistan Relations and the Middle East', *China Report*, vol. 34, nos. 3 and 4 1998.

Young-sook, Nam, 'China's Industrial Rise and the Challenges Facing Korea', *East Asian Review*, vol. 16, no. 2, Summer 2004.

Zhiyong, Shao, 'India's Big Power Dream', *Beijing Review*, 12 April 2001.

NEWSPAPER ARTICLES/REPORTS

Ali, Sardar Aseff Ahmad, 'A New Nuclear Doctrine', *The Nation*, Islamabad, 25 June 1998 in *FBIS-TAC-98-176*, 26 June 1998.

Altaf Gauhar, 'Chinese Wisdom for Pakistan's Benefit', *The Dawn* reprinted in *The Asian Age*, 26 July 1999.

Aneja Atul, 'Sino–Pak Trade Flourishes Through the High Ranges', *The Hindu*, 13 September 1999.

Aneja, Atul, 'China working Towards Consolidation of Xinjiang', *The Hindu*, 10 September 2000.

'Airborne Units Conduct Training Exercise in Tibet', *Xinhua* 29 June 1999 in *SWB FE/3577 G/13* 3 July 1999.

Bagchi, Indrani, 'Changing the Nuke Order', *India Today*, 15 March 2004.

Barbara Starr, 'US Links Chinese Ties to Missile Exports', *Jane's Defence Weekly*, 15 October 1994.

Bedi, Rahul, 'Will the USA Find a Foothold in Kashmir?', *Jane's Intelligence Review,* February 2002.

'Boundary Agreement Between Pakistan and China', *New China News Agency,* 2 March 1963.

Chengappa, Raj with Mohammed Shezad, 'Pakistan's Rogue Scientist', *India Today*, 16 February 2004.

Cheung, Tai Ming, 'Nuclear Deal on Han', *Far Eastern Economic Review*, 6 September 1990.

Commentator's article, 'Troop Withdrawal is the Key to a Political Settlement of the Afghan Problem', *Renmin Ribao*, 26 December, 1985, in the United States Department of Commerce, Foreign Broadcast Information Service: China Daily Report *FBIS-CHI*-85-248.

'Chairman Liu Shao-chi [Shaoqi] Visits Pakistan', *Beijing Review*, no. 14, 1 April 1966.

'Chairman Liu Shao-chi's Speech', *Beijing Review,* no. 14, 1 April 1966, p. 5.

'China gives Pak Terrorist, Seeks Action', *Asian Age*, 18 January 2004.

'China Offers Joint Trade Ventures to Pakistan', *The Dawn*, 26 May 2002.

'China Sets-Off the Biggest Solar Plant', *Pakistan Times*, 17 July 2004.

'China to Help Pakistan in Developing Solar Energy', *Pakistan Times*, 26 March 2004.

'China to Manufacture Mobile Sets in Pakistan', *Pakistan Times*, 7 July 2004.

'China, Pakistan Good Neighbours', *Beijing Review,* no. 27, 6 July 1987.

'China-Pakistan Joint Communiqué' 31 March 1966 in *Beijing Review,* no. 15, 8 April.

'China–Pakistan Reaffirm Air-Links', *China Daily*, 10 September 2003.

'Chinese Close to Sale of Second Nuclear Power Plant to Pakistan', *Financial Times*, London, 8 March 2004.

'Chinese Government Leaders Condemn Indian Expansionism and Aggression Against Pakistan', *Beijing Review,* no. 38, 17 September 1965.

'Commentary on Ethnic Separatism, Religious Activities', *Xinjiang Ribao*, 7 May 1996, *FBIS-CHI-96-100*, 22 May 1996.

'Comments: Angry China Forces Musharraf to Rein Taliban', *POT* (*Afghanistan*), vol. XXV, no. 16 January 2000.

'Comments: China's Concern over Taliban Activities', *POT* (*Afghanistan*), 6 January 2000.

Davis, Anthony, 'Xinjiang Learns to Live with Resurgent Islam', *Jane's Intelligence Review*, vol. 8, no. 9 September 1996.

'Dhaka Airstrip Used by CIA for Covert Operation', *Independent,* Dhaka, 23 April 1999.

Editorial, *Xinjiang Ribao*, 11 October 1990, *FBIS-CHI-90-216*, 7 November 1990.

'Foreign Minister says China agrees on need for Kashmir Settlement', *Radio Pakistan*, 12 June 1999 in *SWB FE/3560 A/7* 14 June 1999.

Gertz, Bill, 'Pakistan-China Deal for Missiles Exposed: Nuclear Ambitions Spur US Concern', *The Washington Times*, 7 September 1994.

———, 'US Has Detected Metals, Electronics on the Way to Nuclear Weapons Lab', *The Washington Times*, 4 June 1998.

———, 'US, China Clash over Missile Deal: Beijing Argues Arms Sales to Pakistan Don't Violate Treaty', *Washington Times*, 4 October 1994.

Han, Nianlong, 'Solid Sino-Pak Ties', *Beijing Review*, Bejing, no. 10, 5 March 1984.

Hu, Xiao, 'Pakistan with China in War on Terrorism', *China Daily* 22 December 2001.

Jacobs, Gordon and Tim McCarthy, 'China's Missile Sales—Few Changes for the Future', *Jane's Intelligence Review*, December 1992.

'Jiang Backs Pak Role in Afghan Peace Aims', *China Daily*, 17 January 2002.

'Jiang Pledges to Forge Pakistan "partnership"', *AFP*, 2 December 1996 in *South China Morning Post*, 3 December 1996.

'Joint Communiqué', *Beijing Review*, no. 20, 17 May 1974.

Koch, Andrew, 'Pakistan Persists with Nuclear Disarmament', *Jane's Intelligence Review*, March 1997.

Krishnaswami, Sridhar, 'China Supplied Missile Parts to Pakistan', *The Hindu*, Tuesday, 7 August 2001.

Lennox, Duncan S., ed., *Jane's Strategic Weapon Systems*, Issue 12, Jane' Information Group, 1990.

Malhotra, Jyoti, 'Mother's Milk', *Indian Express*, New Delhi, 22 July 2004.

Malik, J. Mohan, 'Pakistani Connection', Op-ed, *The Pioneer*, 19 December 2001.

Mann, Jim, 'China Said to Sell Pakistan Dangerous New Missiles', *Los Angeles Times*, 4 December 1992.

Matri, Shimaila, 'From China with Love', *Newsline*, October 2003.

Millhollin, Gary and Gerard White, 'A New China Syndrome: Beijing's Atomic Bazaar', *The Washington Post*, 12 May 1991.

Mohan, C. Raja, 'India and Sino–Pak ties', *The Hindu*, Delhi, 6 November, 2003.

'Navy to be Made 3-Dimensional Force: Khaleda', *The Daily Star*, 29 December 2003.

'New Curbs on Missile Technology Transfer: Washington's Move Against Pakistan–China Cooperation', *The Dawn*, 2 September 2001.

Parthasarthy, G., 'China: An Axis to Grind', *The Pioneer*, 28 August 2003.

POT (*Afghanistan*), 6 January 2000.

'Pak Enhancing Nuke Carrying Capacities', *Press Trust of India*, 12 January 2002.

'Pakistan Navy All Set To Go Nuclear', *Pakistan Observer*, 11 June 2001.

'Pakistan Navy Waiting For Government Nod to Go Nuclear', *Indian Express*, 11 June 2001.

'Pakistan President Meets Chinese Military Delegation', *Xinhua* 6 May 1997 in *FBIS-CHI-97-126*, 7 May 1997.

'Pakistan Prime Minister's "Homecoming to Beijing"' *Beijing Review*, no.10, 11–17 March 1991.

'Pakistan Tests Ghauri III Engine', *Jane's Defence Weekly*, 13 October 1999.

'Prime Minister Discusses Relations with China, Kargil Fighting', *Xinhua* 27 June 1999 in *SBB FE/3573 A/5-6*, 29 June 1999.

Radio Pakistan, 30 June 1999 in *SWB FE/3575 A/5* 1 July 1999.

Ramachandran, Sudha, 'India Frets as China and Pakistan Embrace', *Asia Times*, Web Edition, 23 November 2004.

Reddy, B. Muralidhar 'China May Help Build Strategic Pak Port', *The Hindu* 13 June 2001.

'Sino–Pakistani Ties Prosper', *China Daily*, 19 December 2001.

Sanger, David E. and Eric Schmitt, 'Reports Say China is Aiding Pakistan on Missile Project', *New York Times*, 2 July 2000.

Sciolino, Elaine, 'CIA Report Says Chinese Sent Iran Arms Components', *New York Times*, 22 June 1995.

Singh, Swaran, 'India–China Relations: An Overview', in *World Focus*, vol. 26, no. 3, March 2005, pp. 3–6.

———, 'All Eyes on the Trialogue', *Deccan Herald*, Bangalore, 2 June 2005.

———, 'Border talks Reflect the India–China Relationship', *Global Times*, Beijing, 30 July 2004, p. 18.

———, 'China–India Ties', *World Focus*, New Delhi, October–November–December 2003.

———, 'China–India: Beyond the Bilateral', *World Focus*, Delhi, vol. 25, no. 10–11–12, October–November–December 2004, pp. 37–40.

———, 'Hu Jintao and the Future of Tibet', in *Defence & Technology*, New Delhi, July 2003.

———, 'Russia–China–India: A Strategic Triangle?', in *World Focus*, New Delhi, vol. 24, no.1, January 2003, pp. 12–15.

———, 'Shui: Nan ya zhan zheng zhi yuan' (Water: Cause for War in South Asia?), *Huan Qiu Shi Bao* (Global Times), Beijing, 7 July 2005.

———, 'South Asia's Water Wars' (main article), *Deccan Herald*, Bangalore, 6 July 2005.

———, 'Vajpayee's China Visit: An Overview', *World Focus*, New Delhi, vol. 24, no. 7, July 2003.

———, 'Yi ge 'zhan lue de san jiao' dad an sheng' (The Birth of a 'Big Strategic Triangle'), *Dongfeng Zaobao* (Oriental Morning Post), Shanghai.

Smith, R. Jeffrey and Thomas W. Lippman, *Washington Post*, 8 September 1994.

Smith, R. Jeffrey, 'China Linked to Pakistani Missile Plant', *The Washington Post*, 25 August 1996.

Sneider, Daniel, 'China's Arms Bazaar', *Far Eastern Economic Review*, 18 December 1986.

Suhrawardi, Muzammil, 'Internal Disturbances in China: Religious Organizations Assure Cooperation', *FBIS-CHI-2001-0515*, *Rawalpindi Nawa-i-Waqt*, Tuesday, 15 May 2001.

'The Chinese Connection', *POT* (*Afghanistan*), vol. XXV, no. 2, 3 February 2000.

'The Chinese Connection', *POT* (*Afghanistan*), vol. XXV, no. 1, 6 January 2000.

Weiner, Tim, 'Atom Parts Sold to Pakistan by China, US Says', *New York Times*, 8 February 1996.

Weiner, Tim, 'US Suspects China is Giving Pakistan Help with Missiles', *New York Times*, 26 August 1996.

Xia Yishan, 'Significance of the SCO Foreign Ministers Meeting', *Beijing Review*, vol. 45, no. 5, 31 January 2002.

Zhuqing, Jiang, 'Sino–Pakistan Pledge to Fight the 3 Evils', *China Daily*, 4 November 2003.

WEBPAGE ARTICLES/WEBSITES

Altschul, Jessica, 'China & Pakistan Move Closer on "Official" Nuclear Cooperation', The Jewish Institute for National Security Affairs, available at http://www.jinsa.org/articles/view.html?documentid=2309. (Accessed on 31 January 2004).

Amir, Ayaz, 'Canker in an Ideal Relationship', at http://www.dawn.com, 18 May 2001.

Aneja, Atul, 'Pak. Naval Ships in Myanmar on Eve of Musharaff's Visit' *The Hindu* on indiaserver.com http://www.the-hindu.com 1 May 2001.

'Advantage: Hanoi in Intensifying Geo-strategic Game', at homepage of *Stratfor* at http://www.stratfor.com, 14 February 2001.

'Ancient Silk Road becomes oil route', at http://news3.xinhuanet.com/english/2004-05/19/content_1477138.htm, 19 April 2004.

'Australia and India Mend Ties' Global Intelligence Update, at http://www.stratfor.com/SERVICES/giu2000/071100.ASP

Baruah, Amit, 'Navy Taking Part in Multilateral Exercises' 13 June 2001, http://www.the-hindu.com

Bhatty, Maqbool Ahmad, at http://www.dawn.com/2001/08/06/op.htm

Bhaumik, Subir, 'Bangladesh-Pakistan Joint Naval Exercises; Musharraf's visit to Myanmar: India's Encirclement Begins' 28 April 2001, at http://www.tehelka.com/currentaffairs/apr2001.htm

Bhaumik, Subir, www.tehelka.com/currentaffairs/apr2000/ca04280/musharaff.html

Bodansky, Yosef, 'Beijing Surges for the Strait of Malacca' http://www.freeman.org/m_online/bodansky/beijing/html

Burki, Shahid Javed, 'Among the Giants', at http://www.dawn.com, 5 February 2004.

Burki, Shahid Javed, 'Should We Fear China?' at http://www.dawn.com, 30 December 2003.

'Beijing to Help Set Up Another N-power Plant: Musharraf Gets Warm Welcome in Boao', *The Dawn*, 2 November 2003, available at http://www. dawn.com

'Brief on Gwadar Deep water Port Project', Board of Investment, Government of Pakistan., http://www.pakboi.gov.pk/html/Gawadar_Waterport_project.html

Carnegie Endowment for International Peace, 'World Missile Chart', at http://www.ceip.org/files/projects/npp/resources/ballisticmissilechart.htm

Center for Defence Information, Nuclear Weapons Database, Pakistani Nuclear Delivery Systems, http://www.cdi.org/issues/nukef&f/database/panukes.html

'China and Conventional Weapons Non-proliferation', available at http://www.nti.org/db/china/conpos.htm

'China eyes Breakthroughs in Western Development', *Xinhua*, 8 August 2001, http://www.hartford-hwp.com/archives/55/263.html , 12 August 2001

'China to Built(d) Two New Powerhouses in Thar', *Pak Tribune*, 19 June 2004, Web Edition.

'China, Pakistan Highlight Cooperation', *Xinhua*, 3 November 2003, at http://www.chinadaily.com.cn/en/doc/2003-11/03/content_278040.htm

'China's Current Civilian Technology', available at http://www.rand.org/publications/MR/MR/1292.ch3.pdf

'China's Missile Exports and Assistance to Pakistan' *Center for Non-proliferation Studies, Monterey Institute of International Studies*, July 1999. available at http://www.cns.miis.edu/research/India/china/mpakpos.htm

'China's Missile Exports and Assistance to Pakistan', at http://www.nti.org/db/china/conpos.htm

'China's Nuclear Exports and Assistance to Pakistan' *Center for Non-proliferation Studies, Monterey Institute of International Studies*, August 1999, available at http://www.cns.miis.edu/research/India/china/npakpos.htm

'China's Nuclear Exports and Assistance', at http://www.nti.org/db/china/nexport.htm

'China–Pakistan Joint Declaration', Foreign Ministry of People's Republic of China, http://www.fmprc.gov.cn/eng/zxxx/t40148.htm , 4 November 2003

'Chinese Companies Interested in Investing in Pak Chemical Sector', *Pak Tribune*, 26 May 2004, web edition at http://www.paktribune.com

'Declassified Documents Show That, For Over Fifteen Years Beijing Rebuffed US Queries on Chinese Aid to Pakistani Nuclear Program', at http://www.gwu.edu/~nsarchiv/NSAEBB/NSAEBB114/press.htm

'Defiant Pakistan Threatens to Use Nuke', *Press Trust of India*, 30 May 2002, http://in.news.yahoo.com/020530/20/1p549.html

'Delegation of China Software Industry Association (CSAI) to Pakistan' http://www.pseb.org.pk/ News/csai.cfm

'Detailed Account of China's Missile and Nuclear assistance to Pakistan', The Center for Nonproliferation Studies, Monterey, California, database at www.cns.miis.edu/research/india/china/mpakchr.htm

Economic Survey, 'Foreign Economic Assistance', Pakistan Ministry of Finance, Government of Pakistan, March 2003, pp. 1–20. www.finance.gov.pk/survey/chapter10-fea.pdf

'East Turkistan Terrorist Forces Cannot Get Away With Impunity', *Beijing Review*, vol. 45, no. 5, 31 January 2002.

Faruqui, Ahmad, 'China Card Yet Trump Musharraf', at *Asia Times* (Singapore) 25 May 2002, at http://www.atimes.com/ind-pak/DE25Df02.html

Faruqui, Ahmad, 'China's Defence Policy and Its Implications for Pakistan' web address, http://www.defencejournal.com/2002/feb/china-defence.htm

'Foreign Policy of Pakistan', http://www.embassyofpakistan.org/pb1.php

'Helping China Proliferate', *The Washington Times*, 1 June 2004 at www.washingtontimes.com

'Historical Course in Diplomacy', Editorial, *People's Daily Online Edition*, 14 September1999 http://english.peopledaily.com.cn/China/19990914A127.html

'Hu Jintao Seeks to Cement Cooperation Between China, Kazakhstan', CCTV.COM, at http://www.cctv.com/english/news/TVNews/NoonNews/20030603/100603.html, 3 June 2003.

'India Aims for Influence in Southeast Asia' at homepage of *Stratfor* at http://www.stratfor.com, 29 March 2000.

'India Challenges China in South China Sea', at homepage of *Stratfor* at http://www.stratfor.com, 26 April 2000.

Kagan, Miriam, 'Pakistan Wary of Growing China-India Ties', *Asia Times*, 19 November 2003 at http://www.atimes.com/atimes/South_Asia/EK19Df05.html (Accessed on 30 January 2004).

Kan, Shirlay A., 'Chinese Proliferation of Weapons of Mass Destruction: Current Policy Issues' Congressional Research Service Reports 12056,

June 1998, available at http://www.fas.org/spp/starwars/crs 92056.htm. (Accessed on 3 November 1999).

Kapila, Subhash, 'Bangladesh-China Defence Co-operation Agreement's Strategic Implications: An Analysis', Paper No. 582, 14 January 2003 available at website of *South Asia Analyses Group* at http://www.saag.org.

Khan, Sultan Mohammad, 'The Warmth Cools By', at http://www.dawn.com/events/century/for3.htm

Kondapalli, Srikanth, 'China's Naval Equipment Acquisition', at www.idsa-india

MacDonald, Julia, 'South Asia and South East Asia in 2001', *National Strategy Forum Review*, Spring, 2001 at website of *National Strategy Forum* at http://www.nationalstrategy.com/nsr/v10n3Spring01/100313.htm

Mahapatra, A.B., 'China Acquires a Base in Maldives Against India with Some Help from India', at the website of *News Insight.Net* at http://www.indiareacts.com

Malik, Mohan, 'China's Asia Policy: Implications for Japan and India' at the website of *Virtual Forum on Asian Security* at http://www.arts.monash.edu.au/mai/savirtualforum /PaperMalik1.htm

———, 'India's Dragon delusions', http://www.atimes.com/atimes/South_Asia/EJ17Df03.html

Mingguan, Zhu, 'US Plans on National Missile Defence (NMD) and Theatre Missile Defence (TMD): A Chinese Perspective', paper available on the website of the Centre for Non-Proliferation Studies at http://www.cns.miis.edu/db/Chinaengdocs/Zhu/1999.htm,. (Accessed on 5 June 2000).

Mustafa, Zubeida, 'How Effective is the China Card?' at http://www.dawn.com, 12 November 2003.

Naqvi, MB, 'The Role China is Playing' at http://www.defencejournal.com/2001/feb/role-china.htm

NTI, 'Pakistan Missile Overview', at http://www.nti.org/e_research/profiles/Pakistan/Missile/index_3066.html

'Pak Navy to Acquire 4 Warships from China: Naval Chief', 7 May 2004 available at http://www.paktribune.com

'Pak–China Joint Navel Exercises Begin' at http://www.PakistaniDefence.com

'Pak–China to Discuss Gwadar Port Development' *Navy News, 8 June 2001*, Defence India, at http://www.defenceindia.com/test1.php3? filename=navy.htm

'Pakistan Seeks Chinese Assistance to Boost Vocational Training System', *PakTribune*, 17 September 2004, Web Edition.

'Pakistan, China to Extend Defence Ties: To Hold Regular Naval Exercises Strengthening Defense Capability' available at http://www.paknews.com, 29 May 2004.

'Pakistan's Conventional Military Imports from and Joint Weapons Production with China', SIPRI database on arms transfer at http://projects.sipri.see/armstrade/PAK_MPTS_93-02.pdf

'Pakistan's Ormara Naval Base' *Strategic Affairs* at http://www.stratmag.com/issue/july 15.2000.htm

'Pakistan's Relations with China' available at http://www.forisb.org/pak-majorpowers.html

'Pakistan-China Border to Reopen Next Week', 2 June 2004, http://www.dailytimes.com.pk/default.asp?page=story_1-5-2004_pg7_34

'Pakistani President meets Premier Zhu Rongji' 13 May 2001 at http://www.fmprc.gov.cn/eng/10261.html

'PRC Xinjiang Records Economic Growth', *Xinhua*, 22 March 1996, *FBIS-CHI-96-060*, 27 March 1996.

'President Jiang Zemin Met with Pakistan Chief Executive Officer Pervez Musharraf' 10 September 2000 at http://www.fmprc.gov.cn/eng/5116.html, (Accessed on 10 August 2002).

Raman, B., *Continuing Unrest in Xinjiang*, South Asia Analysis Group, 14 March 1999 www.saag.org/papers/paper41.html (Accessed on 1 February 2004).

Ruisheng, Cheng, 'Sino-Indian Relations after India's Nuclear Tests' 20–2 May 1999 at http://lxmi.mi.infn.it/~landnet/NSA/cheng.pdf

'Relations with Major Powers and Regional Blocs' available at http://www.forisb.org/fpolicy.html

Scobell, Andrew, 'Chinese Foreign Policy and the War on Terror' http://www.asiamedia.ucla.edu/article.asp?parentid=7205, 30 January, 2004.

Scobell, Andrew, 'Chinese Foreign Policy and the War on Terror', at http://www.asiamedia.ucla.edu/article.asp?parentid=7205, 30 January 2004.

State Department Briefing Paper: 'The Pakistani Nuclear Programme', 22 June 1983. In Joyce Battle, *India and Pakistan: On the Nuclear Threshold*, Washington, DC, National Security Archive, 2000, http://www.seas.gwu.edu/nsaarchive/NSAEBB/NSAEBB6/index.

Stockholm International Peace Research Institute (SIPRI) *Data on Arms Transfers*. Available at http://www.projects.sipri.se/armstrade. PAK_MPT_93-02.pdf

Swaine, Michel D. and Ashley J. Tellis, *Interpreting China's Grand Strategy: Past, Present and Future* (Santa Monica: RAND Publications, 2000), Online, www.rand.org/publications/MR/MR1121

'Sino–Pak N-ties Can't be Ruled Out: CIA', *The News*, 15 November 2003 available at http://www.jang.com.pk/thenews/

'Sino–Pakistan Relations', available at http://www.news.xinhuanet.com/english/2003-11/22/content/_1192925.htm

'Sri Lanka, China for FTA, Good Trade Ties with Pakistan', at http://pakistantimes.net/2004/02/27/business1.htm , 27 February 2004.

The Dawn, 2 November 2003, http://www.dawn.com/2003/11/02/top4.htm

'Tracking Nuclear Proliferation 1998: China', at http://www.ceip.org/programs/npp/china.htm

'Tracking Nuclear Proliferation, 1998, China', Carnegie Endowment for International Peace, http://www.ceip.org/files/Publications/Tracking China.asp?p=8. (Accessed on 5 February 2004).

'Uighur Militants Committee for Eastern Turkistan', at http://www.fas.org/irp/world/para/uighur.htm, 5 December 1999.

Vijay Sakhuja,'Sun Tzu's Art of War and Chinese Maritime Ambitions 'at the website of *Peace Forum, Taiwan* at http://www.dsis.org.tw/peaceforum/papers/2003-05/MM0305001e.htm

Waldman, Amy, 'City of Fishermen in Pakistan Becomes a Strategic Port,' *New York Times*, September 2004, Web Edition

Website of Pakistan's Ministry of Foreign Affairs http://www.forisb.org/Pak-majorpowers.htm. (Accessed on 6 June 2000).

Weekly Global Intelligence Update, at homepage of *Stratfor* at http://www.stratfor.com, 3 May 2000.

Wirsing, Robert G., ' "The Enemy of Enemy": Pakistan's China Debate', at http://www.apcss.org/Publications/SAS/ChinaDebate/ChinaDebate_Wirsing.pdf

'Xinjiang Acts as a Bridge to Promote China, Pakistan Trade', Pakistan Times Business and Commerce Desk, http://www.pakistantimes.net/2004/03/03/business2.htmlIbid, 3 March 2004.

'Xinjiang Bridges China, Central Asia', *Xinhua*, at http://english.peopledaily.com.cn/200310/02/eng20031002_125317.shtml, 3 October 2003.

Zedong, Mao, 'On the Rectification of Incorrect Ideas in the Party' 1929 http://www.maoism.org/msw/mao_sw.htm (Accessed on 14 October 2002).

———, 'The Role of the Chinese Communist Party in National War', October 1938 http://www.maoism.org/msw/mao_sw.htm (Accessed on 14 October 2002).

———, *Selected Works of Mao Zedong* http://www.maoism.org/msw/mao_sw.htm (Accessed on 14 October 2002).

Zemin, Jiang, 'Carrying Forward Generations of Friendly and Good-Neighborly Relations and Endeavoring Towards a Better Tomorrow for All' 2 December 1996 at http://www.fmprc.gov.cn/eng/4288.html

The Dawn, 2 November 2003, http://www.dawn.com/2003/11/02/top4.htm

Tracking Nuclear Proliferation 1998: China", at http://www.ceip.org/programs/npp/china.htm

Tracking Nuclear Proliferation, 1998, 'China', Carnegie Endowment for International Peace, http://www.ceip.org/files/Publications/Tracking China.asp?p=6, (Accessed on 5 February 2004).

Uighur Militants Committee for Eastern Turkestan", at http://www.fas.org/irp/world/para/uighur.htm, 9 December 1999.

Vijay Sakhuja, Sun Tzu's Art of War and Chinese Maritime Ambitions, in the website of *Peace Forum*, *Taiwan*, at http://www.dsis.org.tw/peaceforum/papers/2003-03/MAR0305001e.htm.

Waldman, Amy, 'City of Fishermen in Pakistan Becomes a Strategic Port', *New York Times*, September 2004, Web edition.

Website of Pakistan's Ministry of Foreign Affairs http://www.forisb.org/Pakmajorpowers.htm (Accessed on 6 June 2000).

Weekly Global Intelligence Updates, at homepage of *Stratfor*, at http://www.stratfor.com, 1 May 2000.

Wilson, Robert G., "The Enemy of Enemy: Pakistan", China Debate, at http://www.apcss.org/Publications/SAS/ChinaDebate/ChinaDebate_Wilson.pdf

Xinping, [illegible] as a Bridge to Promote China-Pakistan Trade', Pakistan Times Business and Commerce Desk, http://www.pakistantimes.net/2004/03/03/business2.htm, 3 March 2004.

Xinjiang: Bridge [illegible] China, Central Asia', *Xinhua*, at http://english.peopledaily.com.cn/200310/02/eng20031002_125357.shtml, 3 October 2003.

Zedong, Mao, "On the Rectification of Incorrect Ideas in the Party", 1929, http://www.maoism.org/msw/vol1/mao.htm (Accessed on 14 October 2002).

——, "The Role of the Chinese Communist Party in the National War", October [illegible] http://www.maoism.org/msw/[illegible] (Accessed on 14 October 2002).

——, *Selected Works of Mao* [illegible] http://www.marxists.org/[illegible] (Accessed on [illegible] August 2002).

Zhu Rongji, 'Carry Forward Generations of Friendly and Good-Neighbourly Relations and Endeavour Towards a Better Tomorrow', [illegible] December [illegible] http://www.[illegible]38.html.

Index